Laurence Sterne

A Life

Ian Campbell Ross

OXFORD
UNIVERSITY PRESS

Great Clarendon Street, Oxford OX2 6DP

Oxford University Press is a department of the University of Oxford.
It furthers the University's objective of excellence in research, scholarship,
and education by publishing worldwide in

Oxford New York

Athens Auckland Bangkok Bogotá Buenos Aires Calcutta
Cape Town Chennai Dar es Salaam Delhi Florence Hong Kong Istanbul
Karachi Kuala Lumpur Madrid Melbourne Mexico City Mumbai
Nairobi Paris São Paulo Shanghai Singapore Taipei Tokyo Toronto Warsaw

with associated companies in Berlin Ibadan

Oxford is a registered trade mark of Oxford University Press
in the UK and in certain other countries

Published in the United States
by Oxford University Press Inc., New York

First published 2001

British Library Cataloguing in Publication Data
Data available

Library of Congress Cataloging in Publication Data
Data available

ISBN 0-19-212235-5

1 3 5 7 9 10 8 6 4 2

Typeset in Baskerville
by RefineCatch Limited, Bungay, Suffolk
Printed in Great Britain
on acid-free paper by
Biddles Ltd., Guildford and King's Lynn

For

Joyce Mary Ross

and

in memory of

Robert Campbell Ross
(1920–1999)

De mortuis nil nisi bonum . . . 'you are not to speak any thing of the dead, but what is good.' Why so?—Who says so?—neither reason or scripture.—Inspired authors have done otherwise—and reason and common sense tell me, that if the characters of past ages and men are to be drawn at all, they are to be drawn like themselves; that is, with their excellencies, and with their foibles—and it is as much a piece of justice to the world, and to virtue too, to do the one, as the other.—The ruleing passion *et les egaraments du cœur,* are the very things which mark, and distinguish a man's character;—in which I would as soon leave out a man's head as his hobby-horse . . .

(Sterne to Dr *****, 30 January 1760)

Preface

In *Human, All Too Human*—a title any biographer of Sterne might be tempted to borrow—Friedrich Nietzsche wrote that 'Sterne the man seems to have been only too closely related to Sterne the writer: his squirrel-soul leaped restlessly from branch to branch; he was familiar with everything from the sublime to the rascally.' Though he thought Sterne 'the most liberated spirit of all time', Nietzsche was far from happy that the man should have so closely resembled his works. Biographers and critics have often agreed, and from Sterne's own day until ours there have been those who have emphasized the rascally at the expense of the sublime. An anonymous eighteenth-century critic compared Sterne (not wholly facetiously) to the Antichrist, William Makepeace Thackeray wrote that the 'foul satyr's eyes leer out of [his] leaves constantly', and F. R. Leavis memorably dismissed Sterne's great masterpiece, *Tristram Shandy*, in a footnote.* Yet the man and writer who attracted such abuse has also received unrestrained praise and admiration. Sterne's sympathetic contemporaries thought his work indeed 'sublime' and compared him to Rabelais, Cervantes, and Swift. Thomas Jefferson believed Sterne's writings made up 'the best course of morality that ever was written'. In the twentieth century novelists from Virginia Woolf and James Joyce to Milan Kundera and Italo Calvino have vied with each other to pay homage to Sterne's influence on the development of the modern novel.

Sterne has been fortunate in his modern biographers. It was in response to severe Victorian moralists—Thackeray in particular—that Percy Fitzgerald wrote his *Life of Laurence Sterne*, originally published in 1864, reaching its third and final edition in 1906. A fuller, scholarly biography, *The Life and Times of Laurence Sterne*, was first published by Wilbur L. Cross in 1909, finding its final form in the third edition of 1929.

* As 'irresponsible (and nasty) trifling'.

More recently, Arthur H. Cash published his own scholarly biography in two parts, *Laurence Sterne: The Early and Middle Years*, in 1975, and *Laurence Sterne: The Later Years*, in 1986. Alongside these more ambitious works, several shorter biographies deserve mention: among them, Lodwick Hartley's *This is Lorence: A Narrative of the Reverend Laurence Sterne*, first published in 1943, and later reissued as *Laurence Sterne: A Biographical Essay* (1968); Henri Fluchère's *Laurence Sterne: de l'homme à l'œuvre* (1961) and David Thomson's *Wild Excursions: The Life and Fiction of Laurence Sterne* (1972). The leading Sterne scholar of the mid-twentieth century, L. P. Curtis, wrote no biography but his magisterial edition of Sterne's correspondence, *The Letters of Laurence Sterne* (1935), provided more fresh biographical information about the writer than any other single source. Although I have usually gone back to the original magazine reviews of, and pamphlet responses to, Sterne's fiction and sermons, I should also mention two invaluable guides to the contemporary reception of Sterne's work: Alan B. Howes's *Yorick and the Critics: Sterne's Reputation in England 1760–1868* (1958) and *Sterne: The Critical Heritage* (1974). I am pleased to acknowledge my debt to these predecessors and, since I have learned much from them, where I have provided new information or have corrected errors I have done so silently.

In the years since Professor Cash completed his biography students of Sterne have benefited from a number of projects as well as the researches of individuals: from the scholarship of those associated with the ongoing Florida edition of the works of Laurence Sterne (1978–), which has so far published editions of *Tristram Shandy* and of Sterne's sermons, under the general editorship of Professor Melvyn New; from the lifetime devotion to Sterne of the late Dr Kenneth Monkman; and from the editorship by Professor Peter De Voogd of a journal, *The Shandean*, dedicated wholly to Sterne, his works, and their reception. If one might enter a reservation it is—to paraphrase Edward Said writing, in 1984, on Swift studies—that much fine scholarship has been produced in a 'club'-like ambience off-putting to outsiders, where (in the case of Sterne) a small group of academics review not only each others' work but also, on occasion, their own.

The present biography attempts to acknowledge and make accessible the best of recent scholarship on Sterne's life and work, but to do so critically. So, I have gratefully made use of important new materials: for example, the edition of the first part of Sterne's memoir written for his daughter Lydia, based on the holograph manuscript, uncovered among much else in the course of a lifetime's research by Kenneth Monkman;

from external and internal evidence, however, I have rejected many of the works Dr Monkman speculatively attributed to Sterne as not being the work of the writer. Similarly, I have been happy to follow ecclesiastical and theological paths signposted in the Florida edition of Sterne's sermons, but my own reading of the sermons in the light of their contemporary reception has not always persuaded me to accept Professor Melvyn New's conclusions. Besides specific debts to the findings of Sterne scholars, I have learned much from the work of cultural and social historians. I began work on this biography mounted on no hobby-horse but with many competing ideas concerning my subject. It was as I wrote that I found my understanding of Sterne sharpened by studies in the commercialization of eighteenth-century culture, and in the adjacent areas of eighteenth-century notions of literary celebrity and literary authority. Increasingly, Sterne seemed to me to have embodied the duality or tension John Brewer has written of in describing two types among the middling sort in eighteenth-century England: the client of the aristocracy and the entrepreneur in the free market. For the greater part of his adult life until the age of 46, the Revd Laurence Sterne looked anxiously to patrons—to lords temporal and spiritual—for preferment which came slowly at first and, later, not at all. At 46, Sterne haltingly but crucially turned his back on hopes of securing the patronage he had long sought and turned himself, partly to his own surprise, into one of the leading literary entrepreneurs of his day (in the process, ironically enough, securing the very aristocratic patronage that had previously eluded him). The imagination, determination, and skill with which he emerged from decades of frustrated dependency to market himself, along with *Tristram Shandy*, *A Sentimental Journey*, and his sermons, is one of the themes of this book.

Since I first read *Tristram Shandy* I have never doubted that it is one of the world's great comic novels, a book to which it is always a joy to return, and one surpassed by nothing, perhaps, except Sterne's own favourite, Cervantes's *Don Quixote*. Sterne's only other major work of fiction, *A Sentimental Journey*, is scarcely less a triumph of the novelist's art, whether read as comic or sentimental fiction or, with the ambiguity Sterne cultivated, as both together. Nevertheless, I have not attempted to offer exhaustive critical readings of Sterne's novels, and have not listed any of the many fine critical studies of the writer and his work in the select list of works cited. I have been swayed by two thoughts. First, any reader of this biography is likely already to have read Sterne's fiction—and my wish would be that anyone who has not will be led to that pleasure by this book. Secondly, I have written in the confidence that the interest of Sterne's life is not restricted to the fact of his achievements as a writer. That Sterne would never have been the subject of a biography had he not written *Tristram Shandy* or *A Sentimental Journey* is undeniable; that 'ordinary' lives merit literary attention is a conviction I hold as deeply as, I believe, did Sterne. *Tristram Shandy* may, as Samuel Johnson famously remarked, be 'odd', but in its oddity—in its lack of conventional novelistic action or in the tragicomic absurdity of the determining events of Tristram's life—Sterne's work speaks in a radically democratic way of the uniqueness and unique value of each individual's experience. I have tried not to put an unwarranted gloss on Sterne's life by concentrating too narrowly on a few years of literary fame (extraordinary as that fame was) at the expense of those years in which he was, by turns, a soldier's son, a student, a parson, a political journalist, and a farmer—nor by forgetting his chosen or unwilled roles as husband, father, priest, rake, or consumptive. I have celebrated, as Sterne did, the remarkable renown the successful writer enjoyed, but I have not forgotten that his years of fame, no less than the decades that preceded them, were marked by emotional frustrations that his notorious sexual and sentimental liaisons could never subdue. I have quoted comparatively sparingly from *Tristram Shandy* and *A Sentimental Journey* but more extensively from Sterne's less well-known sermons and letters. In quoting widely, as I do, from Sterne's correspondence I have elected to use L. P. Curtis's edition, occasionally supplemented, for particular reasons, by other printings; until the new complete edition of the correspondence currently under preparation by Professor Peter De Voogd becomes available, Curtis remains the best and most easily accessible source. In quoting still more extensively from Curtis's edition of the so-called 'Journal to Eliza', the record of the dying Sterne's daily existence and intense sentimental attachment to the youthful Elizabeth Draper, I indicate my belief that paraphrase is altogether inappropriate to an intense relationship—destructive and life-giving by turns—which had no objective existence outside of the confines of Sterne's imagination or the literary form in which he represented the promptings of his own desires.

So much for intellectual debts—however inadequately recognized here, in the notes, or in my select list of works cited. For their assistance, I am grateful to the staffs of all the libraries in which I worked and thank them here, but would mention in particular the York City Library; the Borthwick Institute, York; the British Library; the Bibliothèque Nationale, Paris; and, above all, the staff of the Library of Trinity College, Dublin, not least Charles Benson and the ever-helpful members of the Department of Early Printed Books. It is also a pleasure to take this opportunity to thank the following for grants awarded and most gratefully received: the Provost's Development Fund, Trinity College, Dublin; the Arts and Social Sciences Benefaction Fund, Trinity College, Dublin; and the Society of Authors.

Personal debts are another matter. For replying to particular queries, I am grateful to Professor Davis Coakley, Dr Kenneth Ferguson, Professor J. B. Lyons, and Dr Fiona Mulcahy. I am especially grateful to Patrick Kelly for reading one chapter of the typescript and offering helpful comments on it. Judith Luna has been the most considerate and encouraging of editors. Among others to whom I owe more general debts of gratitude, I would mention first Maria Pia Ross for her unstinting assistance. Virginia Llewellyn Smith has added friendship and good sense to her formidable editorial skills. Over many years I have enjoyed (and learned from) conversations with Terence Brown, Penny Fielding, Stephen Matterson, and Antoinette Quinn. Ian Small has offered friendship and intellectual stimulation over an even longer period, as well as once more providing help in acquiring materials; I thank him again. A late draft of the book was read by two friends of long standing. Aileen Douglas generously took time away from her own work to offer constructive criticism and helpful suggestions; for these and for her consistent encouragement, I am deeply grateful. Finally, I thank John Valdimir Price who has shared with me his extensive knowledge of the eighteenth century (and other enthusiasms) over more years than either of us would, I suspect, wish to count or perhaps can even believe; I have been fortunate, like Sterne, to have a friend who not only enjoys the same books but who has kept 'a full-spread board, and wore down the steps of his cellar' to my benefit and pleasure. The book is dedicated to my mother and to the memory of my father.

Contents

INTRODUCTION

'Tristram is the Fashion'

One morning in early March 1760 two men met by chance in a street in York. Both in their mid-forties, they were by then old friends, having known each other for almost twenty years. One, a plump, slightly jowly man of affable appearance, was a wealthy landowner, squire of the parish of Stillington, ten miles north of the city. The other, nearly six feet tall, distinctively angular, with a long, sharp nose and thin to the point of gauntness, was an Anglican priest, vicar of two country livings, including Stillington. Stephen Croft, the squire, was setting out for London on private business but paused to ask after the fortunes of his friend. He had good reason, for the recent publication of two slim volumes of comic prose fiction, *The Life and Opinions of Tristram Shandy, Gentleman*, had quite unexpectedly made a local celebrity of the country parson.

The priest, the Revd Laurence Sterne, was unaffectedly delighted by the sudden shift in his fortunes. He had long sought to escape the predictable and uncongenial rural existence to which his modest income and still more modest prospects had restricted him. Even when his fiction became the toast of friends and acquaintances in York and the surrounding countryside, Sterne was not content. Ambition, and a stubborn belief in his work, left him hankering after further success in London, the undisputed centre of English cultural life. To this end, he devised imaginative stratagems aimed at bringing his novel to the notice of influential arbiters of metropolitan taste. Not even in his most optimistic moments, however, could Sterne have imagined that within two months of its first appearance *Tristram Shandy* would become the most talked-about work of English fiction since Samuel Richardson had published *Pamela; or, Virtue Rewarded* to comparable acclaim, two decades earlier.

Stephen Croft was better acquainted than most with the clergyman's ambitions and with the repeated disappointments he had endured over the past many years. Meeting him now, he showed generous delight at the turn in his friend's fortunes and immediately suggested that Sterne accompany him to London. All too familiar with the imprudent vicar's recurring financial problems, Croft even offered pay the cost of his journey: 'in the vulgar Phrase . . . [to] frank him and defray his expenses back.'[1] Handsome as the proposal was, the clergyman hesitated, not out of delicacy but because the timing of the invitation was scarcely ideal. His wife, Elizabeth, was still recovering from a mental breakdown which had led her, some months earlier, to believe herself the Queen of Bohemia; the breakdown, it was whispered, had been caused by her husband's repeated and notorious infidelities. Stephen Croft was not to be put off, however, and he told Sterne bluntly that as he 'cou'd not possibly do her any good by his attendance . . . he had better go along with him.'[2] Thus pressed, and with the single proviso that he should have an hour in which to go home and pack his best breeches, Sterne accepted.

On their arrival in London two days later Sterne joined Stephen Croft as the guest of the latter's daughter and her husband in their house in Chapel Street, close to Hyde Park. The following morning Sterne was missing at the breakfast table. He had left the house early to visit his London publishers, the celebrated booksellers Robert and James Dodsley, in their fashionable shop at the sign of 'Tully's Head', in Pall Mall. Enquiring after *Tristram Shandy*, its author was 'highly flattered, when the Shopman told him, that there was not such a Book to be had in London either for Love or money'.[3]

Such, at least, is the story told many years later by John Croft, brother of Sterne's friend Stephen. John Croft's anecdotes are not always reliable, but there can be little doubt as to the essential truthfulness of his account of this pivotal moment in Sterne's life. Born in 1713, the second child of a younger son of a younger son of a family of Yorkshire gentry, Laurence Sterne had spent his days in an existence familiar enough to others of his class in eighteenth-century England. Possessing the estimable advantages of good birth and education, he entirely lacked the wealth necessary to support the social position he inherited. Like so many of his kind, Laurence Sterne had followed a well-worn path as he attempted to protect his genteel status and secure his future. Orphaned of his father when he was 17, he was able to take a degree at the University of Cambridge thanks to the financial assistance afforded him by a cousin. Having graduated, he took holy orders in the Church of England as soon as he was legally entitled to do so.

After his ordination at the age of 23, Sterne obtained a living in the rural Yorkshire parish of Sutton-on-the-Forest and, for a while, fulfilled his pastoral obligations conscientiously enough. Soon, however, he was called to duties of a different kind. In an age in which the Whig government kept a tight hold on the Church of England, the Anglican clergy were highly politicized and before long Sterne found himself playing a small but prominent part in county politics. Sterne owed his first living to the patronage of his uncle—a powerful church lawyer and a champion of the Whig party interest in Yorkshire. When the time was right Dr Jaques Sterne called upon his nephew to discharge that debt by turning political journalist. So, in the early 1740s, Laurence Sterne took up his pen in support of the campaigns of the Whig candidates in two successive county elections. Before long he was rewarded for his political efforts with a modest share of the preferments the Established Church of the eighteenth century offered to its favoured sons: a prebendal stall in York Minster, soon to be exchanged for another, more lucrative, prebend. Very quickly, however, Sterne found that the savage personal abuse he directed against his Tory opponents in his political journalism had an unwelcome tendency to be returned, with interest, on himself. Dismayed and discouraged, he abruptly turned his back on politics—although he knew that by so doing he would lose the patronage of his now alienated and vindictive uncle and with it his best hope of further advancement in the Church.

Barely 30 years of age, Sterne settled into an altogether quieter, more humdrum existence as vicar of Sutton-on-the-Forest. He acquired a second living, Stillington, but the respectable tedium of a life in a country parish soon led to restlessness. At best, he could be a compassionate as well as conscientious priest: for more than twenty years there were those among the poorer and more vulnerable members of the local community who had reason to be grateful to him for acts of public benevolence and private charity. It was not long, however, before Sterne became intermittently careless of his more routine ecclesiastical duties, so bringing himself into conflict with his respectable country parishioners. Worse still, he gained an unsavoury but deserved reputation as a libertine, a clergyman whose numerous and ill-disguised infidelities brought scandal to the cloth. Only in the pulpit was his standing secure, for the affecting eloquence and apparent spontaneity of his preaching appealed as much to the more demanding urban congregations of York as to the humbler churchgoers of the Yorkshire countryside.

In his late twenties Sterne married Elizabeth Lumley, a young woman from a genteel northern background very similar to his own. In the early years of their marriage Elizabeth would bear a number of children, just one of whom—a daughter, Lydia—would survive infancy. Failing to find emotional or physical satisfaction in his marriage, however, Sterne embarked on a series of adulterous liaisons that he hoped might supplement the scant consolations offered by his relationship with an increasingly unhappy Elizabeth. Such gratification as he found was fleeting; the damage to his moral reputation was more enduring. Unhappy as they were in their personal relationship, however, Laurence and Elizabeth Sterne were at one in their determination to keep up the genteel appearances important to them both. As it became ever more apparent that Laurence's sudden retreat from politics and increasingly sour relations with his uncle had cut him off from the prospect of future ecclesiastical preferment, the Sternes ventured into farming, in a frustrating and ultimately frustrated attempt to supplement an income that never seemed adequate to their expenditure.

Occasionally, in the course of twenty years, some event of national importance—most notably the 1745 Jacobite rebellion—animated the even tenor of a generally staid existence. More frequently there were acute frustrations arising from the fierce but essentially petty-minded politicking characteristic of the venal clerical circles centred on York Minster. For the most part, however, Sterne followed a tranquil, obscure existence in the Yorkshire countryside, living, like many others, a life compounded of small satisfactions and more enduring disappointments. The country parson's leisure hours were filled as predictably as his working life was ordered by the church calendar: for many years, he was later to write, 'Books, painting, fiddling, and shooting were my amusements'.[4] Even the literary talent that had first revealed itself in his political journalism barely distinguished Sterne from many of his clerical contemporaries. He wrote sermons, of course, a little poetry, and, at the end of the 1750s, a short prose satire, *A Political Romance*, also known as *The History of a Good Warm Watch-Coat.* Like his farming, these forays into literature engaged his enthusiasm for a while, but after two decades they had brought him scant notice or reward. Two sermons which made their way into print did not sell well, while his single published poem appeared anonymously and went largely unremarked.[5] Far worse, the witty *Political Romance*, which scathingly but imprudently exposed the rapaciousness of several easily identified members of the Minster clergy, was barely off the press when the archbishop of York hastily intervened to save the blushes of the Church and peremptorily ordered the entire edition to be burned.

It was the publication later that same year of the first two volumes of *Tristram Shandy*, in a small edition of 500 or so copies, printed in York during the last weeks of 1759, that changed Sterne's life—and literary history. From then until his death, just eight years later, Sterne was one of the most celebrated figures of his day, famous not merely among a literary elite but as a celebrity known even to those who never read a word he wrote.

The suddenness and extent of his fame took Sterne by surprise, but he had worked hard to achieve his success. For virtually a year before the first instalment of *Tristram Shandy* went on sale Sterne had been writing and rewriting his work as well as considering, in finely calculated commercial detail, what profit it might bring and how best it might be marketed. Ten months before he travelled south to London with Stephen Croft he had approached Robert Dodsley, the most respected bookseller of the mid-eighteenth century, as a potential publisher. Though Dodsley declined to take Sterne's work on the terms the author first suggested, he did the next best thing by assisting in its publication in York and Dublin, as well as selling copies of the York-printed edition in his London shop.

Once Sterne had copies of *Tristram Shandy* to hand he puffed his work in a letter he wrote himself—though he passed it off as the spontaneous praise of a young singer, Catherine Fourmantel, then his mistress.[6] This letter Catherine sent to her acquaintance David Garrick in London. Three years younger than Sterne, Garrick had long ago left behind his own provincial origins: at 43 he was not only England's leading actor but arguably the most influential arbiter of polite literary taste in the capital. When Garrick rose to the bait and praised the two volumes, Sterne was quickly in contact by means of a letter he now signed with his own name. While still in York, he prompted the actor, playwright, and theatre manager—for Garrick was all three—to consider whether *Tristram Shandy* might not make an admirable 'Cervantic Comedy', assuring him that 'ye 3^{d} & 4th Vol^{s} . . . will be still more dramatick'.[7] That Sterne had never written for the theatre and had indeed not even begun his third and fourth volumes was of no account: 'Half a word of Encouragement would be enough to make me conceive, & bring forth something for the Stage' (*Letters*, 87). What seemed to have worked with the celebrated Garrick might work too with William Hogarth, the most renowned artist of mid-eighteenth century England. So, within a week of his arrival in London Sterne was intimating to an acquaintance that 'I would give both my Ears (If I was not to loose my Credit by it) for no more than ten Strokes of *Howgarth's* witty Chissel, to clap at the Front of my next Edition of *Shandy*' (*Letters*, 99). It was a bold and imaginative ploy on Sterne's part, for few contemporary novels were illustrated—and even fewer by artists of such calibre.[8]

The next edition of his book would be published in London by Robert Dodsley and his brother James, and so anxious was Sterne to obtain for it the added attraction of an illustration by Hogarth that he intimated in some detail just how the artist might be induced to agree. Perhaps, he hinted, an approach might begin: '"Mr Hogarth, I have been with my friend Shandy this morning . . ."' Since Hogarth was as acutely alert to commercial possibility as Sterne, the writer got his illustration, which appeared as a frontispiece to the first London edition of Volumes I and II of *Tristram Shandy*—and in time he persuaded Hogarth to provide a second engraving to illustrate a scene in the fourth volume of his novel.

As the manner of the suggested approach to Hogarth indicates, Sterne had quickly perceived the success he might achieve in London by marketing himself along with his work. Within a matter of days he had become the man of his book. Or, more accurately—and more remarkably—Sterne had become the men of his book, for depending on his audience he was happy to take the part of the facetious Tristram Shandy or the benevolent parson Mr Yorick. In one or other guise he was welcome everywhere, impressing contemporaries with his 'infinite share of wit and goodness, things . . . which are very seldom, indeed, found in any degree together'.[9] Although the same writer noted that it was 'one of the odd qualities of this very odd person, to join contradictions',[10] the assiduity and energy with which Sterne promoted himself and his work together in these early days was widely recognized. When a short biographical account appeared in a new popular journal, the *Royal Female Magazine*, introducing the author to the world as Yorick, people back in York guessed that he had written it himself.[11]

In this case York opinion seems to have been wrong, but it was scarcely unjustified. In January 1760 Sterne himself had openly declared: 'I wrote not [to] be *fed*, but to be *famous*.'[12] The phrase—a pointed reversal of a notorious remark by the actor, playwright, and former poet laureate Colley Cibber, author of the *Apology for the Life of Mr. Colley Cibber, written by himself*—was a clear assertion both of Sterne's literary ambition and superior social status, an affirmation that this new literary celebrity was no hack author but a gentleman. Perhaps, when he penned those words, the prebendary of York believed them to be true. The truth, however, was more complex and more interesting. Indeed, Laurence Sterne himself seems to have lost sight of his avowedly disinterested pursuit of fame within hours of his arrival in London. On the same morning that Sterne had failed to appear at breakfast, Stephen Croft and his son-in-law were travelling along Pall Mall in a coach when they saw him haggling with the booksellers over the price of consigning them the copyright of his work.[13] This he did most successfully, adding to the £250 he gained from the sale of copyright a further £50 for the copies of books already sold. Moreover, Sterne was already negotiating for more than just a second edition to supplement the small, sold-out first edition of the *Life and Opinions*. He was also discussing the publication of two volumes of sermons, designed to take advantage of the popularity of the excellent 'The Abuses of Conscience considered', which he had preached a decade earlier in York Minster and incorporated, to great comic effect, in the second volume of *Tristram Shandy*. As before, Sterne was not entrusting his success to chance. In using the 'Abuses of Conscience' sermon in *Tristram Shandy*, and attributing it to Parson Yorick, Sterne had taken the opportunity to tell the world 'That in case the character of parson *Yorick*, and this sample of his sermons is liked,—that there are now in the possession of the *Shandy* Family, as many as will make a handsome volume, at the world's service,—and much good may they do it'.[14] Fortunately for Sterne, the booksellers had taken the hint and were as enthusiastic about this second literary venture as the author himself.

Sterne was now talking about more money than he had ever possessed in his life. John Croft, who told the story of the early-rising author bargaining with his publishers in Pall Mall, gets the details of these financial transactions wrong—he was writing from memory thirty-five years after the events—but it is easy to credit him in his story that, having reached an agreement, Sterne returned home 'and came skipping into the room, and said that he was the richest man in Europe'.[15] The richest and soon—to take hyperbole a little further—the most famous:

> Sterne's Popularity at one time arose to that pitch, that on a Wager laid in London that a Letter addressed to Tristram Shandy in Europe shou'd reach him when luckily the Letter came down into Yorkshire and the Post Boy meeting Sterne on the road to Sutton pulled off his hatt and gave it him.[16]

In March 1760 Sterne's fame was not quite so extensive, but his own delighted account of his reception among those who, days previously, had not the slightest idea of his existence reveals how quickly it was growing. 'I have the greatest honors paid me, & most civilities shewn me, that were ever known, from the Great; & am engaged allready to ten Noble men & men of fashion to dine' (*Letters*, 96), he boasted a week after he arrived in London. Moreover, his earliest patron, David Garrick, had shown himself willing not merely to speak well of Sterne's book and to help the author in his dealings with the Dodsleys but to assist in introducing Sterne to the best of London society. He also provided him with a free pass to his own box at the Drury Lane theatre for the entire season (a mark of distinction which so impressed contemporaries that it was reported even in the Paris papers[17]).

When not taking advantage of Garrick's generosity, Sterne was entertaining admirers at his new lodgings—'which by the by, are the genteelest in Town' (*Letters*, 102). Just a year after the archbishop of York had insisted on the burning of Sterne's first attempt at prose satire, the bench of bishops, in London for the parliamentary session, sent the country parson their collective compliments. Having failed to gain any significant ecclesiastical preferment in almost two decades, Sterne was quick to make plans to pay a call on each of them in turn. One bishop would go so far as to offer Sterne a 'purse of Guineas', which the author happily accepted, along with much advice as to his future conduct, which he did not. As fortune would have it, Sterne had not been in London for a fortnight when a Yorkshire living close to his own fell vacant due to the death of the incumbent (his own former curate), and he was preferred to it by the patron, the earl of Fauconberg. Yet if Sterne gained this fresh preferment without the need for episcopal patronage, he still required an archiepiscopal signature. Anxious, after so many years of waiting, not to let the prize slip away, Sterne drew up the nomination document himself, presented it to Lord Fauconberg on 28 March, and the following day called on the archbishop of York, in his house in Grosvenor Square, for its completion. It is hard to know how he found the time. To Catherine Fourmantel he wrote that, 'from morning to night my Lodgings . . . are full of the greatest Company—I dined these 2 Days with 2 Ladies of the Bedchamber—then with, Ld Rockingham, Ld Edgecomb—Lord Wichilsea, Lord Littleton, A Bishop—&c &c—I assure you my Kitty, that Tristram is the Fashion' (*Letters*, 102).

In an 'Age of Novelties'[18] this was the highest accolade of all: 'Britons in this age are like the Athenians of old; they are always in search of something new',[19] as one writer on *Tristram Shandy* expressed it. 'Fashion', in Henry Fielding's words, was 'the Governor of this World';[20] it must, as a contemporary economist declared, 'have uncontrolled sway'.[21] In its wake fashion brought Sterne hitherto undreamt-of opportunities. To the author of London's most talked-about book, a man actively considering the imminent publication of a new edition of his work, his new circle of acquaintances must have seemed rich in possibility for a socially and financially rewarding dedication. In dining with Lord Lyttelton, for example, Sterne was in the company of a man who had been a friend of the poet Alexander Pope and the novelist Henry Fielding (who had dedicated *Tom Jones* (1749) to him), and patron of James Thomson, author of *The Seasons* (1730). (If Sterne was impressed by the fact that Lyttelton was himself a published author, whose subsequently celebrated *Dialogues of the Dead* were shortly to appear, he does not mention it—and indeed Sterne seems to have found time to read virtually nothing while in London.) A second notable aristocratic patron of literature with whom Sterne had the honour to dine in these days was Philip Stanhope, the earl of Chesterfield, also a friend of Pope's, as of other writers of Pope's generation such as John Gay, poet and author of *The Beggar's Opera* (1728), and John Arbuthnot. In 1760 a dedication to Chesterfield or Lyttelton would have done any new author great credit. Sterne, however, was aiming higher still, dedicating the second edition of *The Life and Opinions of Tristram Shandy, Gentleman* to no less a figure than the prime minister himself, William Pitt.

At the beginning of 1760 the elder Pitt was at the height of his reputation and popularity following the English military successes against France throughout 1759, the 'Year of Victories', in what would become known as the Seven Years War. 'Though I have no suspicion that the inclosed Dedication can offend you,' Sterne wrote, 'yet I thought it my duty to take some method of letting you see it, before I presumed to beg the honour of presenting it to you next week, with the Life and Opinions of Tristram Shandy' (*Letters*, 103). The confidence of this brief note is decidedly at odds with the feigned modesty of the Dedication itself. 'Never poor wight of a dedicator had less hopes from his Dedication', declared Sterne, 'than I have from this of mine; for it is written in a by-corner of the kingdom, and in a retired thatched house' (*TS*, 'To the Right Honourable Mr. Pitt', [p. 3]). The truth is that Sterne had great and well-founded hopes of his dedication which, in any case, was very probably written in London, not Yorkshire, and was quite certainly not written in a 'retired thatched house' since Sterne had recently moved from his country parsonage to York itself.

In dedicating the first two volumes of *Tristram Shandy* to the 'Great Commoner' Pitt, Sterne seems to glance at his own rise from obscurity to the pinnacle of fame. He had not yet scaled the heights of social aspiration, however. Among those who now befriended Sterne in London was Charles Watson-Wentworth, marquess of Rockingham, lord-lieutenant of the North and East Ridings of Yorkshire and himself a future prime minister. It was Rockingham who, as a lord of the bedchamber, first presented Sterne at Court and took him as part of his grand retinue to

Windsor, where the youthful nobleman was to be installed as a knight of the Garter alongside the hero of the hour, Prince Ferdinand of Brunswick, brother-in-law of Frederick the Great and victor over the French at the Battle of Minden. If he was overwhelmed by all of this, Sterne scarcely showed it—although a hint of provincial awe at the wealth and luxury he was encountering for the first time survives in his noting that the banquet at Windsor was to cost £1,400.[22]

Sterne's immersion in this new world was almost complete. Besides his social engagements in and out of town, Sterne was also sitting for a portrait (now in the National Portrait Gallery in London), executed by England's most fashionable and respected portrait painter, Joshua Reynolds. Before long he was casually excusing himself for the haste in which he was writing to his recent benefactor Stephen Croft, now back in Yorkshire, by mentioning that he had only just returned from an engagement at a concert 'where the D[uke] of Y[ork] perform'd', though he found time to add that 'I have received great notice from him, and last week had the honour of supping with him' (*Letters*, 110–11). A social engagement with royalty was exceptional, but Sterne was hard pressed with flattering invitations: 'I have 14 Engagements to Dine now in my Books, with the first Nobility' (*Letters*, 104), he reported. Towards the end of his life Sterne recorded one of his most vivid memories of the sudden fame his book had brought him. In a letter written seven years after the event he recalled his meeting in 1760 with Allen, Lord Bathurst, dedicatee of one of Pope's most celebrated poems, the third 'Moral Essay'. 'This nobleman', he wrote

> is an old friend of mine.—You know he was always the protector of men of wit and genius; and has had those of the last century, Addison, Steele, Pope, Swift, Prior, &c. &c. always at his table.—The manner in which his notice began of me, was as singular as it was polite.—He came up to me, one day, as I was at the Princess of Wales's court. 'I want to know you, Mr. Sterne; but it is fit you should know, also, who it is that wishes this pleasure. You have heard, continued he, of an old Lord Bathurst, of whom your Popes, and Swifts, have sung and spoken so much: I have lived my life with geniuses of that cast; but have survived them; and, despairing ever to find their equals, it is some years since I have closed my accounts, and shut up my books, with thoughts of never opening them again: but you have kindled a desire in me of opening them once more before I die; which I now do; so go home and dine with me . . . '. (*Letters*, 304–5)

As an intimate of leading writers of an earlier generation, Bathurst was no common reader—and it is hardly surprising that Sterne was so gratified by his attention. It is the more remarkable, then, that in 1760, as for the remainder of his career, Laurence Sterne owed his literary fame not to Bathurst or to personal patronage from any other of the noblemen, politicians, or royalty at whose tables he found so ready a welcome. The secret of Sterne's success lay instead in the skill with which—in collaboration with his booksellers—he reached out to patrons of a different kind: those prosperous middle-class readers who increasingly made up the great bulk of the reading public. These, above all, were anxious to share in the novelty of literary fashion by buying Sterne's novel or his sermons or those works that would, in great profusion, shortly spin off from them. In 1760 Sterne's was no mere *succès d'estime* (though members of the social elite had their part to play); rather, it was a triumph of the writer in the marketplace.

In the spring of 1760 preparations for the first London edition of *Tristram Shandy* continued apace. The first small, York-printed edition having so quickly sold out, James Dodsley acted with dispatch. He paid Sterne £250 for the copyright to the first two volumes, five times what the author had unsuccessfully asked for the previous year. Using more than one printer in the capital Dodsley worked speedily to produce a larger edition of 5,000 copies (ten or more times the size of the York printing). This would appear with a London imprint and with Robert and James Dodsley now proudly declaring themselves to be the publishers of the volumes, called 'The Second Edition' (an earlier Dublin edition having been discreetly overlooked[23]). Sterne had glanced over the sheets of this new edition, and made some few corrections and additions, including the 'Dedication' to William Pitt, but was too busy to do more. The volumes, complete with Hogarth's droll frontispiece, went on sale on 2 April 1760 and sold well enough to require another two London editions before the year was out (two more Dublin editions, one a piracy, also made their appearance in 1760[24]).

Success bred success. By the time the first London edition of *Tristram Shandy* appeared Sterne had also finalized his agreement with the Dodsleys for the publication of two volumes of sermons. In truth, he had laid plans for profiting by the success of his fiction even before leaving York—an advertisement for the sermons had appeared in a local paper as early as the beginning of March.[25] Since Sterne had brought the sermons with him, the booksellers were able to offer them for sale by the last week of May. The two volumes were as carefully marketed as *Tristram Shandy*. Not only did they boast an engraving of the author taken from the Reynolds portrait, but their attractiveness was enhanced in the eyes of the public by an exceptionally prestigious subscription list. Comprising more than 650 names, the list was an eloquent testimony both to the popularity of Sterne and to the entrepreneurial skills of the Dodsleys, who had successfully gained the endorsement of those whom a still greater eighteenth-century entrepreneur, Josiah Wedgwood, would term the fashionable 'legislators of taste'.[26] Those who subscribed included men and women of both rank and achievement. There were dukes and duchesses, over a dozen earls—among them Bathurst, Chesterfield, and Sterne's new patron, Fauconberg—besides lords Lyttelton and Rockingham, the poet laureate William Whitehead, David Garrick, the bluestocking Elizabeth Montagu, both Joshua Reynolds and William Hogarth, the musical historian Charles Burney, the poet and member of parliament Soame Jenyns, William Warburton and six other bishops, and politicians ranging from Charles Townshend, son of Viscount Townshend, to the dissenting radical John Wilkes. Once again, fashion held sway: the sermons proved so popular that a second edition was called for within two months.

What was it about *The Life and Opinions of Tristram Shandy, Gentleman* that had first captivated so many and transformed the life of Laurence Sterne in the space of a few, crowded weeks? Most simply, perhaps, it made readers laugh—often in spite of themselves. A more precise, though still very partial, answer might be that Tristram's fictional autobiography has one of the most arresting opening sentences—baffling and beguiling—in all of English literature:

> I wish either my father or my mother, or indeed both of them, as they were in duty both equally bound to it, had minded what they were about when they begot me; had they duly consider'd how much depended upon what they were then doing;—that not only the production of a rational Being was concern'd in it, but that possibly the happy formation and temperature of his body, perhaps his genius and the very cast of his mind;—and, for aught they knew to the contrary, even the fortunes of his whole house might take their turn from the humours and dispositions which were then uppermost:——Had they duly weighed and considered all this, and proceeded accordingly,——I am verily persuaded I should have made a quite different figure in the world, from that, in which the reader is likely to see me. (*TS* I. i. [p. 5])

Certainly it is hard to imagine any prospective purchaser, however casually drawn to Sterne's work by its title-page, who would not be intrigued by this account by the narrator of his own conception and wish to read further. Evidently the heady conflation of autobiography, heroic romance, mock-medical speculation, and bawdy in a single sentence engaged the attentions of the very first readers, drawing them into a comic narrative seemingly designed at once to raise and then frustrate their expectations. One (enduringly popular) character was introduced only to be killed off immediately, his death marked by the curious, and curiously familiar, lament:

Alas, poor YORICK!

followed by a solid black leaf, in sign of mourning. The further these first readers read on, the more intrigued, amused, and frustrated they became. Neither is it any wonder that readers were sometimes baffled, for the first instalment of Sterne's novel included—among much else—a hero who fails to get himself born throughout two volumes, an ordained jester, a (fictional) marriage settlement, a (real) theological judgement concerning inter-uterine baptism, passed in 1733 by the doctors of the Sorbonne and printed in the original French, my uncle Toby, hobby-horses, the man-midwife Dr Slop, and an excellent if apparently provocative Anglican sermon, read aloud by a servant, Corporal Trim, to an audience of three, one of whom—a Roman Catholic man-midwife—quickly falls asleep (the scene Hogarth opted to depict in his frontispiece). Even in an age notably free in its understanding of prose fiction, *Tristram Shandy* appeared, as Samuel Johnson was later famously to remark, 'odd'.[27]

At times even professional readers were baffled. A reviewer in the prestigious *Critical Review* seemed completely at a loss: 'This is a humorous performance, of which we are unable to convey any distinct ideas to our readers.'[28] Readers perplexed by this admission would not necessarily have found more distinct ideas elsewhere—although they would have found plenty of evidence that this was a book they might want to read for themselves, a work at once amusing and intriguing. In the first months following publication *Tristram Shandy* was variously described in print as 'droll', 'ingenious', and 'entertaining' and accounted 'sensible', 'pathetick', 'humane', 'poignant', and even 'profitable'—that is, morally improving. Sterne himself was likened to comic or satirical writers from Juvenal and Lucian to Rabelais and Cervantes, and, among modern authors, to Swift and Fielding.

Not all was praise. Sterne had been quickly made aware by his first Yorkshire readers—though he must have known it himself—that his work would be accounted indecent, or worse. Such criticism was to make itself felt soon enough. Alongside more favourable evaluations, *Tristram Shandy* was accused of being disfigured by 'wantonness', 'bawdy', 'mean, *dirty Wit*', and 'obscenity', while its author was at best, a 'jester', at worst, 'scabby'.[29] Before he had any idea of how great a success his book would become, and still mindful of the abuse he had suffered nearly twenty years before as a political journalist, Sterne was uneasy about the censure *Tristram Shandy* might receive. He aggressively characterized critics of his work as 'squeamish' (*Letters*, 90), but he nervously exhorted one correspondent ''till you read my Tristram, do not, like some people, condemn it' (*Letters*, 77). Even amid the acclaim accorded him in London, there were moments when he wondered whether he had been right to give his own love of Rabelaisian humour so loose a rein. It was the bishop of Gloucester, Dr William Warburton—author of *The Divine Legation of Moses*, but also editor of the far from uniformly decorous works of Alexander Pope—who, on presenting Sterne with a purse of guineas, added to it an admonition to mend his style. To a man who had spent much of his life in a largely fruitless endeavour to win the favour of ecclesiastical—and lay—patrons, such a warning could not simply be ignored. It is easy to believe that words of advice recently offered by his sensible and well-intentioned friend Marmaduke Fothergill rang in his ears: 'Write & Welcome', but 'get Your Preferment first Lory!' (*Letters*, 76).

To put such prudential considerations behind him was not the work of a moment. In 1760 the propriety of any gentleman's writing for financial gain was not yet beyond dispute—the more so if the gentleman in question was also a clergyman. Earlier in the century, one of Sterne's own favourite authors—Jonathan Swift, dean of St Patrick's Cathedral, Dublin—had turned his face against profiting directly from his extensive writings. Thomas Gray, a near-exact contemporary of Sterne, and a layman, was equally insistent in declining to seek financial reward from the publication of his work, ceding his manuscripts to his publisher gratis.[30] Laurence Sterne, in the first flush of his new-found celebrity, revealed his own anxiety: 'I fear you think me very poor, or in debt', he told one correspondent. Denying that he was driven to the writing of *Tristram Shandy* by want, the struggling parson wrote, in a self-conscious protestation of independence, 'I thank God tho' I don't abound—that I have enough for a clean shirt every day—and a mutton chop—and my contentment with this, has thus far (and I hope ever will) put me above stooping an inch for . . . estate' (*Letters*, 90).

Perhaps it was recurring thoughts of a life lived out in constantly frustrated hopes of preferment and of desires confined within the narrow compass of clean shirts and mutton chops which led Sterne so rapidly to change his mind. At all events, within a few weeks change he certainly did—though it may be that he was forced to recognize how little real choice he had in the matter. On their first appearance the volumes of *Tristram Shandy* printed in York gave no indication even of their provincial origin, still less any hint as to the fact that their author was a clergyman. When that fact became known critical and polite opinion, at least in some quarters, turned hostile; it was the doubtful propriety of a clergyman's authorship of a bawdy novel which particularly exercised Bishop Warburton. Perhaps Sterne might have successfully countered criticism of the indecency of *Tristram Shandy* by the publication of his sermons, had he not chosen to profit from the success of his novel by issuing them under the provocative title of *The Sermons of Mr Yorick*.

Whatever their verdict on the sermons themselves—and despite the fact that half-a-dozen bishops were among the subscribers—reviewers were quick to condemn the impropriety of a clergyman exchanging his gown for a jester's cap. Unable easily to retreat, Sterne determined to stand his ground. Increasingly he put behind him a hesitation to incur the censure of sober clerics like Warburton, and with it his fears of the vituperation that mediocre reviewers and moralizing critics might heap upon him. In the spring of 1760 Sterne accepted that he could not simultaneously enjoy public acclaim and take refuge from its attendant ills. Forced to choose between them, he set his face against the frustrations of his past and elected to accept the abuse plentifully heaped upon him. In so doing Sterne expressed faith in his ability to retain the personal esteem of his new-found aristocratic patrons, while profiting from the commercial possibilities open to him as an author. Even as he half-heartedly endeavoured to retain Warburton's good opinion, prior to the eventual break between them, Sterne could affect to regret the misrepresentation to which his writing had laid him open and to 'wish from my heart, I had never set pen to paper, but continued hid in the quiet obscurity in which I had so long lived' (*Letters*, 116). In truth, he wished no such thing. Informing Stephen Croft in Yorkshire that '[t]here is a shilling pamphlet wrote against Tristram', Sterne added, tellingly, 'I wish they would write a hundred such' (*Letters*, 107).

They did their best. *Explanatory Remarks Upon the Life and Opinions of Tristram Shandy; wherein, the Morals and Politics of this Piece are clearly laid open, by Jeremiah Kunastrokius, M.D.*, published in the last week of April, was followed just over a fortnight later by *The Clockmakers Outcry against the*

Author of the Life and Opinions of Tristram Shandy. Thereafter, the floodgates burst open, deluging the market with imitations, parodies, burlesques, ballads and moral rejoinders. In short succession appeared *The Clockmaker's Political Humbug*, *Yorick's Meditations upon Various Interesting and Important Subjects*, *A Supplement to the Life and Opinions of Tristram Shandy*, *The Life of Jeremiah Kunastrokius*, *The Life and Opinions of Miss Suky Shandy of Bow-Street*, *Tristram Shandy in a Reverie*, and *A Shandean Essay on Human Passions, by Caleb McWhim*.[31] There was also *A Genuine Letter from a Methodist Preacher in the Country, to Laurence Sterne, M.A. Prebendary of York*, later reprinted in a pirated version under the title *A Letter from the Rev. George Whitfield, B.A. to the Rev. Laurence Sterne, M.A.* (though the author was not really the Methodist preacher), which upped the stakes in abusing Sterne and his book by suggesting that *Tristram Shandy* seemed to have been penned by 'the hand of Antichrist himself'.[32]

Writers of all kinds joined the act. Sterne's old university friend John Hall-Stevenson shocked polite readers—Warburton first among them—with two indecent 'Lyrick Epistles'. The *Grand Magazine* published an 'Admonitory Lyric EPISTLE to the Rev. Tristram Shandy'.[33] Sterne's book lent its name to a popular ballad. Before long Sterne was being lampooned alongside one of the first noblemen with whom he had dined after his arrival in London. In parody of Lyttelton's recently published *Dialogues of the Dead*, a pamphlet appeared entitled *Dialogues of the Living: Particulars between the following celebrated Personages, 1. Parson Tristram and the Revd. Mr. Sterne, on the Danger, Sin, and Folly of being Righteous Over-much*. Even broader humour was provided by a number of joke books, going under such titles as *Tristram Shandy's Bon Mots* or *Tristram Shandy's Jests*, which had no more to do with Sterne than the desire to cash in quickly on the success of his work. The most ambitious and audacious attempt to do the same thing was undertaken by a schoolmaster, John Carr, who in September 1760 anonymously published a work entitled *The Life and Opinions of Tristram Shandy, Gentleman*, Volume III, which he attempted to pass off—with some initial success—as being by Sterne himself.

Not everyone who saw in *Tristram Shandy* an opportunity for profit was a scribbler. Like *The Beggar's Opera*, *Pamela*, or *Tom Jones* before it, Sterne's work enjoyed such a degree of popular success as lent itself to rapid commercialization in many forms, so that *Tristram Shandy* (or Tristram Shandy) soon gave its name to a card-game and a soup, and later to a dance and a race-horse.[34]

The celebrity of *Tristram Shandy* seemed to know no bounds. Alongside the commercial frenzy, polite readers kept Sterne's work in the eye of fashion. In the months immediately following publication *Tristram Shandy* and its author were the subject of animated debate among many such readers, including Thomas Gray, Thomas Warton, and Horace Walpole. Copies of the novel reached appreciative readers abroad. At Geneva they improbably delighted the Scots Presbyterian minister the Revd Robert Brown, who wrote to Sterne to enquire whether he were really a clergyman. In Florence, the ageing British minister plenipotentiary, Sir Horace Mann, declared that modern literature was beyond him—but he demanded to receive volumes three and four as soon as they were published. Since many fastidious male readers professed themselves shocked by the Rabelaisian tendencies of Sterne's work, it is perhaps surprising to find that—in defiance of contemporary convention—a number of women, such as Georgina, Countess Cowper, read and enjoyed *Tristram Shandy*. Even those who, like Lady Dorothy Braidshaigh, disapproved of the book, or who, like Mary Delany, felt it better not to expose themselves to the risk of reading it, still wrote about it to their friends.[35] Early reviewers included Edmund Burke (who liked it) and Oliver Goldsmith (who did not).[36] While older readers such as Lord Bathurst and Horace Mann relished the book, it was more predictably popular with irreverent younger readers. Students at Cambridge University, which Sterne had attended almost thirty years earlier, agreed that *Tristram Shandy* was made up of the 'best & truest & most genuine original & new Humour, ridicule, satire, good sense [and] good nonsense'.[37] Their teachers, however, were not always so sure: 'Mark my words,' opined one, 'in the course of twenty years, should any one wish to refer to the book in question, he will be obliged to go to an antiquary to inquire for it.'[38]

In 1760 that critic was very much in a minority. Even those who disliked the book feared its pernicious influence. While the expense of the two volumes—the York edition cost 5*s*. bound, while the second edition published with the Dodsleys' imprint cost 4*s*. sewn—put *Tristram Shandy* (like all other new novels) outside the reach of the less than affluent, the book caused a stir far beyond the bounds of those who had actually read it. In allusion to Walter Shandy's habit of winding up the household clock before joining his wife in bed—which leads, on the night of Tristram's conception, to Mrs Shandy's celebrated question, '*Pray, my dear . . . have you not forgot to wind up the clock?*'—the author of a wittily salacious pamphlet, *The Clockmakers Outcry*, alleged that 'no modest lady now dares to mention a word about *winding-up a clock*, without exposing herself to the sly leers and jokes of the family, to her frequent confusion'.[39] Even the prostitutes who thronged London's streets were said to have taken to enquiring of prospective customers: 'Sir, will you have your clock wound-up?'[40]

Mixed its reception may have been, but the vogue for Sterne's novel in the early 1760s was so great that a hack writer could assert without exaggeration that *Tristram Shandy* 'was dedicated to a minister, read by the clergy, approved of by the wits, studyed by the merchants, gazed at by the ladies, and was become the pocket-companion of the nation'.[41] Among the wits, one newcomer to London, the youthful and ambitious James Boswell, saw the success of Laurence Sterne and his book as an augury for his own future. In some verses he penned in 1760 the 20-year-old Scotsman commented happily on the extent to which Sterne's fictional autobiography had brought its author both literary and social success:

> By Fashion's hands compleatly drest,
> He's everywhere a wellcome Guest:
> He runs about from place to place
> Now with my Lord, then W^th^ his Grace
> And mixing with the brilliant throng,
> He straight commences *Beau Garcon.*
> In Ranelagh's delightfull round
> Squire Tristram oft is flaunting found
> A buzzing whisper flys about,
> Where'er he comes they point him out;
> Each Waiter with an eager eye
> Observes him as he passes by:
> That there is he, do, Thomas! look
> Who's wrote such a damn'd clever Book.[42]

In the spring of 1760 it would have been hard to exaggerate the degree of celebrity achieved either by *Tristram Shandy* or by its author. Following the success of his own novels, Samuel Richardson had written: 'Twenty years ago I was the most obscure man in Great Britain; and now I am admitted to the company of the first characters in the kingdom.'[43] In April 1760 Sterne might have altered twenty years to as many weeks and still said, with perfect justice, the same thing about himself.

The reception accorded him in London in 1760 was something Laurence Sterne would never forget. Indeed, much of what remained of his life—a mere eight years—was spent in trying, often with success, to recapture the heady atmosphere of those weeks. By the end of May, however, having been absent for three months from his three parishes—one of which he had not yet seen—Sterne accepted that it was time to return to Yorkshire. It was to the person best placed to appreciate his changed circumstances that he confided his plans for his homecoming: 'I have bought a pair of horses for that purpose', he told Stephen Croft. His benefactor's brother, John, gives a much fuller version of Sterne's triumphal return in his own anecdotal account. Sterne, he remembered years later, 'sett up a Carriage, and came down into Yorkshire, in a superior style [so] that he soon spent the money which so liberally flowed from the Publick for the produce of his pen and the further sweat of his brow'.[44] Superior Sterne's style certainly was—when he had arrived in York as a young clergyman barely forty gentlemen in the entire city boasted their own carriage.[45] Croft's account is not unmixed with implied criticism of Sterne's extravagance, yet it is honest and accurate in acknowledging that the money the country parson lavished on his return to Yorkshire had been hard earned.

For all his adult life—and like his father before him—Sterne had been in search of personal advancement in a world still largely dominated by long-standing structures of social hierarchy, with their attendant forms of subordination. It was a world in which the hunt for preferment was unceasing and most often unrewarded. What Laurence Sterne, Gentleman, discovered in the spring of 1760 was that he owed his present success and future prospects not, or at least not principally, to long-sought-after aristocratic patronage, but to the previously unthought of—even unthinkable—world of commerce. It was the mid-eighteenth-century commercialization of literature rather than genteel birth or ecclesiastical preferment that brought Sterne both wealth and fame—and with them access to the very centre of the polite world whose fringes he had so long inhabited. Though he arrived suddenly at his destination, Sterne's progress from dependence to independence had been slow. His return to Yorkshire from London in the early summer of 1760 was a triumphal homecoming, but the road he had travelled had been wearisome.

I

Ireland and England, 1713–1738

Clonmel, Dublin, Halifax, and Hipperholme, 1713–1733

Almost half a century previously a very different journey had taken place across the southern counties of Ireland. Along with other members of his regiment and their camp-followers, an impoverished ensign, his heavily pregnant wife, and their infant daughter were making for the small wool-town of Clonmel in County Tipperary. They had recently arrived in Ireland from the French port of Dunkirk, where the regiment had been stationed. The countryside through which they passed on a late November day was not likely to have raised military spirits, still less those of an apprehensive woman close to term. Jonathan Swift, who travelled through Tipperary a few years later, wrote of the sight of 'filthy cabins, miserable, tattered, half-starved creatures, scarce in human shape . . . a bog of fifteen miles round; every meadow a slough, and every hill a mixture of rock, heath, and marsh'.[1] The ensign and his wife making this journey were Roger and Agnes Sterne. Shortly after arriving at their destination Agnes would give birth to her second child and first son, Laurence.

It was on 24 November 1713 that Laurence Sterne came into the world. The circumstances of his birth were not propitious. In a brief memoir that he wrote for his daughter Lydia in September 1758 Sterne was to declare: 'my Birth Day was not ominous to my poor Father, who was that Day with many other Brave Officers broke & sent a Drift into the wide world, with a Wife & two Children.'[2] That Sterne should have been told—and should have remembered—that his birth exactly coincided with the breaking of the regiment is as revealing as the fact that he should have felt it worth repeating. Among several scraps of inaccurate or imperfectly recalled information, this detail is correct. Following a dozen years of fighting, and bitter political controversy in England, the Treaty of Utrecht brought an end to the War of the Spanish Succession in 1713. In line with one of the provisions of the treaty the partial dismantling of the fortifications of Dunkirk began immediately, and the strength of the British army was reduced. Among the regiments disbanded in 1713 was Chudleigh's 34th Regiment of Foot in which the 30-year-old Roger Sterne was serving as an ensign. The order was signed on the very day his first son was born. That son would himself recall the Peace of Utrecht and the breaking of the military on more than one occasion many years into the future. As a political journalist in the 1740s he bitterly denounced those who criticized the notion of a standing army, declaring that: 'As for the Army, it has been complain'd of ever since an unhappy and *deluded* Queen broke Hers, at the Instigation of a *Treacherous* Ministry, to pave the way for the Pretender.'[3] Two decades later still Sterne wrote in *Tristram Shandy* of the effect of these events on Tristam's uncle, Captain Toby Shandy: '*Calais* itself left not a deeper scar in *Mary*'s heart, than *Utrecht* upon my uncle *Toby*'s. To the end of his life he never could hear *Utrecht* mentioned . . . without fetching a sigh, as if his heart would break in twain' (*TS* VI. xxxi. 367).

In 1713 Roger Sterne could have been scarcely less affected, at least by the breaking of his regiment. Reduced to half pay and possessed of no independent fortune, the young officer was obliged to return to his family home in the north of England in search of protection for himself and his wife and young children. With a new born infant to think of, the family delayed their journey for six months until Laurence was thought able to travel with tolerable safety. As a result, it was early in the summer of 1714 that the Sternes finally arrived in Yorkshire. Once there, Roger Sterne had leisure enough to contemplate the consequences of his decision of a few years earlier to leave his mother and siblings in order to try his fortune as a soldier. It was bad enough to be reliant once more on the family he had only recently left in order to assert his independence. More serious was the prospect that stretched before him. Wealthier brother-officers of his own age and younger could hope to advance rapidly in their military careers by acquiring commissions they had the means to purchase. Lacking such means, Roger Sterne would spend the next sixteen years in search of a promotion which would eventually arrive only months before his death in 1731.

For Laurence Sterne, the consequences of his father's situation would be felt throughout his own life. It was not only that his childhood would be harsh and unsettled, a long series of decampments from one barracks, one country, to another, whose most notable points of reference were the births and—usually—the early deaths of brothers and sisters. Nor was it simply that Laurence's boyhood and adolescence would be lived under the shadow of uncertainty as to the availability of financial support such as would enable him to study and eventually take his place in a profession suitable to his family's social position. The true significance of Laurence Sterne's earliest experiences lies in the fact that the greater part of his life, until he published the first volumes of *Tristram Shandy* at the age of 46, was to be spent in a continual struggle to achieve worldly success—an endeavour repeatedly frustrated by insufficient funds and inadequate interest. What he had of both, Laurence Sterne certainly owed to his father's family, but it was due to his father also that he had so little of either. Roger Sterne's career offered a parallel to Laurence's own, and was, in a sense, the cause of it.

The precarious position of Roger Sterne at the time of his son's birth was the more distressing, both to him and to his relations, as the Sternes were a family of some note.[4] Among Roger Sterne's relations were men distinguished in the Church and medicine. Originally from the eastern counties of England, some Sternes had moved north into Yorkshire, while others settled in Ireland, establishing a collateral branch there whose members included both John Stearne (1624–69), the founder of the Irish College of Physicians, and his son, also John (1660–1745), who was Jonathan Swift's immediate predecessor as dean of St Patrick's Cathedral, Dublin, and subsequently bishop of Dromore, and later of Clogher. From among the line of minor gentry who made up the bulk of the novelist's English ancestors one figure stood out. This was Richard Sterne, a cleric of even greater eminence than John Stearne, whose ecclesiastical career culminated in his elevation to the archbishopric of York in 1664.

Born at the end of the sixteenth century, Richard Sterne achieved prominence in the worlds of both the Church and learning. A student of Trinity College, Cambridge, he was subsequently elected a fellow of Corpus Christi College and taught there for a decade. Appointed a chaplain to Archbishop Laud in 1633, Sterne was chosen in the following year by the bishop of Ely to be master of Jesus College, Cambridge, an appointment that was to have significant repercussions in the life of Laurence Sterne. A fervent royalist, Sterne directed not only money but the college plate to the service on Charles I, for which action he subsequently found himself not only stripped of the mastership of Jesus College, but also imprisoned for three years by Oliver Cromwell. When Archbishop Laud was executed in 1645 Richard Sterne was among the clergy, selected from among the archbishop's chaplains, to attend him on the scaffold. Though freed from imprisonment shortly afterwards, Richard Sterne necessarily lived apart from public life until the Restoration of Charles II in 1660, when he was reappointed master of Jesus College. Raised to the episcopate as bishop of Carlisle, Sterne was translated to the See of York four years later, holding it until his death in 1683.

At his death Archbishop Sterne left a large sum of money for the rebuilding, after the Great Fire, of St Paul's Cathedral in London, and established a number of scholarships at both Corpus Christi and Jesus College, Cambridge. It was one of these scholarships, at Jesus College, that chiefly enabled Laurence Sterne to enjoy the invaluable advantages of a university education and a degree half-a-century later. Whatever Richard Sterne's enemies might allege of him—Bishop Gilbert Burnet accused him of using his office for the 'enriching of his family'[5]—Sterne's ancestor was a man of undoubted eminence, distinguished enough for any eighteenth-century gentleman to look to happily as a forebear. In the 'Memoirs' Sterne characterizes his father as 'Grandson to Arch Bishop Sterne',[6] and even once he had begun to gain celebrity on his own account he recalled the family connexion with evident pride when writing to a fellow-clergyman and admirer of *Tristram Shandy*.[7]

Of Archbishop Sterne's thirteen children, three sons survived infancy. Of these, Simon Sterne, the novelist's grandfather, was the third.[8] The portion of the family fortune he inherited—£500 and the remission of his outstanding debts to his father—was sufficient to make him a suitable husband for a local woman, Mary Jaques. Mary was herself heiress to a large estate at Elvington, near York, which had been purchased by her grandfather Sir Roger Jaques, a notable merchant and chief magistrate of York, knighted by Charles I. Simon and Mary Sterne had at least nine children, five sons and four daughters. Roger Sterne, the novelist's father, was the third (and second surviving) son. Laurence himself, then, was born the son of a younger son of a younger son at a time when the English system of primogeniture concentrated most of any family's wealth, and virtually all of its land, on the eldest male. If this were not misfortune enough, Laurence Sterne was also the son of, by eighteenth-century standards, a decidedly imprudent father.

Roger Sterne was born in 1683.[9] When he was 19, his father Simon Sterne died, leaving Roger's elder brother, another Richard Sterne, as head of the family at the age of 22. Richard Sterne lived at Woodhouse, near Halifax, where his father had moved in 1688. His mother, Mary, resided on her own estate at Elvington, where her son Roger continued to live for some time after his father's death. During the winter of 1708–9, when he was already 25, Roger Sterne decided to leave home to join the army. Possibly his decision was affected in some way by the death of his brother Simon earlier in 1708, or perhaps he quarrelled with his family.

Whatever the truth, the reasons for his decision are intriguing, for he enlisted without a commission—the most inauspicious circumstance possible for a young man of his social position. Perhaps, with the nation at war, he hoped to win a field commission.[10] If so Roger's hopes of quick promotion were disappointed, for his commission was finally signed only in July 1710, after he had already seen action in Flanders, serving at the sieges of Douai and Béthune. As a newly commissioned ensign he commanded a platoon at the sieges of Aire, St Venant, and Bouchain, during which the allied forces sustained heavy casualties.

At the age of 27, Roger Sterne was an officer. As an ensign, however, he held the lowliest of commissions and furthermore lacked the financial resources necessary to ensure his promotion in any immediate future. Yet, little over a year later, he married. His wife was Agnes Hobert, described by Laurence Sterne as 'widow of an Officer, I think a Captain, of a good Family'.[11] Agnes Sterne herself, however, was from humbler background than either of her husbands, being the stepdaughter of a sutler, or military provisioner, a man her son would variously describe as a 'noted Suttler' and 'a poor suttler who followed the Camp in Flanders'.[12] The circumstances in which the latter description was written makes this more slighting characterization decidedly suspect, but in either case Agnes's father followed a trade humble enough to make his daughter's social position a considerable contrast with that of the son of a landed gentleman and grandson of an archbishop of York.

To his second account of his father's marriage Laurence Sterne added a curt note with regard to the impecunious ensign's new father-in-law: 'NB (he was in debt to him).'[13] This memoir account, it is true, may well have been tinged with an element of resentment, for in the years before it was written Sterne, exasperated by his mother's financial demands on him, had become estranged from her.[14] Yet whether accurate or not, the reason to which Sterne attributed his parents' marriage vividly indicates the disparity he perceived in the respective social situations of his father and mother. Whatever the truth of the matter, Agnes Hobert's notable qualities of mind or person brought her not one but two officers as husbands. She may have had beauty, for Laurence Sterne later described his elder sister Mary as 'a most beautiful woman, of a fine Figure', while a more impartial observer accounted his younger sister Catherine 'one of the finest women ever seen'.[15] Regardless of the reasons that prompted Roger Sterne to propose marriage to Agnes Hobert, one fact is beyond dispute: the marriage was not, for him, socially advantageous. It was also to prove the prelude to a hard life for Agnes.

The ten months that Agnes Sterne passed with her husband's family after the disbanding of the regiment was perhaps as much a trial for her as for them. Stepdaughter of a sutler and widow and wife of soldiers, Agnes had spent her entire life in military surroundings. The abrupt shift to life in a cottage on her mother-in-law's estate must have been disconcerting. For whatever reason—and there are grounds for believing that her character was not the most amiable—Agnes failed to gain the affection of her newly acquired relations. Nearly twenty years later, after Roger's death, Agnes made the far-from-easy trip from Ireland to England, seeking assistance in transferring her widow's pension from the Irish to the English establishment. She hoped to invoke the assistance of her husband's brother Jaques; in the event, he refused even to see her and she was forced to return home without success.[16]

Despite the uncertainties and possible humiliations involved in living in unfamiliar surroundings in close proximity to a mother-in-law on whom she was financially dependent, the months following the raising of the 34th Foot in July 1715 were scarcely an improvement for Agnes Sterne. The regiment was raised in the face of the imminent threat of a rebellion designed to restore the Stuarts to the throne, and posted to Ireland in order to contain any disturbance there. The entire family, Sterne was later to write, decamped 'Bag & Baggage' for Dublin. In 1715 the Irish capital, with a population of over 100,000, was large by European standards. It was also well garrisoned, the Royal Barracks at Oxmantown Green being capable of holding four regiments each of cavalry and infantry.[17] Within a month of their arrival in Dublin, however, Roger Sterne was ordered back to England. '[I]n a sad Winter, my Mother & her two Children followed him, travelling from Liverpool by Land to Plymouth[1715]. (melancholly Description of this Journy not necessary to be transmitted here)', Sterne wrote.[18] The cause of this rapid change of posting for Roger Sterne's regiment was the complete failure of Jacobites in Ireland to raise popular support for the rebellion, which had begun early in September 1715. Instead, the Jacobite forces in Scotland moved south in the expectation that the predominantly Tory shires of the south-west of England would rise in support of the Pretender. It was to reinforce the Hanoverian forces there that Roger Sterne's regiment was transferred so rapidly to Devon. As Laurence Sterne certainly knew when writing his memoir, the rebels were led by James Butler, duke of Ormonde—who has a role, of sorts, to play in *Tristram Shandy*. In fact, the government in London had acted with such dispatch that Ormonde, bereft of support, did not even attempt a landing. The rebellion was quickly defeated, exemplary punishment meted out to the rebels, and within a year the Sternes were back in Dublin.

By this time the family had once more grown in size; another boy, Joram, had been born in Plymouth. Then began the most settled, and most prosperous, period of Laurence Sterne's boyhood. While his elder brother had inherited their father's estate at Woodhouse, near Halifax, Roger Sterne and his sole surviving brother, Jaques, had been left land which they received when Jaques came of age in 1717. His father's inheritance was quickly disposed of, the lands being mortgaged or sold. The result, Sterne recorded, was that 'My Father took a large house [in Dublin], furnishd it, & in a year and a halfs Time Spent a great deal of Mony'.[19] The Sternes' prosperity was short lived. Roger's improvidence meant that the family was soon dependent once more on his ensign's pay—a total of less than £70 a year. Nor did this more settled period endure much longer: in 1719 'all unhingd again'.[20] This time the regiment was ordered to the Isle of Wight, where it would embark for Vigo as part of an expedition commanded by Lord Cobham in the war against Spain. For a mother and young children even the journey to England was an arduous one. The ship on which they were travelling was driven by bad weather into Milford Haven, and the Sternes finally disembarked at Bristol, from where they proceeded overland to Plymouth, and hence to the Isle of Wight. It is a telling indication of the atmosphere in which Laurence Sterne spent his earliest years that he includes only parenthetically in his account of their journey what must today seem the most distressing feature of it: '(In this Exped[itio]n . . . from Bristol to Ham[p]shire we lost poor Joram, a pretty Boy 4 Years old, of the small Pox.)'[21]

Throughout the period of the expedition to Vigo, which was stormed and captured by the English forces in October 1719, Agnes Sterne and her young family remained on the Isle of Wight. While there Agnes gave birth to her fourth child, Anne, on 23 September 1719. When the victorious English troops returned from Spain, however, Roger Sterne's regiment was sent once more to Ireland. It was from there that Roger was able to send for his wife and children to join him. Caught in a storm on the voyage from the Isle of Wight to Ireland, the ship on which Agnes and her children were travelling sought shelter in a Welsh harbour, although only, in Sterne's account, after his mother had pleaded with the captain. Having remained for a month in Wales, Agnes and her children eventually reached Dublin, from where they travelled south along the coast to the small county town of Wicklow. It was there that they were at last reunited with Roger Sterne who had, by this time, given up his family for lost.

Throughout 1720, by Sterne's own account, the family remained together in the Wicklow barracks, where a third son was born and named Devischer, after Abraham Devischer, a fellow soldier. The career of Abraham Devischer, of Flemish descent, suggests vividly the frustrations experienced by Roger Sterne as a junior officer devoid equally of money and of influential friends. First commissioned in 1711, a year later than Roger Sterne, Devischer was a captain by 1714 and a lieutenant-colonel by April 1720. By contrast, Roger Sterne, despite a decade or more of service, remained a lowly ensign.

After their year in the Wicklow barracks the Sternes 'decamped' for a six-month stay with a relative of Agnes Sterne, a clergyman named Mr Featherstone who lived in the small village of Annamoe, among mountains a few miles inland from the county town. 'It was in this Parish,' Sterne later informed his daughter, 'That I had that wonderful Escape in falling thro a Mill Race whilst the Mill was going—and of being taken up unhurt.——The story is Incredible—But known for Truth in all that part of Ireland, where hundreds of the Common people flocked to see me.'[22] Though Sterne was at pains to assert the authenticity of this 'incredible' tale, one singular circumstance tends to throw doubt on it. A virtually identical story is told of Sterne's great-grandfather Richard, the future archbishop of York. He, indeed, went one better by enjoying a second miraculous deliverance. Not only did he fall into a sluice that carried him unscathed beneath a revolving mill-wheel, he fell also from a church steeple where he was unwisely playing at see-saw. In both cases, the survival of Sterne's illustrious ancestor was attributed to a 'gracious Providence'.[23] When Sterne wrote down the story of his own supposed escape he gave no indication of being familiar with the anecdote concerning his great-grandfather. Is it possible that he had heard the story as a young child and later, growing up away from his family, mistakenly appropriated it to himself? It is certainly conceivable, for the tale is of a kind characteristically associated with those reserved for greatness, and from an early age Laurence Sterne clung to the flimsiest reasons for believing in his own future eminence.

From Annamoe Roger Sterne and his family moved once more to the barracks in Dublin. 'In this year 1721,' Laurence Sterne later recalled, '[I] learnd to write, &c;'[24] he was then in his eighth year. It was at this time too that Anne died. 'This pretty Blossom fell off at the Age of three years in the Barracks of Dublin,' Sterne recalled; 'She Was, as I well remember, of a fine, delicate frame not made to last long, as were most of my fathers Babes.'[25] In 1722 the family was on the move again, this time to

Carrickfergus in County Antrim, on the north side of Belfast Lough. They got no further than Drogheda, some thirty miles north of Dublin. From there they were ordered forty miles west to Mullingar, 'where by Providence we stumbled upon a kind Relation, a Collateral Descendant from Arch Bishop Sterne—who took us all to his Castle and kindly entreated us for a Year'.[26]

The relation so providentially found was a man of whom a humble ensign such as Roger Sterne might well have been in awe: Brigadier-General Robert Stearne, of Tullynally Castle in Westmeath.[27] A brother of John Stearne, bishop of Clogher, Robert Stearne had formerly served in the Royal Regiment of Foot in Ireland, taking command of it in 1712, before leaving the regiment five years later to take possession of his estate in Ireland.[28] The brigadier-general was also governor of the Royal Hospital at Kilmainham, on the outskirts of Dublin: a splendid hospital for military pensioners, built to a design by the Irish surveyor-general William Robinson, after the example of Les Invalides in Paris. The regiment in which Stearne served was an infantry regiment whose royal appellation had been awarded as a distinction for its behaviour at the siege of Namur in 1695. It was at this siege—when English troops under William III regained Namur from the French—that Uncle Toby received the wound in the groin which forced him from army service, worrying the Widow Wadman and forming an important thread in the narrative of *Tristram Shandy*. Robert Stearne had himself been present at the siege of Namur, which he described as 'undoubtedly ye Most desperate that had been made in ye Memory of man'[29]—though he was more fortunate than Uncle Toby, surviving no fewer than '7 Field Battles 15 Sieges, 7 Grand Attacks on Counter Scharps & breaches', without ever losing a drop of blood. In the circumstances, it is scarcely fanciful to believe that the tale of so famous an action was related, more than once perhaps, in a manner likely to have appealed greatly to an 8-year-old boy brought up in military surroundings. Certainly, the interlude remained vividly in Laurence Sterne's memory many years later as a happy change from the life of the barracks. To Roger and Agnes Sterne the stay brought unaccustomed physical comforts and ready access to social circles previously denied them. Roger Sterne may have been an officer and a gentleman, but the social circle of an army ensign in the Ireland of the 1710s and 1720s would have been humble enough. When military duty eventually forced the family to take leave of their most generous relative—one of the very few such that Laurence Sterne was to know in his life—they were, Sterne remembered, 'loadend with kindnesses, &c'.[30]

Welcome as the twelve-month respite had been, life now continued much as before. '[A] most Rueful & tedious Journy had We all',[31] Sterne wrote of their departure. And there was worse ahead than the fatigues of the road. Roger Sterne had earlier travelled south to collect his young son Devischer, who had been sent to nurse in a farmhouse near Wicklow. At the age of 3, Devischer died. Having briefly memorialized his young brother, Sterne continued laconically: 'Another sent to fill his Place, Susan—this Babe too left us behind——in this weary Journy.'[32] In ten years of virtually continual camp-following Agnes Sterne had borne six children, of whom just two were still living. The Sternes were to have one more child, a daughter, Catherine, born in Derry in March 1725. She would survive—eventually to become an unwelcome embarrassment to her brother, who described her as 'most unhappily estranged from me by my Uncle's Wickedness & her own folly'.[33]

The earliest distinct period in Sterne's life was drawing to a close. His first ten years had passed in circumstances far from ideal for any child. His father was frequently absent, at times on active service with the added insecurities that involved. The family had never lived in any one place for more than a year. Instead, Sterne's earliest experiences were of a peripatetic existence, life in barracks being punctuated by frequent journeys—lengthy, arduous, and at times dangerous—by land and sea. At times the noise and colour, the real and reflected glory of military life doubtless excited the young boy, but the memories Sterne retained in later life were more sombre: the births and early deaths of four brothers and sisters. Outside of the barracks the Sternes enjoyed an uncertain social status, briefly affluent but living for the most part in an atmosphere of financial insecurity and partial dependency, at first on Laurence's paternal grandmother and later on distant Irish relatives.

In 1723 or 1724 Laurence Sterne experienced an even more dramatic change in his life: 'the Autumn of that Year or the Spring after, I forget w^{ch}, my father got leave of His Colonel to go to England on purpose to fix me at School. wch he did, near Halyfax.'[34] Laurence would never see Ireland or his father again.[35]

Having settled his son, Roger Sterne left England to return to his regiment in Ireland. His future military career would continue for almost the remainder of his life as disappointingly as before. In 1727 the regiment left Derry for Gibraltar—acquired by Britain under the terms of the Treaty of Utrecht—then under siege by the Spanish. The ensign left his wife and two surviving daughters to the hardships of a life in an Ireland characterized, in the years of his absence, by failed crops and famine, misery, and want. It is unlikely that he saw any of them again. After a difficult voyage Roger Sterne reached his destination on 26 March 1727. Having helped secure the Rock against the attackers, the regiment remained there, subject to unpleasant conditions including outbreaks of dysentery, for three years, as part of a strengthened garrison. While in Gibraltar Roger Sterne fought a duel with a Captain Philips, during which he was run through the body. In one account his antagonist was reported to have struck Sterne with such force as to pin him to the wall; Sterne had apparently the presence of mind to request Philips to brush off any plaster stuck to the point of his sword before withdrawing the blade.[36] Although he survived—'with much difficulty'—it was with an impaired constitution that, his son would write, hastened his death. If, in reading Sterne's affectionate account of his father, it is difficult not to see him as at least a partial model for the good-natured soldier Uncle Toby in *Tristram Shandy*, then is tempting to regard Roger Sterne's encounter with Captain Philips as one of those foolish, uncontrollable occurrences so familiar in the novel—an event whose consequences are out of all proportion to their cause. The duel which so nearly cost Roger his life was fought, Laurence Sterne alleged, 'about a Goose'.[37]

After almost four years in Gibraltar the 34th Foot was ordered to Jamaica, ostensibly to help suppress a rebellion of black slaves, but in fact in an attempt to encourage soldiers to settle there. The regiment landed in February 1731, and Ensign Sterne was part of a detachment dispatched to Port Antonio, on the northern coast of the island. The true situation now became apparent. There was no rebellion; instead the troops, weakened by malnutrition during their long voyage, faced a more deadly enemy—the island itself. The discomforts of an unfamiliar and unhealthy climate were compounded by inadequate barracks and provisions. Within a month a combination of malarial fever and rum was taking a serious toll among the soldiers. The colonel himself died in March, along with many of the officers and men. In such extreme circumstances Roger Sterne at last received the promotion for which he had waited for twenty-three years, being made a lieutenant on 19 March. Whatever elation he may have felt was short-lived. Less than five months later Roger Sterne fell victim to malaria and died, in Port Antonio, on 31 July 1731.[38] He was 48 years old.

In his memoir Sterne relates that his father 'soon fell by the Country fever, wch took away his Senses first, and made a Child of him, and then in a Month or two, he dyed walking about continually without complaining till the Moment he sat down in an Arm Chair, and breathd his Last'.[39]

Thirty-five years after his father had taken his leave of him for the last time at the age of 10, Sterne offered his 10-year-old daughter this account:

> my Father was a little Smart Man—active to the last Degree in all Exercises—most patient of Fatigue and Disappointm^{ts} of wch it pleased God to give him full Measure—He was in his Temper some what Rapid & Hasty—but of a kindly sweet Disposition—void of all Designe; & so innocent in his own Intentions, That he suspected no one, So that you might have cheated him ten times in a Day—if nine had not been sufficient.[40]

Emphasizing as it does the soldier's kindliness, amiability, and innocence, this touchingly warm account recalls Uncle Toby even more strongly (and indeed Sterne was later to have Tristram apply the last phrase of the account to Toby[41]). It is also a description written for his young daughter by a man—little younger than his father had been when he died and himself long made conscious by incurable illness of the precariousness of his existence—who seems to have hoped that a similar filial piety might inform her view of himself. 'I have sent down these particulars relating to my family & Self, for my Lydia, In Case hereafter She might have a Curiosity or a kinder Motive to know them', he noted.[42]

Such details as we know of Roger Sterne—the serving soldier's personal journeys to pick up Devischer from the nurse in Wicklow and to accompany Laurence to school in England, for instance—suggest a notably strong sense of affection for his children. Sterne's brief sketch, however, hints at more than the remembered love of a long-dead father. In characterizing Roger's life as one marked by constant hardship and repeated disappointment, spent in continually deferred hopes of a promotion which arrived only months before his early death, Sterne was also describing his own experience, marked as it had been by a series of failures to achieve success either in his public or private life. As he acknowledged himself, Sterne's recollections were the product of 'a pensive Moode'.[43] A decade later the successful author could imaginatively mend his father's injuries, as he appears to do in three related episodes in *A Sentimental Journey*. In one, 'THE STARLING. ROAD TO VERSAILLES', Sterne included his own family's coat-of-arms, sign of his father's and his own gentility (with the addition of the starling who cries constantly 'I can't get out'),[44] while in both 'THE PATISSER. VERSAILLES' and 'THE SWORD. RENNES', he portrays the loss—and subsequent retrieval—of genteel status. In 'THE PATISSER. VERSAILLES', Yorick hears the story of the Chevalier de St Louis whom he encounters selling pâtés:

> He told me in a few words, that the best part of his life had pass'd in the service, in which, after spending a small patrimony, he had obtain'd a company and the croix with it; but that at the conclusion of the last peace, his regiment being reformed, and the whole corps, with those of some other regiments, left without any provision—he found himself in a wide world without friends, without a livre—and indeed, said he, without any thing but this—(pointing, as he said it, to his croix)—The poor chevalier won my pity, and finish'd off the scene, with winning my esteem too. (*ASJ* 210)[45]

Sterne provides a happier ending to this old soldier's tale than that which awaited his unfortunate father, for the king, hearing the chevalier's story, awards him an annual pension of 1,500 livres. By 1768 Sterne had known great success of his own, but there is good reason to think that the example of Roger Sterne served throughout his son's life as a reminder of the likely frustration of the aspirations and expectations of merit.

The young boy whom Roger Sterne left with his brother's family in England in 1723 was doubtless more sanguine in his ideas of what he might expect from life than the middle-aged Sterne, yet he was surely apprehensive too. Not only had he spent most of his first ten years in a country unknown to his relations, but also in military surroundings equally unfamiliar to them. Moreover, Laurence's uncle, Richard Sterne, who as head of the family took the boy under his protection, had little affection either for his brother Roger or for his nephew, taking responsibility for the latter merely out of a strict sense of family duty. That he took Laurence into his protection at all indicates there was no absolute breach between Richard Sterne and his younger brother, but relations between them appear to have been strained by Roger's imprudent enlistment in the army and his socially disadvantageous marriage. It was at their mother's home in Elvington that Roger Sterne and his young family took refuge after the regiment was reduced in 1713, although Richard was by then head of the family. Nor does Richard seem to have been more helpful than his brother Jaques to Roger's widow Agnes after the lieutenant's death in 1731. Strikingly, the arrangement Roger Sterne came to with his elder brother included the agreement that Laurence would redeem the entire cost of his upkeep and education as soon as he was able to do so.[46] All in all, Richard Sterne was a very different figure from Laurence's father, and it is certain that the warm fraternal friendship of Walter and Toby Shandy, poignantly evoked by Tristram, had no counterpart in Sterne's own youthful experience.

When Sterne arrived in England in 1723 Richard Sterne was living at

Woodhouse, on the River Calder west of Halifax. Daniel Defoe described the surrounding area at length in his *A Tour through the Whole Island of Great Britain* (1724–6), detailing the prosperity of the local textile trade, founded on the plentiful water and coal.[47] In the early eighteenth century Halifax itself impressed contemporaries by its populousness, industry, and wealth, especially on market days.[48] To the young Sterne, who had known Dublin, it would have seemed less remarkable—though he was certainly familiar with the town and its early-fifteenth-century parish church, with its life-size wooden figure of the alms-gathering beggar 'Old Tristram'. Richard Sterne's home, on the other hand, was a far cry from most that Laurence had known: a solid, three-storey house of Tudor origins, commanding extensive views of the Calder valley, its steep hillsides 'spread with houses, and that very thick'.[49] Richard Sterne himself was a considerable landowner and, in consequence, a notable figure in the locality: a governor of schools and workhouses and a justice of the peace. He was also a strong supporter of the Whig prime minister Robert Walpole. Given Richard Sterne's position, his nephew would certainly have acquired by association a social position quite distinct from that he had known as the son of a lowly ensign ageing in the service. The bitterness he later revealed towards his uncle, however, suggests that he was always made aware that he was in Yorkshire on sufferance. If for no other reason, the financial arrangement his father had entered into on his behalf ensured that from an early age Sterne was necessarily conscious of the difference between the socially enviable positions of his uncle and cousins and his own.

In fact, Sterne probably spent little time in his uncle's home at Woodhouse. The school he attended was in Hipperholme, a village with which the Sternes had strong connections: family members were baptized and married in the local Coley Chapel, one of a dozen or more chapels of ease which catered for the thriving population of the exceptionally far-flung parish of Halifax, one of the largest in England.[50] More importantly, Richard Sterne was a governor of Hipperholme School, an obvious reason for his nephew to receive his education there. Perched on the steep slopes of the hills above the river, Hipperholme was far enough from Woodhouse to deter frequent visits. In any case, eighteenth-century school holidays were short, and it is likely that for most of his time there Sterne boarded at Hipperholme.

In an age when the poor standard of teaching was increasingly the matter of comment and complaint, Sterne was fortunate in finding the school under the control of an 'able' master, Nathan Sharpe, who had distant connections with the Sternes.[51] A native of Hipperholme, Sharpe had graduated from Jesus College, Cambridge—the college Laurence Sterne himself would later attend—before returning to take up the post of schoolmaster in 1697. Like other schoolmasters of the day he was an ordained clergyman, who became curate of Coley Chapel in 1703. Thereafter, Sharpe remained in Hipperholme until his death, some thirty years later.

The precise curriculum Sterne followed is not known, but in the early eighteenth century there was remarkably little variation in the education offered by schools of the type Sterne attended. Even much later in the century Yorkshire seems to have been conservative enough in terms of curricular development: the grammar school at Coxwold, where Sterne was vicar in the 1760s, taught only Latin and Greek.[52] Despite the changing needs of a society increasingly devoted to manufacture and trade, the classics were still considered of paramount importance, at least by schoolmasters. Favoured authors included Virgil, Ovid, Horace, Caesar, and Cicero among the Romans, and among the Greeks, Homer and Hesiod. Arithmetic and some geometry were probably taught, perhaps alongside English composition. Pupils who made sufficient progress in their basic subjects may have had the opportunity to study some history, geography, and a little science. Even if they were available, however, it is not certain that Sterne would have been able to take advantage of them, for most subjects beyond those comprising the traditional classical education were taught only to pupils whose parents or guardians were prepared to pay extra. What is certain is that eighteenth-century schools considered it a significant part of their function to instruct their pupils in a due deference, preparing them for the different stations of life they would enter. Whether Richard Sterne would have thought it necessary to have paid any additional fee for supplementary tuition is, at best, doubtful. In the memoir he wrote for Lydia, Sterne does not even mention his uncle, who was to die in 1732, saying merely that he stayed at school with Nathan Sharpe 'till by Gods Care of me, My Cos: Sterne of Elvington became a father to me, & sent me to the University'.[53] It was this cousin, also Richard Sterne, who was to be the dominant figure in the young boy's life after he left his family in Ireland.

If his uncle had social position and a sense of duty, then his cousin Richard offered Sterne affection and friendship. He also had interests that coincided with and perhaps influenced Laurence's own—though not his riding to hounds, an activity which held no appeal to Sterne physically or temperamentally. At Woodhouse there was a library inherited by Richard from his father that Sterne must have envied, while the younger Richard showed an early interest in polite literature, subscribing to Lewis Theobald's edition of Shakespeare while still an undergraduate at Jesus College, Cambridge.[54] Such luxuries were well beyond the reach of Laurence Sterne—and it was only after the success of *Tristram Shandy* that he was at last able to indulge his eclectic taste in books (as he then did with unfeigned delight).[55]

It is not to be imagined, of course, that Sterne did nothing between the ages of 10 and 20 except envy his cousins and compare his lot in life unfavourably with theirs. Yet there are small signs that he never did—perhaps never could—forget the precariousness of his own social position. Sterne's nineteenth-century biographer, Percy Fitzgerald, described a soiled, dirty Latin textbook, *Synopsis Communium Locorum ex Poetis Latinis Collecta*, in which every page was:

> scrawled over with writing, sketches, repetitions of his own name and those of his fellows. Everywhere is repeated 'L.S., 1728,' the letters being sometimes twisted together in the shape of a monogram . . . on nearly every page of this dog-eared volume is displayed some rude drawing or sketch done after the favourite schoolboy rules of art. One curious, long-nosed, long-chinned face has written over it, '*This is Lorence*' . . . . There are owls, and cocks and hens . . . and several . . . soldiers.[56]

If Fitzgerald's account makes these early artistic efforts seem for the most part entirely unremarkable, in retrospect one stands out. Besides depictions of the soldiers among whom he grew up, there is a picture of 'A gentleman', so labelled by the youthful Sterne. Here, it would seem, family history and his youthful environment combined to stimulate Sterne to think from an early age of ways in which he might himself protect his claims to the status of gentleman—threatened by his father's improvidence—and make his own mark on life. From such casually surviving evidence as his defaced Latin textbook, Sterne appears to have been an ordinary enough, if possibly insecure, schoolboy. Young as he was, though, Laurence had ambitions, and by his own later account displayed talents such as might justify them. Writing for Lydia, Sterne insisted that he could not omit mentioning an anecdote of his schooldays with Nathan Sharpe:

> He had the cieling of the school-room new white-washed—the ladder remained there—I one unlucky day mounted it, and wrote with a brush in large capital letters, LAU. STERNE, for which the usher

> severely whipped me. My master was very much hurt at this, and said, before me, that never should that name be effaced, for I was a boy of genius, and he was sure I should come to preferment—this expression made me forget the stripes I had received.[57]

A boy of genius? For many years after leaving school he gave little evidence of genius of any kind. Yet on such scraps, so vividly recalled more than thirty years later, did Laurence Sterne feed his early ambition.

Cambridge, St Ives, and Catton, 1733–1738

In the autumn of 1733, some ten years after he had arrived from Ireland, Sterne finally took his leave of Hipperholme and Woodhouse, travelling south to begin his studies at Jesus College, Cambridge. When he arrived at Cambridge in November 1733 he was already 20, and as such rather older than was the norm for students entering university in the eighteenth century. By Sterne's own account, the reason for the late start to his university studies related to the death of his uncle. Richard Sterne had died a year before in October 1732, leaving his son, the younger Richard, as head of the family. Unlike the loss of his father, who had succumbed to fever in Jamaica fourteen months earlier, his uncle's death is unlikely to have caused Sterne to grieve. Indeed, its timing may have been exceedingly fortunate, for there is no indication that a university education formed any part of the elder Richard Sterne's plans for his orphaned nephew. All of Sterne's gratitude in this regard was reserved for his cousin. Apart from the warm tribute he paid him many years later in the memoir, Sterne was also to contrast the younger Richard's kindness with the distinct lack of sympathy shown him by his one surviving uncle, Jaques. By the time Laurence recalled those days, in a letter written to Jaques in 1751, relations between uncle and nephew were especially sour. Feeling himself once more unjustly treated by his relations, Sterne certainly had no reason to praise Jaques at this juncture, yet the very fact that he was addressing a lengthy and reasoned justification of his own conduct to his uncle suggests that his account of the contrasting behaviour of his cousin and uncle was essentially correct. 'It is not necessary for my Defence,' Sterne declared,

> to go so far back as the loss of my Father Y[r] Brother; Whose Death left me at the Age of 16 [in fact 17] without one Shilling in the World, and I may add, *at that time* without One Friend in it, except my Cosin Sterne of Elvington who became a father to Me, & to whose Protection *then*, I cheifly owe What I now am; for as you absolutely refused giving me any aid at my Father's Death, You are Sensible, without *his*, I should have

> been driven out naked into the World, Young as I was, to have shifted for myself as well as I could. (*Letters*, 34)

What Sterne might have done in these circumstances is a matter of speculation. It is not, however, speculative to note that without education, influence, or money Sterne's life would certainly have taken a very different course.[58] Then, in order to earn a living, he would have been forced to turn his attentions to some comparatively humble occupation, of a kind almost certain to have compromised his social position as a gentleman. Instead, Sterne found himself fortuitously saved from that unwelcome prospect and offered the means to study for a Cambridge degree, which brought with it possibilities of a career in a profession. No wonder, then, that Sterne remained grateful for his cousin's generosity throughout his life or that he retained a lively sense of injury at his uncle Jaques's refusal to help him in a similar manner.

Laurence Sterne was enrolled in Jesus College *in absentia* on 6 July 1733. The choice of Jesus was entirely predictable, for it was the college of which Sterne's great-grandfather had been Master in the seventeenth century and family connections continued to be strong. His cousin Richard had himself recently been an undergraduate—though as a future head of a landowning family he had felt under no obligation to take a degree. More important than reasons of sentiment or tradition, however, was the fact that, among his charities at his death, Archbishop Sterne had established six scholarships—four at Jesus College and two at Corpus Christi—for poor boys who were natives of Nottinghamshire and Yorkshire. Sterne would be eligible for one of these when it became vacant.

In November 1733 Sterne arrived at Jesus College to begin his studies. Then as now, Cambridge was a town dominated both physically and economically by its university. If Daniel Defoe is to be believed, it was also a sober enough environment for the students, for the university authorities were allegedly notably effective in discouraging assemblies, dancing, gambling, sexual intrigue, and general disorder.[59] There was a lively coffee-house culture, however, and Defoe's sober account of student life finds a more animated counterpart in that by Thomas Gray, who arrived at the university as an 18-year-old undergraduate in 1734, the year after Sterne. Not that Gray was complimentary, describing Cambridge as a 'great old town, shaped like a spider, with a nasty lump [Market Hill] in the middle of it and half a dozen scrambling long legs'.[60] Just out of Eton, highly gifted and not a little arrogant, Gray described the university (as he had the town) for the amusement, rather than the edification, of his friend Horace Walpole:

> The masters of colleges are twelve gray-haired gentlefolks who are all mad with pride; the fellows are sleepy, drunken, dull, illiterate things; the fellow-commoners are imitators of the fellows, or else beaux, or else nothing, the pensioners grave, formal sots who would be thought old, or else drink ale and sing songs against the excise. The sizars are graziers' eldest sons who come to get good learning that they may all be archbishops of Canterbury.[61]

Mischievous, even malicious, as it was, Gray's account possessed more than a grain of truth. Cambridge University was not merely dull in the 1730s; it had entered into a decline so steep that by the 1740s the earl of Chesterfield would declare it 'sunk into the lowest obscurity'.[62] Contemporaries concurred that academic standards were generally poor, and student numbers had been falling for decades, being reduced to an annual average of only 144 student matriculations between 1730 and 1739.[63]

The best-known scholar in the university during Sterne's time was the father of a mutual school-friend of Thomas Gray and Horace Walpole. This was Richard Bentley, master of Trinity College for almost forty years from 1700 but energetically engaged, in the year Sterne arrived, in resisting a second attempt by the bishop of Ely to deprive him of the mastership. Though over 70, Bentley was a still-active scholar. Astonishingly productive throughout his life, he had just published his controversial edition of *Paradise Lost* (1732), containing emendations aimed at restoring Milton's supposed original, based on the imaginative supposition that the blind poet had been at the mercy of an inept amanuensis and an unscrupulous editor who, not content with multiplying errors, added lines of his own. Nor was this the culmination of Bentley's scholarly career, for he was to publish his edition of the Latin poet Manilius as late as 1739. Among Bentley's opponents in the Trinity of the 1730s was another literary and religious controversialist, Conyers Midleton, soon to find himself the butt of Henry Fielding's satire in *Joseph Andrews* (1742). A third notable figure in Cambridge was the conservative divine, Dr Daniel Waterland, master of Magdalene College and regius professor of divinity; Sterne would make brief (and enigmatic) mention of his still-popular *Advice to a Student*—first published in 1706—in *Tristram Shandy*.[64]

Altogether less active than any of these was the master of Sterne's own college, Charles Ashton. As a nineteenth-century writer noted laconically,

Ashton's published works 'were not numerous'.[65] He had nonetheless enjoyed a long and outwardly successful academic career, having been elected master of Jesus in 1701—a post he held for over half-a-century—and vice-chancellor of the university in the following year. By the time Sterne arrived at the university, however, Ashton was already something of an anachronism. In the strongly politicized world of eighteenth-century England, Cambridge University was overwhelmingly Whig and Hanoverian in its political affiliations, while Oxford was staunchly Tory and Jacobite (commenting on its decline, Chesterfield was to allege the very existence of the Oxford university 'would not be known if it were not for the treasonable spirit publicly avowed and often exerted there'[66]). Following his accession in 1727 George II acknowledged Cambridge's Hanoverian and Whig loyalties by visiting the university in person and giving money towards the completion of the Senate House. The product of an earlier generation, Dr Charles Ashton was a confirmed Tory. At the time he took up his post as master Jesus College was one of the three largest in Cambridge; when Sterne arrived some thirty years later it was among the smallest.[67] Although the college could boast some distinguished men among its students during Ashton's mastership, they had tended not to remain long. Two of the most notable, Thomas Herring and Matthew Hutton, who would become successive archbishops of York and Canterbury, had been undergraduates at Jesus, but both had moved to fellowships at other colleges soon after they graduated. The philosopher David Hartley, who was an undergraduate and later a fellow, had likewise left in 1730.

Of the college tutors in Sterne's time, the most notable was Lynford Caryl, a future master of Jesus and vice-chancellor of the University; he would be among the subscribers to the first two volumes of Sterne's sermons in 1760. An effective administrator who would succeed in restoring the fortunes of the college, Caryl was an uninspiring if amiable lecturer, notable in later life for a 'sententious brevity of expression'.[68] In fact, the general circumstances prevailing in Cambridge make it doubtful whether Sterne—unable to afford private tuition—received notable stimulation from any teacher there, for few professors or fellows gave formal lectures of any note. The historian Edward Gibbon was writing of Oxford when he alleged, some years later, that 'the greater part of the public professors have for these many years, given up altogether even the pretence of teaching', making his own student days 'the most idle and unprofitable of my whole life'[69]—but while Gibbon exempted Cambridge from the worst of his strictures, others were less generous. In 1728 Jonathan Swift lumped the universities together when writing that from 'some hundred Examples from my own observation' it appeared that young men 'learn nothing more at *Oxford* and *Cambridge*, than to drink Ale and smoke Tobacco'.[70] Daniel Defoe, writing in the same year, concurred: 'young gentlemen are sent to the universities . . . not to study but to drink.'[71] A scarcely more flattering picture was offered by James Miller in some satirical lines written in the 1730s:

> *Half seven Years* spent in Billiards, Cards, and Tippling,
> And growing ev'ry Day a lovelier Stripling;
> With *half* a College Education got,
> Half Clown, half Prig, half Pedant, and half Sot.[72]

Despite such apparent unanimity, it would be wrong to imagine that Sterne himself was careless of his academic progress at Cambridge. One of the merits of Thomas Gray's brief satirical sketch is that it draws attention to the hierarchical nature of the university in the eighteenth century: the division between poorer and wealthier students, between those who had come to study and those whose aim was principally to divert themselves and who, having no need of a qualification, would leave without taking a degree. In an age when the English universities were becoming increasingly aristocratic the gulf between the richest and poorest students could be immense. At one extreme, the eldest son of the duke of Chandos, who went up up to Oxford in 1719, had a private tutor, three servants, and three horses; despite an allowance of £400 a year he managed to run up a debt of over £300 inside eighteen months.[73] At the other, Samuel Johnson had been forced to abandon his university studies in 1731 out of, in Boswell's words, 'irresistible necessity'—in order to take up a teaching post as undermaster at the school in Market Bosworth in Leicestershire at an annual salary of just under £20.[74]

In comparison to Samuel Johnson's impoverished state, Sterne's allowance at Cambridge does not seem entirely negligible, for his cousin Richard gave him £30 a year.[75] Even so such a sum put Sterne among the poorer students, while the fact that he enrolled in the university as a sizar confirmed his inferior status, for Cambridge sizars earned extra money by such humble tasks as waiting at table, while taking their own meals in the buttery to avoid the excessive costs of eating in hall.[76] Wealthier students were easily identifiable as fellow-commoners by the differently coloured gowns they wore, by their access to the college cellars, and by the more dubious privilege of being permitted to dine with the fellows. Only academically—as Gray indicated—were sizars other than an inferior category of student, for it was from among their number and that of the pensioners that scholars were chosen, and it was from the scholars that fellows were elected. Yet despite—or perhaps because of—their devotion to study, sizars were generally looked down upon by more affluent students. Certainly Sterne, aware of his own dependency and dim prospects, felt the disparity between himself and his more fortunate peers.

Despite the concessions made to sizars, and whether through extravagance or the high cost of residence at Jesus College,[77] Sterne's expenses proved greater than his allowance and he was soon forced to borrow. He was fortunate, then, that eight months after his arrival in Cambridge one of the Archbishop Sterne scholarships was freed and Laurence was elected. In this he followed his uncle Jaques and his cousin Richard, and preceded two other cousins. As a scholar Sterne was not permitted to work, but received instead a share of the endowments, which gave him an extra £11 a year, as well as a room and 1*s*. 3*d*. per week for board.[78]

While the award of a scholarship certainly eased Sterne's financial worries, his annual income was still modest and it is probable that, for the most part, his friends were drawn from students in similar circumstances. One much wealthier contemporary—who would later play a significant role in Sterne's life—was John Fountayne, a future dean of York Minster. The disparity in their backgrounds seems to have kept them at a distance as students, for Sterne later described Fountayne merely as a 'College acquaintance'.[79] Sterne probably also knew Joseph Bridges, a student of St John's College four years his junior, who later held livings in and around York and was subchanter of York; Sterne later made him a surrogate for a position he held in the small ecclesiastical court of Alne and Tollerton.[80]

Sterne's later life reveals him to have been a notably sociable man—the gregarious James Boswell was to describe him as 'the best companion I ever knew'[81]—so that it is likely that he was in no way a solitary student at Cambridge. The entirely male character of formal university life, however, could have had limited appeal to a man who in later years showed a marked preference for mixed, or female, company. Nonetheless, it was at Jesus that Sterne formed one of the most significant friendships of his life: with John Hall, later John Hall-Stevenson. Indeed, Sterne's only reminiscence of Cambridge in his memoir was that it was there 'that I commenced a friendship with Mr. H[all,] which has been most lasting on both sides' (*Letters*, 4).[82]

John Hall enrolled in Jesus College in 1735, at the age of 17. Sterne was then 21. Apart from the difference in their ages, there were other important distinctions between the two. Hall enrolled in the college not as a sizar, but as a fellow-commoner. His father, Joseph Hall, was a successful Durham lawyer, while his mother, Catherine, was sister and heir to Lawson Trotter of Skelton Castle, in Cleveland in the North Riding of Yorkshire. John Hall's expectations, in other words, were considerably greater than those of his fellow-student from Yorkshire—and like many others of his background he would leave Cambridge without feeling the need to take a degree. What the two young men had in common, above all, was an enjoyment of literature—especially witty, ribald literature. Among the writers they both enjoyed were older French authors like Rabelais, François Béroalde de Verville, author of *Le Moyen de Parvenir*, and Montaigne, as well as modern English favourites like Swift and his fellow-Scriblerians John Arbuthnot, John Gay, and Alexander Pope. The friendship between Hall and Sterne was one which both would eventually celebrate in their correspondence, where they addressed each other as 'Cosin', and in published works. John Hall-Stevenson is generally taken to be the model for Eugenius in *Tristram Shandy* and *A Sentimental Journey*, and while his was a very modest literary talent, that did not prevent him from becoming a very productive as well as occasionally amusing writer who, in 1760, was quick to celebrate his newly famous friend with a 'Lyric Epistle' entitled 'To my Cousin Shandy, On his Coming to Town'. In his best-known work, *Crazy Tales* (1762), Hall-Stevenson also wrote some verses celebrating Jesus College and in particular the vast walnut tree which stood in the inner court of the College:

At CAMBRIDGE many years ago,
In JESUS, was a Walnut-tree;
The only thing, it had to shew,
The only thing, folks went to see.

Being of such a size and mass,
And growing in so wise a College,
I wonder how it came to pass,
It was not call'd the Tree of Knowledge . . .

Tho', in the midst of the quadrangle,
They ev'ry one were taught their trade;
They ev'ry one were taught to wrangle,
Beneath its scientifick shade.

It overshadow'd ev'ry room,
And consequently, more or less,

> Forc'd ev'ry brain, in such a gloom,
> To grope its way, and go by guess.[83]

Like Sterne, Hall-Stevenson had Yorkshire connections and it may have been these that first drew them together. Local loyalties may similarly have led them into the company of other Yorkshire students, besides John Fountayne and Joseph Bridges. It was possibly at Cambridge that Sterne first became acquainted with Thomas Gilbert, a fellow of Peterhouse (where the fastidious Thomas Gray was writing his reports of Cambridge to Horace Walpole), since Gilbert came from close to Skelton and was later friendly enough with John Hall-Stevenson to dedicate his *Poems on Several Occasions* (1747) to him. Even so, the lack of any evidence of continuing friendships contracted at Cambridge—Hall-Stevenson apart—powerfully suggests that his straitened financial circumstances kept Sterne at a distance from these much wealthier students whose futures seemed destined to be so different to Sterne's own.

When writing the brief memoir for his daughter Sterne was happy to remember Cambridge as the place where he met his 'Cosin' John Hall. In truth, the university also held for him an altogether darker memory. In 1762 Sterne brought the two together when he wrote to Hall-Stevenson from France reminding his friend of the time he had discovered that he was suffering from consumption. The occasion for the letter was a recurrence in Paris of the same frightening symptoms of the tubercular disease he had first known as a student: 'I had the same accident I had at Cambridge, of breaking a vessel in my lungs. It happen'd in the night, and I bled the bed full' (*Letters*, 180). By the 1760s Sterne well knew how sick he was: he had travelled to France for his health, and no subject provides a more continuous thread through the correspondence of his final years. For the young man, in his early twenties, who had already known the deaths of two brothers and two sisters, besides those of his father and uncle, the first unmistakable intimation of his own mortality was doubtless as frightening as it was unwelcome. It was also the prelude to a life characterized thereafter by outward gaiety and inward melancholy.

In January 1737 Sterne's undergraduate career came to an end when he was awarded the degree of bachelor of arts. He left the university, in the words of a later writer, 'with the character of an odd man . . . who had parts if he would use them'.[84] Having left Cambridge, Sterne would only return once more, in the summer of 1740 to take his master of arts degree; this was a formality, but an important one, for the holding of a master's degree was a prerequisite for any clergyman aspiring to become a pluralist.[85] As a graduate Sterne could no longer hold his scholarship. For the first time he was obliged to earn his own living.

In fact, it is doubtful whether Sterne ever considered seriously any alternative to the course he took: ordination in the Church of England. Possibly he was destined for the Church from his boyhood, and it is likely that the Revd Nathan Sharpe had such an eventuality in mind when he predicted in Hipperholme School that Sterne 'should come to preferment'. In the eighteenth century the clerical life was one of a number of familiar options for cadet members of families of the gentry. The others included a commission in the army or navy, entry into one of the professions—law or medicine—or commerce. What was common to each of these possibilities—and what was commonly lamented, not least by the cadets themselves—was that for success in any sphere of life open to them native or acquired ability was rarely enough. The experience of Roger Sterne, whose lack of sufficient funds to purchase a promotion caused him to remain in the lowest of commissioned ranks in the army for twenty years, was likely to have been a sufficient deterrent to his son, even if Laurence had been more physically and temperamentally suited to a military life than was the case. Nor is it at all probable that Sterne considered either the law or medicine as a profession, for the expense involved in training for either would have been prohibitive. Indeed, had he been able to afford a legal education Sterne would almost certainly have acquired one even if he had intended to enter the Church, since his later life, like his writings, show him to have had an unmistakable penchant for the law, and ecclesiastical lawyers like his uncle Jaques were much in demand and hence well able to acquire positions of power and influence for themselves.

The army, medicine, and law aside, there remained trade. The residual prejudice against commerce in the minds of some of the gentry in the first half of the eighteenth century is unlikely to have affected Sterne, for his family had had commercial interests in Yorkshire for some time.[86] The Jaqueses were a family who had made their fortunes in trade and Sir Roger Jaques, who bought the estate at Elvington, married into another family of Yorkshire merchants, the Rawdons. Sterne's uncle, Richard, had close contacts with the business life of Halifax, and himself ran several coal-mines as well as the Sterne mill on the River Calder close by Woodhouse. Perhaps this was the future Richard Sterne designed for his penniless nephew. It is more likely, however, that it was Laurence's lack of money that proved the greatest discouragement to a career in the world of commerce. Certainly, members of the gentry seeking to make their way in some respectable branch of trade were also expected to bring with them some capital. Anyone looking to place a son as apprentice to a London merchant would have needed anywhere between £500 and £1,000, even though once the apprentice had served his term 'he has as much to seek what to do or how to begin his busyness as when he first came'.[87] While it was less expensive to place an apprentice with a Yorkshire merchant, the subsequent problem of inadequate capital remained. Unable to depend on his uncle, Sterne's lack of funds prevented him equally from entering either a profession or substantial business.

Whatever choice of career Sterne might have made had his financial circumstances been different, it is still likely that his future had been all but decided, in consultation with his cousin, by the time he went up to Cambridge. The university produced a large proportion of the English clergy, and the Church was a recognized career for a young man in Sterne's position. Thomas Gray was haughtily but correctly acknowledging as much when he described Cambridge as a place graziers' sons studied to become archbishops of Canterbury, for by mid-century almost half of all bishops came from comparatively humble backgrounds.[88] Even for the industrious and intellectually gifted student, however, the way to preferment was never easy. If, in entering the Church, Sterne was apparently avoiding the frustrations of the military career his father had followed with so little success, then he was entering an organization whose rigidly hierarchical structure was essentially no different from that of the eighteenth-century army. It was Joseph Addison who had most famously made the comparison for his age, when he wrote in *The Spectator* that, like the army itself, the clergy were divided into 'Generals, Field-Officers, and Subalterns'.[89]

Laurence Sterne did, however, enjoy one important advantage denied his father, for the Church was the one place where he could hope for the aid of a close member of his family—his uncle Jaques. In 1737, when Laurence graduated, Dr Jaques Sterne was already archdeacon of Cleveland and precentor of York Minster. Possibly Richard Sterne's willingness to support his cousin financially at university was contingent on Laurence's receiving their uncle's help in finding him a suitable position after graduation, so that he could earn his own living without needing further assistance from the family. Some seventeen years older than his nephew, Jaques Sterne might serve as a model of one kind of eighteenth-century clergyman: clever, intensely ambitious, and decidedly worldly—a 'bon vivant', Bishop William Warburton was to call him.[90] In his early forties when Laurence Sterne took holy orders, he was already well advanced on an ecclesiastical career successful enough to enable him to aid a poor relation.

Jaques Sterne had graduated from Jesus College in 1715.[91] Ordained a deacon in Lincoln in 1717, he took priest's orders three years later in York. By February 1723, when he was still only 26, Jaques was rector of Rise, a small parish in the East Riding of Yorkshire. Six years later he joined the already considerable ranks of pluralists in the eighteenth-century Anglican Church, when he added the living of the neighbouring Hornsea-cum-Riston to his existing parish. A fortnight later he additionally received the prebend of Apesthorpe in York Minster, which he would exchange in 1731 for the wealthier prebend of Ulleskelf. In 1734 he obtained the still-more lucrative prebend of South Muskham in the Cathedral of Southwell, and in November 1735 he became, in his fortieth year, archdeacon of Cleveland and precentor of York Minster. By the time his nephew Laurence was ordained, in other words, Jaques was well able to assist in finding him a suitable cure. Able—and willing, for Jaques quickly saw that Laurence's talents might be turned to his own advantage.

In the memoir Sterne's account of his entry into the Church is laconic: 'I then came to York,' he wrote, 'and my uncle got me the living of Sutton' (*Letters*, 4). In fact, the course of events was a little more complicated, for having been ordained deacon on 6 March 1737 he was licensed on the same day to the curacy of St Ives in Huntingdonshire. This circumstance alone suggests that Sterne had been designed for the priesthood for some considerable period prior to his entry into orders. The minimum age for ordination to the diaconate was 23, and 24 for the priesthood. Sterne was ordained deacon little more than four months after he reached the requisite age (a possible reason for his late entry into Cambridge). In fact, it was not infrequent practice in the eighteenth century for young clergymen of high birth or influence to be ordained deacon and priest within a very short period, sometimes as little as a matter of days, so as to allow them immediately to take possession of a living prosperous enough to support them for the remainder of their life. For Sterne, however, no such living was forthcoming. Instead, he remained in Huntingdonshire for almost a year before returning to Yorkshire, to become assistant curate of Catton on 18 February 1738, at an annual salary of £30.[92] It was a return to an area he had last visited as an infant, for Catton was not far from Elvington and about seven miles from York itself. He would not remain there long. Just over six months later, on 20 August 1738, he was ordained priest.

The circumstances of Sterne's ordination reveal much about the nature of the Established Church in his day. After two decades of Whig government the episcopate was politically engaged and Whig in affiliation (by contrast, no Tory—open to the charge of disaffection to the House of Hanover—had been elevated to the episcopal bench for over a decade). The ready deployment of political interest by senior churchmen went hand-in-hand with an understanding of the bishop's pastoral role which, if less culpable than critics liked to claim, could still in the case of some older prelates suggest a considerable dereliction of episcopal duty. When Sterne was ordained priest, for instance, he did not, as would seem logical, go to York, the northern capital of the English Church. The archbishop of York, Lancelot Blackburn, had carried out no ordinations in person in the archdiocese since 1733, nor would he do so again until his death a decade later (he held no confirmations during his entire tenure of the See between 1724 and 1743). Instead, he gave letters dimissory to ordinands, who subsequently made their way to neighbouring bishoprics—Chester, Lincoln, or Carlisle—or even as far away as London.[93] Sterne himself travelled to Chester, where he was ordained by the Whig, latitudinarian bishop Samuel Peploe.[94]

If the question of Sterne's religious belief is addressed here, after his ordination, then the order is entirely appropriate. Of direct, detailed evidence of the nature of that belief at this time there exists none at all. But if Sterne reveals little indication of personal devotion, either to Christianity or the priestly calling, that does not make him exceptional in his day. Few in the eighteenth century demanded an overt display of religious feeling in an Anglican clergyman, and many were likely to be embarrassed if they found it. Nor did the age expect an over-nice examination of conscience about entering the Church of England primarily for support. The scruples Jonathan Swift experienced in the 1690s on this point set him apart from most clergymen of his age, and even he managed to overcome them, to become a notably conscientious priest.[95] Swift was not unique in his doubts—David Hartley did not take holy orders for just this reason—but few would-be ordinands allowed conscience to divert them entirely from the priesthood simply because they had no compelling vocation.

Certainly, there exists no shred of evidence that Sterne felt any special calling to the priesthood—and after the success of *Tristram Shandy* it was frequently alleged that this clergyman was altogether unfitted for the cloth. Yet if Sterne left few indications of a personal spirituality, then the reason lies as much with the nature of the Christianity he professed as with any shortcomings of his own. For many besides himself, educated in the beliefs first set down in the mid-seventeenth century by the 'latitude-men' or latitudinarians, Anglicanism presented itself as a faith which equally eschewed theological hair-splitting and enthusiasm or evangelical fervour. If, as the latitudinarians argued, religion was natural to man, then morality lay at its heart. Man was social by nature, and his greatest pursuit, as Sterne himself would later preach, was 'after happiness . . . the first and strongest desire of his nature'.[96] Mistaking his object, he might fall into sin, but, thanks to the grace freely available to all—latitudinarianism set its face against Calvinist doctrines of election and predestination—he would discover happiness and holiness to be the same. For the latitudinarians, in other words, Christianity might properly be reduced to a few central truths, easily understood and put into practice. Since even the leading latitudinarian theologians took care to leave religious truth alone when it seemed to exceed the grasp of rational enquiry,[97] it is not surprising to find so little testimony of the nature of Sterne's spiritual beliefs at the time of his ordination. In the event, Sterne would turn out to be a responsible (if fallible) clergyman, whose regard for the central Christian virtue of charity, as well as his ability as a preacher, exceeded that of many of his fellow-clerics.

In any case, at the age of 24, Laurence Sterne was set on a career which would see him through the next two decades of his life. Thanks to the influence of his uncle he acquired, within a week of his ordination, the living of Sutton-on-the Forest, about eight miles north of York on the plain separating the city of York from the moors. It was a signal moment in his life, and Sterne recorded the fact in his own hand in the parish book: 'Laurence Sterne AB was Inducted into y$^{\underline{e}}$ vicarage of Sutton August y^{e} 25$^{\underline{th}}$ 1738.---'.[98]

2

Priest and Husband, 1738–1741

His move to Sutton-on-the-Forest marked the beginning of a fresh start for Sterne. Not only was he embarking on a career, he was also entering a new social and political world. The village of Sutton lay on an abrupt bend on the road leading north from York at a point where another road leads off north-west to the hamlet of Huby, which made part of the parish of Sutton. The forest to which the full name of the parish refers was the Forest of Galtres, of which by that time little remained. Around the village, especially to the north, lay large, open fields. Dominating the village physically and socially were the church and the house of the lords of the manor, the Harland family, to whose close links with Sutton numerous tablets and monuments in the parish church still testify. For most villagers community life centred on the church and Sutton's 'Good convenient Publick House', which was furnished with a large malt kiln for brewing, and which was let to a new publican in the autumn of the year in which Sterne arrived.[1]

Central as the institution of the church might be to village life, a comparison of the vicarage with the Harland house gave a good indication of the relative prosperity of the temporal and spiritual powers of Sutton. The elegant, brick-built Palladian house was a new one, having been put up less than ten years previously, to a design by Thomas Atkinson, as a replacement for an earlier, Elizabethan building. At much the same time as Sterne arrived in Sutton the Harlands were enlarging their home by adding two flanking wings to the central block, prior to embellishing the interior with fine Italian plasterwork. By contrast, the vicarage—which stood facing the Harlands' house, just to the east of the church—was dilapidated. It was also, when Sterne arrived, still occupied by the widow and children of his predecessor as vicar of Sutton, the Revd John Walker, whose death had freed the living for Sterne. Tradition has it that initially Sterne lodged at Church Farm, to the west of the church. A few years after he arrived in Sutton Sterne described the village and its inhabitants in some detail. There were, in 1743, about 120 families in the parish, of which five were Quaker. These had their own Meeting House which attracted some thirty worshippers each Sunday. The parish also contained two 'Petty Schools', one endowed with 20*s*. a year, the other unendowed.[2]

Philip Harland, the local squire, stood as a living reminder to Sterne of his modest status as a clergyman. Just five years older than the new vicar, Harland came from a very similar social background. His family were landed gentry with close contact with the professions. Philip Harland's father, Richard, was in fact a lawyer, living and still practising in York. Philip Harland himself had been educated at Queen's College, Oxford, and had also matriculated at Gray's Inn in London. Politically, the Harlands were Tories and had played an active role for two decades in the opposition to the Whigs under the prime minister Robert Walpole. Sutton was of some importance politically because it had a larger number of enfranchised men than most parishes of its size, with around sixty farmers from Sutton and the neighbouring Huby eligible to vote. These votes, however, were effectively controlled by the Harlands, who had thus helped make the area a stronghold of the Tory (or Country) interest. It was a position which inevitably and immediately brought Laurence Sterne and Philip Harland into conflict.

Throughout his life Laurence Sterne remained, in the family tradition, a supporter of the Whig party. By prevailing political standards—and not least by comparison with his furiously partisan uncle Jaques—he was not a virulent party man. Yet even in his last years when, as the author of *Tristram Shandy*, he welcomed the attentions of Whig and Tory alike, he remained strongly attached to the principles in which he had been educated and on behalf of which he laboured as a political journalist in the 1740s.

How energetic on the Whigs' behalf he might have been had he been financially independent is altogether more difficult to determine. Unlike his fellow-novelists of the mid-eighteenth century, Henry Fielding and Tobias Smollett, Sterne was not active in politics during the years of his fame. Fielding had enjoyed a decade of renown as a dramatist when he wrote for *The Champion* in 1739–40, and was celebrated as the author of *Joseph Andrews* (1742), *Tom Jones* (1749), and *Amelia* (1752) when he started *The Covent-Garden Journal* in 1752; Smollett was similarly well-regarded as author of four novels, including *Roderick Random* (1748) and *Peregrine Pickle* (1751), and as a historian, when he edited the pro-government newspaper *The Briton* in 1762–3. Sterne, by contrast, abandoned party-political writing as soon as he was able—and rather sooner than was prudent for his future career. Perhaps as an ambitious young man looking to make his way in the world Sterne had none of the qualms he would later reveal about meeting the demands contemporary political journalism placed on its practitioners. More likely, he recognized that he had no choice. Penniless clergymen like himself could spend years, decades, or an entire lifetime as humble and socially despised curates on tiny stipends. Thanks to his uncle Jaques, Sterne had acquired a solid living shortly after ordination. The archdeacon of Cleveland, however, was not a man to do anything simply out of family loyalty or affection, especially where the son of his feckless brother was concerned. Jaques Sterne was both an ambitious clergyman and an indefatigable worker on behalf of the Whig interest in the north of England. In itself this did not make the archdeacon unusual in his age. The Established Church was by its very nature political, and its clergy inevitably split between the conflicting political interests of their day. Having been elevated to the See of Bristol in 1735, Thomas Secker—a future archbishop of Canterbury—unselfconsciously noted the political affiliations of his clergy—Whig or Tory—alongside their personal or clerical attributes.[3] When Jaques Sterne obtained the living of Sutton-on-the-Forest for his nephew he was above all gaining a potentially valuable worker for his own party ends. Laurence Sterne's first political task would be to represent the ministerial interest in Sutton and provide a rallying-point for those unwilling to support the Harlands and the Country interest.

However close the connection between ecclesiastical and political life in the eighteenth century, Sterne's duties were not, of course, confined to politics. The young vicar was initially active in all the ways expected of him: he officiated at morning and evening prayer and on church feasts, he preached, celebrated holy communion, performed baptisms, catechized, officiated at weddings, visited the sick and dying, and, when their time came, buried his parishioners. The 'many comfortless scenes [Yorick] was hourly called forth to visit, where poverty, and sickness, and affliction dwelt together' (*TS* I. x. 19) were familiar enough to Sterne himself. For the most part the young priest fulfilled his obligations dutifully enough. In the eyes of Dr Jaques Sterne, however, obligations did not lie exclusively in the parish of Sutton, and Sterne was soon spending much of his time in York. Less than a year after his induction he hired a curate, Richard Wilkinson, to look after the daily parish duties in his absence. Given his own uncertain financial position, it is virtually certain that the move to York was made at his uncle's direction. An election was in prospect and Jaques Sterne required his nephew's pen more immediately to hand.

Even if his presence was demanded in the city, however, it is unlikely that Sterne was unhappy with the move. The York Sterne came to know in the early 1740s was still one of England's great cities, as it had been since the Middle Ages. With a population of around 12,000, it was surpassed in population only by London, Bristol, and Norwich. Separated from the national capital by a journey, along the Great North Road, which still took four days by stage-coach and six by stage-waggon,[4] York also had an important administrative role as the northern metropolis, the castle there being the seat both of county administration and law.

Today it is clear that, during the course of Sterne's lifetime, the city was entering into a slow decline, as previously insignificant towns and villages such as Birmingham, Manchester, and Liverpool or, within Yorkshire itself, Leeds and Sheffield began their rise to prosperity. To Sterne in 1739, however, York appeared at once vibrant and elegant. Still of predominantly medieval appearance, and physically dominated then as now by the great Gothic Minster, the city was an important focus of ecclesiastical and legal life in the north. It was also an important commercial centre and a significant node of communication by water as well as by road, for goods were still transported by ship up the Ouse from the sea in Sterne's lifetime. Socially, York was active in making itself worthy of its continuing contemporary as well as historical importance. The city's civic pride had manifested itself in 1727 in the building of a splendid mansion house for the lord mayor. In the following year the earl of Burlington, a substantial landowner in the county, had drawn up plans for an imposing assembly room (1728–30), based on a re-creation of the 'Egyptian Hall' described by Vitruvius, and a theatre was built in Ingram House in 1734 (it would be replaced by the more substantial Theatre Royal in the following decade). An elegant promenade, the New Walk, laid out along the river in 1733–4, proved so popular an amenity that the corporation had it extended and widened in 1739–40.

Unlike many other provincial centres in eighteenth-century England, York benefited from a close relationship—often cemented by marriage—between the urban professional and merchant class and the county aristocracy and country gentry, a number of whom had town houses there. It was they who provided the public for an active social life, and throughout the year there were regular opportunities to attend concerts, balls, plays, lectures, and the exhibition of travelling novelties. Not all the entertainment available was so elegant, however, and contemporary newspaper advertisements tell of a population variously attached to hunting (the city itself maintained a pack of hounds), cockfighting, bowling, and skittles. Since the assize courts also took place in York twice a year, public executions offered another popular spectacle. In the very month Sterne moved to York the 'notorious Highwayman' Richard Turpin was executed on Knavesmire for horse-stealing; his conduct on the scaffold, where he behaved with 'undaunted Courage' and 'Assurance to the very last', did much to encourage his posthumous reputation as the legendary Dick Turpin.[5] The city was a place also of extensive poverty, with perhaps as many as a third of its inhabitants living at or below subsistence level.

For those who could afford them, however, the city offered a range of attractions unmatched anywhere in the surrounding area. Like other large urban centres, York was increasingly caught up in the consumer revolution of the mid-eighteenth century. In the streets around the Minster there were numerous shops offering an unprecedentedly wide range of fashionable goods for a population able, in growing numbers, to afford them. Many of the goods advertised—books, prints, artists' materials, musical instruments, and sheet music, for example—had particular appeal for Sterne, though for years into the future he would lack the financial means to indulge his interests to any great extent. As an active amateur musician Sterne must have been particularly gratified by the extent of musical activities in York. A fashionable pastime of the gentry who visited the city in the winter, concerts were also a legitimate source of entertainment for the city's many clergymen, whose presence at plays—to say nothing of more boisterous entertainments—was still generally considered a matter of scandal. The directors of the Music Assembly would engage singers and instrumental performers for the whole of the winter season—Italian musicians were held in particular esteem, and during Sterne's first winter in York the Assembly proudly advertised the performances of the 'celebrated Italian singers' Signora Posterla and Signora Chiara Posterla.[6] As in this case, not all of the performers brought to York were quite as celebrated as the organizers of the Music Assembly alleged, but Yorkshire was fortunate in having talented musicians of its own—such as the well-known organist of York Minster John Hebden—who performed regularly. Sterne's own musical preferences seem to have been conservative—his own principal instrument was the bass viola da gamba, shortly to disappear from mainstream European music-making—but York offered plentiful opportunities to hear compositions by popular modern composers such as the Italians Corelli, Vivaldi, and Geminiani, and the German Hasse. By far the most popular composer of the period in York, as throughout Britain and Ireland, was George Frideric Handel, long domiciled in England, without at least one of whose compositions few concerts were complete. York's regular concert-goers also had the chance to hear musical novelties—performances on ancient instruments like the sackbut or unusual 'Foreign Instruments' such as the chalumeau and clarinet.

Despite the general disapproval of the clergy's frequenting the playhouse, it is probable that Sterne—who attended plays regularly in London and in Paris in the years of his fame—took at least occasional opportunities to enjoy York's thriving theatrical life. A playhouse inaugurated in 1734 was replaced, a decade later, by the handsome New Theatre in the Mint Yard. This housed a repertory company which, from the 1730s, had been employed on a salaried basis, offering a winter season of more than two-dozen plays. The dramatic fare itself was that familiar from other eighteenth-century theatres, though the York management made much of any play or performer with a London or Dublin connection. For the most part there was a mix of modern plays and ballad operas, popular works from the Restoration and early-eighteenth-century stage, and a leavening of Shakespeare, usually in 'improved' versions. Sterne could have attended, over the years, performances of such tragedies as Thomas Otway's *Venice Preserv'd*, Nicholas Rowe's *Tamerlane*, and Joseph Addison's *Cato*, Richard Steele's sentimental comedy, *The Conscious Lovers*, and John Gay's *The Beggar's Opera*, as well as popular afterpieces like Gay's *The What d'ye call it.* Shakespeare was represented by, among others, *King Lear and his Three Daughters*, Colley Cibber's version of *Richard III*, *Macbeth*, 'written originally by *Shakespear*, and since altered by Mr. Tate', with 'all the Music, Songs, Dances, Flyings, Sinkings, and other Decorations proper to the Play'[7]—and *The Tempest*, as reworked by Davenant and Dryden. The future creator of Yorick had also several opportunities in the 1740s and 1750s to see the York company perform *Hamlet.*

As elsewhere in mid-eighteenth century England there was a growing interest in the new science, fostered by the success of such works as Benjamin Martin's much reprinted *Philosophical Grammar* (1733) or the translation of Francesco Algarotti's *Il Newtonianismo per le dame* (1737). As a result, the inhabitants of York had frequent opportunities to attend lectures where they could learn more about the revolution taking place in contemporary understandings of the world they inhabited. Of various ventures of this kind, the most ambitious was a series of forty lectures given by Mr Demainbray, in the White Swan Inn in Petergate, covering such topics as mechanics, motion, hydrostatics, pneumatics, magnetism, optics, and astronomy; a ticket for each lecture cost 1 shilling, or 25 shillings for the complete series.[8] For those whose scientific curiosity was more casual, there was a chance in 1745 to see 'one of the greatest Curiosities in the known world': a 'monstrous Stag's Head . . . found in a Peat Moss' near York which, the advertiser declared, was 'supposed to have laid there since Noah's Flood'.[9]

Most celebrated of all York's social events was Race Week, which took place annually in August. Besides the horse-races themselves—which were among the most important of the year in England—there were special concerts, balls, assemblies, and a variety of associated entertainments put on for the benefit not merely of the gentry or citizens of York itself but for the aristocracy of the north of England in general. During Race Week, a contemporary wrote enthusiastically, '*York* shines indeed, when, by the light of several elegant lustres, a concourse of four or five hundred of both sexes, out of the best families in the kingdom, are met together . . . [and] the politeness of the gentlemen, the richness of the dress, and remarkable beauty of the ladies, and, of late, the magnificence of the room they meet in, cannot be equalled, throughout, in any part of *Europe*'.[10] Local pride apart, Race Week offered an occasion for the most prominent and influential members of northern society to meet socially—though it was only in the years of his fame that Sterne was able to take full advantage of the opportunity. Among the advertised attractions in 1739, however, was an important flower show, the Florist-Feast, held at the George Inn,[11] at which one of the two stewards was Sterne's cousin Richard, who doubtless helped the newcomer to York to widen his immediate circle of acquaintance. Even so, Sterne's finances could not have allowed him to take anything like full advantage of his first Race Week, for the daily ticket for the Assembly Room in Stonegate cost half a guinea and even the concert cost 2*s.* 6*d.*, far from insignificant sums of money for the 26-year-old clergyman.

At all events, the sociable Sterne is certain to have found York preferable to the secluded life of a country parson in Sutton-on-the-Forest. He was equally fortunate to have been able to spend the winter of 1739–40 in York rather than in the country, for the winter was a notably harsh one. A big freeze began on 23 December, so intense that the Ouse iced over; within a few days the river was so solid that booths and even a printing press were set up and football matches played on the ice.[12] The freeze, which continued throughout the whole of January, was the most severe to have affected York for half-a-century and prompted the local newspaper, the *York Courant*, to look back to the winters of 1607 and 1614 for comparisons. Nor was the following winter much better. By mid-December 1740 the Ouse had frozen over again, and while the heavy snowfall of 21 December was followed by a quick thaw, this first made roads leading into York impassable and then produced flooding in the city itself, with boats appearing in the city's streets.

It was during the first of these two harsh winters that Sterne was called upon in the double capacity of friend and priest by his Cambridge companion John Hall. Hall was to be married to Anne Stevenson, a north-country heiress who brought her husband a fortune of £25,000, leading him to add her surname to his own. Laurence Sterne married the couple on 7 February 1740. Most likely, by the time Sterne had performed the ceremony, he had also made the acquaintance of a young woman then living with her maid in lodgings in Little Alice Lane in the Minster-Yard. Her name was Elizabeth Lumley, and she would become Sterne's wife. When Sterne first met Elizabeth he was about 26 years old. One of two children of the Revd Robert Lumley and his wife Lydia, Elizabeth Lumley had been orphaned for a decade at the time she met Sterne. The situations of Robert and Lydia Lumley bore a marked resemblance to those of Sterne's own parents. Robert Lumley was the son of a gentleman while his bride, born Lydia Light, was a widow, previously married to Thomas Kirke, a virtuoso and antiquarian of some renown, who died in April 1706. The Lumleys married in September 1711, the same month that saw the marriage of Roger Sterne to Agnes Hobert.

Like Sterne's parents, the Lumleys were not in an ideal financial situation. Robert Lumley had only just graduated from Trinity College, Cambridge, and would not be ordained until December 1712. It was on the income that his wife inherited from her first husband that the couple lived, and at Cookridge Hall, near Leeds, the former home of Thomas Kirke, that they first settled. Two daughters were born to the couple: Elizabeth, who was baptized in October 1714, and Lydia. Eventually Robert Lumley acquired a lucrative living—Bedale in Yorkshire, worth almost £2,000 a year—but by that time the couple found themselves in unmistakable financial difficulties for, like Roger Sterne, Elizabeth's father spent money freely. The Lumleys sold Cookridge to the duchess of Buckingham, and moved to the vicarage at Bedale. Robert Lumley died in 1729 and his wife shortly afterwards. Elizabeth was then 14. Robert Lumley had left his daughters only a much-reduced fortune for their support. Lydia was the first to marry, her husband being another clergyman, the Revd John Botham, rector of Yoxall in Staffordshire. A cousin of the Lumley sisters was Elizabeth Robinson, later to become famous as the bluestocking Elizabeth Montagu.[13] She at least had no high opinion of John

Botham: 'Mrs [Lydia] Botham is at Elford with Lady Andover, which I am glad of,' she wrote waspishly in 1741, 'for poor Lydia has a taste for conversation above the hum-drum mediocrity of her husband's understanding. He has a very good pulpit drone, and gives the whole parish an excellent nap every Sunday with his sermonical lullaby.'[14]

Before the Bothams had been married for many years they were in financial trouble. By 1746 Elizabeth Montagu, as she had then become, was writing more scathingly than ever about Lydia's husband: 'Alas! poor Johnny is such a Johnny that there arises all the difficulty of getting them any preferment. . . . Any exchange from Staffordshire must be advantageous to them, for there, as they unfortunately began with entering into all the expenses that attend a great neighbourhood, they could never have lived in the way they intend doing and may do here.'[15] John Botham was fortunate that same year in being presented with the living of Albury in Surrey by Lord Andover, and was soon trying to stretch the family budget by farming the sixty acres of glebelands at Albury instead of letting them, in order to provide the family with 'grain, fowls, bacon, milk, butter and eggs'. Elizabeth Montagu did not blame her cousin's financial difficulties on John Botham alone, for she recognized that Robert Lumley had brought up his daughters in considerable luxury and seeing a great deal of company, so that Lydia found difficult the transition to living on much-reduced means. It was a situation which would before long become all-too familiar to Laurence Sterne himself.

It was most likely that Elizabeth Lumley's realistic appreciation of her changed circumstances and of the difficulties she might encounter in the future affected her conduct towards Laurence Sterne when he began to pay court to her in the winter of 1739–40. Like many other couples, Laurence Sterne and Elizabeth Lumley probably met in the Assembly Rooms, which they later frequented together. The new assemblies which sprang up throughout England in the 1720s and 1730s provided perfect opportunities for meeting prospective marriage partners. According to one writer, 'knights' daughters' went to assemblies to be 'picked up' (a phrase that Defoe declared he had never seen used in print before).[16] Sterne's more elegant version of his courtship of Elizabeth Lumley forms part of the memoir he wrote for his daughter Lydia, named for both her grandmother and aunt:

> [A]t York I became acquainted with your mother, and courted her for two years—she owned she liked me, but thought herself not rich enough, or me too poor, to be joined together—she went to her sister's

> in S[taffordshire], and I wrote to her often—I believe then she was partly determined to have me, but would not say so—at her return she fell into a consumption—and one evening that I was sitting by her with an almost broken heart to see her so ill, she said, 'my dear Lawrey, I can never be yours, for I verily believe I have not long to live—but I have left you every shilling of my fortune;'—upon that she showed me her will—this generosity overpowered me.—It pleased God that she recovered, and I married her in the year 1741. (*Letters*, 4)[17]

If this is a pleasing account it is also a poignant one, for in the long run the Sternes' marriage was not happy. Yet at the time Laurence Sterne and Elizabeth Lumley must have felt themselves touched by particular good fortune in having found each other, for their courtship was carried on in the shadow of death. Not only was Elizabeth ill with consumption, so too was her suitor. When, at the same time, a friend died, Sterne was prompted to reflect on the suddenness and unpredictability of death. 'I have lost a very valuable friend by a sad accident,' he wrote to Elizabeth:

> and what is worse, he has left a widow and five young children to lament this sudden stroke.—If real usefulness and integrity of heart, could have secured him from this, his friends would not now be mourning his untimely fate.—These dark and seemingly cruel dispensations of Providence, often make the best of human hearts complain.—Who can paint the distress of an affectionate mother, made a widow in a moment, weeping in bitterness over a numerous, helpless, and fatherless offspring?—God! these are thy chastisements, and require (hard task!) a pious acquiescence. (*Letters*, 18–19)

In later years Sterne would write many passages—at times solemn, at others comic (though no less serious)—reflecting on the transience of human life and the 'dark and seemingly cruel dispensations of Providence'. In his letter to Elizabeth he achieved a degree of detachment suitable to a young clergyman, through the expression of conventional pieties. A second death, reported in the same letter, nevertheless brought home to the consumptive the uncertainty of both Elizabeth's life and his own. Anticipating Elizabeth's reaction, he wrote: 'The event was sudden, and thy gentle spirit would be more alarmed on that account' (*Letters*, 19).

The version of his courtship Sterne wrote for his daughter is, we may be sure, true enough in the details he provides (his wife, after all, was at hand to correct any blatant distortion). It was, nevertheless, a prudently edited account. In 1739 Elizabeth Lumley was not the only woman to whom Sterne was making his addresses. On 20 November of that year Sterne wrote to a new friend of his, the Revd John Dealtary, the rector of Skirpenbeck, near Pocklington, in Yorkshire (and, like Sterne, a former student of Jesus College, Cambridge). Sterne began by apologizing for a silence on his part in a correspondence that he had solicited, and then continued:

> I never wishd for your Company so much in my life as Just now. I have a thousand things I want to talk over with you, which are only fit for Conversation, & cannot well be committed to paper: I must let you know thus much; That you have now received a Letter from one of the most miserable and Discontended Creatures upon Earth; Since I writ last to you, I have drawn Miss C—— into a Correspondence: in the Course of which together with her Consistency in acting towards me, since the beginning of this affair; I am convinced she is fixed in a resolution never to marry, and as the whole summ of happiness I ever proposed was staked upon that single Point, I see nothing left for me at present but a dreadfull Scene of uneasiness & Heartachs.[18]

The lover's pains were not of long duration. Later the same winter Sterne was writing sentimental epistles to Elizabeth Lumley while she was away from York, visiting her sister and brother-in-law in Staffordshire:

> My L. has seen a Polyanthus blow in December—some friendly wall has sheltered it from the biting wind.—No planetary influence shall reach us, but that which presides and cherishes the sweetest flower.—God preserve us, how delightful this prospect in idea! We will build, and we will plant, in our own way—simplicity shall not be tortured by art—we will learn of nature how to live—she shall be our alchymist, to mingle all the good of life into one salubrious draught.—The gloomy family of care and distrust shall be banished from our dwelling, guarded by thy kind and tutelar deity—we will sing our choral songs of gratitude, and rejoice to the end of our pilgrimage. (*Letters*, 16)[19]

It would not be long, however, before the harmony would turn to discord, and the pilgrimage would end with Laurence and Elizabeth Sterne making their separate journeys through life.

In the meantime Elizabeth Lumley had reservations about Sterne that may have related to more than their uncertain financial situation. Writing to John Dealtary, Sterne had confessed: 'There is something in my Case very extraordinary and out of the Com̄on Road which I must not venture to Acquaint you with by Letter for fear of accidents & ——.'[20] The sentence could hardly be more tantalizing, and few readers are likely entirely to forgo the pleasure of speculating on what, in Sterne's case, was so extraordinary that it could not be committed to paper. Since there is nothing to aid speculation except the context—following on from the revelation of his unsuccessful courtship of Miss C—— and preceding a wish that Dealtary might enjoy 'a life of uninterrupted Calmness & repose unruffled either with passions or Disappoi[n]tments'[21]—speculation is not especially rewarding. Perhaps Sterne was ready to acknowledge that he had initiated two courtships simultaneously, as would appear to have been the case. At all events, it is likely that Elizabeth Lumley had, whether she knew it or not, some grounds for disquiet about her admirer, besides their mutual poverty. It is possible she did know it, for despite the reticence he displayed in his correspondence with Dealtary, Sterne was habitually indiscreet and his conduct is unlikely to have escaped the attention of local gossips. Certainly, when Matthew Robinson reported the marriage of their cousin Elizabeth in 1741, he wrote to his sister that 'Harry Goddard is here, and informs me that our cousin Betty Lumley is married to a Parson who once delighted in debauchery, who is possessed of about £100 a year in preferment, and has a good prospect of more'.[22] Elizabeth Robinson regarded this information as reliable enough to pass it on, in a letter of her own, though with a discreet change of language and emphasis: 'He [Sterne] was a great rake, but being japanned and married, has varnished his character.'[23]

In the end, all reservations—concerning Laurence's moral character, the lovers' health, and their narrow fortunes—were put aside and Laurence Sterne married Elizabeth Lumley in York Minster on 30 March 1741. By one account, Laurence paid court to his future wife during the space of two years, 'when she as constantly refused him, till at length she asked him the question herself and they went off direct from the [York Assembly] Rooms and were married'.[24] Although this story seems likely to be spurious, it may be that Elizabeth was, in their relationship, the more impulsive of the pair. While Sterne dutifully consulted his uncle in matters concerning his marriage, Elizabeth Lumley had so little reserve about her decision that she declined to have her own fortune settled on her by law, saying that she wished for no better security than her husband's honour.[25] Sterne was suitably impressed by Elizabeth's trust and by the comment of his uncle that 'I was the more bound to take care that the Lady should be no Sufferer by such a Mark of her confidence'. The ceremony over, Sterne noted details of his wedding in the parish register of Sutton-on-the-Forest:

> Laurence Sterne AM. Vicar of Sutton on the Forest and Prebendary of York, was married by the Rev^d.^ D^r^. Osbaldeston Dean of York to Elizabeth Lumley, the 30th. Day of March 1741 (being Easter Munday) in the Cathedral——.[26]

The impending marriage had obviously done wonders for Elizabeth Lumley's health. Her cousin, Elizabeth Robinson, wrote: 'I never saw a more comical letter than my sweet cousin's, with her heart and head full of matrimony, pray do matrimonial thoughts come upon *your recovery*? for she seems to think it a symptom.'[27] Tolerant amusement is not the defining characteristic of Elizabeth Robinson's correspondence, and she shortly becomes more typically acerbic:

> I do not comprehend what my cousin means by their little desires, if she had said little stomachs, it had been some help to their economy, but when people have not enough for the necessaries of life, what avails it that they can do without the superfluities and pomps of it? Does she mean that she won't keep a coach and six, and four footmen? What a wonderful occupation she made of courtship that it left her no leisure nor inclination to think of anything else. I wish they may live well together.[28]

Matthew Robinson evidently felt no need even for the thin veil with which his sister covered her contempt: 'What hopes our relation may have of settling the affections of a light and fickle man I know not, but I imagine she will set about it not by means of beauty but of the arm of flesh.'[29] Still more caustically, he added: 'In other respects I see no fault in the match; no woman ought to venture upon the state of Old Maiden without a consciousness of an inexhaustible fund of good nature.'[30]

In commenting on his cousin's lack of physical beauty Matthew Robinson was, however cruelly, voicing a more widely perceived view of Elizabeth Lumley. One who knew her in later life described her as 'homely'.[31] Yet Elizabeth Sterne brought other, more notable personal qualities to her marriage. She had a 'superior education' and a 'first-rate understanding'—attributes that undoubtedly appealed to Sterne who, throughout his life, showed a strong predilection for the company of intelligent, well-educated women. And while other accounts of Elizabeth Sterne confirm that her stock of good-nature was not unlimited, her fickle, unfaithful husband would give her cause to draw on it extensively during the years of their marriage.

3
Political Journalist, 1741–1742

If Laurence and Elizabeth Sterne had thoughts of quietly settling down to married life in the parish of Sutton-on-the-Forest, they had not reckoned with Dr Jaques Sterne. The archdeacon had other ideas, and was ready to put his nephew to work in earnest for the Whig interest in Yorkshire. Inevitably, Laurence Sterne was acutely conscious of the extent to which his present fortunes and future prospects in the Church depended on his uncle Jaques. Indeed, he had already been given an earnest of what might be in store for him. At the beginning of 1741 he had obtained his first preferment since arriving in Yorkshire when, on 19 January, he was installed prebendary of Givendale in York Minster. As a mark of distinction it was modest enough, for York Minster was well supplied with prebendal stalls, having no fewer than forty-six out of the Anglican Church's approximately 600 prebends.[1] Even so, it was for Sterne the first rung on the ladder of preferment, and gave him a position, however modest, among the elite of the eighteenth-century Established Church. In itself the life of the prebendary was not altogether onerous; one contemporary described it as 'a pretty easy way of dawdling away one's time; praying, walking, visiting;—& as little study as your heart would wish'.[2] Laurence Sterne, though, was well aware of the political obligations his new preferment entailed, and he knew too that the political task awaiting him was not just a way of paying past debts but the surest way to future promotion.

Should Sterne have had doubts of any kind, the example of his uncle was ever before him. As prudent and incisive in his career as his brother, Roger, had been carefree and ineffectual, Jaques followed the family tradition of support for the Whigs with the greatest enthusiasm. As a result he became chaplain and political aide to Lancelot Blackburn, the archbishop of York from 1724, himself an enthusiastic Whig, reputed to have received the archbishopric for having married King George I to his mistress the duchess of Kendal. Even in an age of colourful ecclesiastical careers,

Blackburn's appeared gaudy. He had started in the church in 1681 by accepting a £20 bounty to go as priest to the West Indies, where he was reputed to have served on board pirate vessels, taking his share of the plunder. Nor did his return to England entirely mellow him: one anecdote tells of how, while on a visitation at St Mary's, Nottingham, he asked for pipes, tobacco, and drink to be brought to the vestry 'for his refreshment after the fatigue of confirmation'.[3] As his failure to ordain priests—Laurence Sterne among them—makes plain, the fatigues of his duties sometimes proved altogether excessive to Blackburn.[4] That his energies were otherwise directed is suggested by the contemporary reputation he acquired for profligacy, which gave rise to the posthumously published poem 'Priestcraft and Lust, or Lancelot to his Ladies'. Like Jaques Sterne, Archbishop Blackburn had married, when young, a widow older than himself, and like both the Sternes he did not, it was alleged, prove a model husband. Horace Walpole wrote that Blackburn 'had all the manners of a man of quality, though he had been a bucaneer, and was a Clergyman; but he retained nothing of his first profession, except the seraglio'.[5]

Whatever similarities might have existed between the private lives of Jaques Sterne and his archbishop, Blackburn's career undoubtedly offered a model for his chaplain's own ambitions. Support of the Whigs in the county election of 1727 was followed two years later by Dr Sterne's preferment to the living of Hornsea-cum-Riston.[6] A fortnight earlier he had also received the prebend of Apesthorpe in York Minster, which he would exchange in 1731 for the prebend of Ulleskelf. His active involvement in the election of 1734 brought him the prebend of South Muskham at Southwell Cathedral—worth £400 a year—and appointment in 1735 as archdeacon of Cleveland and precentor of York, the latter post bringing with it the still wealthier prebend of Driffield in place of Ulleskelf.

At the age of 40 Jaques was a churchman of considerable dignity, influence, and wealth. His income from ecclesiastical posts alone brought him over £900 a year—a far cry from the £20 that Laurence Sterne was paying his curate. Jaques Sterne had been hiring curates to serve his various parishes since at least 1730 and had transferred his residence to York, where he purchased the north wing of the Treasurer's Mansion—known as the 'Great House'—in November 1742. This new house he was soon altering and refurbishing with considerable taste and panache. He built a well-proportioned dining-room embellished, most notably around the fireplace, with carved pine woodwork, considered the finest in York.[7] Jaques Sterne, however, did little that was motivated by good taste alone. The other notable feature of the fireplace was a marble plaque featuring

Augusta, wife of Frederick, Prince of Wales, the centre of a rival court to that of his father George II. The archdeacon was hedging his political bets in an unusually elaborate manner, though in the end his hopes, like those of many others, were dashed by the premature death of Frederick in 1751; by the time the young George III ascended the throne in 1760, Dr Sterne was himself dead.

Jaques Sterne had first become active in support of the Whigs shortly after his arrival in Yorkshire, at much the same time as Sir Robert Walpole, the 'Great Man' of contemporary politics and prime minister for two decades, first rose to political pre-eminence. When Laurence Sterne arrived in Yorkshire in 1738 his uncle had long been deeply immersed in the murky waters of local politics. Having found his intelligent, needy nephew an ecclesiastical position close to York, Jaques Sterne was in a position to insist, when the moment should arrive, that Laurence plunge in beside him. For over three years, Sterne swam strongly and successfully with his uncle's party, although, with Walpole's administration becoming increasingly precarious, the current was going strongly against the Whig interest. When eventually Sterne, finding the waters both too dirty and too turbulent for his liking, retreated to dry land, it was to face the wrath of an uncle who, like the Great Man he served, bestowed no favours without intending to exact adequate return.

Sir Robert Walpole had led administrations in England uninterruptedly since 1721, concentrating power in his own hands by a combination of determination, shrewd intelligence, sound policies, and an unsurpassed understanding of the political possibilities of the contemporary system of royal and governmental patronage. During his years in office he drew to himself sufficient parliamentary and countrywide support to see off the greater or lesser threats posed by the Jacobite Pretender, opposition Whigs led by William Pulteney, and a variety of out-of-office malcontents grouped around the ideologue Henry St John, Viscount Bolingbroke. In the process Walpole had also attracted to himself an unprecedented animus, most famously embodied in satirical works by many of the age's leading writers, including Jonathan Swift, Alexander Pope, John Gay, and Henry Fielding. In a range of works from *Gulliver's Travels* to *The Beggar's Opera*, *Jonathan Wild* to the *Dunciad Variorum*, they damned Walpole's manipulation of patronage as corruption, viewed their own neglect as injured merit, and turned their dislike of the 'Great Man' into a moral crusade.

Unlike those Whigs who drifted reluctantly over the years into the Walpole camp when it seemed that the prime minister would never be dislodged, Jaques Sterne had allied himself with the ministerial party from the outset. By the time Laurence Sterne arrived in Yorkshire in 1738 Jaques had had the good fortune and good sense to have supported the ministry for nearly twenty years. In maintaining Walpole in power for so long, Jaques Sterne had played his own modest part.

Since 1716 British general elections had taken place only every seven years. Even so, the expenses of a contested election could be so great that most seats were not fought at all.[8] When a county had two seats, for instance, it was not unusual for the Tories and Whigs to agree to take one each. Yorkshire county politics were not so amiably organized. Until 1727 the Tories held both seats, but in the general election of that year Walpole's supporters succeeded in returning a strong local candidate, Cholmley Turner of Kirkleatham.[9] In 1734 the ministry's supporters in Yorkshire decided to contest both county seats, in an attempt to oust completely the representatives of the Tory, or Country, interest. The 1734 election, in which Jaques Sterne played a leading role in organizing the Whig forces, was bitterly fought, with Archbishop Blackburn sending a circular letter to all his clergy urging them to support the ministerial candidates.[10] In the event, the spoils were divided. The Tories and Whigs each returned a member of parliament for the City of York, while in the county elections Cholmley Turner took one seat, the other going to the young Tory Sir Miles Stapylton. The bitter dispute occasioned by the election did not end with the poll, however, for at enormous expense the defeated Whig candidate in the county election, Sir Rowland Winn, petitioned the House of Commons to overturn the election result in his favour, alleging massive electoral malpractice. Only after eighteen months did the ministry decide to cut its losses and uphold the original result.[11]

Laurence Sterne was still studying in Cambridge in 1734, but so furiously contested an election had left behind a considerable legacy of bitterness and the wounds opened in Yorkshire public life by the election were still unhealed and painful when he arrived in Sutton in 1738. Such was the intensity of feeling that the renewal of party hostilities did not await the succeeding general election. The local newspaper, the *York Courant*, followed national politics closely, regularly, and ritually congratulating or criticizing the local members according to their parliamentary conduct, thereby ensuring that voters knew who had voted, and how, in key parliamentary divisions.

When Laurence Sterne moved from Sutton to York at the end of 1739 political manoeuvring in the city was in full swing. All charitable activity, for instance, took—or was quickly given—a political turn. During the

Great Freeze of 1739–40 corporate bodies and individuals made donations designed to relieve the worst distresses of the city's poor, unable to afford sufficient fuel to keep the cold at bay. The Dean and Chapter of York Minster led the way, with a donation of £20, and the Whig member of parliament for the city, Edward Thompson, quickly followed suit with a personal contribution of 40 guineas.[12] A week later the Tory member for York, Sir John Lister Kaye, made his own personal donation of exactly the same amount. In reporting this fact, however, the *York Courant* did not omit to make political capital of it, for it added that Kaye's was 'an Instance of Generosity the more worth Notice, in regard that Gentleman serves his Country in Parliament without Fee or Reward'[13]—a pointed reference to the fact that Edward Thompson was a government placeholder: namely, Commissioner for the Revenue in Ireland.

If such comparatively minor episodes could be put to active political use, no wonder that a contemporary and much more substantial charitable venture was also politicized. In March 1740 the York County Infirmary opened near Monk Bar, to the north-east of the city of York.[14] The principal instigator of the scheme was the physician Dr John Burton, who would continue to play a role in the life of Laurence Sterne for more than two decades, most famously as the 'squat, uncourtly' Dr Slop of *Tristram Shandy*. John Burton had moved to the city some years previously from Wakefield, and built up a successful medical practice. Alert to the extent of poverty in the northern capital, he published proposals for the building of the hospital. The plan to build the new county hospital was a most characteristic one for the age. Following the founding of three of the great London hospitals—Westminster (1719), Guy's (1723), and St George's (1734)—similiar initiatives were taken in the provinces, with Bristol and Winchester leading the way with county hospitals in 1735 and 1736 respectively. The proposal for a hospital in York was thus part of a movement that would see the foundation of twenty-four provincial hospitals throughout England by 1782. Yet if Burton's project flourished in a largely favourable medical and theological climate (no text was more cited by eighteenth-century divines than 1 Corinthians 13: 13: 'And now abideth faith, hope, charity, these three; but the greatest of these *is* charity'), then it could not be separated either from political intrigue.[15]

Even prior to his arrival in York Burton had been active in the Tory interest, and at the age of 24 had been leader of the Wakefield Tories during the 1734 election. During the poll of that year Burton had led his Wakefield supporters to York, where all voting took place; there he had been a prominent presence, guarding a voting booth personally. So when Burton later accused local Whigs of refusing to support his scheme for the county infirmary he was no disinterested observer. Tories, however, were certainly prominent among Burton's supporters. Philip Harland, squire of Sutton-on-the-Forest, for example, bought in trust for the infirmary the land on which it was built, and was a member of the first board of governors. So too was Sterne's cousin and benefactor Richard, who had broken with the family tradition of support for the Whigs and aligned himself instead with the Tory interest. Meanwhile, the Tory members for both the city and county of York were subscribers to the infirmary, unlike either of their Whig counterparts. When the hospital opened in April 1740 it was staffed not only by Dr Burton but by two other physicians also active in the Tory interest: Dr Francis Drake and Dr John Fothergill.

From the outset, the County Hospital was a success, admitting 430 patients during its first thirteen months of operation, a fact the *York Courant* thought fit to mention immediately beneath a paragraph noting the arrival in York of the Tory candidates in the 1741 election.[16] John Burton, however, was not content to enjoy the mere discomfiture of the York Whigs; he was anxious also to discredit his political opponents. The opportunity soon arose, with Burton claiming that the Whig churchwardens elected during Easter Week planned to divert sacrament money intended for general dispersal to the deserving poor exclusively to needy supporters of their own party.[17]

Whatever the truth of these allegations, no love was lost between the rival political factions in York during the months leading up to the 1741 general election. That election was fought against the background of a general decline in Walpole's popularity, accelerated by the war between Britain and Spain that had begun in 1739. Personally opposed to the conflict, the prime minister had reluctantly bowed to public and parliamentary opinion in its favour after a British seaman, Captain Jenkins, produced his severed ear—allegedly cut off by a member of the crew of a Spanish coastguard vessel who had boarded Jenkins's ship—in the House of Commons. Initially the War of Jenkins's Ear had gone well. In the Caribbean Admiral Vernon achieved a victory at Puerto Bello on 22 November. When news of his success reached York on 18 March 1740 Vernon's capture of the stronghold was hailed by bonfires and the ringing of peals of bells in the city's churches. In the same month as one victory was being celebrated in England, however, the British forces suffered a catastrophic reverse in their inept assault on the port of Cartagena. Among those killed in the resulting massacre was the brother of the city's member of parliament, Edward Thompson, a lieutenant-colonel in the army.[18]

By 1741 Robert Walpole had lost the full confidence of supporters both in and out of parliament. More importantly, he had lost confidence in his own ability to control the situation. Harassed by the opposition at home, the prime minister was engaged in prosecuting a war in which he did not believe, and in which the actions of his military commanders seemed destined to be unsuccessful. Unhappily, it was the conduct of Walpole, his ministry, and the armed forces that the 27-year-old Laurence Sterne found himself obliged to defend, when he was called upon by his uncle to turn political journalist.

The 1741 general election campaign began in Yorkshire some ten months before the poll was finally held. So determined were the Tories to be well prepared that they nominated two candidates to contest the county election on 23 July 1740: the sitting member, Sir Miles Stapylton, and another young man, Charles Howard, Lord Morpeth, son of the earl of Carlisle. Three months later two candidates were likewise chosen to stand in the Country interest in the city election.

The Whig campaign was getting under way more slowly. Cholmley Turner was doubly reluctant to stand: not only did he lack political conviction but he had recently suffered the loss of his only son and heir, who had died eighteen months previously while making the Grand Tour. On 21 April 1741, just four days before the dissolution of parliament, Turner announced that he would not contest the forthcoming election.[19] With only three weeks remaining before polling day the Whigs had no time to find a replacement candidate, and Viscount Morpeth and Sir Miles Stapylton were elected unopposed.

The situation was very different in the York city election. The sitting member of parliament, Edward Thompson of Marston, declared his candidature on 24 October, and just before the poll Sir William Milner, of Nun-Appleton, announced he would stand as a second Whig candidate. In the course of the election both parties spent extravagant sums of money in their efforts to woo voters—Edward Thompson's expenses allegedly amounting to £15,000.[20] Following an exceptionally bitter and violent, as well as unusually expensive campaign, the equal division of seats was maintained, with Edward Thompson retaining his seat and Godfrey Wentworth gaining the other for the Tory or Country interest. In the city, then, the balance of power had been retained, but the loss of a county seat to the Tory party was bad news, not only for local supporters of the ministry but for the administration as a whole. Though Walpole just managed to hold on to power—news of the defeat at Cartagena did not reach England until after the election—he did so with a considerably reduced majority of fewer than twenty seats.

Although the political struggle in the nation as a whole was over for the time being, it was unexpectedly renewed in Yorkshire. On 9 August 1741 the newly elected Viscount Morpeth died of consumption, aged 22. Until Cholmley Turner's belated decision not to stand in the general election had left his party without a candidate, the ministerial interest had been well prepared for electoral battle. In March 1741 they had started a newspaper, the *York Gazetteer*, whose avowed aim was to counteract the advantage held by the Country interest, which controlled the *York Courant*. Owned and edited by the printer Caesar Ward, the *Courant* was politically directed by Dr John Burton and his fellow physician at the infirmary, Dr Francis Drake. Control of the most important news medium gave the conservative interest an important political advantage in York. The founding of the *York Gazetteer*—whose name, recalling those of the London *Daily Gazetteer* and the *London Gazette*, testified to its Whig allegiance—offered the ministerial interest the possibility of offsetting that advantage.

The *York Gazetteer* began as it intended to continue: with a principled avowal of its backers' political sentiments, and an unprincipled attempt to smear their opponents. 'As this Paper is partly set on Foot, to correct the Weekly Poison of the York-Courant,' it declared, ''tis hoped that the Well-Wishers to the Cause of *Liberty* and *Protestantism* will give it Encouragement.'[21] The implication, as even the dullest elector could not fail to understand, was that the only previously existing York newspaper had Jacobite sympathies, supporting arbitrary power and Roman Catholicism. These were the standard charges Whigs levelled against their Tory opponents. They were also charges which would be laid against Dr John Burton in particular by both Jaques and Laurence Sterne—in the case of the former with deadly seriousness, in that of the latter, with comic but more lasting force in *Tristram Shandy*.

Just as the *York Courant* was published by Caesar Ward, though with John Burton and Francis Drake behind him, so the *York Gazetteer* was published for Jaques Sterne by another York printer, John Jackson. On 9 March 1741, the day before the new paper was due to publish its first issue, Jackson suffered a vicious physical attack in York. The person behind the assault was a coal-merchant by the name of John Garbutt, active in the Country interest and known locally as 'General Garbutt'. With a past as dubious as his present behaviour, Garbutt had apparently had in mind more victims than one, for when he appeared before the local magistrates he was bound over to keep the peace 'toward John Jackson the Younger of the City of York printer and Lawrence Sterne of Sutton upon the Forest of York Clerk & all Other his Majesties Liege People'.[22] The linking of Sterne with the printer of the *York Gazetteer* suggests that the young vicar was closely associated with the new ministerial paper from its inception—though despite attempts to identify Sterne's first essays in political journalism in pieces reprinted elsewhere, the earliest piece that may confidently be ascribed to him is a broadsheet reprinting of an article first published in the *Gazetteer* of 16 June 1741.[23]

Written in the aftermath of the general election campaign, the article reveals something more than political grievance, for it deals with the launching of a new coal barge belonging to John Garbutt and named for the two Tory candidates in the city election, Godfrey Wentworth and Sir John Lister Kaye. Describing the launch of *The Kaye and Wentworth*, the *York Courant* had written: 'it is hoped that all the *honest Citizens* will ever remember both the Name of the Vessel, and the great Services done to the Public by the *Master* of it, at the last Election.'[24] Already under obligation to his uncle to attack the Tory interest in York, Laurence Sterne—so nearly the victim of assault by a man thus publicly praised for his conduct during the election—now had a personal reason to engage with his political enemies.

Sterne was not backward, demanding of his readers: 'Whether Those who can stoop to work with so low a Tool as *Garbut*, and when the Work is over can still stoop lower to Thank and Flatter him, have not let fall'n the Mask of Patriotism and discovered under it, more of the Spirit of Slavery than Liberty?'[25] It was a pointed question, for the death of the newly elected Lord Morpeth meant that the electioneering was unexpectedly set to begin again, less than three months after the previous poll. This time the ministerial party was determined to organize itelf adequately. On 29 August—two days before their opponents—the Whigs held a selection meeting and chose as their candidate Cholmley Turner, who had once more been persuaded to offer himself for election. Sterne moved into action on Turner's behalf. His essay of June was reprinted at some time in the late summer or early autumn of 1741, and to it was added a news item dated 31 August, informing voters that John Garbutt had been arrested and imprisoned in York Castle as a returned transportee. If true, this was a grave charge, given Garbutt's role in the assault on John Jackson, since under the terms of the 1718 Act allowing for transportation, any returned transportee convicted of a further crime faced mandatory execution.[26]

For the Country interest the timing of Garbutt's arrest was unfortunate—and may have been far from coincidental. On 1 September the *York Courant* announced the selection of the Tory candidate: 'George Fox, Esq., of Bramham-Park stands Candidate upon the COUNTRY-INTEREST.' In so describing George Fox, however, the *York Courant* was telling less than the full story. As most voters knew—and as Laurence Sterne would soon inform those who did not—George Fox, owner of Bramham Park, was also a considerable landowner in Ireland. The potential incompatibility of these two positions was sufficient, the ministerial interest would allege, to make Fox a wholly unsuitable candidate for election as a member of parliament for Yorkshire.

George Fox came from a well-established Anglo-Irish family. Though born and brought up in England, he had inherited the extensive Irish estates of his uncle in 1724, when he was 28. Fox's connection with Yorkshire was wholly consequent on his marriage in 1731 to Harriet Benson, only daughter and heiress of the recently deceased Lord Bingley, of Bramham Park. As Robert Benson, Lord Bingley had represented the City of York from 1705 to 1713, and had been chancellor of the exchequer before being ennobled in 1713; his fortune amounted to some £100,000 in addition to an income from his estates of £7,000 a year.[27] Although Fox's political career to date been in the south-west of England—where he had represented a Wiltshire constituency since 1731—he acquired such substantial interests in Yorkshire by his marriage that he was being spoken of as a potential candidate for the county as early as 1733.[28] It was the fact that he had other, potentially conflicting interests in Ireland that gave the Whigs the possibility of arguing that he was effectively disbarred from giving unequivocal support to the interests of those he now aspired to represent.

The alleged conflict of interest centred on the wool trade. Along with East Anglia and Lancashire, Yorkshire had long been an important area of English woollen manufacture. At the end of the seventeenth century English manufacturers had recognized the threat posed to their own livelihoods by a strong Irish woollen industry, and had made moves to have it suppressed. In 1699 the English parliament passed an act prohibiting the export of woollen goods from Ireland to any country except England, from which they were effectively excluded by high duties. As a result Irish wool was smuggled abroad, notably to France where lower labour costs allowed French manufactured goods to compete effectively in foreign markets. In the following decades English manufacturers repeatedly petitioned parliament to find adequate means of stopping all British and Irish exports of wool to France. When the Irish parliament discussed wool smuggling in the winter of 1739–40, however, the hostility of its members towards English protectionism ensured that no legislative attempt was made to stop such exports. If the interests of Yorkshire manufacturers were best served by the prevention of Irish wool exports, then, argued the Whigs, George Fox was not the best man to serve those interests. With his estates in Ireland, he might find his private interest and public duty to Ireland lay in encouraging or at least acquiescing in the continued smuggling of Irish wool to France.

The lines of battle for the new election were drawn, then, in the early autumn of 1741. Among the principal issues were matters both of national and local importance: on the one hand, the morality of Walpole's government by patronage and the conduct of the war; on the other, the best interests of the Yorkshire woollen industry. What initially marked the difference between the two parties was that the Tories, conscious of the waning popularity of Walpole and his ministry, concentrated on national affairs. The Whigs, with Sterne as their chief propagandist, sought instead to deflect attention from these by focusing on local interests, and indulging in a sustained personal attack on the Tory candidate.

From the outset the Whigs fought the electoral campaign without scruple. As early as 8 September the *York Courant* published a letter from a Tory apologist from Leeds, known simply by the initials 'J.S.', who solemnly rejected the charge that George Fox was an 'Irishman'[29]—a letter which did nothing to stop the Whigs from repeating the slur on every possible occasion. This dispute was not without an element of farce, for it was Tory backwoodsmen rather than Whigs who were generally (and often with good reason) regarded as xenophobes. Now Tories found the charge of 'foreigner' levelled at their own candidate. 'J.S.' was canny enough to know that it was a charge that must be faced: 'Mr *FOX*, by Marriage to so considerable a Yorkshire Heiress, is possess'd of a great Property in this County; and, living in the Heart of it, in a noble and hospitable Manner, may be justly called a *Yorkshire-Man*.'[30] While thus seeking to affirm George Fox's personal credentials, 'J.S.' strove also to shift the ground of the argument by reference to the parliamentary division on the hotly disputed commercial treaty between Britain and Spain known as the Convention of the Pardo, of which he alleged that 'every Man that voted for it may be said to have forfeited the Title of an *Englishman*'.[31]

'J.S.' 's intervention in the political fray quickly aroused the considerable ire of Dr Jaques Sterne, who set directly about the task of discovering the writer's identity. After investigation, the precentor determined 'J.S.' to be the Revd James Scott, vicar of Bardsey, a parish some eight miles from

Leeds, where Scott lived. An Oxford graduate in his early forties, Scott was among those clergy who disregarded Archbishop Blackburn's endorsement of the ministry and voted Tory during the 1734 general election. Having concluded Scott to be the apologist for the Country interest, Jaques Sterne directed his nephew to respond. Unhappily, as it would turn out, Sterne chose to do so by means of a letter he attributed to an ostensibly disinterested third party, intended for publication in the *Courant*.

Caesar Ward, printer of the *Courant*, was not taken in. On 29 September he published a terse statement of his own:

> *When the Writer of a Letter sent Yesterday to the Printing Office, reflecting upon a worthy Clergyman in this County, and sign'd* J. Wainman, *thinks fit to subscribe* his own Name, *it will be soon enough to insert it; in the mean Time, it may be proper to inform the* Vicar, *who penn'd it, that the Printer of this Paper is not to be impos'd upon by* counterfeited Letters *from* Guisborough, *nor* fictitious Names *in* York.[32]

If Caesar Ward thought his perspicacity might deter Laurence Sterne, he was wrong. Baulked in his attempt to make sport with Scott, Sterne turned to more orthodox forms of political journalism, albeit on terms dictated by his opponents.

That Sterne should have been so quickly forced on to the defensive was owing to the unbounded confidence evinced by the Tories. George Fox had arrived in York on 4 October, after a progress through the East and part of the North ridings where, the *Courant* alleged, he was received with widespread enthusiasm and promises of votes. 'This Extraordinary Success', declared the *Courant*, 'puts it out of Dispute, but that Mr. Fox will be elected by a great Majority.'[33] This was bluster, for the Tory campaign was going so badly that the recently elected Sir Miles Stapylton abandoned Yorkshire for the parliamentary session in London, convinced that the election was lost.[34]

Caesar Ward, meanwhile, remained so confident of victory that he extended an invitation to his political opponents. In the *Courant* of 20 October he declared himself willing '*to preserve that Impartiality, he has constantly observ'd, of inserting any Advertisements relating to the present contested Election, come it from what Quarter it will, provided it is wrote with Decency and good Manners*'.[35] The offer was worded astutely so as to suggest the Country party's repeated boast to be above all factional squabbling and to imply that the ministerial interest might be incapable of writing other than in an indecent and ill-mannered fashion. It also suggests that Ward thought

'J.S.'—who had contributed a second letter to the same issue of the *Courant*—a stronger polemicist than anyone in the Whig camp.

Laurence Sterne was quick to take up Ward's offer, his essay, *Query upon Query; Being an Answer to J.S.'s Letter Printed in the York-Courant October 20, relating to the present contested Election*, first appearing in the *York Courant* on 27 October. Though it was later to be reprinted on three separate occasions[36]—suggesting that contemporaries thought it a strong piece—Sterne's response began weakly. Hampered by Ward's stipulation that he be decent and well-mannered, Sterne flailed around in all directions, sounding both prolix and truculent as he attempted simultaneously to defend Cholmley Turner and smear George Fox. He was more successful in his dismissal of 'J.S.' 's previous letter, declaring contemptuously: 'That out of all the Productions of the Moderns (for one cannot in Conscience suspect the Ancients) of what Climate, Country, or Complexion soever, I challenge you to produce any one Writing, where so long a Chain of undesigned Blunders are link'd together in so narrow a Compass.'[37] Sterne then proceeded to compress his opponent's argument so tightly as to make it appear ludicrous—a rhetorical ploy which, like his invocation of the Ancients and the Moderns, suggests that Sterne have had in mind Swift's *Tale of a Tub*. 'J.S.' 's first point, his opponent alleged, amounted to no more than saying that Cholmley Turner had declined to stand in the general election and that had he not agreed to stand on this occasion there would have been no contest: 'A most admirable and important Conclusion!' Sterne's unsubtle irony here was not entirely unwarranted, since 'J.S.' had indeed argued along just these lines—though the argument was less absurd than it appears today, for in the 1741 general election there had been contests in only four of the forty English counties.

Had Sterne left 'J.S.' behind at this point and turned his attention to Fox his contribution to the political debate might have been rather stronger. Instead, his inexperience led him to attempt a rebuttal of 'J.S.' point for point, paragraph for paragraph. Occasionally he struck a neat, if never dangerous, blow, but his ponderous attack seems motivated more by a desire to wound the Revd James Scott than to strike decisively at the Tory candidate. It was as a fellow-clergyman that Sterne addressed Scott when protesting that 'the throwing out of random Accusations upon a whole Body of Men without the least Proof, the least Shadow of Evidence, is a Piece of Injustice and Barbarity ill agreeing with that Spirit of Meekness and Charity which should be the Characteristic of a *Teacher of Truth*'.[38] Towards the end of his life Sterne was to excuse other dubious aspects of his writing by arguing simply that 'The truth is this—that my pen governs me—not me my pen' (*Letters*, 394). His jibe against Scott's alleged lack of charity was, however, injudicious—and one he would come to regret.

After this clumsy opening, Sterne avoided answering 'J.S.''s queries by posing a further set of questions of his own. Sixteen in all, the queries indicate succinctly the mix of importance of national and local politics evident throughout the 1741–2 Yorkshire campaign. They also reveal Sterne's determination to cast doubt on the merits of Fox's candidacy by argument or innuendo alike. A final query was reserved—most unwisely as it turned out—for a personal attack on 'J.S.'.

In dealing with national issues Sterne was brisk and effective. He defended Walpole's conduct of the war with Spain while characterizing Tory attitudes towards it as duplicitous rather than principled. On the question of corruption Sterne was equally scathing: in response to 'J.S.''s allusion to the defeat in January 1740 of the last Place Bill—designed to limit the offices of profit Walpole had at his disposal—Sterne asked scornfully whether those members of the opposition who brought in the Place Bill really hoped for success. Did they not, he continued, 'wish in their Hearts for the very Places against which They affected to vote?' Confident of having countered 'J.S.''s charges against the ministry, Sterne turned his attention to the rival candidates, praising Cholmley Turner and asking once more whether George Fox was by any means 'a proper Person' to support the interests of the Yorkshire woollen industry when his personal interests were best served by letting his Irish tenants run wool to France?[39]

Sterne would have done well to leave his argument there. Instead, oblivious of the wider needs of the campaign, he was determined to hit personally at 'J.S' who, for that 'blind and extravagant Stroke of Insolence, in daring to call every Gentleman an *Incendiary*, who wish'd for an Opposition the last General Election', deserved 'immediately to be call'd to Account'. In the tense atmosphere of the campaign—especially considering John Garbutt's assault on John Jackson and intended assault on Sterne himself—this last was a dangerously ambiguous phrase.[40]

At its best *Query upon Query* neatly ridiculed the flaccid arguments of 'J.S.', but it contained little likely to sway an uncommitted voter. This was perhaps not its intended purpose, and as an arsenal of arguments for the Whigs and against the Tories and their candidate it certainly offered ministerial canvassers and supporters ammunition enough for local debate. At its weakest, however, Sterne's answer revealed his political and journalistic naivety, suggesting he had decided his principal target to be not George

Fox but 'J.S.'. Sterne's subsequent participation in the election campaign goes far to support such a view.

Away from the journalistic battle, the Whigs were hoping to draw uncommitted voters and wavering Tories to the ministerial interest—to which end they supplemented the usual eighteenth-century electoral standby of bribery with a brazen campaign of blackmail. Dr John Burton was later to allege that a 'little Reverend Time-serving Priest'—most likely Jaques Sterne—had threatened the freeholders of Wheldrake that, if they did not vote for Cholmley Turner, he would demolish part of their parish church at a cost to the parishioners of £600 to £700.[41] Extreme as these tactics were, they appear to have been effective. While the Whigs lost some supporters—unsurprisingly, given the national turn away from Walpole—they gained enough new promises of votes to make their opponents decidedly uneasy.

In so heated a contest, tempers began to fray. Ostensibly the paper war had been conducted as a contest of policies and candidates; now the thinly concealed antagonism between rival writers broke out in open hostility. Sterne, it must be remembered, had published his contributions anonymously, while the Tory polemicist's work, written from Leeds, had merely been signed with the writer's initials. Jaques Sterne, however, had identified 'J.S.' as James Scott. Laurence Sterne had seconded this identification both in the unpublished letter from Guisborough, signed J. Wainman, and by his sneering references to his opponent's lack of the clerical virtues of mildness and charity, for there was only one Tory clergyman with the initials 'J.S.' resident in Leeds: James Scott.

An unsigned contribution to the following week's *York Courant* could, therefore, have done little for the composure of the tyro political journalist, for the writer unambiguously stated that 'J.S.' was not a clergyman but 'a Merchant in the Woollen-Trade'.[42] The assertion was doubly telling, for it not only suggested the imperfect political intelligence of the Whigs, but made light of their oft-repeated fears of the consequences for the woollen industry of the election of George Fox. Still worse was to follow. Although 'J.S.' was not Scott, as the Whigs had thought, the Tory polemicist (whoever he was) had managed to identify his anonymous Whig antagonist as 'Lory Sterne'. The following lines, he asserted, would serve as sufficient answer to all that the author of the last queries had written or could write:

> Let *L——y scribble—what! that Thing of Silk,*
> *L——y that mere white Curd of Ass's-Milk?*

> *Satire or Sense, alas! can L——y feel?*
> *Who breaks a Butterfly upon a Wheel?*[43]

The lines are not perhaps especially apt—Lory Slim, as Sterne would later call himself, was more a stick-insect than butterfly—but the appropriation of Alexander Pope's vicious lines on Lord Hervey was well-judged. Sterne could not even accurately identify his journalistic opponent; what reliance, then, could be placed on the opinions of this political lightweight?

Understandably Sterne was rattled, uncertain whether to believe the denial and how to respond. When he replied to 'J.S.' he did so twice. The first response is contained in a broadside handbill (perhaps deriving from a lost number of the *York Gazetteer*[44]) published on 3 November, and reprinted in the *York Courant* on 10 November. In this reply—hurriedly written in the wake of the unwelcome denial that 'J.S' was a clergyman—Sterne began with mere bluster. It was hard, he alleged to make 'a *serious* Reply to one of the most scurrilous and uncharitable Letters that ever appear'd in a civiliz'd and Christian Country'.[45] Sterne had no difficulty, however, in once more praising Cholmley Turner's virtues, both private and public, along with the conduct of the ministry. As a result, his reply was earnest, ill-focused, predictable, and dull. His second was none of these.

Far from being the fruit of calmer and more studied reflection on how best to retrieve his position, Sterne's second letter is simply abusive. Published in the same issue of the *Courant* as the first, this second reply appeared over the initials 'L.S.'—though it is doubtful that Sterne signed the letter himself. Rather, Caesar Ward seems to have taken understandable advantage of the inexperienced writer's intemperance to place him in the worst possible light, indicating that '*The following Letter is wrote by the same Gentleman that has wrote every Piece that has been inserted in this Paper in vindication of* Cholmley Turner, *Esq*.'. Sterne's letter followed:

> *To the* PRINTER *of the* YORK COURANT.
> SIR,
>
> As J.S. in your last Courant has shown some Marks of Fear and Penitence in denying his Name, and promising never to offend again, it would be almost an Act of Cruelty to pursue the Man any farther; however since he has left the Field with ill Language in his Mouth, I shall send one Shot after him, which, I am confident, is too well founded to miss him.
>
> A certain nasty Animal in *Egypt*, which, I think, *Herodotus* takes notice of, when he finds he cannot possibly defend himself, and prey any

> longer, partly out of Malice, partly out of Policy, he lets fly backward full against his Adversary, and thereby covers his Retreat with the Fumes of his own Filth and Excrement.
>
> As this Creature is naturally very *impotent*, and its chief Safety depends on a plentiful Discharge on such Occasions, the Naturalists affirm, that Self-preservation directs it to a certain Vegitable on the Banks of the River *Nile*, which constantly arms it with a proper Habit of Body against all Emergencies. I am,
>
> *Yours*, L.S.[46]

While certainly livelier than anything the young clergyman had written previously, this letter—influenced perhaps by the lines 'J.S.' appropriated from Alexander Pope—lies directly in the tradition of the vicious personal attacks his critics so frequently directed against Pope himself.[47] Certainly, it was a good deal more abusive than anything 'J.S.' had written.

By printing the letter over Sterne's initials Caesar Ward had shown the clergyman in a poor enough light, but much worse was to follow. The Revd James Scott now broke silence to defend himself from unwarranted attack, thereby adding considerably to Sterne's discomfiture. The letter Scott wrote 'in vindication and support of my own private Character' appeared in the *York Courant* of 24 November. It is simple, straightforward, and strong. Sterne had charged 'J.S.' with being an '*ignorant, scurrilous, uncharitable, proud, insulting Writer, that dare not own my Name*', but, Scott asked:

> what Authority have you for this Libel? Must your own Surmises, without previous Enquiry or due Information who *J.S.* was, necessarily be allowed a sufficient Foundation for you to point him out as a *Clergyman of Leeds*? and consequently to fix the Imputation on me, as those initial Letters can belong to no other? Is this acting consistently with that Spirit of Charity, which you observe indeed justly, but surely without having the least Claim to it yourself, should be the Characteristick of a *Teacher of Truth*?[48]

By turning Sterne's own rash words back against him in this brief series of rhetorical questions, and by denying that he had been involved in so much as a line of the political writing on the present election, Scott made Sterne look wholly in the wrong in the eyes of any uncommitted elector and foolish in the eyes of all. Scott was intelligent enough to know how to make the best use of his advantage. Instead of answering Sterne's call to apologize, he wrote:

> I shall conclude this with expecting that Satisfaction from you; which, as you profess some Regard to Justice and Truth, all the World must allow to be a reasonable Demand from,
>
> *Sir, Yours, &c.*
>
> JAMES SCOTT.[49]

To this powerful, categorical denial Sterne responded promptly but uneasily. In a letter dated 27 November 1741, and published as a broadside, he refrained from repeating directly his allegation while leaving the reader in little doubt that he was still inclined to believe James Scott to be 'J.S.'. Clearly, though, Sterne had no proof to back up his suspicions, or else he would have directly exposed Scott as a liar. What 'evidence' he did produce was at best circumstantial, and in any case susceptible of very different interpretations. Sterne alleged that on the publication of 'J.S.''s first letter a critical reply had been sent to the *York Courant* which Ward refused to print. 'All had been well,' Sterne wrote, 'if the Printer had contented Himself with the true Excuse, "That his natural Tenderness for Nonsense and Abuse would not suffer him to see it ridiculed or detected . . ."'.[50] Instead, he continued, Ward justified his refusal in the *Courant* of 29 September, alleging that the reply 'reflected upon a *Worthy Clergyman*'. As this was a month before *Query upon Query* appeared, Sterne concluded that he had 'a Chronological Argument (which is the strongest kind of Proof) That you are not indebted to *that* Paper for the Imputation'.[51]

Apparently happy that he had won this argument, Sterne turned his divided attentions back to the election itself. On 24 November Caesar Ward had reprinted in the *York Courant* a letter first published ten days earlier in the London newspaper *Common Sense*, attacking the 'Ministerial Hirelings' whom Cholmley Turner numbered among his supporters. Sterne responded in a letter printed in the London *Daily Gazetteer* of 2 December and twice reprinted in the *York Gazetteer* (8 and 15 December). The clash with Ward had unsettled Sterne, however, for while he began temperately enough with a reasoned appeal to voters to judge Cholmley Turner by his political record, he quickly cast argument aside in order to abuse both the 'frantic, Hot-brained' editor of *Common Sense*—the 'Bigotted *Irish* Papist', Charles Molloy—and also the 'foolish blundering' 'J.S.'.[52]

Any hope Sterne might have entertained that he had won his quarrel with 'J.S.' and Caesar Ward was soon dashed. On the same day that his article attacking Molloy appeared in the *York Gazetteer*, Ward intervened once more. What had remained unclear from their previous letters was whether Caesar Ward had offered fresh evidence that 'J.S.' was a clergyman, or had merely implied that Sterne himself—by referring to J.S. as a clergyman in the letter signed 'J. Wainman'—had effectively identified him with the innocent Scott. Sterne maintained the former; Ward equally strenuously asserted the latter. Ward, however, also offered to carry Sterne's 'Chronological Argument' a stage further, alleging that on 28 September he had received an unsigned letter for insertion in the *Courant*, brought by a person who said it had been given him in York Minster for delivery to the printer. Ward read it, found it contained 'several scandalous and false Reflections', and insisted that unless the letter was signed it would not appear in his newspaper. The messenger departed but returned immediately with the letter that now bore the signature 'J. Wainman'. Ward promptly declared that he knew the handwriting to be that of Laurence Sterne. Now he alleged that this letter concluded, in Sterne's hand, '*I am, Rev. Sir,* Yours,' for which reason Ward next day made his reference to the letter 'reflecting upon a worthy Clergyman in this County'.[53] Nor was Ward finished. On 22 October, he continued, a messenger arrived bringing a vindication of Cholmley Turner 'by Way of *Quaere*'. Initially Ward found parts of the letter objectionable, but when the messenger returned with the 'obnoxious Passages' expunged he agreed to insert it in the *Courant.* That same evening, however, Sterne visited Ward in person to correct some mistakes in the letter; the printer handed it to him and Sterne made the necessary corrections. Then, continued Ward, Sterne 'ask'd me, *Why I had objected to any Expressions in it?* to which I gave for Answer, *That they were not Arguments, but personal Abuses*; and I added these Words, *Mr* Sterne, *By an Expression therein, you seem to insinuate, as if* J.S. *the Letter-Writer in the* Courant, *was a Clergyman, I do assure you he is not a Clergyman*'.[54]

Sterne had now been gainsaid twice. First, James Scott had flatly denied that he was 'J.S.', and now Caesar Ward was not merely questioning Sterne's 'chronological' reasoning but asserting that he had unequivocally assured the Whig prebendary that 'J.S.' was not a clergyman.

The conflict was reaching its climax. Faced with Ward's clear statement of his version of the affair, Sterne responded equally bluntly by arranging that a flat contradiction of Ward's story should appear in the *York Gazetteer* of 15 December 1741. The relevant letter appears over the name of the *Gazetteer*'s printer John Jackson, but must have been written with Sterne's approval, and was probably his own work. 'I am desired,' Jackson declared, 'by that Worthy Gentleman [Laurence Sterne], to make use of His Name, and declare for him in a publick and Solemn Manner, That the Assertion of *Caesar Ward* is a downright Falsehood; and that he (Mr.

Laurence Sterne) neither Compos'd that Letter, nor transcrib'd it.'[55] As proof, Jackson continued, the letter—certified upon oath to be that delivered to Ward—was now with the attorney, John Graves, in Petergate, where any interested party might see it. Jackson was further authorized, he said, to deny absolutely in Sterne's name that Caesar Ward assured Sterne that 'J.S.' was not a clergyman. Indeed, two witnesses would swear on oath that when they delivered Sterne's *Query upon Query* Ward had received it with the reflection that 'it was "*Vicar against Vicar*"'.[56]

Just what the uncommitted reader of York—should any by this time have remained—might have made of this is hard to tell. Here were a respectable printer and a young clergyman prepared to attest in print to quite contradictory versions of the same incident. What no one could miss was the fact that between them 'J.S.' and Caesar Ward had raised Sterne to a considerable pitch of fury. It was well for Ward, it was argued in the letter signed with Jackson's name, that he 'did not depose upon *Oath* what he has asserted upon his *Reputation*; for then he might have forfeited both It and his *Ears* together'—an allusion to the contemporary penalty for perjury. This reference, of course, was not just a more explicit threat against a political opponent than the veiled warning to 'J.S.' but also a powerful rhetorical ploy in Sterne's favour. Had Ward made a false deposition on oath he would have been liable to lose his ears. Nevertheless, to make a deposition upon oath that the letter now with John Graves the attorney was the same letter Ward had received was exactly what Sterne had done.

In all the confusion, however, no one who devoted a moment's thought to the matter could have failed to wonder about one point. If Sterne had had nothing to do with the letter in question, how had it come so conveniently to hand when he needed it as proof that his was the true version of events? A letter, written by a third party, two-and-a-half months earlier, intended but rejected for publication in an opposition newspaper on a matter of ephemeral interest, had not only survived but Sterne had located it. In that case he must have known who had written it. If that letter was really by J. Wainman—there were at least two known possibilities: John Wainman, a resident of Pudsey who subsequently voted for Cholmley Turner in the election, and a Joseph Wainman of York—why not produce him to testify to the fact, and thereby clinch incontrovertible victory? If 'J. Wainman' was not the author, then was Sterne not being, at best, disingenuous? Certainly, it is notable that Sterne made no attempt to deny authorship of the letter posted from Guisborough, only of the letter that Ward cited as evidence that it was Sterne alone who had misidentified 'J.S.' as James Scott. It seems equally certain, however, that the letter left for inspection at Graves's attorney's office was at least not penned by Sterne, whose handwriting could not have been unknown in York.

The alternatives, then, are stark. Either Caesar Ward had lied or was mistaken about the handwriting and about having assured Sterne that 'J.S.' was not a clergyman, or Sterne was prepared to perjure himself (and persuade two others to do likewise) rather than back down in his public argument with 'J.S.' and Ward. The most likely answer is that Sterne was lying. Initially, he may well simply have misunderstood Ward when the latter objected to Sterne 'reflecting upon a worthy Clergyman'. Subsequently, it seems probable that—young and inexperienced as he was, under intense pressure from his implacable uncle, and in the wrong about his opponent's identity—Sterne felt himself manoeuvred into a position in which he could do nothing else and still retain credibility. Though speculative, this view helps to explain Sterne's dramatic withdrawal from political activity following the election—a withdrawal effected at the considerable personal cost of incurring the wrath of an unforgiving Jaques Sterne.

If it was a desperate last attempt to come out on top, Sterne's courting of perjury succeeded. Faced with the possibility of being drawn into unpredictable legal proceedings, Caesar Ward decided to abandon the contest between himself and Sterne, declaring that the clergyman's falsehoods and abuse were beneath his notice. To those to whom any sign of weakness looks like an admission of guilt, it should be said that to this feeble rejoinder Sterne apparently made no reply at all. Printer and priest, it would seem, had both had enough.

Not so 'J.S.'. In the 15 December 1741 issue of the *York Courant* he had added to Sterne's discomfiture by applying to him some more lines borrowed from Pope's *Epistle to Arbuthnot*:

> A Wight, who reads not, and but scans and spells;
> A Word-Catcher that lives on Syllables.
> Who shames this Scribler? break one cobweb thro',
> He spins the slight self-pleasing Thread a-new:
> Destroy his Fib, or Sophistry, in vain,
> The Creature's at his dirty Work again,——
> Thron'd in the Centre of his thin Designs,
> Proud of a vast Extent of Flimzy Lines.[57]

On 5 January 1742 he renewed the debate by attacking his Whig opponents as 'the most abandon'd, profligate Set of Fellows, that ever put Pen to Paper, [as they] have not yet had the Impudence to deny',[58] and suggesting that they had still not answered his original queries, 'notwithstanding the many frivolous Attempts, and the Reams of Paper wasted to that Purpose.'[59] The same issue of the *Courant* also included some original verses published under the title of 'A NEW YEAR'S GIFT *for* L——y':

> GRAVE Legends tell, nor is it yet deny'd,
> That old *St. Laurence* on a Grid-Iron fry'd;
> Our young *St. Laurence* is so wond'rous dry,
> I'll wager, that he'd sooner *burn than fry*.
> And, try to *roast* him—he's so lean and sallow,
> 'Tis Ten to One he drops *more T—d than Tallow*.[60]

As he scanned the lines, the reluctant martyr for the Whig cause must have been relieved that the election was now only eight days away. The ministerial interest, aware that the alliance between Tories and opposition Whigs which had marked the 1734 election had broken down, was beginning to be quietly confident that its candidate would emerge triumphant. All that remained for the Whigs was to conduct themselves appropriately—that is, to show all possible generosity to their supporters in matters of food and drink—during the poll which would open on 13 January.

On 11 January Cholmley Turner travelled from Kirkleatham, to be met outside the city walls by a large group of supporters who accompanied him to his lodgings in Castlegate. The following day it was the turn of George Fox to make his entry into the city, on his way to stay with the lord mayor in the Mint Yard. That same day the *York Gazetteer* fired its final shot in support of Cholmley Turner in a letter to the 'Worthy FREEHOLDERS of the Country of YORK' which—the odd swipe at 'J.S.' apart—was a great deal more measured than most of Sterne's recent contributions to the campaign. With Yorkshire in the grip of winter weather both parties doubtless felt an apprehensive chill as they considered the difficulties they faced in bringing in their supporters from the more distant parts of the county—some electors faced a journey of over one hundred miles[61]—especially since the dearth of overnight accommodation in York resulted in a further financial burden for both contenders.

In fact, when the poll formally opened on 13 January York was more crowded than it had ever been. Over 15,000 electors cast their votes during the week-long poll, watched over by agents of the two parties anxious to ensure that each vote cast was valid. Electors were obliged to present themselves at one of the four booths set aside for each candidate. After five days of polling the *York Courant* announced that the ministerial candidate led by over 700 votes, and though Caesar Ward made a final effort to swing any still-uncommitted electors behind the Tory candidate, neither he nor Fox could now stave off defeat. On 21 January the result of the poll for the county of Yorkshire was announced: Cholmley Turner had won. Turner polled 8,005 votes against Fox's 7,049.[62] It was the highest ever poll in the constituency, beating even the previous record in the 1734 general election—an indication of the importance of the election and the vigour with which it had been conducted. Cholmley Turner was once again chaired in triumph through the streets of York to the noisy satisfaction of his supporters.

For the Sternes—uncle and nephew—there were mixed feelings. For both there was the important satisfaction of seeing their candidate victorious and their campaign thereby vindicated—and modern computer analysis suggests that the fierceness of the electoral struggle was not without justification, for even at a time of unpopularity for the government the Whigs managed to attract to their side more independent voters than they lost to their opponents.[63] For the fiercely partisan archdeacon there was the general satisfaction of seeing that the traditionally Tory clergy had at last swung decisively to the Whig interest: of the 346 clergymen who voted, 254 supported Cholmley Turner.[64] With Turner back in parliament with his support, the archdeacon of Cleveland and precentor of the cathedral might also hope that further preferment would come his way.

Yet for Jaques Sterne public success was soon dulled, if not entirely overshadowed, by personal misfortune. Less than a week after the election concluded his wife Catherine died, aged 62. Of Catherine Sterne we know very little; of her husband's feelings for her, even less. The death notice published in the *York Courant* of 2 February is opaquely conventional: 'Last Tuesday died Mrs. Sterne, Wife of the Reverend Dr Sterne, Precentor of the Cathedral, a Lady remarkable for her Piety, Meekness, Charity, and every Qualification that can adorn her Sex; which has render'd her Death regretted by all who had the Pleasure of her Acquaintance.' Our knowledge of Jaques—greedy for rank and riches, places and power—does not, perhaps, inspire us to see his marriage to an affluent widow, sixteen years his senior, as inspired wholly by love. Yet such marriages were not so uncommon in the eighteenth century and could be extremely successful—as Samuel Johnson's marriage to his much-loved Tetty suggests. At all events, it may be doubted that Turner's hard-won election victory gave Jaques very lasting satisfaction.

For Laurence Sterne the campaign had been a period of mixed emotions. At the age of 28, he had been largely responsible for sustaining the ministerial interest's newspaper campaign. He had seen his letters published in the *Gazetteer*, read in York and throughout the county, reprinted in the London papers, and published in the form of broadsides and pamphlets. He was, of sorts, a writer. Of course Sterne could not expect what he had written to survive long.[65] Political journalism, however, was not without its tangible rewards. During the election campaign, the Revd Robert Hitch, a Whig clergyman, fell ill of a fever. He had, it was reported, 'over-heated himself at the strife about obtaining votes for members of Parliament'.[66] On 26 December he died, leaving the prebendal stall of North Newbald vacant. Just over a week later Laurence Sterne resigned the prebend of Givendale and was preferred to that of North Newbald.

Embroiled in controversy, Sterne had little opportunity to dwell at length on this evidence of his improving situation; he was too busy even to attend the induction ceremony in person. With the election over, however, he had leisure to reflect on the cost of his preferment. Despite the Whig success, he could not have taken unequivocal satisfaction in his own performance as a political journalist. He had shown himself able to isolate the national and local issues on which the election would be fought, and adept at repulsing the often leaden-footed assaults of 'J.S.' on the Whig candidate. Yet Sterne had also allowed himself to be deflected from the important battle for Cholmley Turner and against George Fox into what were essentially peripheral skirmishes, first with 'J.S.' and later with Caesar Ward. In these he had emerged less creditably. Whatever his suspicions, and however much Sterne may have felt himself under personal attack, it mattered very little to the campaign whether his Tory antagonist in the *Courant* was or was not the Revd James Scott. Having unwisely made 'J.S.''s identity an issue, Sterne came close to losing all credibility with uncommitted voters.

In the event, Sterne himself recognized that he had indeed pointed the finger at the wrong man. James Scott's denial that he was 'J.S.', together with Caesar Ward's firmness in propagating his version of affairs, made Sterne—and doubtless his uncle, who had first made the misidentification—cast around for another possible suspect. In the *Gazetteer* of 19 January 1742 Sterne gave confident indication that he had identified his antagonist. Using his opponent's technique, he dedicated some verses in the form of a mock epitaph to his adversary:

An EPITAPH.
On the Death of J——k St——n——pe

Since poor J.S. is dead and gone,
Let this be writ upon his Stone.
Here lies J.S.
Devoid of Sense and eke of Strife,
Who in a Fox-Chace lost his Life,
That Tongue alas does now lie still,
That us'd the Strangest Things to tell;
So strange you'd swear 'twas all a Lye,
But for his KNOWN VERACITY.
—Whoo—Whup ye JACKS! ah weep full sore,
That he of Fox Chace says no more.[67]

How Sterne managed at last to identify his opponent (or even whether he was correct in his second guess) is not certainly known, but he was now indicating his conviction that 'J.S.' was the attorney, sportsman, and enthusiastic Tory John Stanhope, of Horsforth near Leeds. Quite why no one had made this identification earlier is something of a mystery, for Stanhope had been an active supporter of George Fox's campaign since at least mid-November.[68] That no denial was apparently offered to this new and transparent identification suggests that this time Sterne had it right, but he must have been well aware that the very identification was an admission of his previous error.

If Sterne had suffered a personal reverse, the minister on whose behalf he had taken up political writing was set to follow suit. His majority much reduced after the 1741 general election, Walpole found it increasingly difficult to manage the House of Commons as he had done for so long. Under attack both within and outside of parliament, the 'Great Man' was gradually deserted by his former supporters. An opposition motion calling for an inquiry into the conduct of the war was defeated in January 1742 by just 253 votes to 250. Whatever comfort he gained from the election of Cholmley Turner in Yorkshire was offset by the loss of another by-election at Chippenham in Wiltshire. After more than two decades as undisputed prime minister, Walpole resigned all his offices on 3 February. When the news reached York four days later, just over a fortnight after Turner's election, Tories rang church bells and the *York Courant* gleefully declared that 'Satisfaction appeared in every honest Face upon an Event so conducive to the true Interest of his Majesty and his Kingdoms'.[69]

Under Spencer Compton, earl of Wilmington, the Whig ministry, survived but with Walpole's resignation came the first real change of political power the nation had known since Sterne was 8 years old. Whether Walpole's fall made his own efforts seem futile it is impossible to say, but it is certain that by March 1742 at the latest Sterne was no longer contributing to the *York Gazetteer.* The *Courant* noted his defection and took the opportunity to remind its readers of Sterne's less successful journalistic efforts, while charging him with cynical self-interest:

L——y's *Reasons for writing no more* Gazetteers

Presuming that to wear the Lawn
I had a just Pretence,
I've scribbled now for one whole Year,
To baffle Common Sense.

I've taken Pains by Logick Rules,
To prove myself an Ass;
Not dreaming what a wond'rous Change
Is like to come to pass.

But now my Pen I've splinter'd quite,
And thrown away my ink,
For 'till I see which Side will win,
I'll neither write nor think.[70]

If the charge of sitting on the political fence was an obvious enough one to make, it soon became apparent that it was not entirely devoid of truth. In July 1742 Sterne experienced the last of the many setbacks he had suffered during his short political career. On the fourth of the month Edward Thompson, the Whig member of parliament for the City of York, died unexpectedly. Such had been the expense of recent contested elections in Yorkshire that the ministerial interest found itself unable to field a candidate, and Sterne found the object of his recent diatribes—the 'Irishman', the 'foreigner', the danger to the Yorkshire woollen industry George Fox—returned to parliament unopposed. There would not be another contested election in the City of York for more than thirty years, nor another contest in the county until 1807.

Sterne's response to what seems to have been the final blow to his self-esteem was swift. On 27 July a letter from him appeared in the *York Courant*:

To the PRINTER *of the* YORK COURANT

SIR,

I find, by some late Preferments, that it may be not improper to change Sides; therefore I beg the Favour of you to inform the Publick, that I sincerely beg Pardon for the abusive Gazetteers I wrote during the late contested Election for the County of York, and that I heartily wish Mr Fox Joy of his Election for the City.

Tempora mutantur, & nos mutemur in illis.

I am, Sir, your penitent Friend and Servant.

L.S.[71]

This is a curious recantation. Most changes of political allegiance, in the eighteenth century no less than in our own, were coupled with solemn and frequently lengthy self-justifications and protestations of principle. Sterne is not merely laconic but, by his opening sentence, appears to go out of his way to live up to the Tory view of him as a man motivated by self-interest. What Sterne intended by his reference to 'some late Preferments' is not certain, although the fact that William Pulteney—for so long the embodiment of principled Whig opposition to Walpole—had abandoned opposition to take his place in the House of Lords as the earl of Bath a fortnight earlier suggests that the young clergyman had the conduct of his betters in mind.

When Sterne wrote his memoir for Lydia he made a brief reference to the bitter quarrel with his uncle which his desertion of Whig factionalism occasioned. The quarrel arose, Sterne wrote, 'because I would not write paragraphs in the newspapers——though he was a party-man, I was not, and detested such dirty work: thinking it beneath me' (*Letters*, 4). Free as it is from overt moralizing, this statement rings true. In 1742, Sterne had very little to gain in ceasing to write at his uncle's behest, and—as was to happen—a great deal to lose. Whatever preferment Sterne obtained was due, as he well knew and was just enough to acknowledge, to Dr Jaques Sterne. What hopes he might have for the future seemed, with a Whig ministry in power, a Whig archbishop, and the heavily Whig clergy at York, to be bound up with the party he had supported so actively. Indeed, despite his changed attitude to George Fox, whom he had so recently reviled, Sterne in no way associated himself with the Country interest or looked in any obvious way towards a future change of political complexion in government. He broke with no Whig friends—except his uncle—and cultivated no new Tory ones (the one close Tory friend he had in York was Marmaduke Fothergill). Although in the first heady flush of celebrity, he might have said, like another Yorkshire vicar more than half a century later:

> Tory and Whig in turns shall be my host
> I taste no politics in boil'd and roast,[72]

Sterne retained powerful Whig sympathies throughout his life. Yet while he might have agreed with Whig policies in 1741–2, Sterne did not like the methods contemporary practice obliged him to use to support those policies in the newspapers. Serious attempts to address pertinent issues, he soon recognized, were not enough. He had to attack and, if necessary, abuse his opponents.

Late in 1742 Sterne was to expound his mature views on party-writing and its abuses at some length in a letter published in the *York Gazetteer* of 2 November.[73] 'Party-Writers of late Years having been so notoriously Scurrilous and Abusive, so aud[a]ciously intemperate in Personal Reproaches and Invectives, not only beyond the Rules of Decency but *Morality*', he begins, 'I am led to make a few Observations upon this great Evil, which, if not by some proper Means restrain'd, will inevitably end in the Ruin of our most *glorious Constitution*.'[74] Sterne's argument is, at heart, simple enough: party-writers must always support their candidate (even when they believe him to be wrong) and attack or preferably vilify their opponents' candidate (even when they are convinced he is in the right). Two years after his death Sterne's acquaintance and fellow-novelist, Richard Griffith, wrote a witty sketch of Sterne as political journalist:

> My uncle then employed me to write a pamphlet, in defence of the ministry. I obeyed his commands, and put the manuscript into his hands. . . . The method I used in that pamphlet was this——I collected together every thing that had ever been objected against the minister, from his first entering into office till that time, and ipse dixited every article, *point blanc*, in the negative——*from my own certain knowledge, and other sufficient authority*. . . . This book of mine has been the *codex*, or *ars politica*, of all ministerial sycophants ever since that æra——for I have scarcely met with a paragraph in any of the state-hireling writers, for many years past, that I could not trace fairly back to my own *code*.[75]

The length and apparent sincerity of Sterne's repudiation of this notion of political writing in 1742 derived from his own experiences, where he had found his own reputation dealt with as unfairly, in his view, as he himself had acted in casting aspersions on the integrity of others. 'If there be Morality in Writing, as there Certainly is, as well as in any other Art, how different is this manner of Writing from it? The Great Law of Morality is, to treat Others, as They wou'd have Others treat them; and which of them wou'd like to be treated with the same Freedom in his Person and Character, as They in their Writing treat Others . . . ?'[76] Not, evidently, Laurence Sterne.

These arguments, however, should not be taken merely as Sterne's belated thoughts. What finally disgusted him with party-political writing were the lies he had told when cornered by James Scott and Caesar Ward. Naively perhaps, he had begun his contributions to the campaign humorously enough—in the letter signed 'J. Wainman'. By the end he found himself embroiled in an angry wrangle in which either he, an Anglican priest, or a respected printer was deliberately lying for small political advantage, and the only doubt was as to which of the two was the guilty party. Herein lies the real significance of Sterne's addressing his recantation to Ward himself. Had he wished merely to placate or ingratiate himself with George Fox, he could have addressed the letter to him rather than including so conventional a compliment to him by way of afterthought. The sincere apologies Sterne offered were as much to Ward as to the public at large, and were Sterne's tacit admission that in abusing Caesar Ward—calling him, in effect, a liar—he had told rather less than the full story. It was the lot of the political journalist to be abusive and abused, and when the election campaign was over Sterne decided he had had enough. What he did not know in July 1742 was how dear a price he was to pay for finding party-writing beneath him. He would have almost two decades in which to count the cost.

4
Sutton and Stillington, 1742–1745

After the intense activity and stress of the election campaign, daily life at Sutton-on-the-Forest offered the weary Sterne the possibility of repose. Like others before and after him in the eighteenth century, Sterne retired to cultivate his garden. He recorded work done during the autumn of 1742 in the parish book:

> Mem^d. That the Cherry Trees & Espalier Apple Hedge were planted in y^e. Garden
> October y^e. 9. 1742. The Nectarines and Peaches planted the same Day: The pails set up two Months before——
> I Laid out in the Garden, in y^e. year 1742
> The Sum of 8: 15.6
> L. Sterne.[1]

The following year he enclosed the orchard and planted there new apple, pear, and plum trees, spending another £5, as he again noted in the parish book. Small as they are, these entries point to one important fact about Sterne's life at the time: the extent to which he saw his future as lying in his own parish rather than in York. As much is confirmed by a belated entry in the Sutton Parish Book, concerning the improvements Sterne had made earlier to the vicarage. When the Sternes finally moved into the house, following their temporary stay at Church Farm, they began to renovate the dilapidated property. Two years after the work had been started Sterne attempted to compute the cost:

	L S D	
Laid out in Sashing the House.	12: 0: 0	Æ Dom: 1741
In Stukoing and Bricking the Hall —	4: 16: 0	——
In Building the Chair House ------	5: 0: 0	——
In building the Parl^r. Chimney -----	3: 0: 0	L. Sterne
Little House ----------------	2: 3: 0	Vicar

> Spent in Shapeing the Rooms, Plastering, underdwrawing [*sic*] & Jobbing—God knows what—— ———————[2]

God might know, but He was not always forthcoming with financial aid. Sterne's cry is the first (to survive) of many that financial embarrassment would provoke in the years ahead.

For all the young vicar's anxiety to remove himself from the world of political manoeuvring which so engaged his uncle, the decision to fix himself in the country was not taken lightly. Sterne would later declare that he and his wife had denied themselves the 'Pleasures and Advantages of a Town Life' for 'prudent Reasons' (*Letters*, 37). They had good cause: Sterne's financial outlay on the Sutton parsonage might appear modest, yet his repairs had cost him more than a quarter of the yearly value of his living. By his own estimate, his income in 1741 amounted to 'a bare hundred pounds', out of which he was obliged, because of his poor health, to keep a curate. Sterne's journalistic activities make it clear that he had not been extremely ill for any extended period during 1741 or early 1742. Even so, his health did not allow him to combine writing in the Whig interest with the daily routine of parish business, especially as regular journeys to Sutton across the plain north of York would scarcely have been advisable for a consumptive, least of all during winter. Sterne had therefore taken on Richard Wilkinson, who was officially admitted to serve as curate in Sutton in December 1740, remaining there for two years. Exactly what Sterne paid Wilkinson is not known, though it is unlikely to have been significantly more than £20 a year—the minimum laid down in Queen Anne's reign by an act of parliament 'for the better Maintenance of Curates'.[3] Even so, the improvements made to the Sutton vicarage, together with the sum he paid his curate, took up half the value of his living, making 1741 an exceptionally expensive year for Sterne.

It was at the time the Sternes settled down in Sutton-on-the-Forest, thereby ridding themselves of the cost of the curate, that their income began to increase. The prebendal stall of North Newbald that Sterne had gained in 1742 in place of Givendale brought him almost an additional £100 annually.[4] This was further supplemented by Elizabeth Sterne's fortune, which paid another £80. Even so, the couple's income fell well short of £300 a year. Moreover, it is clear that Elizabeth Robinson's scepticism about the ability of her cousin and her new husband to live within their income was justified. Sterne had inherited a careless (though hardly carefree) improvidence from his spendthrift father, but Elizabeth Sterne had grown up with rather higher expectations about the fortune that was proper for her. Forty pounds a year, her husband was later to declare, 'would be nakedness to my Wife' (*Letters*, 41)—a remark which suggests a willingness on Sterne's part to accommodate Elizabeth, regardless of the couple's means—and despite a tendency to cupidity on Elizabeth's part which would later seem to many of their acquaintance a destructive rapaciousness.

Returning to Sutton-on-the-Forest meant much more, of course, than immersion in domestic life. Freed from the demands of politics, Sterne was taking up full-time parish duties for the first time for over two years. How congenial he found these—and how seriously he took them—it is hard to know, for the evidence is sketchy and conflicting.

In March 1743 Lancelot Blackburn died, to be succeeded as archbishop of York by Thomas Herring. Earlier in his career Herring had been, among other things, preacher at Lincoln's Inn in London. It was there, in 1728, that he had famously attacked John Gay's *The Beggar's Opera* for its immorality, provoking Jonathan Swift to comment that Gay's work would 'probably do more good than a thousand Sermons of so stupid, so injudicious, and so prostitute a Divine'.[5] The Tory Swift's contempt notwithstanding, Herring was far from stupid or injudicious—David Hume would later be grateful to him for a letter of encouragement following the initial failure of his *History of England*[6]—and if he was 'prostitute' he was so only in the manner of his age. The attack on Gay's anti-ministerial satire was Herring's way of proclaiming both his Whig loyalties and his willingness to enter into political controversy. From being preacher at Lincoln's Inn he proceeded to the deanery of Rochester, before being raised to the See of Bangor in 1737. Once in Bangor, Herring revealed himself as much more than a dependable supporter of the ministry. Unlike one of his recent predecessors in the See, Benjamin Hoadly, who managed never to visit Bangor during the six years he was bishop between 1715 and 1721, Herring spent his summers touring even the remoter areas of the diocese, performing confirmations and ordinations to the ministry.

The pastoral responsibility Herring had demonstrated in Bangor was similarly to distinguish his tenure of the See of York. After his aged predecessor's neglect of the far-flung Archdiocese—which extended beyond Yorkshire to include parts of Nottinghamshire, Lancashire, and Northumberland—the archbishop determined that a thorough survey was necessary. Consequently, he sent out a questionnaire to the diocesan clergy concerning religious observance and practice in the 903 parishes and chapelries in his care. Laurence Sterne's own reply suggests a man who, far from neglecting his duties, was on the contrary scrupulous enough.[7] Having described the population of the parish and its religious composition (there were five Quaker families out of 120), Sterne succinctly described his own activities. Since he had dispensed with the services of his curate following his return to Sutton, Sterne could honestly present himself as being in sole care of his parishioners. 'I do reside personally upon my Cure, and in my Parsonage House,' he replied to one question, adding 'I have no Curate' in answer to another. In response to a further query Sterne revealed that all except one of his congregation were properly baptized and, if of appropriate age, confirmed also. The solitary exception the young vicar described as a 'Quaker Woman whom I have prevailed with to come to Church, but have not been yet able to gain her consent to be Baptized' (*Letters*, 22). Sterne was no enthusiast, and this is perhaps the only instance of active proselytizing which may be attributed to him. Yet in a parish where nonconformity was no major problem—and in a region where Quakerism was well established—even so small an instance is noteworthy.

In the performance of his liturgical duties Sterne presented himself as at least ordinarily conscientious. Both matins and evensong were performed every Sunday, a practice followed in rather fewer than half of the 836 churches referred to in Herring's visitation returns. There were, however, no weekday services, such as were strictly required of the clergy, though few complied. Holy Communion was administered on five Sundays in the year—a slightly above-average frequency in the York archdiocese, for 571 of the 836 churches celebrated the Sacrament quarterly or less. (The Sundays were probably Palm Sunday, Easter Day, Whit Sunday, the Sunday in the octave of Michaelmas, and Christmas Day.) Of the approximately 250 parishioners who might properly communicate, over half actually did so at Easter 1743—an exceptionally high percentage in comparison to parishes elsewhere.[8] Sterne also noted that he gave 'timely Warning' of the Sacrament before it was administered, that he did not request the names of intending communicants beforehand, and that he had never refused the sacraments to anyone who desired them. In reply to a question concerning the catechism, Sterne declared that 'I Catechise every Sunday in my Church during Lent, But explain our Religion to the Children and Servants of my Parishioners in my own House every Sunday Night during Lent, from six o'clock till nine'. That so long a period devoted weekly to the catechism was unusual is evidenced by the concluding sentence of Sterne's reply: 'I mention the Length of Time as my reason for not doing it in Church' (*Letters*, 22). By an account Sterne gave at the end of his life, his rural parishioners certainly had need of intensive catechizing: when a pistol exploded in the hand of Sterne's postillion, the unfortunate man believed his hand blown off and, falling on his knees, began 'Our Father, which art in Heaven, hallowed be thy Name . . . at which like a good Christian, he stopped, not remembering any more' (*Letters*, 390). In fact, while Sterne seems to have been unusually diligent in this particular, he still fell short of the requirements of the canons, which stipulated that catechizing was to take place every Sunday and Holy Day (and not merely during Lent); in 1752 the then archdeacon of Cleveland, Francis Blackburne, insisted on the inadequacy of the practice adopted by Sterne and others: 'whoever shall think fit to limit his Obligations . . . to hearing the Church-Catechism repeated by Rote, and that only for five or six *Sundays* in *Lent*, must put a gloss upon the Text which cannot be justified.'[9]

All in all, however, the picture of Sterne that emerges from the questionnaire is of a priest at once scrupulous and well informed. The weakness of the picture, of course, is that it was drawn by Sterne himself. It is true that Archbishop Herring's final question—asking the clergy for any suggestions they might have toward the better running of the diocese—was left unanswered, which does not suggest a man out to ingratiate himself at all costs. Even so, it is obvious that no young clergyman replying to a questionnaire sent to him by his archbishop was likely to respond in a manner which revealed himself in a poor light, and Sterne was no exception.

However heedful of his parishioners' needs Laurence Sterne may have been, he had one talent in particular much valued in the eighteenth-century Church in general, though doubtless rare enough in rural Yorkshire: he was an excellent and affecting preacher. In an age when sermon-going was as much a popular diversion as a religious duty, Sterne's parishioners were fortunate indeed. His former servant, Richard Greenwood, later recalled that 'the audience were quite delighted with him, & he never preached at Sutton but the [congregation] were in tears'.[10]

Though delivered many years later, this testimony chimes in well with what we know of Sterne as a preacher both from other personal accounts and from those of his sermons—forty-five of them—published during and after his lifetime. For the most part Sterne avoided theological disputation—though he could be keenly anti-Roman Catholic and anti-Methodist on occasion, especially when the attitude of his ecclesiastical superiors made this seem politically expedient.[11] Instead he followed a line common in eighteenth-century Anglicanism, reiterating the importance of good works undertaken as a consequence of faith, underscoring his arguments by eloquently pathetic appeals to his congregations' emotions rather than to their intellect. In this too, Sterne seemed to follow the lead of his superiors in the Church, for Archbishop Herring himself insisted that 'Christianity is more the Religion of the Heart, than of the Head'.[12] In the pulpit itself Sterne's particular gifts came to the fore. To his congregation in the 1740s he seemed to preach extempore. On one occasion, having omitted to bring his sermon with him while preaching in the country away from Sutton, Sterne simply asked for a Bible and 'composed a most excellent sermon which he delivered from a scrap of paper no bigger than his hand'.[13] That he regularly delivered sermons spontaneously is improbable, however, for Sterne shared the general latitudinarian mistrust of the wholly extempore sermonizing associated first with puritanism and later with dissent. Most likely, his popularity as a preacher resulted from a combination of natural eloquence and hard work in the study, based on wide and eclectic reading in the published sermons of other divines. In any case, with a well-stocked mind, a talent for improvisation, and a delivery more dramatic, and certainly more pathetic, than that of neighbouring clerics, Sterne seems quickly to have become the popular preacher Richard Greenwood remembered many years later.

Whatever his natural aptitude for preaching, Sterne's skills were certainly honed by much practice. Throughout the 1740s and 1750s, the Sternes' financial problems led the young vicar to seek out any available means of supplementing an income never adequate to the couple's needs. It was for this reason that he turned to substitute preaching at York Minster. Among the duties of a prebendary was the obligation to preach set turns in York Minister; as prebendary of Givendale Sterne was obliged to deliver sermons there twice yearly. Not all of the clergy with similar obligations were willing or able—the archdiocese was a large one—to fulfill them, however. Hence the opportunity arose for others to supply their place in return for their fee. In the *Intelligencer* Jonathan Swift had described the plight of the impoverished Eugenio, who was forced 'to Preach a Sermon for Ten shillings, to supply his Necessities'.[14] In 1742, and for years thereafter, Sterne was equally necessitous, if somewhat better remunerated. For the sake of the standard fee of £1 Sterne would compose a sermon and then make the journey to York to preach it, in addition to performing the two services held at Sutton every Sunday.

Preparing a sermon for the Minster was certainly a more onerous task than simply preaching to his village congregation. In Sutton-on-the-Forest Sterne acted like virtually every Anglican clergyman in the eighteenth century, borrowing heavily in his sermons from the published works of the great preachers of the present and immediate past, either directly or by means of the commonplace book he seems likely to have kept.[15] The rural congregation to whom Sterne regularly preached were considered to need no great theological insights. It was Swift again who, in *A Letter to a Young Gentleman Lately enter'd into Holy Orders*, spoke for most Anglican clergy in his age, when advising that the basis of preaching was 'first to tell the People what is their Duty; and then to convince them that it is so'.[16] To preach at York Minster, however, was a little more demanding. Though the eight miles separating Sutton from York may not seem a very formidable journey today, the state of the roads could make the journey laborious or even, in bad weather, impossible (on one occasion the condition of the road prevented Sterne from reaching York, even in July). To ride a return journey of sixteen miles between morning and evening service for the sake of £1 suggests that Sterne's financial needs were indeed considerable. If Jaques Sterne's help had enabled his nephew to gain a foothold on the ladder of clerical preferment, Sterne would maintain his position only by dint of his own continuing efforts.

There is some evidence, however, that Sterne's talents in the pulpit were quickly recognized well beyond the Sutton parish boundaries. Three days after his arrival in York Archbishop Herring attended a service in the Minster to mark the sixteenth anniversary of George II's accession. The *York Courant* subsequently reported that a sermon 'suitable to the Occasion was preach'd by the Rev. Mr. Sterne, one of the Prebendaries'.[17] To preach on the anniversary of the king's accession was an honour, but to do so before the new archbishop was a challenge also, for Herring was a protégé of the great pulpit orator William Fleetwood, a successor as preacher at Lincoln's Inn to John Tillotson, and a preacher of whose own sermons it was said that they 'abounded with manly Sense, were animated by the most benevolent Principles, and adorned by his happy Elocution and unaffected Delivery'.[18] As a descendant of one of Herring's predecessors in the See, and a graduate of the same Cambridge college, Sterne was well enough placed to bring himself to the attention of the new archbishop under any circumstances, and to preach a sermon before him immediately after his arrival gave him an excellent opportunity to impress Herring. Sterne's choice of text—'If thou doest well, shalt thou not be accepted? and if thou doest not well, sin lieth at the door' (Genesis 4: 7)—suggests that his attempt to bring himself to the prelate's notice may have been a little too audacious to have served its intended purpose.[19] Certainly, if Sterne was gratified to receive the mark of distinction the invitation to preach suggested, then he appears to have received nothing else. Herring was later to lament that an archbishop's fate was to be deemed 'an inexhaustible Patron' though he might only have 'a slender Patronage',[20] and 'excellent' as Sterne's sermon was reported to have been, Archbishop Herring was to offer the preacher no advancement during his entire tenure of the See of York.

Perhaps Sterne expected none. He had no independent interest, and what little he had once enjoyed was now lost to him as a result of his uncle's implacable hostility. Nor was Sterne's own conduct beyond reproach. A conscientious, politically astute archbishop like Herring would surely soon have uncovered evidence that, as we shall see, Sterne's rakishness did not disappear with his marriage. Moreover, evidence of occasional carelessness even in the performance of his regular duties was also doubtless to hand, for the young priest could be culpably remiss. On one such occasion, an acquaintance reported, Sterne 'was going over the Fields on a sunday to preach . . . it happened that his Pointer Dog sprung a Covey of Partridges, when he went directly home for his Gun and left his Flock that was waiting for him in the Church, in the lurch'.[21] On another, 'a Flock of Geese assembled in the Church Yard at Sutton, when [Sterne's] Wife bawl'd out, "Laurie, powl 'em," i.e. pluck the quills, on which [the congregation] were ready to riot and mob Laurie'.[22] Understandably enough, a vicar so easily distracted from his duties was not always able to depend on the undivided loyalty of his parishioners, and when the ice once broke under him while he was skating one winter on a frozen pond none of them would help to pull him out since, as a third tale has it, 'they were at variance'.[23]

It would be misleading to put too much emphasis on such purely anecdotal evidence, especially since these three stories all derive from the same, sometimes untrustworthy source. It is clear, though, that the young vicar did not settle easily into the ordered life of a rural clergyman. His ever-present financial problems aside, Sterne was far from content in Sutton. Part of the problem lay in the extreme change of circumstances from those he had experienced during his extended sojourn in York. There, the sociable Sterne had enjoyed plentiful opportunities to meet congenial company in the city. No such opportunity existed in Sutton. Instead, Sterne was forced into uneasy proximity to the Oxford-educated, Tory squire of Sutton, Philip Harland. While he was spending most of his time in York, in the company of politically like-minded and convivial friends, leaving his parish to the care of a curate, this presented no great problem. Having abandoned politics and moved back to Sutton, however, the absence of a real social and intellectual equal with whom he could get along amicably was a serious drawback. Certainly, the notorious role Laurence Sterne had played in the 1741–2 by-election campaign, including his abuse of George Fox, now member of parliament for York, cannot have helped their relations. Yet while they were never—like the parson and squire Addison described in the *Spectator*—entrenched 'in a perpetual State of War',[24] the antagonism between Philip Harland and Sterne was sufficient for the latter to note laconically, in his brief memoir: 'as to the 'Squire of the parish, I cannot say we were upon a very friendly footing' (*Letters*, 4). It is likely, indeed, that Philip Harland was by no means pleased to see Sterne back in Sutton, for he appears to have been on altogether better terms with Sterne's curate, Richard Wilkinson. The only two gifts the squire made to Sutton church, as recorded in the parish book, both date from the period of the Wilkinson's curacy:

> The Seven Elm Trees at the Bottom of the Garden, and four in the church yard were the Gift of Phil: Harland Esq: & Planted in the Year 1740.
>
> faithfully recorded by R: Wilkison [*sic*]

> The Arbour and also the Elm Trees in the Garden and Churchyard, were Part of them taken out of Mrs. Wakefield's Garden at Huby & the Rest were the Gift of Phil: Harland Esq: & were planted by Richd Wilkinson curate to the Rev^{d} Mr. Sterne M:A: & Vicar of Sutton in the Year 1740.[25]

No such donations are recorded while Sterne was in residence. It may even be that the preference Harland displayed for Richard Wilkinson affected Sterne's own attitude towards his former curate. Wilkinson's preferment from another Yorkshire curacy to the living of Coxwold—the living Sterne himself would acquire only after the success of *Tristram Shandy*—suggests that he was a capable and conscientious cleric. Yet Sterne went out of his way to record his displeasure at his curate's conduct, appending to the (apparently incomplete) record of baptisms and burials for the year 1741 a testy note: 'N.B. I fear the Register for this Year is defective. By the negligence of The Gentleman who was Curate.'[26]

It is probably wrong, however, to infer that party-political differences—however intensely felt—were the sole source of the disagreement between Sterne and Philip Harland. Richard Greenwood suggested a further reason for the mutual dislike. Sterne, he remembered,

> was for many years at variance with the Harlands, the Squires of his parish—it originated in his determination to give a settlement to a man

> who exercising a trade which required [Apprentices], Mr. Harland thought that thereby an expense might be brought on the parish. Sterne was determined to carry his point, & let the man a farm of [20] £ a year which gave him a settlement, & he never spoke to the Harlands after.[27]

If, as seems likely from Greenwood's testimony, this incident dates from the earliest years of Sterne's residency in Sutton, then the disagreement with Harland may have arisen from the two men's very different sense of what was appropriate to their respective positions, and their shared responsibilities and complementary roles in the governing of village life. Even the one known gesture of apparent goodwill towards Philip Harland made by Laurence Sterne—the gift of a copy of a sermon by him when it was printed in 1747—is decidedly ambivalent, for *Elijah and the Widow of Zerephath* is a charity sermon emphasizing, in no uncertain terms, the Christian duty of the wealthy to provide for those less fortunate than themselves. Unwilling to live in open hostility, unable to live in harmony, the Revd Laurence Sterne and the squire of Sutton existed for perhaps twenty years in what another eighteenth-century novelist memorably described as 'dissent terms of civility'.[28]

In the circumstances, it was fortunate indeed for Laurence Sterne that he received one further preferment in the 1740s. Early in 1744 he acquired a second living. During the winter of 1743–4 the living of Stillington, the parish adjoining Sutton-on-the-Forest, fell vacant by the death of the vicar, the Revd Richard Musgrave. In memoir Sterne made it clear that he owed his preferment not to his estranged uncle but to his wife. 'By my wife's means I got the living of Stillington,' he wrote, 'a friend of her's in the south had promised her, that if she married a clergyman in Yorkshire, when the living became vacant he would make her a compliment of it' (*Letters*, 4). Whether or not it gives the whole story, Sterne's account illuminates how small a role personal merit might play in the distribution of livings in the eighteenth-century Anglican Church.[29] Although pluralism was for long regarded as one of the most widespread abuses of the Established Church of the time—in 1743 the visitation returns showed that 335 of the 711 clergy in the See of York were pluralists—the fact that Sterne's two holdings were adjacent effectively precluded the possibility of any particularly damaging neglect. Sterne was inducted into his new living on 13 March 1744, and did duty in both parishes for nearly twenty years.

Gaining a second living brought Sterne a number of advantages, besides additional responsibilities. Though Stillington was comparatively poor, worth £50 a year at most—only half the value of Sutton—the increase in income could only have been welcomed by the ever-needy and improvident Sternes. Besides the direct increase in income Sterne also gained almost forty acres of land from the living, which together with the church lands of Sutton and Huby gave him a total of about 120 acres.[30] More important than any of these, however, was the fact that Stillington brought Sterne into contact for the first time with a man who was to prove a good and enduring friend. This was Stephen Croft, the squire of Stillington, thanks to whom Sterne would set out for London on one still-distant day in March 1760 to enjoy there the fruits of his success as author of the first two volumes of *Tristram Shandy*. Through Croft, Sterne also acquired a much wider circle of congenial acquaintances. Given his known sociability and the coldness between himself and Philip Harland, Sterne could only have been delighted with his new friends. Just a year older than Sterne, Croft was not only an active Whig but also a man who shared Sterne's diverse interests in painting, music, and literature: in the years to come he would commission Joshua Reynolds to paint his portrait, act as a director of the York Assembly Rooms, and be among the select group to whom Sterne read the earliest draft of what would eventually become *Tristram Shandy*. Croft was also a man of considerable wealth and taste, indicated most obviously in his much-admired rebuilding of Stillington Hall. Contrasting his situation in the two parishes, Sterne paid warm tribute to his friend: 'at Stillington, the family of the C[roft]s shewed us every kindness——'twas most truly agreeable to be within a mile and a half of an amiable family, who were ever cordial friends' (*Letters*, 4). John Croft—whose personal knowledge of Sterne was limited by his long sojourn in Portugal, where he was involved in the port wine trade—wrote that Sterne 'was a constant Guest at my brother's Table'.[31] Our knowledge of his enjoyment of congenial fellowship derives mainly from the years of his fame, but Richard Greenwood described the young Sterne as 'a man of prodigious wit, & the entertainment of every company'.[32] The importance of good conversation to Sterne was enhanced, indeed, by the extent to which he differed in important respects from contemporary norms of male conviviality. As a young man Sterne 'never drank to excess—he usually after Dinner took one glass of wine, of which he drank half, & filled his glass with water for the rest'.[33] Moreover, though he shot regularly he had no time for any other of the older and still commonplace rural pastimes of Yorkshire gentlemen: fox-hunting, horse-racing, horse-breeding, or cockfighting.

Drinking and hunting were, by contrast, precisely the activities enjoyed by Sterne's college friend John Hall-Stevenson. In contrast to the solid, respectable Stephen Croft, Hall-Stevenson also held out to Sterne the tantalizing prospect of companionship of a more facetious and sceptical kind, more attuned to those elements in Sterne's character that his parishioners considered 'crazy, or crackbrained'.[34] Following his marriage, Hall-Stevenson had taken up residence at Skelton Castle, some fifty miles to the north of York. There virtually every feature of life differed notably from Sterne's daily routine. The castle itself was an ancient, moated semi-ruin, habitable only in parts, and thus presented a very different appearance both to the parsonage house in Sutton and to Stillington Hall. In later years Hall-Stevenson celebrated his home in verse as 'Crazy Castle':

THERE is a Castle in the North,
  Seated upon a swampy clay,
At present but of little worth,
  In former times it had its day.

This ancient Castle is call'd CRAZY
  Whose mould'ring walls a moat environs . . .[35]

As early as the year of his marriage Hall-Stevenson was making his home the focus for a group of like-minded friends: intelligent, under-occupied men given to conviviality and country pursuits. One friend later wrote that the master of Skelton 'kept a full-spread board, and wore down the steps of his cellar. His open heart filled his dining-room with choice company'.[36] Choice the company may have been, but Hall-Stevenson's own description of their activities suggests more the essential aimlessness of rural life for those who had no fixed occupation:

Some fell to fiddling, some to fluting,
  Some to shooting, some to fishing,
Others to pishing and disputing,
  Or to computing by vain wishing.

And in the evening when they met,
  To think on't always does me good,
There never met a jollier set,
  Either before, or since the Flood.[37]

Perhaps the jollity was sometimes forced, for Hall-Stevenson later wrote of these years in a very different vein, lamenting that 'ye scantiness of my fortune forced me to vegetate in ye country, and precluded me from every laudable pursuit suggested by ambition'.[38] Some of the jolly set nevertheless had cause to be grateful to Hall-Stevenson for his generosity. One of them was Robert Lascelles, an Oxford graduate, who was in his mid-twenties when he served in the Royal Hunters, a force of irregulars Hall-Stevenson formed in defence of the House of Hanover during the 1745 Jacobite rebellion.[39] Son of a north-country landowner, Lascelles took holy orders in his early thirties only to become Hall-Stevenson's gamekeeper in the mid-1750s; having served as chaplain to an infantry regiment in the 1760s, he eventually became vicar of Gilling West, near Richmond, in 1777, a living he owed to Hall-Stevenson. His devotions, however, seem to have been directed principally to his pipe and the field sports of which he was immoderately fond, and on which he was to write a posthumously published book entitled *Angling, Shooting, and Coursing* (1815).

At Skelton Lascelles was known as 'Panty', short for Pantagruel—a nickname taken from the hero of François Rabelais's earliest work, and indicative of the nature of the society Hall-Stevenson gathered around him. Though no fool, Lascelles was a man of modest achievement, as were two fellow sportsmen, Andrew Irvine and Zachary Moore. Other members of the Skelton circle were more accomplished. Besides the former Peterhouse fellow Thomas Gilbert, who held the nearby living of Skinningrave after 1741, there were two future members of parliament. One was Thomas Scrope of Colby—known at Skelton as Cardinal Scrope—ten years Sterne's junior, who had studied at Oxford and would sit as member for Lincoln from 1768 to 1774; the second was Charles Turner, nephew of Cholmley Turner, a farmer respected for his knowledge by Arthur Young, who had studied both at the Inner Temple in London and at Trinity College, Cambridge, and who would represent Yorkshire in parliament after 1768.

Though most surviving mention of the Skelton set celebrates its sociable nature, there is evidence too of a darker side to its members. Hall-Stevenson himself could be moody and morose. An anecdote first printed in the year after his death tells how the master of Skelton Castle took to his bed because of an east wind, whereupon Sterne hired a boy to climb to the weather-vane atop the Castle and secure it to indicate a west wind, thereby persuading Hall-Stevenson to leave his bed.[40] Like many of the stories which attached themselves to Sterne after his death, the documentary value of this one may be slight. It is certain, though, that Hall-Stevenson would come to regret not only the loss of most of the fortune he had expected to inherit from his father-in-law but also the disappointments of what—'[d]ead to the world, himself, and friend'—he seems to have considered a largely wasted life.[41] A less sympathetic picture emerges of Charles Turner from a prose sketch of him in his later years, written by the playwright George Colman the Younger. Having visited Hall-Stevenson, whom he described as an 'odd, thin figure', Colman met Turner at Kirkleatham in 1775, describing him as 'the most formidable Nimrod in the district', and one who 'persecuted a fox with jovial inveteracy'. When his young son, also Charles, ran into the drawing-room at Kirkleatham with a live mouse, Turner greeted him with the words: 'Bite off his head, Charles'—which the boy promptly did.[42]

An altogether more amiable form of eccentricity characterized the Oxford-educated William Hewett (1693–1766)—the oldest member of the Skelton club (he was twenty years Sterne's senior)—who accompanied the marquess of Granby on his Grand Tour in the 1740s. Like Hall-Stevenson and Lascelles, Hewett took up arms in 1745, becoming colonel of the Leicestershire Volunteers. Even more notably idiosyncratic than others in the group, Hewett was well known, according to Tobias Smollett, 'by the nick-name of Cavallo Bianco, from his appearing always mounted on a pale horse, like Death in the Revelations'.[43] A friend of Voltaire, he brought on his own death by fasting in imitation of the ancients: 'Being taken with a suppression of urine, he resolved, in imitation of Pomponius Atticus to take himself off by abstinence; and this resolution he executed like an ancient Roman. He saw company to the last—cracked his jokes—conversed freely—and entertained his guests with musick.'[44]

Whether or not he was a heretic—as Pope Benedict XIV is reported to have alleged[45]—Hewett was clearly no orthodox Christian, and it is the supposed irreligious nature of the Skelton circle that has given it a degree of notoriety, not least in relation to the religious convictions of the Revd Laurence Sterne. How deserved this is, however, remains open to question. To an extent, Sterne himself must bear some responsibility, for years later he asked Hall-Stevenson to pass on his greetings to the 'Demoniacs'—a name the group probably borrowed from Swift[46]—whom he referred to sardonically elsewhere as the 'household of faith'.[47] While such terminology sits oddly on the lips of an ordained clergyman—and it is true that in the years of his fame more than one friend considered him a sceptic—it by no means supports the more colourful of the speculative accounts which grew up concerning the activities of the circle at Crazy Castle. Certainly there is no evidence to support the notion that Hall-Stevenson's group was some north-country counterpart to the group known as the Monks of Medmenham Abbey, supposedly founded by Sir Francis Dashwood, or the Dublin Hell-Fire Club.[48] In fact it is highly doubtful whether the alleged impiety of Dashwood himself led to anything remotely as lurid—the celebration of black masses, for instance—as the events later imaginatively related in verse and prose by Charles Churchill, in *The Candidate* (1764) or by Charles Johnstone in the second edition of his novel *Chrysal; or, the Adventures of a Guinea* (1766). Much more probable than the idea that Skelton was a centre of rabid freethinking is the likelihood that Hall-Stevenson and his friends shared with Dashwood a mildly daring desire to shock the more staid of their neighbours, coupled with a devotion to Rabelais, symbolized by the (for them) wishful motto '*Fay ce que voudras*' ('Do what you will', the Rule of the imaginary Abbey of Theleme in Rabelais's *Gargantua*).

What is equally open to question is the extent to which Sterne himself was ever a member of the Skelton group in the years prior to his fame. Once he had become a celebrity Hall-Stevenson made much of the friendship that had originated in their student days, and Sterne reciprocated in writing to his 'Cosin Antony'.[49] Yet shortly after Hall-Stevenson had published some verses in praise of Sterne's triumphant arrival in London in March 1760, Sterne himself flatly denied that he had corresponded with Hall in nineteen years. The denial may have been a prudential response to the indecency of the verses themselves, but it is striking that only the slightest evidence survives of more than a continuing acquaintance between the two in the 1740s and 1750s.[50] To later biographers, as perhaps to Sterne himself, the Skelton circle of Hall-Stevenson may have seemed a rich source of amusement and intellectual speculation, but it is doubtful that Sterne enjoyed many opportunities to partake of the society of Crazy Castle in the years before his fame.

The reality, indeed, is likely to have been more mundane. For twenty years or so Sterne's life in Sutton and Stillington centred on those recreations which were increasingly becoming the hallmark of genteel fashion: gardening, painting, music, and reading. Perhaps because he lacked the funds to indulge his real interests, none of these seems to have given Sterne real or lasting satisfaction, however. 'He was not steady to his Pastimes, or Recreations,' John Croft recorded 'At one time he wou'd take up the Gun and follow shooting till he became a good shott, then he wou'd take up the Pencil and paint Pictures.'[51]

Croft's mention of painting is borne out by much of what we know of Sterne's activities and interests throughout his life. Sterne's considerable, if unsystematic, knowledge of painting is evidenced by numerous passages in his correspondence, his fiction, and his sermons. The rapidity with which he had an acquaintance approach William Hogarth for an illustration for

Tristram Shandy perhaps says more for his commercial acuity than his appreciation of the artist's merits, but he was unaffectedly delighted to have his portrait painted by Joshua Reynolds in London and Carmontelle in Paris. He might, as Reynolds himself had done in the *Idler*,[52] satirize the vapid contemporary aesthetic terminology of connoisseurship— 'the expression of *Rubens*,—the grace of *Raphael*,——the purity of *Dominichino*,—the *corregiescity* of *Corregio*' (*TS* III. xii. 144)—but he was familiar with Hogarth's ambitious aesthetic treatise *The Analysis of Beauty* (1753).[53] In *A Sentimental Journey*, Sterne might affect disdain for the common artistic pursuits of the Grand Tourist, but he was quick to report his own delight at having been given private access to the collection of the duc d'Orléans in the Palais Royal in Paris.[54] And though his treatment of Hogarth's 'line of beauty' in *Tristram Shandy* was equivocal, his sermons and novels alike contain scenes so precisely visualized and so delicately imbued with pathos as to bring to mind similarly sentimental compositions of a contemporary master like Jean-Baptiste Greuze. While recurring financial problems limited his ability to purchase pictures until his writing brought him some measure of security, Sterne subsequently delighted in buying prints to decorate his home—and expressed evidently genuine gratitude for a similar gift from a friend. An informed interest in painting does not, however, necessarily make a good artist. Of Sterne's own work, John Croft was dismissive: 'There are severall Pictures of his painting at York,' he noted, adding bluntly, 'such as they are.'[55] Croft may have been correct, however, that Sterne's real artistic talent was as a draughtsman rather than a painter: 'He had a good Idea of Drawing, but not the least of mixing his colours.'[56] These pictures have now all but vanished from sight, but one trace remains to bear out Croft's assertion that Sterne would frequently copy the work of others: a picture of Sterne's friend Thomas Bridges as a mountebank, with himself as the mountebank's assistant, which survives in an engraving, is known to have been copied from a comic broadside entitled *The Infallible Mountebank, or Quack Doctor*. The work, which contains the earliest known portrait of Sterne—by Bridges—finds Sterne sticking very close to his source in his own portrait of his friend.[57] That Sterne himself continued to have some confidence in his artistic judgement, if not ability, is evident from a peremptory and insensitive injunction delivered to his then 16-year-old daughter Lydia in 1764: 'as you have no genius for drawing (tho' you could never be made to believe it) pray waste not your time about it' (*Letters*, 212). Revealing something of the confidence John Croft attributed to her father, Lydia paid no attention to this paternal edict and continued to draw, even allowing herself to be persuaded to attempt some sentimental illustrations for a projected posthumous edition of her father's works in 1769.

As far as music was concerned, Sterne's interest was both real and unexceptional for a man of his time and social background. He played the violin and the bass viol (his own instrument was sold after his death for 6 guineas[58]). The fact that the bass viol was soon to disappear even from domestic music-making suggests that Sterne's tastes were conservative, having been shaped by his own provincial background. All the same, he was a reasonably accomplished amateur performer—and certainly, it would seem, an enthusiastic one:

> Ptr..rr..ing—twing—twang—prut—trut——'tis a cursed bad fiddle.—Do you know whether my fiddle's in tune or no?—trut..prut..—They should be *fifths.*——'Tis wickedly strung—tr...a.e.i.o.u.-twang.—The bridge is a mile too high, and the sound-post absolutely down,—else—trut . . prut—hark! 'tis not so bad a tone.—Diddle diddle, diddle diddle, diddle diddle, dum. (*TS* v. xv. 297)

We have little indication of which composers Sterne favoured in the years before his fame—there is brief mention made in *Tristram Shandy* (III. v) of the sixth of Charles Avison's concertos fashioned from keyboard sonatas by Domenico Scarlatti—but his limited finances necessarily curtailed his ability to purchase expensive sheet music for his own use. We know, however, that in the early 1750s he borrowed from York Minster library works by three composers of previous generations, Henricus Albicastro, Biagio Marini, and Antonio Vivaldi. It is highly likely that, within the limits of his income, he also took advantage whenever possible of the opportunities afforded music-lovers by York's extensive concert programmes. Only during the years of his fame, however, would he have both the opportunity and the means to enjoy first-rate contemporary music in performances of the highest class, such as that he was to hear in the celebrated Bach–Abel concerts in London during the 1760s, one of which he declared to be 'the best Concert I ever had the honour to be at' (*Letters*, 296).

That reading occupied many of Sterne's leisure hours is not surprising—and distinguishes him but little from many other rural clergymen in the eighteenth century. Sterne's taste in literature, however, was unusually eclectic, somewhat backward-looking, and dominated by a preference for idiosyncratic humorous works. That taste had likely been founded in his student days at Cambridge, though he could have had little spare money to buy books—and undergraduates were excluded even from using the university library, let alone borrowing volumes. The books

Sterne particularly favoured in later life, however, were very much those of a kind that appealed also to John Hall-Stevenson, and it may be that the personal libraries of congenial, and wealthier friends first gave Sterne access to the works he would gleefully remember in later life. After his death Sterne's books were sold at auction, but since the auction catalogue contains many books that were not in his library, and omits others he is known to have owned, its value is limited.[59] He had access to the works of highly regarded writers like Shakespeare, another lifelong favourite, even before he left Yorkshire for Cambridge, but among his other preferred authors it is difficult to imagine Sterne reading Rabelais in the house of his uncle, or even of his cousin Richard. It may have been Hall-Stevenson who introduced him to French authors, or they may have become friends after discovering their shared literary tastes.[60] John Croft said of Sterne's literary influences: 'The Books that he studied and drew from most were the Moyen de Parvenir, a small French book, I had it from himself, Montaignes Essays, he affected the style of Rabelais, and particularly Bishop Halls Works which he copied a pie de la lettre.'[61] To this tiny list we can add the Bible, Shakespeare's plays, and Cervantes's *Don Quixote*. In *Tristram Shandy* Tristram apostrophizes 'Lucian . . . my dear *Rabelais*, and dearer *Cervantes*' (*TS* III. xix. 151) and Sterne alludes repeatedly to the Spanish author, as much in his sermons as in his fiction or correspondence. Among other favourites were Erasmus' *In Praise of Folly*, the *Essays* of Bacon, the *Maxims* of La Rochefoucauld, Swift's *A Tale of a Tub*, the periodical papers of Addison and Steele, and such Scriblerian works as the *Dunciad Variorum*, the *Memoirs of Martinus Scriblerus*, and the slighter 'Memoirs of P. P. Clerk of this Parish'. His education had led to familiarity with the classical philosophers, and his profession to a knowledge of the Church Fathers and the sermons of, among many others, John Tillotson, Isaac Barrow, and Samuel Clarke. In modern philosophy, Locke's *Essay Concerning Human Understanding* (1690) was a clear favourite—though his fiction frequently suggests Sterne's familiarity, at least at second hand, with the work of David Hume, especially the *Treatise of Human Nature* (1739–40). As his fiction also reveals, Sterne was nothing if not eclectic in his reading: he was, or would become, familiar with works as diverse as Josephus' *De Bello Judaico*, of the first century AD, Saxo Grammaticus' thirteenth-century *Gesta Danorum*, Henry Swinburne's *A Briefe Treatise of Testaments and last Willes* (1590), Bruscambille's *Prologues tant sérieux que facétieux* (1610), Dr William Warburton's *The Divine Legation of Moses* (1738), and Dr John Burton's *An Essay towards a Complete New System of Midwifery* (1751). Sterne was also particularly fond of two works of encyclopaedic learning: Robert Burton's early-seventeenth-century compendium *The Anatomy of Melancholy* (1621), and Ephraim Chambers's pioneering work of eighteenth-century enlightenment, the *Cyclopaedia* (1728).

With the limited funds at his disposal during his years in Sutton Sterne was unable to form a personal library of any size. That he felt this deprivation keenly is particularly evident from the delight he would exhibit in the summer of 1761, when he eventually had spare money enough to buy some 700 or more books at bargain price.[62] Even so, he did have one resource in those years, besides the libraries of friends. Having become a canon of York Minster at the time he acquired his first prebend in 1741, Sterne also acquired the privilege of borrowing from the library of the Dean and Chapter, which then consisted of some five-and-a-half thousand volumes. Initially at least, Sterne was too occupied with other matters to take advantage of the privilege. Almost six months were to pass before he is recorded as having borrowed any books at all, and even then he did so with an evident eye on his imminent immersion in political writing: he took out two volumes of anti-Roman Catholic tracts in June 1741 and nothing else for twelve months or more. In later years he was to use the Minster Library more extensively and for his own pleasure. Aside from sheet music, Sterne's varied borrowings in the 1750s included more of those encyclopaedic works to which he was drawn throughout his life, among them the *Dictionary Historical and Critical* (1696–7; 2nd English edition 1734–8) by Pierre Bayle, Jean-Frédéric Bernard's *The Religious Ceremonies and Customs of the Several Nations of the Known World* (1731), and early volumes of both *Biographia Britannica: or, the Lives of the most Eminent Persons who have flourished in Great Britain and Ireland, from the earliest Ages down to the Present Time* (1747–66), and *An Universal History, from the Earliest Account of Time* (1747–66).[63]

Restricted access to books can hardly be accounted a self-evident advantage for any writer. Yet Sterne's dependence on the taste of his friends and the holdings of the Minster Library had a marked, and perhaps not wholly negative effect on his own life and work. Temperamentally, there was little chance of Sterne following any one branch of learning or of pursuing any particular study—John Croft's account of the man he knew does not suggest that Sterne would have been likely to emulate a contemporary fellow-cleric such as, say, Gilbert White, whose *Natural History and Antiquities of Selborne* was painstakingly researched and written as its author pursued his clerical duties in the Dorset countryside. Yet if Sterne stuck to no one topic, the knowledge he acquired—however slight—of an unusually wide range of subjects he put to magnificently original use in later years, not least in that profusion of half-serious, half-jesting, and often teasingly recondite allusions that sometimes over-solemn editors and annotators have prided themselves on identifying in *Tristram Shandy*.

By themselves the Bible, Erasmus, Shakespeare, Rabelais, Cervantes, Joseph Hall, Montaigne, Burton, Swift, and Ephraim Chambers form at least the basis of a formidable list of reading. Yet, favourite works and odd allusions aside, we know for the most part remarkably little—his scant surviving correspondence of the 1740s and 1750s is particularly unrevealing—about Laurence Sterne's preferences in literature, especially modern literature. The political journalism of 1741–2 suggests a wide knowledge of Swift's writings, including *A Proposal for the Universal Use of Irish Manufacture*, while Sterne's gift of Berkeley's *The Querist* to a friend suggests that he may have kept up with political and economic questions of interest to him, even when no longer actively engaged in political journalism.[64]

Perhaps the best insight into the kinds of contemporary literature Sterne admired is to be found in the single substantial poem of his to have survived. This is 'The Unknown World', which appeared in one of the leading periodicals of the day, the *Gentleman's Magazine*, in July 1743. Although the existence of the poem would suggest that Sterne wrote other poetry at this period, none of the stylistically diverse works speculatively attributed to him in recent years seems at all likely to have been written by him.[65] 'The Unknown World' is not distinguished, but it is competent and in one respect at least curious—for Sterne's eccentrically employed four symbols: ⊙ for 'world', þ for 'He', ♉ for 'Heaven', and ♃ for 'soul', in the manuscript. The purpose of these symbols is far from clear and was evidently not so at the time of writing either, for the *Gentleman's Magazine* understandably dispensed with them when it published the poem. In Sterne's manuscript version (now lost, but printed by the Yorkshire antiquarian Thomas Gill in the mid-nineteenth century), the first quatrains read:

THE UNKNOWN ⊙
Verses occasion'd by hearing a Pass-Bell,
By^{e} ye Rev^{d} M^{r} St——n.

Hark^{e} my gay Fr^{d} y^{t} solemn Toll
Speaks ye departure of a soul;
'Tis gone, y^{ts} all we know—not where
Or how ye unbody'd soul do's fare.

In y^{t} mysterious ⊙ none knows,
But Þ alone to w^{m} it goes;
To whom departed souls return
To take y^{ir} Doom, to smile or mourn.[66]

If Sterne's leaning towards the curious led him to submit the poem to the *Gentleman's Magazine* in this form, he was soon made aware that the polite magazine readers of the 1740s did not share his taste. The magazine printed the poem, but in conventional typography. It continues:

Oh! by what glimm'ring light we view
The unknown world we're hast'ning to!
God has lock'd up the mystic page,
And curtain'd darkness round the stage!
Wise heaven to render search perplext,
Has drawn 'twixt this world and the next
A dark impenetrable screen,
All behind which is yet unseen!
We talk of heav'n, we talk of hell;
But what they mean no tongue can tell!
Heav'n is the realm where angels are
And hell the *Chaos* of despair!
But what these awful truths imply,
None of us know before we die!
Whether we will or no, we must
Take the succeeding world on trust.
This hour perhaps our Friend is well;
Death-Struck the next he cries, *farewell*!
I die!—and then for ought we see,
Ceases at once to breathe and be.
Thus launch'd from life's ambiguous shore
Ingulph'd in death, appears no more,
Then undirected to repair,
To distant worlds we know not where.
Swift flies the soul, perhaps 'tis gone,
A thousand leagues beyond the sun;
Or twice ten thousand more thrice told,
Ere the forsaken clay is cold!
And yet who knows, if friends we lov'd
Tho' dead, may be so far remov'd;
Only the veil of flesh between,
Perhaps they watch us, tho' unseen.
Whilst we, their loss lamenting, say,

They're out of hearing, far away;
Guardians to us perhaps they're near
Conceal'd in vehicles of air.
  And yet no notices they give,
Nor tell us where, nor how they live;
Tho' conscious whilst with us below,
How much themselves desired to know.
  As if bound up by solemn fate
To keep this *secret* of their *state*,
To tell their joys or pains to none,
That man might live by *Faith* alone.
  Well, let my sovereign if he please,
Lock up his marvellous decrees;
Why should I wish him to reveal,
What he thinks proper to conceal?
  It is enough that I believe
Heav'n's brighter than I can conceive:
And he that makes it all his care
To serve God here, shall see him there!
  But oh! what worlds shall I survey
The moment that I leave this clay?
How sudden the surprize, how new?
Let it, my God, be happy too.[67]

The minor curiosity of its symbols aside, 'The Unknown World' is of particular interest both for the unique insight it offers us into Sterne's earliest literary influences and for the confirmation it affords of the extent to which, even as a young man with a reputation for gaiety, Sterne was preoccupied by death. In its sixty-four lines, divided into quatrains, the poem reflects on the inevitability of death, its frequently inexplicable suddenness, and the mysteriousness of the 'unknown world we're hast'ning to'. Among Sterne's surviving writings of the period, it is closest to the sombre sentiments he expressed in a letter written in the winter of 1739–40, before their marriage, to Elizabeth Lumley, in which he told her of the sudden death of a friend who had left a widow and five children. There, Sterne lamented the 'dark and seemingly cruel dispensations of Providence [which] often make the best of human hearts complain . . . ' before pulling himself up with an apostrophe: 'God! these are thy chastisements, and require (hard task!) a pious acquiescence' (*Letters*, 19).

By the time he came to write his poem, the fact of death had become increasingly familiar to Sterne. The death of siblings and a parent apart, his duties as a priest obliged him frequently to attend dying members of his congregation (in his first two years in Sutton he buried nineteen parishioners, and another ten in 1743). Whether it was this aspect of his calling—his regular presence at deathbeds may have been particularly sobering for a dissolute young man who knew himself to be suffering from a potentially fatal illness—or whether 'The Unknown World' was a more direct response to some particular event in his life, we cannot know. In broad terms, the sentiments of the work chime in well enough with the melancholy which pervades much of Sterne's later and more famous writing, even if it is there generally held in check by a humour always eager to guard against excessive indulgence in lachrymose self-pity. For a poetic meditation on death written by an Anglican priest in the 1740s, the literary influences are individual but not wholly unexpected: Donne's *Devotions* (especially the 'Meditation' (XIV)), Shakespearean soliloquy, and the poetry of Thomas Parnell and Edward Young. By contrast, Sterne eschews almost entirely the intense and severely admonitory speculation of a contemporary work on the same theme such as Isaac Watt's *The World to Come: or, Discourse on the Joys or Sorrows of Departed Souls at Death* (1739).

In particular, the poem suggests Sterne's familiarity with the first part of Edward Young's enormously popular *The Complaint; or Night Thoughts on Life, Death and Immortality*. Young was himself a rural Anglican priest, and his much more extensive (and still-unfinished) poem also used the device of the tolling bell to introduce its theme: 'The Bell strikes *One* . . . | It is the *Knell* of my departed Hours . . .' (I. 54, 58), and may even have suggested elements of the vocabulary Sterne employed in 'The Unknown World'.[68] More intriguingly, Young's poem is partly directed to a youthful rake given the name of Lorenzo. If the still-young Laurence Sterne did indeed read *Night Thoughts*, then the ambitious, reprobate priest can hardly have failed to be struck, at least momentarily, by such lines as '*Lorenzo*, Fortune makes her Court to thee, | Thy fond Heart dances, while the *Syren* sings', or the cautionary 'Beware, *Lorenzo!* a *slow-sudden* Death. | How dreadful that deliberate Surprize? | Be wise to-day; 'tis madness to defer' (I. 387–9). In 1743, and then in his thirtieth year, Sterne might also have remarked on the particular appositeness of Young's line: 'At *thirty* man *suspects* himself a Fool' (I. 416).

In the absence of evidence regarding the extent of Sterne's acquaintance with Young's poem we might not wish to take such speculation too far, and of course it is true that, like Young himself, Sterne drew heavily on earlier sources of literary inspiration. So, while Young's ambitious work is written in blank verse, Sterne's octosyllabic couplets suggest a more direct debt to the couplets Thomas Parnell employed in his widely read meditative poem, 'A Night-Piece on Death' (1721). The influence of a popular poem written over twenty years previously would, indeed, be very much in line with Sterne's often conservative literary taste. Whatever the particular influences on it, however, it is certain that 'The Unknown World' was a poem of a kind likely to find ready acceptance in the 1740s, and Sterne was doubtless gratified to find himself published in so prestigious and widely read a magazine.

So far as the thought of the poem is concerned, however, no reader is likely to feel that it moves smoothly towards a coherent conclusion. Robert Blair, whose *The Grave* was also first published in 1743, reputedly wrote the poem in 1731 but delayed publishing it for fear that it did not become a minister of the gospel. While few readers then or since can have found anything religiously objectionable in Blair's work, Sterne's poem seems barely convinced by its own fideistic argument. It is not that the author does not try, even if such lines as:

> Well, let my sovereign, if he please,
> Lock up his marvellous decrees;
> Why sh^d^ I wish him to reveal
> W^t^ he thinks proper to conceal.
>
> (ll. 53–6)

which represent the Heavenly King as arbitrary monarch, were unlikely to hold unqualified appeal for a mid-eighteenth-century Whig. It is a rationalist, questioning voice which breaks in at the outset of the final quatrain, to ask in tones which do for once appear to speak of personal unease: 'But oh! what worlds shall I survey | The moment that I leave this clay?' In the final couplet the emphasis on faith returns but weakly, and it is hard to believe that any wavering believer reading 'The Unknown World' in 1743 is likely to have found much comfort in it.

Showing affinities with the work of Parnell, Blair, Young, and other 'graveyard' poets, 'The Unknown World' at least allows us the possibility of informed speculation on the kinds of contemporary poetry with which Sterne was familiar in the 1740s. What we have no way of knowing is whether he was also reading the new English prose fiction. There is, in his writing, abundant evidence of Sterne's familiarity with the fiction of earlier writers from the long European tradition of pre-eighteenth-century imaginative prose fiction—Lucian, Rabelais, Cervantes, Bunyan, and others—while John Croft tells us that Sterne was a 'great Admirer' of the pathos of the Abbé Prévost's *Le Doyen de Killerine* (*The Dean of Coleraine*) and the 'naivetè' of Marivaux's *Paysan parvenu.*[69] Sterne was also an enthusiastic admirer of the work of Swift—with a predilection for *A Tale of a Tub* rather than the more popular *Gulliver's Travels*. But there is also less evidence that Sterne had read the work of contemporary novelists than is the case with any other significant writer of prose fiction in the language. Such works, of course, were not available from Sterne's principal resource for books—the York Minster Library. The admiration for French sentimental fictions of the 1730s, such as Prévost's *Le Doyen de Killerine,* is not especially remarkable, since Prévost, like other French novelists—Marie-Jeanne Riccoboni, for example—significantly influenced many eighteenth-century sentimentalists. From brief allusions, it seems likely that Sterne read both Samuel Johnson's *Rasselas* and Voltaire's *Candide* shortly after they appeared in 1759[70]—although as this was also the year in which Sterne was attempting to rework the first two volumes of *Tristram Shandy* to make them acceptable for publication, he was probably as much interested in what booksellers (and their customers) wanted from prose fiction as in the particular works themselves.

Of Sterne's familiarity with other contemporary fiction—the 'new Species of Writing' which so engrossed the English literary world of the mid-eighteenth century—much less may be said with certainty. There is not a shred of hard evidence that Sterne read Defoe's works, for instance—not even *Robinson Crusoe.* The coincidence of names has long suggested Sterne's knowledge of the anonymously published *Life and Memoirs of Ephraim Tristram Bates* (1756), but of any familiarity on Sterne's part with the great outpouring of prose fiction in England in the 1740s and 1750s there is scarcely a trace. In the years in which Laurence Sterne was starting out on his clerical career in rural Yorkshire, Richardson, Henry Fielding, and Tobias Smollett were laying out new paths for English literature. Each was conscious, in very different ways, of the others. Fielding engaged critically with both the morality and rhetoric of Samuel Richardson's *Pamela* (1740) by writing first *Shamela* (1741) and then *Joseph Andrews* (1742), only to respond much more sympathetically to Richardson's *Clarissa* (1748–9) in his final and most pathetic novel, *Amelia* (1752). The young and ambitious Smollett anxiously scoured *Tom Jones* (1749) for hints that Fielding had taken his lead from Smollett's own *Roderick Random* (1748). Even Samuel Richardson, disdainful of so much written by his fellow-novelists, was sufficiently aware of Fielding's work to condemn it (though unread)—and, more positively, he found in such novels as Charlotte Lennox's *The Female Quixote* (1752) prose fiction he was disposed to admire, besides his own. Even if none of these appealed to Sterne, however, there were plentiful works of the 1750s of a kind it seems reasonable to suppose that he would have enjoyed, including Robert Paltock's *Peter Wilkins* (1751), along with *Memoirs of Several Ladies of Great Britain* (1755) and *The Life of John Buncle, Esq.* (1756) by Thomas Amory—a writer, like Sterne himself, later hailed as the 'English Rabelais'.[71]

The lack of precise reference to contemporary fiction in his correspondence is not conclusive, of course, and it may be that Sterne's own sentimentalism fed on that of Richardson, as well as on Prévost's and Riccoboni's, or that the portrayal of Uncle Toby's military campaign on the bowling green takes a hint from Smollett's comic depiction of the garrison of Commodore Trunnion in *Peregrine Pickle* (1751). It may even be that Sterne talked of the emerging fiction of the 1740s and 1750s in conversation with literary-minded Yorkshire friends. We know he shared John Hall-Stevenson's literary tastes, and it would be at the Stillington home of Stephen Croft that he would read—albeit with indifferent success—an early draft of *Tristram Shandy*. As a reader of such periodicals as the *Gentleman's Magazine*, Sterne could not have been unfamiliar with the furious moral controversy aroused by such works as John Cleland's *Memoirs of a Woman of Pleasure* (1748) or Eliza Haywood's *Betsy Thoughtless* (1751). Yet of direct evidence that Sterne drew on, or was even aware of, these or any other works by his contemporaries, there is scarcely a hint.

If Sterne did turn for amusement to the increasingly domestic fiction of the 1740s it was perhaps in search of supplemental satisfactions, for in his private life he was a deeply unhappy man—and unhappy in ways which affected not only his personal relationships but the exercise of his priesthood itself. The story of the Sternes' courtship, as told by Laurence, was a pleasing and even touching one. As much as any man of his time and social position, Sterne had married for love; his account of the courtship suggests a genuine enough passion. But if, as young lovers, Laurence Sterne and Elizabeth Lumley were happy, such felicity as they enjoyed was of short duration. Life in the vicarage at Sutton did not prove easy for two strong-willed people whose improvidence matched ill with expectations already in excess of their fortune. Sterne's decision to abandon party-writing and to settle in Sutton may not have pleased Elizabeth, who must clearly have foreseen not only her husband's limited chances of advancement without the active support of his uncle, but also the threatened tedium of a life largely bereft of the social circle at Sutton Hall. If the couple's frustrations led to quarrels, then Sterne's consequent sexual infidelities only led to more tension.

One kind of frustration seems to have characterized Sterne's relationship with his bride from the outset—at least, if we are to believe a story told by the anecdotist John Seward. On the Sunday following his marriage, Seward alleged, Sterne preached on the text '*We have toiled all the night and taken nothing*'.[72] Near-blasphemous, the story is nevertheless plausible enough, for Sterne had 'but little Superstition to appropriated Expressions', as his Irish acquaintance Richard Griffith would relate many years after.[73] Hester Thrale later recorded an anecdote of Sterne abusing marriage in similarly outrageous terms: when one of his audience dissented, arguing that 'Jesus Christ once honoured a wedding with his presence', Sterne supposedly replied, 'but between You & I Sir . . . that was not the *best* thing he ever did'.[74] Even if true, of course, Seward's story does not necessarily point to the cause of the later, well-documented breakdown in the Sternes' relationship. Writing to his daughter, Sterne understandably makes no reference in his memoir to any disagreement whatever between himself and his wife, still less suggesting any reasons for the discord that certainly characterized the later years of their marriage. There is abundant evidence, however, that their frequent and bitter quarrels resulted, at least in part, from a lack of sexual harmony, resulting in Sterne's flagrant and repeated infidelities, which in turn provoked a further and understandable breach between husband and wife. John Croft reported that Laurence and Elizabeth Sterne 'did not live on the best terms and harmony together, chiefly owing to his infidelity to the Marriage Bed'.[75] Telling confirmation of Sterne's repeated infidelity comes from Richard Greenwood, who served in the Sternes' household for three years after 1742. Greenwood was an old man when the antiquarian Joseph Hunter sought him out in 1807, but he still remembered clearly that, in Hunter's words, he 'used to accompany his master whenever Sterne came to York, & when there he rarely spent a night without a girl or two which Richard used to procure for him. He promised Richard to reward him for keeping these private amours of his secret, particularly from Mrs. Sterne'.[76] Greenwood was appropriately discreet and, he recalled, Sterne kept his side of the agreement.

By his servant's account, however, Sterne's sexual adventures were not confined to the relative security of York. 'Sterne too was continually after his female servants,' Greenwood remembered, '& these things, & sometimes his affairs at York, would come to the ears of Mrs Sterne, and as might be expected great quarrels ensued—During all the time [I] lived with [them], they were upon very ill terms . . .'[77] It is hardly surprising, for John Croft recorded that '[Sterne's] wife once caught him with the maid, when she pulled him out of bed on the Floor and soon after went out of her senses, when she fancied herself the Queen of Bohemia'.[78] While this anecdote is certainly second-hand—Elizabeth Sterne's most serious mental breakdown occurred in the late-1750s when Croft was out of England—it cannot be dismissed altogether. According to Richard Greenwood, when anything produced a difference between him and his wife, Sterne would order Richard to bring out his horse and they would go together to York, on occasion for days at a time, where Sterne 'soon lost all his [cares] in the arms of some more blooming beauty'.[79] It would appear, though, that not all of the beauties in whose arms Sterne sought solace were 'blooming'. By his own testimony Sterne was later treated for a venereal disease (almost certainly syphilis) that most likely had its origin in these years. When Richard Greenwood entered the Sterne household the couple could have been married, at most, for eighteen months.

The failure over several years to have a family did not help the Sternes' marriage. Exactly how many children were born to Elizabeth Sterne is not known. What is certain is that only one would survive beyond the first weeks of life. Recalling his time with the Sternes, sixty years afterwards, Richard Greenwood remembered that Elizabeth 'brought Sterne several children'. Most, he continued, 'died in very early infancy—one a boy lived 3 weeks—Sterne was inconsolable on his death, took to his chamber, and would not leave it of a week'.[80] As this is the only reference to a son born to the Sternes—no mention appearing in either the Sutton or Stillington records—it may be that the elderly Greenwood, after so long a time, was in error. Or the child may have been born elsewhere. Did Elizabeth Sterne leave Sutton for the comparative safety of York to give birth, rather than run the risks of a village confinement? The only two children recorded by Sterne in his own parish book—the first, a daughter, died within a day—were almost certainly born in Sutton, however. Greenwood's 'several' may include stillborn infants, which, following normal eighteenth-century practice, were not included in parish registers, so that Sterne did not record the stillbirth he mentioned bluntly in a letter to the York apothecary, Theophilus Garencieres: 'Mrs Sterne was last Night deliverd of a dead Child . . . She is very weak . . . and is troubled with after Pains' (*Letters*, 45–6).

From his earliest years Laurence Sterne had been as well acquainted as any contemporary man with the painful facts of eighteenth-century infant mortality. Of his parents' seven children, only Laurence and two sisters survived infancy. As a parish priest, his duties in Sutton and Stillington included consoling bereaved parents and burying their offspring. Children—and their mothers—frequently died from complications arising from long, painful labours, or from diseases to which infant children were particularly vulnerable, such as the smallpox Sterne recorded as having been especially fatal in Stillington in the 1750s.[81] Between April 1745 and May 1746 Sterne baptized twelve children in Sutton (a daughter born to Philip Harland and his wife was baptized in York, and may well have been born there). Of the twelve, one girl, Anne Waite, daughter of Robert Waite of New Park, was born on 27 May 1746 and buried by Sterne on 19 November 1748 (another daughter of Robert Waite, also Anne, was baptized by Sterne in June of the year following her sister's death, and buried by him at the age of seven months on 29 January 1750). On 30 July 1745 Sterne baptized a male child, James Wilson, and buried him two days later. At this time Elizabeth Sterne was herself pregnant. On 1 October Sterne proudly recorded the birth of a daughter. The Sutton parish register reads: 'October ye 1st. Born & Baptized Lydia the Daughter of the Reverend M^r^. Sterne Vicar of Sutton & of Elizabeth his Wife, Daughter of the Rev.^d^ M^r^. Lumley late Rector of Bedale.'[82] (A similar, briefer record occurs likewise in the Stillington register.) In a marginal note Sterne added laconically 'died'. In fact, the infant Lydia, named for Elizabeth Sterne's younger sister, died within a day and was buried by her father. It was to be a further two years before, on 1 December 1747, Elizabeth Sterne would again successfully bear a living child: another Lydia, whom Sterne baptized the same day.[83]

The bald record of Lydia's birth and death in the parish register leaves no margin for knowing how Laurence Sterne responded to the loss of his infant daughter. Richard Greenwood's account suggested he took the blow hard. Whether he recalled the deaths of his siblings or turned to such works of consolation as those in which Walter Shandy finds solace for the death of his son, Bobby (*TS* v. iii), is a matter of ultimately unrewarding speculation. Yet, if equally speculative, it is hard not to wonder whether Sterne blamed himself in any way for his wife's inability to bear a child capable of surving the first days or weeks of life. It was at the end of his life that Sterne was treated for what his doctors persisted in diagnosing as a venereal disease—by then, almost certainly tertiary syphilis—despite their patient's equally strong insistence that he had had no sexual relations with any woman, not even his wife, since the early 1750s. Though we cannot know whether Sterne recognized the possibility that the responsibility for the deaths of his stillborn children might lie at his own door, we cannot either ignore the grimly humorous chapters of *Tristram Shandy* devoted to the account of Tristram's disastrous entry into the world, nor the tragicomedy Sterne found in Walter Shandy's response to the death of his eldest son, Bobby.

Whatever the causes of the Sternes' unhappiness in their marriage, the fact remains that the behaviour of the Revd Laurence Sterne cannot be seen in a purely personal light. As vicar of Sutton-on-the-Forest and of Stillington he held a prominent position locally, and there can be no denying that at times he fell far short of what might have been expected of any priest of the Church of England. Since Richard Greenwood's account exists only in the often euphemistic paraphrase of Joseph Hunter, it is hard to be sure of the former servant's attitude to his subsequently celebrated and long-dead master. Greenwood in fact eventually left Sterne's service after an argument between them, yet the intervening years seem to have smoothed away any lingering resentment on the part of the former servant. If so, Greenwood's testimony, unmotivated by malice or even dislike, is the more damaging to Sterne, and not merely as it relates to a husband's—or even a clergyman's—adultery (for Sterne was scarcely the only cleric to have discovered that the bestowal of holy orders did not necessarily mean the loss of illicit sexual desire). According to Greenwood, Sterne 'would frequently be absent many days together' on his visits to York, 'and should Sunday intervene did not return to perform the duties of the day'. Sterne did not, Greenwood averred, 'attend well to the duties of his situation'.[84]

In contrast to the more sober account of himself which Laurence Sterne provided in responding to the questionnaire of Archbishop Herring, anecdotes such as those of Greenwood and Croft suggest him to be a man wholly unsuited by both temperament and moral character to be a clergyman. It is hard to know to what extent Sterne was himself conscious of this unsuitability. In his sermon 'The Abuses of Conscience' he wrote: 'A man shall be vicious and utterly debauched in his principles; exceptionable in his conduct in the world: shall live shameless,——in the open commission of a sin which no reason or pretence can justify;——a sin, by which, contrary to all the workings of humanity within, he shall ruin for ever the deluded partner of his guilt.'[85] If Richard Greenwood and John Croft are to be believed—and there is no reason to doubt them—then Sterne's reputation in York, as in Sutton-on-the-Forest, was certainly compromised. Yet 'The Abuses of Conscience' sermon was preached in York Minster itself, before a congregation which must have included many of the city and county clergy who knew Sterne's reputation. Elizabeth Montagu had heard, before Sterne's marriage, that her cousin's husband had once 'delighted in debauchery'. If now Elizabeth

Sterne back in Sutton had been alerted to her husband's sexual doings in York, it is not likely they had passed unnoticed among the tight-knit clerical community centred on the Minster, a community which included both Sterne's political enemies and his estranged uncle. Did Sterne intend his words from the pulpit as an acknowledgement of his own failings, or was he so blind to the way that others saw him that he simply did not think of their application to himself? It is perhaps easier for us to imagine the former, but we have no way of knowing for certain. In any case, he seems to have done little to change his conduct. Alienated from his influential and vengeful uncle, despised by his political enemies, and an object of suspicion for his moral character, Sterne must have found his prospects for further preferment even bleaker than before—and indeed the truth is that they were.

5
The Jacobite Rebellion, 1745–1746

For three years after his unhappy experience of political journalism in the 1742 by-election Laurence Sterne stayed apart from public life, dividing his time between his house and garden, Elizabeth and his friends, his parishioners at Sutton and Stillington, and his furtive trips to York. Determined as he was to cut himself off from party politics, however, he did not find a total respite from public affairs. In the summer of 1745 the landing in Scotland of Prince Charles Edward Stuart, the Young Pretender, occasioned the greatest threat to the peace and stability of Great Britain since Charles Edward's father, James, had raised the first Jacobite rebellion thirty years previously. Then, in 1715, the Jacobite threat to the newly established Hanoverian dynasty had caused Roger Sterne, and many junior officers like him, to be called from life on half-pay to take up arms again. Now it was the turn of Laurence Sterne to be called from his own, self-willed retirement to exert himself in defence of the House of Hanover and the Church of England.

The '45 had begun quietly, almost innocuously. After an abortive attempt to mount an invasion in the previous year, with the aid of the French who hoped to weaken British armies fighting in continental Europe in the War of the Austrian Succession, Prince Charles Edward set sail in a French privateer from the east coast of France on 4 July 1745, accompanied by a single French warship with 700 men. Separated from even this small force in a brief naval skirmish, the prince landed alone on Eriskay in the Outer Hebrides on 23 July. Nearly a month later, and with still no more than 1,300 hundred men under his command, the prince raised the Old Pretender's standard at Glenfinnan, and proclaimed his father King James III and VIII. In London the government evinced a languid caution in the face of the still-distant rebellion: Edinburgh Castle was provisioned and a small force was sent north from Stirling to check on the state of affairs in the Highlands.[1] The response was inadequate, for the Jacobite troops succeeded in bypassing the 2,000-strong Hanoverian contingent under Sir John Cope and marched south. Having been joined at Perth by both James Drummond, the titular duke of Perth and secretary to the Pretender, and the incisive military commander Lord George Murray, the rebels seized the Scottish capital, isolating the garrison in the castle.

In England life went on normally. York Race Week took place as usual, and on 27 August the *York Courant* reassured its readers that 'there is good Grounds to believe our Apprehensions of Troubles . . . will e'er long blow over'. In London, however, the authorities were beginning to become alert to the threat the rebellion posed. On 31 August the lord chancellor, the earl of Hardwicke, wrote to Archbishop Herring reminding him that 'Archbishops of York had before now drawn the Secular, as well as the Spiritual Sword', adding in a postscript: 'Is it not time for the Pulpits to sound the Trumpet against Popery & the Pretender?'[2] Herring needed no further bidding. 'I thank yr L^{p} for the intimation in your Postscript: so far as my Example or Monitions can go, I will not be wanting in my Duty',[3] he wrote in his reply, and put himself decisively to the task of marshalling the Yorkshire aristocracy, freeholders, and clergy in support of the House of Hanover. His task was not easy, for the Northern Province was not uniformly disposed to rally to the Hanoverian cause. Across the Pennines, Lancashire had a strong Roman Catholic tradition, and the diocese of Chester was considered dangerously Jacobite in its sympathies. Moreover, the loyalty of Yorkshire itself was initially suspect. It was, after all, only a very few years previously that Jaques Sterne—aided and abetted by his nephew Laurence—had encouraged loyal Protestants to detect a covert Jacobite sympathizer in every Tory voter in the elections of 1741 and 1742. Nor could such fears be dismissed merely as a symptom of the precentor's paranoia. Herring himself—no narrow bigot—believed that toleration of Roman Catholics in York had gone too far. He therefore cautioned the lord chancellor that 'ye Numbers & Spirit & Boldnesss of the Papists is such, That their Publick Mass House joins in a manner to the Cathedral . . . & their Audience [is] as large or larger than than of the Protestant Church'.[4] The archbishop believed that the civil powers were to blame for the excessive tolerance shown Roman Catholics in the city, causing the lord chancellor to acknowledge that the intervention of the magistrates was desirable: 'one would think a few Examples would keep such an Enormity under.'[5] Fears of the loyalty of York itself would not have been calmed by the knowledge that two leading Jacobites, the duke of Perth and Lord George Murray, had spent some time in the city before the rebellion.

Fortunately, despite his devotion to the Whig cause Archbishop Herring had been assiduous in cultivating the local Tory gentry and could count on widespread personal support. In the second week of September he met with the principal Yorkshire aristocracy and agreed to call a public meeting, at which proper measures in defence of the Hanoverians and Protestantism might be drawn up. The need for urgency was increasingly apparent. On 21 September the Jacobite army achieved a shattering victory when it routed Cope's English forces at Prestonpans, near Edinburgh, inflicting some 700 casualties while losing barely a dozen men. From his headquarters in the Scottish capital Charles Edward's council of war now determined to advance into England.

In Yorkshire Herring's preparations were proceeding apace. On 22 September he preached a sermon emphasizing the importance of active loyalty to the Crown. The sermon, with a preface exhorting the clergy in particular to rise in defence of their country, was printed and copies circulated throughout the county. News of the defeat at Prestonpans reached York on 24 September, the day that Herring addressed a huge gathering of county gentry, clergy, and city dignitaries at York Castle. At that meeting a loyal association was formed which would be the model for many others throughout England, the assembled gentlemen agreeing that the county should aim to raise £40,000 for the equipping of troops. The role of the clergy—Laurence Sterne among them—was particularly stressed, with the archbishop urging them to 'decline no Pains to instruct and animate your People, nor Expence, according to your Circumstances, to stand up against Popery and Arbitrary Power'.[6] Following the meeting Herring was jubilant: 'I am just come fro̅ the Castle', he wrote to Hardwicke, 'where the Assembly was prodigious, & I am confident, nothing of the sort was ever more unanimous than the Association.'[7] The lord chancellor, in turn, requested Herring not to travel to London for the parliamentary session, but to continue his active role in organizing the county's defence.

Archbishop Herring did so with gusto and with a vehemence surprising in a man usually so temperate and judicious: even in official correspondence he regularly referred to the Jacobites as 'wolves' and 'vermin'. Yorkshire zeal was impressive: 'The Spirit of the County is prodigious, & we are all in motion fro̅ one Corner to the other',[8] reported Herring to Hardwicke. The Lord Mayor of York reported that 'the lowest of the citizens contributed something'[9]—and many Roman Catholics gave to the defence fund, leading Herring to allude darkly to Trojan horses: 'Timeo Danaos et dona ferentes.'[10] Despite his private reservations, however, Herring was a model of public enthusiasm, forever busying himself in every aspect of the preparations to resist a Jacobite advance. When troops were drawn up on the Knavesmire to be reviewed by General James Oglethorpe, the archbishop rode in review alongside. Two years later, he remembered with amusement that 'I set up . . . for something of a Martial Bishop'.[11]

In the city of York the corporation sponsored the organization and equipping of four companies as the York Blues, while the county gathered together local gentry and their servants as the Independents. Among the other troops raised were the Royal Hunters, composed of North Riding gentlemen and their servants and principally organized by Sterne's college friend John Hall-Stevenson. The archbishop regarded them with a certain sardonic amusement:

> Oglethorp is here, & has persuaded thirty or forty young Gentlemen Volunteers to follow him to Berwick, as sort of Hussars, they are to rendezvous on Knavesmire on Mond. morn. have a Ball at Night, & march on Tuesday morn. We must leave it to the General to consider whether a Ball ^will^ inspire or enfeeble his Myrmidons. but Let the Spirit of Defence go forward.[12]

In the midst of all this activity Laurence Sterne was busy himself. Responding to the archbishop's call, he began by making a personal contribution to the defence fund of £10—a far from insignificant sum for one of his means. In Sutton and Stillington he exhorted his parishioners to subscribe likewise, but here the response was muted, and while the latter parish raised £9, the former scraped together a mere £6. 9*s.* 6*d.* Indeed, despite his evident and genuine zeal in endeavouring to mobilize his rural parishioners, Sterne's success was negligible. His own servant, Richard Greenwood, for instance, declined at all costs to add himself to the ranks of the defenders, preferring to leave Sterne's service at Michaelmas 1745, 'having had a few words with his master a short time before in consequence of his refusing to engage as drummer to [Kingston's] Light horse, a regiment of cavalry raised in Yorkshire during the rebellion'.[13] In his refusal Greenwood differed but little from others in the county: notwithstanding the enthusiasm of the gentry, comparatively few ordinary Yorkshiremen were eager to take up arms, at least in the absence of an immediate, discernible threat. Still, if Sterne could not convince his own servant to join in the military defence of the county, we may conclude that he was unlikely to have had great success elsewhere in the village, at least among those not already predisposed to serve.

What remains tantalizingly open to question is whether Sterne himself picked up in defence of the Church of England and the House of Hanover not a sword but a pen. Certainly there was no shortage of literature in prose and verse—addresses, relations, accounts, songs, and epigrams—dedicated by loyal subjects to the defence of Protestantism and English liberty. In York the printer John Hildyard was quick off the mark. Four days after it was delivered, Archbishop Herring's speech of 24 September denouncing the 'present unnatural and detestable rebellion' was on sale—and was sufficiently in demand to be reissued in October as a shilling pamphlet, embellished with a portrait of the prelate.[14] It was Hildyard too who published, in late September, the penny pamphlet *Seasonable Advice to the Inhabitants of Yorkshire*—one of many in recent years to have been speculatively attributed to Sterne.[15] For the most part a rambling catalogue of papist atrocities at home and abroad, the *Seasonable Advice* is interspersed with exhortations to take up arms against the rebel threat, and concludes: 'If You love your Wives and Children, and desire to live with them in Peace and Plenty; Arm, Arm under Your Brave Leaders, and stand up to defend King *George* and your Country; for it is more than probable, if You submit now, You may never hereafter have the Spirit or the Power to defend Yourselves.'[16] Taken in the context of other anti-Jacobite writings of the time the *Seasonable Advice* is entirely unremarkable and, if it should ever be proved to be by Laurence Sterne, would demonstrate only that the 32-year-old Whig clergyman differed in his view of the rebellion remarkably little from the bulk of the Anglican clergy in 1745.

In the excitement of the hour, however, there was a ready market for pro-Hanoverian and, more particularly, anti-Jacobite and anti-Catholic publications. By mid-November John Hildyard himself was announcing a dozen or more in a single advertisement.[17] All were ephemeral, and it is highly unlikely that, with a single, partial exception, anything came from Sterne's pen. The exception, slight in itself, nevertheless gives a glimpse of the naive enthusiasm Sterne shared with his non-clerical friends on the subject of the rebellion. During the autumn John Hall-Stevenson wrote a ballad entitled 'The Royal Hunters' March' in which warfare was represented in the cant of fox-hunting. The ballad took its title from the group of irregulars, 'The Royal Hunters', raised by General James Oglethorpe in York on his way north to meet the rebels, and organized by Hall-Stevenson himself. It opens:

> Since Tencin's Schemes,
> And Charles' Dreams

Disturb our pleasing Toil
  Let us unite,
  And put to Flight
Those Monsters of our Isle.
  The Fox and Hare
  A while we'll spare,
To seek a worthier Prey;
  And all resort
  To noble Sport
Where Glory points the Way.

A version of this ballad published on 16 November by the *Newcastle Journal* has an extra, concluding, stanza:

  Then we will rise,
  And rend the Skies
With Sound of chearful Horn
  And beat the Ground,
  The Country round,
And every Traitor scorn. L.S.

To the ballad there is a note appended: 'N.B. The last Stanza above, sign'd L. S. is an Addition to the Original by a Yorkshire Gentleman.'[18]

If these few lines are all that may, with reasonable certainty, be attributed to the future author of *Tristram Shandy* amid the flood of anti-Jacobite writings in the autumn and winter of 1745–6, then two other items, both of which are mentioned in a single issue of the *York Courant*—that of 19 November—are worth noting. The first is a 'Loyal Song', beginning

O Brother SAWNEY, hear you the News,
  Twang 'em, we'll bang 'em, and hang 'em up all.
An army's just coming without any Shoes,
  Twang 'em, we'll bang 'em, and hang 'em up all.[19]

The song's chorus is to be sung 'to the Tune of LILLIBULLERO'. The second item, appearing on the next page of the *Courant*, is an advertisement:

This Day is Publish'd. (Price 3d.)

Sold by Mess. STABLER *and* BARSTOW, *Booksellers, in* High Ouze-Gate, York, With a curious Frontispiece, engrav'd on a Copper-Plate, fit to be framed and hung up in all Protestant Families.

> THE POPE's dreadful Curse; being the Form of Excommunication of the Church of *Rome*.
> Taken out of the Leger-Book of the Church of *Rochester*, now in the Custody of the Dean and Chapter there. Wrote by *Ernulphus*, the Bishop.[20]

In Volume III of *Tristram Shandy* the unsuspecting Roman Catholic Dr Slop reads out the 'form of excommunication of the church of *Rome*', a copy of which Walter Shandy has procured 'out of the leger-book of the church of *Rochester*', while the staunchly Protestant Uncle Toby whistles 'Lillibullero' as loud as he is able (*TS*, III. x–xi. 134–43).

The writing of *Tristram Shandy*, however, lay well into the future. In the autumn of 1745 the Jacobite Rebellion was no subject for any but the bitterest comedy. On 19 November the *York Courant* published a long article on the conduct of Sir John Cope by 'an Officer of the Army' which concluded:

> *Quaere*, What Rhymes to COPE?
> *Answer* —— —— —— A ROPE.

(Subsequently, both Cope and General James Oglethorpe would be among those officers court-martialled for their failures during the rebellion.)

Despite the enthusiasm and excitement shown in Yorkshire by such groups as the Royal Hunters, Archbishop Herring took a sombre view of events. It had been assumed after its victory at Prestonpans that the rebel army would soon move south across the border to invade England. What was uncertain was whether its route would take it down the west coast or the east. The archbishop's attempts to raise a defence force in Yorkshire seem to have been designed at least in part to discourage the Jacobites from attempting the eastern route, which would have brought them to York itself. Certainly, Herring had no confidence that the enthusiastic but untrained irregulars—whose principal activities had been marching, firing volleys, and drinking numerous loyal toasts—could successfully resist the advance of an already victorious army. Moreover, he had been unsuccessful in his attempts to persuade the government in London to send arms north to York in order that the city could defend itself if attacked. By 22 November he told the lord chancellor that York was 'in no sort of condition to make any resistance, if the Rebels move this way'.[21] Accordingly, he advised the York magistrates that should the Jacobite army take the eastern route they should throw open the city gates to them without hesitation. Personally courageous, Herring saw no point in futile gestures. On the same day the archbishop informed Hardwicke of his intentions: 'As to my own safety I will stay till ye last moment, & if a Scheme of defence of any likelihood can be formd, I will share in ye common Danger.' But, Herring added frankly, 'If not, I know of no Duty that obliges me to run ye hazard of being knocked on the Head or taken Prisoner'. He was ready to escape, he said, at half an hour's notice, and if the rebels took the York road he would endeavour to do so. Should they advance via the western route, Herring insisted, 'I am determind to fix my abode & wait the Fate of ^ & as I may, serve ^ my Country here'.[22]

Others had very different ideas. On the same day that Archbishop Herring was anxiously informing the lord chancellor of his intentions, Sterne's old political antagonist, the Tory stalwart and now-wealthy physician Dr John Burton,[23] set out on a mysterious journey. It was an action that would lead him to the Young Pretender in person—and later to prison and the shadow of the gallows. While keeping the Hanoverian forces guessing as to their exact intentions, the Jacobite army had crossed into England, seized Carlisle, and continued on into Lancashire. On 22 November Dr Burton made it known that he was leaving York to travel to his two estates at Newby in the West Riding, close to the road that would bring the rebel army south. Early the following morning Burton left York and journeyed over fifty miles to Settle—to collect rent owed him, he was later to claim—where he met his estate agent. From him he learned that the Jacobites had set out from Carlisle that day and were advancing by the western route. Instead of retiring hastily, Burton sent news of the Jacobites' route to York by letter, and travelled further westward directly into the path of the rebel army.

What happened thereafter was, and is, a matter of some fact and much conjecture. It is certain that Burton eventually met up with part of the rebel force at Hornby, and that he sent a letter to Hornby Castle where some of the troops were stationed. Shortly afterwards Jacobite soldiers took him—whether under duress or of his own volition—to the castle and later to Lancaster, where he was observed talking to several of the rebels, including the commander, Lord George Murray. Eventually he found his way into the presence of Prince Charles Edward who, along with his secretary, John Murray of Broughton, questioned him. Burton's Whig opponents in York—most prominent among whom was Dr Jaques Sterne—later alleged that their Tory opponent had travelled westward with the deliberate aim of making contact with the rebels, perhaps with the intention of conveying to them money collected covertly by Jacobite supporters in York. (The question of how many Jacobites there really were in York was not, in the end, put to the test, but throughout the autumn of 1745 there seemed to be complete unanimity in the city in support of the House of Hanover; in reading the *York Courant* for the period, for instance, it is easy to forget that this was a Tory paper and the financial support and firm expressions of loyalty from leading Tories in Yorkshire gave the lie to those, such as Jaques Sterne, who alleged that 'Tory' and 'Jacobite' were synonyms.) Burton himself declared that his journey westward from Settle had been prompted by curiosity and a desire to obtain information useful to loyal Hanoverians, but his story failed to convince far less prejudiced men than Jaques Sterne. Archbishop Herring was privately sceptical—particularly since Burton had been allowed to leave the rebel headquarters with two geldings, worth 20 guineas apiece—and characterized the physician as 'of the worst sort, as to Affection to the Government'.[24]

Four years later John Burton would publish his own extended account of his eventful journey in his *British Liberty Endanger'd*, in which he defended his conduct and attacked those whom he claimed to have pursued a spiteful, unjustified, and potentially lethal vendetta against him. In many of its details Burton's account is untrustworthy and contradicted both by the sworn evidence of contemporary witnesses, and even sworn statements by Burton himself.[25] What is not beyond all reasonable doubt, however, is whether Burton was a convinced Jacobite whose sole purpose for making his hazardous journey west from York was to meet up with the Pretender. Even in the heat of the rebellion itself, Archbishop Herring was warning the lord chancellor that 'Burton is a silly Fellow of no mark or likelihood & in my own mind, I am in much doubt whether this Journey of his had not as much or more Folly than Treason in it'.[26] This was a measured, even generous interpretation, since Herring knew that Burton had made at least the acquaintance of leading Jacobites earlier in the decade. Eventually, the most direct evidence against Burton was supplied by John Murray of Broughton, who saved his own life by giving evidence against other rebels, many of whom were subsequently executed. In August 1746, in the Tower of London, Murray testified against Burton:

> This exam[t] being asked whether he recollects a Person called Doctor Burton, being with the Pretender's Army in Lancashire: He saith, he does remember a Person, who, he thinks was a Physician, but cannot recollect his Name: that, this Person came to them at Lancaster, and said that he had been at Hornby Castle: that, he desired this Exam[t] to introduce him to the Pretender, which he did accordingly: that, the said

> Person told the Pretender in this Exam$^{t's}$ Presence, that he came from York: and that there were many Persons there, who would have joined him, if He had come that Way.[27]

Though potentially very damaging, Murray's account of Burton here strongly implies that he had never previously met the physician—which throws doubt on the possibility that Burton had in any way been seriously involved in such discussions between Jacobite sympathizers as took place in York earlier in the 1740s. Whatever really transpired at the meeting with the Young Pretender, however, it is certain that Burton made no independent attempt to leave Lancaster, though he was unguarded, but rather obtained a pass from the duke of Perth and set off for York. By the time he arrived there it was already known that he had had contact with the rebels in Lancaster. Though Burton duly gave an account of himself and of the rebels to interested parties, including the archbishop, it was already apparent that his behaviour, curious at best, had aroused suspicions that would not be easily dispelled.

Most notable among Burton's accusers was Sterne's uncle, the archdeacon of Cleveland. Even by his own account, Burton behaved injudiciously. Having previously protested his complete innocence, he simply laughed at Dr Sterne's suggestion that he be arrested. The archdeacon's antipathy turned to an intense hatred. Soon he had convinced even the archbishop that he had proof that the physician was, as Herring reported to Hardwicke, 'a dangerous & barefaced Traytor, as well as he is a bad man'.[28] For the next eighteen months Jaques Sterne harried the supposed Jacobite so furiously as to make it seem he was determined that Burton should hang. Acting with the grudging support of Archbishop Herring and the approval of the ministry in London, who had reasons of their own to be suspicious of Burton, Jaques Sterne had the physician committed to York Castle and subsequently produced a witness, James Nesbitt, whom he apparently suborned to testify that Burton had uttered treasonable remarks while in prison. Though the witness's credibility was swiftly shattered, Burton remained in prison throughout the winter of 1745–6. Only in March was it finally ordered that he be taken, under arrest, to London.

By the time John Burton arrived in the capital the Jacobite threat had receded, very shortly to disappear for good. After the Pretender's meeting with Burton in Lancaster the rebel army continued south towards the English capital. By 5 December, with the rebels at Derby, only 120 miles from London, the English court made hasty preparations to leave for

Hanover. At this point, however, the Pretender's decision faltered. His army had been enfeebled by the desertion of Scottish Highland troops, and he had received none of the military support he was expecting either from France or from English Jacobites. Confronted by an English army under the duke of Cumberland, third son of George II, the Pretender decided to retreat. On 6 December the Jacobite army began the long march back. In Yorkshire apprehensions were aroused by uncertainty as to the route the rebels would choose. York itself was thrown into uproar by the corporation's panic-ridden decision to shut the city gates and to search the homes of known or supposed 'Papists, Nonjurors, and Suspicious Persons', and to seize the horses as well as any arms they found there. In the event the disintegrating Jacobite army chose to retreat by the route along which it had triumphantly marched so short a time before. As the winter progressed, so the rebels pushed further north. On 17 January 1746 they achieved their final success when they defeated General Hawley's army at Falkirk. Three months later the hungry, exhausted remnants of the Jacobite army were destroyed in half an hour on Culloden moor outside Inverness by the Hanoverian forces under Cumberland.

When news of the victory reached York on 23 April the bells of the city churches were rung, the houses illuminated, and bonfires lighted in the streets in celebration. To his relieved supporters the duke of Cumberland was a hero, and was fêted as such. In London George Frideric Handel composed the oratorio *Judas Maccabeus*, with its celebrated chorus 'See the conqu'ring Hero comes', in his honour. Throughout the country loyal Hanoverians vied to do justice to the duke's military prowess. The York papers advertised commemorative medals in precious metals, dedicated to 'the Darling of the People'. Though it had escaped the passage of the Jacobite army, York was rewarded for its loyalty by a visit from the duke on his return to London. He spent the night of 23 July in the city, and was received at the house of Dr Jaques Sterne by Archbishop Herring and all the leading civic dignitaries, receiving the freedom of the city in a gold box.

In Scotland, by contrast, the notorious savagery with which his troops slaughtered survivors of the rout at Culloden, along with many unfortunates among the local population, earned Cumberland the nicknames of 'Butcher' and 'Stinking Billy'. For Prince Charles Edward Stuart the sobriquet was sweeter—'Bonnie Prince Charlie'—but his lengthy, dangerous escape from Scotland, effected only after five months on the run, was the prelude to an empty life, concluding in drunkenness and political oblivion.

If Culloden and its bloody aftermath proved the end for many of the rebels, for other Jacobite soldiers and supporters the military defeat marked the beginning of their misery. The first prisoners had been seen in York as early as 19 January, when forty-three officers and 149 private men had been held overnight in the Castle, en route for London. Later, other prisoners would be brought south into England on board ship, many dying there, in appalling conditions, of typhus and other diseases, for want of prisons to hold them. In July 1746 an Order in Council decreed that, with the exception of gentlemen or those accused of particularly heinous offences, the prisoners to be brought to trial would be selected by lot. One in twenty only would stand trial for their lives, the others being transported for life as indentured labourers to the colonies in North America and the West Indies. The unluckiest of the rebels were to face trial in London, Carlisle, Manchester, or York.

The York assize opened on Thursday, 2 October, in the Castle, with seventy-five prisoners indicted. Among those who served on the Special Commission of Oyer and Terminer were the archbishop of York, the marquess of Rockingham, Viscount Irwin, Sir Rowland Winn, Sir Miles Stapylton, Cholmley Turner, and Dr Jaques Sterne. The four juries were drawn from a list of thirty-five of the local gentry. The proceedings lasted for two days. Of the seventy-five prisoners, fifty-three pleaded guilty and twenty-two stood trial, of whom five were acquitted. As a result, seventy prisoners were convicted of high treason and sentenced to death. Addressing the condemned men, Lord Chief Baron Parker made what the *York Courant* termed a very pathetic speech before passing the sentence prescribed by law:

> You the Prisoners at the Bar, and every one of you, are to return to the Prison from whence you came; and from thence you must be drawn to the Place of Execution; when you come there, you must be hanged by the Neck, but not 'till you be dead; for you must be cut down alive; then your Bowels must be taken out, and burnt before your Faces; then your Heads must be severed from your Bodies, and each of your Bodies divided into four Quarters, and these must be at the King's Disposal: And God Almighty be merciful to your Souls.[29]

Subsequently, forty-eight prisoners had their sentences commuted to transportation for life. The remaining twenty-two were executed on Knavesmire in three groups, on three successive Saturdays, from 1 to 15 November. The most unfortunate perhaps was James Reid who, notwithstanding the fact he had never borne arms, suffered death for his role as a piper with a Highland regiment.

Laurence Sterne himself may have been present at the trials, and it is possible that he was the author of a pamphlet account of them.[30] At the very least, he would have followed closely the newspaper reports of the trials. Did he take special note of those unfortunates who pleaded in their defence that they had been forced into service with the rebels? And did his mind go back to the previous autumn when he had attempted to force his own servant Richard Greenwood into service with the Royal Hunters?

In comparison with those unfortunates so barbarously executed on Knavesmire, the suspected Jacobite sympathizers in York came off lightly, though Dr John Burton experienced many anxious moments before he was entirely free of the risk of prolonged imprisonment or worse. Undeterred by the failure of his first attempt to provide the prosecution with damning evidence against his political enemy, Jaques Sterne employed a second prisoner, Richard Murth—than whom a less credible witness would have been hard to find—to testify that he had heard Burton express disloyal sentiments while held in York Castle. The archdeacon's second attempt was little more successful than the first. Having failed to provide evidence against Burton, Murth proceeded to fling wild accusations against all and sundry—among those he identified as a rebel-sympathizer was the recorder of York[31]—and finally suggested that he himself was in possession of evidence proving that the entire Country interest was party to a Jacobite plot. For good measure he added that Dr Burton was to have been appointed the Pretender's physician extraordinary in the event of the rebellion's success—though why the prince should have wanted a provincial practitioner with an interest in midwifery in that position was not explained. Regardless of the fact that Murth's information seemed increasingly implausible, Jaques Sterne searched relentlessly for further evidence of Burton's guilt. The archdeacon made no secret of the fact that his motive in pursuing Burton was not merely to add one traitor more to the list of those who suffered in the aftermath of the rebellion, but to put an end to the influence of Burton's party at York.

Fortunately for John Burton, not all Whigs were as vindictive or single-minded as Jaques Sterne. Despite the potentially damning evidence of John Murray of Broughton, Burton was never put on trial. He continued to be held in custody until shortly after the suspension of the Habeas Corpus Act was lifted in February 1747. He was released on bail in March and appeared at York assizes in July, where no evidence was produced against him, at which point he was freed completely—to be preferred, a mere three years later, to a post as commissioner for the Land Tax.[32]

If, in evading the ire of Jaques Sterne, Burton had escaped the uncle, he would not so easily escape the nephew. When Laurence Sterne wrote the first two volumes of *Tristram Shandy*, one of the principal targets of his satire was Dr John Burton, whom he caricatured as Dr Slop, that 'little, squat, uncourtly figure' of a man-midwife, 'of about four feet and a half perpendicular height, with a breadth of back, and a sesquipedality of belly, which might have done honour to a Serjeant in the Horse-Guards' (*TS* II. ix. 84). It is true that in 1759 Sterne was interested in satirizing Burton the man-midwife—author of the *Essay toward a Complete New System of Midwifery* (1751) and the *Letter to William Smellie, M.D.* (1753)—and the physician in virtually no way resembled the grotesque figure of Sterne's imagination. Yet Sterne deliberately reminded the Yorkshire readers for whom *Tristram Shandy* was first written of Burton's dubious activities during the Jacobite rebellion, and their consequences. He made Dr Slop a 'papist'—which Burton was not—and an enemy to the liberty of the press. Sterne also recalled both Burton's imprisonment and subsequent appearance at the York assizes.

In the second volume of *Tristram Shandy* Dr Slop falls asleep during Corporal Trim's reading of a sermon on the text '*For we* trust *we have a good Conscience* '. It was a sermon Sterne himself had preached at the opening of the York assizes of 1750. In it he considered how one might form a proper judgement of 'what is of infinite importance to you not to be misled in,——namely, in what degree of real merit you stand either as an honest man, an useful citizen, a faithful servant to your King, or a good servant to your God'. 'Let CONSCIENCE determine the matter upon these reports,' Corporal Trim reads, 'and then if thy heart condemns thee not, which is the case the Apostle supposes,——the rule will be infallible' (*TS* II. xvii. 105). It is at this point that Dr Slop falls asleep. A little later, the sermon continues:

> human laws not being a matter of original choice, but of pure necessity, brought in to fence against the mischievous effects of those consciences which are no law unto themselves; well intending, by the many provisions made,—that in all such corrupt and misguided cases, where principles and the checks of conscience will not make us upright,—to supply their force, and, by the terrors of goals and halters, oblige us to it. (*TS* II, xvii, p. 106).

Prison and the threat of the gallows were indeed what John Burton had faced for more than two long years between 1745 and 1747, and when Walter Shandy declares at this juncture that he is 'sorry that Dr. *Slop* has fallen asleep before the time of his conviction', few readers in York would have missed Sterne's grim joke.

Whatever Sterne might write more than a decade later, when John Burton was once more a respected and politically active member of York society, he does not seem to have participated personally in his uncle's vicious persecution of the physician. Indeed, the very vehemence of his personal contribution to meeting the Jacobite challenge—as in his fierce endeavour to make Richard Greenwood enlist as a volunteer drummer—was almost certainly intensified by acute anxiety that was not simply political but also private. Elizabeth Sterne was pregnant and very near the end of her term. On 1 October, as hasty preparations for Yorkshire's defence were being made throughout the county, the first Lydia was born. On 2 October Sterne buried her. Whether Sterne responded to this cruel blow as Greenwood tells us he did after a similar loss, by retiring inconsolable to his chamber, we can only surmise. On this occasion he may have attempted to cope with his grief by immersing himself in plans for the county's defence against the Jacobite rebels.

Even in extreme circumstances Laurence Sterne certainly lacked the blind zeal that led his uncle so recklessly to identify any Tory as a Jacobite sympathizer. Yet he was not without considerable prejudice of his own, as he was to demonstrate most tellingly, once the Jacobite cause had been defeated, in an unpleasant article published on 1 July 1746 in the *York Journal: or, Protestant Courant.* In taking up his pen again Sterne doubtless had no sense of breaking his vow not to return to party-writing, viewing his renewed journalistic activity as patriotic rather than factional in inspiration. In London Henry Fielding, with a successful career as a dramatist behind him and more recently celebrated as the author of *Joseph Andrews*, had responded to the national crisis by founding a weekly newspaper in support of the Hanoverians, under the explicit title the *True Patriot.*[33] Even so, Sterne's polemic makes uneasy reading. In his *Protestant Courant* article he sought to cast doubt on the toleration of Roman Catholics in the city of York.

The subject was not a new one. A decade earlier the surgeon Francis Drake, in his ambitious *Eboracum: or, The History and Antiquities of the City of York* (1736), had noted with approval the extent of the tolerance—even encouragement—of Roman Catholics in the city, which he praised as one means of offsetting economic problems arising from the decline of manufacturing.[34] In their turn, Roman Catholics had expressed their recognition of the toleration by a number of friendly and symbolic gestures, including a gift of stone for the restoration of York Minster.[35] Francis Drake, it is true, was scarcely a disinterested observer, for he was himself a Roman Catholic whose Jacobite sympathies would be fully exposed in October 1745 when he would refuse to take the oath of allegiance at the height of the Jacobite rebellion. All the same, York's Roman Catholics had been peacable enough during the rebellion, as all temperate Protestants recognized.

Laurence Sterne would have none of this. Signing himself 'A Commoner', he adopted the persona of a local shopkeeper—a device Swift had memorably and effectively employed in his *Drapier's Letters* (1724–5)—in order to offer thoughts relative to the toleration of Roman Catholics in York. 'A Commoner' declares himself much puzzled that following the city's narrow escape, there are still to be found people who should 'argue in the Favour, should caress, should take within our Bosoms some of those very People, whose Principles, whose Religion and Riches, have been the Means of forming this unnatural Rebellion'.[36] (Did Sterne subsequently note that of the twenty-two unfortunate rebels executed in York in November a mere six were in fact Roman Catholics?) This was a position very close indeed to that of Jaques Sterne, who argued bluntly that 'Papists are necessarily to be suspected of Disaffection'.[37] In similar vein, 'A Commoner' alleged that York's Catholics had celebrated both the early Jacobite victory at Prestonpans and their belated success at Falkirk; but, he went on, '*Culloden* was a Stroke they could never recover; the News of it made them shrink and tremble . . . like *Yorick*'s Skull, they are quite Chopfallen. Where be their Gibes? their Gambols? their Songs? their Flashes of Merriment? Not one now to mock their own Grinning.'[38]

We should not be too distracted by the anticipation of Laurence Sterne's later work to notice that this is pretty nasty writing. The fears of Protestants and Whigs as to what might result from a Jacobite victory were doubtless justified—Fielding's *True Patriot* contained an imagined account of the consequences of the rebel occupation of London in which the Protestant prisoners included both Archbishop Herring and Fielding himself.[39] By the time Sterne was writing, however, the Jacobites were routed and any danger had passed. Not even those more active in the Hanoverian cause than Sterne felt the need to gloat over the massacre at Culloden. Fielding, for instance, found that the *True Patriot* had served its purpose by mid-June and promptly discontinued it. A youthful Edmund Burke noted 'how the minds of people are in a few days changed, the very men who but a while ago, while they were alarmed by his progress so heartily cursed those unfortunate creatures are now all pity and wish it could be terminated without bloodshed'.[40] A scarcely older Tobias Smollett, himself a staunch Hanoverian and no Roman Catholic sympathizer, was sufficiently moved to write 'The Tears of Scotland'—a poem lamenting the brutality of Cumberland's troops which, it was said, 'made every tender-hearted Whig feel himself for moments a Jacobite'.[41] Far from tender-hearted himself, 'A Commoner' soon sounds more like Swift's Modest Proposer than the Drapier, for he will have no truck with arguments that Roman Catholics should be tolerated since their money helps make York '*a rich and flourishing city*'. On the contrary, he declares, 'I can say, with much Truth, that for the twenty Years in which I have been in Business, I have not, during all that Space of Time, taken the Value of five Shillings of their Money'. Therefore, he concludes, 'let us earnestly wish them to retire from us. . . . For this I will venture to say, that as our City has never flourished since they abounded in it, so will it never flourish while they do abound.'[42]

It is more than the twentieth century's experience of the enforced resettlement of religious minorities which should make this uneasy reading, for Sterne was writing at a time when suggestions appeared in print to the effect that all Roman Catholics should be deported or 'like the Jews at Rome' wear a distinguishing mark on their hats.[43] Certainly, no amount of interest in Sterne's early writing or anticipations of his later fiction should be allowed to obscure the fact that his essay is at heart a proposal for the wholesale removal of Roman Catholics from York. If anything, Sterne's likely motivation for his proposal does him less credit than the idea itself. The position he advanced in the summer of 1746 was identical to that of Archbishop Herring, who wrote to the lord chancellor: '[I]t would help if the City of York was cleard as much as possible of Jacobites & Papists. The Trading Towns of our Country are improper places for these Vermin to settle in, but York in all respects, suits them exactly.'[44] In the circumstances, it is hard to resist the thought that, by publicly articulating what the archbishop was known to think in private, Sterne was looking to his own self-interest.

In the event no action was taken against the Roman Catholics. Following the trial of the rebels in the autumn, and the subsequent exemplary executions, the ministry in London showed itself bent rather on a policy of reconciliation than vengeance. The politically astute Herring accordingly moderated his views and let the matter drop. Only Dr Jaques Sterne was implacable. Long after the Jacobite threat had faded, the archdeacon was still harrying Roman Catholics in York. In doing so, he was of course acting entirely in accordance with the law. The penal legislation of the late seventeenth and early eighteenth centuries remained on the statute books, providing often fearsome punishment for offenders—as late as 1767 a Roman Catholic priest named John Baptist Malony was convicted and sentenced to perpetual imprisonment.[45] The focus of the archdeacon's attentions was a convent close by the Micklegate Bar. Belonging to the Institute of the Blessed Virgin Mary, the convent was ostensibly a girls' school but it served also as a centre of worship, its chaplain celebrating mass not only for the nuns and their pupils but for the Roman Catholics of York in general, thereby running foul of the law in several respects. In the winter of 1745–6 the school found itself at the mercy of the York mob, which broke all of its windows and threatened to demolish the building itself. In May 1746 Jaques Sterne was active in his own opposition to the nuns, advising them, through the abbess, to leave York altogether.

For more than four years the archdeacon continued to hound the York nuns, inexorable in his attempt to root out this papist threat to the nation. In 1746 he delivered a charge to the clergy of his archdeaconry which was published the following year under the title: *The Danger arising to our Civil and Religious Liberty from the Great Increase of* Papists, *and the Setting up* Public Schools *and* Seminaries *for the Teaching and Educating of* Youth *in the pernicious Tenets and Principles of* Popery *consider'd*. In the address the archdeacon advanced a conspiracy theory apparently of his own devising, warning the clergy of the zeal of Roman Catholics frustrated by the failure of the rebellion, the secrecy with which they will now operate, and the excellence of the penal legislation against them. 'I am well aware that I have touch'd upon a harsh Topic,' he declared, with good reason, 'I foresee what Resentment I shall draw upon myself from them', but against papist machinations aimed at the re-establishment of the Roman Catholic church in England, Jaques Sterne professed himself to be 'for shewing only a moderate Degree of Zeal in the *Best* Cause, which they exert even to Barbarity in Support of the *Worst*; and I am prepared to receive and despise every Slander'.[46]

At the beginning of 1748 the archdeacon attempted to force Mother Mary Hodshon and the other members of her convent out of their house. The nuns resisted, finding support among fellow Roman Catholics, Catholic sympathizers, and Dr Sterne's own enemies. When it seemed as though the 1748–9 concert season might have to be cancelled for lack of subscribers, the archdeacon was blamed. A correspondent to the *York Courant* declared that the problem arose from 'the restless Spirit of a certain little Doctor, that left unattempted no Methods of Persecution, in his

Power, to banish the Roman Catholic Gentry, who, by spending the Winter here, circulated amongst us many thousand pounds yearly'.[47] Yet for all his efforts Jaques Sterne achieved little in the end. Though he succeeded in having the nuns fined £4. 7*s.* 0*d.* in September 1749, the extent to which he was widely perceived to be conducting a personal vendetta may be gauged by an ironic reference, in the *York Courant*, to 'the famous Cause . . . between a certain Pious Doctor and two Religious Ladies'.[48] Nonetheless, Dr Sterne renewed his attack in 1750 and 1751, with the result that the nuns were fined on two further occasions.

In the end, the archdeacon was hated by his political opponents, considered an embarrassment by the ministry, and at times was treated with ill-disguised contempt by his fellow Anglicans in York. It was Dr Sterne himself who angrily protested in 1750 that one of the hearings relating to the 'Popish Nunnery' was opened by an ecclesiastical lawyer who, 'in a facetious, & I think a not very becoming manner . . . said he was sorry the Clergy of York had occasion to have recourse to such rough methods of making Converts of the Ladies—that the Laws for establishing the Reformation were now grown obsolete & out of date, & the present age too polite & refind to mind or submit to such old unfashionable proceedings' (*Letters*, 427). Neither the implied tolerance nor the urbanity of such sentiments held much appeal for Jaques Sterne, who sneeringly expressed the hope that the judges in the case would not prove 'such fine Gentlemen' as to forget the laws of their country. This was not just a matter, he continued, of 'two or three old women', as apologists had alleged, but a case which would determine 'whether there shal be a Popish Seminary set up, for poisoning the minds of the King's Subjects & drawing them from their Allegiance, in every Town in the Kingdom' (*Letters*, 427). Besides, he added darkly, 'I hope I shal soon have it in my power to prove these innocent Ladies (as some have represented them) guilty of a most treasonable Correspondence, during the late Rebellion, with a Seminary of Jesuits in Scotland & with a Seminary abroad' (*Letters*, 427).

The evidence the archdeacon sought did not apparently emerge, or perhaps his fellow dignitaries at the Minster were less taken with his conspiracy theory. Eventually Jaques Sterne desisted, abandoning his attack on the convent in 1751. The nuns, assured personally by the archdeacon of his decision to end his persecution, gave thanks to God in a Te Deum. Never one to avoid extremes, Archdeacon Sterne subsequently found it expedient to befriend the community and even assist in obtaining financial benefits for them.[49]

The whole distasteful episode is revealing of mid-eighteenth-century attitudes towards Roman Catholicism. While the Penal Laws remained on the statute books, so determined a Protestant as Jaques Sterne, especially if he were a church lawyer, could find ways of harrying those who infringed the law and ensuring they became subject to at least petty penalties. Yet in the case of the Bar Convent such acts were principally inspired by one man, with a small group of supporters. Even in the years immediately following the Jacobite rebellion—whose complex causes certainly included an element of religious controversy—there was no real enthusiasm in the government or the Church to bring the full weight of anti-Roman Catholic legislation to bear on the nuns of York. How little anyone really cared about their presence in the city was amply demonstrated by the eventual assistance afforded them by Dr Sterne himself.

By 1751 Laurence Sterne had long lost interest in the affairs of the Roman Catholic gentry at York. The anti-Roman Catholic prejudice he expressed during his brief intervention in the cause of the archbishop and the archdeacon in the summer of 1746 had, it is true, been very much in line with sentiments expressed in a number of his sermons, not least the most celebrated of all, 'The Abuses of Conscience'. Yet his intervention in the debate on the future of Roman Catholics in York seems likely to have been primarily opportunistic, coinciding so exactly as it does with Archbishop Herring's own views. If so, Sterne was again disappointed, for his contribution brought him no apparent advantage. So, preferring the archbishop's political tact to the archdeacon's zeal, Laurence Sterne ceased to pursue the Roman Catholics once the memory of the Jacobite rebellion receded, declining to be drawn into Jaques Sterne's offensive against the Bar Convent. The temporary alliance between uncle and nephew brought about by the Jacobite threat was short lived. Sterne showed no further interest in party-writing and the quarrel soon renewed itself, though this time on a quite different matter. Laurence Sterne, meanwhile, returned to contemplating his future life in his country parishes.

6

Sutton and Stillington, 1746–1759

The strongest indication that Laurence Sterne had few hopes of further ecclesiastical preferment was his decision to turn farmer. To this end, late in 1744, he acquired the Tindal Farm in Sutton. As vicar of Sutton Sterne already held land in the parish. Along with Elizabeth, he now decided to buy some of his own. Whether attracted to the idea of being landowners—with the connotations of gentility the possession of land held in the eighteenth century—or whether they believed that farming might provide them with an increased income more in line with their needs, the Sternes had obviously considered their decision carefully. On 1 November 1744 they bought the Tindal Farm from a neighbouring clergyman, William Dawson. Evidently by prior arrangement they mortgaged the farm immediately, and within a few days had consolidated their holdings by buying three more pieces from Richard Harland, father of Philip, the squire of Sutton, and leasing two others from Lord Fauconberg.[1]

For a young couple, neither of whom had any real background in, let alone experience of, farming, this was a considerable and exciting venture. Sequestered in Sutton, the Sternes had had plenty of time during the previous two years to observe neighbours and their holdings and to wonder whether they could farm as well or better. As vicar, Sterne was in an unrivalled position to know the yeoman farmers of the parish and to seek their advice, as well as that of such friends as Stephen Croft. The questions he would have asked were principally those relating to the ideal size of holding and the type of farming that would best suit his needs. The answers he received were good ones. If, as seems likely, his holdings now totalled over 300 acres, then the farm was of a size the eighteenth century considered more economically viable than the 100 or so acres he had farmed hitherto. Sensibly, the Sternes went in for mixed farming. This was probably not a difficult decision, for a combination of arable and livestock farming was likely to have been common among their neighbours. The milk cattle the Sternes reared would have provided milk, butter, cream, and cheese for the table, besides a cash surplus—and there may have been beef cattle also. The dung these gave was a ready source of manure for the fields. These in turn provided not only fodder for the cattle but were sown with oats (for animal feed), wheat, and barley—the last being the cereal most commonly used in the north of England for making bread, as well as for malting. Among the by-products of cereal cultivation was sufficient corn left behind after the threshing to fatten poultry in the farmyard, thus providing a source of eggs and an occasional fowl for the table; the Sternes' geese, meanwhile, could feed in the stubble-fields.

Such, at least, was the theory. In practice, farming proved no more successful for the Sternes than for Walter Shandy, whose calculations of the 'prodigious' profits he would make by enclosing the Ox-moor led him to think he would carry all before him. Like Walter, Laurence and Elizabeth Sterne were disappointed at the last—bigger failures apart, even the geese got away—though they persisted in their endeavours until December 1758, when they eventually determined to lease the farm.

That the Sternes were not more successful in their farming may be attributed both to natural circumstances outside their control and to their own inexperience and imprudence. The venture did not start well. In the spring of their very first year on the Tindal Farm a storm of extreme violence caused damage to their anxiously watched crops. Sterne recorded the event in one of only two such entries to be made in the Sutton Parish Book:

> In May 1745
> A Dismal Storm of Hail fell upon this Town, & some other adjacent ones wch did considerable Damage both to the Windows & Corn: Many of the Stones measured six Inches in Circumference———
> It broke almost all the South & West Windows both of this House & my Vicarage House at Stillington———.[2]

In the few surviving letters in which Sterne mentions his farming, the weather predictably figures prominently. Writing in July 1758, he apologized for not having visited his friend the Revd John Blake—an omission he attributed to the 'vile roads & weather, together with the *crisis* of my affairs namely the getting down my crop w^ch^ . . . is now shaking with this vile wind' (*Letters*, 54). Such unseasonable weather necessarily diminished the value of the crop, not only through the destruction caused but by the additional expenses incurred in hiring all available labourers and persuading them to work long hours to minimize damage. A sudden change in the weather, however, produced different problems. Another letter, probably from the same month, reveals Sterne both as a neighbour and as a farming parson. An unidentified friend had evidently enlisted his aid in achieving the best price for his hay. Sterne expressed his willingness to discharge the 'neighbourly Office You stand in want of, to y^{r} Satisfaction', but the task, he went on, would not be easy:

> I have taken proper Measures to get Chapmen for it, by ordering it to be publickly cryed at my two Parishes, But I find a greater Backward-[nes]s amongst my two Flocks in this Respect, than I imagined. This is owing, it seems, to a greater Prospect of Hay & other Fodder, Than there was any Expectation of, about 5 Weeks ago; When, They tell me, y^{r} Crop would have sold for 40 Shill^{s} more Than at present.—I believe there may be some Grounds for this—for all the late mowed Meadows produce plenty, of wch Y^{rs} (wch was cut last Saturday) will be no unacceptable Proof, for they say, You have as much Grass as they could well mow: so that, by their Acc^{t} The Want of the Fodder raised the Value of the Crop.—It is now with the utmost Difficulty, & a whole mornings waste of my Lungs, That I have got two Sufficient Men of Stillington to bid up to what You had offerd—twelve Pounds——I have put them off under the pretence of writing You Word—But in Truth to wait a Day or two to try the Market, & see what more can be got for it—. (*Letters*, 55–6)

Having thus prevaricated with his parishioners on his neighbour's account, the vicar of Stillington urged dispatch. He needed instructions urgently, for the barley crop was almost ready and no labour would then be available for grass-mowing; either Sterne must set men to mow the meadows on his neighbour's behalf or accept the price already offered.

In so clearly laying out the options available, and in attempting every means of achieving the best price for the hay, Sterne was displaying an economic sense, in his neighbour's interest, not always so evident in dealings on his own behalf. John Croft comments on the Sternes' activities: 'They kept a Dairy Farm at Sutton, had seven milch cows, but they allways sold their Butter cheaper than their Neighbours, as they had not the least idea of œconomy, [so] that they were allways behindhand and in arrears with Fortune.'[3]

Given all we know of Sterne's general improvidence, Croft's account rings true enough—though neither the weather nor the Sternes' lack of financial or agricultural expertise was alone to blame for their difficulties.

During the late 1740s Yorkshire was hit by the cattle plague that was sweeping through the entire country. Starting during the famine that afflicted large parts of Europe between 1708 and 1711, the plague reached England, where it wrought maximum damage in 1714. Then concentrated on the area around London, the plague was successfully contained and subsequently eradicated by a programme of slaughtering and the government's compensation of the farmers affected. After some thirty years, however, the plague reappeared and spread rapidly through the southern and midland counties of England, eventually reaching Yorkshire (its seemingly inexorable progress grimly recorded in each succeeding issue of the *York Courant*), despite a renewal of the government policy of compulsory slaughter. From 1746 to 1750 a total of £162,919. 18*s*. 0*d*. was paid by the government in compensation.

How badly Sterne himself might have been affected financially depends on whether his livestock farming extended beyond his dairy herd to beef cattle—the 'black cattle' Defoe noted especially in the region.[4] Even if the Sternes' habitual lack of spare cash had deterred them from deploying limited resources in the more costly raising of beef cattle, however, the all-too obvious effects of the plague must have served to dampen the Sternes' enthusiasm still further as they watched the ruin of their neighbours' livelihoods. As a priest, of course, Sterne was obliged to think of his neighbours' losses as well as his own. What made matters worse for everyone was the complete ignorance of the causes of the plague, making even containment, let alone eradication, problematic. The eighteenth century saw the development of modern scientific farming, yet correspondents were reduced to writing in to the Yorkshire papers to suggest that the infection could be carried 'many Miles, in clouds, by strong Winds', or proffering home-made remedies for infected cattle (one started with 'a Pint of Gin, and a Pint of old Verjuices, in a Quart of Boiling Water').[5] Sterne himself was turning his back on science in favour of religious explanation of the pestilence—at least in the pulpit. Two of his surviving sermons—Sermon XXXII and XLV (one a reworking of the other)—touch on the plague: 'The pestilence amongst our cattle, though it has distressed, and utterly undone, so many thousands; yet what one visible alteration has it made in the course of our lives?'[6] That Sterne actually believed the plague to be a direct result of divine displeasure seems highly unlikely. In fact, the simplest expression of concerned piety is a psalm composed by the Stillington parish clerk and sung by him in church on 28 May 1749. For all its crudity, the psalm is richly evocative of the rural community to which Sterne ministered and preached, torn between religious and scientific explanations of the ruinous misfortunes it faced, and utterly local in its frame of reference:

O Lord we are fearfully Distresst
But Thou canst help us still,
Thou canst if thou wilt do thy best
Let Men say what they will.

For this Distemper are full sad
And Rages in our Town
It is enough to make one Mad.
The like was never Known.

There's old John Crow & Richard Pen
And likewise William Bland
With many more Substantial Men
Now Ruined out of Hand.

And we shall be quite undone
It is no Bout to Strive
And broke up every Mothers Son
As sure as we're Alive.

No Christian Bull or Cow they say
But take it soon or Sine
And it is Tou to one I lay
Good God take care of mine.

For Lord thou know'st we are full poor
So help us for thou can
And we will put our Trust no more
In any Other Man.

The Doctors tho' they all have Spoke
Like Learned Gentlemen
And told us how the Intrails look
Of Cattle Dead & gone

Yeat they can nothing do at all
With all their Learning store
Then Come away thy self O Lord
And Vex us so no More.

But Come with help all in thy Hand
O Come without Delay
And Drive it forth out of the Land
For ever & for Aye.[7]

In retrospect, it seemed to Sterne as if everything had gone wrong with his venture into farming. At the end of his life he cautioned an acquaintance to learn from his own mistakes: 'You are much to blame if you dig for marle, unless you are sure of it.—I was once such a puppy myself, as to pare, and burn, and had my labour for my pains, and two hundred pounds out of pocket . . . a cart load of turneps was (I thought) very dear at two hundred pounds.' By then an old dog, Sterne might reflect ruefully that 'bought experience is the devil', but he could still expostulate with feeling: 'Curse on farming' (*Letters*, 394).

Lacking direct evidence from the early years of Sterne's management of the Tindal Farm, we cannot know how swiftly the lack of success led to disenchantment. The fact that the Sternes did not finally let the farm until 1758, after fourteen years, suggests that they continued for some time to be optimistic about their eventual chances of making their venture profitable. By that time, however, they had been forced to take out a second mortgage with Stephen Croft and John Fountayne, and while Sterne's financial success with the second, London edition of the first two volumes of *Tristram Shandy* enabled him to pay off the first mortgage in June 1760, the second remained unredeemed at his death. Whatever may be true of his attitude to farming during the early years, it is evident that the unpredictability of his agricultural venture turned it eventually into an anxious and exasperating experience. In December 1758, close to the shortest day of the year, Sterne described the farm business that occupied both him and his servants, who:

> set out with a Wagon Load of Barly at 12 o'Clock, & had scarse day to see it measured to the Maltsman—
>
> —I have 4 Threshers every Day at Work, & they mortify me with declarations, That There is so much Barly they cannot get thro' that spe[c]ies before X^{mas} Day—& . . . how I shall manage Matters . . . half distracts my Brain. (*Letters*, 65–6)

It was with understandable, as well as evident, relief that Sterne reported his abandonment of farming. 'I thank God,' he wrote,

> I have settled most of my Affairs—Let my freehold to a promissing Tenent—have likewise this Week let him the most considerable part of my Tyths & shall clear my hands & head of all country Entanglements, having at present only ten p^{ds} [a] year in Land & 7 p^{ds} a year in Corn Tyth left undisposed of, wch shall be quitted with all provident Speed: This will bring me & mine into a narrow Compass—& make us, I hope both rich & happy. (*Letters*, 66)

The pious hope was unfulfilled. The following year was to be decisive in Sterne's life—but if he and his family were never to be uniformly rich, and only intermittently happy, then their lives would not entirely be lived out in the narrow compass they had known for the past two decades.

The fact that the Sternes turned to farming in 1744 did not, of course, mean that the vicar of Sutton-on-the-Forest and Stillington had abandoned his priestly duties. At times, these seem likely to have involved Sterne in complying with obligations about which he must have had acutely conflicting feelings. One was the necessity of being present at the annual visitation of the archdeacon of Cleveland—his uncle Jaques.

Once a year, the town of Thirsk, thirty miles to the north-west of York, would become alive with the clergy and parish officers of the North Riding.[8] It was there in 1747 that Dr Jaques Sterne delivered his charge to the clergy, in which he argued against the toleration of Roman Catholics in York. As for his successor Francis Blackburne, the visitation was an occasion to argue formally for some political position or point of Church discipline important to him. For most who thronged the town it would be a welcome interruption to daily routine, an occasion on which the clergy, parish clerks, and churchwardens of the forty-three parishes of the archdeaconry would gather not merely for business but to renew acquaintance and exchange opinions and gossip over dinner about preferments gained or desired. Much of the business of the ecclesiastical court was routine enough: schoolmasters, physicians, and midwives were licensed and wills were proved. The judge on such occasions might be either the archdeacon himself or a deputy—either Dr William Ward or Ward's deputy, Dr Francis Topham. Dr Topham, who presided regularly in the early years of Sterne's residence in Sutton, was a Yorkshire-born lawyer of just Sterne's age and, like Sterne, a Cambridge graduate. As Sterne watched his uncle's surrogate at work, he—like many another struggling clergyman—must have pondered ruefully on the difference between his prospects and those of his more fortunate contemporaries. Beginning to work in the spiritual courts of the York diocese at the same time as Sterne was setting out in the Church, Topham was already advancing in a career which would conclude with his becoming the leading church lawyer of the northern province. In the process he would invoke the considerable ire of Laurence Sterne, who at the end of the 1750s would turn his attention to Topham in writing *A Political Romance*, the work on York church politics which was to give him confidence in his ability to produce something that might be read and enjoyed beyond the narrow confines of ecclesiastical circles at the Minster.

That Sterne was envious not merely of Francis Topham's comparative eminence in the Church but also of his legal training seems certain, since his own haphazard reading of continental and English jurists—Grotius, Pufendorf, Brooke, Coke, Swinburne, and Selden—is in plentiful, if playful, evidence throughout *Tristram Shandy*, where Topham makes a further appearance as the hair-splitting lawyer Didius at the Visitation dinner. In common with many other clergy of the time, Sterne was in fact appointed a magistrate in the 1740s, thereby enabling him to give some rein to his noted liking for legal argument. His servant, Richard Greenwood, was later to recall that: 'Sterne was a Justice of peace & would often espouse a cause which he was [sure] of bringing thro' at the Quarter Sessions, he could talk down the Lawyer so—this he delighted in.'[9]

Besides this civil commission, Sterne was also active in the spiritual courts. As prebendary of North Newbald he had the further opportunity to indulge in his inclination for the law, when taking his place as judge of the spiritual court there—an office he continued to perform annually until the success of *Tristram Shandy* prompted him to find a surrogate. In sitting in a judicial capacity at North Newbald, however, as in attending the archdeacon's court at Thirsk, Sterne's fondness for the law and legal quibbling had its darker side. Foremost among those who did *not* look forward to sittings of the spiritual courts were the hapless parishioners brought there for trial. Since most—though not all—of the offences considered were sexual in nature, there was doubtless a discernible whiff of titillation, if not prurience, amid the solemn atmosphere of moral disapproval. Chief among the crimes for which parishioners were brought to trial was 'fornication', which, though generally secret enough in its commission, was all too readily detectable in the narrow confines of a pre-contraceptive rural society by its consequences.

Sterne may have enjoyed legal argument, but he must also have been continually aware of the distasteful role into which his office forced him. As parish priest he doubtless had many private occasions to remind parishioners—as Uncle Toby reminds readers—that marriage was ordained 'as a remedy against sin, and to avoid fornication'.[10] In the sermon 'Our Conversation in Heaven' (XXIX), Sterne paraphrases St Paul as he enquires: 'Can that body expect to rise and shine in glory, that is a slave to lust, or dies in the fiery pursuit of an impure desire?'[11] If such sentiments are infrequent in Sterne's sermons, then it may be that the clergyman who had gained an unwelcome reputation for pursuing his female servants found it prudent not too frequently to commend continence to his parishioners.[12] Whatever choice he had in the pulpit, however, was denied him in court. Yet the crime of fornication he had so often been guilty of himself was also that which he was most frequently called upon to judge and punish. The penalty for those convicted could be unpleasant, for it might involve public penance. Some instances of judgements in which Sterne was personally involved survive from the records of the Stillington prebendal court—Stillington was a small spiritual court like that of North Newbald—in the 1750s. In August 1755 Sterne presided at the court. Among those on whom a public penance was enjoined were 'William Johnson and Jane Nelson otherwise Johnson now his wife of the Parish of Stillington'. Despite their subsequent marriage, Jane Nelson's pre-nuptial pregnancy exposed her and her husband to the enforced shame punishment in Stillington parish church. After morning or evening service, on one of three stipulated Sundays in August, the couple were obliged to repeat after Laurence Sterne a declaration of penance beginning: 'WHEREAS, we good Neighbours forgetting our Duties to Almighty GOD, have committed the Crime of FORNICATION together, whereby We have offended Almighty GOD, to the Dangers of our own Souls, and evil Example of others: We do here acknowledge that our said Fault, and hearty Sorrow for the same, desiring Almighty GOD to forgive Us.'[13] In enforcing such a punishment Stillington revealed itself as especially backward, for shame punishments for prenuptial pregnancy and fornication had largely disappeared by 1740 (and for the former would be abolished as an offence by statute in 1787).

William and Jane Johnson might nevertheless have been punished even more severely. Presumably because they had subsequently married, they were obliged to make their declaration in the presence of the churchwardens only, and wearing their 'accustomed Apparel'. A woman unable to achieve respectability by marriage might fare considerably less well. The case of Jane Harbottle, a 'poor woman' of Stillington, shows the rite of penance enjoined in its full and still more repugnant form. When arraigned following the birth of an illegitimate child in 1753, Jane Harbottle had already borne two bastard children, both allegedly to married men. (The baptismal record for 1749 shows Jonathan as 'the child of Th[s] Wood'.) During the Stillington visitation of 1753 a penance was enjoined on Jane Harbottle in respect of the birth of a third illegitimate child—a daughter, Esther. On one of the first three Sundays in September Jane Harbottle was ordered to appear at morning service before the whole congregation, 'being bare-head, bare foot, and bare-leged, having a White

Sheet wrapped about *her* from the Shoulders to the Feet, and a white Wand in *her* Hand'.[14] Immediately after the gospel reading she was obliged to stand on 'some Form or Seat before the Pulpet' and repeat after Sterne:

> WHEREAS, I good People forgetting my Duty to Almighty God, have committed the Detestable Sin of Fornication with *Robert Jepson a Marry'd man* and thereby have justly provoked the heavy Wrath of God against me, to the great Danger of my own Soul, and evil Example of others, I do earnestly Repent, and am heartily sorry for the same, desiring Almighty God for the Merits of Jesus Christ, to forgive me both this and all other my Offences, and also ever hereafter, so to assist me with his Holy Spirit, that I never fall into the like Offence again, and for that End and Purpose, I desire you all here Present, to pray with me, and for me, saying, Our Father . . .

On 8 September Sterne signed the penance, stating that it had been duly performed.

Jane Harbottle, it would seem, accepted the decision of the spiritual court and acted on it obediently and promptly. Not so Robert Jepson. A married yeoman farmer, he too was presented at the 1753 Stillington visitation, 'for the Crime of Adultery by begetting a Bastard Childe upon *Jane Harbotle*'. He refused to perform the act of penance enjoined on him and likewise failed to appear at the visitation of the following year, whereupon Sterne was obliged to excommunicate him. This was not merely a sign of spiritual displeasure. In the eighteenth century the sentence of excommunication took away virtually all of the rights of the guilty party. Henceforth Robert Jepson could not bring a legal action to secure or recover his property, nor could he act as a juryman nor as a witness. He had no right to burial in consecrated ground. Still more alarmingly, he was liable—if served with the writ 'De excommunicato capiendo'—to perpetual imprisonment. Nor was this a wholly idle threat: a case very similar to Jepson's led to a Yorkshire weaver named William Carr lying in prison for over two years for inability to pay the legal fees resulting from his case.[15]

The extent to which sexual irregularities received genuine moral censure in eighteenth-century village life is doubtful. In determining attitudes to pre-marital sexuality or pregnancy, class differences were crucial—with labouring people finding less cause in either for moral censure or self-doubt. Aristocratic attitudes might be extreme: the father of Lord Sandwich opined that 'He that doth get a wench with child and marries her afterwards is as if a man should shit in his hat and then clap it on his head'.[16] Hugh Kelly's popular sentimental novel *Louisa Mildmay, or Memoirs of a Magdalen* (1767), offers a middle-class view of pre-marital unchastity in its protracted examination of the hero's qualms about marrying his bride, the eponymous heroine, after consummating his wedding in a fit of passion on the evening before the ceremony. By contrast with such brutal or baroque sentiments, ordinary people could show a casual disregard for moral strictures and ecclesiastical law alike. When the Revd William Cole recorded in his diary for 1766 an occasion in which he baptized a child and churched its mother in the parlour of his house, immediately after having married its parents in the church, he justified his actions to himself by arguing that 'as the Discipline of our Church, thro' the Practices of the Dissenters, is now so relaxed as to come to nothing, there is no parlying with your Parishioners on any Point of Doctrine or Discipline'.[17] Certainly, in one Yorkshire village in 1743 both parson and churchwardens were afraid to report sexual delinquents to the archdeacon for fear of reprisals from the parishioners, so that William Johnson and Jane Nelson most likely felt sheepish rather than truly shamed—or penitent.

Rather than the moral questions involved, it was the financial implications of bastardy that most perturbed the village community. The risk that the illegitimate child might come on the parish poor rate rather than be supported by its father was the one to be avoided. Legislation passed in 1733 put great pressure on any man alleged by a woman to be the father of her illegitimate child, for he could be arrested to ensure payment for the child's upkeep, should he refuse (or be unable) to marry her. In order to discover the father—or, failing that, a man who could be made to accept responsibility—parish officers often applied whatever pressure they could on the mother. Midwives, for example, might refuse to assist unmarried women in their labours unless they revealed the name of their child's father—a duty imposed on them by the midwives' oath of 1726.[18] In a case such as that of Robert Jepson, who refused to make financial provision for Jane Harbottle's child, the responsibility fell back on the parish. In May 1754 Stillington accepted the responsibility without indulging in excessive generosity. Whereas by law a father could be made to pay between one and seven shillings a week for seven years, Stillington set aside for 'the use of Robert Jibson Childe by botil . . . per week 7 pence'. Despite the mark against him, Robert Jepson was fortunate, being fully reintegrated into the community in later years. In 1762 he became one of the overseers of the poor in the parish—an office to which he was elected by the members of the vestry, who controlled many aspects of village life—serving in the same capacity in 1781 and acting as a member of the jury in 1769.[19]

For Jane Harbottle, the unfortunate mother of Jepson's child, there was no similar distinction. When she died in September 1758 she left to the care of the parish her two surviving children (her second child had died in its third year). Yet Jane Harbottle was shown sympathy by at least one person in the community. As part of her punishment in 1753 she was obliged to go the ten or so miles into York to obtain a copy of her penance. When she set off on her lengthy journey on foot she took with her a letter from the vicar of Stillington to the church lawyer, John Clough:

> Mr Clough
> the Bearer is the poor Woman who was presented at Stillington Visitation, and has left her Child to go & get these said Penances, wch I & Mr Mosely talked so much about. She is as poor as a Church Mouse & cannot absolutely raise a Shilling, To save her Life. so pray let her have the Penance—and as far as the Stamps, I will take care to discharge. If not above 3 or 4 Shillings—
>
> Yrs L. STERNE
>
> *PS*
> Pray dispatch her. That She may not have a 2^{d} Journey as she has a Child to leave—. (*Letters*, 47)

Here we have a brief but vivid glimpse of Sterne's conduct as a village priest. In this casually surving scrap of correspondence, he is revealed as both conscientious and compassionate. Well aware that, unable to pay her fine or legal fees, Jane Harbottle was liable to fall foul of the writ 'De excommunicato capiendo' and find herself imprisoned indefinitely, Sterne defrayed her expenses himself.[20] From the stories retailed by John Croft it is easy to imagine the kind of disagreements the unpredictable, careless Sterne might have had with his respectable parishioners. As the lists of subscribers and their subscriptions to charitable institutions like the York County Hospital regularly published in the York press eloquently testify, the eighteenth century was a great age of public virtue. Sterne's morality was called into question often enough, yet it is not difficult to believe that there were many, like Jane Harbottle, who were grateful for his spontaneous, disinterested acts of private charity.

It was perhaps no more than Sterne expected of himself. In a sermon preached during the 1740s or 1750s, he reflected on the duties of priesthood, and though he did so in general terms, few auditors or readers can have forborne to draw reflexions on the preacher himself:

> [H]ow often do you behold a sordid wretch, whose straight heart is open to no man's affliction, taking shelter behind an appearance of piety, and putting on the garb of religion, which none but the merciful and compassionate have a title to wear. Take notice with what sanctity he goes to the end of his days, in the same selfish track in which he first set out—turning neither to the right hand nor to the left—but plods on—pores all his life long upon the ground, as if afraid to look up, lest peradventure he should see aught which might turn him one moment out of that straight line where interest is carrying him . . .[21]

To which congregation were these words first delivered? Sutton? Stillington? Whatever the answer, Sterne's own rejection of piety void of benevolence is clear enough: 'merciful GOD! that a teacher of thy religion should ever want humanity—or that a man whose head might be thought full of the one, should have a heart void of the other!'[22]

That Sterne later published the sermon containing these reflections was a question of choice; the survival of the brief letter to John Clough concerning Jane Harbottle was a matter of sheer chance. That it should have survived is fortunate, however, for it helps give the lie to a much better-known story which—presenting Sterne as devoid not merely of charity but also of natural affection—once tended to call into question the morality, especially the philanthropic sentimentalism, often admired in *Tristram Shandy* and *A Sentimental Journey*.

The story was that Sterne had scandalously neglected his mother, and refused her financial assistance when she was destitute, thereby condemning her not merely to penury but to the shame and hardship of a debtors' prison. This lurid tale apparently originated with Sterne's Uncle Jaques, to be embellished by John Croft and others before being given wider and memorable currency by Byron. Thereafter it was retailed as fact by writers hostile to Sterne, who condemned his sentimentalism as a sham, a literary affectation wholly at odds with the author's heartless conduct in his own life.

John Croft's account is laconic but to the point: 'Sterne's Mother died in the common Goal at York in a wretched condition, or soon after she was released.'[23] The story of Sterne's relations with his mother from the time he left her to go to school in Yorkshire at the age of 9 or 10 can be most fully reconstructed from an angry letter Sterne wrote in 1751 in protest against the vindictiveness of his uncle Jaques. Twenty years earlier Agnes Sterne was living with her own family in Ireland when the news reached her of Roger Sterne's death in Jamaica. Subsequently she made the journey to England to visit Jaques personally, hoping to secure the aid of her brother-in-law, the rising clerical lawyer, in her desire to draw her annual pension of £20, to which she was entitled as widow of a lieutenant, against the English rather than Irish establishment. Whether because Jaques felt his brother had married beneath him or because he had conceived a personal dislike for Agnes, the visit was unsuccessful. 'I well remember,' wrote Laurence Sterne of this visit, 'she was forced to return back, without having so much Interest as to obtain the favor of being admitted to Your Presence. (not being sufferd even to reach York)' (*Letters*, 35). Without the assistance she had hoped for from Jacques, Agnes Sterne was forced to wait until 1736 before she was able to draw her pension.

Although she was in England, however, Agnes Sterne apparently made no attempt to visit her son, whom she had not seen for eight or nine years. Sterne later recalled his mother's neglect with some bitterness. 'From my Fathers Death to the Time I settled in the World, which was eleven Years, My Mother lived in Ireland—& as during all that time I was not in a Condition to furnish her with Money,—I seldom heard from her' (*Letters*, 35). When she did write she told her son that she was supporting herself by running an embroidery school, leading him to believe that by combining this income with her pension 'she lived Well'.

If Agnes Sterne generally neglected her son, however, she was evidently and understandably assiduous in soliciting the aid of those who might assist her financially. So persistently did she write in the 1740s to beg or demand money that both Jaques Sterne, while still on good terms with his nephew, and Rebecca Custobadie, wife of the register to the Dean and Chapter, warned the recently married Sterne and his wife of Agnes Sterne's 'Clamourous & rapacious Temper'. The young couple lived, Sterne recalled, 'in perpetual Dread of her thrusting herself upon us' (*Letters*, 35–6). Evidently their fear was well-founded, for 'the news that I had Married a Woman of Fortune hastened her over to England' (*Letters*, 35). By the time such news reached Ireland it was doubtless exaggerated, encouraging Agnes Sterne to believe that her own financial difficulties were at an end. Though not poor, Laurence and Elizabeth Sterne were far from wealthy, and when he heard that his mother had arrived at Liverpool, intending to settle herself with her son and new daughter-in-law, Sterne did not hesitate. Forseeing the danger to his marriage of a household containing a mother he hardly knew, taking income away from a wife he had only recently married and whose upbringing had led her to form expectations beyond what his means could satisfy, Sterne determined to forestall her: 'I took Post to prevent her coming nearer

Me,—stay'd three Days with her,—used all the Arguments I could fairly, to engage her to return to Ireland & end her Days with her Own Relations' (*Letters*, 36).

Given such a reply, Agnes Sterne might have wondered, along with the 'best lawyers and civilians in the land', '*Whether the mother be of Kin to her child*' (*TS* IV. xxix. 262). It is, however, a telling indication of how alienated Sterne had become from the parent who had shown so little concern for him throughout the previous two decades that he reveals no sense of a possible incongruity in using the phrase to his uncle. 'I convinced her,' Sterne continued, 'that besides the Interest of my Wife's Fortune, I had then but a bare hundred pounds a year, out of Which my ill Health obliged me to keep a Curate, That we had moreover ourselves to keep, and in that Sort of Decency which left it not in our Powers to give her Much' (*Letters*, 36). During the three days he spent at Liverpool Sterne advanced every means of persuasion open to him. He argued that if he had money it could just as easily be sent to her, and besides £20 in Ireland, where she had family, would go as far as £30 in England, where she knew no one, and in any case there was no way in which Sterne could assist his mother with the inevitable expense involved in moving from one country to the other. Agnes Sterne, however, seems to have accepted her son's financial reasoning no more than his implied rejection of their kinship. Sterne's evidently genuine impatience, born out of a sense of his mother's previous unconcern for him, led him to further tactlessness. 'I concluded,' he later told his uncle, 'with representing to her, the Inhumanity of a Mother *able* to Maintain herself, thus forcing herself as a Burden upon a Son who was scarce able to Support himself without breaking in upon the future Support of another Person whom she might imagine, was much dearer to me' (*Letters*, 36).

Regardless of her own apparent cupidity, Agnes Sterne probably felt entitled to the support of a son not bereft of life's necessities. Sterne evidently felt no comparable sense of filial responsibility. His tactic was to secure himself from further demands at the least possible expense, and so 'summ'd up all those Arguments with making her a present of Twenty Guineas, Which with a Present of Cloaths &c—which I had given her the Day before, I doubted not, Would have the Effect I wanted' (*Letters*, 36). In this, however, as Sterne was obliged to admit, he was greatly mistaken. Though she apparently listened attentively to everything he said, Agnes Sterne had no sooner taken possession of her son's money than she told him 'with an Air of the utmost Insolence': 'That as for going back to live in Ireland; She was determined to Shew me no such Sport—That she found, I had married a Wife who had brought me a Fortune—& she was resolved to enjoy her Share of it, & live the Rest of her Days at her ease either at York or Chester' (*Letters*, 36). So blunt a response may easily be imagined to have infuriated Sterne, who had just parted with 20 guineas he could ill afford. It is another matter whether the reply extenuates his unsympathetic response to Agnes Sterne's understandable desire to end her days in circumstances more comfortable than had been afforded her during the long years of barrack life, or in running an embroidery school in Dublin to supplement a meagre widow's pension. Still, Agnes's resolve amounted to little more than a thinly veiled threat. A decision to settle in York or Chester could only be interpreted as a determination to embarrass her clergyman son close to home, if he would not support her at a discreet distance. Further argument proving of no avail, Sterne took leave of his mother with understandably bad grace, assuring her that 'tho' my Income was strait, I should not forget I was a Son, Tho she had forgot she was a *Mother*' (*Letters*, 36).

Sterne's virtual capitulation, on his mother's terms, had the desired effect of keeping Agnes Sterne away from York, and together with her daughter Catherine, she settled at Chester. By his own account Sterne kept to his promise, though the added financial burden increased the resentment he felt towards his mother. Though Laurence and Elizabeth Sterne were 'kind to her above our power & common Justice to ourselves . . . it went hard enough down with us, to reflect We were supporting both her and my Sister in the Pleasures and Advantages of a Town Life, which for prudent Reasons we denyed ourselves' (*Letters*, 37). This 'weakness,' as Sterne termed it, continued for five years: 'tho' I own, not without continual Remonstrances on my Side, as well as perpetual Clamours on theirs which you will naturally imagine to have been the Case, When all that was given was thought as much above reason by the One, as it fell *below* the expectations of the Other' (*Letters*, 37).

The sense of injustice Sterne experienced all this time was significantly compounded in 1744 by the visit paid him at Sutton by his sister Catherine. Sterne paid for her journey and received her 'with all Kindness'. She stayed for a month or longer, and at the end of her visit 'was sent back at My Own Charge with my own Servant & Horses. with 5 Guineas which I gave her in Her Pocket, & a Six & thirty Piece which my Wife put into her Hand as she took Horse' (*Letters*, 37). Catherine evidently made an impression on the servant who accompanied her on the return journey, for sixty years later Richard Greenwood could recall 'a sister of Sternes visiting them, one of the finest women ever seen'.[24] If Sterne's own account may be trusted, Catherine's fineness was restricted to her outward appearance, for she had been sent to Yorkshire by her mother, who had apparently been apprised of the quarrel between Jaques Sterne and her son, with the express intention of making complaints to the archdeacon about her brother's treatment of their mother and herself. Notwithstanding the kindness shown her at Sutton, this she duly did. 'In what Light she represented so much affection & Generosity,' Sterne later expostulated, 'I refer to Your Memory of the account she gave you of it in her return thro' York; But for very strong Reasons, I believe She concealed from you all that was necessary to Make a proper Handle of us Both; which Double Game, by the by, my Mother has play'd over again upon us, for the same Purposes Since she came to York' (*Letters*, 37).

Sterne felt as deceived and badly treated by his sister as by his mother, yet by his own account he was far from tactful in his dealing with Catherine. It was certainly true, as the young vicar protested, that even as a pluralist and prebendary, he was unable to give his sister a fortune or to maintain her in any great style. Yet the efforts of her brother and his wife to lower her expectations of what station she might hope to occupy in life must inevitably have seemed offensive to Catherine, even if such efforts were, as Sterne coldly maintained, 'the truest Mark of our Friendship'. As recounted by Sterne himself, the various proposals the Sternes made to Catherine went from bad to worse. She must, they said, 'turn her Thoughts to some way of depending upon her own Industry'; if she would, they promised her 'all imaginable Assistance'. Taking a hint from Agnes Sterne's embroidery school, they proposed that Catherine should 'learn the Business of a Mantua-Maker'. Once she was sufficiently adept to set up for herself the Sternes would give her £30 and support her until the business enabled her to become self-sufficient. The proposal was not unreasonable and even, given the Sternes' own financial worries, generous. The alternatives they offered, however, must have seemed considerably less so. Elizabeth Sterne offered to provide Catherine with a complete set of clothes and find her a place in a London milliner's shop, where she might receive £10 a year in wages. Such condescension on the part of her sister-in-law was probably little more acceptable than the Sternes' final suggestion. 'As my Wife had then an Opportunity of recommending her to the family of one of the first of our Nobility,' recalled Sterne, 'She undertook to get her a creditable place in it where she would receive no less than 8 or 10 p^{ds} a Year Wages with other Advantages' (*Letters*, 38). Believing Catherine was ready to fall in with either of the last two suggestions, Elizabeth Sterne obtained the offer of both posts for her. When these were put to Catherine, however, she evinced indignation rather than the anticipated gratitude and rejected both offers 'with the utmost Scorn'. Her brother, she told him, might send his own children to service 'when [he] had any'—a phrase doubtless as wounding to both the Sternes as it was intended to be—but 'for her part, As she was the Daughter of a Gentleman, *she would not Disgrace* herself, but would Live as Such' (*Letters*, 38).

Catherine's arrogance may well have been misplaced, and the Sternes were doubtless tempted to reply that, having rejected their offers, she must live as best she might. Sterne himself could not forget the 'difficulties & Draw-Backs' he faced on beginning to make his own way in the world. There was the repayment of the money his uncle Richard had laid out on his education, food, and clothing for nine years. Fresh in his memory too was the struggle to repay the money he had borrowed over and above the £30 a year his cousin Richard had allowed him at university. The expense of renovating and furnishing the vicarage at Sutton was an even more recent memory. Harsh though it may have been, it is not incomprehensible that Sterne should have felt that his sister's apparent disinclination to support herself by her own efforts 'disengaged me from any further concern'.

It is difficult, though, to withold all sympathy from Catherine. Modestly and prudently as the Sternes prided themselves on living, it was in a manner considerably superior to that to which Catherine was accustomed. That Elizabeth Sterne gave herself considerable airs we know from her cousin Elizabeth Montagu, and her perceived sense of superiority to her husband's family is evident enough in her proposal to Catherine that she go into service. In the course of a month's stay Catherine would have observed that the Sternes were looked up to socially in Sutton, not just by the labourers but by the yeoman farmers as well, and if not on friendly terms with the Harlands, they were the always-welcome guests of the Crofts of Stillington. While she remained the guest of her brother and sister-in-law she would have been treated with more respect than she had ever known. The idea of exchanging the possibility of this life for a place as a milliner's assistant or an upper-servant of the nobility was understandably unappealing. Had he used a little more imagination Sterne might have thought of his own case and his total dependence on his cousin Richard for the university education which had enabled him to support himself in a position appropriate to the son of a gentleman. That their father had been improvident was no more Catherine's fault than his own. Perhaps such considerations did pass through his mind, for though he felt his sister's 'folly' was such as 'might have disengaged Me from any further Concern', yet 'I persisted in doing what I thought was Right' (*Letters*, 38). In future Laurence and Elizabeth Sterne would not support Agnes and Catherine as generously nor as frequently as before, yet they continued to send what they could 'conveniently Spare'.

If Sterne believed he might gain some peace and fulfil his duties as a son by occasional gifts to Chester, he was wrong on both accounts. Piqued by her son's apparent indifference, Agnes Sterne did not merely remain importunate; she also became, in Sterne's own account, increasingly ungrateful for what presents he did make her. She gave others to understand—by insinuation or direct allegation—that her son neglected her and, Sterne reported in 1751 with understandable indignation, 'more than once denyed the Money I have sent her even to My Own Face' (*Letters*, 38). On one such occasion she absolutely denied having received 'a Small Bill drawn for three Pounds by Mr Ricard upon Mr Boldero'. Sterne hastened to investigate:

> I naturally supposed some Mistake of Mr Ricard in Directing—However that She Might not be a Sufferer by the Disappointment, I immediately sent another Bill for as Much More; But withal said as Mr Ricard could prove his Sending her the Bill, I was determined to trace out *who* got my Money, upon which she wrote word back, that She had rec^d^ it herself—But had *forgot it.* (*Letters*, 38)[25]

Exactly how much his gifts amounted to, Sterne could not be certain. 'It is not usual to take rec^ts^ for presents made,' he remarked bitterly, 'so that . . . I have not many Vouchers of that kind' (*Letters*, 38). Still, as close as he could reckon it up, his presents of money, clothes, and other items amounted to not less than £90. Some gifts Sterne had good reason to recall. In December 1747 Agnes Sterne, encouraged by her previously indifferent brother-in-law to report the real or imagined injuries suffered at her son's hands, went to the archdeacon's house in Gray's Court, 'to Complain, She could not get a *Farthing*' from her son. Yet at that very moment, Sterne alleged, 'She carried with her *Ten Guineas* in her Pocket which I had given her but two Days before. If she could *forget* such a Summ I had reason *to remember* it; for when I gave it I did not leave myself One Guinea in the House to befriend my Wife, tho' then within One Day of her Labour & under an apparent Necessity of a Man Mid-wife to attend her' (*Letters*, 39). What Sterne's motives were for so generous a gift under such circumstances he does not say; perhaps he merely wanted to be rid of a mother whose increasing rapaciousness could manifest itself at so inopportune a moment. Yet given Elizabeth Sterne's inability successfully to bear a healthy child—the death of their daughter in 1745 must have been a powerful and disturbing memory to both husband and wife—for Agnes Sterne to have pestered her son at such a time suggests that not all the wrongs of the unhappy relationship between mother and son were on Sterne's side.

By Sterne's own account, moreover, his gift of 10 guineas was not the full extent of his generosity, for he told his mother also that he would give her £8 a year 'whilst I lived'. The possibility that the mother might outlive her consumptive son was evidently real enough and, prompted by the malicious Jaques, Agnes wrote a week after the offer was made—that is, a week after the birth of her granddaughter—that she was determined not to accept her son's offer 'unless I would Settle the eight pounds upon Her out of my Wifes fortune, & chargable upon it In case my Wife should be left a Widow' (*Letters*, 39).

This time Agnes Sterne had gone too far. Sterne absolutely refused such a condition, and three years later his intense indignation at receiving such a demand while his wife was just recovering from Lydia's birth was evident. His wife's fortune, he insisted, was in no way equal to supporting his mother in the event of his death. Moreover, Sterne wrote to his uncle, 'considering how much she has merited at my hands, as the best of Wives, That was I capable of being worried into so cruel a Measure as to give away hers & her Child's Bread upon the clamour which you and my Mother have raised—That I should not only be the Weakest, But the *Worst Man* that ever Woman trusted with all She had' (*Letters*, 39)—a reference to Elizabeth's insistence that her fortune not be legally settled on her but pass directly into her husband's control.[26]

So furious was Sterne with his mother's conduct and Jaques's encouragement of her importunities that, despite their quarrel, he endeavoured to demonstrate to his uncle the utter unreasonableness of Agnes's behaviour. Fearing the possible results of a personal meeting, Sterne wrote to his uncle asking that Elizabeth might present the whole story to Jaques in person. The archdeacon sent word back by Sterne's servant, as Sterne himself later recalled, that he would 'be excused from any Conference with my Wife, But that I might appear before You'. Believing that the only likely outcome of such a meeting was an angry argument Sterne made his excuses in turn, contenting himself with the reflection that he was conscious 'of having done my Duty & of being able to prove I had, when ever I thought fit' (*Letters*, 33). Sterne held to his resolution to keep silent over the matter for three years. In 1751, however, friends told him that Jaques was making further trouble for him—a fact which goaded Sterne to write the long, self-justifying account which is our principal source of information about the unhappy situation. He had discovered that, 'by as Singular a Stroke of Ill-Design as could be levell'd against a Defenceless Man Who Lives retired in the Country & has few Opportunities of Disabusing the World . . . my Mother has moreover been fix'd in that Very place where a hard report might do me (as a Clergyman) the most real Disservice' (*Letters*, 33). Exactly where this was, Sterne does not say. It seems, though, that Agnes Sterne had been committed to prison.

Such at least was the story that began to circulate publicly within a couple of years of Sterne's death in 1768. Philip Thicknesse printed the damaging allegation that Agnes Sterne had been imprisoned for debt in York while her son was 'Wallowing in the luxuries of life, and expences'[27] of London; in fact, Agnes Sterne died before the success of *Tristram Shandy* brought her son his welcome, if precarious affluence. In January 1776 the Revd Daniel Watson, a Yorkshire clergyman, wrote to George Whately, treasurer of the London Foundling Hospital: 'Shall I tell you what York scandal says? viz. that Sterne, when possessed of preferment of 300£ a year, would not pay 10£ to release his mother out of Ousebridge prison, when poverty was her only fault, and her character so good that two of her neighbours clubbed to set her at liberty, to gain a livelihood . . . by taking in washing.'[28] Whatever reliance might be placed on scandal relating to events going back a quarter of a century—and the value of Sterne's living is certainly exaggerated—the story was evidently widely believed in York. John Croft's version is predictably extreme: 'Sterne's Mother died in the Common Goal at York in a wretched condition, or soon after she was released. It was held unpardonable in him not to relieve her, when he had the means of doing it, as a subscription was set on foot for the purpose.'[29] This is certainly incorrect in many of its details; Sterne's mother, if she were imprisoned, must have been so in 1751, yet she lived until 1759, continuing to draw her pension all the while. Richard Greenwood, though, had heard a similar, if less sensational, account of Agnes Sterne's penury: Joseph Hunter recorded that he 'thinks he has heard that his mother was in great distress at York, & that his master would have relieved her, but was prevented by his wife'.[30] (Without endeavouring to excuse Laurence Sterne by blaming his wife, one might find comprehensible Elizabeth Sterne's reluctance to aid a mother-in-law who had already received so much financial aid so ungraciously.) Remarks attributed to Horace Walpole—though published after his death, they have the authentic note of witty malice—gave the story a wider circulation. Of Sterne, Walpole declared that he knew, 'from indubitable authority, that his mother, who kept a school, having run in debt, on account of an extravagant daughter, would have rotted in jail, if the parents of her scholars had not raised a subscription for her. Her son had too much sentiment to have any feeling. A dead ass was more important to him than a living mother.'[31] Lord Byron's reformulation of these words—recalling one of the most famous incidents in *A Sentimental Journey*—remains the most memorable articulation of the charge against Sterne who, Byron declared, 'preferred whining over a dead ass to relieving a living mother'.[32]

By the time Byron wrote those words, more than half a century after the events so freely embroidered had taken place, the undecorated truth lay far behind. Sterne, in fact, was very much perturbed by his mother's imprisonment, even if for reasons that do him no particular credit. As the letter of self-justification he wrote to Jaques Sterne makes clear, he was very concerned about the damage stories of his mother's imprisonment might do to his own reputation. 'I was roused,' he wrote,

> by the advice of my Friends to think of some way of defending myself; which I own I should have set about immediately by telling my Story publickly to the World,—But for the following Inconvenience, That I could not do myself Justice this Way, without doing myself an Injury at the same time by laying Open the Nakedness of my Circumstances, which for ought I knew was likely to make me Suffer more in the Opinion of one Half of the World, than I could possibly gain from the other part of it by the clearest defence that could be made.—(*Letters*, 33).

Faced with such disagreeable alternatives, Sterne turned for help to the friend whom he had first known as a student at Cambridge, John Fountayne, now dean of York Minster, asking him how he might extricate himself from his dilemma. Fountayne's suggestion was that Sterne should meet face to face with both his mother and his uncle, and undertook to do all he could to procure such a meeting. Fountayne fulfilled his promise in January 1751, but Jaques Sterne pleaded pressure of business as a reason for deferring the meeting. Later, by Sterne's account, the archdeacon temporized so resolutely as to force his nephew to pen a 'long and hasty wrote' letter of self-defence. By this time Sterne's resentment at his mother's importunity was equalled by his sense of outrage at being calumnied by his uncle. 'Why,' Sterne demanded of the latter, 'will you interest yourself in a Complaint against your Nephew if You are determined against hearing what He has to Say for Himself?—and if you thus deny him every Opportunity he Seeks of doing himself Justice—is It not too plain, you do not wish to find him Justifyed, or that You do not Care to lose the Uses of such a Handle against him?—' (*Letters*, 34).

Sterne proceeded to the 'true State of the Case' in his defence. Laying aside his 'false modesty,' he stated that were he to die that night his estate would produce a yearly income for his wife and daughter no greater than the £20 his mother received as pension. He concluded:

> *I think I have no Right* to apply one Shilling of My income to any Other Purpose but that of laying by a Provision for my Wife & Child; and That it will be time enough (if then) to add somewhat to my Mother's Pension of 20 p^{ds} a Year, When I have as much to leave my Wife, Who besides, the Duties I owe her of a Husband and the Father of a dear Child has this further Claim; That she, Whose Bread I am thus defending, was the Person, who brought it into the Family, & Whose Birth & Education would ill enable her to Strugle in the World Without it,—That the Other Person, who now claims it from her, & has raised us so much Sorrow upon that score,—brought not one Sixpence into the Family—& tho' it would give me Pain enough to report it upon any Other Occasion That She was the Daughter of no Other than a poor Suttler who followed the Camp in Flanders—was neither born nor bred to the Expectation of a 4th part, of What the Government allowes her, & therefore has Reason to be contented with Such a Provision tho double the Summ would be nakedness to my Wife. (*Letters*, 40–1)

Sterne's letter of self-justification is lengthy, vehement, and in some respects distasteful. It also has the outraged ring of truth and may at least have persuaded Jaques Sterne that persecution of his nephew on this score might eventually rebound upon himself. Though the quarrel between them was never patched up, the archdeacon appears not to have persisted in causing trouble for his nephew, perhaps in acknowledgement of the essential justice of Sterne's case.

In the longer term, however, what Sterne saw as a brave recital of facts in his defence redounded to his direct discredit. To add to the apparent neglect of his mother, he seemed also to be casting a slur on her birth. In fact, it is now known that Sterne's account of his mother's background is essentially accurate. That this is so may provoke further sympathy for Agnes Sterne. With such comparatively humble origins, she had, in her youth, qualities capable of attracting two gentlemen as husbands. Having moved socially upwards, having supported the arduous, peripatetic life of the barracks for so many years, having found herself twice widowed, was she now to slip back, unprotesting, into greater poverty than she had ever known, and in old age too? That Sterne mentions his mother's social origins in such a context is evidence not only, perhaps, of the degree of his exasperation but also of the deeply ingrained social attitudes of his day. If his wife's birth and education gave her certain expectations, Sterne concludes, his mother had no such excuse.

Of Agnes Sterne, after her release from debtors' prison, we know very little. She continued, apparently, to live in York for the remainder of her life and drew her pension, on which, with the occasional aid she received from her son, she lived. Before her death Sterne and his mother were, at least in part, reconciled. In a letter written in 1758 to his friend the Revd John Blake, Sterne wrote: 'I hope my mothers Affair is by this Time ended, to our my Comfort & I trust her's' (*Letters*, 61), and later still he was planning to visit his mother to whom, he wrote, he had 'much' to say. Agnes Sterne died the following year and was buried from the church of St Michael-le-Belfry in York on 5 May 1759.[33] With his sister Catherine there was, unhappily, no reconciliation. According to John Croft, Catherine 'married a Publican in London'.[34] In his memoir Sterne described his sister as 'still living—most unhappily estranged from me by my Uncle's Wickedness & her own folly'.[35]

Sterne's relations with his family were, to say the least, far from ideally happy. That he should have quarrelled with his uncle is, in view of the archdeacon's massive selfishness and vindictive nature, entirely understandable. That he should have suffered an estrangement from Catherine could only, in view of Sterne's poignant account of the deaths of his infant brothers and sisters, have caused him sadness—however much he may have been at fault. The quarrel with his mother was equally pathetic, wherever blame may be laid. Not because Sterne had great love, or even affection, for her; he had not. It was pathetic because the lack of concern he felt that his mother showed for him after he left home aged 9 or 10 was his first real experience of an always frustrated desire for a deep and lasting relationship founded on genuine and reciprocal affection. It was such a relationship that Sterne felt he had missed by his father's absence and early death. He sought it in marrying Elizabeth Lumley, again through his relationship with his daughter, and finally in his celebrated sentimental friendship with Eliza Draper. The desire for such a relationship was never to be fulfilled—he quickly grew apart from his wife, recognized that his love for his daughter would never be reciprocated in the way he desired, and eventually grew to see even the overwhelming intensity of his feeling for Eliza Draper as the delusive produce of an invalid's infatuation.

Laurence Sterne was not the innocent victim of misfortune in his human relationships, yet his own selfishness fed through roots going back at least as far as the lonely years he spent at school in Yorkshire. Separated from his parents, taken in on sufferance by one uncle and neglected by another, aware of how very different was the future awaiting him from that of his more privileged cousins, Sterne was forced to develop a dependence on himself which went against his instinctively outgoing, benevolent nature. The insecurity which led him to place his own needs—financial or emotional, real or imaginary—above the comparable needs of others had its origins in what he felt to have been his abandonment by his mother. No wonder his resentment at her 'Clamorous & rapacious Temper' while he awaited the birth of his own child was so great.

What in calmer moments Laurence Sterne felt about his mother is perhaps best suggested in Tristram Shandy's portrait of Elizabeth Shandy. There is no active malice in the portrait, yet not the slightest indication of any human warmth. The human, if misplaced, feeling that characterizes Walter Shandy, always intent on doing the best for his son yet waylaid by his own ineffectual behaviour, plays no part in the character of Elizabeth Shandy, whose thoughtless question to her husband condemns Tristram from the very moment of his conception. In the entire course of the novel Elizabeth Shandy never addresses a word to her son, nor he to her—and in any very meaningful sense that seems to have been much the fate of Agnes and Laurence Sterne.

Sterne's fiction, though, is neither an attempt at self-exculpation nor even a conscious attempt at self-justification. The question of his alleged hypocrisy, of the divergence between the fictional presentation of sentiment which gained him renown and his supposed lack of real feeling, is a genuine one. That question, however, if tackled honestly, does not wholly discredit Sterne. Byron's pithy reworking of Walpole's sneering comment is frequently quoted—and almost as frequently out of context. For what Byron actually wrote was: 'I am as bad as that dog Sterne, who preferred whining over a dead ass to relieving a living mother; villain—hypocrite—slave—sycophant! but *I* am no better'.[36] It is Byron's savage, dramatic self-censure, not the platitudinous moralizing of Victorian critics, which gets closer to the heart of Sterne. Throughout his fiction Sterne constantly apostrophizes his readers, challenging or slyly nudging us into complicity with him. So often, however, the reader Sterne would address—as with Byron, Baudelaire, or Eliot after him—is the 'hypocrite lecteur—mon semblable'. Few writers have articulated better than Sterne the connection between selflessness and selfishness as spurs to human action. For Sterne, the possibility, held out by Pope, of moving centrally between the extremes of 'mad good nature and of wild self love' barely exists. The Yorick of *A Sentimental Journey* who whines over a dead ass is the Yorick whose vaunted benevolence so often derives elsewhere from motives in which altruistic sensibility and the selfish desire for sexual gratification remain uneasily entwined. For Sterne, not even the best actions are untouched by human fallibility. The Widow Wadman's compassion for the pain Uncle Toby suffers from his groin injury is inseparable from her anxieties for her own future sexual gratification. Toby's benevolent concern for the dying soldier Le Fever and his young son is accompanied by an oath. Unlike the Recording Angel, Sterne's critics have rarely dropped a tear such as might blot out his faults; more often they have acted as the Accusing Spirit—and have not even blushed.

7
Ecclesiastical Politics, 1747–1759

For all his exasperation, Sterne suffered less from the quarrel with his mother and sister, during his years in Sutton and Stillington, than from the many bitter disagreements with his uncle. By the standards of his day Jaques Sterne's comparative eminence in the Church of England was well deserved. His zeal on behalf of the Established Church was matched only by the industry with which he employed his undoubted legal abilities in its service. The worst his archbishop could find to say about him, after all, was that he tended to be a little too warm in pursuing any unfortunate whom he suspected of being less strongly attached than himself to Anglicanism and the House of Hanover. Those who felt the heat of the archdeacon's wrath—Dr John Burton, the recorder of York, or Mother Mary Hodshon and the nuns of the York Convent—would have a rather different view, of course, finding Jaques Sterne a dangerously vindictive antagonist. Such, certainly, was the way he appeared to his nephew, Laurence Sterne. From the moment the latter had accepted his uncle's help, he knew he had incurred a debt he was expected to repay. By abandoning party-political writing in 1742 he had—at least in his uncle's eyes—singularly failed to discharge that debt. While it lasted, the Jacobite rebellion had caused them to form an uneasy alliance. The archdeacon's success in persuading Archbishop Herring to interest himself in bringing the force of ecclesiastical and civil law to bear on York's Roman Catholics had even led Laurence Sterne to take up his pen once more in support of a cause dear to his uncle. The subsequent lack of interest shown by the archbishop and his successor having convinced Laurence Sterne that little was to be gained by pursuing this cause any further, he soon left his uncle to harry the nuns of the Micklegate Bar Convent alone. Given what we know of Jaques Sterne's nature, it is not wholly surprising that the briefly suppressed antagonism between the two men was shortly to break out again—and with renewed virulence.

By the late-1740s, relations between uncle and nephew were so strained as to have become a cause of public comment and even ribald speculation. John Croft later reported it as a matter of fact that Sterne's quarrel with his uncle was not political in origin at all. They fell out, Croft alleged, 'about a favourite Mistress of the Precentors, who proved with child by Laury'. The child was said to be still living when Croft wrote in 1795, and 'to resemble Sterne very much, tho' at the time of their rupture, he gave out as a reason in the publick Coffee House, that it arose from that he wou'd not continue to write periodicall papers for his Uncle'.[1] Croft was writing long after the event, yet the tale cannot be dismissed for that reason alone. Laurence Sterne, we know, was notoriously promiscuous and his uncle little better. In 1744 the *York Courant* printed without comment a Latin epigram, sent in by the suspiciously named 'W. Charnley':

Ad Prae——em quendam

Phillida amas: Bacchis sobolens convicia jactat,
Ne spera ambabus posse placere diu.
Ah! Bacchis nondum didicit spectare lacunar:
Sed dudum hanc artem vir suus edidicit.[2]

Obscure as this must have been for the majority of the *Courant*'s readers, enlightenment was at hand. The following week the same newspaper printed another letter, dated St Andrew's Day, by the transparently fictitious merryandrew 'Tho. English':

> SIR,
> The following Lines are a Translation of the Latin Epigram in your last Paper, as near as I could guess at the Author's Meaning. I declare I know not the Persons to whom it alludes; but, *whoever the Cap fits, let them put it on.*

The proffered translation reads:

MOLLY he loves: But jealous *Sarah growls;*
'Tis hard for one to please two am'rous Souls.
Ah *Sarah!* learn to look and not to see;
Thy Husband long has known that Mystery.

This is immediately followed by four further lines which, notwithstanding the writer's protestations to the contrary, clearly identify the subject of these scandalous verses as the archdeacon:

An A*NSWER to the last Week's* Epigrammatist . . .

YOUR *Epigram* is quite too keen,
  To touch the Fair's Mistakes;
For if it smells not all obscene,
  I never smell'd a *Jaques*.[3]

Whatever the foundation of the story, its odour lingered, for all three verses were subsequently reprinted without comment in the *York Courant* the following April.[4] Of direct evidence that uncle and nephew ever shared a mistress, however, there is none, and whether John Croft preferred to imply a sexual rather than political motive for the split between uncle and nephew from malice or a willing credulity, it is unlikely to be accurate. In 1751 Sterne concluded the long letter to his uncle, written in defence of his own conduct, with a direct reference to their quarrel:

> Notwithstanding the hardest Measure that ever Man received—continued on Your Side, without any Provocation on Mine—without ever once being told my Fault—or Conscious of ever committing one Which deserved an unkind look from You—notwithstanding this, and the Bitterness of ten Years unwearied Persecution . . . I retain that Sense of the Service You did me at my first setting out in the World, Which becomes a Man inclined to be Gratefull, & that I am
>
> Sir
>
> Your once much Obliged
> tho' now, Y^r^ Much Injured Nephew
> LAURENCE STERNE.
>
> (*Letters*, 41)

Even in brief extract, such indignation bespeaks a degree of self-pity on Sterne's part. Moreover, the avowal that he is unconscious of having given his uncle any grounds for the treatment he received may even—if the real cause was indeed a simple refusal to continue writing journalism in the Whig interest—be disingenuous, implying that actions motivated by principle could never deserve such treatment. Yet, writing long before the years of his fame, Sterne could not possibly have known that his letter would survive to be made public, and it is inconceivable that he could have written as he did were there any substance in Croft's version of the cause of the quarrel, since it would have been no more than a provocation to his already enraged uncle to damn him further—at least in private—as a liar.

Even so, in a city the size of York any serious quarrel—whatever its origins—could have significant repercussions. Still more was this true of the much smaller ecclesiastical society centred on the Minster. When that quarrel was between an uncle and his nephew the consequences were necessarily felt by all their mutual acquaintances. As the archdeacon of Cleveland was a far more powerful cleric than his nephew, it was obviously Laurence who had more to lose from their breach. Since his earlier disillusionment with Whig politicking, Laurence Sterne seems to have gone out of his way not to break with any former friends and acquaintances, and these in turn appear to have made the best they could of an awkward situation. Laurence Sterne himself declared of the quarrel with his uncle: 'The Contest between Us, no Doubt, has been Sharp, But has not been made more so, by bringing our mutual Friends into it, Who, in all Things (except Inviting us to the same Dinner) have generally Bore themselves towards Us, as if this Misfortune had never happend' (*Letters*, 25).

From time to time, however, things did not run so smoothly, and Laurence Sterne might find himself all too forcefully reminded of a quarrel in which, in terms of his future prospects, he could only be a loser. One such occasion arose in November 1750, over Sterne's preaching sermons in the Minster in place of colleagues unable or unwilling to preach their turn. Anxious as ever to receive the fees for such substitute preaching, Sterne had just given a sermon in the place of his friend John Fountayne, dean of York Minster, and was ready to preach again in place of a fellow prebendary, Francis Blackburne. To his chagrin, the bookseller John Hildyard, who assisted in finding substitute preachers, bluntly gave Sterne to understand that Blackburne had insisted that, should Laurence Sterne preach, it must be done in such a manner as 'might not Disoblige' the archdeacon.

Sterne was doubly hurt; first for the implied reserve on Blackburne's part; secondly, from the manner in which the reserve was communicated to him. Out of friendship for Blackburne, he declared, he would have declined to preach in his stead, unless certain that such an act could not be construed as an affront to his uncle. As proof, Sterne mentioned that for the past two years he had preached one of the archdeacon's own turns—not, he admitted, 'at his Request, for We are not upon Such Terms', but at the request of a third party, who would scarcely have repeated the invitation had the first substitution given offence. Concerns for Blackburne apart, Sterne was most troubled by the affront offered by a mere bookseller's assumed air of 'much Gravity and Importance'. In one of the earliest surviving anticipations of Sterne's novelistic manner, the indignant prebendary vividly dramatizes the scene. John Hildyard, he wrote:

> beckond me to follow Him into an inner Room; No sooner had he shut the Dore, But with the aweful Solemnity of a Premier who held a Lettre de Chachêt upon whose Contents my Life or Liberty depended—after a Minuits Pause,—He thus opens his Commission. Sir—My Friend the A.Deacon of Cleveland not caring to preach his Turn, as I conjectured, Has left me to provide a Preacher,—But before I can take any Steps in it with Regard to You—I want first to know, Sir, upon what Footing You and Dr Sterne are?—upon what Footing!—Yes Sir, How your Quarel Stands! Whats that to You, you Puppy? But Sir, dont be angry, I only want to know of You, whether Dr Sterne will not be displeased in Case You should preach—Go Look; Ive just now been preaching and You could not have fitter Opportunity to be satisfyed.—I hope, Mr Sterne, You are not Angry. Yes I am; But much more astonished at your *Impudence*. I know not whether The Chancellors stepping in at this Instant & flapping to the Dore, Did not save his tender Soul the Pain of the last Word; However that be, He retreats upon this unexpected Rebuff, Takes the Chancell^r aside, asks his Advice, comes back Submissive, begs Quarter, tells me Dr Hering had quite satisfyed him as to the Grounds of his Scruple (tho' not of his Folly) and therefore beseeches me to let the Matter pass, & to preach the Turn. (*Letters*, 26–7)

Sterne's angry response was to declare that he would not preach and that Hildyard might find a substitute as best he could. Yet, reflecting that Hildyard must have exceeded his instructions from Blackburne and that his impertinence 'had Issued not so much from his Heart, as from his Head', he retracted his refusal and—in characteristically mercurial fashion—parted friends with Hildyard, having promised to preach as arranged.

This trifling incident, animated only by Sterne's imaginative narration, is revealing, for it emphasizes how frequently Sterne was prepared to make the journey from Sutton-on-the-Forest to preach in the Minster and how eager he was to do so. His eagerness and the reasons for it are, in fact, made explicit in Sterne's grateful rejoinder to Archdeacon Blackburne's 'most obliging' reply to his letter:

> As for the future Supply of any of your Vacant Turns, You may be assured I should be willing to undertake them whenever you want a Proxy . . . You would even do me a *Favor* to let me have them—I say a *Favor*, For, by the by, my Daughter will be Twenty Pounds a Better Fortune by the Favors I've rec^d of this kind from the Dean & Residentiaries this Year. & as so much at least is annually to be picked up in Our

> Pulpit, By any Man who cares to make the Sermons—You who are a *Father* will easily guess & as easily excuse my Motive. (*Letters*, 31)

Sterne's financial worries aside, the clash with Hildyard also points to how anxious he was about his standing in York society and how that anxiety was related to his quarrel with his uncle. However much Sterne might wish to be his own man—as in his refusal to write political journalism at Jaques Sterne's behest—his quarrel with so powerful a figure as the archdeacon of Cleveland and precentor of the Cathedral made him the object of some reserve among his fellow prebendaries and liable to what he construed as the impertinence of his social inferiors.

Sterne's relief that he remains on perfectly good terms with Blackburne almost oozes from his second letter. 'I rec[d] the Favor of your most obliging Letter,' Sterne fawned.

> which tho' it was something in Kind of what I expected both from your Character and the Judgment I had pretended to form of You, Yet in *Degree* was so far beyond what I could look for, That I can neither deny myself the Pleasure of thanking you for your Letter, or the Justice of declaring to you the sense I have of the Obligation w[ch] so much Civility and Gentleness have laid me under. (*Letters*, 30)

Excessive as such sentiments appear, Sterne had genuine reason to be obliged to Blackburne, who had earlier shown his goodwill by attempting, though unavailingly, to promote a reconciliation between Sterne and his uncle. To have risked incurring the ill will of one who had already shown himself disposed to be sympathetic was understandably more than Sterne wished to venture. In concluding his letter, he showed himself duly aware of his precarious place in ecclesiastical circles by wishing Blackburne—in a phrase which might have found a place in *Tristram Shandy*—'every Thing this *silly* & uncertain World can procure for the Happiness of You & of your House' (*Letters*, 31).

Sterne's caution and his determination to establish good relations with Blackburne were soon to prove justified. His assurance that the archdeacon would not hold his preaching Blackburne's turn against the latter was, by contrast, decidedly optimistic. On 6 December 1750 Jaques Sterne complained directly to Francis Blackburne of 'M[r] Hildyard's employing the last time the Only person unacceptable to me in the whole Church, an ungrateful & unworthy nephew of my Own, the Vicar of Sutton' (*Letters*, 427), and asking Blackburne to ensure that it would not happen again. Perhaps Blackburne had genuine respect and esteem for Laurence Sterne or perhaps he noted the vindictive archdeacon's order of priorities—an 'ungrateful and unworthy nephew'. At all events, he resisted the interference of Jaques Sterne, allowed Laurence Sterne to preach his next turn, and was still evincing an interest in the welfare of Lydia Sterne after her father's death.

As a result, Sterne seems subsequently to have looked to Blackburne—a gifted, energetic cleric who would shortly succeed Jaques Sterne as archdeacon of Cleveland—as a possible patron. So much is suggested, at least, by the number of Sterne's sermons that combine anti-Roman Catholic with anti-Methodist polemic. The double threat posed by Catholicism and Methodism was one of Francis Blackburne's most cherished notions, to the extent that—however strange it may now seem—he regarded the two as interchangeable if not identical. Blackburne was not alone among Anglicans in being alarmed by the spread of Methodism as John Wesley began his nationwide mission in the 1740s. Nor, in 1745, was he alone in fearing Methodist preachers to be covert Roman Catholics, disguised Jesuits, or Jacobite agitators.[5] All the same, it is striking that such a view should find its way so directly into Sterne's sermons—most notably Sermon XXXVII, 'Penances', where, having excoriated the 'many austere and fantastic orders which we see in the Romish church',[6] Sterne continues:

> Nor is it to be doubted, but the affectation of something like it in our Methodists, when they discant upon the necessity of alienating themselves from the world, and selling all that they have,——is not to be ascribed to the same mistaken enthusiastic principle, which would cast so black a shade upon religion, as if the kind Author of it had created us on purpose to go mourning, all our lives long, in sack-cloth and ashes,——and sent us into the world, as so many saint-errants, in quest of adventures full of sorrow and affliction.[7]

If Sterne did have hopes of finding a patron in Francis Blackburne, then he was to be disappointed. Yet his failure to gain further substantial preferment in the Church, after the two prebends he acquired while writing Whig propaganda, can scarcely have surprised him. Such preferment, he knew, would be dependent on his own talents and political astuteness. That he had the former he did not doubt; that he had the latter was less certain—and Blackburne may not have responded sympathetically to a cleric who so obviously tailored his religious opinions to suit the circumstances.

In one avenue of endeavour, however, Sterne's confidence in his own talents was not misplaced, for his abilities in the pulpit were widely recognized. Nor was he distinguished only in his rural parishes. Forty years after Sterne's death Richard Greenwood could still recall that 'The Minster was crowded whenever it was known that he was to preach'.[8] Perhaps Greenwood exaggerated, but there is no reason to doubt that Sterne was indeed a popular preacher. The £20 Sterne told Blackburne he had put together in a year for his still-infant daughter came from preaching twenty substitute turns which, together with the two sermons his own position as a prebendary required him to deliver, amounted to exactly one in four of the sermons regularly preached in the Minster during the year. Though it seems unlikely that he could have preached so many substitute turns had his sermons not been highly regarded, the strongest indication to this effect lies in the invitations Sterne received to preach on notable occasions, in the Minster and elsewhere.

The first such invitation had been issued on the occasion of the arrival of Thomas Herring to take up his new position as archbishop in 1743. Other invitations followed—and on two separate occasions, the sermons were sufficiently admired to give Sterne the satisfaction of seeing them subsequently in print. On 17 April 1747—it was Good Friday—Sterne preached *The Case of Elijah and the Widow of Zerephath, consider'd* in the Church of St Michael-le-Belfry, as the annual charity sermon delivered to elicit support from the fashionable members of York society, who included the lord mayor, aldermen and, sheriffs, for two charity schools: the Blue Coat school for poor boys and the Grey Coat school for poor girls. To be invited to preach this sermon was a signal honour for Sterne, since the previous year's preacher had been the archbishop himself, Thomas Herring.[9] That his sermon was considered worthy of publication was particularly gratifying, and Sterne remained proud enough of his composition to present a copy of it to Catherine Fourmantel a dozen years later. It has to be said, however, that the vast number of sermons printed in the eighteenth century (over 1,600 separate titles, some of volumes containing thirty or more sermons, appeared between 1732 and 1758 alone) puts the extent of the honour into some perspective. Printed by Caesar Ward for John Hildyard, the sermon was quickly put on sale in the latter's shop in Stonegate, and also in London, at the price of sixpence (though it sold so slowly that copies were still available three years later).

Since *The Case of Elijah and the Widow of Zerephath* is the earliest-known sermon of Sterne's, it has a particular interest for what it reveals of his attitudes to his religion and his priestly calling, to his sermon-giving, and to his own life.[10] Recent scholarship has rightly emphasized the extent to which Sterne's sermons, far from being unique anticipations of either the drama or pathos of his later, fictional writings, share both the theological attitudes and pulpit rhetoric of sermons by his contemporaries. Even so, there is a great deal that is biographically noteworthy in the sermons in general—and in this sermon in particular—besides clear evidence of those features of contemporary pulpit style Sterne admired enough to emulate.

Sterne dedicated the printed version of his sermon to Richard Osbaldeston, then dean of York Minster, who had not only married the Sternes six years previously but had been one of the few constant friends to the vicar of Sutton-on-the-Forest throughout the 1740s. Never effusive, the tribute concludes almost ingenuously with the hope that Osbaldeston will accept the sermon along with 'the motives which have induced me to address it to you; one of which, I cannot conceal in justice to myself, because it has proceeded from the sense of the many favours and civilities which I have received from you'.[11] That Sterne was genuinely grateful we need not doubt, yet his motives were more complex than he suggests. Osbaldeston was a royal chaplain, tutor to the future King George III, and evidently designed for higher things—he would become bishop of Carlisle later in the same year. In dedicating the sermon to the dean, Sterne was not merely acknowledging the past but also looking to the future.

The compliment to Osbaldeston aside, Sterne used his dedication to advert, by way of an awkwardly self-conscious allusion to Pope's *Essay on Criticism*, to the difficulty of preaching a charity sermon with pretensions to originality, confessing himself '*afraid there can be little left to be said upon the subject of* Charity, *which has not been often thought, and much better expressed by many who have gone before: and indeed, it seems so beaten and common a path, that it is not an easy matter for a new comer to distinguish himself in it, by any thing, except the novelty of his* Vehicle'.[12]

For his sermon Sterne took a text—'*And the barrel of meal wasted not, neither did the cruse of oil fail, according to the word of the Lord which he spake to the prophet Elijah*' (1 Kings 17: 16)—forming part of the story of the Widow of Zerephath's selflessness in sharing the last of her food and drink with Elijah in the midst of a famine, and the prophet's subsequent plea to God to raise the Widow's son from death. The appropriateness of text and story to a charity sermon is self-evident, and Sterne was in fact significantly indebted to a work by one of his own favourite authors, Joseph Hall's *Contemplations upon the Principal Passages in the Holy Story*.[13] While such indebtedness was not in itself at all unusual—contemporary preachers' aids provided lists of sermon titles and subjects and the occasions on which the sermons were delivered, so that uncertain preachers might avail themselves 'of the Matter and Arguments of the different Writers upon the same Subject'[14]—the relevance of Sterne's choice of biblical episode to a sermon aimed at eliciting contributions towards the upkeep of charity schools is less immediately apparent.

It is the link Sterne finds which most clearly suggests the personal nature of the sermon he preached on this occasion. Drawing the congregation's attention to the 'great instability of temporal affairs, and constant fluctuation of every thing in this world', Sterne continues:

> What by successive misfortunes; by failings and cross accidents in trade; by miscarriage of projects:——what by unsuitable expences of parents, extravagance of children, and the many other secret ways whereby riches make themselves wings and fly away; so many surprising revolutions do every day happen in families, that it may not seem strange to say, that the posterity of some of the most liberal contributors here, in the changes which one century may produce, may possibly find shelter under this very plant which they now so kindly water.[15]

Since he was preaching in the shadow of York Minster, where his great-grandfather, Richard Sterne, had been archbishop less than seventy years before, Laurence Sterne was surely conscious here of the applicability of these words to his own situation. The results of the 'miscarriage of projects' and the 'unsuitable expences of parents' Sterne had felt throughout his childhood and even in his adult life in his own person, as Roger and Agnes Sterne had slipped far enough downwards in the social scale as to allow a gulf to open up between Roger and his brothers Richard and Jaques. It was thanks only to his own great-grandfather's act of charity in establishing six scholarships for poor boys at Cambridge that Laurence Sterne had been able to attend university at all, and even then only with the charitable assistance, for which he remained intensely grateful, of his cousin Richard. Without these, the prospects for Sterne would have been bleak indeed. Writing to his uncle Jaques four years after preaching his charity sermon, he declared himself to have been, after his father's death, 'without one Shilling in the World, and . . . *at that time* without One Friend in it, except my Cosin . . .' (*Letters*, 34), echoing his own description of poor children as 'utterly cast out of the *way* of knowledge, without a parent—sometimes may be without a friend to guide and instruct them'.[16] Archbishop Sterne, given in Gilbert Burnet's hostile account to the enriching of his own family, could scarcely have imagined that, within half a century of his death, his own great-grandson would have need of the charity he had established.[17] Sterne, by contrast, still remembered at the age of almost 40 the precariousness of his own situation as he struggled to establish himself in the world. Well might he declare that not to do everything to permit the education of those too poor to pay for it themselves was akin to 'exposing a tender plant to all the inclemencies of a cruel season'.[18]

There is, of course, a great deal more to his sermon than self-revelation, advertent or otherwise, yet Sterne's personal engagement in the conventional form of the charity sermon is evidenced throughout by his employment of favourite phrases—'cross accidents' is one—which recur in his writings, often at key moments. It is at the very outset of his comic novel—still lying more than a decade in the future—that Tristram declares that 'I have been the continual sport of what the world calls Fortune . . . That in every stage of my life, and at every turn and corner where she could fairly get at me, the ungracious Duchess has pelted me with a set of as pitiful misadventures and cross accidents as ever small HERO sustained' (*TS* I. v. 10). The inherent unpredictability of human existence—which would become one of the principal themes of the mature writer—is here made the spur to active benevolence on the part of the congregation. Sterne employs rhetorical techniques and ideas which would become characteristic of his own later writing. On occasion, for instance, the preacher appeals to the visual sense of his listeners (and subsequently readers). 'It would be a pleasure to a good mind, to stop here a moment, and figure to itself the picture of so joyful an event . . .', Sterne declares at one juncture, inevitably if incongruously bringing to the mind of the twentieth-century reader the Widow Wadman (*TS* VI. xxxviii. 377), as he exhorts his listeners: 'let any number of us here imagine ourselves at this instant engaged in drawing the most perfect and amiable character, such, as according to our conceptions of the deity, we should think most acceptable to him, and most likely to be universally admired by all mankind . . .'[19] Even more strikingly, when he has conjured up an image of Elijah, set in a scene appropriate for visual representation, Sterne declares that 'It is a subject one might recommend to the pencil [i.e brush] of a great genius'.[20] Sterne, in fact, probably had in mind a particular 'great genius', for the sermon dates from a time when William Hogarth—who would later take another hint from Sterne about an appropriate scene for his talents—was contemplating works on just such subjects for a more ambitious charitable foundation, the London Foundling Hospital, which he and the sculptor Michael Rysbrack were designing to turn into a showpiece for British art. Sterne's own urbane evocation of Elijah—'full of honest triumph in his looks, but sweetened with all the kind sympathy which a gentle nature could overflow with upon so happy an event'[21]—is a suggestive enough anticipation of Sterne's later sentimental manner to remind us that the preacher's representation of the fierce Old Testament prophet—Elijah the Tishbite, slayer of the prophets of Baal—was one very much of and for his own age.

While there is a limit to the extent one would wish to read back into the 1740s preoccupations or turns of phrase Sterne would demonstrate to a wide public only in the 1760s, it is still noteworthy how many characteristic features of his later writing, besides a fondness for pictorialism, are found in this single sermon. The extensive allusion to and quotation from the Bible and different religious writers are to be expected, but the sermon also reveals Shakespearean quotation (here from *The Merchant of Venice*), classical references (Epicurus and Plutarch) mediated through later works (Montaigne's essays), and political allusion (the sermon's pronounced anti-Roman Catholic tone reminds the congregation of the political threat so recently posed by the Jacobite rebellion of 1745–6). Short, fluent, and varied as it is, *Elijah and the Widow of Zerephath* was not an exceptional work for its day, and would certainly never have received the attention given it had its author been other than Sterne. Yet in this sermon it is easy, without forcing the younger writer into the mould of the famous author he would become, to see that Sterne's merits as a 'newcomer' to charity sermons, a preacher still learning his craft, far more obviously anticipate his later characteristics as a novelist than one has any reason to expect. At all events, the sermon served its purpose, drawing over £64 from his audience—far short of the £94 Archbishop Herring's sermon had raised the year before, which was 'the greatest Collection for several Years past'[22] and a sum so much in excess of the norm as to suggest that the congregation responded as much to the eminence of the preacher as to his eloquence; but slightly greater than that raised by any of the preachers in the three succeeding years.

Despite his success, however, it would not be until 1750 that Sterne again received an invitation to preach on a notable public occasion. This sermon was delivered in York Minster to mark the end of the summer assizes in York and, on this occasion the links with Sterne's later fiction could not be stronger. The sermon Sterne preached on Sunday, 29 July, was *The Abuses of Conscience*, destined to become the most celebrated of all his sermons. Not that it provoked any known reaction in York Minster—though the assembled audience of judges and lawyers thought well enough of it to encourage its publication as a sixpenny pamphlet.[23] The eventual fame of *The Abuses of Conscience* lay a decade into the future, after Sterne had perceptively chosen to make it the sermon of Parson Yorick's that Corporal Trim reads to Walter Shandy, Uncle Toby, and Dr Slop while they are awaiting the birth of Tristram himself, in Volume II of *Tristram Shandy*.

For all the criticism his sermons have attracted over two centuries, not least in regard to the extent to which he plundered the printed works of his clerical forebears and contemporaries, Sterne chose well. *The Abuses of Conscience* is undoubtedly among the best of the preacher's surviving sermons, quite apart from the particular uses the novelist would make of it. Less revealing of Sterne's own life than *Elijah and the Widow of Zerephath*, the sermon nonetheless tells us a good deal about the preacher's attitude to his audience, his age, and his sources. For a start, there is a marked contrast between the much greater use of pathos in his earlier charity sermon, designed to elicit contributions for the education of poor children, and the wit of *The Abuses of Conscience*. The latter reveals itself most tellingly at the very opening of the sermon, that celebrated introduction which has too often and quite wrongly been taken to characterize his sermons as a whole.

Sterne preaches to a text from Hebrews 13: 18: '——*For we trust we have a good Conscience,*——'. Having doubtless repeated his text for emphasis, Sterne immediately calls St Paul's words into question:

> TRUST!——Trust we have a good Conscience!——Surely, you will say, if there is any thing in this life which a man may depend upon, and to the knowledge of which he is capable of arriving upon the most indisputable evidence, it must be this very thing,——Whether he has a good Conscience, or no.
>
> If a man thinks at all, he cannot well be a stranger to the true state of this account;——He must be privy to his own thoughts and desires——He must remember his past pursuits, and know certainly the true springs and motives, which, in general, have govern'd the actions of his life.[24]

From the outset, with its dramatic repetition of 'trust', Sterne seizes the attention of his congregation by seeming to question the apostle's words by means of a quibble. And this, apparently, is what he proceeds to do, before eventually clarifying for his audience the whole argument of his sermon which, in turn, he puts forward to gloss the meaning of St Paul's words. 'Conscience', the preacher avers,

> this once able monitor,——placed on high as a judge within us,——and intended, by our Maker, as a just and equitable one too,——by an unhappy train of causes and impediments . . . ——does its office so negligently,——sometimes so corruptly, that it is not to be trusted alone: and therefore, we find, there is a necessity, an absolute necessity, of joining another principle with it, to aid, if not govern, its determinations.
>
> So that if you would form a just judgment of what is of infinite importance to you not to be misled in; namely, in what degree of real merit you stand, either as an honest man,——an useful citizen,——a faithful subject to your king,——or a good servant to your GOD,——call in RELIGION and MORALITY.——Look——What is written in the law of GOD?——How readest thou?——Consult calm reason, and the unchangeable obligations of justice and truth,——What say they?[25]

This is the core of Sterne's sermon, emphasizing the inseparability of religion and morality which, 'like fast friends and natural allies, can never be set at variance, without the mutual ruin and dishonour of them both'.[26] The sermon, which begins by apparently querying Holy Writ, ends by suggesting it to be indispensable to a proper understanding and implementation of secular morality. It is not, however, simply a case of morality needing religion. Sterne argues that the converse is equally true, leading him once more into a strong attack on Roman Catholicism. For a 'general proof' of this, he asks his congregation to consider the history of the Roman Church:

> See what scenes of cruelty, murders, rapines, bloodshed, have all been sanctified by a religion not strictly governed by morality.
>
> In how many kingdoms of the world, has the crusading sword of this misguided Saint-Errant spared neither age, or merit, or sex, or condition.——And, as he fought under the banners of a religion, which set him loose from justice and humanity,——he shewed none,——mercilessly trampled upon both, heard neither the cries of the unfortunate, nor pitied their distresses.[27]

Having considered the effects of separating religion and morality, however, the preacher concludes his sermon, not by confirming values he assumes the Anglican congregation to share, but with words directed very pointedly at his audience of lawyers, including the two judges:

> And in your own case remember this plain distinction, a mistake in which, has ruin'd thousands.——That your conscience is not a

> law;——no,——God and reason made the law, and have placed Conscience within you to determine,——not like an *Asiatic Cadi*, according to the ebbs and flows of his own passions;——but like a *British judge* in this land of liberty, who makes no new law,——but faithfully declares that glorious law which he finds already written.[28]

It was this sermon of which Voltaire, in his essay 'On the Deceptions of Conscience' in the *Philosophical Dictionary* of 1771, asserted that the subject had 'never been better treated'.[29] The sermon is notable both for the way the preacher holds his audience's attention throughout, causing them to focus on the text by taking nothing for granted, and for Sterne's masterly application of the sermon's own moral to the occasion and the congregation. The interrelationship of Church and State can rarely have been more economically expressed.

Yet, despite the extent to which Sterne shaped his attack on the contemporary secularization of morality to suit a particular audience, he had once again drawn heavily on printed sermons by his predecessors, most notably Jonathan Swift.[30] The choice is intriguing, for productive as Swift was, he so disparaged his sermons that a mere dozen of them survive. Moreover, only three of these were published—by Robert Dodsley, future publisher of *Tristram Shandy*—within Swift's lifetime, and then only shortly before his death in 1745. The very fact that only three sermons of so celebrated a writer *had* been published makes it extremely probable, however, that several among Sterne's congregation of lawyers and clerics might have recognized that the preacher was drawing on a work—the sermon is entitled *On the Testimony of Conscience*—by one of the most celebrated churchmen and writers of the century, within six years of its first appearance in print. Sterne's borrowings in his sermons have attracted much commentary and scarcely less criticism, yet given the unembarrassed use he made of Swift's sermon, it is hard to believe that Sterne saw his borrowings from the sermons of others in the light in which subsequent severe moralists have cast them.[31] That Sterne expected his listeners to note his use of Swift's *On the Testimony of Conscience* is doubtful, but in drawing on his eminent and much-admired predecessor he was demonstrating, if only to himself, that he had talent too.

The delivery of an assize sermon and the eventual publication of *The Abuses of Conscience* were, in the confined context of Sterne's life at the time, events of signal importance. Yet he could have found few grounds for optimism that the next decade would bring greater honours or rewards. Days such as that on which he preached to the general approval of a distinguished congregation were few and far between. Indeed, Richard Greenwood's assertion that the Minster was habitually crowded when it was known that Sterne was to preach seems to have involved some belated inflation of the size of the congregation. It was barely three months after the success of *The Abuses of Conscience* that Sterne was back in the Minster in very different circumstances: the (now lost) manuscript of his sermon 'Our Conversation in Heaven' bore the inscription: 'Made for All Saints and preach'd on that Day 1750 for the Dean.—Present: one Bellows Blower, three Singing Men, one Vicar and one Residentiary.—Memorandum: Dined with Duke Humphrey.'[32] Given that Sterne's motive for preaching the dean's turn was the £1 fee it earned him, we may believe that dining with Duke Humphrey— that is, going hungry—may have been an all-too-familiar experience.

Certainly, whatever satisfaction Sterne derived from seeing *Elijah and the Widow of Zerephath* or *The Abuses of Conscience* in print, he would enjoy no such comparable achievement in the decade to follow. Many clergymen with no greater personal interest than Laurence Sterne would have been pleased enough with the preferment that had come their way—a comfortable living was all to which most eighteenth-century clergymen might (or did) aspire. Sterne had received the living of Sutton-on-the-Forest in 1738 when he was 24 years old. In the following twelve years he gained two prebendal stalls, became a pluralist on taking the living of Stillington, and achieved sufficient reputation as a preacher to be asked to deliver several sermons on significant church occasions, two of which were subsequently published. Still, he could never forget that in quarrelling with his uncle he had also squandered his best chance of gaining further significant preferment. If his career in the church was to progress further he needed another patron—and he knew it.

In fact, Sterne enjoyed a considerable stroke of luck. In 1747 the dean of the Minster, Richard Osbaldeston was elevated to the episcopacy as bishop of Carlisle. His successor was a young man, formerly a canon of Windsor, the Revd John Fountayne. By chance the new dean was not unknown to Sterne, for the two had been at Cambridge together, though they are unlikely to have been close friends (Sterne described Fountayne merely as a 'College Acquaintance'). A year younger than Sterne, Fountayne was the son of wealthy Yorkshire gentry and already well set upon a successful career, thanks to the protection he enjoyed from several eminent churchmen within his own family. By the time he became dean of York Minster at the early age of 33 he could number among his relations three bishops, including Thomas Sherlock, the powerful bishop of

London. Such connections enabled Fountayne to rise through the Church—he had previously served as dean of Windsor and of Salisbury—much faster than Laurence Sterne could have hoped, even had he not quarrelled with his uncle. Jaques Sterne, in fact, was the disappointed candidate for the vacant deanship. By quickly aligning himself with Fountayne, Laurence Sterne must have further antagonized his already ill-disposed uncle. Yet, though Sterne at first welcomed Fountayne's arrival, with its promise of the possibility of securing advancement for himself, he would come eventually to resent the dean's failure to reward his efforts as he thought they deserved.

Initially Sterne threw himself wholeheartedly into supporting the new dean. Though he had not previously been assiduous in attendance at the meetings of the chapter, he was present on 24 October 1747 for Fountayne's installation. In turn, Fountayne is likely to have seen his former acquaintance as a potential ally among the Minster clergy.[33] Yet, although Sterne was doubtless glad to find his new dean a man both congenial and already known to him, he was certainly aware that a new period in the Minster's affairs was beginning, in which the patterns of power and influence were far from settled. Thomas Herring, the archbishop, was elevated in 1748 to the primacy of England, as archbishop of Canterbury. He was succeeded in the See of York by another latitudinarian, the bishop of Bangor, Dr Matthew Hutton. If Laurence Sterne was pleased to number the new dean of the Minster among his Cambridge acquaintance, then Jaques Sterne must have found comparable satisfaction in the fact that, like Thomas Herring, Matthew Hutton had been his own fellow-student at Jesus College. It was the archdeacon, in fact, who stood proxy for the new archbishop at the installation ceremony on 29 December 1747.

If Sterne thought that Fountayne would provide him with sufficient protection against the displeasure of his uncle, the elevation to the archbishopric of Matthew Hutton would soon cause him to change his mind. Both archbishop and dean immediately revealed themselves determined to establish the respective rights and privileges of their new situations. These, however, were not clearly defined, and it was not long before the two newcomers found themselves in contention—with the two Sternes, uncle and nephew, in opposed supporting roles.

It was, in fact, Jaques Sterne's persecution of the nuns of St Mary's Convent at Micklegate Bar which acted as a preliminary engagement to more sustained hostilities between Hutton and Fountayne. Dr Sterne was endeavouring to persuade the ecclesiastical court to bring the full force of anti-Catholic legislation against the nuns, despite its evident reluctance to do so. This brought the archdeacon immediately into conflict with the diocesan chancellor, Dr William Herring, a cousin to the former archbishop and a close ally of the new dean, John Fountayne. In his turn Dr Sterne was supported by Dr Francis Topham and by the archbishop himself. The case was messy and long-drawn-out, the court meeting on twenty occasions between May 1748 and November 1749. Such satisfaction as Jaques obtained was restricted to small fines imposed on the nuns and an order that Mary Hodshon, the mother superior, should be seen to conform to the Established Church. For his own part, the archdeacon was accused in court of mistreating the nuns and forced to fight through the courts to recover his expenses in bringing the case, circumstances which perhaps affected his judgement and persuaded him, in 1751, to harass the nuns once more, this time through legal proceedings that dragged on for another year. In his sustained attack on the York nunnery Jaques Sterne could count on the support of Archbishop Hutton against John Fountayne's ally, William Herring. This affair, however, was followed by a more serious engagement in a campaign that culminated in a direct confrontation between the new archbishop and the dean.

In this case hostilities did not result in a death but began with one. In November 1749 the residentiary canon, Samuel Baker, died. Both archbishop and dean had candidates of their own to take his place. Matthew Hutton favoured Dr Francis Wanley, his chaplain, who was related both to the archbishop and, through marriage, to Jaques Sterne. John Fountayne, however, gave preference to William Berdmore, himself related through marriage to William Herring. Of the contenders, Fountayne moved faster to secure the place for his candidate (it was reported that William Herring employed an informant to relay to him immediately news of Baker's death). The morning following Dr Baker's anxiously anticipated demise William Berdmore claimed the position at a chapter meeting convened by the dean. When Archbishop Hutton nominated his candidate twenty-four hours later the place was already filled. Though he protested to the archbishop of Canterbury, Hutton found no better remedy than to attempt a reconciliation with Fountayne, though he was evidently unhappy with Fountayne's conception of the dean's role and authority. Fountayne, meanwhile, was evidently suspicious of the archbishop and his emissary and, with considerable foresight, began keeping a complete record of the correspondence passing between himself and Hutton. Among those who assisted him was Laurence Sterne. The record itself, unused at the time, was to prove significant a decade later, not only for Fountayne and the ecclesiastical power game but for Laurence Sterne's entire future as a writer.

Laurence Sterne was too insignificant a figure in the Church in York to gain significant advantage himself in this ecclesiastical squabble, although by assisting John Fountayne he incurred the displeasure of other principals, not least his uncle, who held grudges deeply. In fact the only preferment of any kind to come Sterne's way at this period was from a quite different source. At the end of 1750 Lord Fauconberg, of Newburgh Priory, presented Sterne with a small favour in his gift when he gave him the commissaryship of the Peculiar Jurisdiction of Alne and Tollerton (small villages close to Sutton), most likely in the hopes of gaining the vicar of Sutton as an ally in his impending endeavour to enclose substantial amounts of land in the area.[34] If so the alliance was secured at little cost, for the fees amounted to no more than £2 a year and Sterne's acceptance of the place depended more on the hope of future favours than on the prestige or expectation of significant financial gain. As it turned out, any hopes he had in this direction were soon thwarted, for when the living of Coxwold, which was in Fauconberg's gift, fell vacant in 1753, Sterne found himself passed over—perhaps because of his known anti-Roman Catholicism, which cannot have endeared him to Fauconberg's Catholic wife Lady Catherine. Most gallingly of all, the living went to Sterne's own former curate, the Revd Richard Wilkinson.

If the commissaryship of Alne and Tollerton was given to Sterne as an anticipation of favours to be received, a second preferment the following year—this time to the Peculiar Court of Pickering and Pocklington—was, by contrast, an indication of support already given by Sterne to John Fountayne. Though more prestigious than the place at Alne and Tollerton, Pickering and Pocklington was not much better remunerated—a fact which rankled with Sterne, for the assistance he now afforded Fountayne extended well beyond backing him in meetings or copying letters for him in his dispute with the archbishop and his supporters. When Fountayne aspired to a doctorate in divinity from his old university in 1751 he determined to acquire it '*per saltum*'. For this purpose he needed to preach a sermon in Latin in the Cambridge university church of Great St Mary's. Unable, or too busy, to compose the sermon—or '*conscio ad clerum*'—himself, Fountayne sought the assistance of Sterne who duly obliged, writing the Latin sermon for him, thus enabling the dean to gain his doctorate.

John Fountayne, it must be said, was not unappreciative of his friend's assistance in Minster politics or in the personal matter of the doctorate.

Perhaps because he could have found others able and willing to assist him, however, he did not value Sterne's help as highly as did Sterne himself. Taken together, the services Sterne rendered Fountayne in the years 1749–51 led him to believe that the dean had an outstanding obligation to him, while Fountayne thought the place of Pickering and Pocklington sufficient recompense. The result was a breach between the two men. After six years of regular attendance at chapter meetings following Fountayne's arrival, Sterne ceased to make the journey from Sutton-on-the-Forest after 1753. Evidently he had been given to understand that there would be no further reward for services rendered. Yet, despite his apparent disenchantment with Fountayne from this time onwards, events transpired in such a way as to draw Sterne back in to decanal politics later in the decade, in circumstances which would crucially alter the entire course of his life.

The starting-point was Fountayne's role in securing for Sterne the commissaryship of Pickering and Pocklington following the death of Dr William Ward. Ward had been commissary (or judge) in many of the spiritual courts, and Francis Topham had long harboured aspirations to succeed him. John Fountayne had other ideas. Besides preferring Sterne to Pickering and Pocklington, he presented the most important peculiar court, that of the Dean and Chapter, to one of Topham's rivals, William Stables. Topham received only places that lay within the gift of the archbishop. These helped make him wealthy but they did not satisfy him, nor did they offer sufficient consolation for what he continued to regard as a breach of good faith towards him on the part of Fountayne.

Although he said little at the time, Topham continued to feel this wound, which festered throughout the 1750s, until it erupted in the *Letter Address'd to the Reverend the Dean of York* in 1758. This was the pamphlet that heralded a brief but fiercely contested paper war, prompting the publication not only of the *Answer to a Letter Address'd to the Dean of York, in the Name of Dr. Topham* (1758) and a *Reply to the Answer to a Letter* in the following year, but much more significantly a little work, *A Political Romance*, by Laurence Sterne.

Even in outline the events behind the quarrel were complex. When Fountayne was preferred to the deanship of York he promised to Topham (or so Topham alleged) the commissaryship of the Dean and Chapter Court. This Fountayne denied, backing up his case with the undoubtedly correct argument that the place was not in the dean's gift but in that of the chapter. Topham suggested that the whole election was a put-up job—though he could offer no corroborating evidence to back up his charge. In attacking Fountayne for failing to give him Pickering and Pocklington, however, Topham changed his position for what he considered firmer ground. This commissaryship *was* in Fountayne's gift, and that he had presented it in 1751 to Laurence Sterne was undeniable.

The affair, though, was still more complicated. In 1749 the then commissary, William Ward, had been asked by another elderly cleric, Dr Mark Braithwaite, to resign Pickering and Pocklington in his favour—an indication, given the unremarkable fees the place commanded, of how poor the rural clergy might be. Ward agreed, on condition that Braithwaite could obtain the consent both of Fountayne and of Francis Topham, to whom he knew the place had been promised. The former was agreeable and, after some hesitation, Topham also finally complied. When Dr Braithwaite found himself so embarrassed financially that he was unable even to take out the necessary patent, Dr Ward appointed him instead his surrogate, thereby giving him access to the fees. Braithwaite, however, had little time left to live, and died sixteen months later. When William Ward himself died the following year, still in possession of Pickering and Pocklington, Fountayne felt under no obligation to give Francis Topham a second chance to succeed. Topham's willingness to cede his turn to Mark Braithwaite Fountayne took as the deed, regardless of Braithwaite's inability to afford the patent. Topham's protests were unavailing, and Pickering and Pocklington went to Laurence Sterne.

Though Topham continued to talk against Fountayne, his vanity—for it was scarcely cupidity—got the better of his judgement. Nor did he give Fountayne sufficient credit for astuteness. On the face of it Topham had a strong case and he evidently made it to anyone who would listen. Fountayne, however, challenged him publicly with fabricating a story to his discredit. When Topham denied it, Laurence Sterne produced incontrovertible proof to the contrary, forcing the discomfited Topham into an admission of the truth of the allegation. Nor had Fountayne finished. When Topham attempted to lessen his responsibility by suggesting that he had possibly misunderstood a letter in which Fountayne had apparently promised him the place, Fountayne requested to see the letter. Topham admitted that he was unable to produce it, upon which Fountayne displayed both a letter of Topham's seeking the dean's aid in securing the place, and his own reply, quite devoid of anything resembling a promise. Francis Topham retired defeated.

Sterne's part in this affair was to support Fountayne and provide testimony forcing Topham into an admission that he had circulated misleading stories about Fountayne around York. Given Sterne's own experience of being caught out in the wrong in the political dispute of a decade earlier, it is probable that he took a certain, not wholly charitable satisfaction at seeing Topham squirming in his turn. Certainly Sterne did not forget the affair, for he would exact more lasting revenge against Topham, portraying him first as the grasping village sexton Trim in *A Political Romance*, and again as the opinionated church-lawyer Didius in *Tristram Shandy*.

Although *A Political Romance*, or *The History of a Good Warm Watch-Coat* would not be written until 1759, it is inseparably linked to the contest of 1749–51 between Archbishop Hutton and Dean John Fountayne, and to the ambitions of Dr Francis Topham. While only Fountayne is likely to have found the dispute settled to his satisfaction, the affair appeared to have been resolved and forgotten, for similar contests were not to recur during Matthew Hutton's tenure of the See of York. The death of Thomas Herring in 1757, however, freed the Primacy of England, and Matthew Hutton soon followed his predecessor at York to Canterbury. The new archbishop of York was Dr John Gilbert, formerly bishop of Salisbury. It was of the news of Gilbert's elevation that Horace Walpole wrote: 'they rung the bells at York backwards in detestation of him. He opened a great table there, and in six months they thought him the most christian Prelate that had ever sat in that see.'[35] Gilbert, in his mid-sixties when translated to York, was in such poor health as caused him to live principally in London—a place of residence in any case much more to his liking than the north of England. All the same, Gilbert was as interested as any of his predecessors in the prerogatives of his new office.

What he discovered did not please him. One of the most sought-after posts among those in the archbishop's patronage was the registrarship of the Exchequer and Prerogative Court. On enquiry, Gilbert discovered that his predecessor, Matthew Hutton, had effectively removed this post from his gift by granting to his chaplain, the Revd Francis Dodsworth, a reversionary patent: that is, a patent given during the lifetime of the then holder which would become effective on his death. Following Hutton's lead, Gilbert gave a further reversionary patent, this time to the Revd Robert Bewley.

Among the interested spectators of all this was Francis Topham. Like his predecessor, Archbishop Gilbert looked to Topham to represent him in his contests with Fountayne and the chapter. For instance, when the archbishop feared that he might have little time left to live he used Topham in a rushed (and unsuccessful) attempt to have his brother inducted as a prebendary. Taking his lead from the example of the archbishop, Topham began his own inquiries into the legality of reversionary patents. Convinced of their validity, he conceived of a similar ploy to secure a post for his own son, Edward, then just 7 years old. His plan was to have his patent as commissary of the Exchequer and Prerogative Court rewritten to include his son's life as well as his own. Believing he could count on the acquiescence of Archbishop Gilbert, Topham approached Fountayne to secure his agreement. Fountayne was not co-operative. The matter came to the attention of the archbishop who, to Topham's disappointment, proved as unhelpful as the dean, declaring that he would not be a party to removing from his successors this piece of their patronage. His own similar act he regarded as exceptional and excused as merely compensating for the loss of patronage he had himself suffered by Hutton's issuing of a reversionary patent to Francis Dodsworth.

Topham's anger knew no bounds. Believing the archbishop to have broken his promise, he spoke openly against him and against Fountayne, whose own allegedly broken promise over the Pickering and Pocklington affair he again recalled publicly. Nor would talk content him. In December 1758 Topham published a pamphlet, *A Letter Address'd to the Reverend the Dean of York; in which is given a full Detail of some very extraordinary Behaviour of his, in relation to his Denial of a Promise made by him to Dr. Topham.* Quite what he hoped to achieve by this is not easy to tell. He can scarcely have forgotten his discomfiture of several years previously at Fountayne's hands, nor have expected the dean to make no response on this occasion. Predictably enough Fountayne replied in kind with *An Answer to a Letter address'd to the Dean of York, in the Name of Dr. Topham.* At this juncture the affair became widely discussed in York, spawning numerous broadsides ridiculing the participants in the affair.

As so often in these years, Laurence Sterne was initially no more than a peripheral figure in the Minster politicking. Now he once again allowed himself to become embroiled in the disputes of others—and on this occasion, in print. Encouraged by Fountayne, or his own ambition, to believe that renewed alliance with the dean might yet gain him future preferment, he began to write *A Political Romance.* These may not, in fact, have been the first words Sterne had penned on Fountayne's behalf in the affair, for Topham's description of *An Answer* as 'the Child and Offspring of Many Parents' indicates his probably accurate belief that Fountayne had enlisted the help of friends, Sterne among them, to rebut Topham's charges. *A Political Romance,* however, was Sterne's own idea and one that offered possibilities he was not slow to exploit with considerable humour and imagination. Sterne worked on the *Romance* with dispatch; the final sections are dated 20 January 1759, and he expected to see it in print by the end of the same month.[36]

The influences behind the *Romance* are not hard to detect. The first, and most important is Jonathan Swift's *A Tale of a Tub*. Though no more than a shilling pamphlet, Sterne's work is, like the *Tale*, made up of several sections: the 'Romance' proper, a 'Postscript', 'The Key', a letter 'To —— ——, *Esq.* of YORK [Caesar Ward, the printer]', signed with Sterne's own name, and a final letter 'To Dr. Topham', again openly acknowledged over Sterne's name. Despite its brevity and modest scope, the pamphlet does no dishonour to his Swiftian model, nor to the other distinguished influences in evidence: among them Boileau's mock-heroic *Le Lutrin* (*The Lectern*), Alexander Pope's facetious 'Key' to *The Rape of the Lock*, and his equally droll *Memoirs of P.P., Clerk of this Parish*.

As with this last work, *A Political Romance* depends on the translation of events in the great world—here the See of York—into that of a country parish, allowing Sterne to create a transparent allegory burlesquing the greed and self-importance of his principal characters. There is the Parson of the Parish (the archbishop), John the Parish Clerk (Dean John Fountayne), and Trim the Sexton and Dog-Whipper (Dr Francis Topham), along with such minor figures as Mark Slender (Dr Mark Braithwaite), William Doe (William Stables), and Lorry Slim (Laurence Sterne himself). The disputed commissaryship of Pickering and Pocklington is represented as an 'old-case-Pair-of-black-Plush-Breeches' which Trim scorns and covets by turn. Sterne's own, conflicting attitudes to this modest preferment are clearly indicated. After ten years of use, he insists, the breeches are worn 'very thin' and not worth 'half a Crown' to their possessor, but Lorry Slim still enjoys their possession since, 'thin as they are, he knows that *Trim*, let him say what he will to the contrary, still envies the *Possessor* of them,—and, with all his Pride, would be very glad to wear them after *him*'.[37]

Although Sterne offers, in an explicitly Swiftian allusion, an account of the '*Battle* of the Breeches', he is at pains to stress from the outset that the breeches are not the real cause of the uproar which disturbs the entire village. The quarrel goes back much further, to the squabble between the Parson of the Parish and Master Trim about an 'old Watch-Coat', which Trim covets. To obtain it, the Sexton takes advantage of the Parson's recent arrival in the village and his indifferent health. This watch-coat—that is, the Exchequer and Prerogative Court—is the real issue of dispute, as the alternative title for his work makes clear: 'The History of a Good, Warm Watch-Coat'.

Initially Sterne intended to have published the *Romance* anonymously. Topham's sneer that Fountayne's answer was, in Sterne's paraphrase, the

'Child of many Fathers' persuaded him otherwise. 'I do here desire', Sterne wrote to Caesar Ward, 'That the Child be filiated upon me, *Laurence Sterne*, Prebendary of *York*.' Although the provenance of *A Political Romance* seems to have been an open secret in York ecclesiastical circles, Sterne's open avowal of authorship rapidly turned into an embarrassment for him.

At first Sterne had been circumspect enough. The quarrel between the Parson and Trim is described in such a way as largely to exculpate Archbishop Gilbert and lay the blame on Topham. Hence, the Parson is 'a Gentleman of a frank and open Temper' who acted 'from the Motive of Generosity' (p. 198). Trim, by contrast, is a 'pimping, dirty, pettyfogging Character' (p. 219), given to 'shifty Behaviour' (p. 197), motivated by vanity and insatiable greed. In one comic and scatological moment he boasts his devotion to the Parson by recalling that less than a fortnight previously he had made a trip to the far end of town 'to borrow you a Close-stool,—and came back, as my Neighbours, who flouted me, will all bear witness, with the Pan upon my Head, and never thought it too much' (p. 203). In the light of such abasement, the Parson is initially willing to cede the Sexton the watch-coat for services rendered, until he discovers in the Parish Book that this same coat had been given by a previous patron of the parish '**to the sole Use and Behoof of the poor Sextons thereof, and their Successors, for ever**' (p. 200). Now law and a desire to protect his own prerogatives assert themselves over simple generosity, and the Parson withdraws his offer of the watch-coat, only to discover that the sexton has pre-empted him by cutting it up to serve as a waistcoat for himself and a petticoat for his wife.

In the course of a few pages dispute follows dispute. The Parson and John the Parish-Clerk become embroiled when Trim puts it into the Parson's head that the Parish-Clerk's desk or lectern in the church was 'four Inches higher than it should be' (p. 205)—though Sterne (remembering he was writing on Fountayne's behalf) insists that the Parish-Clerk, 'bore an exceeding good Character as a Man of Truth' and 'rather did Honour to his Office,—than that his Office did Honour to him' (p. 201). As all sense of proportion gives way to greed and the desire for self-aggrandizement, the entire village—including Lorry Slim—is drawn in, until Trim is given up to public ridicule and left, in the closing lines of the 'Romance' proper, to waddle 'very slowly off with that Kind of inflexible Gravity only to be equalled by one Animal in the whole Creation,—and surpassed by none' (p. 209).

Had Topham been the only butt of Sterne's wit the matter might have smouldered for a while and died out. It had now become clear, however, that not Topham alone but all of the principals in the dispute had become objects of public ridicule. Unwisely, perhaps, Sterne himself suggested as much in the 'Key' he provided. Here we learn that a copy of the 'Romance' was dropped in the Minster-Yard and subsequently picked up by a passer-by who takes it to his political club for discussion. Each member of the club reads the story differently, though each as a political allegory involving a great European power, past or present—hence the work's title, *A Political Romance.* Although none of the town politicians listens to any other, each is convinced by his own interpretation, turning 'the Story to what was swimming uppermost in his own Brain'—an unmistakeable anticipation of the Shandean 'hobby-horse'. In these readings the Parson variously represents King George I, or George II, or Louis XIV, or XV, or the king of Prussia, or the king of Spain, while the Plush-Breeches are understood by turns to stand for Saxony, or Gibraltar, or Sicily, or Spain and the West Indies. Though Sterne is here following Pope's own mischievous 'Key' to *The Rape of the Lock*, in which similarly extravagant political readings of the poem are proffered, his own 'Key' also highlights just how public the ecclesiastical quarrel had become.

No wonder, then, that the dispute between the dignitaries of the Church at York reached the ears of Archbishop Gilbert, who was spending the winter in London. Recognizing how poor a figure both he and the Church cut in the affair, Gilbert summoned John Fountayne and Francis Topham to the capital to discuss the affair. Precisely what was said we can only conjecture—though Topham was certainly as anxious as the archbishop to put a stop to the whole paper war. The result, however, was clear. When Fountayne returned from the metropolis all 500 or so copies of *A Political Romance* were removed from the printers and burned. Such, at least, was the intention. In fact the complete destruction of printed copies of the work did not prove possible and a half-dozen or so examples survived. How fortuitous was even this survival may be gleaned from the fact that Sterne neither possessed a copy himself nor was aware that any had escaped the flames. In December 1761, when making an inventory of his belongings in case of his death abroad, he mentions only what is obviously the manuscript of the work.[38]

Why did Sterne so readily accede to the burning of *A Political Romance*—especially since he seems to have been offered no positive inducement to do so? The most obvious answer is prudence. Prudence was necessary because, as had happened before, Sterne's pen had run away with him. Throughout the *Romance* Sterne had been well aware of the need for tact in his presentation of the Parson, attributing the favours bestowed on Trim to an excess of virtue on the Parson's part: 'A Principle of strong Compassion transports a generous Mind sometimes beyond what is strictly right', he suggests at one point. Set against this overtly laudatory view of his archbishop, however, is a less complimentary view of his attitude to archiepiscopal prerogative.

Trim the Sexton and Dog-Whipper takes his name from the contemporary proverb, 'Trim-tram; like master, like man'.[39] This may have been suggested to Sterne by Jonathan Swift's use of it in tantalizingly similar circumstances, where, writing to the Earl of Orrery, he notes: 'Our B[isho]p Rundle is not yet come over, and I believe his Chaplain Philips is in a reasonable fright that his Patron may fall sooner than any living in the Diocess; I suppose it is Trim Tram betwixt both; for neither have three penny worth of Stamina'[40]—or it may have had still wider currency. Whether Sterne intended the implications of the proverb to be picked up by attentive readers or inserted it as a private joke, his naming of the Sexton misfired. The implication that—in his concern with place and privilege—Topham was taking his lead from the archbishop (or, more correctly, archbishops) was no more flattering to Gilbert than to his predecessor Hutton. It is, however, an entirely accurate reading of the events *A Political Romance* allegorizes. Topham's action, in attempting to rewrite his own patent as commissary of the Exchequer and Prerogative Court in order that his young son might eventually succeed him, was directly inspired by the example of two archbishops in granting reversionary patents to their chaplains, bearing out the proverb 'Like master, like man'.

Since Sterne was, as ever, on the lookout for preferment in 1759, it seems certain that he did not intend publicly to pillory his archbishop. Even if he could not resist the joke of calling Topham by the name of Trim, he may have hoped that the transparent compliments he paid Gilbert would shield him from any suspicion of satire. In turn, Gilbert's motives for encouraging the suppression of *A Political Romance* were doubtless not wholly personal, deriving rather from an understandable desire to limit the damage caused to the See of York. The result was the same. When Fountayne returned to York from visiting Gilbert in London he brought Sterne the unequivocal message that the publication of the *Romance* would result in public rebuke and the archbishop's personal disfavour.[41]

Sterne's motives for writing *A Political Romance* were undoubtedly mixed. A willingness to take the part of Fountayne against Topham merged with the sheer pleasure of writing, of weaving a web of 'twice the Fineness' of anything of Topham's literary spinning and of 'a more curious Pattern' (p. 224). Yet Sterne was also looking to his own self-interest. Initially he hoped Fountayne might at last exercise his patronage and reward him with some real preferment. When it became clear that the publication of the *Romance* would make such preferment less, rather than more likely, Sterne reluctantly acquiesced in his pamphlet being 'committed to the flames'.

How much of a wrench it was, and how greatly his secular hopes depended on the assistance he offered John Fountayne, may be seen in two letters he wrote in 1761, when he was already celebrated as the author of *Tristram Shandy*. In the first he told Elizabeth Montagu at length about the assistance he had afforded Fountayne in his ecclesiastical quarrels, protesting 'I was as much a protection to the Dean of York—as he to me'. This was in the spring of 1761, when Sterne hoped to have placed his uneasy relations with Fountayne on a new footing by writing to him directly to express his sense of grievance. The answer he had received, Sterne told Elizabeth Montagu, 'has made me easy with regard to my View in the Church of York: & . . . it has cemented ⟨a new⟩ the Dean & myself beyond the power of any future breach' (*Letters*, 136). In truth, Sterne was far from easy, for he enclosed a copy of his letter to Fountayne for Elizabeth Montagu to read in order that she might see 'how much & undeserved I have been abused' (*Letters*, 136)—and Elizabeth Montagu was scarcely the confidante one would choose if genuinely anxious to keep any matter a close secret.

Sterne's unease was evidently justified, for within a year he was again writing of Fountayne, this time to his wife and in very different terms. In a memorandum drawn up in advance of his departure for France, Sterne reveals most fully the accumulated resentment of years of failure to attain the preferment he believed he deserved while less talented contemporaries flourished. Worried that he might not have long to live, Sterne was gathering together unpublished works that he hoped might be printed after his death for the benefit of his wife and daughter. Among these was *A Political Romance*, although, Sterne added, 'I have 2 Reasons why I wish it may not be wanted—first, an undeserved Compliment to One [Fountayne], whom I have since, found to be a very corrupt man—I ⟨never⟩ knew him weak & ignorant—but thought him honest'. Aside from undeservedly praising Fountayne, Sterne added that he was unhappy about having placed Topham 'in a ridiculous light—w^{ch}, upon my Soul I now doubt, whether he deserves' (*Letters*, 147).

Nor was it only the unrewarded writing of the *Romance* that still rankled with Sterne:

> My *Conscio ad Clerum*, in Latin wch I made for Fountayne, to preach before the University, to enable him to take his Doctor's Degree—You will find, 2 Copies of it, with my sermons—
>
> —He got Honour by it—What Got I?—nothing in my Life time. then Let me not (I charge you Mrs Sterne) be robbed of it after my death. ⟨my⟩ That long pathetic Letter to him of the hard measure I have re^{d}—I charge you, to let it be printed——Tis equitable, You should derive ⟨som⟩ that good from My Sufferings at least. (*Letters*, 147).

Even allowing for a pardonable self-pity in a man contemplating his possibly imminent death at an early age, the solemn injunction to Elizabeth Sterne suggests not merely how inadequate a recompense for his efforts he considered the commissaryship of Pickering and Pocklington. More than that, and with his talents at last recognized, Sterne was giving vent to frustration and bitterness resulting from decades of neglect. By writing the *conscio ad clerum* Sterne got little or nothing, while Fountayne received his doctorate and the 'Honour' it brought. When he wrote *A Political Romance* in support of the dean, ecclesiastical expediency caused it to be destroyed. Whatever qualms he might subsequently have felt concerning the justice of his parodic account of the Church quarrels in *A Political Romance*, these were insignificant compared to the reluctance with which he acceded to the archbishop's request, conveyed by Fountayne, that his work be destroyed.

An anonymous acquaintance later declared of the burning of Sterne's pamphlet, that 'This was a real disappointment to him; he felt it'.[42] It is easy to believe—yet not all was loss. To set against his disappointment and the subsequent disillusion with Fountayne and the possibilities of advancement offered by patronage, there was real authorial pride in his work: 'It is a Web wrought out of my own brain', he declared, and insisted that his authorship be acknowledged. Even as he was writing Sterne sensed that things could be different—that he might take the lead instead of always playing a supporting role—affirming 'it is high Time for every Man to look to his own' (p. 223). The thought stayed with Sterne. Eight months later—and with *Tristram Shandy* ready to go to the printers—he declared more forthrightly: 'Now you desire of knowing the reason of my turning author? why truly I am tired of employing my brains for other people's advantage.—'Tis a foolish sacrifice I made for some years to a foolish person' (*Letters*, 84). For Sterne the destruction of *A Political Romance* was a decisive moment—and one that, within the space of twelve months, led the 46-year-old author to the writing of *Tristram Shandy* and to fame.

8

Tristram Shandy and the Queen of Bohemia, 1759

In later years Sterne was acutely aware of how important an impetus the writing of *A Political Romance* had been to his future career: 'till he had finished [it] he hardly knew he could write at all, much less with humour, so as to make his reader laugh.'[1] Extravagant as it seems, this assertion represents little more than the bare truth. Certainly Sterne had published a good deal of political journalism, but that was over a decade previously—and comedy was not uppermost in his mind. (Only one stray essay, signed 'Hamlet', published in the *York Journal: or, Protestant Courant* in 1747, hints at the writer Sterne would become, and even this piece, with its *Guardian*-like narrator, is for the most part a tired reworking of the character sketch made popular earlier in the century by Addison and Steele.[2]) Superior by far to all of his earlier writing, *A Political Romance* is a well-managed comic allegory whose composition encouraged Sterne to give freer rein to his imagination. Paradoxically, given its fiery end, it also allowed him to hope that the success that had eluded him for so long in his career in the Church might still be attainable by other means.

So, despite the setback of the suppression of the *Political Romance*, Sterne was quickly at work again. So quickly that he approached Robert Dodsley in London with a proposal for a new book as early as May 1759. Quite what the submitted plan or draft consisted of at this point is uncertain. It seems likely, however, that the work first published in expurgated form by Sterne's daughter Lydia in 1775 as 'A Fragment in the Manner of Rabelais' represents a partial draft of the text Sterne hopefully sent to London in the spring of 1759.[3]

Especially in its unexpurgated state, the 'Fragment' represents an important transitional stage in Sterne's writing of imaginative fiction, being both freer and bawdier than the closely woven allegory of the *Romance*, yet still remaining in essence a prose satire. As in *A Political Romance*, Sterne had taken his lead from his favourite literary works. Most important among these was François Rabelais's *Gargantua and Pantagruel*, which he knew in the extraordinarily imaginative seventeenth-century translation by Thomas Urquhart, later completed by Peter Motteux. Alongside that were two satirical works: François Béroalde de Verville's facetiously indecent *Le Moyen de Parvenir*, and Jonathan Swift's *A Tale of a Tub*. Convinced that God had not created men 'on purpose to go mourning, all our lives long, in sackcloth and ashes', Sterne took heart from the fact that Rabelais, Béroalde de Verville, and Swift were all priests and, in a phrase of Swift's, 'not the gravest of divines'.[4] Like *A Political Romance*, the 'Fragment' centres on clerical life, though here Sterne's satire is aimed not at the scramble for preferment in the Church but at contemporary sermon-making. Since an acquaintance claimed that Sterne's original design in *Tristram Shandy* had been to 'take in all ranks and professions, and to laugh them out of their absurdities',[5] it is likely that the 'Fragment' represents Sterne's first efforts in this direction, beginning with his own profession.

Few aspects of his calling seem to have vexed Sterne more than the composition of sermons. Whether in Sutton and Stillington or in York Minster, congregations looked to the preacher for a stimulating or moving sermon, and the fact that Sterne gained a reputation as a talented preacher perhaps made his task more, rather than less difficult, since his congregations' expectations were higher. Certainly, eighteenth-century congregations were not slow to manifest discontent at dull sermons: even Swift was moved to preach a sermon entitled 'Upon Sleeping in Church'. Yet while the eighteenth-century Church produced a number of great preachers, not all the clergy were committed to producing sermons by the sweat of their own brows. There was nothing necessarily wrong in this, for the devising of sermons on a limited range of approved subjects was not merely condoned but positively recommended: the thirty-fifth of the Thirty-Nine Articles of the Church of England lists twenty-one approved topics for homilies. Moreover, latitudinarian practice had promoted the writing and publication of preachers' handbooks, which met with widespread and distinguished support.[6] It was normal practice for clergymen of the Established Church to make a commonplace book into which they copied the sermons of the most admired preachers of the seventeenth and eighteenth centuries, and even talented and scrupulous clergymen borrowed heavily from the published works of others. For the most part, originality held no absolute appeal either to preachers or their congregations; as Thomas Herring had succinctly observed, Christian morality was 'not made up of many new Discoveries'.[7] Sterne himself, however, was uneasy enough about his own borrowings, or the extent of them, to allude to the question on several occasions.

It is the specific question of when, in sermon-making, borrowing becomes theft that animates much of Sterne's 'Rabelaisian Fragment'. The first chapter (only two survive) opens with one Longinus Rabelaicus delivering himself of his thoughts on how sermon-making might best be methodized:

> My dear and thrice-Reverend Brethren, as well Arch-Bishops and Bishops as the *Rest* of the *Inferior* Clergy! Would it not be a glorious Thing, If any Man of Genius and Capacity amongst us for such a Work, was fully bent within Himself to sit down immediately and compose a thorough-stitch'd System of the KERUKOPÆDIA, daintily setting forth, to the best of his Wit and Memory, & collecting for that Purpose all that is needful to be known & understood of that Art?—— Of what Art, cryed *Panurge*?——Good God! Answer'd *Longinus Rabelaicus* (making an Exclamation, but taking Care to moderate his Voice at the same Time) Why,——of the Art of making all kinds of your theological, hebdomadical, rostrummical, humdrummical what d'ye call'ems [i.e sermons].[8]

Here, Sterne plainly directs his readers to two principal points of literary reference. The first is, of course, Rabelais; the second is Pope—author of the *Peri Bathous* (*On the Art of Sinking in Poetry*), a parodical version of the *Peri Hupsous* (*On the Sublime*) by Longinus—and the entire Scriblerian project in which Pope had engaged alongside Swift, Gay, and Arbuthnot. In the two surviving chapters the influence of Rabelais is systematically pointed up by the names of the group to whom Longinus Rabelaicus addresses his thoughts—Epistemon, Panurge, Triboulet, and Gymnast[9]—though the discussion of the delivery of sermons—especially the fusion of the preacher's physical and spiritual attributes—draws more directly on Swift's account of the Aeolists in *A Tale of a Tub*.

Although the digressive potential of the work is evident from the outset, with Sterne glossing the second chapter as one 'In which the Reader will begin to form a Judgment, of what an Historical, Dramatical, Anecdotical, Allegorical and Comical Kind of a Work, He has got hold of',[10] the two surviving chapters are quite coherent. Chapter 2 opens with an account of Homenas's efforts to write his Sunday sermon:

> HOMENAS who had to preach next Sunday (before God knows whom)—knowing Nothing at all of the Matter——was all this while at it as hard as He could drive in the very next Room: for having foul'd

> two clean Sheets of his own, and being quite stuck fast in the Enterance upon his third General *Division*, & finding Himself unable to get either forwards or backwards—with any Grace——'d—n it,' says He, (thereby Excommunicating every Mother's Son who should think differently) 'Why, may not a Man lawfully call in for Help, in this, as well as any other human Emergency?'[11]

Taking down a volume of Samuel Clarke's sermons from the shelf, Homenas is soon 'transcribing it away, Like a little black Devil', though not without misgivings: 'Tho' I hold all this to be fair and square Yet, if I am found out, there will be the Deuce & all to pay.—'. In fact Homenas quickly comes to an unfortunate end, allowing for one of the most Shandean moments in the entire 'Fragment':

> *What's all that Crowd about, honest Man! Homenas was got upon Dr. Clark's back, Sir——and what of that, my Lad? Why Sir, He has broke his Neck, and fractured his Skull and beshit himself into the Bargain, by a fall from the Pulpit two Stories high.* Alass poor *Homenas*![12]

Although it appears here as generalized satire, the ethics of 'borrowing' from the sermons of others remained a matter close to Sterne's own heart, for he would allude nervously to the question of borrowings when publishing the first two volumes of his sermons in 1760 and later, in *Tristram Shandy*, Yorick inscribes on the first page of one of his sermons, '*For this sermon I shall be hanged,—for I have stolen the greatest part of it*' (*TS* VI. xi. 343).

The allusion to Dr Samuel Clarke as the divine from whom Homenas filches his sermon is equally pointed, for Clarke, a distinguished latitudinarian, twice a Boyle Lecturer and fierce critic of Swift's *A Tale of a Tub*,[13] was a preacher from whose sermons Sterne himself borrowed on several occasions. Even more revealing, however, is the fact that Sterne had originally made Homenas borrow from a sermon by Dr John Rogers, for no better—or worse—reason than to allow him scope for a bawdy joke about Homenas's 'Rogering at it as Hard as he could drive' (this change in his draft representing one of several instances where Sterne seems to have recognized how close he was sailing to the wind in terms of the public acceptability of his work's Rabelaisian humour).

The occasional misgiving aside, Sterne continued his draft in much the same broad satirical strain throughout. Describing the work he sent to Robert Dodsley in May, he declared: 'The Plan, as you <may> will percieve, is a most extensive one,—taking in, not only, the Weak part of the Sciences, in wch the true point of Ridicule lies—but every Thing<,> else, which I find Laugh-at-able in my way.'[14] By this reading, the 'Fragment in the Manner of Rabelais' would represent a development of the satirical account of the Minster clergy in *A Political Romance*, as a prelude to a further broadening of the satire to take in professions and callings other than Sterne's own—even as eventually published *Tristram Shandy* included satirical accounts of the law, medicine, education, and much else (*TS* I. xv and xx). As we know from a second letter Sterne sent to Dodsley in October 1759, the latter had recommended that all local reference be taken out of the book and the satire made more general still, and as the published version of *Tristram Shandy* reveals, Sterne took Dodsley's advice to heart (although some of the material from the 'Fragment' re-emerges in an altered form in the Visitation dinner episode in the fourth volume of the novel).

Between Dodsley's counsel and Sterne's own second thoughts regarding his use of bawdy—which, in the religious context, comes at times dangerously close to blasphemy[15]—*Tristram Shandy* is a very different work from the 'Fragment in the Manner of Rabelais'. If it is not in any simple sense a 'better' one, then it is altogether more up-to-date and accessible and hence—the crucial point for Sterne—more marketable. Sterne's love of Rabelais, Swift, and Pope and his ability to learn from them are in plentiful evidence in the 'Fragment', yet nowhere in the two chapters which survive is there any sense of an engagement with contemporary fiction, that 'New Species of Writing' which Sterne was to exploit with such magnificent success. For all the points of contact between them, the 'Fragment' and *Tristram Shandy* are quite distinct. What is remarkable was how quickly Sterne could rethink and rewrite the work that was to make him famous.

If, as seems likely, Sterne started work on the first version of *Tristram Shandy* after finishing *A Political Romance* in late January 1759, he made rapid progress. By 23 May of that year he was in a position to offer the work to a publisher in London. Sterne's choice of Robert Dodsley suggests, in part, the high value he himself put on his new work. From humble beginnings as a footman, Robert Dodsley had begun to make a name for himself as a poet in his twenties, initially drawing on his experience as a servant and subsequently producing the first of the miscellanies for which he was later celebrated. With the help of Alexander Pope he set up as a bookseller—effectively a publisher in modern terms—at 'Tully's Head' in Pall Mall in 1735. In the course of the next two decades he established himself as one of the leading booksellers of the day, publishing works by, among others, Pope, Young, Gray, Goldsmith, and Johnson. In

1758 Dodsley joined forces with the 29-year-old Edmund Burke to found the *Annual Register*, a review of the past year's events, whose first issue appeared on 15 May 1759, just a week before Sterne approached him with his proposal.

In his letter of 23 May Sterne told Dodsley, ' You will rec^{ve} the Life & Opinions of Tristram Shandy, wch I choose to offer to You first', in a draft suitable for publication in an octavo volume of nearly 250 pages. If Dodsley were to publish the first volume, Sterne assured him, then a second volume would be ready 'by Christmas, or Nov^{r}'. Apart from Dodsley's undeniable prestige, Sterne also indicated that he had a personal reason for offering the publisher his work 'without any kind of Distrust', namely 'your general good Character, & the very handsome Recommendation of Mr Hinksman'.[16] This was John Hinxman, who had worked as an apprentice for Dodsley in London before moving to York in 1757 to take over the late John Hildyard's shop at the Sign of the Bible in the Stonegate.

Sterne's description of the work he was offering Dodsley is revealing of his own uncertainty of aim even as he wrote. Having aligned himself with contemporary satirists in suggesting he would target the 'Weak part of the Sciences' he indicated his ridicule would include 'every Thing <,> else, which I find Laugh-at-able in my way'.[17] The subjectivity implied by the last phrase worried Sterne, for if the world did not share his sense of humour the book would fail. Even as he composed his book in the spring of 1759, such failure seemed a distinct possibility. John Croft was later to relate that when Sterne 'read some of the loose sheets of the Copy of Tristram Shandy to a select company assembled at M^{r} [i.e. Stephen] Croft's for that purpose after dinner, they fell asleep at which Sterne was so nettled that he threw the Manuscript into the fire, and had not luckily Mr Croft rescued the scorched papers from the flames, the work wou'd have been consigned to oblivion'.[18] By May Sterne's understandable nervousness had given way, as he wrote, to a new-found confidence. In a postscript to his letter to Dodsley he alluded briefly to the opinion of his Yorkshire friends and neighbours. 'Some of our best Judges here w^{d} have had me, to have sent [it] into the world—wth cum Notis Variorum', he writes, adding as though in confirmation, 'there is great Room for it', before asserting his own judgement: 'but I thought it better to send it naked into the world.'[19] The idea that *Tristram Shandy* might come with variorum notes serves to emphasize once more the affinities of his first draft with Scriblerian satire; it was evidently as a prose *Dunciad* that the work was received by the Yorkshire friends to whom Sterne read extracts after dinner.[20] Lest he sound too hesitant, though, Sterne also refers with apparent confidence to his work's future success—'(wch such Criticks as this Latitude affords) say it can't fail of'.[21]

Where Sterne seemed understandably less sure of himself was in his manner of approaching Dodsley. When *A Political Romance* was at press he had insisted to his publishers that the pamphlet should be priced at 1 shilling—twice the cost of Francis Topham's *Reply*—and although he acknowledged 'I know you will tell me, That it is set too high . . . [my work], my dear Friend, is quite a *different Story*' (*Letters*, 68). In York Sterne got his way. When he wrote to Dodsley, however, his initial boldness was soon tempered by provincial diffidence: 'The Book will sell', Sterne asserted with assumed confidence, but while asking Dodsley to place a value on his work, he continued: 'tho' I believe the shortest Step is to tell You what I think tis worth myself—wch I hope is 50 pounds.'[22] Here, Sterne overreached himself, and from a second letter he wrote to Dodsley, in the autumn of 1759, we learn that the bookseller had declined to take up the work, at least on the author's terms. The fact is not surprising, for £50 represented a very large sum for a work from an unknown author—Dodsley himself had given Edmund Burke a mere 6 guineas for his *A Vindication of Natural Society* in 1756, and no more than 20 guineas for the copyright to the *Enquiry into the Origin of Our Ideas of the Sublime and Beautiful* the following year. Shrewdly enough, however, Dodsley did not simply reject Sterne's work. Instead, he made a counter-offer of £20, while pleading particular circumstances for his unwillingness to go higher. At the age of 56 Dodsley was, in fact, on the point of retiring from business, leaving the firm in the hands of his brother James, more than twenty years his junior. Combining prudence with tact, Robert Dodsley wrote that the price Sterne asked 'was too much to risk on a single Vol.—which, if it happen'd not to sell, w^d be hard upon [my] Brother'.[23]

It is easy to imagine Sterne's initial disappointment. Dodsley's rejection of his proposal was nevertheless beneficial in the longer term. His reply is lost, but it is evident that Dodsley offered Sterne acute and constructive criticism which the author took seriously, persuading him not merely to reconsider but substantially to rewrite his first draft. Throughout the late spring and early summer of 1759 Sterne set about the process of revision with determination. In revising, he undoubtedly listened to the criticisms of friends and acquaintances to whom he showed his manuscript. More importantly, however, the extensive changes to his original draft represented an effective acknowledgement of the authority of Dodsley as a successful London bookseller, for they were determined above all by the desire to make his work more attractive to a metropolitan audience. Certainly, the postscript to his second letter suggests that Dodsley had told Sterne that his work was too provincial—and that satire (at least personal satire) was now out of fashion. This was prudent advice, well designed for the times: among others, both Lord Lyttelton and William Warburton had recently argued against the prevalence of satire.

So Sterne removed local satire from his work, and considerably softened the bawdy, even downright obscenity, which had marked the 'Fragment in the Manner of Rabelais'. All the same, *Tristram Shandy* is not a chaste book and it is unsurprising to find that even those well-wishers who enjoyed Sterne's humour urged caution on him, 'especially with regard to Prudence, as a divine' (*Letters*, 76). 'You thought in your heart', Sterne was to recall, writing to one anonymous adviser, 'the vein of humour too free & gay for the solemn colour of My coat' (*Letters*, 76). Nor was this cautious acquaintance alone. Sterne revealed that his friend Marmaduke Fothergill, a York surgeon, whom Sterne termed 'My best of Criticks & well wishers', would preach 'daily to Me Upon Your Text—"get Your Preferment first Lory! he says—& then Write & Welcome"' (*Letters*, 76). This was exactly the opposite of what Sterne wished to hear. The enforced destruction of *A Political Romance* and the faded hopes of securing Fountayne's support for progress in his ecclesiastical career were too fresh in his mind. 'But suppose preferment is long acoming (& for aught I know I may not be preferr'd till the Resurrection of the Just)', he demurred with grim humour (*Letters*, 76). Even so, Sterne recognized the soundness of the advice. 'I will use all reasonable caution,' he promised, 'Only with this caution along with it, not to spoil My Book;—that is the air and originality of it, which must resemble the Author—& I fear 'tis a Number of these slighter touches which Mark this resemblance & Identify it from all Others of the [same] Stamp.'

Sterne's rapidly growing sense of confidence in his own judgement is unmistakable, yet he was still perturbed by his vulnerability to accusations of indecency and impropriety. 'I deny I have gone as farr as Swift,' he protested, 'He keeps a due distance from Rabelais—& I keep a due distance from him—Swift has said a hundred things I durst Not Say—Unless I was Dean of St. Patricks—' (*Letters*, 76). Remembering his experience with *A Political Romance*, Sterne toyed with the idea of attempting to cover himself against the criticism of his enemies within clerical circles at York by submitting his new work to the archbishop in advance. Whether he did so is uncertain; if he did, Sterne would have found Gilbert a notably enthusiastic reader but a poor guide to what might be permitted a clergyman. The archbishop was so delighted with *Tristram Shandy* that he supposedly reread the first two volumes every six weeks.[24] So uncensorious a reaction would not be echoed by all readers of *Tristram Shandy*—clerical or lay.

Throughout the summer and early autumn of 1759 Sterne kept himself hard at work, transforming the early draft he had offered Robert Dodsley into the first two volumes of *The Life and Opinions of Tristram Shandy, Gentleman*. It was a busy summer—yet it was made busier still by a crisis in Laurence Sterne's already troubled relationship with his wife. The result was that the ten months that passed between the burning of *A Political Romance* and the publication of *Tristram Shandy* in December 1759 were one of the most fraught periods of Sterne's life.

The relationship between Laurence and Elizabeth Sterne had been troubled for many years. Sterne respected but did not love Elizabeth. Respect drove him, on several occasions throughout his life, to acknowledge freely to others that she had given him no real cause for complaint against her. Yet by the 1750s he no longer found in their relationship either sexual fulfilment or emotional satisfaction. Earlier in their marriage quarrels between them had sent the husband to seek gratification and consolation elsewhere. Since Elizabeth once apparently found Laurence in bed with one of her maids, it seems likely that the purpose of Sterne's sudden journeys to York was clear enough to her. To attempt—or even wish—to apportion blame in these domestic quarrels would be inappropriate. Both Laurence and Elizabeth Sterne were often unhappy in their different ways, confined by their limited income to the life of a small village, and increasingly disappointed in the hopes they had once entertained for their lives.

If only because they had little choice, however, the Sternes remained together for over twenty years, endeavouring to make the best of their situation. At times success or misfortune brought them closer together. Elizabeth's miscarriages and the stillbirths or early deaths of at least two children must have placed their relationship under considerable strain. The birth of their only surviving child, Lydia, on the other hand, enabled the couple to subordinate their differences, at least briefly, to the demands of parenthood. Certainly, both Laurence and Elizabeth Sterne were caring parents—and affection for their daughter is a feature of many of Laurence's letters.

Other events united the Sternes of necessity. The purchase of the Tindal Farm in 1744, for instance, had been a venture carefully considered by both husband and wife. Though it would not in the end be the success they had hoped, their attempts to make a go of farming may have helped smooth the surface of daily life, at least initially.

A common concern for shared friends could also bring the Sternes together. In 1758, for instance, when the Revd John Blake, a decade younger than Sterne and recently appointed master of the Royal Grammar School in York, courted Margaret Ash, both husband and wife took a lively interest in the affair. Fixing a date for a meeting, Laurence Sterne promised that 'from eleven that Day to three, both me & my Rib are at Y^{r} Service, to club our Understandings all together, and I'm sure we shall all be able in 4 hours to digest a much harder Plann & settle it to Y^{rs} & all our Wishes' (*Letters*, 52). In another letter Sterne wrote, 'Be assured we will never fail our friend at any Time much less at a Pinch' (*Letters*, 54), and the use of the first-person plural pronoun is frequently employed at this time—though rare elsewhere in Sterne's letters. In November Sterne told Blake that he and his wife had discussed an aspect of the affair 'a full hour'. Elizabeth Sterne concerned herself sufficiently with her friend's courtship to send not only Blake but also his intended bride a gift from the farm: 'my Wife sends you & Mrs Ash a Couple of Stubble Geese—one for each' (*Letters*, 60), Sterne wrote to Blake in September 1758. This attempt to help smooth Blake's path was evidently no more successful than the letter's own efforts; his prospective mother-in-law declined to give her daughter an adequate dowry and the marriage between Blake and Margaret Ash never took place. Despite his efforts to assist his friend, however, Sterne, is unlikely to have regretted the outcome, for he described Mrs Ash's attempts as 'a Contexture of Plots agst y^{r} Fortune & Person, Grand Mama standing first in the Dramatis Personae, the Lôup Garôu or raw head & Bloody bones to frighten Master Jacky into silence & make him go to bed with Missy, *supperless* and in Peace' (*Letters*, 58).

Even in his dealings with their friend, however, Sterne was behaving in a manner not likely to have brought his wife great peace of mind. The openness with which the couple considered Blake's negotiations with Margaret Ash and her mother found an altogether obscurer counterpart in Sterne's other dealings with his fellow clergyman. The series of letters Sterne wrote to Blake are spiked with private references to concerns—probably financial in some way—Sterne desired to be kept very much hidden from his wife. 'I have transacted my Bristol Affair,' Sterne wrote with more apprehension than confidence, 'The Express (when God sends it) Monsr Apothecary [Theophilus Garencières] will direct as agreed upon between us, & I think I have put the whole into such a train that I cannot miscarry' (*Letters*, 50). Although any attempt to understand this is necessarily tentative, the letter seems to refer to a financial speculation which involved lending money, perhaps at high rates of interest (there seem to have been frequent accounts) in conjunction with John Blake and a Jack Taylor. Although Elizabeth Sterne evidently knew something of the venture, the accounts of which were kept by John Blake, Sterne was anxious to keep details in the dark. 'I tore off the Bottom', Sterne wrote of one of Blake's letters, 'before I let my Wife see it, to save a Lye—However She has since observed the Curtaildment and seem'd very desirous of knowing what it Containd, wch I conceal, & only say 'twas something that no Way concernd *her or me*—So Say the same, If she interrogates' (*Letters*, 54). Such prevarication was repeated later in the affair. Sterne warned Blake that Elizabeth Sterne planned to come to York on the same day as they had arranged to meet with Jack Taylor. 'But if she does twill be of no Consequence to the Affair, as she will dine at Bridges & believes the Meeting concerns ye private Affairs of friend Taylor—' (*Letters*, 59).

Even the little that Sterne told his wife of the affair may have been virtually forced out of him. Certainly, Elizabeth Sterne had good reason in 1758 to be more than ordinarily curious about a letter torn in such a way as to suggest her husband had something to hide. Earlier that year Laurence Sterne had been involved in a village scandal potentially damaging both to his relations with his parishioners and with his wife.

By Sterne's own account, an agent to Lord Fauconberg of Newburgh Priory, named Young, had spread a rumour that Sterne had been speaking openly of an adulterous liaison between two parishioners. The woman in question, Catherine Sturdy, was the wife of a former churchwarden at Sutton-on-the-Forest. The man's identity is unknown, but Sterne wrote to him on 14 March 1758 flatly denying the allegation or that he believed there to be any substance to the story itself. By this time, however, village gossips had brought the tale to the ears of Catherine Sturdy's husband Robert, who was very ill and in poor spirits. The story, Sterne reported, 'prey'd upon him' until Sterne managed to put his mind at rest.[25] Sterne was evidently incensed by the propagation of the story through 'this dirty Village', and challenged Young before witnesses 'with the Baseness of reporting such a Falshood'. Young denied responsibility in his turn, characterizing the tale as 'a Lye invented & spread ab^{t} by a Company of idle Dykers &c, wthout any Hint <of> or Foundation from him. or me', and suggested it to have been done 'by malicious people with no End but to create Disturbance betwixt Mr Sterne & Mr Sturdy'.

There was worse, however. In the same letter, Sterne reported another false allegation of sexual irregularity, this time against himself: 'nam[e]ly,

That In consideration of a favor shown by me in procuring a Farm for an poor Farmer here,—I had lay'[d with] his Wife'. 'This Calumny', Sterne continued, 'was charitably bro[ught to] Mrs Sterne, who only made merry [upon it].'[26] Sterne's denial is strong and forthright. He concludes: 'I am with all Truth, Y^{rs} faithfully'—and there seems no reason to disbelieve his protestations that he had been slandered. Yet in linking the vicar with one tale of sexual intrigue the story attests both to the dislike or resentment Sterne could inspire in the neighbourhood and to village recognition of the weak side of his character. Moreover, given Laurence Sterne's past sexual history, the story can hardly have failed at least to remind an injured wife that her husband's infidelities were public knowledge; at worst, the gossip—whatever Sterne said—may have aroused Elizabeth's suspicion that the story was not without foundation. When, later that same year, Laurence Sterne was again, and rather clumsily, hiding something from his wife, we may wonder whether her thoughts did not turn to the possibility that her husband was, once more, involved in sexual intrigue.

Perhaps they did, for the events of 1758 apparently came to a head in the following year. According to John Croft, Laurence Sterne's sexual conduct resulted in Elizabeth suffering a complete mental breakdown. Mrs Sterne, Croft alleged, 'once caught him with the maid, when she pulled him out of bed on the Floor and soon after went out of her senses, when she fancied herself the Queen of Bohemia'.[27]

As always, Croft's account must be treated with reserve. Even so, most of his stories seem to have had some factual basis, and Elizabeth Sterne's illness can be verified from at least one other source. An anonymous acquaintance of Sterne, whose letter dated 15 April 1760 is an important source of information about his life at around this period, wrote: 'I can say nothing to the report you have heard about Mrs. Sterne; the few times I have seen her she was all life and spirits; too much so, I thought. [Sterne] told me, in a letter last Christmas, that his wife had lost her senses by a stroke of the palsy.'[28]

All that may, with reasonable certainty, be concluded from these different versions is that Elizabeth Sterne did indeed suffer a serious mental breakdown in 1759. John Croft's hostile account seems, at the very least, oversimplified, but it is impossible to rule out the possibility of a connection between Sterne's recurrent infidelities and his wife's illness. Sterne's own attribution of Elizabeth's disordered state to the palsy may reflect either his genuine belief or represent a conscious or unconscious attempt to avert such censure of himself as would necessarily follow the attribution of his wife's illness to his own behaviour.

It is not, of course, impossible that John Croft had information generally kept quiet by Sterne's friends. Certainly, one detail in his anecdote—concerning Elizabeth Sterne's delusion that she was Queen of Bohemia—suggests that he was drawing on an established account of the affair. Croft, though, was not above embellishing any story, however much to the discredit of those it concerned. A more elaborate version of the incident appeared from his pen in 1792 in *Scrapeana*, a short joke book that might, given the quality of Croft's material, have profitably been even shorter. Mrs Sterne, we read:

> fancied herself the Queen of Bohemia. Tristram, her husband, to amuse and induce her to take the air, proposed coursing, in the way practised in Bohemia; for that purpose he procured bladders, and filled them with beans, and tied them to the wheels of a single horse chair. When he drove madam into a stubble field, with the motion of the carriage and the bladders, rattle bladder, rattle; it alarmed the hares, and the greyhounds were ready to take them.[29]

In the version he passed on to Caleb Whitefoord Croft wrote that Sterne treated his wife 'with all the supposed respect due to a crowned head, and continued to practice this farcicall mockery during her confinem^{t} under a Lunatick Doctor at a private house at York'.[30] If Sterne really behaved as Croft alleged, and with no better motive than to exploit the comic possibilities of the pathetic delusions his own behaviour had led to in his wife, then he would certainly deserve the censure Croft would accord him. Yet, whatever germ of truth the tale may contain, the details of the story and Croft's interpretation do not bear close scrutiny.

Versions of the episode current at the time—Croft was writing thirty-five or thirty-six years after the events—find Sterne presented rather as an object of sympathy than of scorn. The Revd Dr Thomas Newton, Jaques Sterne's successor as precentor of York Minster and soon to be bishop of Bristol, wrote to the Revd John Dealtary from London on 4 March 1760: 'I wish Laury Sterne may have more comfort of his wife than he has had.'[31] Such a remark by one closely in touch with events at York suggests that Sterne was in no way generally held responsible for his wife's illness among those who knew him, or who would have been among the first to have heard the worst of a clergyman who had recently aroused resentment enough. Nor is Sterne's attitude towards his wife, as it emerges from letters to different correspondents, consonant with the insensitivity Croft alleged. As much as his wife, Sterne seems deeply to have regretted the failure of their marriage and to have endeavoured, as far as possible, to have compensated for his physical and later emotional infidelities by a scrupulous attention to the material well-being of his wife and the needs of their daughter Lydia. If, before the success of *Tristram Shandy*, he sought refuge from domestic unhappiness with prostitutes in York, the sentimental attachments of the years of his fame may equally well be seen as attempts to find the sexual and emotional satisfaction he craved. Certainly, it is hard not to think of Sterne's own situation when reading his sermon 'The Levite and his Concubine', in which the preacher sympathizes with the Levite who sought a woman 'to share his solitude, and fill up that uncomfortable blank in the heart'.[32] Sterne's own gloss on the biblical text is, it is true, not without an element of wishful thinking, leading him to declare that 'as the Scripture has left us no kind of comment upon it, 'tis a story on which the heart cannot be at a loss for what to say, or the imagination for what to suppose—the danger is, humanity may say too much'.[33] Sterne's parishioners and clerical circles in York may have been less kind, yet Sterne surely deeply felt the sentiments he borrowed for his sermon: '*it is not good for man to be alone*'.[34]

In any case, whatever the causes of Elizabeth Sterne's illness in 1759, it did not deter Sterne from quickly finding consolation elsewhere. By the end of the year he was writing affectionate, very intimate letters to a young singer working on an engagement in York. Catherine Fourmantel seems first to have come to York, along with her mother, in the spring of 1759 to sing in the Assembly Rooms. Given Sterne's love of music, it seems likely that he heard her sing and found means to effect an introduction. The earliest surviving letters probably date from the late autumn of 1759, when Catherine Fourmantel was in York to fulfil a number of engagements; she sang, certainly, on 29 November and 31 December 1759. Sterne's absorption with her is evident from his letters. 'My dear Kitty,' he wrote on one occasion:

> If this Billet catches you in Bed, You are a lazy, sleepy little Slut—and I am a giddy foolish unthinking fellow for keeping You so late up—but this Sabbath is a day of rest—at the same time that it is a day of Sorrow—for I shall not see my dear Creature today—unless you meet me at Taylor's half an hour after twelve—but in this do as You like—I have orderd Matthew to turn thief & steal you a quart of Honey—
>
> What is Honey to the sweetness of thee, who art sweeter than all the flowers it comes from.—I love you to distraction Kitty—& will love you on so to Eternity—so adieu & believe what, time only will prove me, that I am
>
> Y^rs^
>
> (*Letters*, 82–3)

Perhaps because of the unhappy months he had spent during his wife's illness, Sterne threw himself with abandon into this new relationship. The characteristic intimacy of the letters suggests a considerable degree of trust in Catherine Fourmantel's discretion, or a greater degree of infatuation in Sterne. Even in the early stages of their relationship Sterne repeatedly vowed fidelity. One letter concluded with a declaration that he personified a love '*qui ne Changera pas, que en mourant*'; elsewhere he is the 'Affectionate and faithful' Laurence Sterne. That Sterne did not even scruple to sign his full name to compromising billets-doux suggests that his affection for Catherine Fourmantel was fully reciprocated.

What qualities the singer saw in the older, married clergyman we can only surmise. The letters he wrote are full of good humour, and Sterne's ready wit doubtless appealed in a society rather less lively than that to which the singer was used in London. Thanks to the controversy surrounding *A Political Romance* Sterne had acquired a certain notoriety and a reputation as a witty author. Writing—at least Sterne's writing—was certainly one topic of conversation, and perhaps a talent that impressed Catherine Fourmantel. Besides gifts of honey and wine, Sterne presented the singer with a copy of his first printed sermon, *Elijah and the Case of the Widow of Zerephath consider'd*. He may also have read her parts of *Tristram Shandy* as he was composing or revising it, with a view to discovering which qualities were most likely to find ready acceptance among fashionable London novel-readers. Certainly, the fact that he signed one letter 'Yorick' implies that she was quite familiar with his self-portrait as the sentimental parson of the first volume of *Tristram Shandy*.

By tradition, Catherine Fourmantel has been identified with the eroticized figure whom Tristram calls his 'dear, dear Jenny', and though Sterne may well have written these sections before meeting the young singer, there is every likelihood that by the time the book was published he indeed identified her with the new-found object of his affection. It was Catherine Fourmantel with whom Sterne declared himself in love as he revised his book, she to whom he looked for assistance in promoting it in London, and she to whom he wrote most often and with unreserved delight to report the success of his work and his own triumphant reception in the capital.

In the autumn of 1759 that success was no more than a couple of months away. Yet for Sterne the renown that would shortly be his must have seemed at best the wildest daydream—if indeed it was imaginable at all. He had worked hard at revising, as he informed Robert Dodsley in a letter posted from York on 5 October. 'All Locality is taken out of the

Book—the Satyr general,—Notes are added where wanted—& the whole made more saleable—about a hundred & 50 pages added'.[35] Despite the revision and additions that enabled him to produce a text such as would make two volumes rather than the one he had previously offered Dodsley, Sterne did not now ask the publisher to purchase the copyright from him directly. By policy or conviction he acknowledged the justice of Dodsley's refusal to pay £50 for the work of an unknown author, especially since the loss would fall on his brother James who had now taken over the business. 'You need not be told by me, How much Authors are inclined to over-rate their Productions',[36] Sterne wrote, before turning his remark into a graceful compliment to Dodsley.

Instead of having Dodsley purchase the copyright, Sterne proposed 'to print a lean Edition, in 2 small Vols', at his own expense. The edition would be, he suggested, of the size and with the same paper as Samuel Johnson's oriental tale *Rasselas*, which Dodsley had published in April. Sterne's intention was 'merely to feel the Pulse of the World—& that I may know what Price to set upon the Remaining Volumes, from the reception of these'. As encouragement to Dodsley, Sterne repeated that those who had read the book expected its success, and he suggested that he would subsequently 'free myself of all future troubles of this kind [i.e. publication], & bargain with You, if possible for the rest as they come out which will be every six Months'. 'If my Book fails of Success,' Sterne added, 'the Loss falls where it ought to do.' What, precisely, he was proposing was that the first two volumes of *Tristram Shandy* should be printed in York and sent up to London for sale at Dodsley's shop in Pall Mall. Sterne told Dodsley that as he would 'correct every Proof myself, it shall go perfect into the World—& be printed in so creditable a way as to Paper Type etc—as to do no Dishonour to You, who I know never chuse to print a Book meanly'. '[W]ill you patronise my Book upon these Terms,' Sterne enquired, '& be as kind a friend to it as if you had bought the Copy?'[37] Anxiously, he asked Dodsley to reply by return.

A publisher so astute as Dodsley was not likely to have been taken in by Sterne's ingenuous attempt to cast him now as a patron *manqué*. Nevertheless, he agreed to do as Sterne requested. Having thereby effectively secured Dodsley as publisher of his book, the author arranged for the printing of the two volumes of *Tristram Shandy* by Ann Ward, who had taken over the business of her husband Caesar following his death earlier in 1759.[38] These volumes—lacking any indication of their provincial origin and dated 1760—came off of the press probably during the second week of December 1759. By 14 December, Sterne had already dispatched no fewer than eight sets to the 29-year-old Charles Watson-Wentworth, marquess of Rockingham, who had requested them as soon as they were available.[39] The edition was, as Sterne had suggested, a 'lean' one; John Croft claimed it was a mere 200 copies (though 500 has been suggested as a more reliable estimate).[40]

Even this small run involved Sterne in expense beyond his means. Either for the sake of Elizabeth's health or in the (mistaken) anticipation of being preferred to a residentiaryship, Sterne had recently settled his wife and daughter in York, in a house in Minster Yard, thereby worsening his usual financial difficulties. Accordingly he was forced to seek a loan from an acquaintance, William Phillips Lee, to defray the costs of printing. For Sterne to have borrowed in this manner—even if the sum involved amounted to less than the £100 mentioned by John Croft—suggests the extent of the author's faith in the commercial potential of his work. The involvement of Dodsley, coupled with the fact that Lee was willing to advance a significant sum, undoubtedly reinforced the sense of confidence engendered by the favourable comments of local critics.[41] Certainly, Sterne had been active in informing prospective purchasers that publication of his book was imminent. Earlier in the autumn he had plans to ensure that a copy of his book would reach the archbishop of York,[42] and he had even succeeded in attracting the attention of Lord Rockingham (it is not impossible that Sterne had, unsuccessfully, approached him with the idea of dedicating his fiction to this local Yorkshire grandee, lord-lieutenant of the North and East Ridings). Equally importantly, his work was the subject not merely of local knowledge but of eager speculation in York. When one of Sterne's female correspondents told him that she had heard that he was 'busy writing an extraordinary book', he acknowledged the fact while intriguingly urging his correspondent: 'till you read my Tristram, do not, like some people, condemn it.'

Yet despite the pre-publication stir the book was causing in the restricted circles of York, Sterne was not naive enough to believe that his two small volumes would as easily gain favour with a metropolitan audience—at least not unaided. By securing Dodsley as his publisher, even if not on his own preferred terms, Sterne had made a good start. By the third week of December the first advertisement for the book appeared in a London newspaper, the *London Chronicle*, part-owned by Dodsley:

> In a few Days will be published . . . in Two Volumes, Price 5s. neatly bound, The Life and Opinions of Tristram Shandy, Gent. [at] York, printed for and sold by John Hinxman (successor to the late Mr.

> Hildyard) Bookseller, in Stonegate; J. Dodsley in Pallmall, and M. Cooper in Pater-noster-row, London: and by all the Booksellers in Great-Britain and Ireland.[43]

Having done what he could by more conventional means, Sterne now embarked on a piece of self-promotion as ingenious as it was audacious. He wrote out a letter, dated 1 January 1760, in praise of his own book, which he persuaded Catherine Fourmantel to copy and send in her own name to London, almost certainly to David Garrick. At Sterne's behest the singer wrote: 'There are two Volumes just published which have made a great noise, & have had a prodigious Run; for in 2 Days after they came out, the Bookseller sold two hundred—& continues selling them very fast. It is, The Life & Opinions of Tristram Shandy' (*Letters*, 85). As an excuse for writing, Catherine Fourmantel was to tell Garrick that the author was a good friend of hers, to whom she was greatly indebted for having assisted her when she was unknown in York. 'His name is Sterne,' Fourmantel continued, 'a gentleman of great Preferment & a Prebendary of the Church of York, & has a <pro> great Character in these Parts as a man of Learning & wit' (*Letters*, 85–6).

In order further to intrigue Garrick, the letter concludes: 'the Graver People however say, tis not fit for young Ladies to read his Book. so perhaps you'l think it not fit for a young Lady to recommend it however the Nobility, & great Folks stand up mightily for it. & say tis a good Book tho' a little tawdry in some places' (*Letters*, 86). Lest Garrick should feel that this 'witty smart Book' was destined to be merely a provincial success, Sterne not only had Catherine Fourmantel reveal that copies were available in London but added cleverly 'so perhaps you have seen it'—thereby flattering Garrick with the idea that he was aware of everything worthwhile as soon as it was published, while gently making sure that he did not fall behind alleged fashion on this occasion. Since Catherine Fourmantel begins her letter 'I dare say You will wonder to receive an Epistle from me', her acquaintance with Garrick was most probably a slight one—and Garrick may well have seen through the ruse. As it turned out Sterne's anxieties were unnecessary, for his book would very quickly achieve a fashionable success of precisely the kind its author had imagined, and Sterne would need no intermediary to plead his cause in London.

9
Tristram Shandy and Parson Yorick, 1760

From February to December 1759 Sterne had worked tirelessly to achieve success for his new work. He had sought the reaction of his Yorkshire friends and corresponded with Robert Dodsley in London. He had taken the bookseller's initial rejection and suggestions for improvement with good heart, and had substantially rewritten and expanded his fiction. He had found finance and dealt with matters of paper and printing, so as to ensure that the first edition appeared to all possible advantage. Finally, he had endeavoured to draw his book's existence to the attention of as many of those, in Yorkshire and London, as might help it on its appearance in the world.

All of this Sterne had achieved in a period that saw the death of Agnes Sterne and while Elizabeth Sterne was seriously ill as the result of a breakdown. Whatever his feelings about his troubled relationships with his mother and wife, Sterne was acutely aware of the paradox of having written a comic novel in such seemingly unpropitious circumstances. The book was, he told Lord Rockingham, 'every word of it wrote in affliction; & under a constant uneasiness of mind. Cervantes wrote his humorous Satyr in a Prison—& Scarron his, in pain & Anguish—such Philosophers as will account for every thing, may explain this for me'.[1]

For all the effort Sterne invested in his book, he could not guarantee its success. He was fortunate, then, to find in his first reviewer William Kenrick, a sympathetic and perceptive reader. Kenrick noticed *Tristram Shandy* in the appendix to the July–December 1759 volume of the *Monthly Review*, and not only praised it but astutely indicated one of the work's most distinctive features: 'Of Lives and *Adventures*', Kenrick declared, 'the public have had enough, and, perhaps, more than enough, long ago. A consideration that probably induced the droll Mr. Tristram Shandy to entitle the performance before us, his Life and *Opinions*.'[2] Certainly, the recasting of his work as fictional autobiography represented the greatest change in Sterne's drastic revision of his original draft during the previous ten months. In effect, it transformed the author from an eccentric, backward-looking satirist to the foremost contemporary exponent of a peculiarly modern form of writing (so modern that the very term 'autobiography' had not yet made its way into the language[3]). Yet if, in privileging private over public experience, Tristram was joining contemporary writers of many kinds, then, in offering readers his 'Opinions' he seemed intent on outdoing them all. 'As you proceed further with me,' he declared, 'the slight acquaintance which is now beginning betwixt us, will grow into familiarity; and . . . terminate in friendship . . . then nothing which has touched me will be thought trifling in its nature, or tedious in its telling' (TS I. vi. 10). William Kenrick was alert to the dangers Sterne courted in his rejection of 'adventures', noting that the author seemed 'extremely fond of digressions, and of giving his historical Readers the slip on all occasions'.[4] Yet, although he cautioned that 'It would not be amiss . . . if, for the future, he paid a little more regard to going strait forward, lest the generality of his Readers, despairing of ever seeing the end of their journey, should tire, and leave him to jog on by himself',[5] Kenrick avowed his own intention of accompanying Tristram to the end of his tale. The author, he concluded, was 'a writer infinitely more ingenious and entertaining than any other of the present race of novellists. His characters are striking and singular, his observations shrewd and pertinent; and, making a few exceptions, his humour is easy and genuine.'[6]

Sterne could only have been delighted. Yet the tenor of this laudatory first notice quickly found an echo in the reviews which followed. Although the anonymous writer in the January number of the *Critical Review* began by seeming to throw up his hands in exasperation—'This is a humorous performance, of which we are unable to convey any distinct ideas to our readers'[7]—the notice was almost wholly favourable. (Indeed, the single hint of reserve, in which the writer described Uncle Toby, Corporal Trim, and Dr Slop as 'excellent imitations of certain characters in a modern truly Cervantic performance',[8] may be attributed to a tactful desire to pay tribute to the editor of the *Critical Review*, Tobias Smollett, the revised edition of whose *Peregrine Pickle*—to which the reviewer alludes—had appeared in 1758.[9]) For the rest, the writer alerted readers to Tristram's teasingly digressive narrative, and to particularly diverting or eccentric episodes: Uncle Toby's embarrassment in describing the siege of Namur, Corporal Trim's reading of the sermon, and Dr Slop's fall from his horse into the mud after his collision with Obadiah.

Like William Kenrick, the *Critical* reviewer also recognized the novelty of the book and concluded by abbreviating his review, referring readers to the work itself, desiring only that 'they will suspend their judgment till they have dipt into the second volume'.[10] Writing in an admittedly weak imitation of the novel's style, a reviewer for the *London Magazine* was still more enthusiastic: 'Oh rare Tristram Shandy!—Thou very sensible—humorous—pathetick—humane—unaccountable!—what shall we call thee?—Rabelais, Cervantes, what?'[11]

'Sensible', 'humorous', 'pathetick', 'humane', 'unaccountable': this critic did nothing if not suggest the broad scope of Sterne's writing. If early readers were led to *Tristram Shandy* by reviews, then they were surely beguiled into reading further by the extraordinary breadth of subject-matter so variously touched on in the following pages. In *Le Moyen de Parvenir*, one of Sterne's favourite works, François Béroalde de Verville had proclaimed that, in a world full of books—'pretendus livres, cayers, volumes, tomes, œuvres, livrets, opuscules, libelles, fragmens, épitomes, registres, inventaires, copies, brouillards, originaux, exemplaires, manuscrits' (would-be books, copy-books, volumes, tomes, works, booklets, treatises, libels, fragments, abridgements, registers, inventories, copies, day-books, originals, samples, manuscripts)[12]—his own would be 'LE CENTRE DE TOUS LES LIVRES'. In *Tristram Shandy* Sterne seems similarly out to persuade readers that his work too would be the 'CENTRE OF ALL BOOKS'. Those readers would quickly encounter authors familiar and less familiar, old and new: Virgil, Shakespeare, Cervantes, Rabelais, Bunyan, Montaigne, Joseph Hall, and Voltaire, along with the tales of Tom Thumb and Jack Hickathrift, as well as Cicero, Pufendorf, Horace, Locke, Dr James Mackenzie, Saxo Grammaticus, Niccolò Tartaglia, and Dr John Burton—to name a very few—all huddled together according to no immediately obvious plan. Even the familiar might be delusive: 'Pray, Sir, in all the reading which you have ever read, did you ever read such a book as *Locke*'s Essay upon the Human Understanding?——Don't answer me rashly,--because many, I know, quote the book, who have not read it,---and many have read it who understand it not, (*TS* II. ii. 70). Since, like many of his readers, Sterne knew Locke at least partly through popularizations of the philosopher's work, especially in *The Spectator*, it is not entirely clear what considered answer the author himself might have given to Tristram's question.

The first readers, however, were left with many puzzles besides Locke. What was real learning and what was invention? Many assumed that the lengthy judgement by three French theologians concerning the validity of inter-uterine baptism, given in the original French (*TS* I. xx. 49–51) must be a satirical invention—obliging Sterne to add a footnoted reference to his actual source in the second, London, edition of his book. Even the most learned readers were confused: Sir Horace Mann thought the whole book '*humbugging*'—but he wasn't sure. There was good reason. Sterne was a great admirer of encyclopaedias, compilations, and digests—works of popular enlightenment characteristic of the age, from which he borrowed, stole, paraphrased, and misquoted at will. 'It is an age so full of light,' he was later to write in *A Sentimental Journey*, 'Knowledge in most of its branches, and in most affairs, is like music in an Italian street, whereof those may partake, who pay nothing' (*ASJ* 84).[13]

Sterne's amiable metaphor does not entirely conceal the problems his work addresses so lightheartedly. If polite readers and magazine reviewers alike were baffled, then might not any man's—or woman's—opinion be as valid as theirs? Playful as it is, the laughter *Tristram Shandy* provoked was often nervous enough, for not even Sterne's abundant humour can long disguise the fact that virtually every contested area of eighteenth-century life—philosophy, theology, law, politics, gender, education, and medicine among them—has its part in the novel. As books of every description flooded from the nation's presses, no single individual could hope to read even a fraction of the works which booksellers placed before them. How, then, to choose, or know, what was of real value? In so wantonly confusing real with feigned knowledge, Sterne (or Tristram?) was touching on one his age's greatest cultural anxieties: what was it to be an author? One contemporary, Thomas Gray, argued that the true poet required 'a liberal education, with a degree of literature [i.e. learning], & various knowledge'.[14] A writer who had no personal need to ingratiate himself with readers who might be persuaded to purchase his work, Gray was wholly taken aback when he unwittingly produced, in his 'An Elegy Wrote in a Country Churchyard' (1751), a work of immediate popular—and hence commercial—appeal. His response, in 'The Bard' and 'The Progress of Poetry', published in 1757, was to reassert his status as a serious author by penning two ambitious odes widely regarded (to Gray's gratification) as incomprehensible.[15] As Sterne's fellow-prebendary William Mason noted, however, Gray's life was spent in 'that kind of learned leisure, which has only self-improvement and self-gratification for its object'.[16] No wonder, then, that Gray might fear that writing was to be given over to 'slaves and Mercenaries' who made 'gain their principal end, & [who] subject themselves to the prevailing taste of those, whose fortune only distinguishes them from the Multitude'.[17]

It was, however, just the fashionable, upwardly mobile, and affluent audience Gray feared that, to Sterne's delight, so enthusiastically took up *Tristram Shandy*. A contemporary fellow-novelist and cleric, the Revd Francis Coventry, author of *The History of Pompey the Little; or, the Adventures of a Lap-Dog* (1751), had criticized the 'pride and pedantry of learned men, who are willing to monopolize reading to themselves, and therefore fastidiously decry all books that are on a level with common understandings, as empty, trifling and impertinent'.[18] Like Coventry, Sterne rejected such fastidiousness, satirizing pendantry and leaving Tristram to boast that, when read through completely, his 'opinions' will be seen to take in 'all ranks, professions, and denominations of men whatever' (TS I. iv. 7). This was a joke, but a pointed one. Though his work would soon be criticized just as Coventry predicted, Sterne produced in *Tristram Shandy* a book which indeed took for its audience the entire reading public—male and female, young and old, learned and unlearned—giving each member of it liberty to form his or her opinions on the matter it contained.[19] More even than other novels of its time—to say nothing of more prestigious forms of writing—*Tristram Shandy* flattered its readers by assuming their intelligence rather than instructing or preaching at them. In *Tom Jones* Henry Fielding had declared 'every Reader in the World' to be a critic[20]—but he also made it his task to ensure that every reader brought 'correct' standards of critical judgement to bear on his book and on the world. Samuel Richardson might compliment those whom he called those 'Sovereign Judges, my readers', but he acted still more arbitrarily than Fielding in vigorously appealing their verdicts when they differed from his own. Sterne, by contrast, acknowledged with unfeigned conviction that '*De gustibus non est disputandum* . . . there is no disputing against HOBBY-HORSES' (*TS*. I. viii. 12)—and left readers to form their own reflections on his opinions. There would be plenty for them to do. Tristram himself was quick to advertise that, as his 'Life' continued, there would be:

> Accounts to reconcile:
> Anecdotes to pick up:
> Inscriptions to make out:
> Stories to weave in:
> Traditions to sift:
> Personages to call upon:
> Panegyricks to paste up at this door:
> Pasquinades at that: . . .
>
> (*TS* I. xiv. 32)

Sterne knew how to advertise his work well enough. Meanwhile, the

London Magazine thought highly enough of his book to assert that if, as Tristram had promised, he were to continue writing two volumes yearly, he might publish fifty 'abounding with the profitable and pleasant, like these', and still be 'read and admired'. 'Admired!' concluded the notice 'by whom? Why, Sir, by the best, if not the most numerous class of mankind.'[21]

The praise was doubtless gratifying, but Sterne had also judged his market better than the reviewer. His book did more than attract the admiration of a few; it sold well to the many. By the time Sterne arrived in London in March the small York edition was exhausted, and James Dodsley was soon busying himself with a larger, second edition of the first two volumes. Advertised as forthcoming in March, the edition—with a number of corrections and additions, including the dedication to William Pitt, and boasting as frontispiece Simon Ravenet's engraving of the illustration Sterne had successfully solicited from William Hogarth—eventually appeared in early April. Two more London editions were to appear in the course of the year, as well as a pirated Dublin edition.[22] 'Tristram', as Sterne declared delightedly, was indeed 'the fashion'.

What, in retrospect, is most remarkable about the earliest reception of *Tristram Shandy* is that the book appears to have offended no one. This is perhaps surprising, for Sterne's novel opens with striking bawdy—four chapters of it to start with. (Expurgated Victorian editions of the novel would silently cut all four, with their extended comic account of the different preoccupations of Walter and Elizabeth Shandy in the marital bed which result in Tristram's unfortunate conception, allowing the novel to begin at chapter 5, thereby rendering an already challenging narrative virtually impenetrable.) And of bawdy, there was plenty more to come. Yet neither William Kenrick nor the writers in either the *Critical Review* or the *London Magazine* even hinted at the inclusion of anything morally dubious within the pages of the first two volumes. The *London Magazine* thought the book abounded with the 'profitable'—that is, morally instructive—while William Kenrick expressed a 'particular approbation' of the author, not least for having introduced 'an excellent moral sermon' into his book, 'by which expedient', Kenrick added, 'it will probably be read by many who would peruse a sermon in no other form'.[23] By accident or design, Kenrick's comment implicitly linked the Revd Laurence Sterne with an Anglican priest and writer of the previous century. In 'The Church Porch', at the head of his collection *The Temple*, George Herbert had sought to justify his devotion to poetry with the lines: 'A verse may find him whom a sermon flies | And turn delight into a sacrifice.'[24] Sterne, to be sure, was far from sharing the extreme scruples of Herbert, but there is no reason to believe that his inclusion of one of his own sermons into a work of fiction was devoid of all serious intent. Yet it was for just such a perceived lack of moral purpose that Sterne would soon find himself under fierce and sustained attack.

The first hint of a very different response to Sterne's work from those of the *Monthly*, the *Critical*, or the *London* magazines came in a still generally laudatory review in the *Royal Female Magazine*. 'It were to be wished', opined the writer, 'that the wantonness of the author's wit had been tempered with a little more regard to delicacy throughout the greatest part of his work.'[25] This mild demurral—seemingly little more than a token gesture towards contemporary notions of supposed female reticence—was merely a foretaste, however, of a spate of much harsher criticism to come.

Sterne himself had not been oblivious to the possibility that his book would be criticized for its bawdiness, and in letters to friends he defended himself against censure, even before his work was in print. At the end of January, while still in York, he prepared himself against further attack in a formal letter to an unknown acquaintance which, he suggested, might be published at the beginning of the third volume, 'as an apology for the first and second' (*Letters*, 91).[26] Putting on the mantle of the satirist, Sterne claimed his motives for writing to be 'the hopes of doing the world good by ridiculing what I thought deserving of it' (*Letters*, 91). His success in this aim, he declared, he would leave to the judgement of his readers, 'but not to that little world *of your acquaintance*, whose opinion, and sentiments you call the general opinion of the best judges *without exception*, who all affirm (you say) that my book cannot be put into the hands of any woman of *character*'. Yet, although Sterne continued by adding wittily, 'I hope you except widows, doctor—for they are not *all* so squeamish', the tone of his self-defence moves uncertainly between irony and nervous sarcasm. 'But as for the chaste married, and chaste unmarried part of the sex—they must not read my book! Heaven forbid the stock of chastity should be lessen'd by the life and opinions of Tristram Shandy—yes, his opinions—it would certainly debauch them' (*Letters*, 90).

For all his bluster, Sterne's unease was quickly justified—and indeed he could have expected no less. A work with such strong moral claims as *Tom Jones*, for instance, had been attacked a decade earlier for its corrupting tendencies by those who suggested that the earthquakes which hit London in 1750 had been signs of God's displeasure.[27] *Tom Jones* was one of the works Samuel Johnson attacked in his famous *Rambler* essay on prose fiction—written, as Johnson bluntly declared, for 'the young, the ignorant, and the idle'.[28] So too was Tobias Smollett's first novel, *Roderick Random* (1748), and although, undeterred, Smollett published a still bawdier novel, *Peregrine Pickle*, in 1751, a shift in sensibility resulted in the author making a number of prudential cuts in the second edition in 1758. Much of the allegedly indecent material Smollett removed was scatological—involving leaking chamber pots and the like. Sterne's indecency, however, was predominantly sexual—and hence still more liable to the objection that it was morally corrupting rather than merely a violation of good taste. (Later in the decade Louisa Mildmay, heroine of Hugh Kelly's *Memoirs of a Magdalen* (1767), is seduced and ruined by her lover after the couple have spent an evening together reading inflammatory novels: he *Clarissa*, she *Tristram Shandy*.[29]) Even so, the early reviewers not only liked *Tristram Shandy*; they found nothing especially reprehensible in it, and even, on occasion, praised its moral qualities.

Tristram Shandy, of course, had been published anonymously. What happened to change the generally benign, as well as enthusiastic reception the book received was the revelation that its author was a clergyman. The dubious propriety of an Anglican vicar writing a bawdy novel had been made clear to Sterne by friends in York. In the summer of 1759 Sterne had already alluded to the warning he had received 'with regard to the point of prudence as a Divine' (*Letters*, 78). Later in the 1760s the novelist and imitator of Sterne, Richard Griffith, would be still more severe: 'Loose expressions, in a woman, are a double vice, as they offend against decency, as well as virtue; but in a clergyman, they are treble; because they hurt religion also.'[30]

This was the criticism levelled in 1760 against Sterne—and not always in such considered terms. Lady Dorothy Bradshaigh, ardent admirer of Samuel Richardson and his fiction, confessed, in reply to Richardson's aloof query, that she *was* familiar with the word 'Shandy'. 'I did read the short vol^{mes} thro', she admitted, 'and to say the truth, it some times made me laugh.' But, she continued, 'It is a pity a man of so much humour, cou'd not contain himself within the bounds of decency. Upon the whole, I think the performance, mean, *dirty Wit*. I may add *scandelous*, considering the *Man*.'[31]

'*Scandelous*, considering the *Man*': it was a view which, in many different formulations, was to constitute the greatest attack on Sterne, not only during the first months of his fame but throughout the remainder of his life. Given that he had prepared in advance a defence of his work against the charge of indecency, the earliest reviews must have been a relief as well as a delight. Once Sterne appeared in London, however, his calling as an Anglican priest immediately became public knowledge, and subsequent criticism in print and private correspondence rarely failed to advert to the fact. Sterne himself even emphasized the point. In an age when—as James Boswell would disdainfully note—fashionable clergy increasingly tended to avoid 'the appearance of the clerical order',[32] Sterne seems always to have worn black: a feature of his appearance remarked on both by himself and others.[33] Horace Walpole, scarcely the most shockable of men, and one of the readiest to impute sexual motives to any action, drew particular attention to the fact that Sterne was a priest. 'The best thing' in *Tristram Shandy*, he wrote, 'is a sermon—oddly coupled with a good deal of bawdy, and both the composition of a clergyman.'[34] Other commentators were much more severe. A writer to the *Universal Magazine* praised the 'uncommon abilities' of the author but questioned whether the 'moral and useful part' of his work 'justified the use of indecent expressions'. 'Indecent! did I say?', the writer continued:

> Nay, even downright gross and obscene expressions are frequently to be met with throughout the book. . . . It is generally observable that the playhouses are most crouded, when any thing smutty is to be brought on the stage; and the reverend author of this ingenious performance has no doubt used this method as the most effectual, by making it as universally acceptable as possible. But how far it is excusable in any author, especially one who wears the gown, to gratify and promote a prevailing corrupted taste . . . let himself and the world judge.[35]

The world was divided. Oliver Goldsmith attacked Sterne in the *Public Ledger* in an essay entitled 'The Absurd Taste for Obscene and Pert Novels, Such as "Tristram Shandy" Ridiculed', while James Boswell recorded a dispute between Sterne and John Cleland in which the author of *Memoirs of a Lady of Pleasure* (1748), better known as *Fanny Hill*, took exception to Sterne's writings in the harshest terms: 'if you had a pupil who wrote c—— on a wall, would you not flog him?'[36] Others were less censorious. Sterne's own archbishop, John Gilbert, was reputed to have been 'so delighted with the life and opinions of Tristram Shandy, that he read them once every six weeks'.[37] On first reading, Bishop Warburton not only gave Sterne a purse of gold but, according to the precentor of York and future bishop of Bristol Dr Thomas Newton, declared that 'it is wrote, in the very spirit of Rabelais, and has spoke to me highly of it several times, and inquired much after the author, and last Saturday made very honorable mention of it at the Bishop of Durham's before six or seven of the Bishops'.[38] Not all of the bishops present were as taken with Sterne's comedy, however, being, in Newton's words, 'rather offended with the levity of it, thinking it not in character for a clergyman'.[39] What the bench of bishops might enjoy or censure mildly, however, provoked the ire of others. One critic, writing in the *Grand Magazine* in ironical praise of 'that paragon of mirth and humour, *Tristram Shandy*', declared that

> the best of all is—may be you do not know it—*Tristy*'s a clergyman of the church of *England*—smoke the parson!—Did you ever know such a jolly dog of a divine?—He has the finest knack of talking bawdy!—And then he makes such a joke of religion!—What do you think of his introducing a sermon in the midst of a smutty tale, and making the preacher curse and swear by way of parenthesis?—('D——n them all, quoth *Trim*.' There's divinity for you . . . [)][40]

The force, if not the fact of the criticism took Sterne by surprise. Initially, when working to publish and promote his book, he had sought to turn his modest eminence in the Church to his advantage. On first writing to Robert Dodsley, Sterne advised: 'Direct for me, *Prebendary of York*.' In the letter he penned for Catherine Fourmantel to copy to David Garrick he described himself as 'a gentleman of great Preferment & a Prebendary of the Church of York'. His position as a pluralist and prebendary, Sterne initially hoped, would shield him from accusations of being merely a hack writer exploiting the debased public taste in salacious wit for financial gain. It was by indicating that his personal circumstances placed him above the need to write to live—'I wrote not to be *fed*, but to be *famous*'—that Sterne was able most easily, as he thought, to lay claim to principle and to moral purpose in writing.[41]

Far from finding his clerical status an advantage in London, however, Sterne soon found it an embarrassment. The embarrassment only increased when David Garrick reported to Sterne a story which rapidly circulated in the capital: in subsequent volumes of his work, it was said, Sterne intended to satirize William Warburton by making him serve as a model for Tristram's tutor. Garrick's warning was obviously a friendly one, designed to prevent Sterne from attracting to himself unnecessary criticism, for the author of *The Divine Legation of Moses* and editor of Shakespeare and Pope was not only bishop of Gloucester but an inveterate and indefatigable controversialist as well. Sterne denied the truth of the rumour with arch indignation:

> This vile story . . . I felt little from it at first—or, to speak more honestly . . . I felt a great deal of pain from it, but affected an air usual on such accidents, of less feeling than I had . . . What the devil!—is there no one learned blockhead throughout the many schools of misapplied science in the Christian World, to make a *tutor* of for my Tristram? . . . Are we so run out of stock, that there is no one lumber-headed, muddle-headed, mortar-headed, pudding-headed *chap* amongst our doctors?—Is there no one single wight of much reading and no learning amongst the many children in my *mother's* nursery, who bid high for this charge—but I must disable my judgment by choosing a W[arburto]n? (*Letters*, 93).

The denial is witty enough but far from convincing, though Sterne prudently asked Garrick to effect an introduction to Warburton in order that he might deny the story in person.[42] Convinced or not, Garrick sent Sterne's letter to Warburton without delay. The bishop, in turn, replied to Garrick at considerable length, affecting—also not entirely convincingly—to have disbelieved the whole story from the first, and offering, with some apparent nervousness, to befriend the author of *Tristram Shandy*, which he declared he had 'warmly recommended . . . to all the best company in town'.[43]

This, at least, appears to have been true. Horace Walpole related a story virtually identical to that told by Thomas Newton: Warburton, he reported, had 'recommended the book to the bench of bishops and told them Mr Sterne, the author, was the English Rabelais' (although, being Walpole, he embroidered the story by alleging that the bishops had 'never heard of such a writer'[44]). Thomas Newton, however, had also heard the report that 'Tristram is to have his education under the tutorage of Dr. Warburton'.[45] The exact provenance of this story is uncertain but, in spite of Sterne's persistent denials, it seems likely to have been no more than the truth. In a later account, one 'A.B.' wrote that Sterne had been so delighted with the possibilities open to him by making Warburton a model for Tristram's tutor that 'he let the cat out of the bag, by naming it to two or three friends in London', as a result of which it came to Warburton's ears'.[46] When 'A.B.' later taxed Sterne with his untruthful denial, the author allegedly replied that 'the Bishop of Gloucester had brought over a moiety of the old women to his interest'.[47]

In the event, Sterne avoided all extended portrayal of Warburton in *Tristram Shandy*. His encounter with the bishop in London and the brisk correspondence that followed in the summer of 1760 proved significant, nonetheless. While Sterne's ultimate rejection of Warburton's proffered patronage and advice would lead to a complete break in personal relations between the two men—and result in Warburton's unceasing hostility towards the writer—it also led Sterne to see more clearly the direction in which his chances of future success lay. Regardless of Warburton's subsequent change of heart, however, this early episode in London points up once more the extraordinary success Sterne achieved with *Tristram Shandy*, and the equally remarkable fame he himself enjoyed. In the polite literary world of London Warburton's championing of Sterne's book was known and commented on by figures as diverse as David Garrick, Thomas Newton, and Horace Walpole within the space of a few days.

Once he arrived in London in March, Sterne was in personal demand and, in a matter of days, would be accepting invitations from the most fashionable circles in London. Over the next two months he would—as we have seen—meet on familiar terms with the earl of Chesterfield, Lord Lyttelton, the earl of Bathurst, Lord Edgcumbe, Lord Winchilsea, and with members of the Court, attract the notice of the duke of York, and eventually be presented at Court. He would rub shoulders with other men of provincial backgrounds like his own who had similarly achieved success by their own endeavours: among them, David Garrick and Joshua Reynolds. He would be befriended by politicians, from the elderly Tory, Lord Bathurst, to the much younger radical, John Wilkes. The London magazines would print not just reviews of *Tristram Shandy* but biographical accounts of its author. Sterne himself would become almost indistinguishable in the public's mind from his own creations, Tristram Shandy and Parson Yorick. No wonder that James Boswell, himself a newcomer to London in search of fame, should be so enthusiastic an admirer of 'Squire Tristram' and his 'damn'd clever book'. It was, however, that 'damn'd clever book' which not only made Sterne's reputation but did most to damage him, once the fact that he was a clergyman had become widely known.

It might have been supposed, then, that the publication later in the spring of two volumes of his sermons would have helped redress the balance. The truth proved to be quite the reverse. Like *Tristram Shandy*, Sterne's sermons were marketed with care. They were published on 22 May 1760, in two volumes, each bearing two title-pages. The first, audaciously, read 'THE SERMONS OF Mr. YORICK'; the second, more soberly, 'SERMONS BY LAURENCE STERNE, A.M. Prebendary of York, and Vicar of Sutton on the Forest, and of Stillington near York'. Pointedly, publication coincided with Sterne's delivery of a very public sermon to London's senior lawyers in the Serjeants' Inn chapel, the subsequent newspaper account helpfully referring to the preacher as 'the rev.

Mr. Laurence Sterne, editor of Yorick's sermons'.[48] Today sermons seem so unlikely a form of popular reading that it is difficult to imagine the furore their publication caused. The eighteenth century, however, was *the* great age of sermon publishing. Earlier in the century William Fleetwood wrote no more than the truth when he declared: 'There is, indeed, no want of *Printed* Sermons, abundance of *learned* and *useful* ones being daily put out.'[49] In fact, an average of over 230 sermons were published annually between 1700 and 1800. Sampson Letsome's *An Index to the Sermons Published since the Restoration* (1751) indicated that there had been at least 8,800 sermons published in the previous ninety years, while Edward Kimber's index of the *Monthly Catalogue from the London Magazines* indicated that between 1732 and 1758 at least 665 divines had published more than 1,600 titles—some volumes including thirty or more sermons. None of this considerable body of devout writing had previously been attributed to a fictional jester.

Had Sterne published the sermons under his own name alone perhaps the storm of protest he aroused would never have gathered around him. Yet the link between *Tristram Shandy* and the *Sermons* was strong in Sterne's mind, not only because the author wished to exploit the success of his fiction, but because the two works often explore, though with different emphasis, the same themes: providence, fortune, self-knowledge, conscience, right feeling and moral duty. To contemporary religious and literary decorum Sterne made just two concessions. The first, which he may well have been persuaded or obliged to adopt, was to forgo his original intention of calling his volumes, 'The DRAMATIC SERMONS of MR. YORICK. By TRISTRAM SHANDY, Gentleman'——a linking of bawdy fiction, the playhouse, and the pulpit that would certainly have increased the ire of his already enraged critics. The second was to add the second title-page, in order to 'ease the minds of those who see a jest, and the danger which lurks under it, where no jest was meant'.[50] Sterne was not unaware, in fact, of the disapproval that might be awaiting him. In his preface he wrote nervously and not a little disingenuously: 'The Sermon which gave rise to the publication of these, having been offer'd to the world as a sermon of *Yorick*'s, I hope the most serious reader will find nothing to offend him, in my continuing these two volumes under the same title.'[51] However genuinely he entertained them, Sterne's hopes that he might escape censure were quickly dashed.

The first reviewer, Owen Ruffhead, writing in the *Monthly Review*, established his own order of priorities immediately and ominously: 'Before we proceed to the matter of these Sermons, we think it becomes us to make some animadversions on the manner of their publication, which we consider as the greatest outrage against Sense and Decency, that has been offered since the first establishment of Christianity.'[52] Abandoning hyperbole for caricature, Ruffhead continued by imagining Sterne, 'inflated with vanity, and intoxicated with applause' following the success of his 'obscene Romance', as a jester who would now 'mount the pulpit in a *Harlequin's coat*'. Nor was Ruffhead finished: 'Must obscenity then be the handmaid to Religion—and must the exordium to a sermon, be a smutty tale?'[53] Ruffhead's onslaught was directed as much at the age as at the sermons themselves or their author, and in this he was not alone. The *Royal Female Magazine*, for instance, regretted that the 'dissipated taste of the age, leaves little room for hope for much advantage from works, under this serious title'.[54]

What comes as a surprise in the light of such hostile comment is that both these writers, like other contemporary reviewers, praised the substance of Sterne's sermons, often extravagantly. Despite having devoted much of his review to the scandalous mode of publication, Ruffhead declared Sterne's sermons to be 'models for many of his brethren to copy from. They abound with moral and religious precepts, clearly and forcibly expressed.'[55] What Ruffhead did doubt, however, was whether Sterne's offerings could be considered sermons at all, and—like other contemporary readers[56]—he preferred to consider them as moral essays. As such, he accorded them almost unstinting praise:

> we know of no compositions of this kind in the English language, that are written with more ease, purity, and elegance; and tho' there is not much of the pathetic or devotional to be found in them yet there are many fine and delicate touches of the human heart and passions, which, abstractedly considered, shew marks of great benevolence and sensibility of mind.[57]

Similar admiration is not lacking elsewhere in early notices, though only one reviewer saw merit both in the substance of the sermons and the unorthodox manner of their presentation. This was the anonymous writer in the *Critical Review* who declared that: 'It is with pleasure we behold this son of Comus descending from the chair of mirth and frolick, to inspire sentiments of piety, and read lectures in morality, to that very audience whose hearts he has captivated with good-natured wit, and facetious humour.'[58] As if in anticipation of other, hostile reviews, the writer continued:

> Let the narrow-minded bigot persuade himself that religion consists in a grave forbidding exterior and austere conversation; let him wear the garb of sorrow, rail at innocent festivity, and make himself disagreeable to become righteous; we, for our parts, will laugh and sing, and lighten the unavoidable cares of life by every harmless recreation; we will lay siege to Namur with uncle *Toby* and *Trim*, in the morning, and moralize at night with Sterne and Yorick.[59]

Not all of Sterne's critics were narrow-minded bigots, but this sympathetic reaction sets it very much apart from other contemporary reviews of the sermons. The propriety of a clergyman writing, first, a bawdy novel, and secondly, capitalizing on its success by publishing a collection of sermons, came under intense scrutiny. A long, critical dialogue in the *Grand Magazine* in June 1760 allowed full expression of the view that envy and hypocrisy underlay the attacks on Sterne when his authorship of *Tristram Shandy* became known, citing as evidence the contrast between the earliest reviews, which made little of the book's alleged indecency, and the subsequent hostile attacks on Sterne's impropriety. Such judiciousness, however, served only as a prelude to the *Grand Magazine*'s clinching argument that Sterne's clerical calling *did* make all the difference to the way his book should be approached: 'What is only levity in one man, in another may, not unjustly, be stiled obscenity.' The *Monthly* reviewers, the writer continued, 'very properly considered [Sterne's] making his declaration [of authorship] in his *sacerdotal* character, and using it as a recommendation to his *sermons* as an aggravation of the indecency'.[60]

Such a view was not uncommon in the mid-eighteenth century. A few years previously the Scottish clergyman John Home (whose *The Siege of Aquilea* had provided Sterne, newly arrived in London, with his first taste of Garrick's acting) had faced fierce criticism for having written the tragedy *Douglas* and for allowing it to be staged. First produced in Edinburgh in 1756 and in London in the following year, the work was perhaps the most highly regarded tragedy written in two decades, yet many contemporaries regarded the very notion of a clergyman writing for the playhouse as entirely inappropriate. When Samuel Johnson expressed the view that the clergy should exhibit 'a particular decorum and delicacy of behaviour',[61] James Boswell was happy to concur, arguing that clergymen should 'be somewhat more serious than the generality of mankind, and have a suitable composure of manners', arising from a 'due sense of the dignity of their profession'.[62]

Because Laurence Sterne's sense of the dignity of his profession was different from that of many of his contemporaries, however, it should not be too quickly concluded that he had no such sense at all. When the Revd Robert Brown, himself a Scots Presbyterian minister, wrote to his friend John Hall-Stevenson in the summer of 1760 to praise *Tristram Shandy*, he asked for confirmation that Sterne really was a clergyman: 'pray is it really so? or in what part of the Vineyard does he labour?' (*Letters*, 432). In replying, Sterne wrote, with seriousness as well as wit, and with an evidently acute awareness of the extent of public feeling that his conduct was unbecoming a clergyman: 'Be assured I am an unworthy Labourer in the Vineyard—and I verily believe some of the Lords of it, wish me out—being under terrible alarms that I may one day or other do more harm than good in it—' (*Letters*, 122).

Written in the early autumn of 1760, that comment followed on the controversy his sermons had aroused by some three months. Despite the story later told by John Croft, it seems likely that Sterne had been in contact with the Dodsleys before Stephen Croft brought him to London in early March. Certainly it is difficult to imagine the commercially astute author of *Tristram Shandy* putting together a collection of sermons—like Parson Adams in Fielding's *Joseph Andrews* or the Revd Jonathan Dustwich in Smollett's *Humphry Clinker*—and innocently bringing them with him to London, without some prior indication that they would be welcomed by his publishers. In his 'Preface', Sterne wryly recalled the modest success enjoyed by the separate publication of *The Abuses of Conscience* ten years earlier: this, he admitted, 'could find neither purchasers nor readers, so that I apprehended little hazard from a promise I made upon its republication [i.e. in volume II of *Tristram Shandy*], "That if the sermon was liked, these should be also at the world's service"'.[63] When Sterne had first written this in *Tristram Shandy* it was perhaps little more than a joke at his own expense, but the idea seems to have taken root in his mind. In any case, he had certainly laid some plans to publish a collection of sermons even before he had left York: it was in an advertisement in the *York Courant* of 4 March that Sterne recklessly announced the imminent appearance of the sermons under the provocative title of 'The DRAMATIC SERMONS of MR. YORICK. By TRISTRAM SHANDY, Gentleman'. Whether or not they had previously discussed the matter with Sterne, the Dodsleys' principal role in the publication of the sermons most likely consisted in pointing him more surely in the direction of commercial success, persuading him to abandon his original rash thoughts for a title in favour of a somewhat more discreet allusion to his best-selling novel.

Initially the success of Sterne's sermons owed everything to the popularity of *Tristram Shandy*. Yet, as the continuing demand for them during his lifetime and beyond reveals, Sterne was a preacher with a shrewd sense of what contemporary congregations—and sermon-readers—wanted. The two volumes published in 1760 contained fifteen sermons. They may have been Sterne's own choice of what he thought best in his work in the form—or perhaps they represented the sermons that could be rushed into print with the least possible rewriting. There may have been an element of both, for the two volumes appeared speedily enough, yet contain most of the best of the pre-1760 sermons to have survived (subsequent instalments included some sermons delivered after the success of *Tristram Shandy*). Of the fifteen, only one sermon had previously been published: 'Elijah and the Widow of Zerephath', the charity sermon which had first appeared in print in 1747. While the dating of virtually all of Sterne's sermons is extremely problematic—many of them giving predictable signs of having been reworked for delivery on several occasions—some of those in the 1760 collection appear to date from at least as far back as the charity sermon, if not earlier. Sermons such as 'Pharisee and Publican in the Temple' or 'Job's Account of the Shortness and Troubles of Life', with their strong anti-Catholic sentiments, and still more 'Self-examination', which takes issue with both Roman Catholicism and Methodism, probably have their origin in the mid-to-late 1740s. For the most part, though, comparatively little can be deduced from internal evidence alone, and Sterne's strength as a preacher lay in the extent to which his sermons transcend the particular occasions for which they were originally composed to address issues dear to the hearts and minds of eighteenth-century Anglicans.

Sterne himself recognized as much. In his brief 'Preface' he declared, 'I have nothing to add, but that the reader, upon old and beaten subjects, must not look for many new thoughts,—'tis well if he has new language',[64] and echoed his former archbishop, Thomas Herring, when he declared that 'as the sermons turn chiefly upon philanthropy, and those kindred virtues to it, upon which hang all the law and the prophets, I trust they will be no less felt, or worse received, for the evidence they bear, of proceeding more from the heart than the head'.[65] There was nothing exceptional in this; if a touch schematic, Sterne's summary of his sermons as concerned with preaching Christianity through the positive example of good works, undertaken as a consequence of faith, and by appeal to the listener's emotions rather than his intellect, is both accurate and very much in line with a good deal of contemporary latitudinarian sermonizing.

Sterne's desire to appeal to his prospective readers by addressing 'old thoughts' in 'new language' is most immediately evident from the arrangement of the opening sermons of the collection. Sermon I, 'Inquiry after Happiness', treats not merely one of the central concerns of contemporary latitudinarianism but one of the most familiar themes in all of eighteenth-century writing. The opening sentence—'The great pursuit of man is after happiness'—states a perceived truth which, derived from Aristotle and rehearsed in innumerable sermons, could equally have come from Matthew Prior's *Solomon*, Alexander Pope's *An Essay on Man*, Samuel Johnson's *Rasselas*, or any of hundreds of less celebrated works of the previous fifty or so years.[66] Here we find no attempt at novelty but rather a desire to restate familiar truths. (Sterne is here at one with Johnson, who argued that men and women more often needed to be reminded than informed.) In fact, and though his theme is secular as well as religious, ancient as well as modern, Sterne could scarcely be more orthodox. True happiness, he declares, 'is only to be found in religion——in the consciousness of virtue——and the sure and certain hopes of a better life, which brightens all our prospects, and leaves no room to dread disappointments——because the expectation of it is built upon a rock, whose foundations are as deep as those of heaven and hell'. '[E]very man who would be happy,' he concludes, with reference to Solomon and earthly wisdom, '[must] fear God and keep his commandments'[67].

By contrast with the extreme conventionality of this sermon, the second, 'The House of Feasting and the House of Mourning Described', opens with strikingly audacious wit. Sterne takes his text from Ecclesiastes 7: 2, 3—'It is better to go to the house of mourning, than to the house of feasting'—only to open his gloss with the words 'That I deny'. The apparent denial of Holy Writ is powerful, even shocking. It is hard to believe that this sermon could have been preached for Sutton or Stillington; indeed, the continuation, '*for that* is *the end of all men, and the living* will *lay it to* his *heart: sorrow is better than laughter*——for a crack'd-brain'd order of Carthusian monks, I grant, but not for men of the world',[68] suggests a very broad-minded audience indeed. In the *Monthly Review* Owen Ruffhead described the opening as 'pert',[69] and Thomas Gray similarly noted this aspect of Sterne's preaching in the course of an otherwise favourable appraisal, asking Thomas Warton: 'have you read his Sermons (with his comic figure at the head of them)? they are in the style I think most proper for the pulpit, and shew a very strong imagination and a sensible heart: but you see him often tottering on the verge of laughter, & ready to throw his periwig in the face of his audience'.[70]

Sterne's motive, however, was not to offend his congregation or readers but to gain their attention—and by the end of the sermon the preacher has demonstrated abundantly the justice of Solomon's words, making the sermon as a whole entirely orthodox.

Bold as the opening of Sermon II is—and comparable audacity certainly enlivens a number of Sterne's sermons—it is by no means characteristic of the collection as a whole. The fact that Sterne slipped one of them into *Tristram Shandy* should not tempt us too hastily to read the fiction directly back into the sermons. All the same, those sermons were read, as much in 1760 as today, because of the celebrity Sterne had acquired as author of *Tristram Shandy*. Read side by side, in fact, the sermons and fiction throw light on each other, showing up the particular contours of both, while revealing the continuity of certain central preoccupations of Laurence Sterne, as priest and novelist. So, in the sermons Sterne frequently presents a sober yet ultimately optimistic picture of human existence which at times appears as a mirror image of the comic yet sometimes bleak world of *Tristram Shandy*. 'Time and Chance' is the title of the eighth sermon in the 1760 volumes, but its theme—the unpredictability of human affairs—is shared by several others, as it is by *Tristram Shandy*. Sterne the preacher declares that:

> there are some secret and unseen workings in human affairs, which baffle all our endeavours,—and turn aside the course of things in such a manner,—that the most likely causes disappoint and fail of producing for us the effects which we wished and naturally expected from them.—You will see a man, of whom, was you to form a conjecture from the appearances of things in his favor,—you would say was setting out in the world, with the fairest prospect of making his fortune in it;—with all the advantages of birth to recommend him,—of personal merit to speak for him,—and of friends to help and push him forwards: you will behold him, notwithstanding this, disappointed in every effect you might naturally have looked for, from them;—every step he takes towards his advancement, something invisible shall pull him back,—some unforeseen obstacle shall rise up perpetually in his way, and keep him there,—In every application he makes,—some untoward circumstance shall blast it.[71]

Here, in a nutshell, is the world of *Tristram Shandy*: a world in which Tristram invokes 'all the powers of time and chance, which severally check us in our careers' (*TS* IX. i. 485). If Tristram's plight compels the reader's rueful laughter—the novel provides nothing of the pious consolation the preacher habitually offered congregations at his sermons' end—Sterne's view of the world is consistent enough that his description of it as characterized by afflictions, 'brought in, merely by the common cross accidents and disasters to which our condition is exposed',[72] would fit equally his homilies or comic fiction. Indeed, Tristram reveals in the novel's opening pages that he has been born 'into this scurvy and disasterous world of ours' only to find that Fortune has 'pelted me with a set of as pitiful misadventures and cross accidents as ever small HERO sustained' (*TS* I. v. 10). While Sterne the preacher orthodoxly rejects the notion of a world ruled by that 'ungracious Duchess' Fortune, he does not deny the human experience of living in a world which seems subject to time and chance. His difficulty—the central Christian dilemma—is to reconcile his faith in a God 'universally kind and benevolent in all cases and circumstances' with his experience of a world which suggests Him to be quite other. It is a problem much rehearsed by theologians before, during, and after the eighteenth century—and the failure of theodicies in Sterne's time does not distinguish the eighteenth from other centuries. Nonetheless, the century's increasingly overt scepticism—when latitudinarianism itself seemed, to dissenters and evangelical Anglicans alike, to open the way to deism and atheism—renders it unsurprising that some readers of Sterne's facetious fiction should doubt its author's orthodoxy.

No wonder, then, that in his sermons Sterne's acknowledgement of the problem of human suffering should give rise not to attempts to justify the ways of God to eighteenth-century men, but rather to an insistence on the Christian's unchanging duty to alleviate his fellow's distress. In 'Job's Account of the Shortness and Troubles of Life, considered', the preacher reminds his congregation of the recurrence of affliction in human experience at all times and in all places, citing the text, '*Man that is born of a woman, is of few days, and full of trouble:—He cometh forth like a flower, and is cut down; he fleeth also as a shadow, and continueth not*' (Job 14: 1, 2). Such reminders serve a double purpose. First, they assert 'the perishing condition and uncertain tenure of every thing in this world', and serve as exhortations to live a life of piety; secondly, they call forth pathetic set pieces designed to promote active benevolence in the face of want or affliction. 'I think there needs no stronger argument to prove how universally and deeply the seeds of this virtue of compassion are planted in the heart of man,' Sterne declares in 'Philanthropy Recommended', 'than in the pleasure we take in such representations of it.'[73] On this theme—one of the most recurrent in latitudinarian preaching—the sermons make eloquent use of an appeal to sentiment, evoked by episodes of pathos such as would shortly come to be one of the most admired features of Sterne's fiction.[74] Considering the House of Mourning, for instance, the preacher paints a pathetic scene reminiscent (and worthy) of the contemporary genre paintings of Jean-Baptiste Greuze, imagining the place where, perhaps,

> the aged parents sit broken hearted, pierced to their souls with the folly and indiscretion of a thankless child—the child of their prayers, in whom all their hopes and expectations centred:—perhaps a more affecting scene—a virtuous family lying pinched with want, where the unfortunate support of it, having long struggled with a train of misfortunes, and bravely fought up against them—is now piteously borne down at the last—overwhelmed with a cruel blow which no forecast or frugality could have prevented.—O GOD! look upon his afflictions.—Behold him distracted with many sorrows, surrounded with the tender pledges of his love, and the partner of his cares—without bread to give them,—unable, from the remembrance of better days, to dig;—to beg, ashamed.[75]

In such appeals to sympathy, however, Sterne cannot entirely avoid theological problems. Against his sociable view of human nature, he must acknowledge that 'some men have represented human nature in other colours, (though to what end I know not)', leading the preacher to declare 'that the matter of fact is so strong against them, that from the general propensity to pity the unfortunate, we express that sensation by the word *humanity*, as if it was inseparable from our nature'.[76] In such a passage Sterne touches on one of the central difficulties besetting eighteenth-century latitudinarianism. In parenthetically rejecting a Hobbesian view of the state of nature as a state of war, he also comes close to abandoning altogether the view, enshrined in the ninth of the Thirty-Nine Articles, of man as naturally corrupt. And, as the latitudinarians' opponents forcefully argued, if Adam did not fall, Christ's sacrifice served no necessary purpose. Sterne does not confront the problem directly (far more distinguished theologians shied away from the same difficulty), though he seems to acknowledge the difficulty by his tentative reference to humanity '*as if* it was inseparable from our nature'.

Similar moments of theological unease are to be found elsewhere in the sermons, appearing neither as verbal quibbles nor failures of argument but as serious problems of belief.[77] Sermon VII, 'Vindication of Human Nature', for instance, again finds Sterne apparently undecided whether human nature is best understood in terms of the idea of man being made in God's image, or in remembering the extent to which that image has been sullied by the Fall.[78] That Sterne is alert to the difficulties he faces—here he has in mind not only Hobbes but Mandeville and 'so many of the French writers' as well—does much to explain why, ultimately, he tends to evade such problems, subordinating them, in a characteristically latitudinarian fashion, to a more practical theology.

Whatever may have been the truth of his reported extempore preaching from his country pulpit, Sterne appears in his printed sermons as an orthodox preacher ready to offer comfort, hope, or inspiration to his congregations, as he proffers familiar Christian answers to the difficulties of human existence. In the process, however, he touched on questions of doubt which, while they have their origin in scripture, take on a rather different significance when they reappear, in secularized form, among the central themes of his later fiction. One example is the fourth sermon in the 1760 collection, 'Self Knowledge', which takes its text from 2 Samuel 12: 7: '*And Nathan said unto David, thou art the man.*' Sterne comments:

> There is no historical passage in scripture, which gives a more remarkable instance of the deceitfulness of the heart of man to itself, and of how little we truly know of ourselves. . . . To know one's self, one would think could be no very difficult lesson;—for who, you'll say, can well be truly ignorant of himself and the true disposition of his own heart. If a man thinks at all, he cannot be a stranger to what passes there—he must be conscious of his own thoughts and desires, he must remember his past pursuits, and the true springs and motives which in general have directed the actions of his life: he may hang out false colours and deceive the world, but how can a man deceive himself?[79]

Any reader coming to the sermons after reading *Tristram Shandy*—in which the narrator-hero promises 'not only my life, but my opinions also' (*TS* I. vi. 10)—must notice the similarity of concerns between this sermon and Sterne's novel:

> It was a commissary sent to me from the post-office, with a rescript in his hand for the payment of some six livres odd sous.
>
> Upon what account? said I.——'Tis upon the part of the king, replied the commissary, heaving up both his shoulders——
>
> ——My good friend, quoth I——as sure as I am I—and you are you
>
> ——And who are you? said he.——Don't puzzle me; said I. (*TS* VII. xxxiii. 421)

To the facetious novelist, as to the orthodox preacher, the problem presents itself as an apparent paradox: namely, that the only creature 'endowed with reflection, and consequently qualified to know the most of himself',[80] generally knows the least, giving man one of his 'hardest and most painful lessons'. So painful that many, supposing self-knowledge to be a 'divine direction', make it 'the whole circle both of the knowledge and the duty of man'.[81] It is a view which Sterne himself seems often to share. '[L]et us, I beseech you', proclaims the preacher,

> assign and set apart some small portion of the day for this purpose—of retiring into ourselves, and searching into the dark corners and recesses of the heart, and taking notice of what is passing there. If a man can bring himself to do this task with a curious and impartial eye, he will . . . see several irregularities and unsuspected passions within him which he never was aware of,—he will discover in his progress many secret turns and windings in his heart to which he was a stranger, which now gradually open and disclose themselves to him upon a nearer view; in these labyrinths he will trace out such hidden springs and motives for many of his most applauded actions, as will make him rather sorry, and ashamed of himself, than proud.[82]

This is a repeated theme in the sermons.[83] What is striking about such passages is that here Sterne is not, as so often elsewhere, citing or paraphrasing the sermons of other divines, but re-articulating an idea evidently important to him—the impossibility of arriving at true self-knowledge. So, in 'Evil-Speaking' he argues that 'the bulk of mankind live in such a contradiction to themselves, that there is no character so hard to be met with, as one, which upon a critical examination, will appear altogether uniform, and, in every point, consistent with itself'.[84] This, Sterne contends—in a manner which recalls Montaigne, Bayle, or even Hume more than contemporary Anglicanism—is true not only of men over the course of many years: 'the observation is to be made of men in the same period of their lives that in the same day, sometimes in the very same action, they are utterly inconsistent and irreconcileable with themselves.'[85]

If self-knowledge is endlessly elusive, then one reason is that experience too often suggests the relationship between cause and effect in human affairs to be beyond comprehension. 'Time and Chance' is only the most direct of several sermons on a theme (indicated here by the title) close to the heart of preacher and novelist alike. As elsewhere, we need not attribute to Sterne an open scepticism, still less leap hastily into making the novelist our contemporary, for the preacher is again drawing, in the most direct way possible, on Christian teaching. The sermon's text is taken from

Ecclesiastes 9: 11: '*I returned and saw under the sun, that the race is not to the swift,—nor the battle to the strong,—neither yet bread to the wise, nor yet riches to men of understanding, nor yet favour to men of skill,—but time and chance happeneth to them all.*'[86] If this reflects Sterne's view of his own experience in the years before the success of *Tristram Shandy*, then the sermon itself forces upon us the links between his thoughts as a preacher and as the novelist he would become:

> That time and chance,—apt seasons and fit conjunctures have the greatest sway, in the turns and disposals of men's fortunes. And that, as these lucky hits, (as they are called) happen to be for, or against a man,—they either open the way to his advancement against all obstacles,—or block it up against all helps and attempts. That as the text intimates, neither *wisdom*, nor *understanding*, nor *skill* shall be able to surmount them.[87]

In the pulpit Sterne was far from endorsing this vision of a world ruled by blind chance. Only a 'superficial view' of this kind could lead some men 'atheistically' to infer that 'the providence of God stood neuter and unconcerned in their several workings, leaving them to the mercy of time and chance'. '[I]n truth', Sterne counters:

> the very opposite conclusion follows. For consider,—if a superior intelligent power did not sometimes cross and over-rule events in this world,—then our policies and designs in it, would always answer according to the wisdom and stratagem in which they were laid. . . . Now, as this is not always the case, it necessarily follows from Solomon's reasoning, that, if the race is not to the swift, if knowledge and learning do not always secure men from want,—nor care and industry always make men rich,—nor art and skill infallibly raise men high in the world;—that there is some other cause which mingles itself in human affairs, and governs and turns them as it pleases; which cause can be no other than the first cause of all things, and the secret and over-ruling providence of . . . Almighty God . . .[88]

This argument proceeds at much greater length—forming one of the longest paragraphs in any of the sermons—and frequently suggests a preacher ill at ease with his own position. One reason why there are so many instances of events running counter to all probabilities, he suggests, is that God is giving man 'testimony to his providence in governing and dependence upon it, for the event and success of our undertakings', a weak position Sterne attempts to defend by one of his extremely rare footnoted references: here to a sermon by Archbishop Tillotson.[89]

The uncharacteristic appeal to authority is revealing. Four years later John Wilkes would say of Sterne's preaching: 'Tristram pleads his cause well, tho' he does not believe one word of it.'[90] Wilkes goes too far—though it must be acknowledged that he was not the only friend of Sterne's to advance such a view[91]—and it would be truer to say that here Sterne is not writing well though cynically, but is writing poorly, and poorly because he is genuinely engaged in the problems of belief he confronts in his sermon. Despite the assistance of Tillotson, in fact, the sermon's conclusion still suggests how awkward Sterne finds the issues he addresses—and thereby doubtless indicates why he should have returned to them so frequently in his fiction as well as in his sermons. Since it so often falls out in human experience, Sterne avers, that

> the wisest projects are overthrown,—and the most hopeful means are blasted, and time and chance happens to all;——You must call in the deity to untye this knot,—for though at sundry times—sundry events fall out,—which we, who look no further than the events themselves, call chance, because they fall out quite contrary both to our intentions and our hopes,—though at the same time, in respect of God's providence over-ruling in these events; it were profane to call them chance, for they are pure designation, and though invisible, are still the regular dispensations of the superintending power of that Almighty being, from whom all the laws and powers of nature are derived.[92]

If this sounds like a prose paraphrase of Pope's reference to the deity as '[t]he great directing MIND of ALL',[93] then again we should not blame Sterne for revealing unease before what has been perhaps the greatest problem facing Christian belief. Leibniz's optimism, epitomized by his assertion *nihil est sine ratione* ('Nothing is without reason'), had been famously parodied in the year before the sermon was published by Voltaire in *Candide*, and the difficulty was one which to no theodicy—from Milton's *Paradise Lost*, through Pope's *Essay on Man*, to Johnson's *Rasselas*—could provide a satisfying answer.[94]

Sterne himself seems much more at ease in representing particular cases than in dealing abstractly with such theological problems. In Sermon X, 'Job's Account of the Shortness and Troubles of Life, considered', he takes Job as the best example of a man 'qualified to make just and noble reflections upon the shortness of life, and instability of human affairs'.[95] That he intriguingly represents Job, 'who had himself waded through such a sea of troubles', as a type of Hamlet, suggests how the Old Testament figure—the characteristic Christian hero for the eighteenth century—becomes associated with scepticism and self-doubt.[96] In another Job sermon—Sermon XV, 'Job's Expostulation with his Wife'—Sterne emphasizes the heroic status of the individual struggling against misfortune: 'There are few instances of particular virtue more engaging than those, of this heroic cast . . . of a good man involved in misfortunes, surrounded on all sides with difficulties,—yet chearfully bearing up his head, and struggling against them with firmness and constancy of mind.'[97] Through all, the pressure of time is constantly felt. 'With how quick a succession, do days, months and years pass over our heads?'[98] demands the preacher of 'Job's Account of the Shortness and Troubles of Life', anticipating by several—perhaps many—years the moving reflection of Tristram himself: 'Time wastes too fast: every letter I trace tells me with what rapidity Life follows my pen; the days and hours of it, more precious, my dear Jenny! than the rubies about thy neck, are flying over our heads like light clouds of a windy day, never to return more . . . ' (*TS* IX. viii. 498). In the sermon Sterne's rhetorical question is immediately followed by a renewed concern with self-knowledge, with autobiography itself, as he reflects on how our days flee so rapidly, leaving so little impression on us, so that 'when we endeavour to call them back by reflection, and consider in what manner they have gone, how unable are the best of us to give a tolerable account'.[99] Here Christian faith is accounted essential: not because it provides answers, but—Sterne asserts in his conclusion—as consolation for the fact that no answers are to be found. 'When we reflect that this span of life, short as it is, is chequered with so many troubles, that there is nothing in this world springs up, or can be enjoyed without a mixture of sorrow,' Sterne writes, 'how insensibly does it incline us to turn our eyes and affections from so gloomy a prospect, and fix them upon that happier country, where afflictions cannot follow us, and where God will wipe away all tears from off our faces, for ever and ever? Amen.'[100]

If this seems an unlikely conclusion for Sterne, then it points to a notable tension both within his sermons and within Sterne himself. At times the stress on benevolence takes the preacher into the articulation of positions requiring no dependence on revealed religion at all. In 'Vindication of Human Nature' Sterne argues from his text—'*For none of us liveth to himself*' Romans 14: 7—for a human tendency towards altruism. Though he draws extensively on a sermon by Richard Bentley, Sterne compresses Bentley's original in such a way that his own 'demonstration' loses sight of the fact that everything he says applies to all men and not just to Christians—making his final appeal to eschatology, to man's appearance before the 'judgment seat', essentially superfluous. Eighteenth-century and twentieth-century readers have often been at one in finding Sterne's sermons stronger in their moral concerns than in expressions of faith. Yet Sterne himself was frequently at pains to argue for the latitudinarian position that works of charity *are* expressions of religious faith, and—whatever readers may make of the secularism and possible scepticism of the fiction—the first two volumes of Sterne's sermons offer many entirely orthodox expressions, both of faith in a revealed religion and in the importance of grace.[101] So, although not given to frequent use of overt piety, Sterne speaks variously of Christ as 'our Saviour', 'our blessed Saviour', or 'our merciful Saviour'.[102] '[T]here can', he ultimately concludes, 'be no real happiness without religion and virtue, and the assistance of God's grace and Holy Spirit to direct our lives in the true pursuit of it.'[103]

In one sense at least the orthodoxy of the sermons need surprise no one. Anxiously seeking preferment throughout so much of his career in the Church, Sterne was unlikely to compromise his chances of obtaining it by knowingly advancing heterodox views from the pulpit. Equally importantly, his sermons show a notable dependence on the published work of other preachers, that in some cases has been considered as tantamount to plagiarism.

Since much has been made of the issue of the author's borrowings from the sermons of others, it is particularly noteworthy, even quite remarkable, that no contemporary reviewer or reader seems to have commented on these borrowings at all, still less been disturbed by them.[104] Or rather, the one person who was concerned about the borrowings was Laurence Sterne himself. In the 'Fragment in the Manner of Rabelais' he had made the copying of one of Samuel Clarke's sermons by the sermon-thief, Homenas, the matter of his first chapter. While it is possible that he had originally intended this as particular satire, aimed at some fellow-cleric in Minster circles, it is equally likely that he intended no more than a general point likely to have appealed to any preacher with a taste for wit—and to many members of their congregations. On the question of borrowing, contemporary opinion was in any case divided. Forty years earlier, Jonathan Richardson had advanced a position much like Sterne's own (and in remarkably Shandean terms): 'Nor need any Man be asham'd to be sometimes a Plagiary, 'tis what the greatest Painters, and Poets have allow'd themselves in. And indeed 'tis hard that a Man having had a good Thought should have a Patent for it for ever.'[105] (Sterne surely did not know this passage—or he would have borrowed it himself—but he was capable of a decidedly self-reflexive sense of humour at his own expense: when preaching a charity sermon before a polite audience at the London Foundling Hospital in 1761, he would rhetorically dismiss 'the pretences of learning . . . [as] but a sorry object of Pride at the best;—but more so, when we can cry out upon it, as the poor man did of his hatchet,—*Alas! Master,—for it was borrowed*'—a joke which can only be understood if one knows that the remark was itself 'borrowed' from a work by one of his favourite authors, the seventeenth-century writer Bishop Joseph Hall.[106])

While it seems highly unlikely that any of Sterne's original congregation would have detected this borrowing, few by contrast would have been unaware of the fact that virtually every Anglican clergyman of the eighteenth century borrowed from the works of his predecessors at one time or another. The age, it might be said, expected no less. Even so severe and industrious a moralist as Samuel Johnson—himself, though a layman, the author of more than two dozen surviving sermons—merely recommended mildly that every clergyman should try his hand at an original sermon now and again, thereby giving the clearest indication that he considered borrowing all or part of existing sermons entirely acceptable.[107] For many, such borrowings were not merely acceptable but even desirable—for while few of the Anglican clergy had pretensions as theologians, all were concerned to preach orthodox doctrine. Where better, then, to find such orthodoxy than in the works of the most highly regarded preachers of the later seventeenth and earlier eighteenth centuries? In looking to approved models for their sermons preachers were, after all, doing no more than writers of all other literary genres in the eighteenth century tended to do.

Individual clergymen, however, did not imitate or borrow at random; rather, they drew on sermons expressing views congenial to their own. A latitudinarian Whig like Sterne was no more likely to turn to a work by a High Church Tory when preaching the politically charged 30 January sermon in memory of the execution—or martyrdom—of King Charles I in 1649, than he was to look to one by a zealous dissenter. To borrow from approved sources did, however, help ensure that Sterne's sermons do not stray far from accepted doctrine. It was one of the complaints made by many Anglican clergymen—Sterne among them—that Protestant dissenters claimed to preach on the basis of divinely inspired personal revelation: in Sermon XXV, 'Humility', published in 1766, Sterne spoke contemptuously of 'the most illiterate mechanicks, who as a witty divine said of them, were much fitter to *make* a pulpit, than get into one,—[who]were yet able so to frame their nonsense to the nonsense of the times, as to beget an opinion in their followers, not only that they pray'd and preach'd by inspiration, but that the most common actions of their lives were set about in the Spirit of the LORD'.[108] In contrast to such supposed delusion (or fraud), recourse to approved models of pulpit eloquence could appear entirely laudable, and throughout the eighteenth century borrowings were not only widely accepted but even approved.

Or at least—up to a point. What is unusual about Sterne is not that he borrowed heavily in his sermons, but that he subsequently published those sermons and, moreover, did so sufficiently long after they were first composed and delivered that he could no longer be sure himself of the extent of his borrowings. In a letter to the Revd Charles Lawrence, on the subject of borrowings in sermons, Samuel Johnson had wisely recommended: 'Take care to register some where or other, the authours from whom your several discourses are borrowed, and do not imagine that you shall always remember even what perhaps You now think it impossible to forget.'[109] It was advice from which Sterne could certainly have profited. In the 'Preface' to the first two volumes of his sermons in 1760 he alludes to this very difficulty of recollecting sources after a long period. Insisting that none of the sermons had been written with any thought of its being published, Sterne continues:

> I have nothing to add, but that the reader, upon old and beaten subjects, must not look for many new thoughts,—'tis well if he has new language; in three or four passages, where he has neither the one nor the other, I have quoted the author I made free with—there are some other passages, where I suspect I may have taken the same liberty,—but 'tis only suspicion, for I do not remember it is so, otherwise I should have restored them to their proper owners, so that I put it in here more as a general saving, than from a consciousness of having much to answer for upon that score.[110]

If this seems like an instance of the preacher protesting too much, then it is striking that, having been offered every chance to observe borrowings, neither reviewers nor ordinary readers did any such thing. Only Sterne himself seemed concerned, turning his own apparent uneasiness about the extent of his borrowings into a number of jokes in *Tristram Shandy*. Shortly after Corporal Trim has read Parson Yorick's 'The Abuses of Conscience' to the audience in the parlour at Shandy Hall, Tristram asks:

> Can the reader believe, that this sermon of *Yorick*'s was preach'd at an assize, in the cathedral of *York*, before a thousand witnesses, ready to

> give oath of it, by a certain prebendary of that church, and actually printed by him when he had done,——and within so short a space as two years and three months after *Yorick*'s death. (*TS* II. xvii. 113)

Since we know that 'The Abuses of Conscience' itself owed a good deal to Swift's sermon 'On the Testimony of Conscience', this passage is perhaps best understood as a further example of those self-reflexive jokes in which *Tristram Shandy* abounds.

This was not, however, how contemporary readers understood *The Sermons of Mr. Yorick.* For some, as we have seen, the sermons—or at least the manner of their publication—constituted a scandal. For Owen Ruffhead they were better thought of as moral essays. Yet, amid all the controversy, other devout readers saw in Sterne's sermons nothing objectionable whatever. Within two years of their first appearance, three sermons—'Of Evil-speaking', 'The Case of Elijah and the Widow of Zerephath', and 'Job's Account'—were reprinted in a four-volume anthology entitled *The Practical Preacher: Consisting of Select Discourses from the Works of the Most Eminent Protestant Writers: With Forms of Devotion for the Use of Families.*[111] In drawing on 'the most eminent Protestant writers' *The Practical Preacher* cast its net widely, and the collection contained sermons by many of the most notable divines of the previous hundred years. There were sermons by both Samuel Clarke and John Rogers—the two preachers whose sermons Homenas copies, in successive drafts of the 'Rabelaisian Fragment'—as by well as by John Tillotson, Thomas Sherlock, and John Sharp, while divines as diverse as the High Church Jacobite Francis Atterbury and the celebrated latitudinarian Benjamin Hoadly were also included. As a maker of sermons Sterne was in distinguished and varied company. In the 'Advertisement' to *The Practical Preacher* the aims of the collection are described as being:

> to promote the Interests of rational and manly Piety. The Sermons contained in it are not upon Points of curious and intricate Enquiry, nor upon the topics of any particular Sect or Party, but upon the most interesting practical Subjects. Their general Tendency is to enforce Moral and Christian Virtues by Christian Motives; to shew, that Religion tends to the Perfection of our reasonable Natures; that it is our highest Honour, and our highest Interest.[112]

As a brief description of Sterne's own output of sermons this could hardly be bettered. The appeal is to reasoned acceptance of the central tenets of (Anglican) Christianity, untroubled by the finer points of theology, and anxious to assert that the often fierce divisions of early-eighteenth-century

Anglicanism had no place in the 1760s. While implicitly allowing the existence of a laudable secular morality, the 'Advertisement' subordinates this to the superior claims of the Christian religion—to be understood, of course, as the doctrine of the Established Church.

In the early summer of 1760, such respectability must have seemed to Sterne very far away. He was contented, nonetheless. Even before publication the literary success of *The Sermons of Mr. Yorick* was all but secured, for the volumes boasted an extraordinarily impressive list of subscribers, more than 650 in all, including members of the nobility, politicians, clergy, and notable writers. Graced by an engraved frontispiece taken from a portrait of Sterne by Joshua Reynolds—one of the clearest signs of his new-found celebrity—the sermons were also a resounding commercial success. Published on 22 May, the first edition sold out so quickly that a second appeared on 21 July—and there would be no fewer than six further editions during Sterne's lifetime, making the sermons more commercially successful than even *Tristram Shandy* itself.

By the time the sermons appeared Sterne must have come to expect no less than complete success. From the time of his arrival in London early in March until the end of May his celebrity knew no bounds. Sterne's ingenuous delight in his sudden fame is most vividly detailed in his letters, but in none more so than those he wrote to the singer Catherine Fourmantel, who had remained in York to complete her engagements at the Assembly Rooms. It was to his 'dear Kitty' that he wrote on 8 March, following his journey to London with Stephen Croft, to tell her that 'I have arrived here safe, & sound, except for the Hole in my heart, which you have made, like a dear enchanting Slut as you are' (*Letters*, 96). His intention on the day he wrote was to take lodgings in either Piccadilly or the Haymarket, and he promised he would give Kitty the address before sealing his letter: 'I shall wait for . . . the return of the post with great impatience—so write my dear Love without fail' (ibid.).

The letters Sterne wrote to Catherine Fourmantel in the spring of 1760 provide us with an especially illuminating account of the writer emerging from the obscurity of a distant rural parish into the brilliance of the very highest social circles in the metropolis. They also reveal a more disturbing aspect of his character, adding a victim to the story of his success.

Sterne had met Catherine Fourmantel when she came, with her mother, to perform in the York Assembly Room concerts of 1759–60. At the end of 1759 Elizabeth Sterne—still suffering from the mental breakdown which had struck her earlier in the year—moved, along with her husband and their daughter, from Sutton to a house in the Mint Yard in York. Sterne's relationship with Catherine Fourmantel nevertheless developed quickly and incautiously. The parson presented the singer with a copy of his sermon *Elijah and the Widow of Zerephath*:

> [Not] merely because it was wrote by myself,—but because there is a beautiful Character in it, of a tender & compassionate Mind in the Picture given of Elijah. read it my dear Kitty, & believe me, when I assure You, that I see something of the same kind & gentle disposition in your heart, which I have painted in the Prophet's—which has attach'd me so much to you & your Interests, that I shall live and dye your
>
> Affectionate & faithful
> LAURENCE STERNE
>
> (*Letters*, 83–4)

Despite the risk of further scandal, Sterne made constant arrangements to see Catherine, sometimes at the house of a friend. Soon he had no scruples about committing to paper even more extravagant sentiments: 'I love you to distraction Kitty—& will love you on so to Eternity' (*Letters*, 83).

Three months may pale in relation to Eternity, but by the end of March 1760 Sterne's life in York must have seemed to him another existence—which, in a sense, it was. The sentiments of Sterne's first letter dated four days after his arrival in London, remain those familiar from the letters he had written to Catherine Fourmantel in York: 'my dear dear Girl let me assure you of the truest friendship for you, that ever Man bore towards a Woman—where ever I am, my heart is warm towards you & ever shall be, till it is cold for ever' (*Letters*, 97). Catherine had refused to receive a male visitor unwelcome to Sterne—though not necessarily to herself—and a jealous Sterne thanks her profusely for it, avowing he 'would give a Guinea for a Squeeze of y^r hand', instead of remaining 'solitary & alone'. Sterne was not solitary for long. Soon he was telling her: 'My Lodgings is every hour full of your great People of the first Rank who strive who shall most honour me—even all the Bishops have sent their Complim^t[s] to me, & I set out on Munday morning to pay my Visits to them all. I am to dine w^h Lord Chesterfield, this week &c &c—and next Sunday Ld Rockingham takes me to Court' (*Letters*, 101). Sterne's social round continued. It was to Kitty that he related the kindnesses shown him by David Garrick, to whom she had effected an introduction in the first place, and to Kitty that he revealed the news of his preferment to Coxwold. Now there was little chance of finding himself alone: 'from morning to night my Lodgings . . . are full of the greatest Company', he wrote; 'I dined these 2 Days with 2 Ladies of the Bedchamber—then with, L[d] Rockingham, L[d] Edgecomb—L[d] Wilchelsea, Lord Littleton, A Bishop—&c—&c—' (*Letters*, 102).

As Sterne's social success increased, however, so his concern for Kitty diminished. At first he was anxious for news of her and of her expected arrival in London, in order that she might share in his triumph. Rapidly, though, Sterne's letters turned to notes whose very brevity speaks eloquently of the pressure of his social engagements. 'I have snatch'd this single Moment, tho' there is Company in my rooms to tell my dear dear Kitty . . . tha[t] I am hers for ever & ever' (*Letters*, 101), Sterne wrote on one occasion. Subsequent letters echo the hurry. 'Tho' I have but a moment's time to spare' (*Letters*, 102), one letter opens, while in another Sterne says bluntly: 'I have not a Moment to spare' (*Letters*, 104). By April Sterne was embarked on an impressive round of social engagements. Thomas Gray wrote to Thomas Warton: 'Tristram Shandy is still a greater object of admiration, the Man as well as the Book. One is invited to dinner, where he dines, a fortnight beforehand.'[113] At the end of March and beginning of April Sterne was sitting for Joshua Reynolds; the result is the great portrait (now in the National Portrait Gallery in London) of the writer sitting pensively at a table, his head resting on his hand. Later in April Lord Rockingham took Sterne to court, and in the following month invited him to be part of his retinue when he was installed Knight of the Garter at Windsor, where Sterne was presented to the young duke of York, brother to the future King George III.

In the early weeks after Sterne's departure for London Catherine Fourmantel must have been delighted to receive the vivid letters in which so many sudden and unexpected triumphs were related with such relish. Yet if many people saw much of Laurence Sterne during the spring of 1760, Catherine Fourmantel did not. While her professional engagements constrained her to remain in York, Sterne professed disappointment but consoled them both: '[T]hese separations, my dear Kitty, however grievious to us both—must be—for the present—God will open a Dore, when we shall sometime be much more together, & enjoy Our Desires without fear or Interruption' (*Letters*, 104). Ambiguous as this particular letter is, it appears that Sterne was actively contemplating the possibility he might one day marry Kitty Fourmantel. Elizabeth Sterne was still ill and he may not have expected her to live long. He had already written to Catherine Fourmantel: 'I have but one Obstacle to my Happiness now left—& what that is, You know as well as I' (*Letters*, 102), and later declared passionately: 'I pray to God that You may so live and so love me as one Day to share in my great good fortune' (*Letters*, 104). However they may appear in retrospect, the sentiments were surely genuine—if only because Sterne, enjoying his new-found celebrity, must have been alert to the possibility that such indiscretions could be held against him.

To read through the surviving letters Sterne wrote to Catherine Fourmantel in the spring of 1760 is, however, to follow the rapid decline of Sterne's feelings for her. Their situation, suddenly, had been entirely reversed. In York the youthful Catherine had for Sterne the glamorous attraction of being a concert singer from London. In London Sterne was the celebrity—far more widely known and fêted than Catherine Fourmantel could ever hope to be. Even her continuing presence in York was due to the fact that she had received word of her failure to secure an engagement in the Ranelagh pleasure gardens during the forthcoming season.

If Catherine Fourmantel entertained any real feelings for Sterne, her hopes that they might share a future together were very soon to be dashed. While separated from him in York she received his continual, if hasty, protestations of love and devotion. When she finally arrived in London she received, instead, a ticket to the theatre. 'My dear Kitty,' Sterne wrote, 'As I cannot propose the pleasure of your Company longer than till four o'Clock this afternoon, I have sent you a Ticket for the Play, & hope you will go there that I may have the Satisfaction of hopeing you are entertained' (*Letters*, 107). The young woman's attractions for Sterne were fading fast: 'my dear Kitty. I was so intent upon drinking my Tea with you this afternoon that I forgot I had been engaged all this week to visit a Gentleman's family, on this day . . . I will however contrive to give my dear friend a Call at 4 o'clock—tho' by the by I think it not quite prudent . . . ' Sterne did, it is true, add: 'but what has prudence my dear Girl to do with Love?' (*Letters*, 108–9), but Catherine Fourmantel would have needed to be very naive not to see the direction in which things were going. Courted by the best London society, Sterne must have realized the impossibility of being seen too often in the company of a young singer. To be the author of a bawdy book was one thing, but as a married clergyman to have, or appear to have, an openly acknowledged mistress would have put Sterne decisively beyond the pale of polite society. The last surviving letter from Laurence Sterne to Kitty amounts to nothing more than an excuse for not having seen her: 'If it would have saved my Life, I have not had one hour or half hour in my power since I saw You on Sunday—else my dear Kitty may be sure I sh^{d} not have been thus absent.—Every Minute of this Day & to morrow is pre[e]ngaged, that I am as much a Prisoner as if I was in Jayl'

(*Letters*, 109). The ardent lover of York, who insisted on Catherine being at home on Tuesday at seven, was now an absent lover.

By writing to Garrick, Catherine had helped Sterne gain entry to the most fashionable London circles. In entering them, Sterne had left Catherine behind, and she would be heard of, in Sterne's life, no more.[114] After both of their deaths, however, Catherine Fourmantel came back to haunt Sterne, for in the account of a one-time possessor of their letters—preserved by Catherine in her lifetime—Kitty Fourmantel, jilted by Yorick, lost her senses and was confined to a madhouse.[115] There exists no confirmation of this lurid tale, and the possibility that she served as a model for the beautiful Maria of Moulines of *A Sentimental Journey*, driven to madness by the absence of her lover, as the writer further alleged, must be doubted. That Sterne, in the first weeks of his fame, treated Catherine Fourmantel badly, may not.

The late spring and early summer of 1760 was almost certainly a difficult time for Catherine Fourmantel. It was also the most joyous period Sterne had ever known. He could not remain in London indefinitely, however, no matter how many dinner invitations continued to appear. In mid-May, he wrote to Stephen Croft indicating an intention to remain in London until the publication of his *Sermons*, and then to return to Yorkshire. The author's delight at his continuing celebrity and commercial success are manifest. Excusing once more his 'hasty scrawl', Sterne informed Croft that he had 'just come from a Concert where the D[uke] of Y[ork] perform'd—I have received great notice from him, and last week had the honour of supping with him' (*Letters*, 110–11). Yet, even notice by royalty could not detain him indefinitely, and he was making serious preparations for a stylish return. For his journey, he told Croft, he had bought a pair of horses to pull his new chaise, and—given the tale of Parson Yorick's rural rides on his 'lean, sorry, jack-ass of a horse' (*TS* I. x. 16)—it is no wonder that, many years later, John Croft could still recall the story of Sterne's triumphant journey back to the Yorkshire countryside he had left in such very different circumstances a few short months before.

10

Coxwold and London, 1760–1761

Everything we know about Sterne's visit to London in the spring of 1760 suggests that he returned home giddy with success. Yet he was acutely aware too of the need to consolidate that success, and secure his fame. He had told Robert Dodsley that he would produce a new instalment of *Tristram Shandy* every six months and although this optimistic—and perhaps commercially ruinous—proposition was soon forgotten, Sterne set himself to work on the continuation in the first days of June. Immediately he met with a check, for he found himself drawn into a brisk exchange of letters with Bishop William Warburton. Though an irritating distraction from the task in hand, this correspondence was ultimately instrumental in persuading Sterne that he might (and must) lay aside long-cherished hopes of ecclesiastical patronage in order to make his own way in the world. 'I am just sitting down to go on with Tristram,' Sterne began, adding, 'the scribblers use me ill, but they have used my betters much worse, for which may God forgive them' (*Letters*, 112). This last remark was a reference to the allegations that Sterne intended to satirize Warburton in *Tristram Shandy*. Instead, he presented the bishop with a copy of his *Sermons*—thanking him effusively for 'the generosity of your protection, and advice to me' (*Letters*, 112).

Sterne's deferential tone was evidently motivated by a desire not to give unnecessary offence—and had the bishop been content with the response the subsequent relations between the two might have been very different. Instead, the deference encouraged Warburton to proffer more unwanted advice. Warburton was then staying at Prior Park near Bath, home of Ralph Allen—the friend of Henry Fielding and dedicatee of *Amelia*—and he used his leisure to reply to Sterne at length. Warburton's avowed desire was to reclaim Sterne as a moralist. 'You have it in your power', he opined, 'to make that, which is an amusement to yourself and others, useful to both', but he cautioned Sterne also that 'you should above all things, beware of its becoming hurtful to either, by any violations of decency and good manners'. This was advice Warburton evidently felt Sterne needed, for he admitted: 'but I have already taken such repeated liberties of advising you on that head, that to say more would be heedless, or perhaps unacceptable' (*Letters*, 113).

Acceptable or not, Warburton scarcely paused before expostulating at length on the indecency of the two poems published in April 1760 as *Two Lyric Epistles: one to my Cousin Shandy, On his coming to Town; and the other To the Grown Gentlewomen, The Misses of* ***. Their author, Warburton declared, 'appears to be a monster of impiety and lewdness,' adding, 'yet such is the malignity of the scribblers, some have given them to your friend Hall; and others, which is still more impossible, to yourself' (*Letters*, 113). Warburton's pretended care for the reputation of Sterne and Hall-Stevenson was disingenuous enough, for the master of Crazy Castle was indeed the author of the *Two Lyric Epistles*, and Warburton's insinuation that the first poem put Sterne in 'a mean and ridiculous light' was designed to create a breach between Sterne and his friend. To bolster his own opinions Warburton had called on Garrick to urge Sterne to prudence, and he concluded by expressing his own Addisonian ideals of the proper function of the writer, who would—like Garrick—be one who 'has availed himself of the public favour, to regulate the taste, and, in his proper station, to reform the manners of the fashionable world; while by a well judged œconomy, he has provided against the temptations of a mean and servile dependency, on the follies and vices of the great' (*Letters*, 113).

Sterne replied to Warburton's letter immediately and respectfully, yet with a notable independence of spirit:

> Be assured, my lord, that willingly and knowingly I will give no offence to any mortal by anything which I think can look like the least violation either of decency or good manners; and yet, with all the caution of a heart void of offence or intention of giving it, I may find it very hard, in writing such a book as 'Tristram Shandy', to mutilate everything in it down to the prudish humour of every particular. I will, however, do my best; though laugh, my lord, I will, and as loud as I can too. (*Letters*, 115)

His first laugh was at Warburton's expense, for he mischieviously intimated his own supposed belief that the first of the *Two Lyric Epistles* had in fact been written by Garrick. As to the magazine writings on him, such as that in the April issue of *the Royal Female Magazine* to which Warburton had alluded, Sterne responded:

> These strokes in the Dark, with the many Kicks, Cuffs & Bastinados I openly get on all sides of me, are beginning to make me sick of this foolish humour of mine of sallying forth into this wide & wicked world to redress wrongs, &c, of wch I shall repent as sorely as ever Sancha Panca did of his in following his evil genius of a Don Quixote thro thick & thin—but as the poor fellow apologized for it,—so must I. '*it was my vile* fortune & my *Errantry & that's all that can be said* on't[']. (*Letters*, 116)

Perhaps—but now, more than ever, Sterne accepted that he must needs pay the price of his longed-for fame. Certainly, his last feeble protestation of a desire to have remained a private rather than public figure rings hollow indeed: 'I wish from my heart, I had never set pen to paper, but continued hid in the quiet obscurity in which I had so long lived: I was quiet, for I was below Envy—& yet above Want; & indeed so very far above it, that the idea of it never once enterd my head in writing' (*Letters*, 116). Having delivered himself of this insincere protestation,[1] Sterne seems to have determined to defer to the bishop no more, drawing to a close in a manner ambiguously balanced between respectful submission and open satire. Reporting a visit paid him by Richard Osbaldeston, the former dean of York and now bishop of Carlisle, Sterne mentions that he had asked Osbaldeston about Warburton's health and, in particular, 'how far the Waters had relieved you under the pain & indigestion you complaind of'. The fact that Sterne was expressing concern for the bishop's flatulence, arising from biting off more than he could easily chew, is unlikely to have escaped Warburton, any more than the ambiguity of Sterne's concluding good wishes for 'happiness in this world and in the next' (*Letters*, 116). Yet, undeterred, the bishop persisted in a further, rapidly sent letter in which he repeated his admonishments and exhortations to be governed by 'honour, virtue, and religion'. He also seems to have taken quite seriously Sterne's professed desire for a return to his former quiet existence: 'Notwithstanding all your wishes for your former obscurity, which your present chagrin excites, yet a wise man cannot but choose the sunshine before the shade' (*Letters*, 119).

Faced with such platitudes Sterne decided he had had enough and made no reply, allowing the rapid exchange of correspondence to lapse. Instead, he wrote to a female admirer, Mary Macartney, making tart reference to Warburton's missives: 'Lord defend me', he wrote, 'from all litterary commerce with those, who indite epistles as Attornys do Bonds, by filling up blanks, and who in lieu of sending me what I sat expecting—a

Letter—surprize me with an Essay cut & clip'd at all corners' (*Letters*, 117). Subsequently Sterne referred to Warburton with even less respect or even caution: 'the Bishop of Glocester, who (to be sure) bears evils of this kind—as no man ever bore'em, has wrote me a congratulatory Letter thereupon—the Summ total of all wch is—Tht we bear the Sufferings of other people with great Philosophy—I only wish <I> one could bear the excellencies of some people with the same Indifference' (*Letters*, 118).[2]

Sterne apparently could not, for he never re-established personal relations with Warburton. Turning his back on the possibility of the very ecclesiastical patronage he had so earnestly sought in the past, he made instead a sly, imprudent reference to the bishop in the fourth volume of *Tristram Shandy*: 'What a rate have I gone on at,' declares Tristram, 'curvetting and frisking it away, two up and two down for four volumes together, without looking once behind, or even on one side of me, to see whom I trod upon! . . . But your horse throws dirt; see you've splash'd a bishop' (*TS* IV. XX. 237). The result was that Warburton spoke against the second instalment with some force, and although he found slightly better words for the fifth and sixth volumes at the end of 1761, he showed only increased hostility to the book's author, telling Richard Hurd, future author of *Letters on Chivalry and Romance* (1762) and successively bishop of Lichfield and Worcester: 'The fellow himself is an irrecoverable scoundrel.'[3]

In the summer of 1760 Sterne cut his losses, abandoned his fruitless correspondence with Warburton, and turned to other concerns. Having reached York at the end of May, he had almost almost immediately made the fifteen-mile journey north-east, via Sutton-on-the-Forest and Stillington, to take possession of his new living. At the extremity of the plain north of York, Coxwold stood on the edge of the moors. The village centred on the fifteenth-century church of St Michael, then in need of repair, something Sterne would attend to in the following year. Though small, the village boasted both a grammar school and a modest village school, devoted to ensuring that the parish children had the required degree of functional literacy.[4] Newburgh Priory, the Fauconbergs' impressive if ungainly house, lay beyond Coxwold to the east (in fact, Sterne's first contacts with the family came at an unhappy juncture, for his patron's wife, Lady Catherine, had died in London on 29 May). To the north-east were the remains of the Gothic Byland Abbey, a late-twelfth-century Cistercian foundation which had fallen into ruin subsequent to the sixteenth-century suppression of the monasteries. Of more immediate interest to Sterne was the house he and his family were to occupy. Like much of the village it was late medieval in origin—an enormous chimney at the east end survives from that period—but had been much altered over the course of the previous three centuries. Though it was not a parsonage house, being rented from Lord Fauconberg, Sterne was to effect further additions and changes of his own, helping to give the house the attractively idiosyncratic appearance it retains today.[5]

Initially Sterne seems to have taken pleasure in the fruits of his preferment. Coxwold's situation was far preferable for the tubercular priest than the lower-lying Sutton-on-the-Forest, and in any case novelty always attracted Sterne. He began to plan changes to his house in order to accommodate his wife and daughter and give himself a suitable study in which to write. As he had done almost two decades earlier at Sutton, Sterne also set to work to improve his garden. In response to an enquiry from an admirer, he declared that any letter addressed to himself as 'Prebendary of York' would find him labouring in the vineyard, 'either pruneing, or digging or trenching, or weeding, or hacking up old roots, or wheeling away Rubbish' (*Letters*, 122). Though Sterne doubtless thought himself a labourer worthy of his hire, his fatigues would not be of long duration.

Domestic concerns apart, there was much else to be done. Lord Fauconberg needed Sterne's assistance to complete the long-standing enclosure scheme at Sutton, where the earl held substantial amounts of land; Sterne obliged promptly, and the matter was effectively complete within six weeks of his arrival. There was also the need to make the acquaintance of his parishioners and to socialize with those of suitable standing in the village. Lord Fauconberg's rank—he had been elevated to an earldom in 1756—probably stood in the way of any real intimacy. Coxwold was not London, and however free Sterne's relationships with the aristocracy had been there, especially when he was 'Shandying it', social distinctions counted for much more in the Yorkshire countryside. Throughout the remainder of his life, in fact, Sterne was careful to cultivate good but never excessively familiar relations with Fauconberg and his family. At all events, Fauconberg was never to Sterne what Stephen Croft had been at Stillington—and there was no other neighbour of comparable rank. Given the clamour of his arrival down in Yorkshire, Sterne's presence must have made many in the quiet village wary enough. Four months after his arrival the village grammar-schoolmaster, the Revd Robert Midgley, waspishly reported Sterne to be 'Eloquent *in* the pulpitt & not at all mute out of it'.[6]

Midgley was not alone in his reservations, for dutiful as Sterne was to his new patron, he was less conscientious in fulfilling his responsibilities with regard to humbler neighbours. Parish affairs at Sutton and Stillington remained in the hands of William Raper, the unqualified curate Sterne had appointed in the summer of 1759 at the time of his move to York. Ill-educated, Raper had done nothing to win the respect of the local communities—quite the reverse[7]—yet Sterne would make no attempt to remedy the situation for another year.

More striking than such indifference to the parishioners among whom he had lived for twenty years, however, is the degree to which Sterne was intent on putting all past frustrations and disappointments behind him. For two decades he had sought preferments, however modest, wherever they might be had. Having obtained places within the spiritual courts, he had also—by several accounts—thoroughly enjoyed the opportunities these positions offered of indulging his weakness for the law. Now, within the space of a year or so, he effectively abandoned his preferments—or at least the responsibilities that went with them. At both North Newbald and Alne and Tollerton he appointed substitutes to deal with outstanding business, delayed by his own neglect. More strikingly still, in the light of the furore surrounding Sterne's appointment there, he found no time even to act as commissary of the Peculiar Court of Pickering and Pocklington. That he was too disgusted to convene the court in 1759, following the enforced destruction of *A Political Romance*, is perhaps understandable—and might have been excused on the grounds of Elizabeth's serious illness. That he consolidated the work of four visitations—one each in Pickering and in Pocklington in both 1759 and 1760—into a single session, to which he sent a substitute, indicates eloquently how completely he now saw his future to lie in a quite different road from the ecclesiastical byways he had frequented for so long. Sterne did, in fact, appear once more in person as commissary at Pickering and Pocklington—in the summer of 1761—but never thereafter.

In his repudiation of the many petty frustrations he had endured for so long, Sterne's unaccustomed access to a supply of ready money certainly played a part. While he had been in London in May Stephen Croft had advanced Elizabeth Sterne 10 guineas for her immediate needs. In early October, when he received the fees due him as Vicar of Stillington, Sterne immediately repaid the loan. Even when his income would not meet his expenses, as would still happen frequently in the future, he retained a concern that his wife should want for nothing material. Otherwise, Elizabeth's recovery from her mental breakdown seems to have done nothing to improve their relationship. Neither did the petering out of Sterne's relationship with Catherine Fourmantel. Sterne was soon in flirtatious correspondence with other, more socially desirable women, including, in that summer of 1760, Mary Macartney, soon to marry a future governor of Jamaica, and 'My Witty Widow, Mrs. F[enton]'.[8] A passing reference by Mary Macartney to 'conjugal Squabbles' suggests that the state of the Sternes' marriage was common knowledge. Sterne's only extended reference to Elizabeth in his surviving correspondence at this time occurs in a letter written in Latin to John Hall-Stevenson. It is not complimentary—and suggests how unhappy both partners in the marriage must have been. 'I don't know what's the matter with me,' Sterne confessed, 'but I'm more sick and tired of my wife than ever—and possessed by a devil urging me to town . . . a lecherous devil that won't leave me alone, for since I'm no longer sleeping with my wife, I'm more lustful than I can bear—and so mortally in love—and foolish . . .'[9]

This letter was written in December 1760, by which time Sterne's delight in the novelty of Coxwold had long disappeared. It was work on the third and fourth volumes of *Tristram Shandy* that kept him so long in Yorkshire. In truth, he had worked hard at the continuation throughout the summer and autumn. Although, following the interruption of Warburton's correspondence, he was still working at the beginning of the third volume at the end of June,[10] by early August it was complete. Initially at least, Sterne may have felt his pathway straightforward enough. The second volume of his work had concluded with Corporal Trim's reading of the sermon to Walter Shandy, my uncle Toby, and Dr Slop, who are sitting in the parlour while Elizabeth Shandy is in labour in an upstairs bedroom. The most important task in volume III would be to get the hero born—something duly accomplished, though not without plentiful digression. If so much was clear, however, the masterful chain of tragicomic events Sterne sets in motion is a tribute to his ability to weave together the humorous and sentimental threads of his book. So, Tristram is finally brought into the world by the maladroit man-midwife Dr Slop who, mistaking Tristram's head for his hip, crushes the child's nose with his newfangled obstetrical forceps. The results are catastrophic. First Slop must improvise a bridge, using a piece of whalebone from the stays of the servant Susanna, in an attempt to restore the infant hero's mangled nose. Tristram almost forgotten, the bridge becomes the source of poignant comic misunderstanding between the distraught Walter and the ineptly sympathetic Toby. Walter's attempt to redeem his son's misfortune, determining to give him the 'fortunate' name of Trismegistus, is frustrated by his inability to put on his breeches quickly enough, leaving Susanna to run down the gallery with the name in (and partly out of) her head, so that the curate, assured that the expiring child is to be christened '*Tris*—something', baptizes him 'Tristram'—a name Walter holds in particular contempt. If, in summary, this is black farce, then the pathos with which Sterne depicted the disappointed Walter's reaction—'My father lay stretched across the bed as still as if the hand of death had pushed him down, for a full hour and a half, before he began to play upon the floor with the toe of that foot which hung over the bed-side' (*TS* iv. ii. 219)—both recalls the inconsolable Sterne after the death of one of his children (in James Greenwood's vivid retelling) and allows for the extended account of the touching relationship between Walter and Toby, a relationship poised between sympathetic identification and total mutual incomprehension.

That Sterne was happy with his new instalment is evident from a remark made in a letter to the 'witty widow': 'I think there is more laughable humour,—with equal degree of Cervantik Satyr—if not more than in the last' (*Letters*, 120–1). Anxious as he was to finish his continuation, Sterne was soon given a further spur to industry for, in the autumn, he discovered he had a rival. In September a work purporting to be the third volume of *Tristram Shandy* appeared in print in London. Written by a London schoolmaster, John Carr, it seemed likely enough to deceive the public for Sterne to publish a disclaimer denying all knowledge of the imposture, and declaring that his own continuation would again appear from R. & J. Dodsley in London, and John Hinxman in York.

The extent to which Sterne's circumstances had changed in barely six months is glaringly apparent from his uncontainable anxiety to return to London. For twenty years, he had sought further preferment in the Church and in March he had pressed his suit on both Lord Fauconberg and Archbishop Gilbert, in his haste to confirm his preferment to Coxwold. Having acquired and taken possession of the living, he could scarcely wait to escape from the rural seclusion it offered in order to return to the social round of London. Though his departure was several times delayed, he finally reached the capital once more on 6 December. In his letter to Hall-Stevenson, he denied that his haste was in any way motivated by vanity or the desire of once more being the centre of attention.[11] All the same, Sterne immediately took up where he had left off in the spring. The visit he paid to Archbishop Gilbert on the following day may have been a courtesy call, but it was also an earnest of Sterne's intention of rejoining the social world. Writing to Stephen Croft on Christmas Day, the priest forbore any mention of that Christian feast in favour of informing his friend that 'I have been in . . . a continual hurry since the moment I arrived here—what with my books, and what with visiters, and visitings' (*Letters*, 126). Writing the following month, he grumbled complacently that 'I never dined at home once since I arrived—am fourteen dinners deep engaged just now, and fear matters will be worse with me in that point than better' (*Letters*, 128).

On this visit Sterne threw himself into metropolitan life with the same delight as the previous year, but with greater facility. His Yorkshire friends had expressed doubts about the more audaciously bawdy sections of Sterne's continuation of *Tristram Shandy*—notably 'Slawkenbergius' Tale'—which they had read or had read to them. Sterne's London audience, or at least that part of it disposed to be sympathetic to him, had no such qualms. Sterne himself found it easier to concur with these than to pay overmuch heed to provincial reservations. To Stephen Croft the author wrote:

> I am not much in pain upon what gives my kind friends at Stillington so much on the chapter of *Noses*—because, as the principal satire throughout that part is levelled at those learned blockheads who, in all ages, have wasted their time and much learning upon points as foolish—it shifts off the idea of what you fear, to another point—and 'tis thought here very good—'twill pass muster—I mean not with all—no—no! I shall be attacked and pelted, either from cellars or garrets, write what I will—and besides, must expect to have a party against me of many hundreds—who either do not—or will not laugh. 'Tis enough if I divide the world. (*Letters*, 126).

The circumstances in which Sterne found himself were markedly changed. Nine months earlier he had been indebted to Stephen Croft for the opportunity to visit the capital. Now he was able to pass on the London news to Croft in York. The death of George II on 25 October 1760 led to the accession to the throne of the late king's grandson. George III was a young man—just 22—and an idealist. He gave early indications that he took his position very seriously, and Sterne recorded his practice of rising early, riding out with his brothers, and devoting himself subsequently to business, trying to make himself easily available to petitioners without leaving them at the mercy of those surrounding the throne. Sterne's graceful compliment to the king and his brother, the duke of York, in the fourth volume of *Tristram Shandy*, published in January 1761, doubtless reflected his genuine admiration; the compliment relates to Walter Shandy's lucubrations concerning the naming of his son, of whom he asserts that, 'heaven is witness! that in the warmest transports of my wishes for the prosperity of my child, I never once wished to crown his head with more glory and honour, than what GEORGE or EDWARD would have spread around it' (*TS* IV. viii. 223). Under the guidance of the Scots peer the earl of Bute, the new monarch was making an attempt to turn himself into the Patriot King imagined by Henry St John, Lord Bolingbroke, in his opposition writings of the 1730s. Bolingbroke's anti-Walpole politics—his advocacy of an end to the widespread system of patronage Walpole had developed and exploited—he presented as a campaign against corruption. Sterne drily reported George III's attempts to put Bolingbroke's opposition morality into practice: 'The K[ing],' he wrote, 'seems resolved to bring all things back to their original principles, and to stop the torrent of corruption and laziness' (*Letters*, 126).

Sterne also reported to Stephen Croft details of furious arguments raging over the malign influence supposedly exercised by the earl of Bute, a close adviser of the young king's mother, and over William Pitt's conduct of the war in Germany. Though he had dedicated the first London edition of volumes I and II of *Tristram Shandy* to Pitt less than a year previously, Sterne was now caught between waning admiration for the prime minister and a desire to speak well of the friends of the young monarch. So he expressed his view of the rivalry between Pitt and Bute and their respective followers in terms reminiscent of Gulliver's account of the Big-endians and Little-endians in Lilliput: 'we shall be soon all Prussians and Anti-Prussians, B[ute]'s and Anti-B[ute]s, and those distinctions will just do as well as Whig and Tory—and for aught I know serve the same ends' (*Letters*, 126). With public opinion shifting against the war, now in its fifth year, Sterne wrote to Croft on 17 February 1761 that,

> We had the greatest expectations yesterday that ever were raised, of a pitched battle in the H[ouse] of C[ommons], wherein Mr. P[itt] was to have entered and thrown down the gauntlet, in defence of the German war.—There never was so full a house—the gallery full to the top—I was there all the day—when, lo! a political fit of the gout seized the great combattant—he entered not the lists. (*Letters*, 129)

Despite Pitt's absence, a fierce debate ensued, with those for and against the continuation of the war equally in evidence. Observing the proceedings, Sterne must have been reminded, when comparisons were drawn with the conclusion of the War of the Spanish Succession, both of his own father and of uncle Toby. One of the speakers argued that 'the reasons for wishing a peace now, were the same as at the peace of Utretch [*sic*]—that the people behind the curtain could not maintain the war and their places too, so were for making another sacrifice of the nation, to their own interests.—After all—the cry for a peace is so general, that it will certainly end in one' (*Letters*, 129).[12]

To pass on news from the capital to his Yorkshire friends was certainly gratifying to Sterne. Nothing, however, more vividly indicates his changed circumstances than the fact that, after so many fruitless years of seeking to obtain the ear of others, the writer now found himself cultivated for the influence he might exercise—and by none other than his old patron Stephen Croft. Croft's son (also Stephen), a junior officer in the Royal North Britain Regiment of Dragoons, was in search of promotion. The young cornet's father sought Sterne's aid and—doubtless mindful of his own father's frustrated hopes for promotions throughout his career—he promised to do his best: 'My friend, Mr. Charles T[ownshend], will be now secretary of war—he bid me wish him joy of it, though not in possession.—I will ask him—and depend, my most worthy friend, that you shall not be ignorant of what I learn from him—believe me ever, ever, Yours, L.S.' (*Letters*, 130). How dependable a patron Sterne proved to be, however, is uncertain. A month later, he was writing to Stephen Croft playing down his influence with the secretary of war and suggesting that the state of the war made the present moment unpropitious for further intercession. Stephen Croft received his desired promotion later in the year, but the absence of any mention of it in his letters suggests that Sterne played no significant part in the affair.

In fact, for all the pleasure Sterne took in his new eminence—real or imagined—he had other, more pressing matters to occupy him. The third and fourth volumes of *Tristram Shandy* appeared on 28 January 1761. The nervousness he had revealed a year earlier about the moral censure his book might provoke—in the wake of his correspondence with Bishop Warburton—had given way to a determination to defy all public criticism. It was just as well. If the first two volumes had risked censure, then the second instalment seemed positively to invite it. Besides Tristram's narrative of the mishaps surrounding his birth, the volumes contained Slawkenbergius' tale of the well-endowed stranger whose enormous nose sets all Strasbourg aflutter, and the tale of Phutatorius and the hot chestnut that falls into his breeches at the visitation dinner. Just three weeks after publication the author could reveal that 'One half of the town abuse my book as bitterly, as the other half cry it up to the skies', but he added with satisfaction, 'the best is, they abuse and buy it, and at such a rate, that we are going on with a second edition, as fast as possible' (*Letters*, 129–30).

How much of Sterne's apparent self-confidence was real and how much affected is more difficult to gauge. As his Stillington friends had feared, volumes III and IV provoked real outrage. In London it was alleged that 'All the Bishops and Clergy cry out shame upon him,'[13] and there was even a report that Sterne had been forbidden the Court. Accurate or not, there seems to have been some truth in the fact that Sterne's admiration for the young King George III was not reciprocated. When the novelist was presented at Court it was alongside the Revd Alexander Cruden, author of the celebrated *Concordance to the Bible.* Cruden was received with great marks of royal favour and thanked for his services to the cause of religion. When the Revd Laurence Sterne was presented, however:

> the King made so slight a bow, that the disappointed Author told the noble Lord by whom he was presented that he was confident that the King could not have distinctly heard his name, and begged to be presented a second time. On his name being again announced, the King replied to the Nobleman, 'My Lord, you have told me so already'.[14]

Sterne, meanwhile, was stung into denying all rumours that his personal character had suffered:

> I thank God . . . I have never yet made a friend, or connection I have forfeited, or done ought to forfeit—but on the contrary, my true character is better understood, and where I had one friend last year, who did me honour, I have three now.—If my enemies knew that by this rage of abuse, and ill will, they were effectually serving the interests both of myself, and works, they would be more quiet—but it has been the fate of my betters, who have found, that the way to fame, is like the way to heaven—through much tribulation—and till I shall have the honour to be as much mal-treated as Rabelais, and Swift were, I must continue humble; for I have not filled up the measure of half their *persecutions*. (*Letters*, 132)

The renewed allusion here to his fellow-clerics Rabelais and Swift reveals once more not only the author's own points of reference but also the fact that the renewed attacks on *Tristram Shandy* centred not simply on its indecency per se but on the impropriety of a clergyman writing such a book. In an unsigned review in the February number of the *Monthly Review*, Owen Ruffhead referred to the generally favourable reception accorded by the magazine to the first two volumes of *Tristram Shandy*, recalling his own praise of the author as 'infinitely more ingenious and entertaining than any other of the present race of Novelists'.[15] The compliment, however, was merely a preface to a long, hostile review. No one, Ruffhead suggested, could have supposed the work would have been so fashionable; still less could anyone have imagined its author to be a 'Dignitary' of the Church of England, 'had not the wanton brat been publicly owned by its reverend Parent'.[16]

Conscious of the objection that there had been little complaint about the content of Sterne's novel until its author's clerical calling had been revealed, Ruffhead continued:

> It is true, that in some degree, it is our duty, as Reviewers, to examine books, abstracted from any regard to their Author. But this rule is not one without exception: for where a Writer is publicly known, by his own acknowlegement, it then becomes a part of our duty, to animadvert on any flagrant impropriety of character . . . there is a certain faculty called *Discretion*, which reasonable men will ever esteem; tho' you, the arch *Prebend* Mr. *Yorick*, alias Tristram *Shandy*, have done all in your power to laugh it out of fashion.[17]

Ruffhead even invoked Thomas Hobbes's *Leviathan* against Sterne on the importance of discretion, before changing tack and levelling instead the more dangerous charge of 'DULLNESS'. 'Yes, indeed, Mr. Tristram, you are dull, *very dull*.' The complaint is expanded throughout the second part of the review which, alleging volumes III and IV to be, on the whole, 'not only scandalously indecent, but absolutely DULL', concludes with the 'friendly admonition' that Sterne leave off writing altogether.

Two months later Sterne's fellow-novelist Tobias Smollett, writing in the *Critical Review*, gave a much more balanced account of the second instalment, in the course of which he noted the importance of Rabelais as a model for Sterne. (Others agreed, and those who had no relish for *Gargantua and Pantagruel* had little taste either for Sterne.[18]) Despite some reservations elsewhere, Smollett expressed particular admiration for the characters of Walter Shandy, uncle Toby, and Corporal Trim, declaring that 'incoherent and digressive as it is, the book certainly abounds with pertinent observations on life and characters, humourous incidents, poignant ridicule, and marks of taste and erudition'.[19] Even among Sterne's admirers, however, reaction was mixed. Bishop Richard Hurd found volume IV to be 'full as humorous' as the first two—but he declared volume III to be 'insufferably dull and even stupid'.[20] What Hurd could not deny, even as he enjoyed parts of Sterne's work, was its indecency; the author, he wrote, does not seem 'capable of following the advice given him: "*of laughing in such a manner as that Virgins and Priests might laugh with him*"'.[21] Not all ecclesiastical readers were as backward in expressing their reservations as Hurd. Mark Hildesley, bishop of Sodor and Man, replying to the severely critical remarks on Sterne's work of Samuel Richardson—who had protected himself by not reading volumes III and IV and only glancing at the first two—suggests a more general reaction:

> Your Strictures, Good Sir, upon the indelicately witty Yoric,—From the little I accidentally Read of Shameless-Shandy—(for that little was enough to forbid me to read more) I believe to be very just . . . That Spiritual Men, & ecclesiastical Dignitaries Shoud Countenance & Encourage Such—a Production, & such—an Author, is hardly Capable of any sort of Defence.[22]

Others were equally negative. Even the usually sympathetic Dr Thomas Newton, bishop of Bristol, thought volumes III and IV to be 'more gross and offensive' than the first instalment, and reported adverse public reaction: 'All the graver part of the world are highly offended; all the light and trifling are not pleased'.[23]

What no one could deny was that, with his continuation of *Tristram Shandy*, Sterne had kept himself firmly in the public eye.[24] In the midst of the controversy he was invited to preach a charity sermon at the London Foundling Hospital. George Whateley, the treasurer of the Hospital, requested Sterne to preach for half an hour, though the fatigue of speaking in public, which was soon to persuade him to leave off preaching almost entirely, led Sterne to suggest that a short sermon would be just as effective in raising funds for the Hospital, since it was no more than a reminder to the audience of its Christian duty, being strictly 'useless where men have *wit enough* to be honest'. In any case, he accepted the invitation and, on Sunday, 3 May, preached the sermon 'The Parable of the Rich Man and Lazarus Consider'd' (later to appear in the fourth volume of his sermons in 1766) to a large and distinguished audience. The subsequent collection raised £55. 9*s*. 2*d*. for the charity's funds.[25]

A few days later Sterne received a further indication of the extent of his fame. On 9 May the Society of Artists held an exhibition which included Joshua Reynolds's great portrait of Sterne, as well as both Simon-François Ravenet's original drawing after the Reynolds portrait, which had in turn served for the frontispiece for *The Sermons of Mr. Yorick*, and Edward Fisher's mezzotint of Sterne.[26] (Had Sterne been in London during the following year's exhibition of the society he could have admired George Stubbs's painting of the racehorse Tristram Shandy.[27])

Socially too, Sterne's life was as active as ever. Back in February he had told Stephen Croft of a planned visit to John Spencer, shortly to be created Viscount Spencer of Althorp, and of a grand assembly to be given by the countess of Northumberland at Northumberland House. Sterne dined with Elizabeth Montagu and made the acquaintance of her friend Elizabeth Vesey, the first of the blue-stocking hostesses, who had begun her fashionable intellectual gatherings in the early 1750s, with whom he began to correspond in his most sentimental manner.

After a full six months in London Sterne returned home to Yorkshire in June. Given the nostalgia for the delights of a rural existence—the Horatian *beatus ille* theme—that pervades so much eighteenth-century writing, Sterne's reaction to country retirement makes ironic reading. The attractions of Coxwold had quickly disappeared, to be replaced by a distaste for the restrictions of country life. 'I rejoice you are in London—rest you there in peace', he wrote to John Hall-Stevenson, adding:

> here 'tis the devil.—You was a good prophet.—I wish myself back again, as you told me I should . . . the transition from rapid motion to absolute rest was too violent.—I should have walked about the streets of York ten days, as a proper medium to have passed thro', before I entered upon my rest.—I staid but a moment, and I have been here but a few, to satisfy me I have not managed my miseries like a wise man—and if God, for my consolation under them, had not poured forth the spirit of Shandeism into me, which will not suffer me to think two moments upon any grave subject, I would else, just now lay down and die. (*Letters*, 139)

Though he tried to bolster his own spirits—suggesting that in half an hour he would doubtless be 'as merry as a monkey—and as mischievous too, and forget it all'—not even Sterne's willingness to surrender to the spirit of his own fictional creation could mask the very real sense of the difference between his life as a celebrity in London and the round of priestly and domestic duties which were his lot in Coxwold. Nothing in Coxwold pleased him: the weather was as bad as a 'bleak December', he lamented, expressing once more the desire to be back in London: 'Curse of poverty, and absence from those we love!—they are two great evils which embitter all things' (*Letters*, 139).

As though struck by the force of what he had written—how little time ago had he declared that he wrote 'Not to be *fed*, but to be *famous*'—Sterne drew back. Poverty, he now acknowledged, was no overwhelming problem, and 'as for matrimony, I should be a beast to rail at it'. Elizabeth, he told his friend, was 'easy' again with their life, but, he added darkly, 'the world is not so'. Reports of the bad relations between Elizabeth and himself were obviously well known, not only in Yorkshire but also in London. Certainly they had reached the ears of Elizabeth's cousin: Elizabeth Montagu upbraided Sterne with a report that he had spoken badly of his wife in public. Sterne defended himself, asserting that he had always given his wife 'the Character of as moral & virtuous a woman as ever God made'. Moreover, he added: 'What Occasion'd Discontent ever betwixt us, is now no more—we have settled Acc^ts^ to each others Satisfaction & honour—& I am persuaded shall end our days with out one word of reproach or even Incivility' (*Letters*, 136).

'Without one word' would have been scarcely less accurate. During the winter of 1760–1 Sterne was so busy with his social life in London that he found no time even to write to Elizabeth at home in Yorkshire. As an afterthought to a long letter to Stephen Croft he requested his friend: 'Pray when you have read this, send the news to Mrs. Sterne' (*Letters*, 133). In Sterne's version, it was only public tattle that persuaded the couple to spend some time together. Were it not for the scandal, Elizabeth 'declares herself happier without me', Sterne told Hall-Stevenson, adding that the decision had been made not in anger but from experience and good sense.[28] Indeed, Elizabeth already had plans to rid herself of her husband decently by finding a wealthy young man to whom Sterne might act as tutor on the Grand Tour.

In the meantime Sterne had work to do. 'To-morrow morning, (if Heaven permit) I begin the fifth volume of Shandy', he wrote to Hall-Stevenson at the end of June. A month later he told his friend, 'I go on with Tristram', while on 21 September he wrote to a female correspondent, again from Coxwold: 'I am scribbling away at my Tristram. These two volumes are, I think, the best.—I shall write as long as I live, 'tis, in fact, my hobby-horse: and so much am I delighted with my uncle Toby's imaginary character, that I am become an enthusiast' (*Letters*, 143). His earlier doubts about the critical reaction to his work had been cast aside, Sterne wrote: 'I care not a curse for the critics—I'll load my vehicle with what goods *he* sends me, and they may take 'em off my hands, or let them alone' (*Letters*, 140).

The summer of 1761 was a prosperous period for Sterne, one when the 'curse of poverty', as he had termed it, was lifted from him. 'I have bought seven hundred books at a purchase dog cheap—and many good,' he wrote jubilantly to Hall-Stevenson in July, 'and I have been a week getting them set up in my best room here' (*Letters*, 142). Moreover, he was able to enjoy in full the pleasures of York Race Week in August and to visit John Hall-Stevenson and his friends at Crazy Castle. Nor was Sterne alone in enjoying the rewards of his fame. Having been abandoned for so long, Elizabeth and Lydia at last benefited from Laurence's success. Sterne purchased a chaise for his wife and a pony for his daughter: gifts which left all three happy (as the consequent absence of Elizabeth and Lydia gave Sterne himself some much-needed peace in which to write). The continuation of *Tristram Shandy* even briefly became a family venture, for Sterne reported that 'my wife knits and listens as I read her chapters', and Lydia, now in her fourteenth year, assisted her father by copying new material.

In the autumn there was more general celebration. On 22 September the coronation of the young George III took place in London, at Westminster Abbey. Coxwold celebrated by roasting an entire large ox, 'with his Head on and Horns gilt',[29] after which the bells were rung to summon the villagers to church. There Sterne preached from memory a sermon on the text 'And they sware unto the Lord with a loud Voice, and with Shouting, and with Trumpets, and with Cornets. And all Judah rejoiced at the oath.' Sterne's sermon was well judged for the festive occasion, not only for the text but also for the story of King Abijah and his succession by Asa, from which it was taken. The tale of a war-torn kingdom returned to peace and prosperity under a youthful new monarch found an obvious parallel in the present-day hostilities against France that had begun in 1756. Lest this seem too remote to the immediate concerns of his rural congregation, Sterne concluded with an elegant admonition: 'In vain shall we celebrate the day with a loud voice, and with shouting, and with trumpets,—if we do not do it likewise with the internal and more certain marks of sincerity,—a reformation and purity in our manners.'[30] Presumably the reformation did not start immediately, for as the earl of Fauconberg's steward, Richard Chapman, informed his lordship:

> about 3 o'Clock the Ox was cut up and Distributed Amongst at least 3000 People, after which two Barrils of Ale was Distributed amongst those that could get nearest to 'em, Ringing of Bells Squibs and Crackers Tarr Barrills and Bonefires, &c and a Ball in the Evening Concluded the Joyfull Day.[31]

If the Coxwold villagers enjoyed themselves, Sterne's own enjoyment of the festivities was tinged with disappointment that he was not in London to enjoy the coronation celebrations there, as he confessed in a letter written to an acquaintance who had the good fortune herself to be in the capital for the occasion.[32]

This, however, was impossible, for besides his ecclesiastical duties Sterne was busy with the continuation of *Tristram Shandy* throughout the summer and into the autumn of 1761. Too busy, for—as he later wrote—he suffered a severe haemorrhage: 'hard writing in the summer, together with preaching, which I have not strength for, is ever fatal to me' (*Letters*, 150). In an attempt to prolong his life Sterne determined to attempt a cure by travelling to the warmer climate of the south of France. Though Elizabeth Sterne's hope that her husband might find a place as a 'bear-leader', or travelling tutor, was not fulfilled, by September Sterne was actively planning a trip abroad.

Most important among the concerns of the pluralist Sterne was the need to find curates for his various parishes. For this Sterne needed the permission of his archbishop, though such permission was routinely granted to those travelling for their health. At Sutton and Stillington, Sterne settled on the Revd Marmaduke Callis, a man in his late twenties, who was appointed in September 1761 at a salary of £32—receiving in addition permission to live rent-free in the vicarage at Sutton. Though intended to compensate Callis for the modest salary he was to receive, the concession was one that Sterne—and more particularly his wife, daughter, and successor in Sutton—would come to regret: in 1765, while Callis was still in residence, the vicarage would burn down, leaving the question of liability for repairs still unresolved at Sterne's death.[33] For Coxwold, Sterne found James Kilner, who began to serve in October or November 1761, when Sterne left Coxwold for London. Kilner was already in his mid-thirties but, lacking a degree (and even a university education), he had failed to be ordained a priest and was currently serving as a humble usher, or assistant master, at Coxwold School. He received the still more modest annual salary of £30. His ecclesiastical responsibilities taken care of, Sterne made arrangements also for his friend Stephen Croft to look after his personal affairs, and engaged Lord Fauconberg's agent, Richard Chapman, to follow suit at Coxwold.

Having so settled his affairs in Yorkshire, Sterne left for London towards the end of November, taking with him the fifth and sixth volumes of *Tristram Shandy*. He did so, perhaps, a little more apprehensively than the year before. For the first time he would have to do without the assistance of the Dodsleys. That this was Sterne's own decision seems unlikely. Possibly the Dodsleys themselves, acutely sensitive to the market, thought that the book had had its day.[34] Much more probably, the brothers were uneasy about the continuing bawdy of Sterne's novel and his evident determination to face out all censure. In 1759, it seems certain, Sterne *had* accepted Robert Dodsley's advice to tone down some of the indecency characteristic of the first draft of *Tristram Shandy*. Now, emboldened by his success, Sterne determined to press ahead in his own way—his own way including the chapter 'Upon Whiskers' (*TS* v. i. 276–9), the ludicrous account of Tristram's accidental circumcision by the falling sash-window (*TS* v. xvii. 301), and the tale of uncle Toby's amours, leading to the page left blank for the reader to paint a picture of the 'concupiscible' Widow Wadman, 'as like your mistress as you can——as unlike your wife as your conscience will let you—'tis all one to me——please but your own fancy in it' (*TS* vi. xxxviii. 376–7). His only apparent concession to prudence was, at a late stage in the production of the continuation, to remove the third of three mottoes from the title-page. This had read 'Si quis Clericus, aut Monachus, verba joculatoria, risum moventia sciebat anathema esto', or 'If any priest or monk know jesting words exciting laughter, anathema upon him'. Given the widespread voicing of criticism that *Tristram Shandy* was an improper book for a priest to have written, Sterne perhaps accepted that the motto was unnecessarily provocative—though it still appeared on the title-page of a Dublin edition of Volumes V and VI which was published more or less simultaneously with the English edition,[35] and when a second English edition of the volumes appeared in 1767, Sterne reinserted the motto.

Whatever the precise circumstances and the reasons for them, Sterne now broke with Robert and James Dodsley whom he had first approached back in 1759, and who had done so much to ensure his celebrity in 1760, as author both of *Tristram Shandy* and of the *Sermons of Mr. Yorick.* In their place he turned to Thomas Becket and Peter Dehondt, the booksellers with whom he would remain linked professionally for the remainder of his life. Initially his arrangement with them was similar to that he had agreed with Dodsley in 1759, by which Sterne himself took some of the risk in publishing, buying paper and arranging for the printing of the two volumes by the notable London printer William Strahan.[36]

It seems likely that the details of this agreement were far from settled when Sterne left for London, yet progress was quickly made so that T. Becket and P. A. Dehondt were named as publishers of the fifth and sixth volumes of *The Life and Opinions of Tristram Shandy, Gentleman* in the newspaper advertisements which first appeared on 17 December. The two volumes themselves were on sale less than a week later, on 22 December. Perhaps to assure the public that his book still merited the protection of those who had patronized it on its first appearance, Sterne added a dedication to John, Viscount Spencer, who would become one of his closest and longest-standing aristocratic friends. Astutely, Sterne added:

> I beg your Lordship will forgive me, if, at the same time I dedicate this work to you, I join Lady SPENCER, in the liberty I take of inscribing the story of *Le Fever* in the sixth volume to her name; for which I have no other motive, which my heart has informed me of, but that the story is a humane one. (*TS* v. [273])

Whatever his heart may have informed him, Sterne's head was undoubtedly guided not merely by gallantry but by commercial acumen; if Lady Spencer accepted the dedication, who could doubt but that the new volumes were suitable for female readers of the greatest sensibility? In fairness, however, it must be said that Sterne was not wholly cynical in his relations with the Spencers, who remained loyal friends to him: he made a fair copy of the Le Fever episode to present to Lady Spencer,[37] and when Lord Spencer presented the writer with a silver inkstand three years later, he responded in a manner at once simple and eloquent: 'I wish I knew how to than[k] You properly for your obliging present; for to do it with all the sense I have of your obliging goodness to me, would offend You; and to do it with less—would offend myself. I can only say to Lord Spencer "*That I thank him* . . ." ' (*Letters*, 258–9).

In 1761, however, Sterne's commercial sense was evident in everything to do with his latest volumes. To protect himself against imitation and forgery, Sterne took the extraordinary step of personally signing every copy of volume V. The *Critical Review* thought the ploy unnecessary:

> Mr. S.—— might have saved himself the trouble of signing his name to each volume of this performance . . . as it would be impossible for any reader, even of the least discernment, not to see in the perusal of half a page, that these volumes can be the production of no other than the original author of Tristram Shandy.[38]

Sterne, however, had good reason to fear the undiscerning purchaser. John Carr's purported continuation of *Tristram Shandy* had taken in some readers when it appeared in September 1760, and though a spurious work published in 1766 purporting to be the ninth volume fooled few, Richard Griffith's fictional *Posthumous Works of a Late Celebrated Genius* would be regarded as genuine on its publication in 1770. Even in December 1761 itself, a pamphlet published in London under the title *Life and Amours of Hafen Slawkenbergius, Author of the Institute of Noses* was advertised as being printed 'in the Size and Manner of Tristram Shandy, in order that so valuable a Supplement may be preserved by being bound at the End of the Sixth Volume'.

The *Critical Review*'s notice was, moreover, decidedly ambiguous. 'Here', averred the writer, 'we find the same unconnected rhapsody, the same rambling digression, the eccentric humour, the peculiar wit, petulance, pruriency and ostentation of learning'[39] of the previous instalments. If Sterne's novel had captivated readers in 1760 by its novelty, then these volumes, the *Critical Review* implied, were simply more of the same. The *Court Magazine* expressed the lukewarm view that 'those who are fond of the other volumes, may probably have pleasure in reading these',[40] while other reviewers simply found that they had nothing to say of the continuation that had not been said of the earlier volumes. That novelty had its limits was suggested even more economically in private by James Boswell, once Sterne's foremost admirer, who wrote of the volumes: 'We have just a succession of Surprise, surprise, surprise'[41]—and declared that he would read no more.

Like Boswell, the *Critical* reviewers thought that Sterne had written himself out and expected these volumes to be the last. Nevertheless, the continuation attracted praise and censure, along with mere indifference. The censure focused predictably enough on the novel's indecency and on the peculiar impropriety of the fiction being the work of a clergyman. Doubtless intriguing readers by reference to a 'ridiculous disaster which happened to Tristram Shandy in his infancy, and which we think rather too impure to be repeated',[42] the *Critical Review*'s relentless irony could have left few in doubt that Sterne's Rabelaisian humour was in full evidence, even as it asserted Sterne himself to be no match for the French original. Even this reviewer, however, acknowledged (rather vaguely it is true) that the volumes contained 'much good satire on the follies of life; many pertinent remarks on characters and things; and some pathetic touches of nature, which compels us to wish the author had never stooped to the exhibition of buffoonery'.[43]

The wish was echoed by other notices which, again like the *Critical Review*, singled out the episode of the death of Le Fever for particular praise. This, said the *Critical Review*, 'is beautifully pathetic, and exhibits the character of Toby and his corporal in such a point of view, as must endear them to every reader of sensibility'.[44] In the *Monthly Review*, John Langhorne—himself an ordained clergyman—concurred, citing the episode at length and commenting that it 'does greater honour to the abilities and disposition of the Author, than any other part of his work'. Langhorne's is, in many ways, one of the finest contemporary reviews of

Tristram Shandy, certainly of the fifth and sixth volumes. Without abusing Sterne, Langhorne makes it abundantly clear that he has real and appropriate reservations about the writing of indecent literature by a priest of the Church of England:

> Have we not then a right to complain, if a person, by profession obliged to discountenance indecency, and expressly commanded by those pure and divine doctrines he teaches to avoid it; ought we not to have censured such a one, if he introduced obscenity as wit, and encouraged the depravity of young and unfledged vice, by libidinous ideas and indecent illusions?[45]

Langhorne's is a modest and moderate complaint against aspects of Sterne's book unbecoming a priest. Sterne though had thrown all caution to the wind. The licentiousness many deprecated in his writings was now allegedly characteristic of his private conduct. Samuel Johnson is recorded as having declared himself to have been in Sterne's company on just one occasion, 'and then his attempt at merriment consisted in his display of a drawing too indecently gross to have delighted even in a brothel'.[46] Johnson, who had little time for Sterne as a man or writer, perhaps exaggerated the indecency of the drawing produced. All the same, the painter Henry Fuseli—not the primmest of men—was shocked, when he met him, by Sterne's language.[47] A still coarser anecdote survives concerning Sterne's delight in sexual innuendo: 'An old Dowager asked Sterne how old he was. He answer'd Quatre Fois, Madame, shewing her he knew that she meant to find whether he was able to gratify her'.[48] Whatever the truth of these stories, it is difficult to imagine that Sterne could have achieved or sustained his extraordinary social success if such behaviour were characteristic of him.

Wit and licentiousness are so inseparably a part of *Tristram Shandy*, however, that it is perhaps surprising how many readers were willing, even if reluctantly, to overlook such passages in order to enjoy what they truly admired in Sterne: his talent for pathos. Having elaborated his objection against Sterne's indecency, John Langhorne changed tack, arguing that since Sterne had published *The Sermons of Mr. Yorick* he had 'been of opinion that his excellence lay not so much in the humorous as in the pathetic; and in this opinion we have been confirmed by the . . . story of Le Fever. We appeal to the Heart of every reader whether our judgment is not right?'[49] It was a perceptive question, for while most reviewers concentrated on Sterne's wit, whimsy, and indecency, it was precisely the pathetic that the generality of readers came to value in Sterne's work, the more so as the decade (and the century) went on. By some, at least, it was valued immediately. One female reader, who read the two volumes within days of their appearance, shed tears at the story of Le Fever, and wrote to tell Sterne that the thought of the accusing spirit flying up to heaven's chancery with the oath (in volume VI, chapter viii) was 'sublime'. Thanking her for the compliment, Sterne was pleased—and vain—enough to confide that 'my friend, Mr. Garrick, thinks so too' (*Letters*, 150).

Delighted as the novelist certainly was by the approbation of his readers, illness allowed him little respite. On Christmas Eve 1761—two days after publication of the volumes—Sterne was actively making preparations for his journey to France. Checking his accounts he found himself in need, and scribbled off a direct note to David Garrick: 'upon reviewing my finances, this morning, wth some unforeseen expences—I find I should set out with 20p^{ds} less—than a prudent man ought—will You lend me twenty pounds' (*Letters*, 146). Fortunately for Sterne, Garrick obliged at once and, with his purse prudently if not copiously filled, Sterne sat down to order his affairs against the possibility, as he wrote bluntly to his wife, 'I should die abroad'.

Despite the couple's troubled past, Sterne's thoughts were all for Elizabeth's comfort—and he left a memorandum relating to his financial affairs with Elizabeth Montagu to be passed to Elizabeth Sterne in the event of his death. His estate Sterne estimated at £1,800 or more, together with around £200 from his livings, and whatever the sale of his library and the publication of his work might fetch. He instructed Elizabeth as to those writings of his that remained unpublished, and advised her how she should invest the proceeds from them, adding a strong warning that, if Lydia should marry, his wife should 'upon no Delusive prospect, or promise from any one . . . leave Y^{r} self DEPENDENT; reserve enough for y^{r} comfort—or let her wait y^{r} Death' (*Letters*, 147).

Foremost among his unpublished works, Sterne indicated, were more sermons—sufficient to fill another three volumes (though he advised selecting just enough for two). There were also bundles of letters, now in Coxwold, York, and in the trunk in London in which he had deposited the sermons, 'to be sifted over, <for> in search of some either of Wit, or Humor—or what is better than both—of Humanity & good nature' (*Letters*, 146). Such letters, Sterne continued, would make up a further two volumes, and, he added, 'as not one of 'em was ever wrote, like Popes or Voitures to be printed, they are more likely to be read'. In addition there was the picture of 'the Mountebank & his Macaroni'—the portraits Sterne and Thomas Bridges had painted of each other—which, Sterne indicated, 'is in a Lady's hands, who upon seeing 'em,—most cavallierly declared She would <not> never part with them—And from an excesse of Civility—or rather Weakness I could not summon up severity, to demand them' (*Letters*, 148). His mind concentrated by the thought of his possibly imminent death, Sterne had the foresight to write the lady's name on a card which he sealed in an envelope, giving Elizabeth Montagu discreet hints as to how to blackmail her, should she be still reluctant to hand over the picture in the event of Sterne's demise.

Finally, Sterne reminded Elizabeth, there was also 'the Political Romance I wrote', though he hoped that it would not be necessary to publish this, given his ridicule of Francis Topham whom Sterne now believed he had wronged, and 'an undeserved Compliment' to John Fountayne. The mere thought of Fountayne—'a very corrupt man'—powerfully reminded Sterne of past resentments, and he drew his wife's attention to the Latin sermon he had written to enable Fountayne to take his Cambridge doctorate in divinity. 'He got Honour by it—What got I?', Sterne complained. The success he had achieved for himself temporarily forgotten, Sterne had written what he described as a 'long pathetic Letter', outlining the hard treatment he had received at Fountayne's hands. 'I charge you,' he wrote to Elizabeth, 'let it be printed—Tis equitable, You should derive <som> that good from My Sufferings at least' (*Letters*, 147).

The memorandums were dated 28 December 1761. If they make gloomy reading, there was good cause. Writing to a friend three days later, Sterne confessed he was 'very ill, having broke a vessel in my lungs' (*Letters*, 150). Having settled his affairs, there was no reason to linger, and in the first week of January, Sterne set off for France.

II
France, 1762–1764

Paris, 1762

To enter France from England in 1762 was no simple matter, for the two countries were still at war. Sterne was fortunate in being able to accompany George Pitt—recently appointed envoy to the court at Turin—travelling via Chatham to Dover where the diplomatic party took ship.[1] Making his way south from Calais, Sterne reached Paris in mid-January. He had barely arrived, however, when report spread in London that he had died. Though quickly scotched, the rumour was credible enough that in mid-February *Lloyd's Evening Post* published a poem that both eulogized the writer and acknowledged the controversy that had surrounded his work:

> STERNE! rest for ever, and no longer fear
> The Critic's malice, and the Wittling's sneer;
> The gate of Envy now is clos'd on thee,
> And Fame her hundred doors shall open free;
> Ages unborn shall celebrate the Page,
> Where hap'ly blend the Satirist and Sage;
> While gen'rous hearts shall feel for worth distrest;
> Le Fevre's woes with tears shall be confest;
> O'er Yorick's tomb the brightest eyes shall weep,
> And British genius constant vigils keep;
> Then, sighing, say, to vindicate thy Fame,
> 'Great were his faults, but glorious was his flame'.[2]

The generosity of spirit the poem evinces is pleasing, but the elegiac note was quite misplaced. Far from having succumbed to his illness, Sterne found himself rejuvenated—so that instead of quickly pushing on southwards, he remained in Paris for no less than six months.

Alongside with London, mid-eighteenth century Paris was one of the two greatest cities of Europe, with a population approaching 900,000. It was also the first major resort for British and Irish tourists once they had crossed the Channel. Few left the city without paying a visit to its principal sights: the Louvre, the Luxembourg, the Tuileries, the Palais-Royal, and the Gobelins tapestry factory among them. Sterne's own motive for so greatly prolonging his stay was quite different. To his surprise and delight, the author found himself as lionized in the French capital as he had been in London two years earlier. 'Well! here I am, my friend,' Sterne wrote to David Garrick at the end of January, 'as much improved in my health for the time, as ever your friendship could wish, or at least your faith give credit to—by the bye I am somewhat worse in my intellectuals, for my head is turned round with what I see, and the unexpected honours I have met with here' (*Letters*, 151).

Sterne's description of the honours accorded him in Paris as 'unexpected' was no false modesty. When Adam Smith visited Paris the following year he took the precaution of asking his friend David Hume to 'Make my Compliments to all the men of Genius in France who do me the honour to know anything about me'.[3] Sterne had made no such preparations. Yet he wrote delightedly to Garrick that 'Tristram was almost as much known here as in London, at least among your men of condition and learning, and has got me introduced into so many circles ('tis comme a Londres)' (*Letters*, 151). Whether Sterne realized it or not, his work was known almost exclusively by reputation: one sceptical English observer declared that there were 'not five people in Paris possess'd of a Tristram Shandy, nor one of those who are, who pretends to understand it'.[4] The first (and then only partial) translation of *Tristram Shandy*, by J.-P. Frénais, would not appear until 1776, with the entire work becoming available only in 1785.[5] Sterne's novel made an especially tardy appearance in French, but a marked delay was not unusual for, among the English fiction published in French translation during the months Sterne spent in Paris, Edward Kimber's *Joe Thompson* had first appeared in English in 1751 and Henry Fielding's last novel, *Amelia*, now adapted by the sentimental novelist Marie-Jeanne Riccoboni, in 1752. Much more quickly available, by contrast, were the first two volumes of Frances Sheridan's masterpiece of sensibility, *Memoirs of Miss Sidney Bidulph* (1761), adapted as *Mémoires à servir à l'histoire du vertu* by no less a writer than the abbé Prévost.

In the absence of a French translation of *Tristram Shandy*, Sterne's reputation among the wider reading public in France was dependent on the extensive reporting in French magazines of the stir that his work had caused in England. As early as April 1760 the *Journal Encyclopédique* had written:

> c'est ici le monstre d'Horace. Des pensées morales, fines, délicates, saillantes, solides, fortes, impies, hazardées, téméraires: voilà ce que l'on trouve dans cet Ouvrage . . . La vivacité de son imagination, le feu de ses portraits, le caractère de ses réflexions, tout plait, tout intéresse & tout séduit.[6]
>
> (here is Horace's monster. Moral, fine, delicate, outstanding, solid, strong, impious, hazardous, daring: such are the thoughts to be found in this work . . . the liveliness of its imagination, the fire of its likenesses, the nature of its reflections: all are pleasing, engaging, seductive.)

Should this encomium have been thought inadequate, the writer also noted English admiration for Sterne's work and clinched his demonstration of the author's extraordinary celebrity by revealing that Sterne had received a prosperous living from a nobleman and free passes for the theatre from David Garrick.

It was enough to persuade the French that 'Tristram is a great Genius in his own Country',[7] and some of the most powerful and cultured men in Parisian society were quick to invite Sterne to their gatherings. 'I have just now a fortnight's dinners and suppers upon my hands', Sterne told Garrick, instancing invitations he had received from Michel-Étienne Lepeletier, comte de Saint-Fargeau and advocate-general to the *parlement* of Paris, the *philosophe* Baron D'Holbach, the Graf von Limburg-Styrum, dean (and later prince-archbishop) of Speyer, and Claude de Thiard, comte de Bissy, who asked that the author be introduced to him.

Of all the invitations Sterne accepted, the most intriguing was certainly that extended by the Baron D'Holbach. Enormously wealthy, D'Holbach entertained lavishly in his house on the rue Royale (now the rue des Moulins, near the church of St Roch). There his guests included Diderot, Grimm, Marmontel, Suard, Naigeon, and the abbés Raynal and Morellet. These were no ordinary social gatherings, for not only was D'Holbach's coterie a notable centre of advanced Enlightenment thought but D'Holbach in particular had a reputation as an atheist.[8] One regular guest, the 'Great Infidel' himself, David Hume, was initially taken aback by the atmosphere of the gatherings, which were notorious among contemporaries for the anti-religious conversation.[9] Even Edward Gibbon, another of Holbach's guests, declared himself unable to approve 'the intolerant zeal of the philosophers and Encyclopedists, the friends of d'Olbach and Helvétius . . . [who] laughed at the scepticism of Hume, preached the tenets of atheism with the bigotry of dogmatism and damned all believers with ridicule and contempt'.[10] The fact that Sterne felt so much at home among what he termed this 'joyous sett'—gives some circumstantial weight, at least, to the possibility that he was himself tempted by contemporary religious scepticism.

Or perhaps he just enjoyed the attention. 'The French love such a nonsensical fellow as I am', he confided to a friend,[11] and six weeks later he was just as engaged socially as when he had first reached the capital:

> I was last night at Baron de Bagg's concert; it was very fine, both music and company; and to-night I go to the Prince of Conti's. There is Monsieur Popelinière, who lives here like a sovereign prince; keeps a company of musicians always in his house, and a full set of players; and gives concerts and plays alternately to the grandees of this metropolis; he is the richest of all the farmer[s-general]; he did me the honour last night to send me an invitation to his house, while I stayed here—that is, to his music and table. (*Letters*, 155)

Such invitations were not the only marks of distinction Sterne received. The comte (soon to be duc) de Choiseul paid him a notable compliment, as he was quick to write to David Garrick: '*Qui le diable est ce homme là*—said Choiseul, t'other day—ce Chevalier Shandy—You'll think me as vain as a devil, was I to tell you the rest of the dialogue—whether the bearer knows it or no, I know not—'Twill serve up after supper, in Southampton-street, amongst other small dishes, after the fatigues of Richard the IIId' (*Letters*, 157). Meanwhile the duc d'Orléans commissioned Louis Carogis, known as Carmontelle, to paint a watercolour sketch of Sterne to add to his collection of celebrated visitors to Paris, who included David Garrick and David Hume (and would soon embrace the 7-year-old Wolfgang Amadeus Mozart, on his first visit to Paris with his father, Leopold, in the winter of 1763–4). The duke, Sterne told Garrick, with barely concealed delight, 'has suffered my portrait to be added to the number of some odd men in his collection; and a gentleman who lives with him has taken it most expressively, at full length—I purpose to obtain an etching of it, and send it you' (*Letters*, 157–8).

For an author whose work was so little known in France, the reception accorded Sterne was indeed remarkable. Sterne's response to his unexpected celebrity was to consider how best he might capitalize on it. To this end, he contemplated the publication of a polemical exchange between himself and Claude-Prosper-Jolyot de Crébillon, son of the famous playwright, Prosper-Jolyot de Crébillon. Crébillon *fils* was a novelist whose *Égarements du coeur et de l'esprit* (1736) Sterne knew; he was also a sceptic and admirer of David Hume, to whom he dedicated a novel. As described to Garrick, Sterne's was a cynically commercial venture:

> Crebillion has made a convention with me, which, if he is not too lazy, will be no bad *persiflage*—as soon as I get to Thoulouse he has agreed to write me an expostulat[o]ry letter upon the indecorums of T. Shandy—which is to be answered by recrimination upon the liberties in his own works—these are to be printed together—Crebillion against Sterne—Sterne against Crebillion—the copy to be sold, and the money equally divided —This is good Swiss-policy. (*Letters*, 162)

It may be that Crébillon proved as lazy as Sterne feared, or perhaps the scathing review accorded the third and fourth volumes of *Tristram Shandy* by the *Journal Encyclopédique*, which described Sterne's work as 'filth upon filth' (*saletés sur saletés*)[12] made the idea of any defence seem less attractive. In any case, the project seems to have gone no further.

While in Paris Sterne did not spend all of his time with French acquaintances. He had taken lodgings in St Germain-des-Près and found himself in company with 'about fifteen or sixteen English of distinction, who are now here, and live well together' (*Letters*, 152). These included the 13-year-old Charles James Fox and his tutor, the youthful Irishman George Macartney—shortly to be knighted prior to becoming British envoy to the court of Catherine the Great at the age of 27. With them, Sterne visited Versailles and—despite his later, fictionalized denial—made some attempt to see as many of the tourist sights as possible. In *A Sentimental Journey* Yorick boasts that he has 'not seen the Palais royal—nor the Luxembourg—nor the Façade of the Louvre—nor have attempted to swell the catalogues we have of pictures, statues, and churches'.[13] Sterne, by contrast, appears to have visited the capital's principal monuments and the many private houses and palaces to which he was given privileged access.[14]

If Sterne was concerned not to appear too much like every other English traveller, however, he was equally anxious to distinguish himself from the unconditional admiration of Paris he thought characteristic of the French themselves. In volume VII of *Tristram Shandy* he was to poke fun at the French boast that '*they who have seen Paris, have seen every thing*' when Tristram, insisting that 'they must mean to speak of those who have seen it by day-light. As for candle-light—I give it up', laboriously enumerates, by district, the 900 streets of Paris, concluding:

> In the quarter of the *Luxembourg*, sixty two streets.
> And in that of St. Germain, fifty five streets, into any of which you may walk; and that when you have seen them with all that belongs to them, fairly by daylight—their gates, their bridges, their squares, their

> statues----and have crusaded it moreover through all their parish churches, by no means omitting St. *Roche* and *Sulplice*---and to crown all, have taken a walk to the four palaces, which you may see either with or without the statues and pictures, just as you chuse—
>
> ——Then you will have seen——
>
> ——but, 'tis what no one needeth to tell you, for you will read it yourself upon the portico of the Louvre, in these words,
>
> EARTH NO SUCH FOLKS!—NO FOLKS E'ER SUCH A TOWN
> AS PARIS IS!—SING, DERRY, DERRY, DOWN.
>
> (*TS* VII. xviii. 401–2)

Making his first trip abroad at the age of 48, Sterne in fact delighted in the attractions of Paris and took a close interest in public affairs. During his stay, two very different events stood out. The first was the debate that would lead to the expulsion of the Jesuits from France in 1764. Under attack throughout Catholic Europe, the Jesuits—one of those 'fanatick orders' Sterne had attacked in his sermons[15]—had already been expelled from Portugal in 1759, and in the course of the next decade would suffer a similar fate throughout most of Europe and the French and Spanish colonies of America before the order was eventually suppressed by Pope Clement XIV in 1773. In France the debate was conducted with such a welter of pamphlets both attacking and defending the Society of Jesus that its only rival as a topic of conversation, Sterne slyly reported, was the comic opera. Sterne himself kept abreast of the controversy and in a letter to Lord Fauconberg, written in April, recommended the recently published *Compte Rendu des Constitutions des Jésuites*, a fiercely anti-Jesuit work by Louis-René de Caradence de la Chatolais. Less than a month after Sterne left Paris, an *arrêt* in large letters proscribing the Society was posted throughout the streets of the capital. The expulsion of the Jesuits from France and her territories was ultimately to find its way into *Tristram Shandy*, where Tristram, going to visit the college of the Jesuits in Lyons to see their Chinese library, finds himself sentimentally detained at the Tomb of the Two Lovers, which he finds to be just as well, '*for all the* JESUITS *had got the cholic*—and to that degree, as never was known in the memory of the oldest practitioner' (*TS* VII. xxxix. 426).

The second extraordinary event of Sterne's stay in Paris was the great fire that destroyed the Foire de St Germain, very close to Sterne's probable lodgings in the rue Jacob, hard by the church of St Germain. It was the biggest fire seen in Paris for many years—though it was shortly to be followed by the destruction of the Opéra in the rue Saint-Honoré, close to the Palais-Royal, in April 1763. Sterne described the destruction of the fair, which opened each year on 3 February, in a letter to his wife:

> A terrible fire happened here last night, the whole fair of St. Germain's burned to the ground in a few hours; and hundreds of unhappy people are now going crying along the streets, ruined totally by it . . . They compute the loss at six millions of livres, which these poor creatures have sustained, not one of which have saved a single shilling, and many fled out in their shirts, and have not only lost their goods and merchandize, but all the money they have been taking these six weeks. (*Letters*, 154)

Sterne does not mention, and when writing perhaps did not know, that more than goods were lost in the conflagration. Another contemporary account mentions that among those who lost their lives were spirit-drinkers burned to death in a fireball that erupted when flames reached the alcohol.[16] Even so, in a moment of reflection rare in his correspondence with his wife, Sterne recounts an episode related to the fire, in a manner that would not be out of place in *A Sentimental Journey*: '*Oh! ces moments de malheur sont terribles*, said my barber to me, as he was shaving me this morning; and the good-natured fellow uttered it with so moving an accent, that I could have found it in my heart to have cried over the perishable and uncertain tenure of every good in this life' (*Letters*, 154).

Sightseeing and socializing apart, Sterne also began his stay by attending the theatre and opera regularly, making a point of reporting on them both in his letters, especially to David Garrick. He enthused over Claire-Joseph-Hippolyte Legris de Latude, called Clairon, who reigned as a leading actress at the Comédie Française for more than two decades. He had seen her in the title-role of Claude-Guimard de la Touche's *Iphigénie en Tauride*, of a performance of which a French contemporary wrote: 'Mlle Clairon évoqua du sein des morts l'ombre d'*Iphigénie en Tauride* ou plûtot Iphigénie elle-même' ('Mlle Clairon called forth from the bosom of the dead the shade of *Iphegenia in Tauris*, or rather of Iphigenia herself').[17] Sterne concurred: 'she is extremely great' (*Letters*, 152), he told Garrick, though he thought Marie-Françoise Dumesnil even finer. How much Sterne actually understood of the plays he attended so assiduously is less certain, for his French, never good, was at this time decidedly poor. Perhaps it was for this reason that the initial attractions of the French theatre soon wore thin for him. Although, writing at the end of January, he reported his intention of going with a party of friends to see the noted comic actor Pierre-Louis Dubus *dit* Préville in Louis de Boissy's comedy,

Le Français à Londres, two months after his arrival in Paris, Sterne was jokingly admitting to Garrick: 'The French comedy, I seldom visit it—they scarce act any thing but tragedies.' In any case, as Sterne had hinted in relating the Jesuit controversy, the principal centre of theatrical activity in the Paris of 1762 was not the legitimate stage but comic opera, which had been revitalized following the much-publicized reunion of the Opéra Comique with the Comédie Italienne, achieved by royal command on Wednesday, 3 February. 'The whole City of Paris is *bewitch'd* with the comic opera', Sterne reported without enthusiasm in March, promising to send over some examples of the operas to Garrick, along with another novelty, the verse satire *Le Sallon*, by Alexis Piron.

Sterne's known friendship with England's most celebrated actor was not always an advantage. 'I have been these two days reading a tragedy, given me by a lady of talents, to read and conjecture if it would do for you' (*Letters*, 162), Sterne wrote in mid-April, at a time when most of his English friends and acquaintances had left Paris. In fact the play, Diderot's *Le Fils naturel* (1757), had already been translated into English by Elizabeth Griffith—the Irish sentimental novelist and wife of Sterne's future acquaintance, Richard Griffith—and would be printed by Dodsley in 1767 as *Dorval, or the Test of Virtue.* Sterne was not enthusiastic: 'It has too much sentiment in it, (at least for me) the speeches too long, and savour too much of *preaching*— . . . it is not to my taste—'Tis all love, love, love, throughout . . . so I fear it would not do for your stage' (*Letters*, 162).

If Sterne regretted that *Dorval*'s theatricality was compromised by its 'preaching', he was, by contrast, surprisingly happy to discover the extent to which French preaching might be theatrical —'surprisingly' because in his earliest published sermon Sterne had vigorously attacked Catholicism precisely on the grounds that, 'with all its scenical decorations and finery, [it] looks more like a theatrical performance.'[18] Now Sterne was delighted to find Catholic worship enlivened by histrionics:

> I have been three mornings together to hear a celebrated pulpit orator near me, one Père Clement, who delights me much; the parish pays him 600 livres for a dozen sermons this Lent; he is K[ing]. Stanislaus's preacher—most excellent indeed! his matter solid, and to the purpose; his manner, more than theatrical, and greater, both in his action and delivery, than Madame Clairon, who, you must know, is the Garrick of the stage here; he has infinite variety, and keeps up the attention by it wonderfully; his pulpit, oblong, with three seats in it, into which he occasionally casts himself; goes on, then rises, by a gradation of four steps, each of which he profits by, as his discourse inclines him: in short,

> 'tis a stage, and the variety of his tones would make you imagine there were no less than five or six actors on it together. (*Letters*, 154–5)

A sustained interest in the dramatic, which characterizes so much of Sterne's letter-writing from Paris, goes considerably beyond what might be expected even of a correspondent of David Garrick or of one who, like Sterne, had been himself a preacher notable for his pulpit manner. With increasing frequency—and increasing confidence—Sterne took on a role of his own, to meet the wishes of an audience of friends and acquaintances who desired him to resemble Tristram as closely as possible. 'Be it known,' Sterne wrote to Garrick in March, 'I Shandy it away fifty times more than I was ever wont, talk more nonsense than ever you heard me talk in your days—and to all sorts of people.' A month later he was again telling Garrick that 'I Shandy it more than ever' (*Letters*, 157, 163).

Sterne, of course, had long acknowledged—indeed encouraged—the public identification of himself with his fictional character. Now he increasingly exploited that identification. Jean-Baptiste-Antoine Suard declared: 'jamais un auteur et ses ouvrages ne se sont ressemblés davantage: les lire ou le voir et l'entendre, c'était presque la même chose' ('never have an author and his works resembled each other, more closely: to read them or to see and hear him was almost the same thing').[19] In his *Mémoires Historiques sur la vie de M. Suard* Garat offers a peculiarly striking example both of what was expected of Sterne and how far he was prepared to go to oblige his public. Stopping one day in front of the statue of Henri IV on the Pont-Neuf, Sterne was quickly surrounded by a crowd attracted by his behaviour, whereupon he turned round crying, 'Why are you looking at me? All of you, follow me', and dropped to his knees before the statue, persuading the crowd to do likewise. Garat, commenting that Sterne had seemingly forgotten that Henri IV was a *French* king, misses the point—though what that point was is decidedly ambiguous.[20] The monarch before whose statue Sterne was kneeling had, it is true, famously granted liberty of worship to Protestants in 1598 by means of the Edict of Nantes, yet he was also the monarch who, more infamously, had himself renounced Protestantism in order to claim the French throne, with the dictum 'Paris vaut bien une messe'. By kneeling in homage, was Sterne—who knew his history well enough—proclaiming his adherence to the Protestant faith, dramatizing a cynical willingness to adopt any identity willed on him, provided the rewards were great enough, or—as so often—delighting in the ambivalence of his actions?

Whatever the truth, Sterne understood just as well in Paris in 1762 as he had in London two years previously how ample might be the rewards of literary success coupled with sociability and a ready wit. In the fictionalized account of his Paris visit he later offered in *A Sentimental Journey*, Sterne insisted on Yorick's tendency to accommodate himself to the will or opinion of others: 'For three weeks together, I was of every man's opinion I met.—*Pardi! ce Mons. Yorick a autant d'esprit que nous autres.—Il raisonne bien*, said another.—*C'est un bon enfant*, said a third.—And at this price I could have eaten and drank and been merry all the days of my life at Paris . . . ' (*ASJ*, 266). Eventually Yorick finds this a 'dishonest *reckoning*' and grows ashamed of it, but for Sterne the rewards of 'Shandying it' proved to be real enough. Nor were those rewards simply material. Indeed, in reading his letters from Paris, it is easy to overlook just how ill the consumptive writer had been. Sterne himself had not forgotten, however. '[I] verily do believe', he told Garrick, 'that by mere Shandeism sublimated by a laughter-loving people, I fence as much against infirmities, as I do by the benefit of air and climate' (*Letters*, 163). That his renewed health derived at least in part from his own sense of well-being was tacitly recognized by the physicians he consulted. Seeing so remarkable an improvement in their patient in the first three weeks of his stay in the French capital, they advised him to remain in Paris rather than continue his projected trip to the south of France. Yet, however great the improvement, Sterne did not feel well enough to return home, and the same physicians who encouraged a prolonged stay in Paris were equally against his notion that he might remain in the French capital until the end of May and then return to England via Holland. Enlarging upon the theme, Sterne reported in April that had he remained in London during what had been 'a most dismal foggy winter, I had certainly been six weeks ago in my grave' (*Letters*, 159). The doctors in Paris, he added, foresaw similar dangers the following winter if he did not allow time for his lungs to strengthen by spending it in Toulouse, free from coughs and colds: 'after this,' Sterne reported, 'they say, they shall look upon my Cure as compleat' (*Letters*, 159).

Whether or not he was reporting his physicians' advice exactly—and it is hard to credit that he could have believed this last, optimistic prognostication—Sterne insisted that he had an additional reason to accept his physicians' advice. In the same letter in which he reported on his health to Lord Fauconberg (who, as Sterne's patron, had a legitimate interest in a clergyman whose projected absence of a few months was turning into one of perhaps a year and a half), he related the poor health of his daughter, Lydia, who, back in Yorkshire, was 'in a declining way with this vile Asthma of hers' (*Letters*, 160). The decline had continued over three winters, Sterne declared, and unless something more than 'bare Medecines' could be found for her, she would be lost. Something more, of course, suggested a winter in a warmer climate, and Sterne had fixed on Toulouse, where plans to hire a 'little house w^{h} a large Garden, in the pleasantest part of the Town' were already evidently far advanced. If Sterne himself felt better, he protested, he would return home after fixing his wife and daughter in Toulouse; if not, he would stay there as well and make his way home in May of the following year. Given the fact that Sterne had begun making plans for renting a house in Toulouse *before* consulting Lord Fauconberg, it is unlikely, however, that he seriously considered returning to Coxwold immediately. In the event, any lingering thoughts that he might come straight back after settling his family were soon dispelled. After five months of gradual improvement he was attacked by a fever which resulted in a relapse, 'so that I have lost in ten days all I have gain'd since I came here' (*Letters*, 164).

As a result of this setback Sterne determined to leave for Toulouse as soon as his family could join him. Here his contacts proved invaluable. Though a reader of Sterne's Paris correspondence would have no inkling of the fact, England and France remained at war, as they had been for the previous six years. In *A Sentimental Journey* Yorick declares that 'I had left London with so much precipitation, that it never enter'd my mind that we were at war with France',[21] so that he had no passport. While the account of his application for a passport in *A Sentimental Journey* is certainly fictionalized, Sterne did procure one with remarkable speed—in a letter to Garrick, he declared, it 'goes on swimmingly' (*Letters*, 151).[22] He made his decision to proceed south only in April, yet was able to report by 12 May that the comte de Choiseul had sent him passports for Elizabeth Sterne and Lydia. In his application Sterne had powerful support—d'Holbach, Limburg, and Lepeletier seconded his request—but Choiseul's dispatch seems to have represented a genuine regard for Sterne; when the duke of Buccleuch, accompanied by his tutor Adam Smith, was preparing to travel to Toulouse in January 1764, the introductions to Toulousain polite society Choiseul apparently promised were not readily forthcoming, notwithstanding the fact that the war was over.[23] The matter of the passports was in fact now of some importance to Sterne, who was anxious to leave as soon as possible and expressed the hope that his wife and daughter would be with him by mid-June.

In the event, communications and travel were so slow that Elizabeth and Lydia Sterne did not arrive in the capital for almost two months. The intervening period was marked both by Sterne's attempt to wind up his affairs in Paris and by a series of letters detailing the material arrangements to be made for the family's stay in France. Among the business he transacted was a request to Thomas Becket, his new publisher, to supply his French friends with the English books they wanted. For Diderot, for instance, he asked that Becket send:

> All the Works of Pope—the neatest & cheapest Edition—(therefore I suppose not Warburtons)
> The Dramatick Works of Cibber—& Cibbers Life—
> Chaucer
> Tillotson's Sermons—the small edition—
> All Lock's works.
> the 6 Vols. of Shandy.
>
> (*Letters*, 166)

These last were to be a gift from Sterne to Diderot, who read them almost immediately—'I am reading the maddest, the wisest, the gayest of all books', he wrote to Sophie Volland in September[24]—and eventually wrote a Shandean work of his own, *Jacques le fataliste et son maître.* As a gesture of reconciliation, Sterne also sent two small valuable snuffboxes, one filled with garnets, the other containing his portrait, to be forwarded to his wife in York. The letters written to Elizabeth subsequent to his decision to winter in Toulouse suggest a changed mood on Sterne's part, being by turns practical and solicitous. In part, they are full of instructions as to what purchases his wife and daughter should make in London—gentlemen's watches for gifts, pins, needles, a 'strong bottle-skrew', and a silver coffee-pot, a copper tea-kettle, watch-chains, knives, a cookery book, among others—and what they should defer buying until their arrival in Paris. Elsewhere, Sterne repeatedly fusses as he offers suggestions as to how Elizabeth and Lydia might travel most comfortably:

> For God sake rise early and gallop away in the cool—and always see that you have not forgot your baggage in changing post-chaises—You will find good tea upon the road from York to Dover—only bring a little to carry you from Calais to Paris—give the Custom-House officers what I told you—at Calais give more, if you have much Scotch snuff—but as tobacco is good here, you had best bring a Scotch mill and make it yourself, that is, order your valet to manufacture it—'twill keep him out of mischief.—I would advise you to take three days in coming up, for fear of heating yourselves—See that they do not give you a bad vehicle, when a better is in the yard, but you will look sharp—drink small

> Rhenish to keep you cool (that is if you like it.) Live well and deny yourselves nothing your hearts wish. So God in heav'n prosper and go along with you—kiss my Lydia, and believe me both affectionately,
>
> Yours,
>
> L. Sterne
>
> (*Letters*, 170)

This was in mid-May; a fortnight later Sterne was still sending practical instructions about Scotch snuff and repeating his advice about the need to travel in the coolest part of the day, instancing the case of a friend whose party intended to travel from four to nine in the morning and not venture out again till six in the evening. Yet the thought of seeing Elizabeth and Lydia again prompted Sterne's tenderest feelings for them both. 'Write and tell me something of every thing,' he asked at the end of May, 'I long to see you both, you may be assured, my dear wife and child, after so long a separation' (*Letters*, 171). In mid-June he was urging them to do everything necessary for their ease of mind, adding—a trifle effusively, given his recent relations with his wife—'I wish I was with you to do all these offices myself, and to strew roses on your way' (*Letters*, 176).

The most important item Sterne purchased was a chaise—not an easy item to find when those available were being sent for the use of the army. He was evidently well pleased with his purchase: 'you will be in raptures with your chariot', he told his wife. It does not, however, sound the most comfortable of conveyances:

> You will wonder all the way, how I am to find room in it for a third—to ease you of this wonder, 'tis by what the coach-makers here call a cave, which is a second bottom added to that you set your feet upon which lets the person (who sits over-against you) down with his knees to your ancles, and by which you have all more room—and what is more, less heat—because his head does not intercept the fore-glass little or nothing—Lyd and I will enjoy this by turns; sometimes I shall take a bidet—(a little post horse) and scamper before—at other times I shall sit in fresco upon the arm-chair without doors, and one way or other will do very well. (*Letters*, 173)

Elizabeth Sterne and Lydia eventually arrived in Paris on Thursday, 8 July, well pleased with the speed of their journey and with the experiences it had afforded them. They were soon sightseeing and doubtless buying the silk, blonds, and gauzes which a female acquaintance had advised Sterne were best purchased in the French capital, where they were both 'very beautiful and cheap' (*Letters*, 172). Having had no alternative but to accept York as their metropolis for so long, Elizabeth and Lydia could hardly have been other than delighted with the sights and sounds of Paris. They were not, however, permitted to stay long. Already anxious to be making his way south, Sterne wrote to his wife that a week or ten days would be enough for their visit to the French capital. By the time his wife and daughter arrived he had a more urgent reason for wishing to be on his way. 'About a week or ten days before my wife arrived at Paris', he wrote to John Hall-Stevenson, 'I had the same accident I had at Cambridge, of breaking a vessel in my lungs. It happen'd in the night, and I bled the bed full.' Believing he was likely to bleed to death, Sterne sent for a surgeon who, using the standard treatment in such cases, bled him at both arms. '[T]his saved me', Sterne reported, but he lay speechless in bed for three days, and it was a further week before he ventured out. 'This with my weakness and hurrying about made me think it high time to haste to Toulouse' (*Letters*, 180).

The journey from Paris to the south-west lasted three weeks and, undertaken in high summer, was made in the worst possible conditions. 'We have had four months of such heats that the oldest Frenchman never remembers the like,' Sterne would tell Hall-Stevenson, ''twas as hot as *Nebuchadnezzar's oven*, and never has relaxed one hour' (*Letters*, 180). In an account of his journey written to his Paris banker Robert Foley, Sterne sounded less like Yorick the Sentimental Traveller and more like the Tobias Smollett of the *Travels through France and Italy*, whom he was to parody as the perpetually discontented Smelfungus in *A Sentimental Journey*. To Foley, Sterne complained:

> In our journey we suffered so much from the heats, it gives me pain to remember it—I never saw a cloud from Paris to Nismes half as broad as a twenty-four sols piece.—Good God! we were toasted, roasted, grill'd, stew'd and carbonaded on one side or other all the way—and being all done enough (*assez cuits*) in the day, we were eat up at night by bugs, and other unswept out vermin, the legal inhabitants (if length of possession gives right) of every inn we lay at. (*Letters*, 182–3)

The route Sterne followed is almost certainly that taken by Tristram in his journey through France, described in volume VII of *Tristram Shandy*: 'FONTAINEBLEAU, and SENS, and JOIGNY, and AUXERRE, and DIJON the capital of Burgundy, and CHALLON, and Mâcon the capital of the Mâconese' (*TS* VII. xxvi. 409), and hence to Lyons. From Lyons, with its medieval clock in the cathedral, its *History of China* in the Jesuit library, and the Tomb of the Two Lovers—all of which Tristram, characteristically, fails to see—the route lay along the banks of the Rhône to Avignon where, as a good Protestant, Tristram ignores the Papal Palace that completely dominates the town, declaring there to be nothing to see 'but the old house, in which the duke of Ormond resided' (*TS* VII. xli. 427). Any reader of Sterne is likely to regret that his letters contain so few hints of his reactions to the places he visited or the countryside through which he passed. The probable reasons for his reticence are hinted at, however, in the Avignon section of volume VII of *Tristram Shandy*, where Tristram wittily strikes a cautionary note all too appropriate for the travel-writers of the eighteenth century (and beyond):

> I think it wrong, merely because a man's hat has been blown off his head by chance the first night he comes to Avignion,——that he should therefore say, 'Avignion is more subject to high winds than any town in all France:' for which reason I laid no stress upon the accident till I had inquired of the master of the inn about it, who telling me seriously it was so——and hearing moreover, the windyness of Avignion spoke of in the country about as a proverb—I set it down, merely to ask the learned what can be the cause. (*TS* VII. xli. 428)

From Avignon Sterne headed for Nîmes—one of the principal attractions for British tourists, with its Roman amphitheatre and the Maison Carrée, one of the finest of all surviving Roman temples—and on across the plains of Languedoc. In describing his progress Sterne insisted in his letters on two points: it was hot and uncomfortable. Yet this journey provided not only a fruitful source of inspiration for the continuation of *Tristram Shandy*, but gave Sterne the germ of an idea which he would eventually develop into the Sentimental Traveller in *A Sentimental Journey through France and Spain*. In *Tristram Shandy* he would metamorphosize his experiences in his 'PLAIN STORIES':

> How far my pen has been fatigued like those of other travellers, in this journey of it, over so barren a track—the world must judge—but the traces of it, which are now all set o' vibrating together this moment, tell me 'tis the most fruitful and busy period of my life; for . . . by stopping and talking to every soul I met who was not in a full trot—joining all parties before me—waiting for every soul behind—hailing all those who were coming through crossroads—arresting all kinds of beggars, pilgrims, fiddlers, fryars—not passing by a woman in a mulberry-tree without commending her legs, and tempting her into a conversation with a pinch of snuff——In short, by seizing every handle, of what size

> or shape soever, which chance held out to me in this journey—I turned my *plain* into a *city*—I was always in company, and with great variety too; and as my mule loved society as much as myself, and had some proposals always on his part to offer to every beast he met—I am confident we could have passed through Pall-Mall or St. James's-Street for a month together, with fewer adventures—and seen less of human nature. (*TS* VII. xliii. 430)

To the stretch of road between Nîmes and Lunel belongs the final episode of volume VII of *Tristram Shandy*, the encounter with Nannette. Equivocal, like so many others, the scene contrasts the idealized rustic simplicity of the Languedocian peasant[25] with the cultured yet fallible worldliness of Tristram who, at the very instant of admiring the spontaneous courtesy of Nannette, finds his own good-nature at odds with his sexual desire for her:

> A sun-burnt daughter of Labour rose up from the groupe to meet me as I advanced towards them; her hair, which was a dark chesnut, approaching rather to a black, was tied up in a knot, all but a single tress.
>
> We want a cavalier, said she, holding out both her hands, as if to offer them——And a cavalier ye shall have; said I, taking hold of both of them.
>
> Hadst thou, Nannette, been array'd like a dutchesse!
>
> ——But that cursed slit in thy petticoat!
>
> Nannette cared not for it.
>
> We could not have done without you, said she, letting go one hand, with self-taught politeness, leading me up with the other.
>
> A lame youth, whom Apollo had recompenced with a pipe, and to which he had added a tabourin of his own accord, ran sweetly over the prelude, as he sat upon the bank——Tie me up this tress instantly, said Nannette, putting a piece of string into my hand——It taught me to forget I was a stranger——The whole knot fell down——We had been seven years acquainted.
>
> The youth struck the note upon the tabourin—his pipe followed, and off we bounded——'the duce take that slit!'
>
> The sister of the youth who had stolen her voice from heaven, sung alternately with her brother——'twas a Gascoigne roundelay.
>
> VIVA LA JOIA!
> FIDON LA TRISTESSA!
>
> The nymphs join'd in unison, and their swains an octave below them———

> I would have given a crown to have it sew'd up——Nannette would not have given a sous——*Viva la joia!* was in her lips——*Viva la joia!* was in her eyes. A transient spark of amity shot across the space betwixt us——She look'd amiable!——Why could I not live and end my days thus! Just disposer of our joys and sorrows, cried I, why could not a man sit down in the lap of content here—and dance, and sing, and say his prayers, and go to heaven with this nut brown maid? (*TS* VII. xliii. 431–2)

Prudence overcoming sentiment and desire, Tristram 'dances off', and his route—'from Lunel to Montpellier——from thence to Pesnas, Beziers . . . Narbonne, Carcasson and Castle Naudairy' (*TS* VII. xliii. 432)—brings him, as the same route would have brought Sterne, into the city of Toulouse.

Toulouse and Montpellier 1762–4

In 1762 Toulouse was a sizeable city by eighteenth-century standards, with more than 40,000 inhabitants. Lying mainly on the right bank of the Garonne—with the suburb of St Cyprian across the river linked to the old town by the splendid and recently built Pont Neuf—the city had just begun to expand beyond the city walls. In important respects Toulouse bore comparison with York. Not only was it a major regional centre—capital of the French south-west, as York was of the north-east of England—but it too was the seat of an important archbishopric (besides the most important *parlement* outside of Paris). It was under the influence of two successive archbishops that Toulouse would in the course of the 1760s develop quays and impressive gardens and walks to the north-east of the old city, as York had in the 1730s. In addition, Toulouse could boast a university and a cultural life epitomized by its four academies.

Sterne's choice of Toulouse, however, had been determined less by any of these factors than by the low cost of living relative to other towns in the south of France. It also helped that he had a contact in the city—the abbé Macarthy (to whom he was perhaps introduced by John Hall-Stevenson, who had spent some time in Toulouse in 1759)—who prepared for the Sternes' arrival by renting them a house. Although there was considerable inflation in Toulouse during the 1760s, with staples such as wheat commanding prices equal to or even higher than those at Paris, Sterne found the overall cost of living very reasonable. Above all, he was delighted with his accommodation, which was certainly more spacious than any he and Elizabeth had enjoyed during their married life. 'They were,' he wrote,

> most deliciously placed at the extremity of the town, in an excellent house well furnish'd, and elegant beyond any thing I look'd for—'Tis built in the form of a hotel, with a pretty court towards the town—and behind, the best gardens in Toulouse, laid out in serpentine walks, and so large that the company in our quarter usually come to walk there in the evenings, for which they have my consent—'the more the merrier.'—The house consists of a good *salle à manger* above stairs joining to the very great *salle à compagnie* as large as the Baron D'Holbach's; three handsome bed-chambers with dressing rooms to them—below stairs two very good rooms for myself, one to study in, the other to see company.—I have moreover cellars round the court, and all other offices. (*Letters*, 183)

From the same landlord, Sterne continued, he had acquired the use of a country house just two miles from the town and, he added with delight, 'what do you think I am to pay for all this? neither more or less than thirty pounds a year—all things are cheap in proportion—so we shall live for very verry little' (*Letters*, 183).

Material considerations aside, however, the choice of Toulouse was an uncomfortable one, for the city was in the grip of intense Roman Catholic fervour which, giving rise to a corresponding anti-Protestant feeling, resulted in one of the eighteenth-century's most notorious outbursts of religious bigotry. In 1761 the sieur Jean Calas, a noted Protestant tradesman at Toulouse, was charged, together with his wife, of murdering his eldest son, who was taking religious instruction prior to converting to Roman Catholicism. The very night before his reception into the Roman communion, it was alleged, Calas and his wife had strangled their son with their own hands, following a council at which a group of assembled Huguenots had resolved on the murder. Toulouse was soon ablaze with anti-Protestant sentiment. Before Calas's trial François Rochette, a 26-year-old apothecary and Protestant minister, was seized together with his secretary by soldiers as they journeyed to celebrate some marriages and baptisms. Tried for having performed the duties of a minister, having preached, performed baptisms, marriages, and having celebrated communion in defiance of French law, they were sentenced to death on 18 February 1762 and executed the following day. Rochette, whose father and grandfather had reportedly also been hanged as Protestant ministers, declined all attempts to persuade him to apostasize on the scaffold, but when he attempted to speak to the assembled crowd the military drummers drowned out his voice, and the hangman pushed him so violently that his words were lost as he began to strangle.

Nor was this the only fatal sentence carried out that day. While Rochette had been awaiting trial three fellow-Protestants attempted his rescue from prison. Henri de Grenier, seigneur de Coumelle, and two younger brothers, both named Jean, were convicted of sedition, carrying arms, and attempting to free Rochette from royal custody, with the result that the three men were beheaded immediately after the hanging of the pastor they had hoped to rescue. One local chronicler, Pierre Barthès, who described their bravery and 'obstinacy' in the face of death, reported that the crowd which gathered to watch the executions was so large that the place de Salins where the scaffold was erected could not contain it, nor were there sufficient places at the windows or on the roofs of the surrounding houses for those drawn by the 'novelty' of so uncommon an execution.[26]

Jean Calas soon found his own martyrdom. Less than a month later, on 9 March 1762, he was convicted of the murder of his son and sentenced to die on the following day. The decreed punishment was fearful. Calas was condemned to be broken alive on the wheel and left there for two hours before being strangled; subsequently his body was to be burned and the ashes scattered to the winds. The execution took place in the place St-Georges, after Calas refused to recant. Calas's widow—reportedly born in London—was banished for life along with two others; her younger son, charged with complicity in his brother's murder, was merely imprisoned, after agreeing to sign an act of abjuration.

Just five months after Calas met his barbaric end the Revd Laurence Sterne arrived in Toulouse to spend the first winter of his convalescence. That he makes no mention whatsoever of the case is all the more remarkable, not just because he had frequently preached in the past against Roman Catholic intolerance which had led 'helpless wretches' to 'undergo the massacres and flames to which a false and a bloody religion had condemned them',[27] but because the Calas affair quickly became an Enlightenment *cause célèbre*, taken up by numerous writers, Voltaire and Adam Smith among them.[28]

Although no Protestant died for his faith while Sterne was in Toulouse, the bloody executions continued, faithfully reported by Barthès. On 7 September 1762 a murderer, broken on the wheel in the place St-Georges, died screaming; the executioner being ill, his place was taken by an assistant who, striking his victim awkwardly, half smashed the unfortunate man's skull. Among other executions—by hanging or breaking—which took place during Sterne's residence, two youths—a 17-year-old in November and an 18-year-old in March—died on the wheel for murder.[29]

Again Sterne makes no mention of such events, though it is impossible that he could have remained unaware of them. His total silence on such matters is particularly intriguing, for foreign injustice and barbarity usually provoked comment—if only in the form of patriotic self-congratulation—from the least sentimental of English travellers. As a result, it is hard not to speculate on how Sterne—the Anglican clergyman, the Whig polemicist, the anti-Jacobite and scourge of papists in the 1740s, the creator of uncle Toby who could not even harm a fly—responded to such instances of French Roman Catholic justice.

Perhaps, as a visitor to France, Sterne preferred (or, in time of war, thought it prudent) not to comment on such matters in his correspondence with friends in England. In fact—and in contrast with his account of Paris—very little of the public life of Toulouse finds its way into his correspondence. But there were other reasons, too, for Sterne was once more very ill. 'For six weeks together, after I wrote my last letter to you,' Sterne told Hall-Stevenson in October, 'my projects were many stories higher, for I was all that time, as I thought, journeying on to the other world' (*Letters*, 185). Having recovered from his last haemorrhage in Paris, he was now suffering from an illness called the 'Baraquette', characterized by a very heavy cold and agonizing sore throat, and responsible for the deaths of 'a prodigious number' of victims, of all social ranks and age.[30] The medical profession's helplessness in the circumstances did little for Sterne's confidence. 'The physicians here are the errantest charlatans in Europe, or the most ignorant of all pretending fools,' he complained to Hall-Stevenson, adding that:

> I withdrew what was left of me out of their hands, and recommended my affairs entirely to Dame Nature—She (dear goddess) has saved me in fifty different pinching bouts, and I begin to have a kind of enthusiasm now in her favour, and in my own, That one or two more escapes will make me believe I shall leave you all at last by translation, and not by fair death. (*Letters*, 185–6)

Not all were so fortunate. Among the many deaths that took place during these weeks, two made a particular impact on the city. Soon after the family's arrival the death of a Jacobin (i.e Dominican) priest, Father Azéma, revered for his piety, brought scenes of public devotion remarkable even for 'sainte' Toulouse; when the body was displayed in the Jacobins' church, it had to be protected from devotees among the large crowd who attempted to tear the clothes from the corpse and take them away as relics. Shortly afterwards the marquis de Maniban, president of the *parlement* at Toulouse, also died. Aged 77, and having served as president for forty-two years, the marquis was the first president to die in office since 1688. For three days and nights bells throughout the city were rung incessantly in sign of mourning, and the burial was accompanied by the most elaborate funeral ceremonies.[31]

Sterne was too ill to observe these ceremonies in person. He was also sick on 18 September, when Toulouse marked the victory of the prince de Condé over the prince of Brunswick with a solemn Te Deum in the Church of St-Étienne. Since the prince's victory represented the defeat of a British ally, Elizabeth and Lydia must have observed with mixed feelings the bonfires lit throughout the city in celebration. Even when Sterne was once more restored to health, however, his reticence over public matters is remarkable. He describes neither the ceremonial entry into the city of monsieur de Bastard, the new premier of the Toulouse *parlement*, nor the reception held by him on 15 November which terminated in a magnificent exhibition of fireworks in the place de l'Hôtel de Ville. Sterne is even silent—at least in his surviving correspondence—concerning the 'Basoche'—an ancient festivity, held so infrequently that the previous one had taken place as long ago as 1729, in celebration of the birth of the Dauphin. In 1762 the Basoche—held once more in honour of the new president of the *parlement*—involved the crowning of an elected 'King' who, for many days, rode, sceptre in hand, through the city streets along with his richly garbed followers, to the apparent delight not only of the citizens but of numerous visitors drawn to Toulouse by the spectacle. The whole celebration climaxed in a sumptuous ceremony in the Augustinian church, in whose nave a velvet-covered throne, decorated with silver, had been erected. A vast choir sang throughout and at intervals were accompanied by organ, cymbals, trumpets, drums, and fifes.[32] A final surprising omission from his letters written at Toulouse, though, is attributable to a temporary absence from the city, for Sterne was visiting a friend in the country when, their cholic taking another turn for the worse, the Jesuits were finally expelled from Toulouse on 26 March 1763, their church and house closed up, and the sale of their furnishings announced by bills posted throughout the town.

That Sterne so conspicuously ignored the public life of Toulouse even after his return to health was, in truth, the result of increasing disenchantment with his surroundings. With *Tristram Shandy* untranslated, Sterne was quite unknown in the provincial city. He was accorded neither the acclaim nor honour with which he had become familiar in Paris as well as London, his presence unacknowledged by the *capitouls*, or the

Jeux Florissans, the Toulousian academy of the arts. By mid-October, just two months after his arrival, Sterne was already protesting that he had enough of the city. Though he professed to think Toulouse as good as any town in the south of France, he declared it not to his taste. Certainly, he was disappointed in his hopes of finding a substantial English-speaking community there. Most of the English and Irish residents of Toulouse had left after the outbreak of hostilities with France, at the insistence of the French authorities, only a few having been allowed to remain for humanitarian reasons. Those who had obtained police permission to stay were predominantly Irish Roman Catholics, whom the French authorities did not perceive as a threat to national security. The fact that Sterne's command of the French language was poor did not help: 'I splutter French so as to be understood', he admitted (*Letters*, 178). (Less kindly, Richard Phelps, in reporting the French understanding that Sterne was a 'great Genius' in his own country, had added, 'and he would very probably be so in this, if he would learn to speak before he attempts talking'.[33]) As a result Sterne was bored, thinking the French platitudinous, their character admitting of little variety and no originality. Though they were civil enough, he asserted, civility itself 'wearies and bodders one to death—If I do not mind, I shall grow most stupid and sententious' (*Letters*, 186).

The result was that Sterne was restricted to his family and a tiny circle of English-speaking friends. The introverted nature of this society is well indicated in a letter to his banker, Robert Foley, written on 8 December 1762, when Sterne reported that they were all 'pra[c]tising a play we are to Act here this X^mas^ Holy days'. Nine days later he elaborated: 'You will scarce believe the news I tell you—There are a company of English strollers arrived here, who are to act comedies all the Christmas, and are now busy in making dresses and preparing some of our best comedies—Your wonder will cease, when I inform you these strollers are your friends with the rest of our society, to whom I proposed this scheme [as a] *soulagement*' (*Letters*, 191). Sterne's use of *soulagement* ('solace') does not suggest that he had found much in Toulouse or its inhabitants to entertain him. Instead, he threw himself into the preparations for the play-acting with zest. The plays chosen for performance were Susannah Centlivre's *The Busybody* (1709), and Vanbrugh and Cibber's *The Provok'd Husband; or A Journey to London* (1728)—the latter a still-popular comedy Sterne could have seen performed in York in the 1750s,[34]—which was now adapted to fit the company's own situation, under the title *A Journey to Toulouse.* 'Thus my dear Foley,' Sterne wrote, 'for want of something better we have recourse to ourselves, and strike out the best amusements we can from such materials' (*Letters*, 191).

If Sterne was bored, however, his wife and daughter were enjoying themselves. The provident Elizabeth, much impressed by the cheapness of Toulouse, was already planning to stay for a further winter, much to her husband's disgust. This opposition of wishes, he confessed resignedly, 'tho' it will not be as sour as lemon, yet 'twill not be as sweet as sugar candy' (*Letters*, 186). 'Miss Shandy', meanwhile, was 'hard at it with musick, dancing, and French speaking, in the last of which she does *à marveille*, and speaks with an excellent accent, considering she practices within sight of the Pyrenean Mountains' (*Letters*, 186). Even the pride Sterne took in Lydia's accomplishments, though, was not sufficient to reconcile him to an extended stay in Toulouse. He was anxious to spend two or three months in the foothills of the Pyrenees, but his wife would not hear of additional expense. Sterne assumed authority—'But she may talk—I will do my own way, and she will acquiesce without a word of debate on the subject' (*Letters*, 186)—but nevertheless stayed where he was, yearning for his English friends and soliciting their correspondence.

The Treaty of Paris having brought an end to the war in February 1763, Sterne might have hoped for an increase of English-speaking companions. In the event he had one less. The story of his selfless care of a young fellow-consumptive, George Oswald, in the weeks before Oswald's death is, like that of his kindness to the unfortunate Jane Harbottle of Stillington, one which allows us to glimpse Sterne's practice of the benevolence his writings commend. The illegitimate younger son of a Scottish diplomat and merchant, George Oswald had, like Sterne, travelled to the south of France in search of health. Like others, he had tried various resorts and physicians (in Montpellier he had been treated without success by the same physician, Antoine Fizès, who would shortly arouse the ire of Tobias Smollett[35]). In February 1762 it was clear that Oswald was dying and, together with the Irish Roman Catholic priest the abbé O'Leary, Sterne had him moved to a house in the country, where he was seen by a number of physicians who professed themselves unable to do anything for him. For a while, Sterne kept this news from Oswald until, sensing how short a time his friend had to live, he performed the duty of, as he termed it, the 'Messenger of Death'. Sterne related that Oswald 'rec^{d} the news in ^such^ a manner as would put Philosophy, wth all its Cant, to the blush—. "God's will be done," my good friend, said he without any emotion, but that of religion—& and taking hold of my hand, he added that he was more grateful for this last act of friends^{p} & thank'd me more for it, than for all the others he had rec^{d}.'[36] Having presented Sterne with his pocket-watch as a tribute, Oswald died on 1 March.

The death of Oswald, and the impotence of physicians to prevent it, further depressed Sterne's hopes that anything of real value was to be gained by prolonging his stay in France. Within a fortnight he was actively considering an early return to England. On 12 March 1763 he apologized to Thomas Becket for not having written sooner by explaining that he had hoped to be in England by April, though he now accepted that this was impossible. He kept himself busy by writing a further instalment of *Tristram Shandy*. Before the idea of using his own experience of foreign travel occurred to him, or at least before he began writing volume VII, Sterne had continued with the story of uncle Toby—not quite in a straight line indeed, but with sufficient sense of direction to 'have got [Toby] soused over head and ears in love' (*Letters*, 186), as he had told Hall-Stevenson back in October. He likewise reported at that time that he had 'many hints and projects for other works'—an allusion, perhaps, to the materials that would turn eventually into volume VII of *Tristram Shandy* and, later still, into *A Sentimental Journey*. Certainly, he was well advanced in the next volumes of *Tristram Shandy* by March, when he hoped to bring them with him on his return to England. Becket's revelation that the fifth and sixth volumes of *Tristram Shandy* were selling slowly worried Sterne, however, and he asked anxiously for an '*exact account*' of what Becket had left. Though he declared that 'I have no doubt upon my mind of the edition selling off' (*Letters*, 191–2), his anxiety surfaces, albeit in jocular fashion in the eighth volume of his book, where Tristram asks rhetorically: 'Is it not enough that thou art in debt, and that thou hast ten cart-loads of thy fifth and sixth volumes still—still unsold, and art almost at thy wit's end how to get them off thy hands [?]' (*TS* VIII. vi. 439). He could not have been greatly reassured by Becket's answer to his letter, for of the 1,173 sets remaining unsold at the last count—2,827 having been previously accounted for—only 182 had been purchased, leaving 991, or almost a quarter of the total edition, still unsold.[37]

This unwelcome confirmation of his gloomy financial prospects had an immediate effect, prompting Sterne to consider ways in which they might be improved. If Becket had no hope of *Tristram Shandy* selling well, then 'my Sermons are ready with a months Labour, when I see a seasonable Occasion for their appearance' (*Letters*, 192). It was anxiety about money, rarely absent in Sterne, that prompted the unmistakable hint of blackmail with which he concluded his letter: 'I sh^{d} much sooner chuse you sh^{d} publish them, or what else I write, than any other' (*Letters*, 192). Sterne signed off with the words, 'I am truely y^{r} friend', but there were, he hinted, other booksellers in London should Becket protest too much about *Tristram Shandy*'s disappointingly slow sale.

By the late spring of 1763 Laurence Sterne had given up thoughts of an early return home. The decisive moment came at the beginning of May, when he sought permission to extend his absence from Coxwold. The request was made to Archbishop Robert Drummond, who had succeeded John Gilbert in 1761 following the latter's death. Lydia's health had improved, he told the archbishop, but he himself remained ill,

> having since the first day of my arrival here been in a continual warfare with agues, fevers, and physicians—the 1st brought my blood to so poor a state, that the physicians found it necessary to enrich it with strong bouillons, and strong bouillons and soups a santé threw me into fevers, and fevers brought on loss of blood, and loss of blood agues—so that as *war begets poverty, poverty peace*, &c. &c.—has this miserable constitution made all its revolutions; how many more it may sustain, before its last and great one, God knows—like the rest of my species, I shall fence it off as long as I can. (*Letters*, 195)

While Sterne expressed the hope of returning to England in the spring of 1764, he also believed he would never preach again. He had preached too often already, he told the archbishop, and were his age to be computed by the number of sermons he had delivered, 'I might be truly said to have the claim of a *Miles emeritus*', adding that were a Hôtel des Invalides established for preachers he would ask the archbishop's aid to become a pensioner. The author of *Tristram Shandy* concluded with a sombre yet discreetly allusive note, expressing the hope that Drummond's indulgence would allow him to add 'a few quiet years to this fragment of my life' (*Letters*, 196).[38]

Sterne now intended to leave Toulouse in the first week of June for the resort of Bagnères-en-Bigorre in the Pyrenean foothills, expecting to find there 'much health and much amusement from the concourse of adventurers from all corners of the earth' (*Letters*, 193). As importantly, Sterne hoped to turn the experience into material for his fiction. The temptation to send Tristram to Spain was predictably strong in so fervent an admirer of Cervantes, and Sterne wrote: 'I shall cross the Pyreneans, and spend a week in that kingdom, which is enough for a fertile brain to write a volume upon' (*Letters*, 198). It is hard not to regret that, like so many of Sterne's plans, this quixotic notion came to nothing. As restless as ever, he was also planning still further ahead. He had hopes of crossing with his family by boat to Leghorn, and of spending the following winter in Florence before returning home via Paris in the following April. '[B]ut this is a sketch only,' Sterne concluded, 'for in all things I am governed by circumstances—so that what is fit to be done on Monday, may be very unwise on Saturday' (*Letters*, 193–4).

Besides his health, the most important circumstance governing Sterne was money. Scarcely a letter was written without some allusion to his uncertain finances, and Sterne's money worries dominate his correspondence with his banker, Robert Foley, throughout the spring and early summer. At the end of April, he was asking Foley to advance him, 'for a few posts or so', 80 guineas he was expecting from York in a couple of weeks. Immediately on receipt of these funds, he explained, the whole family would leave for the foothills of the Pyrenees. Three weeks later, he wrote again to Foley in the same manner: 'It is some disappointment to me that you have taken no notice of my letter, especially as I told you we waited for the money before we set out for Bagnieres,—and so little distrust had I that such a civility would be refused me, that we have actually had all our things pack'd up these eight days, in expectation of receiving a letter' (*Letters*, 196). The Sternes' bags were to remain packed for some time further, for it was not until 9 June that Foley replied, prompting a generous apology from the evidently relieved Sterne. Three days later Sterne wrote again, enclosing £50 and a prudential compliment: 'When I write the history of my travels—Memorandum! I am not to forget how honest a man I have for a banker at Paris' (*Letters*, 198).

In the end, the stay at Bagnères-de-Bigorre made possible by the arrival of money proved unsuccessful. The resort was dull, with few of the attractions Sterne had anticipated. Much more seriously, Sterne reported that the thinness of the Pyrenean air brought on continual haemorrhaging and 'all the Tribe of evils insident to a pulmonary Consumption' (*Letters*, 205). As a result he did not make his projected trip to Spain, but occupied himself instead with projecting journeys for the future, and in attempting to fix on a place of residence for the following winter. A letter written from Bagnères in mid-July shows him still perturbed by the financial implications of the slow sale of the fifth and sixth volumes of *Tristram Shandy*. Thomas Becket had settled with Elizabeth Sterne, in her passage through London on the way from York to Paris, but the bookseller had sold a further 182 sets and Sterne reminded him that he had written in April asking for £20: 'but not having heard a word from You Since in answer, or any Intimation from Mr Foley my Banquer that he had rec^d^ the Summ, I suppose by some Accident or Mistake, my Letter never yet found its Way to You' (*Letters*, 199). Perhaps Becket responded more readily to the excuse Sterne offered than to the implied threat of his previous letter, for he evidently replied to Sterne's satisfaction.

Given his ill health, Sterne's difficulty in finding a place to pass the following winter was particularly irksome. He crossed the south of France so often, he declared, 'that I ran a risk of being taken up as a spy', though as a result he 'jogg'd [himself] out of all other dangers' (*Letters*, 205). Along with his wife and daughter he visited Aix-en-Provence and Marseilles, but found objections to both. Aix was another parliament town, 'of which Toulouse has given me a surfeit' (*Letters*, 202), he wrote, while Marseilles was impossibly expensive, both for accommodation and the daily cost of living. Instead the Sternes fixed on Montpellier, 'where things are moderate enough—tho' a third dearer than at Toulouse' (*Letters*, 201).

Sterne's constant preoccupation with money and the need to winter economically had its grim side. The choice of Montpellier had been determined partly by its long-standing reputation as a suitable resort for invalids: especially, in the words of *The Tatler* more than half a century previously, for 'Persons who have a Disorder in their Lungs'.[39] No sooner had he arrived in Montpellier, however, than he discovered that the town 'had a bad Character of late years, as the grave of consumptive people'. All he could do was to hope for the best, declaring resignedly: 'I see nothing yet to terrifye me upon that score' (*Letters*, 200).

The Montpellier of the 1760s was small, but notable both for its ancient university and for the modern additions to the city. Tobias Smollett, who was there at the same time as the Sternes, wrote in *Travels through France and Italy* that: 'The town is reckoned well built, and what the French call *bien percée*; yet the streets are in general narrow, and the houses dark.'[40] For entertainments there was a 'tolerable concert' twice a week, and a theatre during the winter months. One of Montpellier's principal attractions for Sterne, besides its cheapness, was a more substantial English-speaking community than that of Toulouse. Montpellier was a popular resort with English travellers, and especially, despite its reported reputation, with invalids. It was to this very popularity, however, that Smollett attributed the fact that it was one of the most expensive towns in the south of France. The inhabitants of Montpellier, he noted acerbically, 'affect to believe, that all the travellers of our country are grand seigneurs, immensely rich and incredibly generous; and we are silly enough to encourage this opinion, by submitting quietly to the most ridiculous extortion, as well as by committing acts of the most absurd extravagance'.[41] Smollett was notoriously ready to believe himself imposed upon by mercenary foreigners wherever he went, but James Boswell, who visited Montpellier two years later on his way back home from Italy, confirms Smollett's view.[42]

When Sterne arrived in Montpellier in the autumn of 1764 he found four or five families who turned out to welcome him. Among the city's permanent residents was a Scots merchant and banker, Alexander Ray, who had already earned Sterne's gratitude by allowing him substantial credit (£200 according to Sterne, who may, however, have been attempting to impress Robert Foley in Paris). In fact Sterne never touched the money, probably for fear of being unable to repay it. Banker to many British visitors, Ray was a familiar figure in Montpellier and a man well liked and respected. Smollett described him as 'a gentleman of great probity and worth, from whom I have received repeated marks of uncommon friendship and hospitality',[43] while Boswell found him 'a free, sensible, good-humoured man with a variety of agreeable knowledge'.[44]

To judge from his own correspondence, Sterne seems to have been harder to please. When the arrival of Lord Rochford, en route to take up the post of British ambassador in Madrid, brought him news of his friends, Sterne wrote wistfully to Robert Foley in Paris: 'I suppose you are full of English.'[45] Instead, Sterne lamented, 'we are here, as if in another world, where unless some stray'd Soul arrives, We know nothing of what is going on in y^rs'.[46] In fact, Sterne saw more people than his laments would imply. He certainly knew Tobias Smollett and his wife Anne, who, in turn, kept company with Elizabeth and Lydia Sterne. It is difficult, however, to imagine that the blunt Smollett, endlessly curious about the past and present states of the cities he visited, warmed to Sterne, especially if the latter was 'Shandying' it, and Sterne's subsequent caricature of him as the 'learned Smelfungus' in *A Sentimental Journey* suggests scant regard in that direction either. They may, nonetheless, have been brought together by mutual friends, for both would have been at home with William Hewett, the eccentric friend of John Hall-Stevenson, one of the Demoniacs of Crazy Castle and now in his early seventies, whom Smollett described as 'one of the most original characters upon earth'.[47] If we may depend on *Humphry Clinker*, where Hewett appears as a friend of Matthew Bramble, this was no vain boast: among the stories Smollett includes is an anecdote in which Hewett, on the Capitol in Rome, 'made up to a bust of Jupiter, and, bowing very low, exclaimed in the Italian language, "I hope, sir, if ever you get get your head above water again, you will remember that I paid my respects to you in your adversity" ', prompting Pope Benedict XIV, to whom these remarks were reported, to laugh, saying, 'Those English heretics think they have a right to go to the devil in their own way'.[48]

Another friend of John Hall-Stevenson's to visit Montpellier during Sterne's stay was Jean-Baptiste Tollot, a native of Geneva, who had accompanied Hall-Stevenson from that city to Toulouse in 1759, and whom Sterne had met in Paris in 1762. Now he was accompanying two Yorkshiremen, Thomas Thornhill of Fisby and his brother George. When they arrived in Montpellier they found the Sternes with Hewett and some other English visitors: 'j'eu je vous l'avoue baucoup de plaisir en revoiant le bon et agreable Tristram, qui me parut etre toujours a peu prez dans le meme etat ou je l'avois laissè a Paris' ('I must tell you that I had the great pleasure of again seeing the good and agreeable Tristram, who seemed very much the same as he was when I left him in Paris').[49] Tollot gathered from Sterne that the writer would have enjoyed himself more at Toulouse without his wife, but added that though she made him pass some bad moments he bore all their disagreements with angelic patience.

It was clear by now that, despite his expressed reluctance, which was more on Lydia's account than Elizabeth's—'I wish my girl in England' (*Letters*, 210)—Sterne would leave behind both wife and daughter when he eventually returned home. As early as the end of September he had indicated as much to Lord Fauconberg. His wife, he wrote, 'being a great Œconomist', wished to return to Toulouse with Lydia, where she believed that they could save as much in one year as would keep them in clothes for seven. '[M]y system', declared Sterne, 'is to let her please herself—so I shall return to Coxwould alone' (*Letters*, 201). He told Robert Foley the same thing a few days later, though making no mention of the financial reasons for the separation and suggesting that Montauban rather than Toulouse was Elizabeth's preference for the winter. Tollot, meanwhile, had been told that the two women wished to stay in France 'pour *finir* Miss Stern'.[50] In writing to Lydia herself from Paris, however, Sterne insisted that only concern for her health persuaded him to allow her to remain behind with her mother.

Whatever real weight this last reason had with Sterne, in comparison to the renewed tension in the marriage, it was for reasons of economy that Elizabeth Sterne and her daughter chose to remain in France. Sterne's financial difficulties multiplied during the autumn and winter of 1763–4, and his attempts to borrow money to see him through this period prompted much ingenuity and the exploitation of all his literary talent in correspondence. Writing to Robert Foley to thank him for an arrangement which gave Sterne the right to draw on Foley's correspondent at Toulouse for 1,500 livres, Sterne came laughably close to suggesting that the long-suffering banker was importunate in his attempts to lend the author money. But, 'as I knew the offer came from your heart,' Sterne wrote, 'I made no difficulty of accepting' (*Letters*, 202). The extent of his financial embarrassment was becoming increasingly apparent, however whimsically he endeavoured to conceal it. Just seven weeks later Sterne solicited the loan of 50 pounds from a man he had never met—John Mill, a London merchant. '[N]ow it seems a little paradoxical,' he confessed, 'when I have so many friends and wellwishers I live with as Brothers, I should rather take this Liberty with a friend whose face I never yet saw—but the truth, upon running ove[r] the List over in my mind, I found not one, I could take such a Liberty with, wth less pain of heart—which is all the apology I will make', though apparently feeling that this might not do, he added that his first visit on returning to London would be to Mill, 'to bring along wth me, (at least) the Interest in ten thousand thanks—& for the Capital, The whole Shandean family will stand bound—You shall be paid the very first Money God sends' (*Letters*, 204, 205). Whether Mill found Sterne's anticipated source of income sufficient guarantee to advance the loan we do not know.

Sterne had luck elsewhere, however. Having written to Lord Grosvenor, a subscriber to the first four volumes of the *Sermons*, with a similar request for £50, Sterne was understandably delighted to receive the loan of a hundred. 'No body but Lord Grosvenor would have thought of such a Thing—', he wrote, with less hyperbole than usual, 'You may take my word, my Lord, That a Man must have a *good* heart before he can have a *generous* one—and that to have a generous one, A Man must live so as to *Afford* to consider the public more than himself' (*Letters*, 206).

Pressing as they were, Sterne's financial perplexities were not the greatest of his worries. The year 1764 began badly for him. On 5 January he started to write a letter to Robert Foley and broke off to ride out south-west of Montpellier, in the direction of Pézénas. He returned home in a shivering fit and was confined to bed with a fever for ten days. 'I have suffered in this scuffle with death terribly,' he confessed, 'but unless the spirit of prophecy deceive me—I shall not die but live' (*Letters*, 208). He had lost faith in the efficacy of both the climate and the physicians at Montpellier to restore his health. The air, he now believed, was too sharp. Montpellier's climate in winter disappointed other British travellers besides Sterne. Smollett reported that a few days after his arrival it rained incessantly for the best part of a week, 'leaving the air so loaded with vapours, that there was no walking after sun-sett without being wetted by the dew almost to the skin'.[51] Boswell, who was there in December 1765, reported that 'The frost was so intense that I thought myself in Russia. I had great pleasure in being able to say that I had felt much severer cold in the south of France than I had ever felt in Scotland.'[52] And if Sterne found the weather bad, then the doctors were worse. 'My physicians', he wrote, 'have almost poisoned me with what they call *bouillons refraichissants.*—'tis a cock flead alive and boiled with poppy seeds, then pounded in a mortar, afterwards pass'd thro' a sieve—There is to be one crawfish in it, and I was gravely told it must be a male one—a female would do me more harm than good' (*Letters*, 210).

Sterne's disillusion met with few compensations elsewhere. The delighted anticipation he had once shown towards his first trip to the continent had long since given way to disenchantment. 'I am preparing to leave France,' he wrote to one correspondent, 'for I am heartily tired of it—That insipidity there is in French characters has disgusted your friend Yorick' (*Letters*, 209). Given the popular images of the two traveller-novelists who coincided in Montpellier, it is amusing to find the genial Yorick and irascible Smelfungus exchanging roles. While Smollett had looked forward to the gathering of the States of Provence in January, when Montpellier 'will be extremely gay and brilliant',[53] Sterne complained that: 'The states of Languedoc are met—'tis a fine raree-shew, with the usual accompanyments of fiddles, bears, and puppet-shews.—I believe I shall step into my post-chaise with more alacrity to fly from these sights, than a Frenchman would to fly to them . . . I shall be in high spirits, and every step I take that brings me nearer England, will I think help to set this poor frame to rights' (*Letters*, 210). The man who had left home two years previously in search of health now needed to return to England to regain it.

Sterne's stay in France had been costly, and he was leaving behind a much-loved daughter along with a little-loved wife. What he did have to take back with him to England, however, was enough experience for use in a further volume of *Tristram Shandy* and the germ of what would eventually become *A Sentimental Journey*.

When he left Montpellier Sterne did not return home directly but passed some time in Paris. Despite still straitened circumstances—his correspondence shows him anxious about his credit and the disappointingly slow sale of the latest instalment of *Tristram Shandy*—he was able to lodge in the expensive Hôtel d'Entragues in the rue Tournon, a few yards from the Luxembourg Palace, as a guest of Tollot or the Thornhills, with whom he travelled. Tollot had earlier told Hall-Stevenson in a letter of his plan to find Sterne a good room in the same hotel as his own party, where the impoverished writer might also eat with his friends whenever he wished.

Sterne was appropriately grateful. When he described his lodgings in a letter to Lydia, he spoke warmly of his hosts: 'they are good and generous souls' (*Letters*, 212). Sterne also paid daily visits to John Hall-Stevenson's uncle Lawson Trotter, a Jacobite who had fled England following the failure of the 1745 rebellion. Although he was, in theory, a dangerous acquaintance, Sterne did not scruple to visit him 'without much, or indeed any precaution'. Indeed, Trotter was visited by many English visitors to Paris, 'as well by In's as Out's', as is well-evidenced by two dinners Sterne attended, at which his fellow-guests included the marquess of Tavistock, heir to the duke of Bedford, and the son of the British ambassador.

It was the ambassador himself who occasioned one of the two most notable incidents that occurred during Sterne's second visit to Paris. Despite his earlier determination never to preach again, Sterne was prevailed upon to deliver a sermon in the ambassador's chapel on the occasion of the first service there, on 25 March 1764.[54] Recently arrived in Paris, the earl of Hertford had just taken and sumptuously furnished the 'magnificent' Hôtel de Brancas, near the Louvre, at the junction of the rue de l'Université and the rue de Bourbon: 'It occupied the curiosity, formed the amusement, and gave a subject of conversation to the polite circles of Paris, for a fortnight at least' (*Letters*, 219). When the day arrived for the first service in the chapel, Lord Hertford asked Sterne if he would preach. Etiquette alone required that he accept, but there was, in any case, no danger of a refusal, for Sterne was delighted to be once more a centre of attention. Mischievously, he chose for his text the fifteenth verse of 2 Kings 20—'And he said, What have they seen in thine house? And Hezekiah answered, All *the things* that *are* in mine house have they seen: there is nothing among my treasures, that I have not showed them'—'an odd subject your mother will say' (*Letters*, 212), Sterne wrote to Lydia. By the time word of the sermon reached London the choice of text was maliciously reported not merely as odd but as a deliberate insult to Lord Hertford. The affront derived from the fact that Sterne's sermon supposedly included the rebuke Isaiah delivered to Hezekiah for showing the royal treasures to the Babylonian ambassadors, which concludes, as Sterne reported it in a letter to William Combe: 'And Hezekiah said unto the Prophet, I have shewn them "my vessels of gold, and my vessels of silver, and my wives and my concubines, and my boxes of ointment, and whatever I have in my house, have I shewn unto them: and the Prophet said unto Hezekiah, thou hast done very foolishly"' (*Letters*, 219).

If Sterne really paraphrased the Old Testament account in this manner in the pulpit, then his intimation that his choice of text was merely unlucky does not stand up to scrutiny. The paraphrase is a decidedly satirical one—even allowing for the fact that Sterne is drawing on three separate sources in 2 Kings 20, 2 Chronicles 32, and Isaiah 39. Though Sterne told William Combe that, 'as the text is a part of Holy writ that could not give offence', the most offensive words appear nowhere in Scripture. In fact, the printed version of the sermon which appeared in 1766 is quite different from Sterne's sly account to William Combe—though the alteration may have been made for prudential reasons, leaving open the possibility that Sterne did choose to offer his provocative version of scripture before his urbane Paris audience.[55] Undoubtedly he was capable of such effrontery, and whether or not the preacher chose to glance at the new ambassador and his palatial residence, he certainly took the opportunity of aiming a witty dart at another member of the congregation in the chapel. This was David Hume, the philosopher and historian, two years Sterne's senior and at the time acting as secretary to the ambassador and tutor to his son. '[A]s the Chaldeans were great searchers into the secrets of nature,' Sterne affirmed:

> especially into the motions of the celestial bodies, in all probability they had taken notice at that distance, of the strange appearance of the shadow's returning ten degrees backwards upon their dials, and had enquired and learned upon what account, and in whose favour such a sign was given; so that this astronomical miracle, besides the political motive which it would suggest of courting such a favourite of heaven, had been sufficient by itself to have led a curious people as far as Jerusalem, that they might see the man for whose sake the sun had forsook his course.[56]

It was not a passage likely to have gone unremarked by the author of the essay 'Of Miracles' (1748)—nor, indeed, by any other member of the congregation, to whom Hume's reputation as the 'Great Infidel' was well known. In fact, despite the 'scurvy misrepresentations', no one seems to have been seriously offended by the sermon. 'Lord Hertford did me the honour to thank me for it again and again', Sterne was able to report with understandable delight, and even David Hume 'favoured it with his grace and approbation' (*Letters*, 219).[57]

Later that same day Sterne and Hume were both guests at a dinner hosted by Lord Hertford, during which, according to rumours that quickly circulated in London, the parson and the sceptic had quarrelled. Sterne was quick to quash such gossip, writing in a letter home:

> The story . . . which you heard related, with such an air of authority, is like many other true stories, absolutely false. Mr. *Hume* and I never had a dispute—I mean a serious, angry or petulant dispute, in our lives:—indeed I should be most exceedingly surprized to hear that *David* ever had an unpleasant contention with any man;—and if I should be made to believe that such an event had happened, nothing would persuade me that his opponent was not in the wrong: for, in my life, did I never meet with a being of a more placid and gentle nature; and it is this amiable turn of his character, that has given more consequence and force to his scepticism, than all the arguments of his sophistry.—You may depend on this as a truth (*Letters*, 218).[58]

The origins of the tale of the supposed dispute lay, Sterne surmised, in 'a little pleasant sparring' at dinner, but that, he insisted, was characterized by 'good-will' and 'urbanity' on both sides. 'I had preached that very day at the Ambassador's Chapel, and *David* was disposed to make a little merry with the *Parson*; and, in return, the Parson was equally disposed to make a little mirth with the *Infidel*; we laughed at one another, and the company laughed with us both' (*Letters*, 218).

While we have no account of the occasion from Hume, there is no evidence of the least ill-will between the two men. In 1773, five years after Sterne's death, the Scottish philosopher referred to *Tristram Shandy* as the 'best Book, that has been writ by any Englishman these thirty Years' (though he rather tarnished the praise by adding 'bad as it is').[59] Sterne himself was later to incorporate a pleasing anecdote concerning himself and Hume—perhaps deriving from the same dinner at Lord Hertford's—into *A Sentimental Journey*:

> A prompt French Marquis at our ambassador's table demanded of Mr. H——, if he was [John] H[ume] the poet? No, said H——mildly——*Tant pis*, replied the Marquis.
>
> It is H——the historian, said another——*Tant mieux*, said the Marquis. And Mr. H——, who is a man of excellent heart, return'd thanks for both.[60]

Sterne's second visit to Paris also revealed a side of his personality hidden during the long months he had spent with his family in the south of France, supporting the understanding of Tollot that the writer would have enjoyed himself more there had his wife been elsewhere. Without Elizabeth Sterne to restrain him Sterne led a very different life, encouraged to dissipation as he was by friends, most notably John Wilkes, then at the height of his notoriety. Born the son of a distiller in 1727, Wilkes had married at the age of 22 an heiress ten years his senior. Subsequently he had pursued a dissolute life, characterized in the public imagination by his membership of the Hellfire Club, or the Monks of Medmenham Abbey. In order to participate in public life Wilkes outwardly conformed to the Church of England (though his family background was in Dissent), and he was elected to parliament in 1757. Wilkes took a prominent part in opposing the ministry of Lord Bute in 1762 and 1763. Along with the clergyman and satirist Charles Churchill, he founded and edited a newspaper which, under the name of *The North Briton*, presented an open challenge to the ministerial paper, *The Briton*, edited by Tobias Smollett. On 23 April 1763 Wilkes published the celebrated (or infamous) No. 45, in which he attacked ministerial policy through the speech delivered from the throne by George III four days earlier—an act which led to his imprisonment. After the Lord Chief Justice, in a famous ruling, rejected the legality of general warrants, Wilkes was set free. His release notwithstanding, however, he was subsequently expelled from parliament on the hypocritical grounds of having composed an obscene poem, *An Essay on Woman*, in parody of Pope's celebrated *Essay on Man*. Forced into exile in France, he was officially *persona non grata* in diplomatic circles in Paris, but Wilkes was renowned for his personal charm and was apparently present in the embassy chapel when Sterne preached there.

Already known to Wilkes in London, Sterne shared many of his political views, both on the perceived arrogance of Lord Bute—the '*Scotch* horse [which] cannot bear a saddle upon his back' of *Tristram Shandy* (v. 11. 280)—and on the shortcomings of the Treaty of Paris. In Thomas Becket the two men also shared a publisher. Moreover, Sterne was doubtless amused by the fact that the notes to *An Essay on Woman* were written in parody of William Warburton's notes to his 1751 edition of Pope—though he could scarcely have endorsed the blasphemous or heterodox aspects of Wilkes's poem.[61] Certainly he spent considerable time with Wilkes in Paris, for writing to Charles Churchill on 10 April 1764 Wilkes declared: 'Sterne and I often meet, and talk of you.' He continued: 'We have an odd party for to-night at Hope's, two lively, young, handsome actresses, Hope and his mistress—Ah! poor Mrs Wilkes!!!'[62]

Whether he might have added 'poor Mrs Sterne!!!' is tantalizingly uncertain. The composition of the party scarcely encourages belief that Sterne was present in any spiritual capacity. In 1767 Sterne was to assert that he had had no sexual relationship with any woman, even his wife, in two decades—though there are ample hints to the contrary throughout his correspondence, with John Hall-Stevenson and David Garrick among others.[63] Whether on this occasion his failings were of the flesh or merely of the spirit, Sterne's susceptibility to the attractions of other women certainly surfaced again in the absence of his wife. In May he wrote to John Hall-Stevenson:

> I have been for eight weeks smitten with the tenderest passion that ever tender wight underwent. I wish, dear cosin, thou couldst concieve (perhaps thou can'st without my wishing it) how deliciously I canter'd away with it the first month, two up, two down, always upon my hânches along the street from my hôtel to hers, at first, once—then twice, then three times a day, till at length I was within an ace of setting up my hobby horse in her stable for good an all. I might as well considering how the enemies of the Lord have blasphemed thereupon; the last three weeks we were every hour upon the doleful ditty of parting—and thou mayest concieve, dear cosin, how it alter'd my gaite and air—for I went down and came like any louden'd carl, and did nothing but mix tears, and *Jouer des sentiments* with her from sun-rising even to the setting of the same. (*Letters*, 213)

The sentimental liaison ended, Sterne revealed, when the unknown woman left for the south of France. '[And] to finish the comedie,' Sterne concluded, 'I fell ill, and broke a vessel in my lungs and half bled to death. Voila mon Histoire!' (*Letters*, 213).

Sterne's stay in Paris was almost at an end. 'We have been talking and projecting about setting out from this city of seductions every day this month', Sterne confessed in a letter to Hall-Stevenson on 19 May, adding that: 'We are now setting out without let or hindrance and shall be in London ye 29th, Dijs, Deabusque volentibus' (*Letters*, 214). And, since neither gods nor goddesses willed otherwise, Sterne set off on 24 May, along with the Thornhills and Tollot, from what he crudely termed 'foutre-land'. Yet, even as he left, his often disparaging view of France softened: 'we ought not to abuse it—for we have lived (shag, rag and bobtail), all of us, a most jolly nonsensical life of it' (*Letters*, 214).

12
England, 1764–1765

By the time he set foot in England once more Sterne's 'most jolly nonsensical life' in France had lasted for no less than two years and four months. Even so, he was in no immediate hurry to return to Coxwold. Instead, he preferred to remain in London, where he stayed with the Thornhills—probably in Thomas Thornhill's house in Berkeley Square. There he took up the threads of his social life and managed a short visit out of town to Lord Ligonier, now commander-in-chief of the army in Great Britain, who years before had served in the same campaigns as Roger Sterne. Despite his determination to renew old friendships, however, Sterne was too busy to call on all of his acquaintances or to enjoy to the full the amusements of the capital (hence he missed the concert featuring the 8-year-old Mozart which took place at Ranelagh at the end of the month). When he eventually took leave of London, he explained his departure in an apologetic letter to Elizabeth Montagu: he was going down to Yorkshire, he told her, 'to write a world of Nonsense—if possible like a man of *Sense*' (*Letters*, 216).

What Sterne did not intend to do on his return to Yorkshire was to take up in earnest his priestly duties at Coxwold. Replying to one of a list of enquiries circulated by Archbishop Drummond, he wrote: 'I have a residing Curate—and always shall have one, as I fear I shall never be in a condition to do duty myself' (*Letters*, 217). Sterne remained in bad health throughout the summer and autumn of 1764. In October he spoke of 'long & obstinate coughs, & unaccountable hemorrages in my lungs, & a thorough relaxation of the Organ (or something worse) in consequence of them' (*Letters*, 229). Removing himself from all parochial duties was one of the measures he took to protect himself from the worst effects of his illness. To Robert Foley, he had written in August: 'you will certainly see me at Paris the week following, for now I abandon every thing in this world to health and to my friends' (*Letters*, 222). Once again he insisted that he would preach no more: 'the last sermon I shall ever preach, was preach'd at Paris' (*Letters*, 222). This was to prove not quite true, for Sterne would be persuaded to mount the pulpit again—but only on the most extraordinary occasions.

Whatever his resolve, Sterne was not yet a free man. James Kilner, who had served as assistant curate at Coxwold for the previous two and a half years, had never been ordained priest. 'By some mistakes or other, either on his side or mine,' Sterne confessed to the archbishop, 'some thing has ever prevented his obtaining Priest's Orders' (*Letters*, 217). The principal cause of the failure was poverty. Already in his mid-thirties when he became unofficial curate to Sterne, Kilner had not attended a university, still less taken a degree. He had been a deacon for five years, and had previously served in cures in four different counties, to no great material advantage to himself. In Coxwold he served as assistant curate while continuing to act as usher in the village school run by the Revd Thomas Newton. When asking his archbishop's permission to extend his stay in France in May 1762, Sterne had implied that Kilner would be a candidate for priest's orders at the next ordination and duly gave him such reference as he could for a man he scarcely knew. Kilner had been recommended by the last clergyman he had assisted 'as a scholar, & a moral Man', he carried out his duties at Coxwold without complaint, and Sterne concluded with the hope that Kilner would give Drummond 'all possible Satisfaction' (*Letters*, 164). Though Sterne had done his part Kilner did not get off to the best of starts, for prior to delivering Sterne's sealed letter to the archbishop he opened it—a fact Drummond duly recorded in noting Kilner's case.

Kilner, in fact, had reservations of his own. 'My Lord,' he wrote to the archbishop on 6 September 1762,

> I am inform'd by a Letter lately come into our Neighbourhood from him, that Mr Sterne is at Thoulouse, has recover'd his Health very much, & purposes to return to England wth ye first Spring.——I hope y^{r} Grace will dispense wth me in Statu quo till then . . . I have been in several poor Places, & in frequent Journyings, among People who now & then ought to have us'd me more liberally; so that my Pocket has been kept low.[1]

At this time Kilner's total income was just over £40 a year. To the archbishop, He explained, 'Licensing might embarrass me, as my Ability is yet but weakish'.[2]

When Kilner did wish to take Holy Orders in the following year, he found that Sterne's testimonial was not sufficient for the archbishop. Even in 1764 Drummond was not convinced of Kilner's merits, for Sterne was driven to pressing his curate's case hard to him. So hard, in fact, that he later apologized for giving a personal recommendation in relation to the period when he was abroad and was therefore in no position whatever to give such a testimonial. Still, he insisted in a letter of 30 October, Kilner's character

> in this parish is very good; and that the man is well liked as a quiet and an honest man, & withal as a good reader and preacher: I think him so myself; and had it not been impertinent, <gi> to speak to a point, of which your Grace is this moment going to be a Judge—I believe him a good Scholar also—I do not say, a graceful one—for his bodily presence is mean; & were he [to] stand for Ordination before a popish bishop—The poor fellow would be disabled by a Canon in a moment. (*Letters*, 229)

Kilner was eventually ordained priest on 4 November 1764, and was licensed the following day as assistant curate of Coxwold, on Sterne's nomination, at a salary of £30 a year. The whole episode is a telling illustration of the plight of the poorer clergy in the eighteenth century, and—always allowing for the considerable differences in the personal attainments of Kilner and Sterne—indicates how much Sterne owed both to his cousin Richard, who had enabled him to go to university, and to his uncle Jaques, during his early years in the Church.

Having settled his parish affairs Sterne intended to turn to the major task awaiting him during the summer of 1764: the continuation of *Tristram Shandy*. As so often, however, he allowed himself to be distracted repeatedly. In July or early August he travelled to Harrogate. Later in August he was at York for Race Week, where he met up with friends old and new, including John Hall-Stevenson and the Thornhills. Finally Sterne visited Scarborough in September, reporting that he had 'been drinking the waters ever since the races, and have received marvellous strength, had I not debilitated it as fast as I got it, by playing the good fellow with Lord G[ranby] and Co' (*Letters*, 226).

Like other English spa towns, Scarborough was a popular resort in the mid-eighteenth century, especially for the opportunities it offered both sexes to socialize. Smollett gave a brief account of it later in the 1760s in *Humphry Clinker*:

> Scarborough, though a paltry town, is romantic from its situation along a cliff that overhangs the sea. The harbour is formed by a small elbow

> of land that runs out as a natural mole, directly opposite to the town; and on that side is the castle, which stands very high, of considerable extent . . . . At the other end of Scarborough are two public rooms for the use of the company, who resort to this place in the summer, to drink the waters and bathe in the sea; and the diversions are pretty much on the same footing here as at Bath. The Spa is a little way beyond the town, on this side, under a cliff, within a few paces of the sea, and thither the drinkers go every morning in dishabille. . . . Betwixt the well and the harbour, the bathing machines are ranged along the beach, with all their proper utensils and attendants.[3]

Among the company at Scarborough were William Petty, the earl of Shelburne, who had served under Granby when the latter was commander of the British troops in Germany between 1759 and 1762, and perhaps William Hewett. It was at Scarborough that Smollett placed Hewett's meeting with Matthew Bramble in *Humphry Clinker*: 'He came hither to Scarborough, to pay his respects to his noble friend and former pupil, the M[arquess] of G[ranby], and, forgetting that he is now turned of seventy, sacrificed so liberally to Bacchus, that next day he was seized with a fit of the apoplexy, which has a little impaired his memory; but he retains all the oddity of his character in perfection.'[4]

Besides 'playing the good fellow' with his friends, Sterne was cultivating another sentimental friendship with a young woman during the summer of 1764. She was Sarah Tuting, whom Sterne had first met during the York Race Week in 1760. The daughter of George Tuting, of Newmarket, a horse-racing enthusiast, Sarah Tuting had passed most of her life in racing circles. She was on the point of travelling to Italy for her health, and Sterne recommended her warmly to Robert Foley as 'a lady known and loved by the whole kingdom' (*Letters*, 222). On the following day, 26 August 1764, Sterne wrote to Sarah Tuting herself.

> Well! once more adieu!—farewell! God be with you! in this long journey may no thorn grow near the path you tread; and when you lie down, may your pillow, gentle Sally, be soft as your own breast; and every dream be tinged with pleasures which hearts like yours are only destined to inherit—so get well, dear Lady, mere[ly] not to lose y^{r} birth right *here*—& do not die to enter upon it too soon hereafter. (*Letters*, 223–4)

Sterne could not resist mingling irony with sentiment, however, for he added: 'This is mere Selfishness; and Yet I thought I was writing the most sentimental Letter that ever the hand of true gallantry traced out—and o'my conscience I still believe I am—but I wait to be accused before I justify' (*Letters*, 224). Such frivolity apart, Sterne's letter is shot through with a sense that, as invalids, he and Sarah Tuting share a common fate, and he proffered advice for her coming journey: 'The heart must be chearful and free from desires during all this Pilgrimage in search of health—no hard jostlings in your journey must disturb either body or mind one moment—if you have left a Philander—think not about him' (*Letters*, 224). Just over a month later Sterne acknowledged Foley's attentiveness to Sarah Tuting, about which she had written to her admirer, though he added, 'Surely *she needed no* recommendation' (*Letters*, 227).

Sterne's circumstances in the summer of 1764 did not allow him to dwell exclusively on his friendship with Sarah Tuting. Financial affairs intruded persistently as he anxiously attempted to reconcile the growing needs of his wife and daughter in France with his own dwindling resources. Since arriving back in Yorkshire Sterne had sent £100 in instalments to Thomas Selwyn, out of which Foley was to take what was owed him and place the rest on account. His wife, Sterne reckoned, would draw on Foley for up to 100 louis d'or before March the following year to supplement the hundred he had left with her. Elizabeth Sterne was intending to spend no more than 5,000 livres in the course of the year, and 'you shall always have money before hand of mine', Sterne was careful to assure Foley—though he added, with an assumed nonchalance that is unlikely to have escaped the banker, 'twenty pound this way or that makes no difference between us' (*Letters*, 222). By the end of September Sterne sounded less sanguine. He had heard from his wife, then at Montauban, that she had immediate need of £50; if Foley would send an order to his correspondent at Montauban to pay her in cash, Sterne would reimburse him within three weeks. 'But as her purse is low,' he added, 'for God's sake write directly' (*Letters*, 228).

Throughout the autumn of 1764 his letters constantly reveal urgent financial perplexity. On 11 November he told Foley that he had previously sent a bank bill for £30 to Becket in London, and on the day of writing sent a further bill for £52 10*s*., with instructions that the money be remitted to Foley. When he arrived in London in five weeks' time, Sterne assured his banker, Foley would receive more money, but 'if Mrs Sterne, before I get to London, sh^{d} have Occasion for 50 Louis—be so kind as to honour her draught upon You' (*Letters*, 231). Just five days later Sterne wrote again. His wife had been importuning Foley for money that she believed Sterne had remitted to Paris for her use. Sterne apologized, insisting that he had already written

> to set Mrs. S[terne] right in her mistake—That you had any money of mine in your hands—being very sensible that the hundred pounds I had sent you, thro' Becket's hands, was but about what would balance with you. The reason of her error was owing to my writing her word, I would send you a bill in a post or two for fifty pounds—which, my finances falling short just then, I deferr'd—so that I had paid nothing to any one—but was however come to York this day, and I have sent you a draught for a hundred pounds—in honest truth a fortnight ago I had not the cash—but I am as honest as the king (as Sancho Pança says) *only not so rich*. (*Letters*, 223–4)

As though conscious that wit alone might not suffice, Sterne assured Foley on 29 September that everything would be settled by Christmas, when he intended to be in London with the continuation of *Tristram Shandy*. He knew, at least in broad terms, what the next two volumes of his work would contain—being well equipped with 'nature & Travel', as he had told Elizabeth Montague back in June. Yet for all the financial pressure on him, he could summon up little enthuasiam for writing. Even after his visits to York and Scarborough he was more inclined to pleasure than industry. 'I rejoice you have been encamp'd at Harrogate,' he had told Hall-Stevenson in late September, adding regretfully, 'by now, I suppose you are decamp'd—otherwise as idle a beast as I have been, I would have sacrificed a few days to the god of laughter with you and your jolly set' (*Letters*, 226). Instead he retired reluctantly to the solitude of his house at Coxwold—'my Philosophical Hut', as he termed it—to complete the latest instalment of his novel. He was already thinking ahead, though. If blessed with good health he intended to winter in London; if not, he would push on to Paris instead.

Despite the air of irrepressible optimism he habitually assumed when writing about financial matters, Sterne was acutely conscious that he would have difficulty supporting a second continental journey. Casting around for possibilities, he told Hall-Stevenson that he hoped he might become a 'bear-leader' or travelling-tutor to a young nobleman. In principle the plan was good, for the financial rewards available to distinguished tutors were considerable indeed. In the same year Adam Smith was receiving no less than £500 per annum (later extended by a pension for life of £300) for acting as tutor to the duke of Buccleuch. This, it is true, was quite exceptional and the personal austerity, which together with his formidable intellect, made Smith an ideal tutor for his 17-year-old charge formed no part of Sterne's character. In fact, the plans he jestingly outlined for his putative charge—'[if] I can persuade some *gros* my Lord to take a trip . . . I'll try if I can make him relish the joys of the *Tuileries, Opera Comique*, &c.' (*Letters*, 228)—were a little too close to the truth, and doubtless go a long way to explaining why this particular scheme came to nothing.

Sterne's enthusiasm for returning to France suggests that he had entirely forgotten how discontented he had been there just nine months previously. The dull, unsociable life at Coxwold became more oppressive still as he imaginatively re-created his travels while writing his account of Tristram's adventures abroad. Moreover, the prospect of visiting France without his wife in tow was particularly appealing. At all events, mention of his efforts with *Tristram Shandy* brought to mind thoughts of his friends in the French capital:

> You will read as odd a Tour thro' France, as ever was projected or executed by traveller or travell Writer, since the world began.
>
> —tis a laughing good temperd Satyr against Traveling (as puppies travel)—Panchaud will enjoy it—I am quite civil to the parisiens—et *per Cosa,*—You know—tis likely I may see'em again—& possibly this Spring. (*Letters*, 231)

What Sterne seems to have had in mind, as his '*per Cosa*' suggests, was travelling further south, and within a week he was telling Robert Foley of his plans to go Italy 'this year'—though he qualified this by adding, 'at least I shall not defer it above another' (*Letters*, 234).

By mid-November the continuation of *Tristram Shandy* was all but complete. Sterne, though, found little time for leisure. He had already postponed an invitation to visit Hall-Stevenson at Skelton because of the pressure of parish business. ''Tis a church militant week with me, full of marches, and countermarches—and treaties about Stillington common, which we are going to inclose' (*Letters*, 232). This was the second enclosure with which Sterne had been concerned; in the first—in 1759—3,000 acres of land in the parish of Sutton were enclosed. At Stillington, where the enclosure eventually took in some 1,400 acres, the process was a lengthy one, not finally completed until February 1768, just a month before Sterne's death. He had also found his time taken up with visitors: a friend from London, and others who were perhaps guests of Lord Fauconberg's at Newburgh Priory: 'I have been *Miss-ridden* this last week by a couple of romping girls (*bien mises et comme il faut*) who might as well have been in the house with me, (tho' perhaps not, my retreat here is too quiet for them) but they have taken up all my time, and have given my judgment and fancy more airings than they wanted.—These things accord not well with sermon making' (*Letters*, 233). Finding virtue as well as repose in solitude, Sterne was for once content to remain in 'sweet retirement' in Coxwold until December. 'I wish you was sat down as happily, and as free of all worldly cares' (*Letters*, 234), he wrote to Robert Foley uncharacteristically—and somewhat provocatively, since he still owed the banker money.

In the end Sterne put himself hard to writing, for he arrived in London before Christmas as he had planned, bringing with him the manuscript of the continuation of *Tristram Shandy*. This was published, as volumes VII and VIII of the complete work, by Becket and Dehondt at the end of January 1765. Surprisingly, given the comparative failure of his previous instalment, Sterne showed no obvious anxiety about the critical reception of these latest volumes. Perhaps he was confident that the novelty of the account of Tristram's journey to France, as he flees England after Death has coming knocking at the door, would restore the popularity of his book. Or he may have decided once and for all that whatever the reviewers' response might be, his aim was to succeed with the public. If so, he must have been particularly gratified by the success he enjoyed, despite lukewarm notices in the magazines. By mid-March he could tell Garrick in a letter that 'I have had a lucrative winter's campaign here—Shandy sells well' (*Letters*, 235).

All the same, Sterne looked hard at the reviews to see what, exactly, the reviewers admired and what they did not. Predictably, there was further censure of what was variously termed the 'ribbaldry',[5] the 'want of decency',[6] or—more bluntly—the 'obscenity'[7] of Sterne's writing. Since the seventh volume contained the decidedly bawdy story of the abbess of Andoüillets and the novice Margarita, and the eighth the teasing account of the Widow Wadman's attempt to discover exactly where Toby had been wounded in the groin, Sterne could scarcely have expected it otherwise. Much worse from Sterne's point of view, some criticized the work as dull or meaningless. One reviewer spoke of 'incoherent stupidity',[8] another thought the seventh volume contained 'an unconnected, unmeaning, account of our author's journey to France'.[9] None of this was enough to stop some writers again attempting weak pastiches of Sterne's style in their reviews. Nor, however, did it stop Ralph Griffiths, for all his reservations, from constructing a dialogue in which he paid Sterne the heartiest of compliments:

> Reviewer. Admirable!—Mr. Shandy, you understand the art, the true art of travelling, better than any other mortal I ever knew or

> heard of! O! what pleasure, what a delightful exercise of benevolence have I lost, by not keeping company with you, all the way from Avignon!
>
> SHANDY. Fun?—banter?—irony?—eh?
>
> REV. Irony!—no,—by this hand! Tristram! thou has won my heart also—What a social soul! We will never suffer a cross word between us again— . . .
>
> SH. Now you grow quite good-natured—I'll shew you the manuscript of my eighth volume; and you shall be introduced to the sweet widow Wadman.
>
> REV. I'm extremely glad we've met with your worthy Father again, and that good soul—your Uncle Toby; with the honest Corporal, and Obadiah—for I've a sincere regard for the whole family . . . .[10]

Nor was Griffiths finished. Having previously compared Sterne's talent to that of Joshua Reynolds, he suggested a further comparison with Samuel Richardson. The occasion was the story of the mote in Widow Wadman's eye in chapter 24 of volume VIII:

> REV. Never was any thing more beautifully simple, more natural, more *touching*! O Tristram! that ever any grosser colours should daub and defile that pencil of thine, so admirably fitted for the production of the most masterly pictures of men, manners, and situations!—*Richardson*—the delicate, the circumstantial RICHARDSON himself, never produced any thing equal to the amours of Uncle Toby and the Widow Wadman . . . .[11]

This was praise indeed, if somewhat unexpected in its point of reference (at least Richardson's death in 1761 had shielded the writer himself from the ignominy of the comparison). Griffiths concluded, however, by alluding to John Langhorne's sympathetic review of volumes V and VI,[12] published a full three years earlier:

> One of our gentlemen once remarked in *print*, Mr. Shandy—that he thought your excellence lay in the PATHETIC. I think so too. In my opinion, the little story of Le Fevre has done you more honour than every thing else you have wrote, except your Sermons. Suppose you were to strike out a new plan? Give us none but amiable or worthy, or exemplary characters, or, if you will, to enliven the drama, throw in the *innocently humorous* . . . . Paint Nature in her loveliest dress—her native simplicity. Draw natural scenes, and interesting situations—In fine, Mr. Shandy, do, for surely you can, excite our passions to *laudable* purposes—awake our affections, engage our hearts—arouze, transport,

> refine, improve us. Let morality, let the cultivation of virtue be your aim—let wit, humour, elegance and pathos be the means; and the grateful applause of mankind will be your reward.[13]

Like Langhorne, Griffiths was a critic who had real reservations about aspects of Sterne's work, yet this is generous as well as incisive criticism. It would be an oversimplification to say that Sterne took to heart everything Griffiths had to say, for he insisted in indulging his love of the sexually ambivalent phrase or situation right to the end of *Tristram Shandy*. All the same, he acknowledged the force of Griffiths's arguments in the more studied cultivation of sensibility in his final work, *A Sentimental Journey through France and Italy*.[14]

In the short term, however, it was financial success that concerned Sterne most. As he told Garrick, he also had plans to publish two further volumes of sermons, which he intended should double his profit from the sale of *Tristram Shandy*. The sermons would not, in fact, appear until the following January, but Sterne was already delightedly anticipating a large and prestigious subscription list. Although no longer publishing with the Dodsleys, Sterne had mastered the commercial lesson they had taught him. As Josiah Wedgwood—whose factory would turn out large quantities of marble and plaster busts of Sterne after the writer's death—was to declare: '*Fashion* is infinitely superior to merit . . . and it is plain from a thousand instances if you have a favourite child you wish the public to fondle and take notice of, you have only to make a choice of proper sponcers.'[15] It was through just such a choice of proper sponsors that the Dodsleys had helped ensure the success of the first two volumes of his sermons, and the second instalment too, Sterne determined, would go into the world 'with a prancing list *de toute la noblesse*—which will bring me in three hundred pounds, exclusive of the sale of the copy' (*Letters*, 235).

Understandably, Sterne revealed all the delight one might expect of a man who had spent much of the previous six months calculating the precise state of his finances and writing letters—supplicatory and placatory by turns—to his banker, in order not to leave his wife and daughter in penury. '[W]ith all the contempt of money which *ma façon de penser* has ever impress'd on me,' Sterne averred, 'I shall be rich in spite of myself' (*Letters*, 235). The remark was at once ingenuous and untactful, for Garrick, to whom Sterne was writing, had more reason to be pleased with the improvement in his friend's finances than the writer apparently recalled. The sum of £20 that Sterne had borrowed in December 1761 prior to setting out for France had never been repaid, and Garrick testily reminded Sterne as much in his reply. Sterne effusively protested his innocence of any intention of reneging on his debt, signing off:

> adieu!—I love you dearly—and Y^{r} Lady better.—not hobbi-horsically—but most sentimentally & affectionately.
>
> for I am Y^{rs} (that is, if you never say another word ab^{t} this scoundrel 20 p^{ds})
>
> with al the Sentim^{ts} of Love & friendliness you deserve from me—. (*Letters*, 237)

The fact of money in hand and the prospect of more to come now brought Sterne back to thoughts of travel. This time there was no need to include a young 'my Lord' in his vision of the projected trip, for he would lay out a portion of his earnings in a tour round Italy. 'In the beginning of September I quit England, that I may avail myself of the time of vintage, when all nature is joyous, and so saunter philosophically for a year or so, on the other side of the Alps' (*Letters*, 235). His trip would give him further material to work on, besides further profits. In Italy, he told Garrick, 'I shall spring game, or the duce is in the dice' (*Letters*, 235).

Sterne's high spirits owed much to his thankfulness for being back in London, where he was again enjoying metropolitan life to the full. In particular, he was again taking full advantage of Garrick's generosity in offering him the freedom of the Drury Lane theatre, greatly enlarged since his last visit. 'I have frequently stept into your house—that is, as frequently as I could take the whole party, where I dined, along with me,' he reported to Garrick, continuing, 'This was but justice to you, as I walk'd in as a wit' (*Letters*, 235). In the end, and in marked contrast to previous visits to the capital, Sterne did not find London's pleasures unalloyed: 'I lead such a life of dissipation I have never had a moment to myself which has not been broke in upon, by one engagement or impertinence or another' (*Letters*, 234), he confessed to Garrick in March and, apparently taking up the suggestion of Elizabeth Montagu, went the following month to drink the waters at Bath.

Even with the success of the new instalment of *Tristram Shandy*, financial matters were never far from Sterne's mind, and he was constantly forced to exercise his ingenuity to alleviate new problems as they arose. Elizabeth Sterne had drawn on Robert Foley for a further £100 and Sterne, commenting on the fact, wrote simply: ''tis fit you should be paid it that minute—the money is now in Becket's hands' (*Letters*, 238–9). He also asked Foley to send him his account so that he might promptly discharge the balance, adding 'I have made a good campaign of it this year in the field of the literati—my two volumes of Tristram, and two of sermons, which I shall print very soon, will bring me a considerable sum' (*Letters*, 239).

The idea of an unprecedently prestigious and profitable subscription list had now taken firm hold in Sterne's mind. The best way to ensure it, he had decided, was to turn entrepreneur and solicit subscriptions himself. 'Almost all the nobility in England honour me with their names', Sterne told Foley, with only a touch of hyperbole:

> and 'tis thought it will be the largest, and most splendid list which ever pranced before a book, since subscriptions came into fashion.—Pray present my most sincere compliments to lady H[?ertford] whose name I hope to insert with many others.—As so many men of genius favour me with their names also, I will quarrel with Mr. H[um]e, and call him deist, and what not, unless I have his name too.—My love to Lord W.—Your name, F[oley] I have put in as a free-will offering of my labours—your list of subscribers you will send—'tis but a crown for sixteen sermons—Dog cheap! but I am in quest of honour, not money. (*Letters*, 239)

The truth was very different. The man who had written *Tristram Shandy* not to be fed but to be famous was again in search both of honour and money. The inclusion of Foley's name was transparently less a tribute to friendship than to the services the banker had rendered him in the past—and those Sterne hoped he would render in future as an agent drumming up subscribers in Paris. In fact, if he made the effort Sterne hoped for, Foley had only mixed success. Lord Warkworth (the possible 'Lord W.' of Sterne's letter) subscribed to the third and fourth volumes of the sermons, but the name of Lady Hertford (almost certainly 'Lady H.') did not appear among the subscribers until the eventual, posthumous publication in 1769 of volumes V, VI, and VII of her father's sermons by Lydia Sterne, while David Hume was apparently prepared to take the risk implied in Sterne's jocular threat, for his name is likewise absent.

While hard-headedly promoting his far-from-complete volumes of sermons, Sterne was also devoting himself more tenderly to affairs of the heart. That his many sentimental friendships were not all instigated by Sterne is evident from an answer he wrote to a Mrs. F—— whom he had met in Bath: 'and pray what occasion, (either real or ideal,) have You Madam, to write a Letter from Bath to Town, to enquire whether <the> Tristram Shandy is a married Man or no?—and You may ask in Your turn, if you please, What occasion has Tristram Shandy gentleman to sit down and answer it?' (*Letters*, 240). For the first, Sterne declared, his admirer must answer to her own conscience; for the second, it is the lady's beauty, incapable of being withstood by 'one of Tristram Shandy's make and complexion'. Indeed, he continued, 'If T. Shandy had but one single spark of galant[r]y-fire in any one apartment of his whole Tenement, so kind a tap at the dore would have <lighted> call'd it <up> all forth to have <seen> enquired What gentle Dame it was that stood without—good God! is it You M^{rs} F—! what a fire have You lighted up! tis enough to set the whole house in a flame' (*Letters*, 240). It may not be inappropriate to surmise that Sterne burnt less furiously than he would imply. The hesitant, hyperbolic gallantry here goes some way beyond the usual run of his sentimental correspondence. Sterne, moreover, was uneasy about where Mrs. F——'s admiration might lead. '"*If Tristram Shandy was a single Man*" —(o dear!) . . . *If* thou wast a single Man—bless me, Mad^{m}, this is downright wishing for I swear it is in the *optative Mood* & no other' (*Letters*, 240). Faced with such wishing, Sterne sketched a humorous self-portrait, at once lubricious and unappealing:

> except that I am tolerably strait made, and near six feet high, and that my Nose, (whatever as an historian I say to the contrary), is an inch at least longer than most of my neighbours—except that—That I am a two-footted animal without one Lineament of Hair of the beast upon me, totally spiritualized out of all form for conubial purposes—let me whisper, I am now 44—and shall this time twelve-month be 45 [Sterne was in fact 51]—That I am moreover of a thin, dry, hectic, unperspirable habit of Body—so sublimated and rarified in all my parts That a Lady of y^{r} <penetration> Wit would not give a brass farthing for a dozen such: next May when I am at my best, You shall try me—tho I tell You before hand I have not an ounce & a half of carnality about me—& what is that for so long a Journey? (*Letters*, 241)

However seriously Sterne or his correspondent took sentiments so facetiously expressed, there remains no evidence that this relationship, at least, went any further, either by letter or in person.

Sterne's tangled dealings with women are illuminated more clearly by another friendship at this time—though on this occasion his acute unease is understandable. Lady Anne Stuart, third daughter of the earl of Bute—the minister Sterne had lampooned in the fifth volume of *Tristram Shandy*—had married Lord Warkworth, the future duke of Northumberland, in July 1764 at the age of 18. In the following August she was present at the Assembly Rooms in York where she most probably met Sterne. By April 1765, he was writing to her, from a coffee-house, in terms that suggest a genuine infatuation:

> Why would you tell me you would be glad to see me?—Does it give you pleasure to make me more unhappy—or does it add to your triumph, that your eyes and lips have turned a man into a fool . . . the weakest, the most ductile, the most tender fool, that ever woman tried the weakness of—and the most unsettled in my purposes and resolutions of recovering my right mind.—It is but an hour ago, that I kneeled down and swore I never would come near you—and after saying my Lord's Prayer for the sake of the close, of not being led into temptation—out I sallied like any Christian hero, ready to take the field against the world, the flesh, and the devil; not doubting but I should finally trample them all down under my feet—and now I am got so near you—within this vile stone's cast of your house—I feel myself drawn into a vortex, that has turned my brain upside downwards. (*Letters*, 242–3)

Sterne had purchased a box ticket to attend a benefit night at Drury Lane, he told Lady Warkworth, but if she is alone at seven and would suffer him to spend the evening with her, he would attend her instead. He will dine in Wigmore Street nearby and will remain there until seven o'clock. 'If I hear nothing by that time I shall conclude you are better disposed of—and shall take a sorry hack, and sorrily jogg on to the play—Curse on the word. I know nothing but sorrow—except this one thing, that I love you (perhaps foolishly, but) most sincerely' (*Letters*, 243).

If a letter written by Sterne some two to three weeks later may be credited, the author did not meet with absolute discouragement. Yet, however foolishly in love Sterne thought himself to be, he had not lost all sight of social realities and he was already, at the time of writing, back in York—to have remained, he protested, would have 'dis-*Order'd* the Priest' (*Letters*, 245). His prudence was not misplaced. Lady Warkworth, or Lady Percy as she was styled from 1766, suffered the discovery of letters from other admirers, and in March 1768 made an assignation with a Mr F—— in which she injudiciously told him that he would be safe since her husband would be away all day. Following a further intrigue, her husband divorced her in 1779. Her subsequent career was no less notorious, with few of her many admirers proving as prudent as Laurence Sterne.

Even if he took fright at the apparent willingness of the young wife of a leading nobleman to encourage his epistolary advances, Sterne was increasingly deceiving himself as well as others, as he became locked into a cycle of ever more quixotically sentimental friendships with young women. 'I myself must ever have some dulcinea in my head—it harmonises the soul—', he wrote, 'and in those cases I first endeavour to make the lady believe so, or rather I begin first to make myself believe that I am in love—but I carry on my affairs quite in the French way, sentimentally' (*Letters*, 256).

Back once more in Coxwold, Sterne was immediately forced to abandon sentimental concerns for matters less susceptible of imaginative manipulation. He had suffered a further haemorrhage: 'Hall left me bleeding to death at York,' he wrote, 'of a small vessel in my lungs—the duce take these bellows of mine' (*Letters*, 248). Recovering quickly, however, he was soon keenly anticipating future pleasures. Writing to the young Lord Effingham, Sterne looked forward to the prospect of meeting him in August at the York Races. Effingham, then a 19-year-old serving soldier—and a future Governor of Jamaica—was an acquaintance of a number of Sterne's friends, including John Hall-Stevenson, Thomas Scrope, and John Blaquière, later to be chief secretary of Ireland.

As so often, Sterne's relationship with Effingham was not void of self-interest. The letter he wrote in May 1765 served primarily to thank Effingham for adding his name and his mother's to the forthcoming volumes of his sermons, and mention of a possible meeting at York Races led Sterne bluntly to insist that he had solicited more than his Lordship's name: 'next to the pleasure of getting my five and forty shillings out of your hands—I know nothing that will give me more delight than to see you in the *flesh*' (*Letters*, 248). Yet, for all his anxiety to accumulate subscriptions, the parson was moved for once to put his finances at risk by gently reproving the young nobleman and giving him a piece of Christian advice: 'cura valetudinem tuam diligenter—as a means to which, keep your body in temperance, soberness and chastity—which is a quotation from the Church Catechism, which with all your good memory I fear your Lordship sometimes forgets' (*Letters*, 248).

Sterne, in fact, had good reason to heed his own advice on the importance of health, especially following his recent haemorrhage. Yet, having so earnestly solicited subscriptions, he was soon working hard at writing or revising sermons for his new volumes. Despite having attended the Visitation at Thirsk and having presided at Alne and Tollerton, he was still far enough advanced by July to have hopes that the two volumes might be ready for the printer in mid-September. Conscious of his public reputation, Sterne very deliberately conceived of the new instalment of sermons as a redemptive counterpart to the continuation of *Tristram Shandy*—at least as far as the critics were concerned. To a friend, Thomas Hesilrige, he wrote:

> Have you seen my 7 & 8 graceless Children [i.e volumes VII and VIII of *Tristram Shandy*]—but I am doing penance for them, in begetting a couple of more ecclesiastick ones—which are to stand penance (again) in their turns . . . to keep up a kind of balance, in my shandaic character, & are push'd into the world for that reason by my friends with as splendid & numerous a List of Nobility &c—as ever pranced before a book, since subscriptions came into fashion. (*Letters*, 252)

Inevitably, Sterne added: 'I should grieve not to have your name amongst those of my friends—& in so much good company as it has a right to be in—so tell me to set it down—and if you can—Lord Maynards. . . . If any occasions come in y^{r} Way, of adding 3 or 4 more to the list; y^{r} friendship for me, I know will do it.' But, Sterne went on anxiously, 'You must take their crowns—& keep them for me till fate does me the courtesy to throw me in y^{r} Way' (*Letters*, 253). How many occasions may have come Hesilrige's way is not known (and he failed to elicit a subscription from his great-uncle, Lord Maynard, the lord-lieutenant of Sussex); nevertheless, Hesilrige did subscribe himself—and not only to the third and fourth volumes of the *Sermons* but to the posthumous volumes as well, and to *A Sentimental Journey*.

The approaching end of labours on his the third and fourth volumes of the *Sermons of Mr. Yorick* allowed Sterne to turn his mind once more to his projected visit to Italy. His plan was to leave England in September and winter in Rome and Naples. 'L'hyvere <de> a Londres ne vaut pas rien, pour les poumones,' he told Hesilrige in July, 'a cause d'humiditè et la fumè dont l'aire est chargèe' ('A London winter does nothing for the lungs, because the air is heavy with dampness and smoke') (*Letters*, 253). In the same month Sterne suggested in a letter to Foley that he would be in Paris in September. Again he owed Foley money, but was able for once to suggest that this was the banker's fault for having failed to provide Sterne with an up-to-date account that could be paid from moneys Becket was holding. The relatively healthy state of his finances was of considerable moment to Sterne. He had abandoned all hopes of finding some nobleman to whom he might act as tutor on his travels. 'As to the project of getting a bear to lead,' he told a friend, 'I think I have enough to do to govern myself—and however profitable it might be (according to your opinion) I am sure it would be unpleasurable' (*Letters*, 257). He was far from carefree in expressing such sentiments, however, for he added: 'Few are the minutes of life, and I do not think that I have any to throw away on any one being' (*Letters*, 257).

Sterne did not make an exception to this maxim even for his wife and daughter, for he now planned to spend nine or ten months in Italy and to visit Elizabeth and Lydia in France on his way home. Lydia had been much in his thoughts recently, for he had received a proposal of marriage to her from an elderly and apparently wealthy French admirer. In contrast to the general French view of the importance of sentiment in love—'*l'amour* (they say) *n'est rien sans sentiment*' (*Letters*, 256) Sterne wrote—the motives of Lydia's admirer appeared above all mercenary. Sterne's peremptory response, however, set a precedent for generally unsympathetic dealings with anyone who showed a romantic interest in Lydia. Apparently without consulting his daughter's inclinations at all, he abruptly declined the offer on her behalf. In a letter to a friend Sterne complained of his daughter's suitor in terms that combine financial reserve with a leering innuendo which might almost justify Thackeray's strictures on his fellow-novelist.[16] It is a letter that suggests as much about the relations of the middle-aged Sterne with younger women as about Lydia's unknown admirer:

> Without any ceremony . . . he wrote me word that he was in love with my daughter, and desired to know what *fortune* I would give her at present, and how much at my *death*—by the bye, I think there was very little *sentiment* on *his side*—My answer was 'Sir, I shall give her ten thousand pounds the day of marriage—my calculation is as follows—she is not eighteen, you are sixty-two—there goes five thousand pounds—then Sir, you at least think her not ugly—she has many accomplishments, speaks Italian, French, plays upon the guittar, and as I fear you play upon no instrument whatever, I think you will be happy to take her at my terms, for here finishes the account of the ten thousand pounds'—I do not suppose but he will take this as I mean, that is—a flat refusal. (*Letters*, 256)

Of this particular suitor, no more was heard.

If Sterne showed dispatch in dealing with one matter, the burning down of the parsonage house at Sutton in the summer of 1765 was not so speedy of resolution. The house, on which he had lavished such attention in the early 1740s, had been occupied since 1761 by Sterne's curate, the Revd Marmaduke Callis, and his wife. The fire had started in the end of the parsonage nearest the church, but was spotted quickly and apparently brought under control and extinguished without doing much damage.

The following day, however, despite the precaution of an overnight watch on the house, the fire found its way to the other end of the parsonage, where it burnt so furiously that it could not be contained and the entire building was lost. 'How these fires happened is not known', reported the *York Courant*[17] but Sterne had his own version. 'I have had a parsonage house burnt down by the carelessness of my curate's wife,' he told his friend John Wodehouse; 'as soon as I can I must rebuild it, I trow—but I lack the means at present' (*Letters*, 256–7). In fact Sterne was never to find the means, and the shell of the building remained abandoned to become, after the author's death, a source of severe trouble to his widow and daughter, as well as a vexation and source of expense to his successor as vicar of Sutton.[18] In the summer of 1765, though, Sterne affected great indifference towards his misfortune. 'I am never happier than when I have not a shilling in my pocket,' he wrote to John Wodehouse, with a blithe disregard for the truth: 'Adieu my dear friend—may you enjoy better health than me, tho' not better spirits, for that is impossible' (*Letters*, 257).

However strong his spirits, Sterne's body was increasingly weak. 'I find I must once more fly from death whilst I have strength' (*Letters*, 257), he wrote of his projected journey, and expressed the hope that the air of Naples would effect a cure. Frustratingly, he was again forced to postpone his departure. For all his earlier optimism, he was making slow progress on his sermons, probably as a result of his illness, and was still composing those works he hoped would underwrite his travel. Eventually he decided that his health would allow him to delay no longer, and he left Coxwold without having completed the sixteen sermons he had planned for his new volumes. The truth was that Sterne was exhausted, and could write no more: 'I have drained my ink standish to the bottom.'[19]

As a result, he consigned not the promised sixteen but only twelve sermons to Thomas Becket. This was three fewer than had been gathered in the first two volumes of the sermons, and even then the number was made up by the inclusion of 'The Abuses of Conscience' from volume II of *Tristram Shandy*. Sterne had also promised his publisher a preface, but though he claimed this was written, he told Becket that it would be better omitted. In fact Sterne was already in Paris, and so was abroad when the third and fourth volumes of the *Sermons of Mr. Yorick* were eventually published on 18 January 1766.

Despite the care Sterne had originally intended to dedicate to his new collection—to judge by the careful shaping of the opening—the two volumes as they appeared reveal an eclectic choice among the compositions available to him. Sermons of comparatively recent composition included the Foundling Hospital sermon of 1760, a sermon preached in September 1761 for the coronation of George II (this was not 'Asa: A Thanksgiving Sermon', preached at Coxwold, which for some reason was omitted from the collection), and that delivered in the ambassador's chapel in Paris in the summer of 1763. Other sermons—especially those directed against the abuses of Roman Catholicism and Methodism—seem likely to date from much earlier: the late-1740s or early 1750s, when Sterne was still hoping to find a patron in Archbishop Herring or Dr Francis Blackburne. Most surprisingly, Sterne omitted a number of sermons which later readers have judged superior to those he chose to print, including 'Search the Scriptures', which in its discussion of the beauty and literary merit of Holy Scripture was especially well adapted to the taste of the 1760s.

When they appeared the sermons boasted a subscription list as impressive for the most part as Sterne had hoped. Pointedly, however, no bishop subscribed on this occasion (though Voltaire, Diderot, and D'Holbach did). The volumes themselves met with a mixed reception, made more predictable by reviewers' insistence on reading them with *Tristram Shandy* very much in mind. The *Critical Review* found that '[t]he author of *Tristram Shandy* is discernible in every page of these discourses. They who have read the former will find in the latter the same acute remarks on the manners of mankind, the same striking characters, the same accurate investigation of the passions, the same delicate strokes of satire, and the same art in moving the tender affections of nature.'[20] To see so complete a correspondence between Sterne's fiction and his sermons may seem forced—though, given the praise lavished on the sermons, Sterne was unlikely to have objected. Such perceptions were widespread, however. The *Critical Review* suggested that 'the author sometimes forgets the dignity of his character, and the solemnity of a christian congregation, and condescends, on the most interesting topics of religion, to excite a jocular idea, or display a frivolous turn of wit'.[21]

If this appears equally excessive as a response to Sterne's newly published sermons, then it also suggests a common perception of the gravity of the preacher's office. Sterne himself, in his sermon 'National Mercies considered', preached in 1761 or 1762, had warned against the dangers of a tendency to substitute 'wit . . . raillery and mirth' for 'arguments and sober reasoning' in the treatment of the 'mysteries of . . . religion'.[22] While his admonition seems wholly devoid of self-irony, he could hardly have been surprised to find that others were more sober in their expectations of what was appropriate to the pulpit than he was himself. In the *Monthly Review* William Rose wrote: 'Whether all the sermons contained in these two volumes were preached or not, we cannot inform our Readers. We would willingly believe, for the sake of the Author's credit, that they were not: there is an air of levity in some of them, altogether unbecoming the dignity and seriousness of pulpit-discourses.'[23] Even more forthright in their repudiation of Sterne's pulpit performances were William Cowper and Sarah Scott. The former confessed that, 'though I admire Sterne as a man of genius, I can never admire him as a preacher', while the latter wrote tersely: 'surely such stuff was never published.'[24]

Despite such comments, contemporary reviewers were by no means uniformly hostile to the substance of his sermons. What, in their different ways, each objected to was Sterne's passing off of what they considered moral essays as sermons. Though an admirer of Sterne's good humour and philanthropy, William Rose began with a demurral, commenting: 'His sermons, if they must all be called by that name, contain many pertinent and striking observations on human life and manners: every subject, indeed, is treated in such a manner as shews the originality of his genius, and as will, in some measure, soften the severity of censure, in regard to his ill-timed pleasantry and want of discretion.'[25] William Cowper was more direct, declaring that Sterne 'mistakes the weapon of his warfare, and fights not with the sword of the Spirit for which only he was ordained a minister of the Gospel, but with that wisdom which shone with as effectual a light before our Saviour came as since, and which therefore cannot be the wisdom which He came to reveal to us'.[26] Yet Cowper himself accounted Sterne 'a great master of the pathetic', and declared that 'if that or any other species of rhetoric could renew the human heart and turn it from the power of Satan unto God, I know no writer better qualified to make proselytes to the cause of virtue than Sterne'.[27] Cowper's insistence on the centrality of revelation to Christianity marks him out from many other commentators on Sterne's sermons in the 1760s, yet other, less evangelically inclined critics concurred in preferring to regard those compositions as, at best, moral essays. More negative was Samuel Johnson who, on being shown Sterne's *Sermons* by an acquaintance in his home town of Lichfield, abruptly enquired: 'Sir . . . do you ever read any others?' When his hapless companion mentioned the names of Sherlock, Tillotson, and Beveridge, among others, Johnson replied: 'Ay, Sir, *there* you drink the cup of salvation to the bottom; here you have merely the froth from the surface.'[28]

The comment—and it is uncertain to which volumes of the sermons Johnson was referring—is harsh, yet one not wholly at odds with the reservations expressed by others (which might give readers today pause before they too easily accommodate Sterne even to the admittedly broad and placid stream of mid-century latitudinarianism). Occasionally, indeed, the sermons in the 1766 volumes offer apparent justification for such views. Initially, at least, Sterne seems to have pointed up rather than played down the witty or ingenious elements of the sermons—as early as May 1765 he had already decided to open the third volume with 'The Character of Shimei', whose subject, he insisted to the earl of Effingham, was 'so truly Shandean, that no after-wit would bring me off' (*Letters*, 247). Moreover, he placed all of those sermons—'The Case of Hezekiah and the Messengers', 'The Levite and his Concubine', and 'Felix's Behaviour Towards Paul, examined'—with especially arresting openings at the beginning of the same volume. Equally, he seemed willing rather to court than discourage criticism by entitling one of his sermons 'Advantages of Christianity to the world'. The sermon opens in a manner that must have brought to the mind of many readers Swift's ironical *Argument against abolishing Christianity*, especially since the preacher appears to acknowledge that it cannot be demonstrated that the morals of the world have been improved to any extent by Christian revelation. In fact, Sterne's method here, as elsewhere, is designed first to provoke indignation in order to calm it subsequently; certainly the sermon concludes with an entirely orthodox emphasis on free will and the individual's freedom to accept or reject Christian revelation.

Many, if not most of the sermons rehearse the importance of Christian teaching to secular morality in an entirely unexceptionable manner. Once more Anglican doctrine is bolstered by attacks on both Roman Catholicism—'Consider popery well; you will be convinced, that the truest definition which can be given of it, is——That it is a pecuniary system, well contrived to operate upon men's passions and weakness, whilst their pockets are o'picking'[29]—and Methodism: 'a republication, with some alterations of the same extravagant conceits' as characterized seventeenth-century enthusiasm.[30] (Sterne's apparently greater familiarity with Quakers, acquired through their long-time presence in his Yorkshire parishes, seems to have instilled in him an unusual degree of tolerance for some Protestants who strayed outside the Anglican fold; though he insisted that, like Methodists, Quakers were 'collateral descendents from the same enthusiastic original' who 'believe the Holy Ghost comes down upon their assemblies, and *moves* them without regard to condition or sex, to make intercessions with unutterable groans',[31] he nevertheless pointedly refers to them benignly as 'a harmless quiet people'.) As a counterpart to attacks on non-Anglicans, Sterne is, on appropriate occasions such as the accession of George III, warm in praise not merely of Anglican teaching but of the Reformation, the Glorious Revolution, and the Established Church in England.[32]

As with the earlier volumes, there are also repeated hints of deeply personal reflections scattered throughout undatable sermons. 'The History of Jacob, considered' takes as its subject a story that leads easily enough into an account of individual disappointments at the hands of those to whom one might look for comfort and support. Yet though Sterne does not stray far from the story of Jacob as told in Genesis, it is hard not to sense a personal note when he reflects: 'the avarice of a parent,—the unkindness of a relation,—the ingratitude of a child,—they are evils which leave a scar',[33] or again, in his sour reflection on matrimony: 'Listen, I pray you, to the stories of the disappointed in marriage:—collect all their complaints:——hear their mutual reproaches; upon what fatal hinge do the greatest part of them turn?—"They were mistaken in the person" '—a distinctly unbiblical (and uncharitable) passage, despite the subsequent allusion, via 1 Peter 3: 1–4, to the proper subjection of wives to husbands and of a wife being '*the ornament of a meek and quiet spirit*'.[34] It would be wrong, though, to suggest the possible application of such sentiments to Sterne's unhappy relations with his mother, his uncle, and his wife without noting that such passages seem to bring out a profoundly personal note of another kind. Drawing directly on the New Testament rather than on any intermediate source, Sterne apostrophizes his congregation:

> ——Dear inconsiderate Christians! wait not, I beseech you . . . take a view of your life now;—look back, behold this fair space capable of such heavenly improvements—all scrawl'd over and defaced with——
>
> ——I want words to say, with what—for I think only of the reflections with which you are to support yourselves, in the decline of a life so miserably cast away, should it happen, as it often does, that ye have stood idle unto the eleventh hour, and have all the work of the day to perform when night comes on, and no one can work.[35]

'The night cometh, when no man can work': the words, from the gospel of St John, which Samuel Johnson had engraved on his watch, suggest once more the biblical underpinning of Sterne's preoccupation in his fiction with the passing of time,[36] most notably in passages whose substance (though here secularized and sexualized) might come from any Anglican moralist, from John Donne to Johnson himself:

> Time wastes too fast: every letter I trace tells me with what rapidity Life follows my pen; the days and hours of it, more precious, my dear Jenny! than the rubies about thy neck, are flying over our heads like light clouds of a windy day, never to return more——every thing presses on——whilst thou art twisting that lock,——see! it grows grey; and every time I kiss thy hand to bid adieu, and every absence which follows it, are preludes to that eternal separation which we are shortly to make.——
>
> ——Heaven have mercy upon us both! (*TS* IX. viii. 498)

If there is one truly controversial sermon in the second instalment of *The Sermons of Mr. Yorick* then it is 'The Prodigal Son', which—despite an orthodox opening—shifts direction abruptly and disconcertingly midstream. The retelling of Christ's parable begins with an imaginative and pathetic account of the prodigal's leaving home, which culminates in the reflection that 'Nothing so powerfully calls home the mind as distress. . . . Gracious and bountiful GOD! Is it not for this, that they who in their prosperity forget thee, do yet remember and return to thee in the hour of their sorrow?'[37] Having reached this climax, however, the sermon concludes with a lengthy and quite unexpected digression on travel and on the Grand Tour which must inevitably have provided further ammunition for those who thought Sterne's efforts, at best, moral essays.

Sterne was fortunate that they thought nothing worse. The subject of travel, and specifically the Grand Tour, was, it goes without saying, a commonplace in later-seventeenth- and eighteenth-century writing, whether as a matter of serious consideration, as in John Locke's *Some Thoughts Concerning Education* (1693), or as satire, as in the fourth book of Pope's *Dunciad* (1744).[38] Sterne, whose original idea for *Tristram Shandy* apparently involved 'travell[ing] his Hero . . . all over Europe . . . to return Tristram . . . a compleat English Gentleman',[39] had prepared his sermons for publication in the same year which saw the appearance of volume VII of *Tristram Shandy*, with its account of Tristram's tour. More to the point, however, were Sterne's own plans to leave England once more for France and Italy. Breaking abruptly as it does in the middle, 'The Prodigal Son' gives every indication of having been substantially altered from the version in which it had first been delivered. Most likely, while toying with the notion of covering his own travelling expenses by finding a young gentleman to escort, Sterne conceived of the idea of inserting into his sermon some sober reflections on the qualities ideally demanded of a travelling tutor as a form of self-advertisement. Certainly, the portrait he proffered of the 'able pilot' who would guide the young tourist through the perils of Europe and bring him safely home bears more than a passing (if discreetly sanitized) resemblance to Sterne himself. Knowledge is important, Sterne concedes, but not sufficient in itself, for youth should rather 'be escorted by one who knows the world, not merely from books—but from his own experience:—a man who has been employed on such services, and thrice made the *tour of Europe, with success*'.[40] Such a tutor must not be one who merely knows the details and costs of 'every stage from Calais to Rome' or one furnished with introductions to the literati, but rather one who understands that 'Conversation is a traffick' and that young travellers must bring knowledge (or a knowledgeable tutor?) with them if they are to avoid the many pitfalls awaiting the unwary.

'The Prodigal Son', then, is an advertisement for Sterne's merits as a travelling tutor. Happily for him, those contemporary letters in which he discusses his hopes of finding such a post were unknown to the wider public in 1765. What reviewers, already suspicious of Yorick's sermons, would have made of Sterne and 'The Prodigal Son' had they been able to read them is not a matter of happy contemplation.

In the end, Sterne's abandonment of his hopes of finding a pupil to escort was at least in part due to an honest appraisal that he did not himself possess the ideal qualities of a travelling-tutor. It was just as well. Having completed his collection as best he was able, and urgent in his desire to leave England for warmer and healthier climes, Sterne found himself so ill that initially he could not even reach London to deliver his sermons to the publisher. Instead, he determined to go first to York, 'to recruit myself of the most violent spitting of blood that ever mortal man experienced' (*Letters*, 258). If it was so ordained, he explained, he would rather die at York than in a post-chaise on the road to London.

13
France, Italy, and England 1765–1767

At the beginning of October 1765, a full month later than he had hoped, Sterne finally left Coxwold. Fortunately he made a rapid recovery from the illness that had made him fear for his life, and remained only briefly at York before heading south to London. For once, even the metropolis could not detain him—though the demands of fashion distracted him from gloomier thoughts. Sterne's only surviving letter from his stay is a brief, hastily written note to Robert Foley in Paris, asking that he order a bag-wig for him—'la plus jolie—la plus gentille'—exclaiming, 'It is a terrible thing to be in Paris without a perriwig to a man's head' (*Letters*, 260). As befitted a clergyman, Sterne seems invariably to have dressed in a sober manner even when abroad—as may be seen, for instance, in Carmontelle's portrait of him at Paris in 1762—yet he was unable to avoid deferring to French custom in the matter of wigs.[1] Most British travellers of the period commented on the meticulous attention Frenchmen devoted to their appearance. Even Tobias Smollett, who ridiculed the tendency of the French to wear over-elaborate dress on the most unsuitable occasions, as when hunting, admitted that: 'The good man, who used to wear the *beau drap d'Angleterre*, quite plain all the year round, with a long bob, or tye perriwig, must here provide himself with a camblet suit trimmed with silver for spring and autumn, with silk cloaths for summer, and cloth laced with gold, or velvet for winter; and he must wear his bag-wig à la pigeon.'[2] So it was that Samuel Johnson, whom Boswell found on his first visit to him wearing a 'little, shrivelled, unpowdered wig, which was too small for his head',[3] submitted during his trip to Paris with the Thrales to wear a 'Paris-made wig of handsome construction'.[4] Sterne, in fact, may have been embarrassed by the unfashionable wig he wore on his arrival in Paris in 1762. Two years earlier Boswell had written of Sterne's 'wig centauric, formed with care | From human and equestrian hair',[5] and Yorick's experience—when the barber 'refused to have any thing to do with my wig: 'twas either above or below his art: I had nothing to do, but to take one ready made of his own recommendation'[6]—was perhaps a reflection of his own. Certainly the matter intrigued Sterne, leading Tristram to surmise that French barbers claimed the dignity of gentlemen by virtue of their trade: 'forasmuch as *the periwig maketh the man*, and the periwig-maker maketh the periwig——ergo . . . we shall be Capitouls at least—pardi! we shall all wear swords——' (*TS* VII. xvii. 400).

Sterne's journey from London to Paris took five days. He travelled to Calais, where he rested for some time at the Hôtel d'Angleterre, a handsome and elegantly furnished inn owned by Pierre Dessin, whom Sterne celebrated (much to the advantage of his trade in later years) in *A Sentimental Journey*. Dessin, whom Sterne privately characterized as 'a Turk in grain' (*Letters*, 177), had previously held the lease of the Lyon d'Argent, at which Elizabeth Sterne was advised to put up on her way to Paris in 1762. The inn having burned down in October 1764—that fire and one the previous month having been allegedly started by Dessin himself—Dessin solicited subscriptions from English travellers so successfully that he was able to purchase the substantial house he would call the Hôtel d'Angleterre. It was in Calais also that Sterne set what justly became one of the most celebrated sentimental set-pieces in *A Sentimental Journey*: the story of Parson Yorick's encounter with the Franciscan friar, Father Lorenzo ('The Monk. Calais' and 'The Snuff-Box. Calais', *ASJ* 70–5, 95–103). The episode opens with Yorick determining in advance to give nothing to the mendicant, only to find himself shamed by the courteous resignation with which the friar accepts his refusal; subsequently Father Lorenzo offers Yorick a pinch of snuff, leading the pair to exchange snuffboxes, Yorick subsequently guarding the friar's 'as I would the instrumental parts of my religion, to help my mind on to something better' (*ASJ* 101). The episode offers one of the most sympathetic portrayals of a Roman Catholic religious in mid-eighteenth-century English fiction and is particularly remarkable both for its implied critique of Anglicanism's usual insistence that only the 'industrious' or 'deserving' poor merited charity and for the considerable shift it denotes in Sterne's personal response to Roman Catholicism, in contrast with the anti-Catholic tone of his political journalism and the many anti-Catholic sermons he preached in the 1740s and 1750s.

Assuming Yorick's itinerary in *A Sentimental Journey* to have been that followed by the author himself, Sterne proceeded from Calais to Paris by way of Montreuil, Nampont, and Amiens. Intending to stay just long enough to see old friends—especially the Baron D'Holbach and Diderot—before continuing his journey, Sterne was delighted to find a number of

Englishmen in Paris, among them John Wilkes, the actor and playwright Samuel Foote, and Horace Walpole.

Walpole was less pleased, recording the occasion of their meeting with characteristic *hauteur*: 'You will think it odd', he wrote to Thomas Brand on 19 October, 'that I should want to laugh, when Wilkes, Sterne, and Foote are here; but the first does not make me laugh, the second never could, and for the third, I choose to pay five shillings when I have a mind he should divert me.'[7] More to Walpole's taste was John Fitzpatrick, the earl of Upper Ossory, whom Walpole considered 'one of the properest and most amiable young men I ever knew';[8] later a member of the Literary Club, the earl was also an admirer of Sterne, a subscriber to the third and fourth volumes of the sermons and to *A Sentimental Journey*, and purchaser, after Sterne's death, of Reynolds's first portrait of the writer. Another future subscriber to *A Sentimental Journey* whom Sterne found in Paris was Lord William Gordon, a son of the duke of Gordon. Finally there was John 'Fish' Craufurd, source of the episode 'The Case of Delicacy' which concludes Sterne's work; Craufurd's footman, John Macdonald, who was at the last to have his own part to play in Sterne's story, called him 'one of the gayest young gentlemen and the greatest gambler that ever belonged to Scotland'.[9]

Whatever the attractions of Paris or the company he found there, Sterne was soon on his way south. He enjoyed an 'agreeable' journey as far as Lyons, where he stayed a week in the company of about a dozen of his countrymen, including the radical clergyman, the Revd John Horne Tooke—a 'joyous time,' he wrote, 'dining and supping every day at the commandant's' (*Letters*, 262).[10] Despite the promising start, Sterne's journey began to go less smoothly after he had left Lyons for Turin. Having fled England to avoid the damp, he found himself marooned at the town of Pont de Beauvoisin:

> at present I am held prisoner in this town by the sudden swelling of two pitiful rivulets from the snows melting on the Alps—so that we cannot either advance to them, or retire back again to Lyons—for how long the gentlemen who are my fellow-travellers, and myself, shall languish in this state of vexatious captivity, heaven and earth surely know, for it rains as if they were coming together to settle the matter. (*Letters*, 262)

Eventually the waters eased, and eight days later Sterne was again writing to Isaac Panchaud, this time to tell him that 'After many difficulties I have got safe & sound—tho eight days in passing the Mountains of Savoy'

(*Letters*, 263). The crossing of the Alps, especially so late in the season, was no easy matter for eighteenth-century travellers—as Yorick notes in *A Sentimental Journey*, where he remarks on the *desobligeant* which had 'been twice taken to pieces on Mount Sennis' (*ASJ* 87). The crossing of Mont Cenis was, in fact, the object of fascination to numerous British travellers, among them James Boswell—who described the prospect as 'horridly grand'[11]—Edward Gibbon, and Samuel Sharp (traditionally the Mundungus of *A Sentimental Journey*[12]). In his *Letters from Italy* Sharp wrote:

> the passage into *Italy* is composed of a very steep ascent . . . the descent on the *Italian* side is not so steep as that on the side of *Savoy*. . . . Both going and returning, when you arrive at the foot of the mountain, your coach, or chaise, is taken to pieces, and carried upon mules to the other side, and you yourself are transported by two men, on a common straw elbow chair . . . fixed upon two poles, like a sedan-chair.[13]

Having arrived in Italy Sterne found himself in much the same situation as on the other side of the Alps. The whole of the countryside between Turin and Milan was under water following exceptionally heavy rainfall. The enforced stay of a fortnight's duration was scarcely a hardship, however, for mid-eighteenth-century Turin was the flourishing and elegant capital of the Kingdom of Savoy.[14] It was also a hospitable city, and Sterne had barely arrived before he was reporting that 'I am very happy—and have found my Way into a dozen houses already' (*Letters*, 263).[15] Sterne was even presented to King Charles Emmanuel III of Sardinia, presumably through personal contacts, for he could scarcely have been known in Turin, even by reputation (Sterne's popularity in Italy, except among a very few cosmopolitan men of letters, had to await Ugo Foscolo's celebrated translation of his final work, published under the title *Viaggio sentimentale di Yorick lungo la Francia e l'Italia* in 1813[16]). Gibbon described the court as 'bigotted, gloomy and covetous', though being received there surely flattered Sterne's vanity. Sterne is also likely to have enjoyed the gossip for which the court was noted,[17] yet he may not have found himself always at ease with the Piedmontese he met. Even James Boswell, whose progress through Italy was far from chaste, found Turin a shock; visiting the city the year before Sterne, he wrote: 'amongst the thoroughbred libertines of Turin to have sentiment is to be a child.'[18]

Sterne found few fellow-countrymen in Turin, but got on well with those he did encounter—Sir James Macdonald and a Mr Ogilvy. Sir James Macdonald, of Sleat on the Isle of Skye was then 23 years old, a descendant of the Lords of the Isles, a Gaelic-speaker, and one of the most highly regarded and promising young men of his day. He had gained an enviable reputation as a scholar at Eton and Christ Church, Oxford, and was admired by, among others, Madame du Deffand, Baron Grimm, and his fellow-countrymen David Hume and Adam Smith. Even the hard-to-please Horace Walpole described him as 'a very extraordinary young man; for variety of learning' (though he added sourly, 'He is rather too wise for his age, and too fond of showing it'[19]). For others Macdonald was distinguished not only for his wit and learning but also for his love of poetry, music, and painting. He may have been drawn to Sterne in particular as a fellow-invalid. Grimm wrote of him that his health did not permit him to hope for a long career, and that his passion for study tired him. At all events, he and Sterne evidently found each other congenial company for they agreed to pursue their journey southward together. When they left Turin on 28 November Sterne wrote that 'We have spent a joyous fortnight here, and met with all kinds of honours, and with regret do we both bid adieu, but Health on my side, and good sense on his, say 'tis better to be at Rome' (*Letters*, 265).

Not that Rome was quickly reached: 'I have been a month passing the plains of Lombardie, stoping in my Way at Milan, Parma, Plac[e]nza, Bolognia', Sterne reported (*Letters*, 265). How long he and Macdonald stayed at the cities they visited en route is uncertain, though the fact that their journey took them through several states must have proved of considerable interest to Macdonald, if not to his companion: in the mid-eighteenth century Milan was capital of the Duchy of Milan, under Austrian domination, while Parma and Piacenza were the administrative centres of two Spanish-controlled duchies, and Bologna formed part of the Papal States. Though we are left to speculate, Yorick's references in *A Sentimental Journey* to Milan—then a city of some 100,000 inhabitants—certainly suggests an extended visit there. In the 1760s Habsburg Milan was increasingly open to Enlightenment influences, and it is likely that a celebrated English writer would have been a source of interest, even if his work were unknown at first hand. In the year prior to Sterne's visit Pietro Verri, assisted by his brother Alessandro and the economist and jurist Cesare Beccaria, had started *Il Caffè*, a newspaper modelled on the English periodicals of half-a-century before, the *Tatler* and the *Spectator*. When Alessandro Verri visited London in 1768 he was particularly anxious to meet Sterne, declaring that his friends would never forgive him otherwise.[20]

Among those literati whom Sterne is known to have met in Milan was the priest and poet Giancarlo Passeroni, whom he encountered in the rooms of the minister, Count Firmian. The same age as Sterne and, like him, possessed of illustrious friends, Passeroni presented, in other respects, a marked contrast to the English visitor. Eminently modest, declining gifts and honours, Passeroni preferred to live in respectable poverty, admired and esteemed for his exemplary life. His most important work, a poem of 101 cantos entitled *Il Cicerone*, appeared between 1755 and 1774 and won high praise in its day from, among others, Rousseau. Characterized by a tendency to digressions that take over from the ostensible subject-matter, *Il Cicerone* offers certain parallels to *Tristram Shandy*. Passeroni, indeed, understood Sterne to acknowledge that *Il Cicerone* had given him the idea for his novel, with the result that the poet-priest incorporated an account of their meeting into his poem:

> E già mi disse un chiaro letterato
> Inglese, che dalla mia stampita
> Il disegno, e il modello avea cavato
> Di scrivere in più Tomi la sua vita;
> E pien di gratitudine, e d'amore
> Mi chiamava suo Duce, e Precettore.[21]

> (And once a noted English writer told me that from this work of mine, he had taken the design, the model for writing his own life in several volumes and, full of gratitude and affection, called me his leader and teacher.)

What basis this might have in fact is difficult to judge. Sterne was certainly capable of elegant and imaginative flattery, though it is difficult, given his near total lack of Italian, to conceive how he could have paid Passeroni such an extravagant compliment in that language (they could, of course, have conversed in Latin or French), still less have been influenced by the writer's work.

Sterne himself, despite his intention to publish an account of his travels, kept no journal or other record of his tour. When Alessandro Verri visited him in London shortly before the latter's death, Sterne told him that he had not made any written record while travelling in Italy but would write his book 'a suo capriccio' ('at whim'). Though he intended to represent his experience of Milan in *A Sentimental Journey*, he told Verri that he would make up his adventures to suit the purposes of his fiction.[22] Verri also understood Sterne to be already engaged in writing his *Viaggio sentimentale d'Italia* but, if he had begun, nothing of the work—interrupted by his death soon after Verri's visit—survives, barring one displaced Milanese adventure in the published volumes of *A Sentimental Journey*:

> I was going one evening to Martini's[23] concert at Milan, and was just entering the door of the hall, when the Marquesina di F*** was coming out in a sort of a hurry—she was almost upon me before I saw her; so I gave a spring to one side to let her pass—She had done the same, and on the same side too; so we ran our heads together: she instantly got to the other side to get out: I was just as unfortunate as she had been; for I had sprung to that side, and opposed her passage again—We both flew together to the other side, and then back—and so on—it was ridiculous; we both blush'd intolerably; so I did at last the thing I should have done at first—I stood stock still, and the Marquesina had no more difficulty. I had no power to go into the room, till I had made her so much reparation as to wait and follow her with my eye to the end of the passage—She look'd back twice, and walk'd along it rather side-ways, as if she would make room for any one coming up stairs to pass her—No, said I—that's a vile translation: the Marquesina has a right to the best apology I can make her; and that opening is left for me to do it in—so I ran and begg'd pardon for the embarrassment I had given her, saying it was my intention to have made her way. She answered, she was guided by the same intention towards me—so we reciprocally thank'd each other. She was at the top of the stairs; and seeing no *chichesbeo* near her, I begg'd to hand her to her coach—so we went down the stairs, stopping at every third step to talk of the concert and the adventure—Upon my word, Madame, said I when I had handed her in, I made six different efforts to let you go out—And I made six efforts, replied she, to let you enter—I wish to heaven you would make a seventh, said I—With all my heart, said she, making room—Life is too short to be long about the forms of it—so I instantly stepp'd in, and she carried me home with her—And what became of the concert, St. Cecilia, who, I suppose, was at it, knows more than I.
>
> I will only add, that the connection which arose out of that translation, gave me more pleasure than any one I had the honour to make in Italy. (*ASJ* 172–3)

It was on his return through Milan that Sterne had a less happy connection with a servant, which he incorporated—with sly sexual innuendo—into Tristram's experiences:

> My shirts! see what a deadly schism has happen'd amongst 'em—for the laps are in Lombardy, and the rest of 'em here—I never had but six, and a cunning gypsey of a laundress at Milan cut me off the *fore*-laps of five—To do her justice, she did it with some consideration—for I was returning *out* of Italy. (*TS* IX. xxiv. 521)

In the early part of his Italian journey Sterne found the climate just as he would have wished, the weather 'as delicious, as a kindly April in England' (*Letters*, 266). Further south, however, he was less fortunate, for before reaching Florence he was '3 days in crossing a part of the Apenines coverd with thick snow—sad transition!' (*Letters*, 266). At Florence Sterne halted once more, intending a three-day visit to dine with Sir Horace Mann, British envoy to the Grand-Duchy of Tuscany. Mann was a long-time resident of Florence, who had taken up his post there in 1740 and would remain in the Tuscan capital until his death at the age of 85 in 1786. He had initially expressed enthusiasm for Sterne's work. 'You will laugh at me, I suppose,' he wrote to Horace Walpole, his correspondent for over half a century, 'when I say I don't understand *Tristram Shandy*, because it was probably the intention of the author that nobody should. It seems to me *humbugging* . . . It diverted me, however, extremely, and I beg to have as soon as possible the two other volumes which I see advertised in the papers for next Christmas.'[24] The continuation had pleased him much less: 'Nonsense pushed too far becomes insupportable',[25] he had written. Still, Sterne was doubtless well received, for Mann was a celebrated host whose 'most serious business', in the words of Edward Gibbon, who had passed through Florence a year before, 'was that of entertaining the English at his hospitable table'.[26] Sterne's acquaintance Louis Dutens would declare that he 'scarcely ever knew a man whose conversation afforded so inexhaustible a fund of pleasing instruction'.[27]

Sterne left only slight record of his activities in Florence, though it seems certain that he paid at least brief visits to the city's principal sights. These included the Tribuna in the Uffizi palace, which held not only the Medici Venus but also the celebrated classical statue of *l'arrotino*, otherwise known as the 'listening slave', which he had introduced into volume V of *Tristram Shandy* in his description of Mrs Shandy eavesdropping at the door.[28] It was in Florence too that Sterne met the artist Thomas Patch, who lived directly opposite Horace Mann. Then in his early forties, Patch had worked in Florence since 1755 after being forced to leave Rome following a homosexual indiscretion. It was he who famously painted a grimly comic portrait of the consumptive Sterne as Tristram Shandy coming face to face with Death—recounted in the opening chapter of volume VII—a painting from which Patch subsequently made two different etchings. Whether detained by the artistic riches of the city or, as is more probable, the company, Sterne evidently enjoyed himself, for he stayed twice as long as he had originally envisaged and was eventually driven south only by the intense cold.[29]

When Sterne left Florence, it was with the intention of spending a fortnight in Rome before moving on to Naples. In the Eternal City, he told Isaac Panchaud, he would stay just long enough to 'tread the Vatican, and be introduced to all the Saints in the Pantheon' (*Letters*, 266). With a population then at around 150,000, Rome was the principal attraction for most eighteenth-century Grand Tourists, drawn there by the classical heritage their education had taught them to revere. Sterne's principal response to the city, by contrast, was disappointment at the small number of English visitors he found there. One resident he did meet, however, was the sculptor Joseph Nollekens, who executed the celebrated bust of Sterne which became the artist's favourite among his works (it was said to have pleased him 'even to his second childhood');[30] exhibited in London in 1767, the bust was subsequently mass-produced in marble and plaster as one of the many items of Sterneana sold to an eager public after the writer's death.

In forbearing to offer thoughts on the decline and fall of classical Rome Sterne was exceptional among eighteenth-century literary travellers; his interests, however, lay in the present. Architecturally, the city was distinguished in the mid-eighteenth century by the baroque building around the Quirinale, and in the area between the Piazza Navona and the Capitol, as well as for that most theatrical piece of town planning, the Piazza di Spagna and the Spanish Steps, close to the Trevi Fountain, completed just four years previously. Having visited the Vatican, however, Sterne surely also made his intended excursion to the Pantheon, for it was there that he placed Yorick's encounter with Smelfungus—a fictionalized portrayal of the querulous Tobias Smollett of the *Travels through France and Italy*. Smollett, fiercely independent of mind in his account of all he saw, had written in the *Travels*: 'I was much disappointed at the sight of the Pantheon, which after all that has been said of it, looks like a huge cock pit, open at the top. . . . I am not one of those who think it is well lighted by the hole at the top . . . I visited it several times, and each time it looked more and more gloomy and sepulchral.'[31] Sterne's satirical portrait of Smollett is a good example of what he meant when he told Verri that he would improvise on his own experience of travel in *A Sentimental Journey*, for Smollett—whom Sterne had last seen in Montpellier two years previously—had left Italy before his arrival. A celebrated meeting between Yorick and Smelfungus nevertheless makes its way into *A Sentimental Journey*:

> I met Smelfungus in the grand portico of the Pantheon—he was just coming out of it—'*Tis nothing but a huge cock-pit*, said he—I wish you had

> said nothing worse of the Venus of Medicis, replied I—for in passing through Florence, I had heard he had fallen foul upon the goddess, and used her worse than a common strumpet, without the least provocation in nature. (*ASJ* 117–18)

By late January or early February 1766 Sterne was finally in Naples. Like other English travellers, he was delighted from the outset, writing to Lydia that 'I find myself infinitely better than I was—and hope to have added at least ten years to my life by this journey to Italy—the climate is heavenly, and I find new principles of health in me' (*Letters*, 267).[32]

Naples under the Bourbons was a teeming and flourishing city of around 400,000 inhabitants. The Villa di Portici (1736), the San Carlo Opera House (1737), the Capodimonte Palace (1738), and the Albergo dei Poveri (1752) were all comparatively recent additions to the urban fabric, part of the work undertaken by Carlo III shortly after his accession to the throne. Across the Bay of Naples, Mount Vesuvius was spectacularly active. The extent of contemporary fascination with the eruption is well illustrated both by numerous written accounts by travellers of many nationalities and by a host of paintings, while in the shadow of the volcano the excavations of Pompeii and Herculaneum were already under way (as was their commercial exploitation).

For Sterne, characteristically, none of this was as important as the fact that Naples was also full of English visitors. He was able to renew his friendships with Sarah Tuting and met Lady Anne Clifford, daughter of the countess of Newburgh and widow of Count Joseph James Mahony; he also began a new friendship with Sir William Stanhope, brother to the earl of Chesterfield. As in Florence, he was received by the British envoy, in this case, the Honourable (later Sir) William Hamilton, who had been appointed British envoy extraordinary and plenipotentiary to the Court of Naples in 1764. In marked contrast to his reticence over the classical sights of Rome, Sterne professed himself delighted with the modern diversions of Neapolitan life: 'We have a jolly carnival of it—nothing but operas—punchinellos—festinos and masquerades' (*Letters*, 269). Carnival at Naples was a principal attraction for visitors. Edward Gibbon, who had been present during the previous year's festivities reported that the carnival was 'most brilliant', leaving him no time to breathe between 'balls, operas, Assemblies and dinners'.[33] On the day Sterne described his surroundings so cheerfully to John Hall-Stevenson, he was going to a masquerade given by the Principessa Francavilla, which 'is to be superb'. Eleonora Borghese, the Princess Francavilla, was wife to the grand chamberlain to Ferdinand IV—who had succeeded his father in 1759—one of the seven great offices of the Kingdom of Naples. Immensely rich, the prince had leased the imposing Palazzo Cellamare and refurnished it magnificently in the French style; his gardens, stocked with a profusion of exotic plants, were the finest in Naples. The entertainments could be equally exotic—the prince's household included a dwarf—and it was in the gardens that Casanova was taken, along with Sir William Hamilton and Elizabeth Chudleigh, the then self-styled duchess of Kingston, to view the spectacle of a very fat middle-aged priest, the abbé Paolo Moccia di Fruttamaggiore—a fine classicist, author of admired Latin epistles and a Greek prosody—throw himself entirely naked into water, whereupon he rose, without making the slightest movement, and floated like a 'planche de sapin' ('a spruce plank').[34]

Whether Sterne was similarly privileged is not known—though the sight would surely have delighted him—but the Carnival festivities of the Francavillas were considered the finest in Naples, with exceptional music and masques. Samuel Sharp described the entertainment outside of the Carnival season during his visit just two months before Sterne's:

> The Prince of *Franca Villa* keeps a kind of open table every night, with twelve or fourteen covers, where the *English* of any figure are at all times received with the greatest politeness . . . the Princess of *Franca Villa* this season gave three [balls] in one week, where the company amounted to seven or eight hundred people each time.[35]

Most importantly for Sterne, however, his long journey to Naples seemed to be answering its principal aim. His health was improving and, he reported delightedly, 'here I am, as happy as a king after all, growing fat, sleek, and well liking—not improving in stature, but in breadth—' (*Letters*, 269).

If Naples during Carnival was a far cry from Coxwold, it was also very different from the conditions in which Sterne's wife and daughter were living during the winter of 1765–6. Elizabeth and Lydia Sterne had left the south of France and settled in Tours. The unhappy result of this change of situation is revealed in a letter Sterne wrote to Lydia shortly after his arrival in Naples: 'Sorry am I that you are both so afflicted with the ague, and by all means I wish you both to fly from Tours, because I remember it is situated between two rivers, la Loire, and le Cher—which must occasion fogs, and damp unwholesome weather—therefore for the same reason go not to Bourges en Bresse—'tis as vile a place for agues' (*Letters*, 267). There were financial problems too. Five days later Sterne wrote to Robert Foley requesting that he send Elizabeth money immediately: 'she sends me word she has been in want of cash these three weeks—be so kind as to prevent this uneasiness to her—which is doubly so to me' (*Letters*, 271). He asked Foley to allow Elizabeth Sterne £100 with which to begin her year; insisting that he himself had made scant use of his letters of credit, having drawn little more than 50 louis at Turin, the same in Rome, and a few ducats in Naples.

Sterne was also considering his return journey to England. On 3 February he asked Lydia to write to him in Rome telling him of her new place of residence, and assuring her of his intention to visit her in May, wherever she was. Though once more disdainful of a 'little French admirer' of Lydia's, Sterne was otherwise full of paternal affection: 'if I live,' he told her, 'the produce of my pen shall be yours—If fate reserves me not that—the humane and good, part for thy father's sake, part for thy own, will never abandon thee!' (*Letters*, 268). These were words that Lydia, who published the letter in her collection of Sterne's correspondence, must have reflected on with some bitterness in the years of financial embarrassment that followed her father's death. In the winter of 1766, however, Sterne felt well-disposed even towards Elizabeth: 'If your mother's health will permit her to return with me to England, your summers I will render as agreeable as I can at Coxwould—your winters at York' (*Letters*, 268). Despite such show of concern for his family, however, it took no more than two days before Sterne had rejected his original intention of taking a ship from Leghorn to Marseilles as a prelude to visiting Lydia, and was instead considering the repeated proposals of Henry Errington, of Sandhoe, Northumberland, that they return home together via Rome, Venice, Vienna, and Berlin.[36]

Of Errington, who was a Roman Catholic, Sterne wrote to John Hall-Stevenson: 'I have known him these three years, and have been with him ever since I reach'd Rome; and as I know him to be a good hearted young gentleman, I have no doubt of making it answer both his views and mine—at least I am persuaded we shall return home together, as we set out, with friendship and good will' (*Letters*, 269). Sterne was already serious enough to ask Hall-Stevenson to procure him a letter of introduction to Lord Stormont, British ambassador in Vienna, 'importing that I am not fallen out of the clouds' (*Letters*, 269). Three days later the attractions of a journey back to England subsidized by Errington were so strong that Sterne was reassuring Robert Foley of his creditworthiness by telling him that he was to return home with 'a gentleman of fortune' (*Letters*, 271), and he used the same phrase in a letter to Richard Chapman, his agent in

Coxwold and steward to Lord Fauconberg, written on 17 March.[37] Among those he left behind was the companion of his journey south Sir James Macdonald, who was 'just recovering a long and most cruel fit of the rheumatism'. The recovery was slow, and he remained in Naples until April. Unlike Sterne, however, Macdonald did not live to return home, dying at Frascati, in the hills outside of Rome, on 26 July 1766.

Sterne eventually left Naples with Errington, intending to pass Holy Week in Rome. Their journey was not without incident, for the road was notoriously bad: Henry Ellis, famous for attempting the North-West Passage, told Edward Gibbon he would rather circumnavigate the globe than travel from Rome to Naples.[38] In writing to thank the British envoy for his hospitality, Sterne told William Hamilton that he and Errington had 'had a voyage of it by Mount Cussino, full of cross accidents, but all was remedied along the road by sporting and Laughter' (*Letters*, 273). The pair dined and supped at the Benedictine monastery of Monte Cassino, where they were treated, Sterne recorded, 'like Sovereign Princes'. They arrived in Rome by eleven o'clock on the morning of Saturday, 15 March, 'without bodily hurt except that a Dromedary of a beast fell upon me in full Gallop, and by rolling over me crushed me as flat as a Pankake' (*Letters*, 273).

During Easter week Rome was a popular place of resort for English travellers. Whereas, during Carnival, Sterne reckoned there were twenty-five English at Naples and scarcely a third of that number in Rome, he reported that those still in Naples would soon 'decamp'. One of those who followed Sterne north was Samuel Sharp, who wrote in his *Letters from Italy* that, 'were a man to choose a month in the year to spend at *Rome*, I would recommend that month, in which the Holy Week is included'.[39] Sterne wrote from Rome to an acquaintance in Paris on Easter Sunday, 30 March 1766:

> I am much recover'd in my health, by the Neapolitan Air—I have been here in my return 3 Weeks, seeing over again wt I saw first in my way to Naples . . . We have pass'd a jolly laughing winter of it—and having changed the Scene for Rome; We are passing as merry a Spring as our hearts could wish. I wish my friends no better fortune in this world, than to go at this rate—haec est Vita dissolutorum. (*Letters*, 275)

Sterne was still intent on pursuing his way home with Errington via Venice, where they hoped to be for the Ascension; they planned to continue via Vienna, Dresden, Berlin, Hanover, and Holland, he wrote, though 'Whether we come back to Paris is not yet settled'.

For whatever reason—perhaps the death on 16 March of Lady

Stormont, wife of the British ambassador in Vienna—Sterne's plans changed dramatically. Errington altered his determination to visit the imperial capital, and he and Sterne parted company, perhaps on no very good terms.[40] Sterne reluctantly reverted to his original intention, and in mid-May paid a visit to his wife and daughter in France. Elizabeth and Lydia Sterne were guests of Gabriel-François de la Noüe-Vieuxpont, comte de Vair, who was living in the house of a friend, the chevalier de Fontette, at Fontette, close to Dijon in Burgundy. Writing to Hall-Stevenson, Sterne described the

> delicious Chateau . . . where I have been patriarching it these seven days with her ladyship, and half a dozen of very handsome and agreeable ladies. . . . This is a delicious part of the world; most celestial weather, and we lie all day, without damps, upon the grass—and that is the whole of it, except the inner man (for her ladyship is not stingy of her wine) is inspired twice a day with the best Burgundy that grows upon the mountains, which terminate our lands here. (*Letters*, 277)

After a mere week's visit, however, Sterne was already restless, and he determined to continue on to England, leaving behind his wife and daughter. 'Never man has been such a wildgoose chace after a wife as I have been—after having sought her in five or six different towns, I found her at last in *Franche Comté*—Poor woman! she was very cordial, &c. and begs to stay another year or so' (*Letters*, 277). If his relations with Elizabeth brought Sterne little pleasure, then Lydia—now 19—gave him more satisfaction: 'Lydia pleases me much—I found her greatly improved in every thing I wish'd her' (*Letters*, 277). Altogether he was happy and optimistic:

> I am most unaccountably well, and most accountably nonsensical—'tis at least a proof of good spirits, which is a sign and token given me in these latter days that I must take up again the pen.—In faith I think I shall die with it in my hand, but I shall live these ten years my Antony, notwithstanding the fears of my wife, whom I left most melancholy on that account. (*Letters*, 277)

Sterne's intention was to travel home as quickly as possible; he hoped to be in Paris in two days and back in London to celebrate the king's birthday on 4 June. Whether or not he succeeded, his return was rapid enough. Despite his repeatedly expressed desire to see D'Holbach, Diderot, and his other Parisian friends, Sterne did not on this occasion remain in the French capital long enough even to meet the new wife of Robert Foley, whom the banker had married less than six months previously. Instead, he was back in London by mid-June and in Yorkshire by the end of the month.

Installed once more in Coxwold, Sterne's first concerns were, as usual, financial. Elizabeth was already asking for more money, and her husband directed Isaac Panchaud to send her 50 pounds, adding:

> I have such an entire confidence in my wife, that she spends as little as she can, tho' she is confined to no particular sum—her expences will not exceed three hundred pounds a year, unless by ill health, or a journey—and I am very willing . . . that she should draw for fifty or a hundred pounds extraordinary, that it and every demand shall be punctually paid—and with proper thanks; and for this the whole Shandean family are ready to stand security. (*Letters*, 278–9)

He had good cause for concern that Elizabeth should not be left without funds for, as he told Panchaud, his wife had been 'very poorly—and my daughter writes to me with sad grief of heart that she is worse' (*Letters*, 279).

Sterne's speedy return to Coxwold had been prompted above all by a desire to work on the continuation of *Tristram Shandy*. In fact a multitude of small tasks awaited him: 'A thousand nothings, or worse than nothings, have <snatch'd> been every day snatching my pen out of my hands', he lamented, adding, however, 'I take it up to day in good earnest' (*Letters*, 281). For once resisting the temptation of a visit to Scarborough with Hall-Stevenson, Sterne applied himself to the task in hand. '[A]t present', he told a correspondent on 23 July, 'I am in my peaceful retreat, writing the ninth volume of Tristram' (*Letters*, 284). More significantly, his imagination was taken with the idea of a new work, which would eventually become *A Sentimental Journey*. He therefore declared that he would publish just one volume of *Tristram Shandy* on this occasion, so as to be able to begin the four volumes of his new book in the new year—after which 'I shall continue Tristram with fresh spirit' (*Letters*, 284).[41] If the chronology Sterne recorded in the novel is to be believed, however, progress in writing was scarcely rapid. The passage, 'And here am I sitting, this 12th day of August, 1766, in a purple jerkin and yellow pair of slippers, without either wig or cap on' (*TS* IX. i. 486) occurs in the very first chapter of the ninth volume. Even so, Sterne was content. 'What a difference of scene here!' he commented, contrasting Yorkshire unfavourably with the lands through which he had travelled; 'But with a disposition to be happy, 'tis neither this place, nor t'other that renders us the reverse.—In short each man's happiness depends upon himself—he is a fool if he does not enjoy it' (*Letters*, 284).

It was while Sterne was working on *Tristram Shandy* that he received a letter remarkable for its indication of his fiction's growing reputation as a moral work and its readers' belief in its capacity for effecting reform. Ignatius Sancho, then in his mid-thirties, was born on board a slave-ship in 1729. One of an estimated 14,000 or 15,000 blacks in mid-eighteenth-century London, he had been butler to the duke of Montague, who had left him a legacy and annuity enabling him to open a chandler's shop.[42] Sancho was taken up by London polite society because of his enthusiasm for music, painting, and literature. Author of some poetry and a tract on the theory of music, he was later to be the subject of a well-known painting by Thomas Gainsborough, given wider circulation through an engraving by Bartolozzi. Sancho's letter to Sterne, written on 21 July 1766, concerned the West Indian slave trade:

> I am one of those people whom the vulgar and illiberal call '*Negurs.*'—The first part of my life was rather unlucky, as I was placed in a family who judged ignorance the best and only security for obedience.—A little reading and writing I got by unwearied application.—The latter part of my life has been—thro' God's blessing, truly fortunate, having spent it in the service of one of the best families in the kingdom.—My chief pleasure has been books.—Philanthropy I adore.—How very much, good Sir, am I (amongst millions) indebted to you for the character of your amiable uncle Toby!—I declare, I would walk ten miles in the dog days, to shake hands with the honest corporal—Your Sermons have touch'd me to the heart, and I hope have amended it.[43]

Sancho had not written merely to praise Sterne, however. He had been inspired by a passage in 'Job's Account of the Shortness and Troubles of Life, considered', published in the second volume of Sterne's *Sermons* in 1760: 'Consider slavery—what it is,—how bitter a draught, and how many millions have been made to drink of it.'[44] Now Sancho asked Sterne if he might not give 'one half hour's attention' to the African slave trade with the West Indies: 'That subject, handled in your striking manner, would ease the yoke (perhaps) of many.' In passable imitation of Sterne's pathetic style, Sancho concluded: 'Dear Sir, think in me you behold the uplifted hands of thousands of my brother Moors—Grief (you pathetically observe) is eloquent;—figure to yourself their attitudes;—hear their supplicating addresses!—alas!—you cannot refuse.—Humanity must comply.'[45]

That Sancho should address this plea to Sterne is a telling indication of how the writer's much-criticized work was increasingly regarded by sympathetic contemporaries as a powerful exhortation to moral improvement and even practical social reform. Sancho makes the point that, with the exception of Sterne and Sarah Scott, author of *The History of Sir George Ellison* (1766), none of Sancho's favourite writers 'has drawn a tear' for black slaves (what Sarah Scott, who had been so appalled by the third and fourth volumes of Sterne's sermons, might have thought of being linked with him in this way may only be conjectured). In the 1760s the slave trade was approaching its height, with nearly two-and-a-half million slaves in European colonies in the New World, over 400,000 of them in the British West Indies alone.[46]

Sterne replied promptly to Sancho's letter, indicating that by a strange coincidence he had just completed a 'tender tale' of the sorrows of a poor, friendless negro girl when he received Sancho's letter in recommendation of so many of her brethren and sisters. '[B]ut why *her brethren*? or yours, Sancho!—any more than mine?' Sterne proceeded:

> It is by the finest tints, and most insensible gradations, that nature descends from the fairest face about St James's, to the sootiest complexion in africa: at which tint of these, is it, that the ties of blood are to cease? and how many shades must we descend lower still in the scale, 'ere Mercy is to vanish with them?—but tis no uncommon thing, my good Sancho, for one half of the world to use the other half of it like brutes, & then endeavour to make 'em so. (*Letters*, 286)[47]

The fact that the version of the letter Sterne copied into his letter book shows some slight revision of the text he sent to Ignatius Sancho (eventually printed by Lydia Sterne in her edition of her father's correspondence) suggests that from the outset he had an eye on publication. If so, he was evidently prepared to take a public stand on an issue that was by no means fashionable in the 1760s, when the principal agitation against the slave trade was confined to Quakers. In the event, the story to which Sterne referred in his reply to Sancho—if ever fully written—could not be woven into the finished fabric of *Tristram Shandy*'s final volume. The Moorish girl was not forgotten, however, and a brief sentimental episode survives:

> WHEN Tom, an' please your honour, got to the shop, there was nobody in it, but a poor negro girl, with a bunch of white feathers slightly tied to the end of a long cane, flapping away flies—not killing them.——'Tis a pretty picture! said my uncle Toby—she had suffered persecution, Trim, and had learnt mercy——
>
> ——She was good, an' please your honour, from nature as well as

> from hardships; and there are circumstances in the story of that poor friendless slut that would melt a heart of stone, said Trim; and some dismal winter's evening, when your honour is in the humour, they shall be told you with the rest of Tom's story, for it makes a part of it——
>
> Then do not forget, Trim, said my uncle Toby.
>
> A Negro has a soul? an' please your honour, said the Corporal (doubtingly).
>
> I am not much versed, Corporal, quoth my uncle Toby, in things of that kind; but I suppose, God would not leave him without one, any more than thee or me——
>
> ——It would be putting one sadly over the head of another, quoth the Corporal.
>
> It would so; said my uncle Toby. Why then, an' please your honour, is a black wench to be used worse than a white one?
>
> I can give no reason, said my uncle Toby——
>
> ——Only, cried the Corporal, shaking his head, because she has no one to stand up for her——
>
> ——'Tis that very thing, Trim, quoth my uncle Toby,——which recommends her to protection——and her brethren with her; 'tis the fortune of war which has put the whip into our hands *now*——where it may be hereafter, heaven knows!——but be it where it will, the brave, Trim! will not use it unkindly.
>
> ——God forbid, said the Corporal.
>
> Amen, responded my uncle Toby, laying his hand upon his heart. (*TS* IX. vi. 493)

Modest though it is, Sterne's response to Ignatius Sancho shows up both the writer's liberal sympathies and his alertness to shifts in public mood. Unfashionable in 1767—twelve years earlier even David Hume had declared himself 'apt to suspect the Negroes to be naturally inferior to the Whites'[48]—the sentiments Sterne expressed were very soon to find an echo far beyond the advanced Enlightenment circles to which they had been previously confined. In 1772 Lord Chief Justice Mansfield delivered a verdict which was understood to make slavery illegal in Britain. The passage from the sermon which had first attracted Sancho's attention was reprinted, under the title 'Slavery', in *The Beauties of Sterne* (1782), and imaginative writers, from Thomas Day in 'The Dying Negro' (1773), to Helen Maria Williams in *Peru* (1784), would attack slavery by promoting sympathy for its victims in their work. Josiah Wedgwood struck a medallion against the slave trade, whose emblem—a kneeling African in chains, surmounted by the Sternean legend: 'Am I not a man and brother?'—was copied onto fashionable consumer items such as cups, plates, and jewellery. The move towards abolition was slow, but although British participation in slave traffic would continue for forty years after Sterne's death, public opinion moved increasingly against it until the passing of an abolition bill put a virtual end to the Caribbean slave trade in 1807.[49]

Sterne continued at Coxwold, working on the continuation of *Tristram Shandy*, throughout the summer and autumn of 1766. As usual there were pleasant distractions, notably York Race Week in August. On this occasion Sterne preached a sermon to a fashionable congregation that included the duke of York. Even on his return to Coxwold, however, writing did not come easily, hampered as he was by unwelcome interruptions. Once more money was a problem, aggravated now by Elizabeth Sterne's illness. On 21 September he requested Isaac Panchaud to remit fifty louis d'or to his wife whenever she might ask for it, but he added, 'pray be so good as not to draw upon Mr. Becket for it (as he owes me nothing)' (*Letters*, 288)—a sure indication that few, if any, of the remaining sets of volumes V and VI or VII and VIII of *Tristam Shandy* had been sold. Sterne told Panchaud that his wife was very ill, and that he was himself contemplating a trip to France around Christmas in the company of a young nobleman. 'I cannot think of her being without me,' he wrote, 'and however expensive the journey would be, I would fly to Avignon to administer consolation to both her and my poor girl' (*Letters*, 288). For several weeks Lydia's letters contained few grounds for optimism concerning her mother's health. 'My daughter says her mother is very ill,' Sterne told Robert Foley on 25 October, 'and I fear going down fast by all accounts—'tis melancholy in her situation to want any aid that is in my power to give' (*Letters*, 289). Would Foley send another 30 guineas, besides the £50 already remitted, Sterne asked, assuring him that he had sent a bank bill to Becket. Apparently preparing his banker for future financial embarrassment, however, he added, 'surely had I not done so, you would not stick at it—for be assured, my dear F[oley] that the first Lord of the Treasury is neither more able or more willing (nor perhaps half so punctual) in repaying with honour all I ever can be in your books' (*Letters*, 289).

November brought better news, Lydia writing that her mother seemed out of danger. Elizabeth Sterne had hired a chateau at Vaucluse near Avignon, celebrated as the home of Petrarch. The location evidently appealed to Lydia, who gave an account of it in one of her letters to her father. Sterne responded suitably: 'I envy you the sweet situation . . . the Fountain of Vaucluse, by thy description, must be delightful' (*Letters*, 301). He added, 'Petrarch's tomb I should like to pay a sentimental visit to', thereby casting himself, wittingly or unwittingly—since Petrarch died and was buried at Arquà in northern Italy—in the part of Tristram on his fruitless visit to the Tomb of the Two Lovers in Lyon (*TS* VII. xxxii, xl).

In his letters to Isaac Panchaud Sterne characteristically abandoned sentiment for hard-headed business sense, giving an extended account of the chateau in the hope of persuading the banker what a fine economist his wife was: it is 'really pretty', he wrote, 'on the side of the Fountain of Vaucluse—with seven rooms of a floor, half furnished with tapestry, half with blue taffety, the permission to fish, and to have game, so many partridges a week, &c.' (*Letters*, 289). As to the price, Sterne demanded: 'guess! sixteen guineas a year—there's for you P[anchaud].' He added that his wife would have need of a further 100 guineas at the end of December, which he asked Panchaud to remit. Sterne himself would be in London by Christmas week and would then arrange that Panchaud be repaid: 'I am going to ly in of another child of the Shandaick procreation, in town—I hope you wish me a safe delivery' (*Letters*, 290). Elizabeth Sterne, meanwhile, was well enough not only to have taken possession of her new house but was also making plans to spend Christmas at Marseilles—the city the Sternes had rejected as a home for the winter of 1763–4 on account of its 'dearness of living'.[50]

The improvement in Elizabeth Sterne's health did not last long. A week before Christmas her husband wrote to John Hall-Stevenson that he was threatened every hour with a journey to Avignon to see his wife who was very ill, and who 'I suppose is going the way of us all' (*Letters*, 291). Sterne's supposition was premature, however—and the absence of references to her illness in subsequent correspondence suggests that she recovered sufficiently for Lydia no longer to consider her in any immediate danger. While Elizabeth Sterne's health remained poor for the remainder of her life, she would still outlive her husband by some years.

His wife's illness, however, was not the end of the 'chapter of evils' of which Sterne complained in his letter to Hall-Stevenson. 'I'm tormented to death and the devil, by my Stillington Inclosure' (*Letters*, 291), he wrote. Three thousand acres of land in the parish of Sutton-on-the-Forest were enclosed in 1759, and Stephen Croft had been involved for some time in the lengthy process of enclosing lands at Stillington. Now the Dean and Chapter had made an application to parliament for the enclosure of Stillington Fields and Stillington Common. Eventually some 1,400 acres were enclosed at Stillington, by act of parliament (6 George III, c. 16), one of 4,000 similar acts which saw 6.8 million acres of land in England and Wales—some 21 per cent of the total cultivated land—enclosed between 1750 and 1830, changing the face of the countryside. Both as vicar of

Stillington and as a landowner Sterne had a close interest in the enclosure and was engaged in numerous meetings before his subsequent involvement in consequent legal detail. For Sterne the principal benefit accruing from the process was the commutation of tithes of wool and lamb to allotments of land.[51]

Harassed by his wife's illness, financial problems, and the demands of the enclosure scheme, even the well-intentioned civility of Lord Fauconberg and his family seemed to Sterne to 'oppress me to death'. He longed to see Hall-Stevenson, 'but whilst I'm tied neck and heels as I am—'tis impracticable' (*Letters*, 291). Worst of all, he was still trying to finish the ninth volume of *Tristram Shandy*, which again centres on Widow Wadman's obsessive desire to know where, exactly, Uncle Toby had received his painful wound in the groin. Though it was going on 'busily', he was not happy with it: 'what I can find appetite to write, is so so.'[52]

The long-projected visit to London, when it eventually came, was a considerable relief to Sterne. Yet even there he could not escape his responsibilities entirely. The first letter he wrote from the capital, on Tuesday, 6 January, was to Lord Fauconberg to report on a meeting he had had on his patron's behalf prior to setting off for London, concerning the new turnpike direct from York to Helmsley. Sterne's journey to the metropolis had been made in appalling weather conditions—'a terrible Hurricane of Wind & snow', that affected the entire route; ''twas one continued storm all the way, & many stages had we to plough through Snow up to the horses bellies' (*Letters*, 292). The journey was so difficult that he was only at Barnet on the third night, finally reaching London on 6 January. A rapid thaw was deceptive, for a renewed snowfall left the streets four inches deep in snow and the weather turned intensely cold. 'I could scarse lay in bed for it', Sterne reported. A full week later he wrote that there was 'a dead stagnation of every thing, & scarse any talk but about the Damages done over the Kingdome by this cruel Storm' (*Letters*, 296).

Having finally arrived in London Sterne took lodgings in the rooms in Old-Bond Street, close to Piccadilly, that he would continue to occupy, when in the capital, until his death. The large sitting-room and bedroom was let by Mrs Mary Fourmantel, a widow with a high-class business in hair accessories (she was not, apparently, related to the singer Catherine Fourmantel). No sooner had he arrived than Sterne learned by letter of the difficulties of his friend William Combe, who had just left England for France. Then in his mid-twenties, Combe was an aspiring poet who, long after Sterne's death, would finally achieve renown as author of the verses which, together with Thomas Rowlandson's illustrations, made up *The*

Tour of Dr Syntax in search of the Picturesque (1809)—a work parodying the current fashion for such picturesque travels as those of John Gilpin. Less admirably, Combe also achieved a certain notoriety as forger of a number of letters he attributed to Sterne.[53] Sterne was quick to speculate on the reason for Combe's hasty departure for France: '[I]s it some nasty scrape of gallantry?' he wrote, 'or a more cleanly one of simple Love?'[54] If the latter, Sterne continued, in a manner that indicates why he should have inspired the affection of so many friends, 'I'll put off my Cassoc & turn Knight Errant for you, & say the kindest things of you to Dulcinea that Dulcinea ever heard' (*Letters*, 294). Yet amid the whimsical good nature of his letter, Sterne did not avoid more serious, if delicately phrased advice, for in bidding Combe farewell he concluded, in terms similar to those he had earlier employed to Lord Effingham—Combe's contemporary at Eton—'I heartily wish your happiness—seek it where you will, my dear Sir, You will find it no where, but in Company with Virtue and Honour' (*Letters*, 294).

Disregarding his own advice, Sterne himself was soon in the company of the decidedly unvirtuous William Douglas, earl of March and the future fourth duke of Queensberry, known both for his role in the development of horse-racing and for his sexual intrigues. In 1767 Douglas was at the centre of the entourage of the duke of York, but Sterne was no longer as impressed by the nobility as he had been seven years previously when he enjoyed the first fruits of his unexpected celebrity: he went away from the company, he wrote to Lord Fauconberg, no wiser than he had come.

Even so, there was plenty to enjoy in London—the theatre, concerts, and assemblies—besides the Court. Sterne reported dutifully to the ladies of the Fauconberg family back in Coxwold, so that they might share vicariously in the attractions of metropolitan life. Notable among these for Sterne in 1767 were the celebrated concerts directed at Carlisle House, in Soho Square, by Theresa Cornelys. A former singer, Cornelys was also mother of an illegitimate child by the Venetian adventurer Giacomo Casanova who, having been present at a night-long ball in 1763, described Carlisle House as 'digne de la maison d'un prince' (it was also rather more profitable, for the receipts that night had totalled more than 1,200 guineas).[55] Though Sterne might have resisted the comparison, there was considerable similarity between the socially ambitious and financially successful author and Theresa Cornelys, whose entertainments had captivated aristocratic circles and made her wealthy into the bargain. She was, in fact, an impresario of rare imagination. Having separated her masquerades from her more serious musical enterprises after 1764, she was promoter of the first successful professional concerts in London, directed by Johann Christian Bach—eighteenth and youngest child of Johann Sebastian—and Karl Friedrich Abel. It was of one of these that Sterne described enthusiastically as 'the best assembly, and the best Concert I ever had the honour to be at' (*Letters*, 296). The concerts had an especial appeal for Sterne, because Abel, while also a proponent of new music, was the last great European virtuoso on the viola da gamba, the instrument Sterne himself played.

All in all, the first two months of 1767 proved a busy time for Sterne. The ninth volume of *Tristram Shandy* had been advertised as early as 8 January, though the author was still revising proofs at the time. 'I am all this week in Labour pains; & if to Day's Advertiser is to be depended upon shall be safely deliver'd by tuesday' (*Letters*, 294). In fact publication was delayed for a further fortnight, and the final instalment of Sterne's work did not appear until Thursday, 29 January. Like the first London edition of the first and second volumes, the single volume bore a dedication to William Pitt, now Lord Chatham. Something of the social distance Sterne had travelled since 1760 is apparent in the familiar and ribald tone he employed: 'I should lament from my soul, if this [dedication] exposed me to the jealousy of their Reverences; because, *a posteriori*, in Court-latin, signifies, the kissing hands for preferment—or any thing else—in order to get it (*TS* IX. 'A DEDICATION TO A GREAT MAN', 483),—a Hogarthian touch that would have been unthinkable for Sterne only a few years previously.

Notwithstanding his earlier doubts, Sterne thought the ninth volume well received. Enquiring of Isaac Panchaud whether the book had yet reached Paris, he reported happily, ''tis liked the best of all here' (*Letters*, 300). Whatever Sterne himself believed, however, the truth was rather different. For a start, an anticipated fall in demand led to an edition of only 3,500 copies, rather than the 4,000 copies printed of the previous two instalments.[56] Moreover, the critical reception was generally lukewarm, with reviewers again complaining that Sterne's once-novel work had grown stale and tiresome. Even Ralph Griffiths, who had written with such enthusiasm of the previous instalment, found his patience tried by Sterne's disregard of his advice to rely on pathos alone. Noting, in the *Monthly Review*, the comparisons made between Sterne and Cervantes or Rabelais, Griffiths affected to have discovered 'his *real* prototype,—HARLEQUIN', making *Tristram Shandy* itself the 'PANTOMIME OF LITERATURE'.[57] While he found occasional episodes to praise, Griffiths's severe conclusion spoke of his disappointment with Sterne: 'O what pity that Nature should thus capriciously have embroidered the choicest flowers of genius, on a paultry groundwork of buffoonery!'[58]

For the most part reviewers seemed to have resigned themselves to Sterne's irrepressible taste for bawdy—(the volume ends defiantly with a story of 'A COCK and a BULL', which Parson Yorick declares to be 'one of the best of its kind, I ever heard' (*TS* IX. xxxiii. 539). So, the *Gentleman's Magazine* took comfort in the fact that, while Sterne must certainly plead guilty to 'gross indecency', then 'indecency does no mischief, at least such indecency as is found in *Tristram Shandy*; it will disgust a delicate mind, but it will not sully a chaste one'.[59] The wider public did not always agree, and to some the ninth volume proved intolerable. A letter-writer to *Lloyd's Evening Post* complained bitterly:

> Nothing sure disgraces the present age more, than to see a Clergyman continuing to give us, without any animadversion, up to the *ninth* volume of a bawdy composition. The same hand, that one day gives us the most *pathetic* Sermons, the next gives us the most feeling compositions, to rouse our sensitive appetites; to inflame with lust, and debauch and corrupt our youth of both sexes. . . . Surely our Spiritual Rulers must *frown* at such things.[60]

Some readers were intent on making sure that their 'Spiritual Rulers' *did* frown, for a petition was sent to the archbishop of York, urging that he take steps to 'deter this wanton Scandal to his Cloth from proceding in this Lewd Ludicrous manner as he has long done to the shame & Disgrace of his Sacred Order & to the detriment of Society'.[61]

Amid the disconcerting mixture of indifference and moral outrage inspired by *Tristram Shandy*, Sterne's concerns were all for his new book. As with volumes III and IV of his sermons, Sterne was soon soliciting subscriptions from friends and acquaintances of repute for his projected *A Sentimental Journey*. Seeking French subscribers, he wrote to Isaac Panchaud that

> the undertaking is protected & highly encouraged by all our *Noblesse*— & at the rate tis subscribed-for, will bring me a thousand guineas (au moins)—twil be an Original—in large Quarto—the Subscription half a Guinea—if you can <let me> procure me the honour of a few names of men of Science or Fashion—I shall thank you—<but> they will appear in good Company, as all the Nobility here almost have honoured me wth their Names. (*Letters*, 300).

In writing to Panchaud Sterne was not being strictly truthful. He had not yet begun his new work—'I have laid a plan for something new, quite out of the beaten track', he wrote on 20 February (*Letters*, 301)—and the account of the degree of support he enjoyed was certainly exaggerated. In part, he was again attempting to reassure Panchaud that he need not fear for the security of future loans. At least Sterne's finances were in better shape than they had often been in the recent past—particularly because the author had received an advance of £205. 17*s*. 0*d*. from his publisher against the profits to accrue from sales of the ninth volume of *Tristram Shandy*. Financial worries remained, nonetheless, especially with regard to Sterne's wife and daughter in France.

Lydia Sterne was now 19 years old and sufficiently fluent in French to be translating some of her father's sermons into that language with the aid of a neighbour, the abbé de Sade. The abbé was a younger son of the then marquis de Sade, and uncle to the most notorious holder of that title. A former vicar-general to the archbishop of Toulouse and Narbonne, he had also enjoyed the salon life of Paris, though he had retired in 1752 to his home near Vaucluse, where he pursued a study of Petrarch in the endeavour to identify the Laura of the sonnets with the wife of one of his ancestors, Hugues de Sade. From one of Sterne's letters it appears that Lydia was once present during repartee between the abbé and his notorious nephew that aroused Sterne's disgust; 'I am out of all patience with the answer the Marquis made the Abbé,' he wrote, ''twas truly coarse, and I wonder he bore it with any christian patience' (*Letters*, 301).

For all his worries about money, Sterne's correspondence suggests a continual, if sometimes impatient concern for the material well-being of both his wife and daughter. From his advance he supplied Elizabeth with 'a hundred Guineas (*or* pounds) I forget w[ch]' (*Letters*, 299), as he informed Isaac Panchaud with studied nonchalance. When Lydia subsequently wrote to plead poverty, Sterne replied with evident, and apparently justified testiness: 'Why do you say that your mother wants money?—whilst I have a shilling, shall you not both have ninepence out of it?' (*Letters*, 301). He repeated requests that his wife be sent 100 louis, when she passed Christmas at Marseilles, and when Lydia's guitar was broken he asked Panchaud to find someone in Paris to buy her another of a kind she was unable to find in Marseilles: 'it must be strung with cat gut & of 5 Cords—si chiama in Italiano, La Chitera de cinque corde . . . would you be so good to my Girl as to make her happy in this affaire' (*Letters*, 303).

One can only hope that Lydia was gratified by such small pleasures, for in affairs of greater moment things were not always proceeding well. After having so decisively rejected the first proposal of marriage his daughter had received, Sterne received another in 1767. In writing to Panchaud, he spoke of an 'advantagious offer at Merseilles—he has 20,000 Liv^{res} a year—& much at his ease—So I suppose Md^{lle} with Madame ma femme will negotiate the Affair' (*Letters*, 300). The tone of this letter certainly suggests that Lydia was not adverse to her wealthy admirer, yet if so she or her mother may have handled the affair badly, for Sterne's correspondence contains no further mention of the proposal and no marriage resulted. If the affairs of the heart were going ill for the daughter, however, it was a very different matter for the father.

14
London, 1767

It was in January 1767 that Sterne first met Mrs Elizabeth Draper, the 22-year-old wife of Daniel Draper, an official of the East India Company. Elizabeth Draper was born at Anjengo on the Malabar Coast on 5 April 1744, the daughter of May Sclater, an East India Company official, and his wife Judith, daughter of Charles Whitehill, who became chief of the settlement at Anjengo.[1] May Sclater died in 1746, aged 26, when Elizabeth was 2, and she was orphaned of her second parent two years later when Judith Sclater died. Cared for by their grandfather, Elizabeth and her younger sisters, Mary and Louisa, grew up in India until they were sent to England to be educated, when Elizabeth was about 10. Even by eighteenth-century standards 'education' is perhaps too grand a word for Elizabeth's experience. The girls, she was to write, 'were never instructed in the importance of anything, but one world[ly] point, that of getting an establishment of the luxurious kind, as soon as possible. A tolerable complexion, an easy manner, some degree of taste in the adjustment of our ornaments, some little skill in dancing a minuet and singing an air are the *summum bonum* here.'[2] Elizabeth Sclater returned to India in 1757 to the home of her grandfather, now in Bombay. Within a year of her return she gave evidence of having learned her single lesson well, and married, at the age of 14, a man seventeen years her senior. Daniel Draper was already well set on a career that would take him, among other locations on the subcontinent and beyond, to Tellicherry, Surat, and Bombay, where he eventually rose to the position of second in council.[3]

The Drapers had two children: a son was born in 1759 and a daughter two years later. In 1765 Daniel and Elizabeth Draper sailed to England with the aim of settling their children there to be educated. Having travelled the country on visits to relatives and spas, Daniel Draper returned to India, leaving not only his children but also his wife, who remained to settle the children in school and to regain her own health. The former task was soon accomplished, while Elizabeth's search for full health took the form of further visits to relations and friends by whom, in her own account, the young woman was much admired for her beauty and accomplishments.

Among Elizabeth Draper's friends were Commodore William James and his wife Anne, both of whom Laurence Sterne knew and greatly esteemed. Commodore James, he told Lydia, 'possesses every manly virtue—honour and bravery are his characteristicks', while his wife was 'one of the most amiable and gentlest of beings' (*Letters*, 301). Of modest origins, William James had enjoyed an adventurous and successful career subsequent to running away to sea at the age of 12. He entered the service of the East India Company in 1747 when in his twenties, and rose to become commander-in-chief of the Company's naval forces. The age was one in which great fortunes were to be made in India, and if James's contemporary Robert Clive was exceptional in leaving England virtually penniless and returning with a fortune of more than £40,000 a year, then there were many who amassed in India wealth of a magnitude they could have hoped for nowhere else. James himself acquired both a formidable reputation for skill and valour and a fortune large enough to enable him to retire to England before he was 40.

Once home he purchased Park Place Farm at Eltham, and a substantial London home in Gerrard Street in Soho. It was at the latter that Sterne first met Elizabeth Draper. Despite their differences of age, background, and social standing, Sterne became quickly infatuated with Elizabeth, or 'Eliza,' as he always called her. In his earliest surviving letter to her, probably written in the January of 1767, he was already confessing that he is 'half in love', and added 'I ought to be *wholy so*—for I never valued, (or saw more good Qualities to value,)—or thought more of one of Y^r^ Sex than of You' (*Letters*, 298). Along with this note he sent Eliza a copy of his books: 'the Sermons came all hot from the heart—I wish that could give em any title, to be offer'd to Y^rs^——the Others came from the head—I'm more indifferent ab^t^ their Reception——' (*Letters*, 298).

If not infatuated, Eliza Draper was at least willing to entertain her admirer's sentimental overtures. They soon adopted pet names for each other; he was the 'Bramin', she the 'Bramine', a gesture towards Sterne's priestly calling and Eliza's Indian background. 'The Brahmins', Eliza wrote, 'are easy, plain, unaffected sons of simple nature—there's a something in their Conversation & Manners, that exceedingly touches me.'[4] At 22, and having spent virtually all of her life in a distant colony, Elizabeth Draper was flattered to be noticed by such a celebrity as Sterne. Yet as a married woman, mindful of social proprieties, she did not respond without reserve to her unexpected admirer. When she was slightly indisposed Sterne was not admitted to see her, and though he protested by letter that 'a friend has the same right as a physician', he anticipated Eliza's reply: 'The etiquettes of this town (you'll say) say otherwise' (*Letters*, 299).

Whatever caution Elizabeth exercised was much needed, for Sterne himself was remarkably indiscreet. Within a few weeks of their first meeting news of her husband's passion for Eliza had reached the ears of Elizabeth Sterne in the south of France. Lydia reported that her mother had expressed a desire to hear no more of the matter and had asked her officious correspondent to drop the subject entirely. Nonetheless, on 23 February 1767 Sterne responded defensively to Lydia, who had taxed her father on the subject in no very delicate terms. 'I do not wish to know who was the busy fool, who made your mother uneasy about Mrs. [Draper],' he wrote, adding acerbically, ''tis true I have a friendship for her, but not to infatuation—I believe I have judgment enough to discern hers, and every woman's faults' (*Letters*, 301).

Perhaps he had, but the reader will look hard and long in Sterne's correspondence before finding evidence that Elizabeth Draper had faults at all. In writing to Eliza herself Sterne only once hints a shortcoming, and even then merely as a prelude to an extravagant compliment: 'you want nothing but firmness, and a better opinion of yourself, to be the best female character I know' (*Letters*, 309). More often he praised Eliza without reserve, and in any company in which she unhappily chanced not to be present. At a dinner given by the octogenarian Lord Bathurst—one of the author's earliest admirers—on a day when Eliza was unwell, Sterne talked of her 'an hour without intermission'. Bathurst heard him with so much pleasure, Sterne reported, that 'the good old lord' toasted Eliza's health three times and expressed the hope that he might live long enough to be introduced as a friend of Sterne's 'fair Indian disciple', and to see her 'eclipse all other nabobesses as much in wealth, as she does already in exterior and (what is far better) in interior merit' (*Letters*, 304). With only one other person—'and of sensibility'—present, Sterne passed a 'most sentimental' afternoon till nine o'clock, and, he confessed to Eliza, 'when I talked not of thee, still didst thou fill my mind, and warmed every thought I uttered' (*Letters*, 305).

Sterne's sudden and near-total absorption in Eliza must be viewed in the light of two facts. First, severe and protracted illness had made the writer emotionally vulnerable. Secondly, Sterne knew he must soon lose Eliza, for Elizabeth Draper was planning her return to her husband in

India—and would finally leave England in April, a mere three months after she and Sterne first met. The knowledge that their time together was limited did much to intensify his emotion, driving him to fantasize on a future in which they might be reunited. He insisted that Eliza must write during their separation—and perhaps the most remarkable (and characteristically eighteenth-century) feature of their celebrated friendship was that it was conducted almost entirely through their letters. From Eliza, as earlier from Lydia, Sterne demanded artless letters: 'Write to me, my child, only such. Let them speak the easy carelessness of a heart that opens itself, any how, and every how, to a man you ought to esteem and trust. Such, Eliza, I write to thee,—and so I should ever live with thee, most artlessly, most affectionately, if Providence permitted thy residence in the same section of the globe' (*Letters*, 306).

The premonition of the loss he would suffer by Elizabeth Draper's departure affected not only Sterne's feelings towards her, but made him more sensitive to his separation from his own family. In a lachrymose letter to his daughter—self-pitying yet still poignant in Sterne's very lack of self-control—he lamented:

> I am unhappy—thy mother and thyself at a distance from me, and what can compensate for such a destitution?—For God's sake persuade her to come and fix in England, for life is too short to waste in separation—and whilst she lives in one country, and I in another, many people will suppose it proceeds from choice—besides I want thee near me, thou child and darling of my heart. (*Letters*, 307)

Whether his wife and daughter were moved by this sudden and unexpected appeal in quite the way Sterne apparently hoped is doubtful, however, for he continued ingenuously by suggesting that the real cause of his distress was not the family separation but the illness of 'the dear friend I mentioned in my last letter' (ibid.). This was an illness so severe, at least in his imagination, that although Sterne expressed fervent hopes for Eliza's recovery, he also copied out for Lydia a verse epitaph he had composed in anticipation of her imminent demise. 'I was with her two days ago,' Sterne went out, 'and I never beheld a being so alter'd—she has a tender frame, and looks like a drooping lily, for the roses are fled from her cheeks—I can never see or talk to this incomparable woman without bursting into tears—I have a thousand obligations to her, and I owe her more than her whole sex, if not the world put together' (*Letters*, 307–8). Unsurprisingly, such sentiments did not bring about a rapid reconciliation between Laurence Sterne and his wife. The feelings of both Elizabeth and

Lydia Sterne must have been mixed, however, for the entire letter—one of the most disorganized in all of Sterne's correspondence—reveals how ill he was himself. 'Say all that is kind of me to thy mother,' Sterne concluded, 'and believe me my Lydia, that I love thee most truly' (*Letters*, 308).

In the absence of other evidence it is difficult to know whether Sterne's fears for Elizabeth Draper were well founded or the product of a distraught imagination. Certainly, his letters to her were a little more tactful than those written to his daughter. ''Tis melancholy indeed, my dear, to hear so piteous an account of thy sickness! Thou art encompass'd with evils enow, without that additional weight! I fear it will sink thy poor soul, and body with it, past recovery—Heaven supply thee with fortitude!' (*Letters*, 308–9). On the day he wrote Sterne had passed the afternoon with Anne James, in whom he was fortunate to find a sympathetic and patient confidante. 'Mrs. James, and thy Bramin, have mixed their tears a hundred times, in speaking of thy hardships, thy goodness, thy graces. 'tis a subject that will never end betwixt us' (*Letters*, 309). Sterne's attitude to Eliza reveals itself in this letter, as in others, as an uneasy mixture of the amorous, paternal, and pastoral. 'Reflect, Eliza,' he wrote, 'what are my motives for perpetually advising thee?' (ibid.). The answer was his fund of affection for her, affection which led him to see her very differently from the way she was perceived by others: 'I wish I could inspire you with a share of that vanity your enemies lay to your charge (though to me it has never been visible); because I think, in a well turned mind, it will produce good effects' (ibid.).

Elizabeth Draper was by now receiving more from Sterne than letters and advice. Heedless of his continuing financial worries, he presented her with anything he thought might give her pleasure: gifts which included a pair of globes—terrestrial and celestial—which had been newly advertised by George Adams, instrument-maker to George III, at prices ranging from 5 to 28 guineas. When Elizabeth Draper asked Sterne to speak to Johann Zumpe about the tuning of her square piano, he gave her a tuning hammer and pliers for twisting the piano wires. He bought iron screws for the globes and ten brass screws for hanging clothes. 'I purchased twelve,' Sterne added, 'but stole a couple from you, to put up in my own cabin, at Coxwould.—I shall never hang, or take my hat off one of them, but I shall think of you' (*Letters*, 310). In preparation for Eliza's departure for India Sterne had also written to a pilot in Deal, asking that he supply her with the best armchair in the town. 'Would I could, Eliza, so supply all thy wants, and all thy wishes!', Sterne wrote; 'It would be a state of happiness to me' (ibid.). Believing that this might be the last letter Eliza would receive before her departure, Sterne, adopting the priestly guise of Yorick, invoked the protection of the 'God of Kindness', that 'Being whom thou hast wisely chosen for thy eternal friend' (*Letters*, 311).

Before she left Elizabeth Draper must surely have felt in need of divine assistance, for Sterne's anxiety magnified the undoubted dangers of the long sea voyage to India to the extent that he could scarcely envisage her safe arrival. 'Gracious and merciful God! consider the anguish of a poor girl,' Sterne wrote tactlessly to the poor girl herself, 'Strengthen and preserve her in all the shocks her frame must be exposed to. She is now without a protector, but thee!' (*Letters*, 312). Whatever apprehensions she had about the voyage awaiting her, they could hardly have been lessened by Sterne's invocation, especially as he ended his prayer, with presumably unconscious gloom: 'Save her from all accidents of a dangerous element, and give her comfort at the last' (ibid.).

Tact was the least of the qualities of the fevered letters Sterne wrote to Eliza immediately before her departure. No sooner had he praised the 'unaffected sweetness' in a miniature of her he had commissioned from the artist Richard Cosway, than he confessed that 'When I first saw you, I beheld you as an object of compassion, and as a very plain woman' (ibid.). 'You are not handsome, Eliza,' Sterne continued with increasing directness,

> nor is yours a face that will please the tenth part of your beholders,—but . . . I scruple not to tell you, I never saw so intelligent, so animated, so good a countenance. . . . A something in your eyes, and voice, you possess in a degree more persuasive than any woman I ever saw, read, or heard of. But it is that bewitching sort of nameless excellence, that men of nice sensibility alone can be touched with. (*Letters*, 312–13)

If Elizabeth Draper was capable of receiving such remarks as the compliments Sterne evidently intended them to be, she was indeed possessed of at least some of the sensibility her admirer so freely attributed to her.

This letter of Sterne's, however, suggests that he had lost almost all touch with any world but a fantasy one of his own imagining. He invoked Eliza as his muse, but a muse, apparently, who might be rented by the hour. 'Were your husband in England, I would freely give him five hundred pounds (if money could purchase the acquisition) to let you only sit by me two hours in a day, while I wrote my Sentimental Journey.' Lest this be thought prodigal, he added: 'I am sure the work would sell so much better for it, that I should be re-imbursed the sum more than seven times told' (*Letters*, 313). The curious precision in the passage (£500 for just *two* hours a day, to be returned *seven*-fold) suggests a man whose fantasy world—part scriptural, part account-book—has become so elaborate as to exclude any sense of self-awareness, let alone self-irony.

The obsessive concern with Eliza so characteristic of Sterne's behaviour at this period is nowhere better illustrated than in his repeated attacks on the Newnhams, members of a family of wealthy London merchants who were friends of Elizabeth Draper and the Jameses. Why he took so intense a dislike to the Newnhams is not clear, though it is difficult to avoid the suspicion that they advised Elizabeth Draper to be more cautious in her friendship with Sterne, lest their relationship become the subject less of prurient gossip than of outright scandal. Certainly he wrote of the Newnhams that 'They are bitter enemies of mine, and I am even with them', continuing, 'La Bramine assured me they used their endeavours with her to break off her friendship with me, for reasons I will not write, but tell you' (*Letters*, 369).

To his exasperation, Elizabeth Draper refused to give up her 'worthless' friends at Sterne's behest. As a result he spoke against them with a vehemence entirely disproportionate to any reasonable cause. 'I would not give nine pence for the picture of you, the Newnham's have got executed,' he expostulated (apropos of nothing in particular). 'It is the resemblance of a conceited, made-up coquette' (*Letters*, 313). Here Sterne came perilously close to the very character given Elizabeth Draper by the less sympathetic of her acquaintance. Lest the bad taste of the Newnhams be insufficient inducement to drop the friendship, Sterne brought Anne James to his assistance. She has been trying to avoid the importunate Newnhams, Sterne reported, for fear that if she allows the least acquaintance she will never get rid of them. 'She begs I will reiterate my request to you, that you will not write to them. It will give her, and thy Bramin, inexpressible pain' (ibid.).

This was quite simply a lie. Anne James had said nothing of the sort to Sterne and, as far as can be judged, continued her friendly relations with the Newnhams. The deception, however, seems to have succeeded with Eliza, and was not immediately discovered by Anne James. It came to light only because Sterne confessed it in a letter to a friend—Anne James's request 'was merely a child of my own brain, made Mrs. J[ames]'s by adoption, to enforce the argument I had before urged so strongly' (*Letters*, 369). The friend to whom Sterne confessed this had himself made the mistake of intimating his intention of effecting an introduction to the Newnhams, apparently as a result of Anne James having described them as 'sensible' and 'amiable' people. Sterne was unforgiving. 'I despise them,' he wrote, 'and I shall hold your understanding much cheaper than I now do, if you persist in a resolution so unworthy of you' (ibid.). In confessing his deception, Sterne appears guilty but not at all remorseful. 'Do not mention this circumstance to Mrs. J[ames],' he asked, ''twould displease her'.

Fortunately for Sterne, who was to owe much to Anne James in the last months of his life, it seems that she did not learn of the deception during his lifetime. Presumably, however, she read his confession when Lydia published the letter in her collection in 1775, and may well have been made aware of it earlier. Certainly, some awareness of Sterne's subterfuge seems to have come to the notice of both Anne James and Eliza Draper, as may be seen from the reserve the latter was to express a number of years later: 'I was almost an idolater of his worth, while I fancied him the mild, generous good Yorick we had so often thought Him to be.'[5] Elizabeth Draper, meanwhile, may or may not have broken off her relationship with the Newnhams, but in either case she had the discretion to avoid mentioning them further in writing to her determined admirer.

Sterne's correspondence in these last days of Elizabeth Draper's stay in England—while her ship, the *Earl of Chatham*, waited for favourable conditions to set sail—reveals him in an intense state of anxiety. No occurrence was too small to perturb him. The presence on board Eliza's ship of a young soldier, already attached to her companion Hester Eleonora Light, makes Sterne surmise that he will soon attach himself to Eliza herself, 'because thou art a thousand times more amiable' (*Letters*, 315). When Eliza, perhaps searching for uncontroversial subjects, informed Sterne that her cabin is to be painted, the news appalled him. It would be much better, he declared, if the cabin were simply washed down: 'Paint is so pernicious, both to your nerves and lungs,' he insisted, that it will 'destroy every nerve about thee. Nothing so pernicious as white lead. Take care of yourself, dear girl; and sleep not in it too soon. It will be enough to give you a stroke of an epilepsy' (*Letters*, 315–16). It was fortunate for Elizabeth Draper that she does not seem to have been of an unduly nervous disposition.

Though he was to be separated from her physically, Sterne did not intend to lose all contact with Eliza. He directed her to gather all of his letters in chronological order, and to sew them together. 'I trust they will be a perpetual refuge to thee,' he wrote, 'and that thou wilt (when weary of fools, and uninteresting discourse) retire, and converse an hour with them, and me' (*Letters*, 316). In his own estimation at least, those letters contained 'much advice, truth, and knowledge', though they were most distinguished by the 'loose touches of an honest heart' which would speak to Eliza more than the 'most studied periods; and will give thee more ground of trust and reliance upon Yorick, than all that laboured eloquence could supply' (ibid.). In a sustained attempt to convince Eliza of how much she meant to him, Sterne quite forgot his wife and daughter. 'Remember,' he wrote desperately, 'that while I have life and power, whatever is mine, you may style, and think, yours' (ibid.). Eventually, in the same letter, he did remember his daughter: 'I will live for thee, and my Lydia—be rich for the dear children of my heart—gain wisdom, gain fame, and happiness, to share with them—with thee—and her, in my old age' (*Letters*, 316–17). Agitated, as time ran out for posting his letter, Sterne concluded with the determination to 'recommend thee to Heaven, and recommend myself to Heaven with thee, in the same fervent ejaculation, "that we may be happy, and meet again; if not in this world, in the next."—Adieu' (*Letters*, 317).

Despite the dramatic air of finality, this impassioned farewell was to prove an anticlimax. Poor weather conditions prevented the *Earl of Chatham* from sailing, and Sterne was able to send further letters to Eliza. The news that her illness was worse cheered him a little, since he hoped it might mean she would be forced to remain in England, perhaps for another year. If, Sterne pondered on paper, Daniel Draper were the generous, humane man Eliza had described, he would surely applaud rather than censure her decision to remain. Indeed, Sterne wrote that he had been 'credibly informed' that her husband's only real objection to Elizabeth Draper's remaining longer in England was a fear that she might run up debts which he would be obliged to meet and, Sterne continued, with self-induced indignation, 'that such a creature should be sacrificed for the paltry consideration of a few hundreds is too, too hard!' (*Letters*, 318). In the same vein he indulged an extravagant fantasy that he might buy Eliza from her husband. 'Oh! my child, that I could, with propriety indemnify him for every charge, even to the last mite, that thou hast been to him! With joy would I give him my whole subsistence—nay, sequester my livings, and trust the treasures Heaven has furnished my head with, for a future subsistence' (ibid.). While allowing that Eliza owed much to her husband, and something also to appearances and the opinion of others, Sterne insisted that she owed more to herself and, if she were to continue ill, should leave Deal and return to London. Then, in order that she recover her health, they might travel together to France and join Elizabeth Sterne and Lydia to make 'parties of pleasure' there or in Italy.

The air of quasi-paternal solicitude that Sterne adopted was not unalloyed with rather different feelings. 'I begin to think you have as many virtues as my uncle Toby's widow,' he wrote sportively, adding ambiguously, 'I don't mean to insinuate, hussey, that my opinion is no better founded than his was of Mrs. Wadman; nor do I conceive it possible for any *Trim* to convince me it is equally fallacious' (ibid.). Having taken sexual innuendo as far as the Widow Wadman, Sterne continued, in an effortful transition: 'Talking of widows—pray, Eliza, if ever you are such, do not think of giving yourself to some wealthy nabob—because I design to marry you myself' (*Letters*, 318–19). This, Sterne insisted cheerfully, was no mere fancy: 'My wife cannot live long . . . and I know not the woman I should like so well for her substitute as yourself' (*Letters*, 319); ''Tis true,' he added, with a rare touch of returning wit, 'I am ninety-five in constitution, and you but twenty-five—rather too great a disparity this!—but what I want in youth I will make up in wit and good humour—Not Swift loved his Stella, Scarron his Maintenon, or Waller his Sacharissa, as I will love, and sing thee, my wife elect!' (ibid.).

To take these letters to Eliza as a literal record of Sterne's mental or physical state at this time is, of course, dangerous. The ailing author of *Tristram Shandy* had become an accomplished master at giving highly studied writing the appearance of complete spontaneity. In asking Eliza to gather together his correspondence in order—as in comparing himself to Swift, Scarron, and Waller—he seems to have had in mind eventual publication, if only following his death. Yet the effects of the pulmonary tuberculosis from which he had suffered for over thirty years were increasingly apparent, and the mercurial shifts of mood had, at least in part, a physical origin. Sterne's agitation was the prelude to a serious physical collapse. 'My dear Eliza!', Sterne began his next letter,

> I have been within the verge of the gates of death.—I was ill the last time I wrote to you; and apprehensive of what would be the consequence.—My fears were but too well founded; for in ten minutes after I dispatched my letter, this poor, fine-spun frame of Yorick's gave way, and I broke a vessel in my breast, and could not stop the loss of blood till four this morning. I have filled all thy India handkerchiefs with it.—It came, I think, from my heart! (*Letters*, 320)

Weak and exhausted, Sterne fell asleep to wake two hours later with his shirt wet with tears. He had dreamed, he told Eliza, that his spirit had flown to her in the Downs and that she had come to administer what consolation 'filial affection' could bestow; 'Dear girl! I see thee,—thou art for ever present to my fancy . . . Blessing attend thee, thou child of my heart' (ibid.).

The last letter Sterne wrote to Eliza before she eventually set sail for India speaks poignantly of the progress of his consumption as, from one paragraph to another, his mood swings from remembered sorrow to renewed hope.[6] 'My bleeding is quite stopped, and I feel the principle of life strong within me', Sterne wrote. He had awoken hungry and eaten breakfast with a good appetite. 'I write to thee with a pleasure arising from that prophetic impression in my imagination, that "all will terminate to our heart's content"' (ibid.). For a writer whose work expresses so frequently and so eloquently the unpredictability of life, these were optimistic sentiments indeed—even if Sterne attributed his pleasure to an impression in his imagination rather than to rational or religious conviction. That impression came from Eliza's faith that 'the best of beings (as thou has sweetly expressed it) could not, by a combination of accidents, produce such a chain of events, merely to be the source of misery to the leading person engaged in them' (ibid.).

Was Elizabeth Draper even remotely aware of how unerringly she had gone to the very heart of Sterne's own doubts? If an all-powerful, ever-present God exists, and is the 'best of beings', why does He allow accident, mere chance, so often to intervene in human life? *Tristram Shandy* is the finest comic expression of such questioning in eighteenth-century literature. As a conscientious priest, Sterne had, for years, endeavoured in his sermons to rationalize his own doubts, and give hope to his congregations, through the articulation of orthodox Anglican belief. Now he clung to the words of Eliza Draper, who avoided such doubts by means of a simple, unreflective faith. For a brief moment that faith sufficed. 'The observation', he wrote, 'was very applicable, very good, and very elegantly expressed. I wish my memory did justice to the wording of it' (ibid.). The substance of the remark having been accepted, however, it was immediately forgotten as Sterne digressed into extravagant praise of Eliza's epistolary style. Her letters he declared to have shown to half the (admiring) literati in London. Possessed of beauty, goodness, and accomplishments, Sterne wrote, Eliza must be Nature's peculiar care—'the best and fairest of all her works' (*Letters*, 321).

After so many false conclusions, this really was to be Sterne's last letter to Eliza before she set sail. The *Earl of Chatham*, Sterne read in the papers, had reached the Downs and the wind was fair: 'Cherish the remembrance of me; think how I esteem, nay, how affectionately I love thee, and what a price I set upon thee.' Sterne bade Eliza be hopeful, to sing 'any little stanza on the subject' every morning, together with the devotion of a hymn. He offered Eliza one further emphatic piece of advice:

REVERENCE THYSELF.

. . . I am, and shall be, the last to deplore thy loss, and will be the first to congratulate and hail thy return.—

FARE THEE WELL!

(*Letters*, 321)

Sterne would not see Eliza again. She did not return to England until 1777, after unsubstantiated charges of adultery against her brought to an end her marriage to the allegedly abusive Daniel Draper. In the meantime the *Earl of Chatham* sailed from Deal on 3 April 1767. Left alone, Sterne consoled himself by plotting Eliza's homeward voyage, but even at his most optimistic—imagining Eliza at Madras by the end of July—he did not hope to receive news of her safe arrival in Bombay before the following February.

He did not neglect Elizabeth Draper in her absence, however. From April to August he kept a record of his activities and feelings—day by day, even hour by hour—which he intended to send to Eliza when she had reached India. She in turn was to keep a similar record of her daily life, for Sterne's benefit.[7]

Some of Sterne's work is lost, but what survives (the greater part), is prefaced by a note: 'This Journal wrote under the fictitious Names of Yorick & Draper—and sometimes of the Bramin & Bramine—but tis <a Copy> a Diary of the miserable feelings of a person separated from a Lady for <whom he had> whose Society he languish'd—' (*Letters*, 322). Sterne's attempt to adhere to the agreed concept of the journal resulted in a work that is exemplary for his age: a detailed record of the minutiae of daily life, shot through with the excesses of extravagant emotional turmoil. The result is a remarkable portrait of the artist as a sick man. The very first entry brutally juxtaposes emotional and material experience. The decision that both he and Eliza should keep a diary meant, Sterne wrote:

> the Sun has not more constantly rose & set upon the earth, than We have thought of & remember'd, what is more chearing than Light itself—<Thou dear> eternal Sunshine! <of my heart> Eliza!—<how> dark to me is all this world without thee! & most heavily will every hour pass over my head, till that is come wch brings thee, dear Woman back to Albion. dined with Hall <this> &c—at the brawn's head. (*Letters*, 322)

Bathetic as the juxtaposition appears, it is wholly appropriate, for however willing Sterne's spirit was to dwell in the realms of fancy, his flesh was distressingly weak. For his supper with Hall-Stevenson, Sterne recorded that he paid 'a severe reckoning all the night' and rose 'tottering & feeble'. So ill was he, that despite a serious attempt to keep a daily record of his activities, he confused the day of the week and the date of his entries for an entire week, writing a day behind throughout this time. His entry for 'Munday. Ap: 15'—actually Tuesday, 14 April—begins: 'worn out with fevers of all kinds but most, by that fever of the heart with wch I'm eternally wasting, <since> & shall waste till I see Eliza again—dreadful Suffering of 15 Months!—it may be more' (*Letters*, 323). Sterne now gave way to his melancholy. He remained at home reading Eliza's letters and professed no interest in other company or diversion. 'What a change, my dear Girl, hast thou made in me!' (ibid.), he wrote with some justice—and indeed the transformation of the gregarious author who revelled in the delights of metropolitan society in 1760 into the solitary man who mourned Eliza's departure in 1767 could hardly have been greater. Sterne's mental dejection was matched, and most likely caused by, bodily debility. He went to bed with a high fever, and was so ill on rising that he could not go to visit Anne James to enjoy the pleasure of a sentimental conversation about Eliza. He was at this time treating himself with patent medicines—notably James's Powders, an alleged remedy producing a strong diaphoretic effect, invented by Dr Robert James, and extravagantly praised in his last novel, *Amelia*, by Henry Fielding, who died not long after.[8]

Even in the midst of very real illness, however, Sterne was capable of attitudinizing—or perhaps incapable of not attitudinizing. Thus, he told Eliza that he had 'leand the whole day with my head upon My hand; sitting most dejectedly at the Table with my Eliza's Picture before me—sympathizing & soothing me—O my Bramine! my Friend! my—<future Wife> Help-mate!' (ibid.). Later that same day Sterne dramatized the meal he ate alone:

> I have just been eating my Chicking, sitting over my repast upon it, with <no> Tears—a bitter Sause—Eliza! but I could eat it with no other—when Molly spread the Table Cloath, my heart fainted with in me—one solitary plate—one knife—one fork—one Glass!—O Eliza!—twas painfully distressing,—<I look'd> I gave a thousand pensive penetrating Looks at the Arm chair thou so often graced on these quiet, sentimental Repasts—& Sighed & laid down my knife & fork,—& took out my handkerchiff, clap'd it across my face, & wept like a child. (*Letters*, 323–4)

In the absence of word from Eliza, Sterne sought solace in rereading his own journal, and evidently thought well of this particular scene.[9] Little more than a fortnight later he gave a slightly different version of it in his entry for 2 May, adding, on this occasion, a speaking part for Molly: 'I never bring in the Knives & forks, added She, but I think of her [Eliza]—There was no more trouble with you both, than w^h one of You—I never heard a high or hasty word from either of You—You were surely made, added Molly, for one another' (*Letters*, 336).

Sterne could not always be alone, however, and he increasingly sought consolation for Elizabeth Draper's absence where he could. He found it above all in the sympathetic company of Anne James. In fact, both Anne James and her husband truly appear to have been the 'faithful friends' of whom he frequently wrote warmly to Eliza. When he failed to appear at their house one Sunday—a day they habitually entertained—Anne James's fears that Sterne's condition had deteriorated led her to send her maid to enquire after him. For her solicitude, he returned 'most sentimental thanks', and he wrote to Eliza in a crescendo of effusive gratitude: 'She suffers most tenderly for Us, my Eliza!—& We owe her more than all the Sex—or indeed both Sexes <put together> if not, all the world put together' (*Letters*, 326). The Jameses indeed showed exemplary patience as well as friendship for Sterne, supporting him in his unhappiness despite his uncontrollable tendency to burst into tears on any occasion. Such tears were evidently contagious, for Anne James would sometimes end up crying too: 'I weep <i[ng]> for You both, said she (in a whisper,) for Elizas Anguish is as sharp as yours—<&> her heart as tender—her constancy as <single> great—heaven <will> join Your hands <shortly> I'm sure together!' (*Letters*, 325). Thoughout this lachrymose scene, Sterne revealed, William James remained in the same room, reading a pamphlet on the affairs of the East India Company.

Even the Jameses could not always console Sterne, however. It was Anne James, for instance, who gave him a second-hand account of Daniel Draper and his allegedly detestable behaviour at Bombay which, Sterne wrote, 'sunk my heart' (*Letters*, 324). When company could do nothing for his state of mind, he took refuge in solitude and his imagination. On 16 April he sent for a chart of the Atlantic, in order that he might the better conjecture where Eliza might be day by day; on 18 April he was happy to accept Commodore James's estimate that the *Earl of Chatham* would by then have reached Madeira. 'I shall trace thy track every day in the Map, & not allow one hour for contrary Winds, or Currents (*Letters*, 325)', he wrote. On the previous day he had purchased a copy of Robert Orme's *History of the Military Transactions of the British Nation in Indostan*; 'why?—Let not my Bramine ask me—her heart will tell her Why I do this, & every Thing—' (*Letters*, 324).

Loneliness and physical debility brought Sterne to new depths of depression. The priest did not even attend church on Sunday, 19 April, Easter Day. His brief journal entry for the most joyful feast in the Christian calendar concluded laconically: 'all day at home—in extream dejection.' Two days later, he was suffering from a fever brought on, so he wrote, by Eliza's departure: 'I am very ill—very ill for thee.' His doctors declined to accept Sterne's self-diagnosis but blamed his condition on taking James's Powders and on his foolhardiness at 'venturing out on so cold a day' (*Letters*, 328). In writing later to William and Anne James, Sterne declared that his physicians must be wrong, for 'I am certain that whatever bears that name must have efficacy with me' (ibid.). However, the doctors could do nothing for Sterne except bleed him—he lost 12 ounces of blood—in order to quieten him. This treatment produced no benefit, and when Sterne awoke on the following morning he was able to get up only with the utmost difficulty, so that his physician ordered him back to bed, where he was bled once more. The result was near disaster: the bleeding was uncontrolled; 'my arm broke loose, & <lost> I half bled to death in bed before I felt it' (*Letters*, 326). Even in this condition, however, Sterne found strength to slight his old antagonists: replying to a card from Anne James urging him to take care of his health for the sake of his friends, especially Eliza, Sterne added triumphantly 'not a word from the Newnhams!' (*Letters*, 327).

In response to enquiries sent by the ever-concerned Jameses, Sterne reported his condition in some detail. 'God knows,' he told them, 'I am not able to give a good account of myself, having passed a bad night in much feverish agitation' (*Letters*, 328). This pattern was to be repeated for some days. On 23 April Sterne noted in his journal: 'a poor night. and am only able to quit my bed at 4 this afternoon' (*Letters*, 329)—a bare entry representing his apparent determination to fulfil his promise to write every day. Sterne's condition was now giving rise to fears for his life, for he recorded that during the course of the day he was visited in bed by no fewer than forty friends (though he may have exaggerated the number, since he was anxious to assure Eliza that her visit would have been worth them all). By 24 April, however, Sterne himself felt that his end was near. The complete entry for the day reads: 'So ill, I could not write all this morning—not so much, as Eliza! farewel to thee;—I'm going——' (ibid.).

In the event, not only were Sterne's fears unfounded but the day was to prove a turning-point in this bout of illness. He spent an easier night, and on the following day was able to write: 'am a little better—So Shall not depart, as I apprehended' (ibid.). As he recovered his health, so too Sterne recovered his sense of the ridiculous, even when the 'whimsical' story he had to tell Eliza—'as comically disastrous as ever befell one of our . . . family—Shandy's Nose—his *na*me—his Sash-Window are fools to it' (ibid.) —was at his own expense. The injury resulting from catching cold and taking James's Powders fell, Sterne recorded:

> upon the worst part it could,—the most painful, & most dangerous of any in the human Body—It was upon this Crisis, I call'd in an able Surgeon & with him an able physician <,—> (both my friends) to inspect my disaster—tis a venerial Case, cried my two Scientifick friends.—'tis impossible. at least to be that, replied I—for I have had no commerce whatever with the Sex—not even with my wife, added I, these 15 Years—You are xxxxx however my good friend, said the Surgeon, or there is no such Case in the world—what the Devil! said I, without knowing Woman—we will not reason ab^{t} it, said the Physician, but you must undergo a course of Mercury,—I'll lose my life first, said I,—& trust to Nature, to Time—or at the worst—to Death,—so I put an end with some Indignation to the Conference; and determined to bear all the torments I underwent, & ten times more rather than, submit to be treated as a *Sinner*, in a point where I had acted like a *Saint.* Now as the father of mischief w^{d} have it, who has no pleasure like that of dishonouring the righteous—it so fell out, That from the moment I dismiss'd my Doctors—my pains began to rage with a violence not to be express'd, or supported.—every hour became more intollerable—I was got to bed—cried out & raved the whole night—& was got up so near dead, That my friends insisted upon my sending again for my Physician & Surgeon—I told them upon the word of a man of Strict honour, They were both mistaken as to my case—but tho' they had reason'd wrong—they might act right—but that sharp as my sufferings were, I felt them not so sharp as the Imputation, wch a venerial treatment of my case, laid me under—They answerd that these taints of the blood laid dormant 20 Years—but that they would not reason with me in a matter wherein I was so delicate—but Would do all the Office for wch they were call'd in—<&>namely, to put an end to my torment, wch otherwise would put an end to me.—& so have I been compell'd. to surrender myself—& <so> thus Eliza is your Yorick, y^{r} Bramine—your friend with all his sensibilities, suffering the Chastisement of the grossest Sensualist—Is it not a most ridiculous Embarassm^{t}, as ever Yorick's Spirit could be involved in— (*Letters*, 330)

This is a most vivid, as well as ridiculous anecdote, and quite extraordinary for a man who, twenty-four hours before, had good grounds for believing himself to be dying. It also provides a revealing glimpse into the care Sterne took in his apparently spontaneous writing, for he not only told Eliza that it would make a fine episode in Tristram Shandy's life—a suggestion that he had not entirely given up the idea of a continuation—but also divulged that the writing of it had taken him three sittings. Certainly, he was pleased with the end result—which 'ought to be a good picture—I'm more proud. That it is a true one' (ibid.)—for he repeated it, virtually verbatim, in a letter to Lord Shelburne a week later.[10] Sterne also appears to have related the incident to his wife, doubtless inspired, as he told Eliza, by 'the purest consciousness of Virtue'.

The entire incident—so much to Sterne's apparent disadvantage if not discredit—is remarkably pertinent to a consideration of Sterne's life and his work alike. If we are to believe the assertion (which is the foundation of the whole story) that he had had no sexual relationship, not even with his wife, in the previous fifteen years, we are left with a portrait of a man whose behaviour changed radically within a relatively short space of time. The profligate priest of Richard Greenwood's account, whose domestic dissatisfaction or sexual appetite led him to court scandal by visits to prostitutes in York at a time when he held a prebendal stall in the Minster, turned in the course of the 1740s from promiscuity to sexual abstinence. If Greenwood is correct, the Sternes' marriage was in difficulties from its earliest years, but as Lydia was born in 1747, Sterne's sexual relationship with his wife evidently survived Elizabeth's detection of her husband's adultery, only to be broken off in the early 1750s. While this chronology would square with Sterne's present assertion, it is certainly at odds with other evidence: the letter he wrote in Latin to John Hall-Stevenson in 1760—alleging that it was sexual desire that was driving him to London—and with scattered references in letters to or from David Garrick and John Wilkes, to say nothing of what we might reasonably surmise, on the basis of the surviving letters, about Sterne's relationship with Kitty Fourmantel.

The exact nature of Sterne's sexuality might be a matter of prurience or idle curiosity were it not for the pervasiveness of the theme of impotence in Sterne's work. In *Tristram Shandy* the virility of Walter Shandy is in doubt from the opening page, while Uncle Toby's potency is a matter for unending speculation, given the wound he has sustained in the groin, whose exact nature gives so much anxiety to the Widow Wadman. Following his unfortunate childhood accident with the falling window-sash after the maid Susanna, finding no chamber-pot under the bed, has encouraged him to '**** *** ** *** ******' (*TS* v. xvii. 301), Tristram becomes so much the object of speculation as to his physical integrity that the exasperated Walter expresses the view that to quieten gossip he must needs exhibit his son at the market cross. At the very last even the Shandy bull, kept 'for the service of the Parish', is found in 'no way equal to the department' (*TS* ix. xxxiii. 539). The recurring motif of impotence in his writings is further emphasized by the frequently invited (if dangerous) identification of Sterne with his fictional creations, so that in *A Sentimental Journey* we find Yorick's encounter with the grisette, which concludes: '. . . then I have only paid as many a poor soul has *paid* before me for an act he *could* not do, or think of' (*ASJ* 243). Inevitably, such episodes focus attention on the ambiguous sexuality of Sterne in his later years, and such matters as his quickness to impute impotence to his daughter's elderly French admirer in 1765. While various speculative possibilities present themselves, none can be considered at all certain. From 1760 onwards Sterne was a very public figure, and a priest whose literary success depended on not overstepping too far the bounds of common decency. The degree of furtiveness which marks his often ambivalent references to sexuality in his correspondence might allow us to infer a psychic cause of Sterne's possible impotence. It is possible too that Sterne might have contracted not only syphilis in York in the 1740s but also gonorrhoea, passing either or both on to his wife, who suffered a number of miscarriages and stillbirths—another potential source of guilt which might have resulted in impotence. So far as the disease itself was concerned, the recurrence of the symptoms of syphilitic infection after two decades was in no way out of the question, whatever Sterne may have believed.

So much is speculation, yet such speculation is unavoidable, above all because it is impossible not to wonder about Sterne's motives in telling this story to the 23-year-old woman he claimed he wished to marry. Did he really believe that such an account would make no difference whatever to their relationship? Or does the entire story suggest how completely all Sterne's talk of marriage belongs to the realm of fantasy? It is impossible to be sure, yet one thing is certain: the entire episode and its retelling gave Sterne new strength and new hope: 'Every thing convinces me, Eliza,' he wrote, 'We shall live to meet again—So—Take care of y^{r} health, to add to the comfort of it' (*Letters*, 330).

Despite the distress caused by Eliza's absence, Sterne was fortunate in possessing many solicitous friends, besides the ever-concerned Jameses. The knocker was continually sounding as cards were sent and enquiries made after him; 'my room [is] allways full of friendly Visiters' (ibid.), he reported. As the cures his physicians prescribed took effect, Sterne even became reconciled to what he continued to think of as their mistaken diagnosis. He was still extremely feeble, however, having taken nothing more in a week than water-gruel, until he ate some mackerel and boiled fowl at the solicitation of John Hall-Stevenson. Even in the company of one of his oldest friends, however, Sterne did not forget Elizabeth Draper, and he drank a toast to her everlasting peace and happiness with the first glass of wine he tasted. And when Hall-Stevenson departed, leaving him alone once more, Sterne reported that he flew to his journal 'to tell thee, I never prized thy friendship so high, or loved thee more' (*Letters*, 331). He penned a further lengthy paragraph and more before he finally slept at three in the morning.

Weakened though he was, Sterne had survived another crisis in his illness and was again making plans for the future. His physical state would keep him in London for at least three weeks more, he wrote, for he thought it hazardous to start a journey to Yorkshire in less. For virtually the first time since he arrived in London in March 1760 society held little attraction for him. Instead, he co-operated in his cure in order to hasten his return to what he now thought of as the consolatory solitude of Coxwold. By Sterne's own account his doctors were pleased with their patient's progress; they 'stroked their beards, & look'd ten per C^{t} wiser upon feeling my pulse, & enquiring after my Symptoms' (*Letters*, 332), though they insisted that he continue on a course of Van Swieten's corrosive mercury (the usual, unpleasant contemporary treatment for venereal disease). Yet still it was Eliza's absence that most affected Sterne, as he never ceased to protest. His landlady, Mrs Fourmantel, and Molly sympathized with Sterne, for 'they thought I was broken hearted, for She [Molly] never enterd the room <but> or passd by the door, but she heard me sigh heavily—That I neither eat or slept or took pleasure in any Thing as before, except writing— —' (*Letters*, 333).

Sterne was able to do little else. On the third day after he had survived the crisis of his illness he was still so weak as to be unable to walk across the room and back without fatigue. Instead, he contemplated his portrait of Eliza: 'I have it *off by heart*—dear Girl—oh tis sweet! tis kind! tis affectionate! tis—thine my Bramine—I say my matins & Vespers to it—I quiet my Murmurs, by the Spirit which speaks in it—"all will end Well my Yorick"' (ibid.). The near-sacrilegious description suggests just how sick he was, yet it was to his obsession with Eliza that Sterne attributed his gradual recovery. After a night filled with dreams of her, Sterne awoke 'comforted & strengthend' sufficiently to visit Anne James, who sympathized with him fulsomely. The exertion required—both physical and emotional—was as much as he could stand, and he could only reach the street door, he said, with difficulty. When he eventually reached his Bond Street lodgings once more it was to spend the remainder of the day on the sofa—the prelude to a relapse which the following day had Sterne again anxious for his life.

So rapidly did his health fluctuate, however, that he was well enough on the next day to receive visitors. One day later still, on 1 May, he went to St James's Park where he encountered an old acquaintance—perhaps Lady Warkworth—whom he designated 'Sheba', and with whom he enjoyed an arch exchange of pleasantries based on their previous relationship:

> I thank'd Sheba, very kindly [for her enquiry after his health], but w^th^out any emotion but what sprung from gratitude—Love alas! was fled with thee Eliza!—I did not think Sheba could have changed so much in grace & beauty—Thou hadst shrunk <the good girl> poor Sheba away into Nothing,—but a good natured girl, with out powers or charms—I *fear* your Wife is dead, quoth Sheba——no, you don't *fear* it Sheba said I—Upon my Word Solomon! I would quarel with You, was you not so ill—If you knew the Cause of my Illness, Sheba, replied I, you w^d^ quarrel but the more with me—You lie, Solomon! answerd Sheba, for I know the Cause already—& am so little out of Charity with You upon it—That I give You leave to come & drink Tea with me before You leave Town—you're a good honest Creature Sheba—no! you Rascal, I am not—but I'm in Love, as much as you can be for y^r^ Life—I'm glad of it Sheba! said I—You Lie. said Sheba, & so canter'd away. (*Letters*, 335)

In the course of narrating a single incident Sterne had transformed himself from a pining invalid on the verge of death into the witty sentimentalist of the days before he knew Elizabeth Draper. Eliza's influence hangs over the whole scene, nevertheless, and Sterne used the encounter with Sheba to insist again on the single-mindedness of his passion for Eliza: 'O My Eliza, had I ever truely loved another (w^h^ I never did) Thou has long ago, cut the Root of all Affection in me—& planted & waterd & nourish'd it, <for> to bear fruit only for thyself' (ibid.).

If Sterne could, on occasion, write himself into health, the power of the pen was fallible. After his visit to the park, he spent two hours, from eight till ten, at Ranelagh and, perhaps unsurprisingly, returned home ill. The following day, fearing a further relapse, he sent for a doctor who confined him again to the sofa—no great hardship, for Sterne was unable to walk, stand, or sit upright without aggravating his condition. To add to his discomfort he continued to give strong evidence by his symptoms that he was suffering from a venereal ailment, and he was accordingly treated for such by his physician (on 5 May Sterne was dosing himself with 'l'*Extraite de* Saturne . . . (a french Nostrum)'). '[W]as I not conscious I had had no Commerce with the Sex these 15 Years,' Sterne wrote, 'I would decamp to morrow for Montpellier . . . where Maladies of this sort are better treated' (*Letters*, 336). Though he would not, of course, travel to the south of France to cure a malady he could not have, Sterne toyed with the idea of going abroad anyway, for the sake of the climate and the improvement it would work on his constitution. Such moments of optimism were few. Increasingly, he found himself incapable not merely of physical but even of mental exertion. An attempt to write a letter to Lord Shelburne failed when Sterne passed the evening instead lost in an imaginary re-creation of Eliza's journey to India, whose difficulties and dangers his imagination magnified to such an extent that Eliza's very survival seemed improbable. Only 'the hand of Providence' could protect her from the manifold perils of sea and climate.

Sunday, 3 May, brought a renewed crisis for Sterne. 'What can be the matter with me!' he exclaimed, 'Some thing is wrong, Eliza, in every part of me—I do not gain strength; nor have I the feelings of health returning back to me; even my best moments seem merely the efforts of my mind to get well again' (*Letters*, 337). The answer, Sterne reflected, was clear: he could not reconcile himself to the thought that he might never see Eliza again. In this frame of mind he determined he must get to Anne James in order to restore his tranquillity by conversation with his sentimental friend. When he arrived he was unable, he recorded in the journal, to say more than three words, 'thro' utter weakness of body & mind' (*Letters*, 338). On his return he could not climb the stairs to his rooms unaided. All the same, he was cheered by Anne James's suggestion that he might send a letter to Eliza overland, and although the post office refused to accept his letters he found a merchant willing, for the not-inconsiderable cost of 30 shillings, to take the letters to Aleppo and on to Bassorah (Basra), leading him to hope that Eliza might hear from him before Christmas.

Anne James's idea had a doubly beneficial effect on Sterne. First, the thought that it was not entirely impossible to contact Eliza made him less agitated, and secondly, it persuaded him to write to Eliza immediately, thereby dissuading him from going out. For two days he remained at home, writing to Eliza and seeing friends. On 6 May he dined out for the first time since the onset of this bout of illness, more than three weeks previously, although he declined to go to the concert at Carlisle House, arguing that he could enjoy at home 'a More harmonious evening' with Eliza than he could hope for at Soho with J. C. Bach. Even now Sterne was far from well. He continued 'poorly', and for three days recorded that he was 'unaccountably disorder'd'. Nonetheless, he was gradually reintegrating himself into normal social life. The knowledge that he intended to return to Yorkshire as soon as his health would permit him to travel led many of his contemporaries to invite Sterne to dine before he left. '*Man delights not me—nor Woman*' (*Letters*, 339), he wrote plaintively in the journal—but he accepted the invitations anyway.

Having recovered some degree of good health, Sterne became so quickly taken up with receiving and returning visits that his combined journal entries for a period of almost a fortnight—from 4 to 16 May—take up rather less space than the record of many single days earlier on. By 16 May his failure to write, despite the frequently reiterated protestations of his suffering while separated from Eliza, was so marked that Sterne excused his neglect by citing Eliza's behaviour as precedent, declaring that he was 'Taken up all day with worldly matters, <as> just as my Eliza was the week before her departure' (ibid.). In her absence he endeavoured to mollify Eliza by intimating that his conversation that day with Countess Spencer had centred wholly on Mrs Draper's many merits.

Little in the journal, however, so clearly proclaims Sterne's renewed health and interest in life as a brief letter he wrote that same day to Ignatius Sancho. Having established contact with Sancho, Sterne was now using him to garner subscriptions for *A Sentimental Journey*. He thanked him for adding the names of the duke and duchess of Montagu, and their son, but added that there was a further task he might perform, which was to drum them for their subscription money. To avoid keeping accounts—for which Sterne claimed to have little talent—and because of his ill health, he wished to be sure of having his money before leaving town. He had made plans to leave London, Sterne added in a postscript, but he would remain an extra day in order to dine with Lord and Lady Spencer.

With the gradual recovery of bodily health, the enjoyment Sterne derived from social engagements seemed to overcome his sense of deprivation caused by Eliza's absence. 'At Court', opens the entry for Sunday, 17 May, and while Sterne immediately added, 'every thing in this world seems in Masquerade, but thee dear Woman—and therefore I am sick of all the World [b]ut thee' (*Letters*, 341), the afterthought is decidedly unconvincing. Though he continued to present his experience in terms of how greatly he was missing Eliza—packing, for instance, is 'tormenting' because Molly speaks all the while of 'poor Mrs Draper— . . . how good a Lady!—How sweet a temper!—how beautiful!—how genteel! . . . She says however . . . tis Impossible not to be in Love with her——' (ibid.)—Sterne was quite prepared to alter the facts to present himself to Eliza to best advantage. The entries for 20 and 21 May are revealing:

> 20—Taking Leave of all the Town, before my departure tomorrow.
> 21. detaind by Lord & Lady Spence[r] who had made a party to dine & sup on my Acc^{t}.
>
> (*Letters*, 341)

Although Sterne insisted that he was 'Impatient to set out for my Solitude', he was rather less anxious to do so than he pretended, for he knew perfectly well on 20 May that he was not leaving the following day, having mentioned the engagement to Ignatius Sancho almost a week previously. Still, Sterne was returning to Coxwold, forsaking the social world with its 'few treacherous supports—the feign'd Compassion of one—the flattery of a second—the Civilities of a third—the friendship of a fourth—they all deceive', in favour of 'retirement, reflection & Books'—and, of course, thoughts of Eliza, Sterne's 'second self' (*Letters*, 342). A self-conscious leave-taking of the town in favour of rural retirement was scarcely an unfamiliar pose in the eighteenth century—although exceptional for Sterne—and he thought well enough of the passage in the journal to copy it immediately into a formal letter to the earl of Shelburne.[11] In a letter written to John Talbot Dillon on the morning of his departure spontaneity reasserted itself: 'my chaise stands at my door to take and convey this poor body to its legal settlement.—I am ill, very ill—I languish most affectingly—I am sick both soul and body—it is a cordial to me to hear it is different with you' (*Letters*, 344–5).

His journey home was neither difficult nor excessively long, yet Sterne bore it badly; he was, he declared, 'ill—and dispirited all the Way' (*Letters*, 346). 'What a Creature I am!', he wrote on the day of his departure. All week he had longed to be on his way; now he found himself 'ready to bleed' in leaving the place where he had met Eliza. The usual sentimentality of the journal gave way to a more robust and witty tone in a brief note to John Hall-Stevenson, in which Sterne presented himself travelling home in very different terms: 'I have got conveyed thus far,' he wrote from Newark on 25 May, 'like a bale of cadaverous goods consigned to Pluto and company—lying in the bottom of my chaise most of the rout, upon a large pillow which I had the *prevoyance* to purchase before I set out' (ibid.).

Yet beneath the humour there was a more serious note, commanding sympathy precisely because for once Sterne does not ask for it. 'I am worn out,' he wrote, 'but press on to Barnby Moor to night, and if possible to York the next.—I know not what is the matter with me—but some *derangement* presses hard upon this machine—still I think it will not be overset this bout' (ibid.). In an attempt to avoid any such overset, Sterne rested for two days at Brodsworth near Doncaster, family home of Archbishop Drummond. Not only was it an apostolic precept that bishops be given to hospitality, but Drummond, the son of an earl, had a private fortune which enabled him to entertain splendidly. Sterne recorded that he was 'kindly nursd & honourd', and he returned the hospitality of the archbishop, his wife, and his sister by showing them Eliza's portrait, and relating 'a short but interesting Story of my friendship for the Original' (ibid.). On the seventh day after leaving London Sterne finally arrived back at Coxwold.

15
Coxwold and London, 1767–1768

The journey from London to Coxwold took its toll. For two days Sterne was confined to bed, 'so emaciated, and unlike what I was' that he did not believe he would survive. '[A]dieu dear constant Girl—adieu—adieu,' he wrote, adding haltingly, 'Remember my Truth <31> to thee and eternal Fidelity—Remember <w> how I Love—remember What I suffer.' Sterne concluded a joint entry for 28 and 29 May by once more expressing his feeling that he owned Eliza: 'Thou art mine Eliza by Purchace—had I not earn'd thee with a better price.——' (*Letters*, 346–7).[1] For his venereal complaint too, Sterne was paying dear. Having suspended his cure in London after suffering from 'terrible Cholicks', he started again on a course of corrosive mercury: a 'deadly poyson, but given in <Kunastrokius> a certain preparation, not very dangerous' (*Letters*, 341). The deletion of 'Kunastrokius', an awkwardly intrusive allusion to the first volume of *Tristram Shandy*, suggests that Sterne had been consulting Dr Richard Mead's *A Mechanical Account of Poisons*, in an attempt to understand his prescribed course of treatment—though what he found there is unlikely to have reassured him.[2] Nor would Sterne accept his doctors' diagnosis, complaining that they 'have got it into their Nodelles, That mine is *an Ecclesiastick Rhum* as the french call it—god help em! I submit as my Uncle Toby did, in drinking Water, upon the wound he rec^{d} in his Groin—*Merely for quietness sake*' (*Letters*, 347).

Two days later, he received news that promised little quietness in the near future. A letter arrived from Lydia indicating that she and her mother intended to return to England for a while. Ostensibly undertaken for Sterne's benefit, the visit was not to be without strings. Sterne must promise not to detain them past the following April, after which they would return to France where both mother and daughter had decided to settle permanently. He agreed; Elizabeth and Lydia Sterne would take lodgings and stay from October to April. When they left again it would be 'for good and all', he surmised, adding 'Every thing for the best! Eliza' (ibid.).

Although this last phrase suggests that Sterne had not entirely abandoned the comforting fantasy that Eliza and he might one day marry, the journal entry continues in a more bitter vein, as he reflected on the motives behind his wife's decision to return home to see him. It would be a visit neither of friendship nor form, he wrote, but 'of pure Interest—to <get on> pillage What they can from me' (ibid.). Elizabeth Sterne had eyes on a small estate belonging to her husband worth £60 a year, which she intended to sell, investing the proceeds to give them a yearly income of £200, to be continued whichever of the three should live longest. 'I'm truely acquiescent,' Sterne wrote, 'tho' I lose the Contingency of surviving them—but 'tis no matter—I shall have enough—& a hundred or two hundred Pounds for Eliza when ever She will honour me with putting her hand into my Purse' (*Letters*, 348).

Throughout the entry Sterne displayed, by turns, self-pity, generosity, affection, and wild optimism: 'I am not sorry for this visit, as every Thing will be finally settled between us by it . . . & th[e]n, I will think Eliza, of living for myself & the Being I love as much!' (ibid.). The sense of imagined injury remained strong, however, with Sterne lamenting that he would be pillaged, during the visit of his wife and daughter, of 'a hundred small Items by them—wch I have a Spirit above saying, *no*-to; as Provisions of all sorts of Linnens—for house use—Body Use—printed Linnens for Gowns—Magazeens of Teas—Plate, (all I have (but 6 Silver Spoons)[)]—In short I shall be <pluck> pluck'd bare' (ibid.). Plucked bare, that is, of all but Eliza's portrait and her gifts to him, besides the furniture of his 'thatch'd Palace':

> and upon those I set up Stock again; Eliza what say You, Eliza! shall we join our *little Capitals together*?—will Mr Draper give us leave? he may safely—if y^{r} *Virtue* & Honour are only concerned,—'twould be safe in Yoricks hands, as in a Brothers—I w^{d} not wish Mr Draper to allow you above half I allow Mrs Sterne—Our Capital would be too great . . .' (ibid.)

As expressed in the journal for Eliza, the notion that Daniel Draper might agree to his wife's return to England, with an allowance, in order that she and Sterne might live together as brother and sister at Coxwold, only hints at the extent to which Sterne was living in an imaginary world of his own creation. When he came to repeat the idea in a draft letter to

Daniel Draper himself, it is evident than he had passed from consoling, private fantasy into the realm of blind self-delusion:

> Sir
>
> <It is out of th>
>
> <to> I own, it S^{r}, that the writing of a Letter to a gentleman I have not the honour to be known to, & <upon (wch Wh>—a Letter likewise upon no kind business (in the Ideas of the world) is a little out of the common course of Things—but I'm so myself—& the <reason of m> Impulse wch makes me <write> take up my pen—<is all of a piece> is out of <of> the Comon Way too—for [it] arises from the honest pain I should feel, in <avowing such an><having & cherishing so great an> so great esteem & friendship <for Mrs Draper> & Esteem as I bear <I have for your Lady—, for Mrs Drapers,> If I as I do for Mrs Draper,—<& not> If I did not wish & hope to extend it to <the Husban Partner I of her pleasures> Mr Draper also.—I <am> fell <really dear Sir> in Love with y^{r} Wife—but tis a Love, You would honour me for—for tis so like that I bear my own daughter who is a good creature, that I <can> scarse distinguish a difference betwixt it—The moment I had—<th> would have been <the last, I would—>
>
> that moment would have been the last <of my acq^{ce} with my friend (all-worthy as she is)—>
>
> I wish it had been in my power to have been of true use to Mrs Draper at this Distance from her best Protector——I have bestowed a great deal of pains (or rather I sh^{d} [say] pleasure) upon her head—her heart needs none—& her head as little as any Daughter of Eve's——I wish I could make myself of any Service to <her, M^{rs} D whilst I at this distance—> whilst She is in India—& I in the world—<and it would ill answer the purpose & Spirit of this Letter, if,>
>
> for worldly affairs, I could be of none—
>
> & indeed less, than any it has been my fate to converse wth for some years,—<such as my good fr—God preserve her!—>—I wish you dear Sir, many years happiness <with>
>
> —<I pray> Tis a part of my Litany, to pray <to heaven for> for what I fear she well her health & Life—& <I hope God.>—She is too good to be lost—& I would out [of] pure zeal to [take] a pilgrimage to Mecca to seek a <specifick> Medcine. (*Letters*, 349–50)

With its false starts and multiple emendations, this poignant letter reveals all too clearly Sterne's awareness—as the draft crumbles before him—of the absolute impossibility of formulating any such proposal in a remotely acceptable manner. Certainly no subsequent draft survives, and it is exceedingly improbable that the letter was ever sent.

As his fantasy faded, Sterne became increasingly concerned that Elizabeth Sterne's imminent arrival would place considerable restraints on his behaviour, allowing him less time for reveries of any kind. If he should be able to continue with his journal at all, he wrote, it would only be in snatches and by stealth—and he was already heartily wishing that the summer and winter were past. Encouraged by Sterne, his friends were sympathetic. 'You cannot conceive', he wrote, 'how much & how universally I'm pitied, upon the Score of this unexpected Visit from France—my friends think it will kill me' (*Letters*, 351).

With increasing frequency, he turned to the imagination, not merely as a source of consolation but as a refuge. It was indeed manifest for Sterne, as one of his favourite authors had written, 'what mighty Advantages Fiction has over Truth; and the Reason is just at our Elbow; because Imagination can build nobler Scenes, and produce more wonderful Revolutions than Fortune or Nature will be at Expence to furnish'.[3] Accordingly, Sterne sought solace in solitude, where thoughts of Eliza could transform an indifferent world into one sympathetic to his own feelings. The perspective would brighten up, Sterne wrote, and 'every Tree & Hill & Vale & Ruin abt me—smiles as if you was amidst 'em' (*Letters*, 352). Yet he was unable to sequester himself in this consoling landscape for long. If happiness was indeed, as Swift had written, 'the perpetual Possession of being well deceived',[4] then Sterne's inability to deceive himself perpetually left him a prey to moments of intense dejection. '[D]elusive moments!', he wrote of his periods of happiness, 'how pensive a price do I pay for you—fancy sustains the Vision, whilst She has strength—but Eliza! Eliza is not with me . . . I wak<ing>e from my delusion to a thousand Disquietudes, which many talk of—my Eliza!—but few feel' (ibid.). None of which prevented Sterne from imagining, while decorating a small apartment in his house on the following day, that he was preparing it for Eliza herself. He would continue to enrich the simple, elegant room, he wrote, until Fate would permit him the joy of leading Eliza into it. 'Oh my Eliza!', he exclaimed, 'I shall see thee surely Goddesse of this Temple,—and the most sovereign one, <of> of all I have—& of all the powers heaven has trusted me with' (ibid.).

The constant drive towards hyperbole and the generally high-flown flights of rhetoric in the journal might seem to make Sterne's reference to powers entrusted him by heaven merely one more instance of an inveterate tendency to invoke celestial metaphors when he had exhausted terrestrial ones—the Brahmine has become a goddess. Yet it would be misleading to think that his invoking of God was entirely devoid of genuine religious feeling. Repeatedly, in the course of the journal, the unhappy priest seeks divine consolation for his human miseries. Frequently the God who emerges from a reading of the journal bears a startling resemblance to the ideal sentimentalist—a celestial, omnipresent Anne James, ever ready to listen to Sterne's distresses and offer consolation. Yet the characterization of the deity as the man of feeling par excellence was not unique to Sterne in the eighteenth century—and he implies a real sense of himself in emotional extremity. 'I have but one small anchor, Eliza! to keep this weak Vessel of mine from perishing—I trust all I have to it—as I trust Heaven, which cannot leave me, without a fault, to perish.—may the same just Heaven my Eliza, be that eternal Canopy wch shall shelter th<ee>y head from evil *till we* meet' (*Letters*, 351). Appropriately enough, marine metaphors recur as Elizabeth Draper continued on her voyage (on 2 June Sterne calculated that after some two months she would have rounded the Cape of Good Hope): 'Thus—Thus my dear Bramine are we tost at present in this tempest—Some Haven of rest will open to us. assuredly—God made us not for Misery<!> and Ruin—he has orderd all our Steps—& influenced our <Love> Attachments for what is worthy of them—It must end well—Eliza!—' (*Letters*, 352). His trust in divine benevolence was doubtless sincere, but the Revd Laurence Sterne's substitution of 'Attachments' for 'Love' suggests a degree of doubt as to exactly how far he might attribute his devotion to Mrs Elizabeth Draper to God's will.

What is certain is the close connection between Sterne's physical and emotional well-being. At the end of the first week of June he described his rural life in terms of a pastoral idyll. Coxwold, he told a friend, was

> a land of plenty. I sit down alone to venison, fish and wild fowl, or a couple of fowls or ducks, with curds, and strawberries, and cream, and all the simple plenty which a rich valley under (Hambleton Hills) can produce—with a clean cloth on my table—and a bottle of wine on my right hand to drink your health. I have a hundred hens and chickens about my yard—and not a parishioner catches a hare, or a rabbet, or a trout, but he brings it as an offering to me. (*Letters*, 353)

Sterne was taking the air regularly in his post-chaise and declared that he felt better for the cure to which he had so reluctantly submitted in London: 'Begin to recover, and sensibly to gain strength every day—and have such an appetite as I have not had for some Years—I prophecy I shall be the better, for the very Accident which has occasiond my Illness, & that . . . I shall have more health and Strength, than I have enjoy'd these ten Years—' (*Letters*, 354).

In part, Sterne's renewed optimism was attributable to the more cheering of the fantasies in which he indulged himself. Instead of imagining the various perils to which Elizabeth Draper would be subject on her voyage to India, he mapped out a progress by which she would reach Bombay, obtain her husband's permission to return to England, set sail, and be back in England by September 1768. Sterne himself would not leave his rural retreat for London until March—'for what have I to do there, when (excepting printing my Books) I have no Interest or Passion to gratify' (*Letters*, 355)—returning to Yorkshire in June to await Eliza's arrival. Quite how seriously even Sterne himself took this romantic vision of an untroubled future is hard to judge, but he was certainly devoting himself in a practical manner to easing the way to share his life with Elizabeth Draper. He was trying to negotiate the sale of his estate, the profits of which would keep his wife and daughter in France and enable Sterne to 'purchace peace to myself—& a certainty of never having it interrupted by Mrs Sterne—who when She is sensible I have given her all I can part with—will be at rest herself' (ibid.). His wife's desire to turn the proceeds into French annuities, Sterne told himself, was the clearest possible indication of her intention to reside permanently abroad. The question of where his wife might settle continued to perturb him, nonetheless. Despite the reasonable contention of John Hall-Stevenson that it mattered little where she lived so long as husband and wife agreed to live apart, Sterne responded that though it was just the argument he would himself have used to anyone else, 'tis an Idea wch won't do so well for me' (ibid.). The English Channel and a fortune invested in French funds seemed to him surer barriers than any other to the unwelcome disturbance of his peace.

Against such pragmatic concerns Sterne set an imaginative world within which he immersed himself. 'I have return'd from a delicious Walk of Romance, my Bramine,' he wrote on 12 June,

> which I am to tread a thousand times over with You swinging upon my arm—tis to my Convent—& I have pluckd up a score Bryars by the roots wch grew <up> near the edge of the foot way, that they might not scratch or incommode you—had <you> I been sure<ty> of y^{r} <pass> taking that walk with me the very next day, I could not have been more serious in my employm^{t}—dear Enthusiasm! (*Letters*, 356)

The 'Convent' to which Sterne referred was his own description of the extensive ruins of Byland Abbey, which he transformed into a ghostly retreat peopled with the shadowy inhabitants of his own imagination.

While it is easy to think of the Convent as one more instance of

Sterne's surrendering to fantasy under the pressure of unwelcome realities, the creative nature of this enterprise led him away from solipsism to a social world. In elaborating his fantasy he began increasingly to present it to an audience. Nor was his imagined readership made up solely of Eliza. The fullest account of the Convent appears in a letter Sterne wrote, most probably in mid-June:

> I am just now return'd from one of my nightly visits; & tho' tis late, for I was detain'd there an hour longer than I was aware of, by the sad silence and breathlessness of the night, and the <delusio[n]> subject (for it was yourself) which took up the conversation—yet late as it is, I cannot go to bed without writing to you & telling you how much, and how many kind things we have been talking abou[t] you these two hours—Cordelia! said I as I lay half reclined upon her grave—long—long, has thy spirit triumphed over these infirmities, and all the contentions to w^{ch} <the> human hearts are subject—alas! thou hast had thy share—for she look'd <me th> I thought, down upon me with such a pleasurable sweetness—so like a delegated Angel whose breast glow'd with fire, that Cordelia could not have been a stranger to the passion on earth—poor, hapless Maid! cried I—Cordelia gently waved her head—it was enough—I turn'd the discourse to the object of my own disquietudes—I talk'd to her of <Lady ******> my Bramine: I told her how kindly nature had formd you—how gentle—how wise—how good—(*Letters*, 360)

The long letter in which this passage occurs was apparently sent to Elizabeth Draper. Earlier, however, Sterne had also sent a virtually identical letter to a noblewoman whom he addressed as Lady ****** or the Countess of ******. In redirecting it to Eliza, Sterne had merely added the inscription 'My dear Bramine', and substituted the same or similar terms in place of 'Countess', 'Lady ******', or 'My dear Lady'. What is most striking here is not simply that he should have repeated material from one letter in another, but that in the same month as he was expressing most pathetically the sense of loss he was experiencing through having been separated from Eliza, he was writing with interchangeable intimacy to another woman.

No wonder that the letter has been called 'the most compromising document that remains to us in Sterne's autograph'.[5] Certainly, if we assume that Sterne intended his protestations of love to be accepted with equal seriousness by both women, we can hardly do less than accept that he was flagrantly duplicitous. Reading the letter alongside the journal begs the question of how much—if any—of the latter work we can consider as the genuine effusion of real passion, or even infatuation. The question is not easily answered. When L. P. Curtis wrote that this letter is the most compromising document 'that remains to us', he was not indulging in innuendo but stating the literal truth. After Sterne's death his widow's brother-in-law, the Revd John Botham, went through the writer's papers, burning everything he did not think it proper that Elizabeth or Lydia Sterne should see. Lydia herself wrote of her mother's knowledge that there were found among the papers some 'which ought not to have been seen no not even by his Daughter' (*Letters*, 434). The papers, quite apart from any other value they might have had for our knowledge of Sterne, would almost certainly have allowed us to evaluate more accurately the letter in question.

Exactly in what fashion Sterne wrote to the numerous women with whom he enjoyed sentimental liaisons is something of which we know all too little. Yet there are elements in this letter which sound discordant in the context of the journal and which indicate an altogether more playful mood than that cultivated by the sentimentalist. '[P]ray when you first made a conquest of T. Shandy did it ever enter your head what a visionary, romantic, <did> kind of a Being you had got hold of? When <Lady ******> the Bramine sufferd so careless and laughing a Creature to enter her <roof>, did she dream of a man of Sentiments, and that, She was opening the door to such a one, to make him prisoner for Life' (*Letters*, 361). The self-characterization as Tristram is itself highly unusual in the journal, where Sterne prefers the guise of Yorick or the Brahmin, and suggests a reversion to a mood more familiar from the time before he met Eliza Draper—the time, that is, in which we may assume that he had met Lady ******. The concluding paragraph of the letter opens in a quite inappropriate manner for a missive intended for Eliza:

> now in answer to all this, why have I never rec^{d}—one gracious nod, <conveyed thro'> from You? why do you not write to me? is writing painful? or is it only so, to me? dear Lady write anything and write it any how, so it but comes from y^{r} heart, twil be better than the best Letter that ever came from Pope's head. (*Letters*, 362)

Such sentiments—the commonplaces of Sterne's exhortations to his correspondents on writing, emphasizing the importance of spontaneity—are markedly at odds with anything else he had written to Eliza since the earliest days of their friendship. This alone would seem to suggest that the letter was at first wholly directed to the Countess ******, who would have accepted the declarations of passion as the inspiration of whimsy and not of love, as Sterne had intended.

Most likely it was the success of the pathetic set-piece, the Cordelia episode, that led Sterne to readdress the letter to Eliza, regardless of the unsuitability of much of the remainder of it to her situation. Sterne frequently used extracts from the journal in writing to other correspondents. The fact that he repeated material need not be taken here as deviousness but as a common trait among letter-writers. Nor is such a supposition at odds with his own stress on spontaneity, for he admits in the journal itself that his writing is far from being uncrafted. Sterne consoled himself in Eliza's absence not only by writing the journal but also by regularly rereading it. He was certainly given to incorporating passages from the journal in subsequent letters, and was still rereading it as late as February 1768, for in a letter written then he quotes a substantial passage from his entry for 13 June 1767. Such copying or reworking was natural enough to the writer, and if any duplicity was involved in the central case, it was in assuming that Eliza would take literally the sentiment he had originally intended playfully for Lady ******.

Whatever the truth, the success of this small creative act enabled Sterne to set about a more ambitious task: the writing of *A Sentimental Journey*. The seeds of his final work had been long germinating in his mind. As early as the autumn of 1762 he had written to John Hall-Stevenson from France that he had 'many hints and projects for other works' besides *Tristram Shandy* (*Letters*, 186). Since he was not more specific, it may well be that there was a hint of bravado here on Sterne's part, for the fifth and sixth volumes of his novel were not selling well and he was anxious to reassure himself that waning public demand for one book would not spell the end of his success as a writer. From the outset, however, he had evidently considered some kind of travel work as part of his future plans. It is perhaps significant that when he first approached Robert Dodsley back in 1759 two of the works he mentioned in his letter were Voltaire's *Candide* and Samuel Johnson's *Rasselas*, both unconventional works of fictional travel. In volume I of *Tristram Shandy*, the narrator makes mentions of his tour abroad as tutor to the son of Mr Noddy in 1741—though disappointingly Sterne did not finally follow up this particular hint. A plan, considered in 1763, to send his hero to Spain also came to nothing, but Sterne's own experience of travel in France between 1762 and 1764 provided the basis of volume VII of *Tristram Shandy*. It was the critical reception—or part of it—to this volume which, more than anything, seems to have focused his mind on the idea of his travel book. In the

Monthly Review, it will be remembered, Ralph Griffiths had written: 'Admirable!—Mr. Shandy, you understand the art, the true art of travelling, better than any other mortal I ever knew or heard of!'[6] Such encouragement, reinforced by his second experience of continental travel in 1765–6, made up his mind. By the end of July 1766 he was declaring that 'Never man . . . has had a more agreeable tour than your Yorick', and indicating that he would write only one volume of *Tristram Shandy* that year before turning to a new work in four volumes.

Despite extreme ill-health and mental dejection, Sterne took the writing of *A Sentimental Journey* very seriously. He had both a title and a plan for the book by the beginning of 1767, though his emotional involvement with Eliza led him to defer its writing. In February 1767 he had told his daughter that 'I shall not begin my Sentimental Journey till I get to Coxwould—I have laid a plan for something new, quite out of the beaten track' (*Letters*, 301). Commencing in June, he was 'beginning to be truly busy' at the work in early July. What had coloured his original plan for the work was his relationship with Eliza. In mid-June he was working on the first section of the new book and, as he wrote, immortalizing there the miniature portrait of Eliza she had presented to him before she left for India. The significance he attached to the early inclusion in *A Sentimental Journey* of Eliza and the portrait is evident from an extended and prescient passage in the journal for 17 June:

> I have brought y^{r} name *Eliza*! and Picture into my work—where they will remain—when You & I are at rest for ever—Some Annotator or explainer of my works in this place will take occasion, to speak of the Friendship wch Subsisted so long & faithfully betwixt <the> Yorick & the Lady he speaks of—Her Name he will tell the world was Draper—<a b> a Native of India—married there to a gentleman in the India Service of that Name—, who brought her over to England for the recovery of her health in the Year 65—where She continued to April the year 1767. It was ab^{t} three months before her Return to <Bombay> India, That our Author's acquaintance & hers began. <with her> Mrs Draper <She> had a great Thirst for Knowledge—<She>—was handsome—<gentle> genteel—engaging—and of such gentle dispositions & so enlightend an understanding,—That Yorick, (whether he made much Opposition is not known) from an acquaintance—soon became her Admirer—<her partiality to him, so> they caught fire, at each other at the same time—& they w^{d} often say, <their Affection> without reserve to the world, & without any Idea of saying wrong<,> in it, That their Affections for each other were *unbounded*—<except by a

> ... of honour & Virtue>—M[r] Draper dying in the Year xxxxx—This Lady return'd to England, & Yorick the Year after becoming a Widower—They were married—& retiring to <his preferment> one of his Livings in Yorkshire, where was a most romantic Situation—they lived & died happily.—and are spoke of with honour in the parish to this day—— (*Letters*, 358–9)

This romance-like evocation of their relationship acted powerfully on Sterne. Increasingly, he would become intent less on transcribing his feelings than on fictionalizing them. That he retained some hopes that Eliza really would return to England, and that the death of their respective spouses would free them to marry, is not impossible. He was distinctly conscious, however, that he was no longer writing either from a sense of imperfectly controlled fantasy or to encourage Eliza. He was writing a kind of fiction, and he knew it. 'How do you like the <?account> History, of this couple, Eliza?—is it to your mind?—or shall it be written better some sentimental Evening after your return—tis a rough Sketch—but I could make it a pretty picture, as the outlines are just—we'll put our heads together & tr<ie>y what we can do' (*Letters*, 359). The very substitution of the more neutral 'account' by the consciously literary 'History' suggests Sterne's conception of what he has written, but he goes on directly to acknowledge that the version of the story he has committed to paper makes it impossible for him to send it to Eliza (as he had promised), though he would retain it for her return: 'This last Sheet has put it out of my power, ever to send you this Journal to India ... If I can write a Letter—I will—but this Journal must be put into Eliza's hands by Yorick only' (ibid.).

Sterne's readjustment of his relationship with Eliza coincided with—and was probably the result of—a marked improvement in his health. On 19 June he declared that 'I never was so well and alert, as I find myself this day ... you never saw me so Young by 5 Years' (*Letters*, 363). Now he faced his wife's return with much greater equanimity than had previously been at his command, marvelling at her readiness to travel a thousand miles in either direction, from ill will, not good, 'to see how I do, <—> & whether I am fat or lean'. He was even ready to wish his wife already at Coxwold, if only that 'She might the sooner depart in peace' (ibid.). The ambiguity of this last phrase was far from playful, for Elizabeth Sterne was ill herself. To travel from southern France to Yorkshire was not likely to improve her condition, but Lydia reported that she was determined to visit her husband at Coxwold. Now, recalling his wife's earlier proposal not to leave

France until she felt herself near to death, Sterne tastelessly committed to writing a barely concealed hope: 'surely this journey is not prophetick!' (ibid.).

Such speculations did not, however, detain him long, for he was ready to pay a visit himself—to Hall-Stevenson at Crazy Castle, where he intended to stay for ten days. He had left off his medicines and felt, he said, perfectly well. Leaving Coxwold on 22 June, and stopping at York that night, Sterne reached Skelton the following day. He took with him on his visit both *A Sentimental Journey* and his journal. The visit passed in a 'course of continual visits & Invitations' (*Letters*, 364). Sterne now displayed Eliza's portrait whenever an opportunity arose, and was gratified, while dining with a large party the following day, to find it 'highly admired' (*Letters*, 365). Not all of the visitors were perfectly adapted to his current frame of mind, however. The visit for dinner of Peter Lascelles—'Bombay Lascelles'—recently retired from his position as a naval captain with the East India Company, produced the exasperated reflection from Sterne: 'What a stupid, selfish, unsentimental set of Beings are the Bulk of our Sex! by Heaven! not one man out of 50, informd <either> with feelings—or endow'd either with heads or hearts able to possess & fill the mind <of . . . . > of such a Being as thee, with one Vibration like its own' (*Letters*, 364–5). Though Sterne made no mention of it at the time, Peter Lascelles had earned his displeasure by more than mere failure to respond with the requisite degree of enthusiasm when Eliza was brought into the conversation. Rather, Lascelles—probably responding to Sterne's request for first-hand information about the Drapers in Bombay—had told him something he had rather not have heard. What exactly this was—even whether it related to Daniel Draper or to Eliza herself—remains a matter of conjecture, but it was to perturb an anxious and easily jealous Sterne for many weeks. Yet, however 'unsentimental' he found Lascelles the encounter was not altogether fruitless for, putting his dislike aside, the ever-pragmatic Sterne successfully solicited a subscription from him for *A Sentimental Journey*.

In the end, though, Sterne's visit to Crazy Castle was less successful than he had hoped. Two days after his arrival 'company and dissipation' had combined to determine him to cut short his visit and return home after a week instead of ten days. He slept badly, dreaming that Eliza was a widow but that she married the captain of her ship. He awoke in a fever, and was ill the following day. That morning he wrote that he was set on riding himself into better health 'and better fancies'. Along with Hall-Stevenson he took his chaise to the beach at Saltburn-by-the-Sea, where 'we dayly run races in our Chaises, with one wheel in the Sea, & the other <i> on the Sand' (*Letters*, 366). It was not enough, and the next day Sterne returned to Coxwold. 'O 'tis a delicious retreat! both from its beauty, & air of Solitude; & so sweetly does every thing ab^{t} it invite y^{r} mind <of> to rest from its Labours—and be at peace with itself & the world—That tis the only place, Eliza, I could live in at this juncture' (*Letters*, 366–7).

Sterne's moods still fluctuated rapidly. On his first day back in Coxwold he imagined Eliza inhabiting his cottage with him; on the second he tormented himself by imagining that Daniel Draper's behaviour to his wife would be so different from what she had previously experienced that she would not return to England at all. Convinced once more that Eliza would come back, Sterne dwelt instead on the time that must elapse before they were reunited: 'the Space between is a dismal Void—full of doubts, & suspence' (*Letters*, 368). It was now the end of June, just three days short of three months since the *Earl of Chatham* had sailed for India. 'I have got over this Month—so fare wel to it, & the Sorrows it has brought with it,' Sterne wrote, adding gloomily, 'the next month, I prophecy will be worse—' (ibid.).

'But who can foretell what a month may produce—Eliza' (*Letters*, 370). The opening words of the entry for the following day show Sterne expressing an optimism wholly at odds from the lugubriousness of the preceding entry. The contrast is so abrupt that we might question whether a concern for literary effect was not overcoming any desire on Sterne's part simply to record his changing moods. The entry, however, continues in a manner which again suggests his emotional heights and troughs to be closely related to his physical well-being. 'I am perfectly recoverd,' he enthused, 'or more than recover'd—for never did I feel such Indications of health <and . . . > or Strength & promptness of mind' (*Letters*, 371).

Even the impending visit of his wife hung less heavily over his head than hitherto, not least because Hall-Stevenson had persuaded him to allow Elizabeth no more than £1,500 to be invested in the French funds to produce £150 annually, the residue for her needs coming directly from Sterne himself. It was the uncertain date of his wife's arrival that most perturbed him. 'Hear nothing of her,' he recorded on 4 July, 'so am tortured from post to post, for I want to know certainly *the day &* <our> hour of this Judgment' (*Letters*, 372). He was, he continued, 'pitied by every Soul, in proportion as her Character is detested—& her Errand known—She is coming, every one says, to flea poor Yorick or slay him—& I am spirited up by every friend I have to sell my Life dear, & fight valiantly in defence both of my property & Life' (*Letters*, 373).

The characterization of Elizabeth Sterne is harsh, but the sympathy his friends and acquaintances had for her husband seems genuine enough, and by no means merely a polite response to his own complaints. When Alessandro Verri learned of Sterne's death, he wrote regarding Elizabeth and Lydia that 'mi dicono che sono due vere diavole inquiete e maldicenti' ('I'm told they are two really restless malicious devils').[7] The judgement is severe, especially on Lydia, but so widely unpopular was Elizabeth Sterne that when, after her husband's death, a collection of more than £700 was made, the sum was directed solely towards the author's daughter rather than his widow. Elizabeth Montagu wrote to her sister that Ann Morritt of York, who organized the collection, 'had promised the Subscribers it should be converted into an annuity for the girl for . . . Mrs. Sterne was so little loved or esteemed there would not have been a single guinea given if that condition had not been made'.[8]

However little affection Sterne retained for his wife, he was not inclined to be vindictive. 'Now my Maxim, Eliza, is quietly in three [words]—"Spare my Life, & take all I have"'. If this would not suffice, he continued, there could be no living in the same country with her, and 'If she will not betake herself to France—I will' (ibid.). But such thoughts, he continued, were no more than his fears, for he believed that Elizabeth would be as impatient to leave England as he would be to see her go. When he discovered from Lydia that no letter of his had reached his wife and daughter in France, Sterne was dismayed. 'This gives me concern,' he confessed, 'because it has the Aspect of an unseasonable unkindness in me—to take no notice of what has the appearance at least of a Civility in desiring to pay me a Visit' (ibid.). Besides, he continued, Lydia had done nothing to deserve ill of him and 'tho' her mother has, I w^{d} not ungenerously take that Opportunity, which would most overwhelm her, to give any mark of my resentment'. 'I have besides,' he added, somewhat contradictorily, 'long since forgiven her' (ibid.). Forced as it appears, Sterne's tolerance was helped by his wife's renewed promise that she would settle permanently in the south of France; as a result he wrote a letter of 'Consolation & good will', encouraging her to leave immediately so as to reach York in time for the races in mid-August.

Having done his duty to wife and daughter, Sterne could now consult his own desires. He indulged himself anew in his fantasy of life with Eliza in Coxwold: '[E]re every thing is ripe for <*wishes* > our Drama,—<will> I shall work hard <for> to fit out & decorate a little Theatre for us to act on—but not before a crouded house—no Eliza—it shall be as secluded as the elysian fields—retirement is the nurse of Love and kindness' (*Letters*,

374). This seems still to have been a genuine enough sentiment, for Sterne recorded that though he had received half-a-dozen letters pressing him to join friends at Scarborough, he had, he said, 'found pretences not to quit You *here*—and sacrifice the many sweet Occasions I have of giving my thoughts up to <thee> You' (ibid.). Whether or not he exaggerated the amount of time he passed in thinking of Eliza, he attributed his failure to write an even more extensive journal to his other pressing concerns: 'a Book to write—a Wife to receive & <live> make Treaties with—an estate to sell—a Parish to superintend—and a disquieted heart <to> perpetually to reason with, are <an> eternal calls upon me' (*Letters*, 376). This passage, it must be said, is taken virtually verbatim from a letter written a week earlier to a friend, when the calls were adduced as reasons for not joining his friends in Scarborough.

Eliza apart, Sterne's days were indeed well filled during the final summer of his life. His preoccupation with the anticipated arrival of his wife and daughter is certain. The estate had to be sold by then, and he was evidently keen to obtain the best possible price (he had received an offer of £2,000 for it on 4 July). Parish business, though he made little mention of it, remained a continual call on his time—and the very fact that we hear nothing of Sterne's failure to fulfill his pastoral obligations is the surest sign that he did not neglect them. If all this were insufficient, Sterne was also busy composing.

Having begun work on the first pages of *A Sentimental Journey* in mid-June, he was now writing steadily. 'Hail, Hail! my dear Eliza,' he began the entry in his journal for 3 July, 'I steal something every day from my sentimental Journey—to obey a more sentimental imp<luse>ulse <to> in writing to you' (*Letters*, 372). The following day, he recorded: '—get on slowly with my Work—but my head is too full of other Matters—yet I will finish it before I see London—for I am of too scrupulous honour to break faith with the world—great Authors make no scruple of it—but if they are great Authors—I'm sure they are little Men' (*Letters*, 373). When he wrote a letter to Commodore and Mrs James on 6 July, he told them: 'I am now beginning to be truly busy at my Sentimental Journey—the pains and sorrows of this life having retarded its progress—but I shall make up my lee-way, and overtake every body in a very short time' (*Letters*, 375).

For almost two months Sterne revealed little about his progress, though he encouraged his publisher, Thomas Becket, by revealing that 'some Genius[e]s in the North declare it an Original work, and likely to take in all Kinds of Readers,' adding only, 'the proof of the pudding is in the eating' (*Letters*, 393). At the request of friends, he began to allow repeated sampling, and took the manuscript of his work with him when he went to spend ten days at Scarborough in the second half of September. The Irish novelist Richard Griffith read or heard it there, and subsequently wrote to his wife and fellow-novelist Elizabeth that Sterne:

> has communicated a Manuscript to us, that he means soon to publish. It is stiled a Sentimental Journey through Europe, by Yoric. It has all the Humour and Address of the best Parts of Tristram, and is quite free from the Grossness of the worst. There is but about Half a Volume wrote of it yet. He promises to spin the Idea through several Volumes, in the same chaste Way, and calls it his *Work of Redemption*.[9]

Though slower than he had hoped, progress was sustained, for Sterne was determined to finish a publishable section of the book before he visited London. By 15 November, he was 'fabricating at a great rate' (*Letters*, 401); four days later he wrote to a friend that, 'I am in earnest at my sentimental work' (*Letters*, 402). The physical as well as mental effort was enormous. Nine days later he complained that he had 'worn out both his spirits and body with the Sentimental Journey—'tis true that an author must feel himself, or his reader will not—but I have torn my whole frame into pieces by my feelings—I believe the brain stands as much in need of recruiting as the body' (*Letters*, 402). The level of emotional intensity at which Sterne was living during these months is suggested by his response to reading an autobiographical manuscript by Richard Griffith, who told his wife that Sterne 'actually dropped Tears as he went on'.[10] Eventually forced to abandon his plan to be in London by Christmas, Sterne nevertheless completed two volumes by then, allowing him to leave almost immediately, arriving in the capital on the first day of 1768.

All through the summer, while Sterne had struggled with *A Sentimental Journey*, he continued to describe in his journal the physical and emotional details of his daily life. He was, he told Eliza, 'as melancholly & sad as a Cat; for want of you', adding that he had himself such a cat, which sat beside him through the day, purring to his sorrows, '& looking up gravely from time to time in my face, as if she knew my Situation' (*Letters*, 376–7). (However much this owes to invention, it cannot escape notice that the sympathetic cat later changes sex: 'I sit here alone as solitary and sad as a tom cat, which by the bye is all the company I keep' (*Letters*, 390).) Sterne reflected ruefully, 'poor Yorick! to be driven, wth all his sensibilities, to these resources' (*Letters*, 377). His other means of coping with his loneliness were more familiar. Having arranged his cottage with Eliza in mind, he turned his attention to the garden, where he was making a 'sweet' pavilion in a retired corner. He continued to imagine where, exactly, Elizabeth Draper might be on her voyage to India. At the end of June he allowed her a further month at sea before arriving at Madras. By 10 July he wrote that he could no longer suffer her to be on the water, and decreed that 'in 10 days time [he had first written '5' and then struck it out], You shall be at Madrass . . . on the 20th therefore Ins^{t} I begin to write to you as a Terrestrial Being'. Tellingly, he added, 'I must deceive myself' (*Letters*, 377). In fact Sterne's self-deception concerned more than Eliza's whereabouts, for in the same entry of 10 July he uneasily revealed that there had been more than he had earlier acknowledged to account for his evident dislike of Peter Lascelles. He sought solace in his by now habitual refuge: 'I have just kissed y^{r} picture, even that sooths many an anxiety' (ibid.).

In truth, Sterne had anxieties enough. 'I'm pierced with the Ingratitude and <unfeeling «disapp»> unquiet Spirit of a restless unreasonable Wife whom neither gentleness or generosity can conquer', he recorded angrily on 11 July. Elizabeth Sterne had been 'waging War with me, a thousand miles off', Sterne continued, bombarding him with letters as often as three times a week during the previous month. 'I have offer'd to give her every Shilling I was worth, except my preferment,' Sterne wrote in exasperation, 'to be let alone <to die> & left in peace by her' (*Letters*, 378). Even noting the barely controlled self-pity of Sterne's first thoughts, it appears that Elizabeth Sterne was indeed becoming importunate, doubtless sensing and being wounded by Sterne's neglect and evident desire to be rid of her. She gave her husband to understand that she would insist on an additional £400 before she would agree to settle permanently in France. 'Gods will be done,' wrote Sterne resignedly, 'but I think she will send me to my grave'. In addition to her increased demand Elizabeth Sterne had deferred her visit for a further two months, much to his annoyance; 'it keeps me in eternal Suspence all the while—for she will come unawars at last upon me—& then adieu to the dear sweets of my retirement' (ibid.).

In fact retirement was not doing Sterne the good he had imagined, and recording in the journal his anger at his wife's demands exacerbated rather than relieved his distress. He could not 'eat or drink or sit still & write or read', he lamented, but would only walk 'like a disturbed Spirit' in his garden. Sterne's friends were concerned for him. He received repeated invitations to escape his melancholy by joining in company, and when Hall-Stevenson sent over to Coxwold on purpose to fetch him he finally gave in.

No amount of company, however brilliant, could entirely deflect

Sterne's thoughts from Eliza. Indeed, if we believe the journal, he habitually made the absent Eliza the focus of conversation. 'Your picture has gone round the Table after supper', Sterne wrote, adding that even the ladies present, 'who hate grace in another, seemd struck with it in You' (*Letters*, 379). So pleased was he with the reception of her portrait that he enthused: 'I verily think my Eliza I shall get this Picture set, so as to wear it, as I first proposed—ab^{t} my neck—I do not like the place tis in—it shall be nearer my heart' (*Letters*, 379–80). It is indeed around Yorick's neck that Eliza's portrait appears in *A Sentimental Journey*.

The congruence of Sterne's journal and his new fiction—both written in the guise of Yorick—suggests that, however it began, the journal can only be accepted as an accurate record of Sterne's life with extreme reservations. In the very effective juxtaposition of entries for separate days Sterne reveals the altogether superior artistic control over his material of which he was capable once restored to better health. Increasingly, there are signs of him writing not merely for others besides Eliza, but even for an audience such as would have relished *Tristram Shandy* above *A Sentimental Journey*. Having charmed Elizabeth Turner with the miniature of Eliza, Sterne continued: 'O my dear Lady, cried I, did you but know the Original—but what is she to you, Tristram—nothing; but that I am in love with her—et ceetera——said She—no I have given over dashes—replied I——' (*Letters*, 379).

When he left Crazy Castle Sterne brought John Hall-Stevenson home with him to Coxwold. They stayed barely long enough for Sterne to note with satisfaction Hall-Stevenson's admiration of the improvements he had made, before leaving for Harrogate. On the way the pair broke their journey to pass the day with the archbishop of York—'this good Prelate, who is one of our most refined Wits—& the most of a gentleman of our order', Sterne wrote, apparently with an eye on the eventual publication of the journal. Certainly this estimate of Drummond, emphasizing the archbishop's urbanity and wit at the expense of more spiritual qualities, is very much in line with Drummond's own sense of values (he once reproved an enthusiastic evangelical, the Revd Richard Conyers, with the startling admonition that 'Were you to inculcate the morality of Socrates, it would do more good than canting about the new birth').[11] At all events, Sterne and Hall-Stevenson surely enjoyed themselves, for the archbishop's table was noted for 'champagne wit, and champagne wine'.[12] Sterne went on to record that the archbishop told him he loved him and had a high value for him, and 'such an Opinion of my head & heart that he begs to stand Godfather for my next Literary production' (*Letters*, 380). Sterne was delighted and promptly added Drummond's name to the list of subscribers to *A Sentimental Journey*.

Sterne remained at Harrogate Spa, drinking the waters for a week—'to no effect'—and comparing the women there unfavourably with Eliza.[13] However this may be, it is notable that he made only one entry in the journal during his entire stay—the first time he had failed to write for so long a period since he had begun the diary back in April. Even the single entry concludes in a way more reminiscent of *A Sentimental Journey*—its ostensible sensibility ironically qualified by incongruous juxtaposition than the earlier journal entries: 'I Love thee Eliza, more than the heart of Man ever loved Woman's—I even love thee more than I did, the day thou badest me farewel!—Farewell!—Farewell! to thee again—I'm going from hence to York. Races—' (*Letters*, 381). If the bathos of Sterne's epistolary leave-taking suggests that the combination of better health, plentiful diversion, and lengthening absence had enabled him to achieve a degree of detachment from Eliza, then such detachment was not to last for long. When he reached York on 27 July he found packets of letters from Eliza, which had just arrived from São Tiago in the Cape Verde islands which the *Earl of Chatham* had reached as long ago as 2 May. Immediately shutting himself in his bedchamber, Sterne ordered that he be denied to all visitors, and spent the evening and the following day until dinner reading and rereading Eliza's journal. 'I read & wept—and wept and read till I was blind—then grew sick, & went to bed—& in an hour calld again for the Candle—to read it once more'. The account, Sterne wrote, was 'most interesting . . . the most endearing one, that ever tried the tenderness of man . . . as for my dear Girls pains & her dangers I cannot write ab^{t} them—because I cannot write my feelings or express them any how to my mind . . .' *Ill love thee for the dangers thou hast past*' (ibid.). Eliza had not, in fact, found herself either among the anthropophagi or men whose heads did grow beneath their shoulders—though she petulantly described the island of São Tiago as 'the vilest Spot of earth I ever saw & inhabited by the ugliest of Beings'[14]—and Sterne's allusion to dangers referred to the illness from which she had suffered in the Cape Verde islands. Her illness apart, Elizabeth Draper could scarcely have hoped for a better voyage: it had been 'a Charming passage', she wrote to her cousin Thomas Limbrey Sclater, 'fair winds and fine Weather all the way.—Health too, my friend, is once more return'd to her enthusiastic Votary. I am all life and air and spirits—who'd have thought it . . . ?'[15] Not, certainly, Laurence Sterne, who now received another letter from Eliza—dated eighteen days after the previous one—in which she gave him further details of her ill health, which he passed on to Anne James: 'continual & most violent rhumatism all the time—a fever brought on with fits—and attended with Delirium: & every terrifying symptome—the recovery from this <left> has left her low—and emaciated to a Skeleton' (*Letters*, 388). Only in the last three or four days' entries did Elizabeth Draper record some improvement in her health, at last giving her admirer modest grounds for optimism about the outcome of her illness.

Following the receipt of her letters, Sterne was immediately thrown back into total absorption with Eliza. 'I now want to have this week of nonsensical Festivity over,' he wrote, 'that I may get back, with thy picture wch I ever carry ab^{t} me—to my retreat and to Cordelia' (*Letters*, 382). Cordelia's sudden reappearance in the journal—for the first time in several weeks—suggests how much Sterne was moved by hearing from Eliza again. 'O my Eliza!', Sterne enthused, 'thou writest to me with an Angels pen—& thou wouldst win me by thy Letters, had I never seen thy face, <&> or known thy heart' (*Letters*, 384). Nor was his sense of irritation at York Race Week a mere affectation, for he returned home to Coxwold on the fifth day after arriving at York. Once there he reread Eliza's letters repeatedly and felt 'a sympathy above Tears—I trembled every Nerve as I went from line to line—& every moment the Acc^{t} comes across me—I suffer all I felt, over & over again' (ibid.).

Sterne was not helped by his wife's continuing demands. Elizabeth Sterne—'& I wish I could not add my Daughter (for she has debauch'd her Affections)', he wrote, before deleting the comment on Lydia—was using him 'most unmercifully' (ibid.). His friends advised him to fly from her, but where, he asked reasonably enough, could he go? The bishop of Cork and Ross, Dr Jemmett Browne, suggested Ireland and offered him a place in his diocese. Though grateful, Sterne was not convinced. The bishop, he wrote, 'is the best of feeling tender hearted men—knows our Story—sends You his Blessing—and says if the Ship you return in touches at Cork (wch many India men do)—he will take you to his palace, till he can send for me to join You—he only hopes, he says, to join us together for ever' (ibid.).

If Sterne was anxious to leave his present home, he was certainly not without offers of livings elsewhere. The day after recounting the kindness of Jemmett Browne, he told Eliza that he had the offer of exchanging two Yorkshire preferments for a living in Surrey worth £350 a year, but added 'if a Mitre was offer'd me, I would not have it, till I could have thee too, to make it sit easy upon my brow' (*Letters*, 386). A less fanciful worry for Sterne than whether he should accept a bishopric was the arrival of his wife. He could think of nothing else and, he added, 'at present all I can write would be but the History of my miserable feelings' (*Letters*, 387).[16] His bitterness at what he construed as Elizabeth Sterne's depredations filters through even into a letter he wrote in mid-August to Anne James, to whom he ordinarily wrote most sentimentally. 'Here's Complaisance for you,' he declared,

> I went 500 Miles the last Spring, out of my Way, to pay my Wife a weeks Visit—and she is at the expence of coming post a thousand miles to return it—What a happy pair!—however, *en passant*, She takes back sixteen hundred p^{ds} into france with her——and will do me the honour, <every thing> likewise to strip me of every thing I have—
>
> —except Eliza's Picture. (*Letters*, 389)

Despite this characteristically pathetic self-portrait, Sterne was writing the following day in his witty, whimsical style to John Hall-Stevenson. He had been unable to stir abroad except on foot for a week, he revealed, after his postillion had suffered an accident when a pistol exploded in his hand. The postillion, immediately assuming his whole hand to be lost, 'instantly fell upon his knees and said (Our Father, which art in Heaven, hallowed be thy Name) at which, like a good Christian, he stopped, not remembering any more of it—the affair was not so bad as he at first thought, for it had only *bursten* two of his fingers (he says)' (*Letters*, 390). Here the lighter tone of the letter reflects not only the fact that it recounts the misfortunes of someone other than himself, but also a fresh improvement in Sterne's health. 'I never have been so well since I left college,' he wrote, 'and should be a marvellous happy man, but for some reflections which bow down my spirits—but if I live but even three or four years, I will acquit myself with honour' (ibid.). As so often before, though, the improvement in Sterne's health was short-lived; within ten days he was again feeling ill and, what was worse, spitting blood.[17]

The reflections that bowed down Sterne's spirits perhaps concerned his behaviour towards Elizabeth, for he wrote in a notably conciliatory fashion to Lydia on 24 August. When his wife and daughter arrived in England, Sterne told them, 'I will shew you more real politesses than any you have met with in France, as mine will come warm from the heart' (*Letters*, 391). Elizabeth and Lydia Sterne had in fact been enjoying the *fêtes champêtres* given by the marquis de Sade. Though having little in common with de Sade's later activities, except a decidedly perverse sense of humour, the entertainments were exotic enough by English provincial standards for Lydia to detail the marquis's hospitality at some length. Sterne replied, as he was doubtless expected to, with some shock:

> The follying of staying 'till after twelve for supper—that you two excommunicated beings might have meat!—'his conscience would not let it be served before.'—Surely the Marquis thought you both, being English, could not be satisfied without it.—I would have given not my gown and cassock (for I have but one) but my topaz ring to have seen the *petits maitres et maitresses* go to mass, after having spent the night in dancing. (*Letters*, 391)

Perhaps fearful of the extent to which his wife and daughter had been corrupted by French customs, Sterne assumed an authority scarcely warranted by his long neglect of them: 'Another thing I must desire—do not be alarmed—'tis to throw all your rouge pots into the Sorgue before you set out—I will have no rouge put on in England' (*Letters*, 391–2). As compensation, Sterne encouraged both Lydia and her mother to take the chance to buy whatever they wanted during their stop in Paris: 'tis an occasion not to be lost.' They must also write to him from Paris, so that 'I may come and meet you in my post-chaise with my long-tailed horses', Sterne insisted, adding, 'and the moment you have both put your feet in it, call it hereafter yours' (ibid.)—having apparently forgotten that he had earlier promised the same post-chaise to Eliza.[18]

If the reflections that bowed down his spirits concerned rather his relations with women other than his wife, then two letters written in September 1767 throw some light on the subject. The first, to a woman addressed solely as Hannah, reveals Sterne at his most facetious—the letter is very much the product of Tristram rather than Yorick:

> Ever since my dear H[annah] wrote me word she was mine, more than ever woman was, I have been racking my memory to inform me where it was that you and I had that affair together . . . Now I cannot recollect where it was, nor exactly when—it could not be the lady in Bond-street, or Grovesnor-street, or —— Square, or Pall-mall.—We shall make it out, H[annah] when we meet—I impatiently long for it. (*Letters*, 393)

Whether Sterne's uncertainty was genuine or merely feigned, his reputation as a man of affairs seems considerably to have exceeded the facts. 'People think I have had many,' Sterne admitted, 'some in body, some in mind, but as I told you before, you have had me more than any woman—therefore you must have had me, H[annah], both in mind, and in body' (ibid.).

One of those who evidently thought of Sterne as a man of many affairs was Sir William Stanhope, to whom Sterne wrote on 19 September 1767. 'My dear Sir,' he opens, 'You are perhaps the drollest being in the universe—Why do you banter me so about what I wrote to you?—Tho' I told you every morning I jump'd into Venus's lap (meaning thereby the sea) was you to infer from that, that I leap'd into the ladies beds afterwards?—The body guides you—the mind me' (*Letters*, 394). As a comment about his life as a whole, the remark does not hold—and Sterne himself could hardly have pretended otherwise. As an account of his motivation in the last years of his life, it is most probably true. Not that Sir William Stanhope was greatly to be blamed for misconstruing his meaning, for Sterne's noted willingness to play whatever role the public wished must have led to considerable confusion, in the minds of those who did not know him well, as to the real nature of his relationships with women. Willingness to shock even his admirers is evident enough from an anecdote related, it seems likely, with an eye on future publication. 'A very agreeable lady arrived three years ago at York, in her road to Scarborough—I had the honour of being acquainted with her, and was her *chaperon*—all the females were very inquisitive to know who she was—"Do not tell, ladies, 'tis a mistress my wife has recommended to me—nay moreover has sent her from France"' (*Letters*, 403).

Here, as on other occasions, Sterne implied that any misunderstanding of his character stemmed from a reprehensible confusion of the author with his creation: 'The world has imagined, because I wrote Tristram Shandy, that I was myself more Shandean than I really ever was—'tis a good-natured world we live in, and we are often painted in divers colours according to the ideas each one frames in his head' (*Letters*, 402–3). Though he may well, on occasion, have been frustrated by an over-readiness on the part of others to confuse him with his fictional creation, his complaint is disingenuous at best. For years Sterne had been happy to take up a place both in English and French society by playing, with considerable relish and success, the role of Tristram or Yorick as the mood took him or the situation demanded, exploiting to the full the moral ambiguity his impersonation permitted.

Writing to Sir William Stanhope, Sterne alluded ambiguously to such previous relationships as that referred to by his correspondent, when recounting the circumstances in which he had written to Hannah and his ignorance of her identity. Having playfully decided who she was not, Sterne concluded: 'Enough of such nonsense—The past is over—and I can justify myself unto myself—can you do as much?—No faith!—"You can feel!" Aye so can my cat, when he heard a female caterwauling on the house top—but caterwauling disgusts me. I had rather raise a gentle flame, than have a different one raised in me' (*Letters*, 394). Given the nature of the complaint for which Sterne had so recently been treated by his physicians, the innocence of the relationships to which he had earlier alluded is doubtful, at best. Yet disconcertingly, Sterne continued by denying all sexual wrongdoing. 'Now, I take heav'n to witness,' the priest began, 'after all this *badinage* my heart is innocent' (ibid.). It is simply, he declared in a Tristram-like metaphor, that his pen has galloped away with him, and the 'truth is this—that my pen governs me—and not me my pen'. While it is not impossible that such a claim could be an easy means of self-exculpation, it rings true. *Tristram Shandy* itself is constructed on just such a principle of moving rapidly from one idea to another, in shifting from the serious to the light-hearted, of exploiting the possibilities for bawdy in the most innocent of ideas. It seems entirely consonant with Sterne's ways of thinking and writing that he should take the same delight in such rapid transitions in his correspondence, and that the bawdy to be found there is evidence more of mental alertness than moral laxity. Certainly, Sterne was anxious not to be misunderstood. In a further letter to Sir William Stanhope, written eight days later, he affirmed: 'my Sentimental Journey will, I dare say, convince you that my feelings are from the heart, and that that heart is not of the worst of molds—praised be God for my sensibility! Though it has often made me wretched, yet I would not exchange it for all the pleasures the grossest sensualist ever felt' (*Letters*, 395–6).

On 1 October 1767 Elizabeth and Lydia Sterne at last arrived in York. Sterne was there to greet his wife and daughter and to accompany them to Coxwold. He was delighted to see Lydia and was careful to give no overt sign of displeasure at Elizabeth's presence. When writing on a financial matter to Panchaud he deviated from his usual businesslike tone to reveal proudly that Lydia seemed 'transported' with the sight of him, and he continued: 'Nature . . . breathes in all her composition; and except a little vivacity—which is a fault of the world we live in—I am fully content with her mother's care of her'. (With a tact not always characteristic of him, Sterne was careful, in writing to Panchaud, not to blame Lydia's vivacity on her stay in France.) Excusing himself for this familiar intrusion into a business letter, Sterne wrote merely, ''tis natural to speak of those we love' (*Letters*, 396). A similar pride is in evidence in the letter Sterne wrote to Commodore and Anne James on 3 October, the day after the Sternes arrived at Coxwold. 'My girl has return'd an elegant accomplish'd little slut,' Sterne declared, adding what might be construed as a compliment to her mother: 'my wife—but I hate to praise my wife—'tis as much as decency will allow to praise my daughter' (*Letters*, 398).

By the end of the visit, Lydia had made an even deeper impression on her father: 'She is a dear good Creature—affectionate, and most elegant in body, and mind—she is all heaven could give me in a daughter' (*Letters*, 400). He wrote to the Jameses that Lydia had also received many advantageous proposals of marriage in France, so would settle there with her mother. Sterne's unexpected benevolence towards his wife may have been partly due not only to the fact of actually seeing her again rather than merely dreading her arrival, but also to the recognition that his apprehension had been exaggerated. Elizabeth Sterne had not, he discovered, arrived solely with the intention of plaguing her husband, and had indicated her intention of leaving Coxwold within a month or two to winter in York. Sterne would then be free to go to London at the beginning of January.

By the time his wife and daughter departed arrangements between the three of them had been resolved to their mutual satisfaction. Characteristically, Sterne found that he was not untouched by nostalgia. Elizabeth was to retire to France, where she would remain for the rest of her life: 'I have conquerd her,' Sterne wrote, though with no sense of triumph, 'as I w^{d} every one else, by humanity & Generosity—& she leaves me, more than half in Love wth me' (*Letters*, 399). Her health was too poor for her to have optimism that she might return to England, so that Sterne knew his parting with the woman he had married twenty-six years previously was likely to be his last. 'God bless,' he wrote, '& make the remainder of her Life happy', though he could not resist adding wryly, 'in order to w^{ch}, I am to remit her three hundred guineas a year' (ibid.).

Busy with his work on *A Sentimental Journey* and preoccupied with the arrangements for the visit of Lydia and Elizabeth, Sterne had added nothing to his journal since 4 August. Yet the freedom their departure allowed him led to no resumption of the journal. Instead, he penned his final entry. Having briefly related both his wife's visit and spoken of her decision to remain abroad, he put an end to his rhapsodical work with the briefest of codas: '—And now Eliza! Let me talk to thee—But What can I say, <—> of What can I write—But the Yearnings of heart wasted with looking & wishing for th<ee>y Return—Return—Return! my dear Eliza! May heaven smooth the Way for thee to send thee safely to us, & soj[ourn] for Ever' (*Letters*, 400).[19]

Whether by this belated change to the first-person plural pronoun, Sterne intended to refer to all of Elizabeth Draper's friends in England, or merely to himself and the cat, he had evidently overcome his infatuation. Indeed, Eliza's name is remarkable for its virtual absence in subsequent correspondence. Even in writing to Anne James on 12 November, as in his earlier letter of 30 October to her and her husband, Sterne makes no mention of Eliza. Expressing a lively sense of his obligations to the Jameses, he now linked them and their fifteen-month-old daughter, Elizabeth Anne, not with Eliza but with Lydia. Similarly, it was with Lydia rather than Elizabeth Draper that he associated Anne James in writing of his new work: 'My Sentimental Journey will please Mrs. J[ames], and my Lydia—I can answer for those two' (ibid.). In writing to another friend, Sterne made the apparent substitution of Lydia for Eliza literal. Having mentioned the bishop of Cork and Ross's offer of a living in Ireland, and the offer of the Surrey living, he stated that he would not go unless his wife and daughter would accompany him. 'I live for the sake of my girl,' Sterne now wrote, copying a passage from his journal entry for 3 August, but changing Eliza's name to Lydia's, 'and with her sweet light burthen in my arms, I could get up fast the hill of preferment, if I chose it—but without my Lydia, if a mitre was offered me, it would sit uneasy upon my brow' (*Letters*, 406). Once more, Sterne would not, without the woman he loved, accept a bishopric if they offered it to him ('they won't', the hard-headed Lydia might have responded).

Such fantasizing apart, Sterne's sense of renewed loss was genuine. When Lydia had been gone a week, he wrote: 'My heart bleeds . . . when I think of parting with my child—'twill be like the separation of soul and body—and equal to nothing but what passes at that tremendous moment', though even here he could not avoid adding wittily, 'and like it in one respect, for she will be in one kingdom, whilst I am in another' (ibid.). It seems entirely reasonable to speculate that the sensible advice Sterne offered to his friend A. L——e in mid-November 1767 was the fruit of his own experience. His friend was deeply unhappy in loving a woman who, though admired by many, would pay no attention to any. Why, Sterne asked pragmatically, should his friend believe he might succeed where dukes had failed? 'I pity you from my soul,' Sterne wrote, 'but we are all born with passions which ebb and flow (else they would play the devil with us) to different objects—and the best advice I can give you, L——e, is to turn the tide of yours another way' (*Letters*, 402).

Sterne himself was still writing hard, though uncertain as to when he might complete the two volumes he now intended. His wife's visit, he complained, had set him back a month. All the same, he hoped to be in London by Christmas or the New Year. 'I am going to ly-in; being at

Christmas at my full reckoning,' he told Sir George Macartney, lately returned from his post as envoy extraordinary at the court of Catherine the Great at St Petersburg, 'and unless what I shall bring forth is not *press'd* to death by these devils of printers, I shall have the honour of presenting to you a *couple of as clean brats* as ever chaste brain conceiv'd—they are frolicksome too, *mais cela n'empeche pas*' (*Letters*, 405). Sterne also took the opportunity to put Macartney's name on the list of subscribers to *A Sentimental Journey*; Sir George took the hint handsomely and subscribed for five sets on imperial paper.

Intriguing as it is, Sterne's description of *A Sentimental Journey* in his letter to Sir George Macartney is only one of several, and various, accounts he gave to friends. 'It is a subject which works well, and suits the frame of mind I have been in for some time past', he wrote; 'I told you my design in it was to teach us to love the world and our fellow creatures better than we do—so it runs most upon those gentler passions and affections, which aid so much to it' (*Letters*, 400–1). So, at least, he told Anne James, concluding with a graceful compliment to both her and her husband: 'Adieu, and may you and my worthy friend Mr. J[ames] continue examples of the doctrine I teach'. At much the same time, however, Sterne wrote a brief letter to Hannah in his whimsical vein, in which he again referred to *A Sentimental Journey* as a work which 'shall make you cry as much as ever it made me laugh—or I'll give up the Business of sentimental writing—& write to the Body' (*Letters*, 401). Jocular as it is, the remark suggests once more the close relationship between laughter and tears as impulses behind Sterne's sentimental fiction, throwing light on the rapid and subtle shifts of mood which characterize *A Sentimental Journey*—and which have given rise to greatly differing readings of it. The difficulty of knowing exactly what one's feelings are—the recognition that the self that feels instinctively for a fellow-creature, in misfortune or otherwise, can never be identical with the self reflecting on, or analysing, the instinctive response informs Sterne's shifting comments on his work at the time he was writing it. It is a work which had its origins in emotion—''tis true that an author must feel himself, or his reader will not' (*Letters*, 402)—but from which the writer may detach himself sufficiently to laugh, although his aim may be to make his readers cry that they may learn compassion for others.

With a view to stimulating controversy in advance of publication, Sterne appears to have gone out of his way to foster different views of his new work. Writing on 28 November to the earl of——, he declared of *A Sentimental Journey*: 'If it is not thought a chaste book, mercy on them that read it, for they must have warm imaginations indeed!' (*Letters*, 403). It is hard to believe that he was entirely serious. Rather, he seems to have become increasingly sensitive to the abuse his work had attracted from readers who felt obliged to adopt in public a disapproving stance at odds with their private morality. Thanking an American enthusiast, Dr John Eustace, who had gifted him a 'shandean' walking stick, Sterne expressed his exasperation with those 'unconverted' readers, whom he termed 'Hypocrites and Tartufe's':

> Your walking stick is in no sense more *shandaic* than in its having *more handles than one*—The parallel breaks only in this, that in using the stick, every one will take the handle which suits his convenience. In *Tristram Shandy*, the handle is taken which suits their passions, their ignorance or sensibility [while] a true feeler always brings half the entertainment along with him. His ideas are only call'd forth by what he reads, and the vibrations within, so entirely correspond with those excited, 'tis like reading *himself* and not the *book*. (*Letters*, 411)

Whatever the justice of his case, Sterne had obviously taken a beating too many from the critics, for he hoped that his new work might allow for an accommodation: 'the women will read this book in the parlour, and Tristram in the bed-chamber' (*Letters*, 412).

Even as he discussed his new work Sterne was acutely conscious of the precariousness of his life, and was thinking carefully about a posthumous edition of his letters. This, he estimated, would bring in at least £800, thereby providing support for his wife and daughter. Among the various and varied recipients of letters Sterne mentions are Marmaduke Fothergill, his surgeon friend in York, Hall-Stevenson—whom Sterne declared to have received hundreds of letters from him, though written 'in too careless a way' (*Letters*, 407)—Garrick, Mary Macartney, the countess of Edgecumb, and many others. Collected, the letters would make four small octavo volumes and would sell well, Sterne believed. It was a suggestion for which Lydia would be grateful and which, after her father's death, she would later act on with determination.

Sterne, meanwhile, was again dangerously ill. To the Jameses he wrote that he had been suffering from 'a fever, & bleeding at my lungs, which ha<s>d confine<me>d me to my Room three weeks' (*Letters*, 408). By the time he wrote that letter on 28 December he was sufficiently improved in health to travel, and was already in York on the first stage of his journey to London, which he would undertake with Hall-Stevenson. For the first time since 10 August Sterne mentioned Eliza in a letter to the Jameses. His sentiments were simultaneously extravagant and perfunctory—having suggested that his illness was 'a sort of sympathy' for the Jameses' affliction, caused by the illness of their daughter, he added, as though by way of afterthought, 'and I make no doubt when I see Eliza's Journal, I shall find She has been ill herself at that time'. He continued in like vein: 'I am rent to pieces with Uncertainty ab^{t} this dear friend of ours—I think too much—& intereste myself <too> so deeply by My friendship for her,—that I am worn down to a Shadow—to this I owe my decay of health—but I can't help it' (ibid.). Though Sterne's sentimental diagnosis of the cause of his illness does not convince, his concluding allusion to the state of his health suggested how ill he was. 'I am weak my dear friends, both in body & mind,' he wrote, 'so god bless you—Youl see Me enter like a Ghost—so I tell you before hand, not to be frighten'd' (*Letters*, 408–9).

Sterne did not exaggerate. He was so sick when he arrived in the capital that he could not leave his lodgings. He retained a spark of optimism, all the same: 'I continue to mend, and doubt not but this, with all other evils and uncertainties of life, will end for the best' (*Letters*, 409). Sterne was fortunate in having Commodore and Anne James as friends, and he knew it. In writing to the earl of —— he declared that, 'If your Lordship is in town in Spring, I should be happy if you became acquainted with my friends in Gerrard-street—you would esteem the husband, and honour the wife' (*Letters*, 403). Sterne saw the Jameses' house in Soho as a place to which he could retreat whenever he wished. Uncertain whether he could accept an invitation to one of their regular Sunday evening gatherings, he wrote: 'If I cannot, I will glide like a shadow uninvited to Gerrard Street some day this week, that we may eat our bread and meat in love and peace together' (*Letters*, 409). As an acknowledgement of their generous hospitality and valued friendship he attempted to do the Jameses small favours, having already written from Coxwold to ask 'What can I send you that Yorkshire produces? tell me—I want to be of use to you, for I am, my dear friends, with the truest value and esteem, your ever obliged, L. STERNE' (*Letters*, 375). Though no longer a subscriber to the Carlisle House assemblies, Sterne made great efforts to find the Jameses a ticket for the first gathering of the new year. He also helped Anne James with her drawing—he had made her a present of colours and an easel the previous April—and was busying himself with borrowing a print for her to copy. While he was teaching Anne James to paint, she was herself being painted. The fashionable Benjamin West produced a portrait of her which Sterne found admirable: 'he has caught the character of our friend—such goodness is painted in that face, that when one looks at it, let the soul be ever so much un-harmonized, it is impossible it should remain so' (*Letters*, 412).

Sterne too was sitting for his portrait—again by Joshua Reynolds. That this would be a final portrait—it fact it would remain unfinished at Sterne's death—must have been equally obvious to painter and subject. Though he had pulled back from the brink of death on many previous occasions—and still enjoyed brief periods of remission—company now tired him. A gift of wine from Elizabeth Montagu brought the response that it would 'restore to me what I have lost—w^{h} is a little strength—which I usually regain in as short time, as I lost it; I am absolutely this morning free from every bodily distemper that is to be read of in the catalogue of human infirmities' (*Letters*, 414). Despite her frequent acerbity Elizabeth Montagu was continually solicitous, and although she was already a subscriber, Sterne exceptionally went so far as to give her an imperial paper copy of *A Sentimental Journey* before publication. In response to one of her letters of enquiry after his health, he confessed: 'I am ill—very ill—Yet I feel my Existence Strongly, and something like revelation along with it, which tells, I shall not dye—but live—& yet any other man w^{d} set his house in order' (*Letters*, 416). Instead Sterne was writing again, a 'most comic' romance he told Elizabeth Montagu. 'I brave evils,' he asserted in recollection of *Tristram Shandy*, 'et quand Je serai mort, on mettra mon nom dans le liste de ces Heros, qui sont Morts en plaisantant' ('and when I am dead, my name will be placed in the list of those heroes who died in a jest') (ibid.).

A Sentimental Journey through France and Italy. By Mr. Yorick, to which Sterne had devoted hard months of work in the most difficult circumstances throughout the preceding summer and autumn, finally appeared under the imprint of Becket and Dehondt on 27 February 1768. Despite the ill health which had dogged its writing, Sterne still found energy enough to make some small corrections while the book was at press.[20] His work's appearance gave Sterne understandable satisfaction, though his plans for the subscription list were only partly realized: instead of the 650 or so who subscribed to the second instalment of the sermons, *A Sentimental Journey* attracted just 334 subscribers. Lydia, however, reported that the book was admired by every one in York, and in reply Sterne commented, 'tis not vanity in me to tell you that it is no less admired here' (*Letters*, 417). Yet he was not deceived by this last instance of worldly success; 'what is the gratification of my feelings on this occasion?' he wrote; 'the want of health bows me down, and vanity harbours not in thy father's breast' (ibid.). He would not live to see more than, at most, one printed notice of his book.

When *A Sentimental Journey* finally appeared Sterne was suffering from a 'vile influenza', and though he was quick to reassure Lydia—'be not alarm'd, I think I shall get the better of it'—he knew he had little time left. '[I]f I escape,' he wrote, ''twill not be for a long period' (ibid.). When Richard Griffith met Sterne at Scarborough in the previous September he had been amazed by his continuing survival: '[h]is living for Ten Years past was a Miracle, and that he should live for Twenty Years to come was the only *Miracle*, I fancy, that he believed in.'[21] Now Sterne was thinking seriously of his death, especially insofar as it would affect Lydia. Elizabeth Sterne had evidently heard that, should he die first, her husband intended to put Lydia under the protection of Eliza Draper. Lydia wrote to her father on the subject, but he denied the intention vehemently. 'No, my Lydia!', he replied, ' 'tis a lady, whose virtues I wish thee to imitate, that I shall entrust my girl to—I mean [Anne James] . . . from her you will learn to be an affectionate wife, a tender mother, and a sincere friend' (ibid.). Sterne's resentment flared briefly at what he took to be his wife's misrepresentation of his love for Lydia, but he was no longer disposed to bear grudges. 'I think, my Lydia, that thy mother will survive me,' he wrote, adding, 'do not deject her spirits with thy apprehensions on my account' (*Letters*, 418). He sent gifts of a necklace and buckles not only to his daughter but also to his wife; 'My girl cannot form a wish that is in the power of her father, that he will not gratify her in—and I cannot in justice be less kind to thy mother'. The kindness of his friends remained constant, Sterne assured Lydia, though he expressed the wish that he might have had his daughter to nurse him. 'Write to me twice a week, at least,' he conjured her, 'God bless thee, my child, and believe me ever, ever thy Affectionate father, L. S.' (ibid.). They were the last words Sterne would address to his daughter.

Only one subsequent letter of Sterne's survives, and is perhaps the only one he wrote, for he was now critically ill. 'Your poor friend is scarce able to write', he told Anne James, 'he has been at death's door this week with a pleurisy'. His doctor treated him by bleeding and vesication. 'The physician says I am better', Sterne wrote doubtfully, adding, 'God knows, for I feel myself sadly wrong' (ibid.). So weak was he that he was forced to stop a dozen times in writing rather fewer than a dozen lines. The Jameses remained close to him until the end. William James had visited the day before Sterne wrote, and the dying man begged him to come again. 'I want to ask a favour of him, if I find myself worse—that I shall beg of you, if in this wrestling I come off conqueror' (*Letters*, 419), Sterne continued more hopefully; but he had little confidence that this time he could defeat his old antagonist. Instead he asked that, in the event of Elizabeth Sterne's death, Anne James would act the part of mother to Lydia. 'You are the only woman on earth', he wrote pointedly, 'I can depend upon for such a benevolent action'. Commodore James, he was sure, would be as a father to his child. He invoked blessings on his friend and asked that, 'If I die, cherish the remembrance of me, and forget the follies which you so often condemn'd—which my heart, not my head betray'd me into'. Sterne concluded by asking that Anne James should commend him to her husband, 'as I now commend you to that Being who takes under his care the good and kind part of the world.—Adieu' (ibid.).

Laurence Sterne died in his Old Bond Street lodgings at four o'clock in the afternoon of Friday, 18 March 1768. He was 54 years of age. It was a death as close to the one he had imagined as any man could in reason have expected. In the seventh volume of *Tristram Shandy* Sterne had written:

> WAS I in a condition to stipulate with death . . . I should certainly declare against submitting to it before my friends; and therefore, I never seriously think upon the mode and manner of this great catastrophe, which generally takes up and torments my thoughts as much as the catastrophe itself, but I constantly draw the curtain across it with this wish, that the Disposer of all things may so order it, that it happen not to me in my own house——but rather in some decent inn——at home, I know it,——the concern of my friends, and the last services of wiping my brows and smoothing my pillow, which the quivering hand of pale affection shall pay me, will so crucify my soul, that I shall die of a distemper which my physician is not aware of: but in an inn, the few cold offices I wanted, would be purchased with a few guineas, and paid me with an undisturbed, but punctual attention——(*TS* VII. xii. 395)

Sterne himself died in just such circumstances: in lodgings, with no friends by, but properly attended by a nurse. Fortuitously, there was also a witness of literary bent. John Macdonald, footman to Sterne's Scottish friend John Crauford, arrived at Old Bond Street at his master's bidding to enquire after Sterne. The dying author had been the subject of the conversation around the dinner table.[22] In his memoirs Macdonald described his visit: 'I went into the room, and he was just a-dying. I waited ten minutes; but in five he said: "*Now it is come.*" He put up his hand as if to stop a blow, and died in a minute.' Macdonald returned with the news to Crauford and his guests. 'The gentlemen', he reported, 'were all very sorry, and lamented him very much.'[23]

EPILOGUE

'Alas, poor YORICK!'

De mortuis nil nisi bonum . . . 'you are not to speak any thing of the dead, but what is good.' Eight years before his own death Sterne had rejected the sentiment as justified neither by reason nor scripture.[1] Given the controversy that had characterized his public life in the intervening period, it would have been impossible for the commentary that followed on Sterne's death to be unadulterated praise. Public comment and private judgement, both on the man and his work, were often in conflict—though the praise of his admirers could be generous in the extreme.

Sterne's death coming so soon after the publication of *A Sentimental Journey*, the book's first reviews were understandably influenced by the fact. Only the first of the two notices by Ralph Griffiths in successive issues of the *Monthly Review* seems to have been written before news of that death became public knowledge. In the circumstances it is the more striking that Griffiths found much to admire. Making reference to his review of the seventh and eighth volumes of *Tristram Shandy*, he noted with evident satisfaction: 'Now, Reader, did we not tell thee . . . that the highest excellence of this genuine, this legitimate son of humour, lies not in his humorous but in his pathetic vein?—If we have not already given proofs and specimens enough, in support of this opinion, from his *Shandy*, his *Sermons* . . . we could produce more from the little volume before us.'[2] In particular Griffiths singled out the episode of Yorick's meeting with the monk in Calais: 'What an affecting, touching, masterly picture is here!'[3]

Eulogy soon changed to elegy. 'Alas poor Yorick!', began the second part of Griffiths' notice, in the April issue of the *Monthly Review*, which found much else to praise in the *Journey*: 'What delicacy of feeling, what tenderness of sentiment, yet what simplicity of expression are here!', he wrote of Yorick's encounter with the Fille de Chambre (*ASJ* 187–91)—declaring that *A Sentimental Journey* was Sterne's 'best production:——though not, perhaps, the most admired of his works'.[4] Like other reviewers, Griffiths concluded by alluding to the Recording Angel's tear blotting out Sterne's faults, and other writers likewise made reference to his death in appropriately Shandean terms. 'Our Sentimentalist having lately made a journey to that country *from whose bourne no traveller returns*, his memory claims at least as much indulgence as our duty to the public permitted us to allow him when alive',[5] began the *Critical Review*'s notice in March. It is hardly surprising, though, that this notice was decidedly unsympathetic in its assessment of Sterne's *Journey*, for the journal founded by Tobias Smollett was unlikely to respond warmly to a work which unfairly (if amusingly) ridiculed Smollett as the perpetually discontented Smelfungus. In any case, the *Critical Review*'s estimate of the book was uncharacteristic of the general tenor of the reviews. The *Political Register*'s reviewer complemented rather than endorsed Ralph Griffiths' opinion by declaring 'an original vein of humour' to be Sterne's chief merit, but concluding that by adding to it 'the moral and the pathetic' he had produced, in *A Sentimental Journey*, his best work.[6]

The view was shared by individual readers. Horace Walpole, who had expressed fastidious disdain for *Tristram Shandy*, read *A Sentimental Journey* immediately following its publication and praised it as 'exceedingly good-natured and picturesque', with 'strokes of delicacy'.[7] Elizabeth Montagu too considered *A Sentimental Journey* to be Sterne's best work, though she added, 'I cannot say it was suitable to his serious profession'.[8] Other critics carried such moral criticism much further, uncompromisingly rejecting both the man and his works. In some cases this was simply a question of paying off old grudges, as when—little more than a fortnight after his death—William Warburton vindictively dismissed Sterne as 'the idol of the higher mob' and 'common jester to the many'.[9] By contrast, Elizabeth Carter, who acknowledged that she had not read, and probably never would read, his works, showed a sternly Johnsonian moral sense when asserting that Sterne's sentiment involved a dangerous confusion of right and wrong. Such responses to *A Sentimental Journey* became, in time, much more elaborate, as in Vicesimus Knox's lurid comment that 'Many a connexion, begun with the fine sentimentality which Sterne has recommended and increased, has terminated in disease, infamy, madness, suicide, and a gibbet'.[10] Fanny Greville, godmother to Frances Burney, offered her own complementary, yet equally direct criticism of Sterne: 'A feeling heart', she averred, 'is certainly a right heart; nobody will contest that: but when a man chooses to walk about the world with a cambrick handkerchief always in his hand, that he may always be ready to weep either with man or beast,—he only turns me sick.'[11]

In fact, the distance from the praise of Griffiths or Walpole to the criticism of Knox or Greville was not great, for both sets of reactions depended on an increasing tendency to read *A Sentimental Journey* as though Sterne had quite left comedy behind in quest of the pathetic (only a few short years before the 'English Rabelais' had seemed the very embodiment of 'WIT and HUMOUR'[12]). Rightly or wrongly—and today the book appears much less an unapologetic advocacy of sentiment than a searching comic critique of sensibility and its excesses—Griffiths's preference for pathos over humour would be echoed by others. The Irish novelist Henry Brooke, who began his *The Fool of Quality* (1765–70) under the influence of the facetious humour of *Tristram Shandy*, soon abandoned this in favour of moralizing sentiment (leading, in the next century, to Charles Kingsley's praise of the book as containing more that was 'pure, sacred, and eternal' than any work of literature since Spenser's *The Faerie Queene*[13]). Other writers took sensibility as their starting-point. Henry Mackenzie's *The Man of Feeling* (1771) was only the most celebrated of the many hundreds of sentimental novels to appear in the wake of Sterne's success. In the years following his death, Sterne himself was increasingly read almost exclusively as a sentimentalist—the Rabelaisian aspects of his work becoming progressively unfashionable—a tendency encouraged by the publication, in 1782, of *The Beauties of Sterne.*[14] In this immensely popular and often reprinted work—it went through thirteen editions by 1799—the pathetic or sentimental tales of *Tristram Shandy*, the *Journey*, and the *Sermons* were torn from their contexts and rearranged for the most exquisite emotional effect. The result was to reduce the possibility of ironic or even equivocal readings of such episodes as 'The Dead Ass' at Nampont, the meeting of Yorick with Maria of Moulines and her goat, or indeed any articulation of the simple rural idyll that sensibility encouraged but which the author had long ago rejected in his own life. Sterne himself, though, had suggested that *A Sentimental Journey* would teach its readers 'to love the world and our fellow creatures better than we do' (*Letters*, 401). The tears his book drew forth from its admirers were now celebrated not simply as signs of individual sensibility, but as evidence of the 'sympathizing principle, by which we are led, as by a secret charm, to partake the miseries of others', transforming feeling into a cohesive force, and making of isolated individuals a social whole—the very doctrines, in other words, variously advanced, in secular or religious terms, over the course of the previous half-century by latitudinarian divines and by moral philosophers from the earl of Shaftesbury through Francis Hutcheson, David Hume, and Lord Kames to Adam Smith.[15] The cult of sensibility

Sterne's writings did so much to encourage was remarkably tenacious, in prose and verse: Wordsworth's first published poem was the 'Sonnet, on seeing Miss Helen Maria Williams weep at a Tale of Distress'.[16] Only slowly did the cult come under sustained critical scrutiny, as its devotees increasingly indulged the cultivation of personal feeling without recognizing a concomitant need to translate sympathy into practical acts of philanthropy. So Mary Wollstonecraft, whose early work extols the power of sentiment, and literary sentiment in particular, eventually turned decisively away from it in favour of the power of reason, arguing that 'misery demands more than tears' and that 'soft phrases, susceptibility of heart, delicacy of sentiment, and refinement of taste, are almost synonymous with epithets of weakness . . . those beings who are only the objects of pity and that kind of love, which has been termed its sister, will soon become objects of contempt'.[17]

Even so, it was only the transformation that sensibility had wrought in eighteenth-century culture, especially male culture, that enabled Wollstonecraft to take her final critical stand. In any case, such considered critiques of the cult of sensibility lay in the future. In the immediate wake of Sterne's death David Garrick expressed the general public mood in his unaffectedly eloquent epitaph for the writer:

> Shall pride a heap of sculptur'd marble raise,
> Some worthless, unmourn'd titled fool to praise;
> And shall we not by one poor grave-stone learn
> Where genius, wit, and humour sleep with *Sterne*?[18]

In 1768 Garrick's question was far from rhetorical. Following his death in his lodgings, Sterne's funeral took place on 22 March in the fashionable church of St George's, Hanover Square. His body was subsequently interred in a new graveyard, belonging to the parish of St George's but situated beyond Tyburn, during a ceremony attended by no more than two or three mourners. A little more than a year after his death a report appeared in the *Public Advertiser* to the effect that shortly after the burial Sterne's remains had been stolen by body-snatchers and sold for dissection at one of the universities.[19] The story was disseminated widely, so that almost forty years later Sterne's servant from his days in Sutton recalled that 'it was generally believed in the village that his corpse became a subject for the surgeon's knife'.[20] By the most convincing account the dissection took place at Sterne's old university, Cambridge, under the direction of the professor of anatomy there, Charles Collignon.[21] In one of several, not always consistent eighteenth-century accounts, the Shakespearean scholar and editor Edmond Malone noted that he had spoken to someone who 'was present at the dissection' and who assured him that 'he recognized Sterne's face the moment he saw the body'.[22] The dissection proceeded but, given the fact that Sterne's corpse had been recognized, the body was later taken back to London for clandestine reburial.

Neither Elizabeth Sterne nor Lydia was in London at the time of the writer's funeral, nor for some time after. Moreover, their financial embarrassment was notorious; the archbishop of York himself described them, just eight days after Sterne's death, as 'most distressed objects, [who] have a Scene of unhappiness opened to them, wch it will be difficult for the best-intentioned to prevent' (*Letters*, 433). It is no wonder, then, that no memorial to Sterne was commissioned by his wife and daughter. In the following year, however, two freemasons erected to his memory a stone inscribed with the words 'Alas! Poor Yorick'. In so doing, they intended to honour a man whom they perceived to share their belief in 'mutual benevolence' and 'friendly feeling', a man whose work manifested the very sociability they themselves professed as masons.[23] Though less than eighteen months had passed since the author's death the exact location of the grave had been already lost, so that the inscription on the stone noted merely that 'Near to this Place | Lyes the Body of | The Reverend Laurence Sterne, A.M.'. For 200 years no other monument marked the whereabouts of Sterne's uneasy resting-place.

Nor was it any wonder. All efforts by Sterne's former friends and admirers after his death were directed towards ensuring a decent settlement for Elizabeth and Lydia Sterne. Despite his own efforts, Sterne had failed to manage successfully the profits of his writing. In reply to a letter from Elizabeth Montagu, the archbishop of York had alluded discreetly to the possibility that the deceased clergyman's wife and daughter might apply for a 'small pension of £6 or £8'.[24] Though he acknowledged the sum to be a 'trifle', it is a telling indication of how poor the Sterne women were perceived to be. The actual situation was not quite so bad but, recalling Sterne's repeated references to his wife's needs in respect of his mother's and sister's in the 1750s, or indeed his own continual anxiety in his last months that wife and daughter should want for nothing, the situation into which Elizabeth and Lydia were thrust by his death was an unhappy one. That situation, as the archbishop bluntly told Elizabeth Montagu, was exacerbated by the 'ruinous' state of the parsonage house at Sutton-on-the-Forest, unrepaired following the fire there in 1765. Although he expressed the hope that Sterne's successor—the Revd Andrew Cheap, who had been installed a week after Sterne's death—would show the 'compassion due to the Widow and orphan', he could make no promises. When Elizabeth Sterne rejected the suggestion that she make a compromise payment of 100 guineas to Cheap, the archbishop was exasperated with her, as, in no uncertain terms, was the new vicar of Sutton, who recorded his comments in the Parish Book.[25] Elizabeth Sterne's persistence paid off, however, for in the end Andrew Cheap accepted 60 guineas.

Elizabeth Montagu's urgent plans to assist her cousins were only the beginning of a sustained endeavour to put Elizabeth and Lydia Sterne on a sound financial footing. It was an effort that involved many people known and unknown to Sterne. That it continued for several years testifies both to the affection and esteem in which his friends and admirers held the deceased writer, and to a dogged determination by Elizabeth and Lydia that they should retain the social status they thought rightfully theirs. The task was not easy, since the Sterne women and their would-be benefactors had very different ideas of what was appropriate to their status. Elizabeth Montagu's comment to her sister, the novelist Sarah Scott, is eloquent: 'The only thing for these people would be to board in a cheap place, but my good cousin is si tracassiere [so interfering], she puts every Town into a combustion in a month.'[26]

Elizabeth Montagu acted on behalf of her cousin out of principle, not affection: 'Mrs. Sterne is a woman of great integrity and has many virtues,' she wrote on another occasion, 'but they stand like quills upon the fretfull porcupine, ready to go forth in sharp arrows on the least supposed offence.'[27] Few, in fact, had a truly good word for either Elizabeth or Lydia. Elizabeth Sterne's brother-in-law, the Revd John Botham—the husband of her sister Lydia—complained that Sterne's daughter had written to him 'in a dictating manner'[28]—an assertion given some credibility by the fact that Lydia's surviving business letters are at times rather more curt than was perhaps politic in the circumstances.[29]

The Sternes, meanwhile, complained in their turn—and as regards John Botham, with much better reason. Lydia had asked her uncle to send all of Sterne's papers to her and her mother in York. Instead, Botham read them through and, as Lydia wrote, 'burnt what he did not think proper to communicate to us.—'.[30] In this instance—and her father had not yet been dead a month—filial piety competed in Lydia with concern for the future well-being of herself and her mother:

> [I]t was not mama's intention that any one shou'd read my Father's papers. well knowing that there was some amongst them which ought

> not to have been seen no not even by his Daughter nor sh^{d} I have wish'd to see one of them! mama is very much chagrin'd at this for notwithstanding she can perhaps rely on Mr Botham's secrecy yet it grieves that even he should be so well acquainted with certain anecdotes. but to burn any paper was very wrong.[31]

Nor was this all, for Botham failed to observe Elizabeth and Lydia's request that he sell off Sterne's clothes and personal effects to the best advantage, despite Lydia's sensible argument that 'many of his friends would have been glad to have purchased his trinkets at even more than their value only because they once belong'd to Mr Sterne'.[32] Neither did he present Sterne's gold snuffbox to John Hall-Stevenson, who was particularly anxious to obtain it as a memento. Finally, Botham peremptorily refused to hand over the money he had raised by selling Sterne's effects until the details of the estate had been worked out more clearly.[33]

It was fortunate that Lydia had better news from outside of the family. In Yorkshire a collection had been started, the earliest contributor being the marquess of Rockingham, who had first extended his patronage to Sterne back in 1759 by purchasing eight sets of volumes I and II of *Tristram Shandy*, and who now subscribed 50 guineas.[34] Once the Whig magnate had set the fund rolling, others rapidly followed suit.[35] Since nothing less than 5 guineas was accepted, Lydia was able to fend off any suggestion that she and her mother were considered as destitute objects of charity, declaring the collection 'an *honour* to Mr Sterne's memory & no small one to us & cannot lessen us in the eyes of the world'.[36] Lydia was also very much her father's daughter, for in relating all this to her aunt she added: 'would to God it may succeed, if *you approve of it.* and in case you do my dear Madam may we hope that you will second our friends endeavours in the south as they will do yours in the North!'[37]

Eventually the fund in the north raised more than £700. In relating this information to her sister Sarah Scott, Elizabeth Montagu specified that it was 'for Miss Sterne': the subscribers having been promised 'it should be converted into an annuity for the girl for . . . Mrs. Sterne was so little loved or esteemed there would not have been a single guinea given if that condition had not been made'.[38] Lydia herself was not exempt from criticism from her benefactors, however, one of them begging Elizabeth Montagu 'to advise Miss Sterne not to affect witt, a desire of being distinguished that way she says has ruined the whole family'.[39] Lydia anxiously denied any such affectation;[40] nevertheless, in indicating an intention to allow her £20 annually, Elizabeth Montagu tartly expressed the hope that her generosity 'will give my advice more weight'.[41]

Lydia Sterne was certainly not ungrateful for the efforts made on her behalf: 'how gracious, how merciful is God to us!', she exclaimed, 'what comfort he has sent us what friends has he rais'd us up!'[42] She was equally and understandably delighted in December to receive a charmingly unpretentious letter from Lady Spencer, telling her that John 'Fish' Crauford had made a separate collection among Sterne's friends, averring that 'it would give him pleasure to be of any service to his family for his sake'.[43] The subscribers included, besides Crauford himself, Charles James Fox, the earl of Upper Ossory, the duke of Roxburgh, the earl of Shelburne, and Commodore William James, each of whom contributed 10 guineas; among those giving 5 guineas was 'Mr Hume the Historian'.[44] The total subscription amounted to £108. 15*s.* 0*d.*

Lydia's gratitude for the efforts made on their behalf seems wholly genuine, yet neither she nor her mother was apt to leave everything to Providence. Much earlier in the year the women had sold off all of Sterne's effects—'his furniture a Cow, & some hay included 56^l^ his Chaise, & horses 60^l^ his Books 80'—but once outstanding debts had been paid the balance amounted to only £22. Worse, creditors were still appearing: 'last night we rec^d^ a Bill from a person in York. for wine the summ 25^l^ and the other day we rec^d^ a Bill for Shoes from London.'[45] In order to make ends meet the women had agreed to vacate their lodgings in York during Race Week for the sum of 5 guineas, a considerable saving on their annual rent of £20.

Such minor economies were all very well, but Elizabeth and Lydia Sterne needed a much larger sum of money in hand if they were to fulfil their aim of returning to France with an annuity sufficient to support them in a befitting manner. Their greatest resource—as Sterne himself had recognized as far back as 1761, on the eve of his departure for France in search of health—was the novelist's unpublished compositions and his correspondence. Since then, of course, Sterne had published a further two volumes of his sermons. At that time, ill as he was, he had excused the small number of sermons—just twelve instead of the sixteen he had promised his publisher—by unwisely declaring that no further sermons would be published, except 'the sweepings of the Author's study after his death'.[46]

Undeterred, Lydia Sterne—still only 21 years old—set herself the task of seeing these 'sweepings' into print. Within months of her father's death, her efforts were well under way. She had sent all the sermons she could find to John Hall-Stevenson, asking for his assistance in preparing them for publication. Evidently she had not read them very carefully, for Hall-Stevenson indicated that at least one of them had already appeared in an earlier volume; moreover, his own first reading of those she had sent revealed several passages common to sermons already published. Lydia had, nevertheless, given astute thought to how the remaining sermons might be marketed. Since there were eighteen sermons in all, they could be divided into three volumes of six sermons each. 'I think you judge rightly', Hall-Stevenson added, 'to fix the price at three half crowns, then make a bargain to clear your subscription, and sell the Copy.'[47] If Lydia had not read the unpublished sermons with ideal care, Hall-Stevenson had evidently not looked attentively at those already published, for he recommended that Lydia approach Thomas Becket who, he declared 'was certainly mistaken when he told me, your father had assured him, that he had nothing but the Sweepings of his study, in the Sermon way'—manifestly failing to recognize the phrase as Sterne's own. In a sense, however, Hall-Stevenson was right, for while some of the remaining sermons are weak, others are as strong as any Sterne wrote. Becket, however, was unconvinced, and after protracted negotiations offered Lydia terms so unfavourable as to persuade her to approach William Strahan, who had printed the fifth and sixth volumes of *Tristram Shandy* for Becket and Dehondt after Sterne had left his original publishers, the Dodsleys. Lydia wrote indignantly:

> I enclose you Mr. Beckett's proposal—when he last offer'd £400 for the copyright he insisted on no such terms as these—this affair of not offering them to anyone else must be managed with the greatest caution—for you see he says that he will not take them if offer'd elsewhere. He will be the judge of the quantity and quality—& insists on a year's credit . . . my mother and myself . . . had rather anyone had them than Becket—he is a *dirty fellow*.[48]

Strahan was presumably discreet as well as hard-headed, for eventually he and his partner Thomas Cadell collaborated with Becket in the publication of the final three volumes of sermons, which appeared in 1769 under the decorous title of *SERMONS by the Late Rev. Mr. STERNE*; a second edition followed later the same year. The subscription list of over 700 names prefixed to the sermons once more bears witness both to the esteem in which Sterne and his writings were held and to the indefatigable efforts of Lydia and her mother to ensure their own well-being.

Further evidence of the latter continued, indeed, for several years to come. Although in 1769 Lydia and Elizabeth Sterne returned to France, we know that Lydia made strenuous efforts to persuade John Wilkes and John Hall-Stevenson to write a biographical account of her father. In one letter she begged Wilkes for 'three lines with a promise of writing Tristrams life for the benefit of his widow and Daughter', bolstering her entreaty by pleading that Isaac Panchaud's failure—he went bankrupt with debts of £70,000—'has hurt us considerably—we have I fear lost more than we in our circumstances could afford to lose'.[49] Though she had no way of knowing it, Lydia's choice was an unhappy one, for John Wilkes was given to failing to complete what he had begun, having abandoned both an edition of the poems of his friend Charles Churchill, and a history of England, of which he completed only the introduction. Four months later she was writing to John Hall-Stevenson in even more pathetic terms, though in this case she evidently overplayed her hand, for the plan came to nothing.

Undaunted, Lydia turned to a different project: the publication of an edition of her father's letters. In truth, she and her mother were in need. They had first settled in Angoulême, but by March 1770 had determined on 'going a little further south where we may live cheaper'.[50] Their choice fell on Albi, of which Lydia wrote: 'the situation . . . is pretty . . . but there is little society. and the little there is, is scarce worth the trouble of searching after.'[51] As time went on the Sternes made many economies, yet Lydia's letters, especially to Elizabeth Montagu, remain full of hints concerning their poverty—and gratitude when her godmother or some other well-wisher acted upon those hints.

Although it is sometimes difficult to distinguish matters of record from veiled hopes of further assistance, Lydia's letters reveal that the health of both women was poor. Lydia described herself as 'in bad health and . . . very thin',[52] and Elizabeth was worse, having suffered an epileptic fit which left her permanently unwell. When the 24-year-old Lydia received, and accepted, a proposal of marriage from Jean-Baptiste-Alexandre-Anne Médalle, a Roman Catholic four years her junior, in 1772, she wrote a distressed letter to Elizabeth Montagu outlining the hard financial conditions imposed by her prospective father-in-law, and begging that her godmother transfer the £30 she gave the two women annually to Elizabeth Sterne alone. Elizabeth Montagu obliged without hesitation, though she was clearly unhappy at the prospect of Lydia's marriage. In particular, she reproached her for giving no indication of her fiancé's social standing—something Lydia had doubtless omitted because her husband-to-be was the son of a minor tax collector—a *receveur de décimes*—in the customs at Albi.[53] She had also omitted to mention that she was pregnant—which was just as well, for Elizabeth Montagu could not, in any case, forbear reflecting at length on Lydia's imprudence:

> all you give your friends is that you are going to marry a man of a different Religion, and to reduce your Mother to almost beggary, both these things you confess. You seem at the same time to declare steadfastness in Religion and Filial piety to your parent. My dear cousin the actions not the words are what shall decide the judgment of God and man . . .[54]

Having written to tell Elizabeth Montagu her news in late March, Lydia Sterne abjured Protestantism and married Médalle in April.[55] The haste was understandable, for she gave birth to a son, Jean-François-Laurens, little more than three months later, on 6 August 1772. Elizabeth Sterne survived her first grandchild by less than a year, dying in Albi in July 1773. Later that same year Lydia bore a second son, who died before his fifth birthday. Jean-François-Laurens—known as 'Laurent'—would die in 1783, aged 11.[56]

The future of Mrs Médalle, as she now styled herself, lay in France. Yet she returned to England once more, in 1775, and revealed herself as determined as ever to make the most of the scanty resources her father had left her. As before, she enlisted the help of Laurence Sterne's closest friends, this time to put together a collection of his letters. Financial necessity having taken precedence over Lydia's personal dislike for him, Thomas Becket would be the publisher. A note dated 23 June shows David Garrick still good-naturedly lending his influential assistance: 'Mr Garrick presents his compliments to Mr^{s} Fenton & will take it as a particular favour if she will permit Mr Becket to publish the letter of Sterne she is in possession of, among the remains which are preparing for the press of that very singular genius.'[57] Where there were gaps, Lydia was ruthless. The writer Hannah More noted in 1776:

> Mrs Medalle (Sterne's daughter) sent to all the correspondents of her deceased father, begging the letters which he had written to them; among other wits, she sent to Wilkes with the same request. He sent for answer, That as there happened to be nothing extraordinary in those he had received, he had burnt or lost them. On which, that faithful editor of her father's works sent back to say, that if Mr. Wilkes would be so good as to write a few letters in imitation of her father's style, it would do just as well, and she would insert them.[58]

For the most part, modern Sterne scholars have been as readily shocked as the very proper Hannah More at Lydia's willingness to allow imagination to take the place of record in this case. It is hard, though, not to feel sympathy for a woman who, with few resources, was so determined to guarantee her own future and that of her young family, while keeping up the appearances of gentility in her enforced exile. Certainly, it is easier to sympathize with Lydia Sterne than with William Combe who, in his *Philosopher in Bristol* (1775), wrote 'if the love of gain . . . entirely envellopes all traits of feeling and delicacy of sentiment . . . I bless heaven that I am not a man of merchandize'[59]—yet still managed to pass off a volume containing his own forgeries as genuine letters of Sterne.[60] If an understandable desire to eke out her scanty materials to fill the maximum number of volumes—eventually there would be three in all—persuaded Lydia to one dubious expedient, then a further deception on her part must be attributed, at least partly, to filial piety. Passages from her father's journal to Eliza, and perhaps one or more letters written originally to her, were redated and readdressed to her mother—causing problems for biographers and, in Sterne's ostensible employment of the term 'sentimental' a full decade before it became fashionable usage, to lexicographers as well.[61]

Since Lydia Sterne was at times a poor editor by modern standards, her sins of commission and omission have been frequently noted. Yet it was she and she alone who prompted the publication of what letters—114 in all—she could find, and she who first published, albeit in a more decorous version than the original, what she termed 'A Fragment in the Manner of Rabelais', as well as the slight 'An Impromptu' and the 'Memoirs' her father had written for her on the eve of his great fame.[62] Regardless of her motives—and there can be no doubt that they were primarily financial—her achievement was to help foster continuing interest in her father and his writings. Certainly others were ready to cater to the public taste for Sterne's private correspondence in the 1770s. Still living in India, Eliza Draper had thought fit to publish *Letters from Yorick to Eliza* in 1773, and *Sterne's Letters to his Friends on Various Occasions* appeared two years later. The first of these comprised letters written by a married clergyman to the wife of another man, encouraging more criticism of Sterne for, as the *Gentleman's Magazine* phrased it, 'such cicisbeism is always unsafe';[63] the second included just twelve letters, most of which were forged, probably by William Combe. As a result, neither could adequately present the private Sterne to the public. The selection of letters offered by Lydia Médalle, however, did just that. As in the past, Ralph Griffiths was the most perceptive, as well as sympathetic, of reviewers:

> The Letters of Sterne . . . will reflect no disgrace on his memory. They are genuine, and they will serve to assist us in forming a more competent idea of the character of the celebrated Yorick, than we could with certainty collect from the writings which were published by himself. He seems, in almost every Letter, to have written from the heart. His immediate situations, and feelings, rather than his genius, appear to have always guided the pen of his correspondence; and we see in the recesses of private life, the man who so conspicuously shone in the public capacity of an Author.[64]

In the first flush of success, in 1760, Laurence Sterne had written delightedly to Catherine Fourmantel, alerting her to the print taken from Sir Joshua Reynolds's portrait of him which was to act as frontispiece to the first two volumes of *The Sermons of Mr. Yorick*, and adding gleefully: 'so I shall make the most of myself, & sell both inside & out' (*Letters*, 105). Lydia Médalle did not print that letter in her collection, but she was clearly her father's daughter for the same idea had occurred to her. An elegant frontispiece to *Letters of the Late Rev. Mr. Sterne* shows her next to, and dominating, a bust of her late father; the print, by James Caldwell, is taken from a painting by the fashionable artist Benjamin West.[65]

Having returned to France, Lydia Médalle died in 1779 at Toulouse, where she had first stayed with her parents as a 15-year-old; she was 32. She had outlived by a year the second woman for whom, in his final years, Sterne showed genuine affection. Eliza had returned to her husband, Daniel Draper, in Bombay in 1768, and had subsequently accompanied him to Tellicherry and Surat, before returning to Bombay in 1772. In the following year the couple parted for good, following unsubstantiated allegations of her infidelity, and Eliza sought the protection of her uncle in Masulipatam. Although relations between them became strained, Eliza Draper maintained contact with Anne James and, in a lengthy, rambling, and at times fatuous letter written from Bombay in the spring of 1772 endeavoured to defend her conduct in relation to her sentimental friendship with Sterne. Her much-professed concern for Elizabeth and Lydia Sterne did not, however, prevent her from speaking ill of Sterne's wife nor, as we have seen, from publishing a selection of Sterne's correspondence with her as *Letters from Yorick to Eliza*. She returned to England in 1777, but her life thereafter was sickly and short. Having travelled in desperate search of health to Hot Wells at Bristol, she died there in August 1778 and was buried in the north aisle of Bristol Cathedral, where a memorial tablet to her is still to be seen.

For two centuries Sterne's own grave was marked only by the pious offering of the masons, placed in the general vicinity of that plot from which the writer's remains had been seized by body-snatchers and to which his dissected skeleton had been so surreptitiously returned. Sterne's real memorial during that time was his reputation as a writer. Never uniformly admired and sometimes vilely abused, Sterne and his work were nevertheless capable of commanding the most extraordinary respect. Thomas Jefferson, future president of the United States, proclaimed that 'The writings of Sterne . . . form the best course of morality that ever was written'.[66] The editor of *The Beauties of Sterne* appropriated his author's account of the scriptures and applied it to Sterne's own works which, he declared, contained: 'Sublime and noble passages, which, by the rules of sound criticism and reason, may be demonstrated to be truly eloquent and beautiful. There is something in them so thoroughly affecting, and so noble and sublime withal, that one might challenge the writings of the most celebrated orators of antiquity to produce any thing like them.'[67]

The Beauties of Sterne represents one small instance of the commercialization of the man and his writings which Sterne had done so much to foster during his lifetime, and which heralded the more general commercialization of writers and writing whose effects have remained with us to this day. The first 'complete' *Works* of Sterne appeared in Dublin in 1775; a London edition of the *Works* in ten volumes followed in 1780. To these literary tributes were added prints of the author and his writings, including illustrations of scenes from *Tristram Shandy* and *A Sentimental Journey* by, among several others, John Nixon, Michael Angelo Rooker, and Henry Bunbury;[68] there was also an engraving by William Ryland taken from Angelica Kauffmann's *Maria*, depicting Maria of Moulines from *A Sentimental Journey*, which was 'circulated all over Europe . . . in an incalculable variety of forms and dimensions . . . and . . . transferred to numerous articles of all sorts and sizes, from a watch case to a tea waiter'.[69]

In the course of time Sterne's person and writing attracted the homage that nineteenth- and twentieth-century literary piety increasingly paid to genius: popular and scholarly biographies, new editions of the novels (at times abridged or bowdlerized), translations,[70] critical books by the score, and articles in their thousands; since 1989 a scholarly journal has been entirely dedicated to Sterneana.[71] The first scholarly edition of Sterne's collected works, published in twelve volumes in 1904, will soon be superseded by the completion of a counterpart for the twenty-first century.[72] To find that his work would indeed be 'read, perused, paraphrased, commented and discanted upon——or to say it all in a word . . . be thumb'd over by Posterity' (*TS* IX. viii. 497), as he had once jokingly suggested, would undoubtedly have pleased Sterne's spirit.

The influence of Sterne's writings on the imagination of those who came after him would surely have pleased him still more. In the half-century after his death writers throughout Europe—among them Diderot in France, Jean Paul in Germany, Ugo Foscolo in Italy, and Pushkin in Russia—had paid creative homage. Even as his bawdy fell into increasing disrepute among his fellow-countrymen and women, Sterne found a champion in Byron, who wrote of his own masterpiece, *Don Juan* (1819–24), 'I mean it for a poetical T[ristram] Shandy'.[73] If Charles Dickens was unusual in mid-nineteenth-century England in his admiration of Sterne's humour and sentiment alike, across the Atlantic in Brazil Machado de Assis found a poignant and witty counterpart to Tristram's narration of his experiences before birth in his *Memorias postumas de Braz Cubas (Epitaph of a Small Winner)* (1880). In 1830 Goethe admired Sterne's freedom of spirit, thought *A Sentimental Journey* 'inimitable' (though everywhere imitated), and declared of *Tristram Shandy* that 'My admiration has increased and is increasing with the years'.[74] If Goethe honoured Sterne as the most liberated spirit of his century, Nietzsche thought him 'the most liberated spirit of all time'.[75] Nietzsche's favourite novel, *Tristram Shandy* was soon widely admired as a key modernist text *avant la lettre*. Describing *Work in Progress* (later *Finnegans Wake)*, James Joyce declared his book's elements to be 'exactly what every novelist might use: man and woman, birth, childhood, night, sleep, marriage, prayer, death . . . Only I am trying to build many planes of narrative within a single aesthetic purpose. Did you ever read Laurence Sterne?'[76] Considered in such terms, it is not surprising that the post-revolutionary Russian formalist critic Viktor Shklovskiĭ could claim *Tristram Shandy* to be the 'most typical novel in world literature'.[77] Virginia Woolf, meanwhile, suggested *A Sentimental Journey* to be 'more true to life than to literature'[78]—and looked to Sterne as she strove in her own novels to break free of constrictive nineteenth-century modes of fictional representation. Conscious of the importance Sterne has held for novelists from Beckett and Borges to Nabokov and Salman Rushdie, Italo Calvino acknowledged *Tristram Shandy* as the 'undoubted progenitor of all the avant-garde novels of our century'.[79] Sterne himself, who swore not to confine himself to 'any man's rules that ever lived', might have preferred the accolade of Milan Kundera, who acknowledged him as the writer who taught the world to see the novel as a '*great game*'.[80]

Sterne's restless spirit must surely be appeased. Whether the writer's corporeal fate would have pleased him equally is another matter. In a rare act of piety the late Kenneth Monkman succeeded in 1969 in locating Sterne's bones in the burial-ground belonging to St George's, Hanover Square, then due to be lost to development, and had them reinterred in a grave next to St Michael's Church in Coxwold.[81] Having spent so much of his adult life aspiring towards the worldly success his writing finally brought him, Sterne now lies in an otherwise obscure country churchyard in a village he was usually anxious to leave for the sociable world of London. No mute inglorious Milton, Sterne showed no desire in his lifetime to join in death a village community to which he was connected only by a tardy act of aristocratic patronage of the kind that had long eluded him. Time and chance, though, have conspired to play one final trick on Sterne. Across the road, not far from the graveyard, his former home, now fancifully known as Shandy Hall,[82] is a shrine to the writer where, for the price of the entrance fee, the public can pay homage to one of modernity's first respectable and respected commercial writers. Inside and out, alive and dead, Sterne continues to be sold. His fate would certainly have amused and perhaps, after all, not entirely displeased him.

Notes

Introduction

1 John Croft, 'Anecdotes of Sterne Vulgarly Tristram Shandy', *The Whitefoord Papers*, ed. W. A. S. Hewins (Oxford, 1898), 227.

2 Ibid.

3 Ibid.

4 *Sterne's Memoirs: A Hitherto Unrecorded Holograph Now Brought to Light in Facsimile*, ed. Kenneth Monkman (Coxwold: The Laurence Sterne Trust, 1985), 22 (hereafter cited as *Memoirs*).

5 The poem is 'The Unknown World' published in *The Gentleman's Magazine* in 1743; see below pp. 110–14. Dr Kenneth Monkman speculatively attributed to Sterne a number of poems which appeared in the York papers in the 1740s; none of the attributions is wholly convincing and some are quite implausible; see Kenneth Monkman, 'Sterne and the '45', *The Shandean*, 2 (1990), 45–136.

6 There is no proof that Catherine Fourmantel was Sterne's mistress, but the amorous intimacy of his correspondence with her in 1759–60, so different in tone and content from the sentimental correspondence he engaged in with several women in subsequent years, suggests that their relationship was sexual; see below pp. 210–11 and 245–9.

7 *Letters of Laurence Sterne*, ed. Lewis Perry Curtis (Oxford: Clarendon Press, 1935), 87; hereafter cited in the text as *Letters*.

8 In 1760 Tobias Smollett's third novel, *Sir Launcelot Greaves*, was being serialized in *The British Magazine*, with illustrations by Anthony Walker (it is believed to be the earliest illustrated serialized novel); Sterne was perhaps aware of Smollett's illustrated translation of Cervantes's *Don Quixote* (1755), whose third edition of 1756 had a further six illustrations by Hogarth. See also Ronald Paulson, *Hogarth*, 3 vols. (Cambridge: Lutterworth Press, 1993), esp. iii. 276–84, and Jennifer Uglow, *William Hogarth: A Life and a World* (London: Faber and Faber, 1997), 623–5.

9 *Tristram Shandy's Bon Mots, Repartees, odd Adventures, and Humorous Stories . . .* (London, 1760), 3–4.

10. Ibid. 4.

11 Dr John Hill, 'A Letter to the Ladies Magazine', *Royal Female Magazine* (Apr. 1760), repr. in *The London Chronicle*, 7 (3–6 May 1760), 434–5; see also Wilbur L. Cross (ed.), *Works of Laurence Sterne*, 12 vols. (London: The Jenson Society, 1906), vi. 33–46.

12 'To Dr. *****', *Letters*, 88–91 (90); as L. P. Curtis argued, the letter was almost certainly written with publication in mind.

13 *Whitefoord Papers*, 227–8.

14 Laurence Sterne, *The Life and Opinions of Tristram Shandy, Gentleman*, ed. Ian Campbell Ross (1983; rev. edn., Oxford and New York: Oxford University Press, 2000), II. xvii. 114; further references are to this edition and are given parenthetically in the text as *TS*.

15 *Whitefoord Papers*, 228.

16 Ibid. 231; in 1762 Sterne himself

directed a correspondent to write to him at Toulouse as '*Monsieur Sterne gentilhomme Anglois*', adding airily, 'twill find me' (*Letters*, 186).

17 *Journal Encyclopédique*, 3: 1 (1 April 1760), 157.

18 The phrase is William Warburton's, *The Divine Legation of Moses* (London, 1738), 'Dedication', p. ii.

19 *Alas! Poor Yorick! or, a Funeral Discourse* (London, 1761), 36.

20 Henry Fielding, *The True Patriot*, 1 (5 November 1745), in *The True Patriot and Related Writings*, ed. W. B. Coley (Oxford: Clarendon Press, 1987), 103.

21 N. Foster, *An Enquiry into the Present High Price of Provisions* (London, 1767), 41; quoted by Neil McKendrick, 'Introduction', in Neil McKendrick, John Brewer, and J. H. Plumb, *The Birth of a Consumer Society: The Commercialization of Eighteenth-Century England* (London: Europa, 1982), 11.

22 *Letters*, 107.

23 Kenneth Monkman, '*Tristram* in Dublin', *Transactions of the Cambridge Bibliographical Society*, 7 (1979), 343–68.

24 Kenneth Monkman, 'Bibliography of the Early Editions of *Tristram Shandy*', *The Library*, 5th series, 25 (1970), 11–39; id., '*Tristram* in Dublin', and 'Bibliographical Descriptions', appendix 5 of Melvyn and Joan New (eds.), *The Life and Opinions of Tristram Shandy, Gentleman*, 3 vols. (Gainesville, Fla.: University Press of Florida, 1978–83), 907–38.

25 *York Courant*, 4 Mar. 1760.

26 See Neil McKendrick, 'Introduction', in Neil McKendrick, John Brewer, and J. H. Plumb, *The Birth of a Consumer Society*, 43.

27 James Boswell, *Life of Johnson*, ed. R. W. Chapman, rev. J. D. Fleeman (Oxford: Oxford University Press, 1970), 696.

28 *Critical Review*, 9 (January 1760), 73.

29 *Royal Female Magazine*, 1 (Feb. 1760), 56, cited in Alan B. Howes (ed.), *Sterne: The Critical Heritage* (London and Boston: Routledge & Kegan Paul, 1974), 53; [Owen Ruffhead], *Monthly Magazine* (May 1760), 30; *Universal Magazine of Knowledge and Pleasure*, 25 (Apr. 1760), 190, cited in *Sterne: The Critical Heritage*, 63; Lady Dorothy Bradshaigh to Samuel Richardson, letter of June 1760, cited in *Sterne: The Critical Heritage*, from A. D. McKillop, *Samuel Richardson: Printer and Novelist* (1936), 182; A *Letter from the Rev. George Whitfield, B.A., to the Rev. Laurence Sterne, M.A.* (London, 1760), 2.

30 As a sign of changing times, it should be noted that after Gray's death an animated discussion took place between his editor, the poet and precentor of York, the Revd William Mason, and Horace Walpole, genteel author, printer, and publisher, concerning the doubtful propriety of Gray's attitude; in the 1750s, however, even novelists might think writing for profit beneath them, so that the *Monthly Review* for June 1752 repeated the assertion of the Irish Huguenot army agent, William Chaigneau, that he had sought no 'pecuniary Indulgence' from the bookseller for his manuscript (see also William Chaigneau, *The History of Jack Connor* (Dublin, 1752), p. iii).

31 For the fullest account of the reaction to the first two editions of *Tristram Shandy* and the first edition of the *Sermons*, see Alan B. Howes, *Yorick and the Critics: Sterne's Reputation in England, 1760–1868* (New Haven: Yale University Press, 1958), esp. pp. 1–12, and *Sterne: The Critical Heritage*, esp. pp. 46–107.

32 *A Letter*, 2; a similar attack occurs in *The Clockmakers Outcry*, 10.

33 *Grand Magazine*, 3 (June 1760), 317–19.

34 See Howes, *Yorick and the Critics*, 2, quoting *Gentleman's Magazine*, 30 (June 1760), 289; *Grand Magazine*, 3 (June 1760), 290–3; *London Magazine*, 30 (May 1761), 269; George Stubbs exhibited a painting of a horse called Tristram Shandy at the Society of Artists of Great Britain, held at Spring Gardens, Charing Cross, on 17 May 1762 (see Sir Walter Gilbey, *Life of George Stubbs, R.A.* (London, 1898), 'Appendix C', 177.

35 See letter of Lady Dorothy Bradshaigh to Samuel Richardson, June 1760, in *Sterne: The Critical Heritage*, 90; *The Autobiography and Correspondence of Mary Granville, Mrs. Delany*, ed. Augusta Waddington Hall, Lady Llanover, 3 vols., 1st series (1861), iii. 588; letter of 24 Apr. 1760.

36 See Edmund Burke in *Annual Register* (1760), iii. 247; Oliver Goldsmith, 'Chinese Letters, *Public Ledger* (30 June 1760), Letter 53, repr. as *The Citizen of the World* (1762); see Arthur Friedman (ed.), *Collected Works of Oliver Goldsmith*, 5 vols. (Oxford: Clarendon Press, 1966), ii. 221–5.

37 Brit. Mus. Add. MSS 39929, fo. 1, quoted by Curtis, *Letters*, 87, n. 4.

38 B. N. Turner, 'An Account of Dr. Johnson's Visit to Cambridge, in 1765', *New Monthly Magazine*, 10 (1818), 389.

39 *The Clockmakers Outcry* (London, 1760), 42.

40 Ibid.

41 *Alas! Poor Yorick!* (London, 1761), 19–21.

42 James Boswell, 'A Poetical Epistle To Doctor Sterne [,] Parson Yorick [,] And Tristam Shandy', Bodleian MS. Douce 193, 11[r].

43 Richard Graves, 'Trifling Anecdotes of the Late Ralph Allen, Esq. of Prior Park, near Bath', *The Triflers* (London, 1806), 68, quoted in T. C. Duncan Eaves and Ben D. Kimpel, *Samuel Richardson* (Oxford: Clarendon Press, 1971), 537.

44 *Whitefoord Papers*, 229.

45 Francis Drake, *Eboracum: or, the History and Antiquities of the City of York* (London, 1736), 241.

Chapter One

1 *The Correspondence of Jonathan Swift*, ed. Harold Williams, 5 vols. (Oxford: Clarendon Press, 1963–5), iv. 34.

2 *Memoirs*, 2–3.

3 *York Courant*, 10 Nov. 1741, [p. 1].

4 For Sterne's family, see Percy Fitzgerald, *Life of Laurence Sterne*, 3rd edn. (London: Chatto & Windus, 1906), esp. chap. 1; J. W. Clay, 'The Sterne, Family', *Yorkshire Archaeological Journal*, 21 (1911), 91–107; Wilbur L. Cross, *The Life and Times of Laurence Sterne*, esp. chap. 1; *Letters*, esp. 1–5 and nn. *passim.*; David Thompson, *Wild Excursions: The Life and Fiction of Laurence Sterne* (London: Weidenfeld & Nicolson, 1972), 53–5; Arthur H. Cash, *Laurence Sterne: The Early and Middle Years* (London: Methuen, 1975), esp. chap. 1 (henceforth cited as *EMY*); *Memoirs*, *passim.*

5 Gilbert Burnet, *History of his Own Time* (London, 1724), i. 590.

6 *Memoirs*, 1.

7 See the letter of 9 Sept. 1760 to the Revd Robert Brown, *Letters*, 121–3 (122); Sterne deleted the mention of his grandfather attending Archbishop Laud at his execution in his copy of the letter to Brown, perhaps recalling belatedly that his correspondent, a Scottish Presbyterian, was unlikely to have had great respect for Laud.

8 For Simon Sterne, see *Letters*, 5, n. 1, Cash, *EMY* 4–5, 11–12, and Richard Forrester, 'Uncle Jaques Sterne', *The Shandean*, 4 (1992), 197–233 (199).

9 He was baptized on 19 July 1683 at Upper Helmsley in Yorkshire; see Upper Helmsley parish register (Borthwick Institute PR U/Hel 1). This reference, which makes Roger some nine years older than previously believed, was first noted by Forrester, 'Uncle Jaques Sterne', 230, n. 5.

10 See Arthur H. Cash's suggestion to this effect, *EMY* 8

11 *Memoirs*, 1; Agnes Hobert's husband was probably Edward Hobart, promoted lieutenant in 1705, who apparently died in 1709; see *Memoirs*, pp. xix-xx, n. to p. 1, ll. 2–4.

12 *Memoirs*, 1; *Letters*, 40.

13 *Memoirs*, 1.
14 See below, pp. 154–67.
15 *Memoirs*, 3; James M. Kuist, 'New Light on Sterne: An Old Man's Recollections of the Young Vicar', *PMLA* 80 (1965), 549.
16 See Sterne to Jaques Sterne, letter of [5 Apr. 1751], *Letters*, 35.
17 Maurice Craig, *Dublin 1660–1800: A Social and Architectural History* (Dublin: Allen Figgis, 1969), 94.
18 *Memoirs*, 4.
19 Ibid. 4–5.
20 Ibid. 5.
21 Ibid.
22 Ibid. 9.
23 See *The Diary of Ralph Thoresby, F.R.S.*, 2 vols. (London, 1830), i. 154; the story was perhaps not so very unusual, for Daniel Defoe tells a very similar tale in *A Tour through the Whole Island of Great Britain*, Letter VIII, (1724–6; repr. Harmondsworth: Penguin, 1971), 458.
24 *Memoirs*, 11.
25 Ibid. 7.
26 Ibid. 11.
27 This identification was first made by David Thomson in *Wild Excursions*, 53 ff; for Robert Stearne, I have followed 'An Account of the most Remarkable Transactions w[h] Brigad. Stearne has been Engaged in with the Royal Regiment of Foot in Ireland', National Library of Ireland Ms 4166 (Phillipps MS 13285); the manuscript is bound and regularly paginated.
28 Robert Stearne is identified as brother of John in *The Grand Juries of the County of Westmeath 1727–1853*, 2 vols. (Ledestown, 1853), 306–7; I am most grateful to Dr Kenneth Ferguson for this reference.
29 Ibid. 34.
30 *Memoirs*, 11.
31 Ibid.
32 Ibid.
33 Ibid. 13.
34 Ibid.
35 Few of his contemporaries were aware that Laurence Sterne had been born in Ireland. Though the memoir written for Lydia draws attention to the fact, Sterne only mentioned his Irish background in one letter; denying at length a report that he had 'ridiculed my Irish friends at Bath' in 1765, he concluded: 'Besides, I am myself of their own country:—My father was a considerable time on duty with his regiment in Ireland; and my mother gave me to the world when she was there' (*Letters*, 250). The letter in which this passage occurs was, however, allegedly addressed to, and first published by, William Combe, who certainly forged some of the letters he attributed to Sterne; Professor Curtis, however, accepted this letter as genuine. For Sterne as an Irish writer, see below, 'Epilogue', p. 430 and n. 76.
36 Percy Fitzgerald, *The Life of Laurence Sterne*, 2 vols. (London, 1864), i. 79.
37 *Memoirs*, 14.
38 For Roger Sterne's posting to Jamaica and death, see PRO: CO 91/1, PRO: CO 137/19, ff. 16, 25–7, and PRO: WO 25/18, 45 and C.O. 137/53 ff. 336, 368, cited and quoted in part by Curtis, *Letters*, 8, n. 20.
39 *Memoirs*, 14.
40 Ibid. 15.
41 *TS* VI, xxix. 365–6; see also *Memoirs*, pp. xxviii-xxix, n. to p. 15, ll. 1–5.
42 *Memoirs*, 2.
43 Ibid. 15.
44 For an account of the Sterne family coat-of-arms, see Laurence Sterne, *A Sentimental Journey through France and Italy*, ed. Gardner D. Stout, Jr. (Berkeley and Los Angeles: University of California Press, 1967), 205, n. to ll. 37–40; further references are to this edition and are given parenthetically in the text as *ASJ*.
45 'THE SWORD. RENNES' picks up the same theme, relating the story of a Breton nobleman who resigns his nobility, goes to Martinique for twenty years, where he makes a fortune, subsequently returning to France to reclaim his sword and his nobility. Though a clergyman,

Sterne seems to have been attached to the sword as a sign of his own gentility: he wore George Oswald's sword after the latter's death (see below, pp. 296–7), and was portrayed wearing clerical garb and a sword in Thomas Patch's painting of Tristam's encounter with Death in *TS* VII. i.

46 *Letters*, 39–40.

47 Defoe, *A Tour through the Whole Island*, esp. Letter VIII. See also John Smail, *The Origins of Middle-Class Culture: Halifax, Yorkshire, 1660–1770* (Ithaca: Cornell University Press, 1994).

48 Defoe, *A Tour*, 496–7.

49 Ibid. 491.

50 Defoe believed it the largest of all: see ibid. 494–5.

51 *Memoirs*, 13.

52 *Letters*, 217; *York Courant*, 25 Aug. 1761. See also Paul Langford, *A Polite and Commercial People: England 1727–1783* (1989; repr. Oxford and New York: Oxford University Press, 1992), 79–84, and Geoffrey Holmes, *Augustan England: Professions, State and Society 1680–1730* (London: Allen & Unwin, 1982), chap. 3.

53 *Memoirs*, 13.

54 John Nichols, *Illustrations of the Literary History of the Eighteenth Century*, 8 vols. (London, 1817–58), ii. 222; letter of Revd Styan Thirlby to Mr Theobald, 'Camb. Jesus College, May 7, 1729'.

55 See below, p. 265.

56 Fitzgerald, *The Life of Laurence Sterne*, 10; see also Cornhill *Magazine*, NS 19 (1892), 482.

57 *Letters*, 3–4; Sterne did not include this story in the first part of the 'memoir' he wrote for Lydia in 1758 but set it down only after he had demonstrated his 'genius' with the publication of *Tristram Shandy*; references to the second part of the 'memoir' are to L. P. Curtis's edition in *Letters*, and are given parenthetically in the text.

58 For the difficulties facing young men in Sterne's position see Edward Hughes, *North Country Life in the Eighteenth Century: The North-East, 1700–1750* (1952; repr. London: Oxford University Press, 1969), 105 ff.

59 Daniel Defoe, *A Tour through the Whole Island of Great Britain*, 107–8.

60 Gray to Horace Walpole, 31 Oct. 1734: *Horace Walpole's Correspondence*, 13, ed. W. S. Lewis, George L. Lam, and Charles H. Bennett (New Haven: Yale University Press, 1948), 58.

61 Ibid. 58–9.

62 Philip Stanhope, Lord Chesterfield, *Letters from Lord Chesterfield to Alderman George Faulkner, etc., being a Supplement to his Lordship's Letters* (London, 1777), 23.

63 John Cannon, *Aristocratic Century: The Peerage of Eighteenth-Century England* (Cambridge: Cambridge University Press, 1984), 45.

64 *TS* VI. xi. 343.

65 *DNB* i. 647.

66 Stanhope, *Letters from Lord Chesterfield to Alderman George Faulkner, etc.*, 23.

67 D. A. Winstanley, *Unreformed Cambridge: A Study of Certain Aspects of the University in the Eighteenth Century* (Cambridge: Cambridge University Press, 1935), 186; for Jesus College during Sterne's time there see Arthur Gray and Frederick Brittain, *A History of Jesus College, Cambridge* (1960; rev. edn. Cambridge: Silent Books, 1988).

68 Gilbert Wakefield, *Memoirs of the Life of Gilbert Wakefield* (London, 1792), 62–4.

69 Edward Gibbon, *Memoirs of my Life*, ed. Betty Radice (Harmondsworth: Penguin, 1984), 76.

70 Jonathan Swift and Thomas Sheridan, *The Intelligencer*, ed. James Woolley (Oxford: Clarendon Press, 1992), no. 9, p. 122.

71 Daniel Defoe, *Augusta Triumphans* (London, 1728), 4.

72 James Miller, *On Politeness* (London, 1738), p. 11, ll. 202–5.

73 C. H. C. and M. I. Baker, *The Life and Circumstances of James Brydges, first Duke of Chandos* (Oxford: Clarendon Press, 1949), 100–3; and Cannon, *Aristocratic Century*, 56.

74 Boswell, *Life of Johnson*, 45–57; Walter

Jackson Bate, *Samuel Johnson* (London: Chatto & Windus, 1978), chap. 8 *passim.*

75 *Letters*, 40.

76 Winstanley, *Unreformed Cambridge*, 201–3.

77 Ibid. 201.

78 Jesus College archives, TRU. 3. 1, quoted by Cash, *EMY* 46 n. 1.

79 *Letters*, 33.

80 *Letters*, 59, n. 7.

81 Boswell, quoted by Frederick A. Pottle, *James Boswell: The Earlier Years 1740–1769* (London: Heinemann, 1966), 67.

82 The reminiscence occurs in the second part of the memoir, written during the years of his fame; for further discussion of Sterne's relationship with Hall-Stevenson in the 1740s and 1750s, see below, pp. 102–5.

83 John Hall-Stevenson, 'My Cousin's Tale of a Cock and a Bull', *Crazy Tales* (London, 1762), 16–17.

84 *Tristram Shandy's Bon Mots, Repartees, Odd Adventures, and Humorous Stories*, 5.

85 Norman Sykes, *Church and State in the XVIIIth Century* (1935; repr. New York: Octagon Books, 1975), 147–8.

86 It is not impossible that Roger Sterne entertained a strong aversion to trade, however; certainly, his apparent attachment to military honour, like his son's account of his father, suggests that his otherwise inexplicable decision to join the army as an ensign might have resulted from an outright refusal to go into business of any kind.

87 Hughes, *North Country Life in the Eighteenth Century*, 104.

88 Holmes, *Augustan England*, 91.

89 *The Spectator*, ed. Donald F. Bond, 5 vols. (Oxford: Clarendon Press, 1965), no. 21 (24 Mar. 1710–11), i. 88.

90 William Warburton to Ralph Allen; 'Two Letters of Bishop Warburton', *Surtees Society*, 124 (1915), 194.

91 See Richard Forrester, 'Uncle Jaques Sterne', *passim.*

92 Diocesan Registry, York. Institutions (Commissions) 1731–42: Inst AB 11A, p. 24.

93 S. L. Ollard and P. C. Walker, 'Archbishop Herring's Visitation Returns', *Yorkshire Archaeological Society* (1928–31), p. xii; Norman Sykes, *Church and State in England in the XVIIIth Century*, 99

94 For Peploe's political allegiances, see S. W. Baskerville, 'The Political Behaviour of the Cheshire Clergy, 1705–52', *Northern History*, 23 (1987), 74–97, esp. 83–4.

95 'However, although his fortune was very small, he [i.e. Swift] had a scruple of entring the Church meerly for support'; Jonathan Swift, 'Family of Swift', *Miscellaneous and Autobiographical Pieces, Fragments and Marginalia*, ed. Herbert Davis (Oxford: Basil Blackwell, 1962), 194.

96 Sermon 1, 'Inquiry after Happiness', *The Sermons of Laurence Sterne*, ed. Melvyn New (Gainesville, Fla.: University Press of Florida, 1996), iv. 3, in *The Florida Edition of the Works of Lawrence Sterne*, vols. iv (Text) and v (Notes); further references to Sterne's sermons are to this edition, cited as *Sermons.*

97 In his *Exposition of the Thirty-Nine Articles*, Bishop Gilbert Burnet restricted himself, in dealing with the Holy Trinity, to the comment that 'if God has declared this inexplicable thing concerning himself to us; we are bound to believe it, though we cannot have any clear Idea how it truly is' (Article I, 37); in a letter, the leading latitudinarian, John Tillotson, then archbishop of Canterbury, congratulated Burnet by affirming that 'In the article of the Trinity you have said all, that I think can be said upon so obscure and difficult an argument'; see Isabel Rivers, *Reason, Grace, and Sentiment: A Study of the Language of Religion and Ethics in England, 1660–1780* (Cambridge: Cambridge University Press, 1991). For latitudinarianism and Anglicanism more generally, see also Norman Sykes, *Church and State in the XVIIIth* Century; Philip Harth, *Swift and Anglican Rationalism* (Chicago: University of Chicago Press, 1961); Gerard Reedy, SJ, *The Bible and Reason: Anglicans and Scripture in Late Seventeenth-Century England* (Philadelphia:

University of Pennsylvania Press, 1985); and Gordon Rupp, *Religion in England, 1688–1791* (Oxford: Clarendon Press, 1986).

98 The York Diocesan Registry records his collation to Sutton on the Forest on 24 August 1738; Institutions (Commissions) 1731–42, p. 29.

Chapter two

1 *York Courant*, 4 Sept. 1739, [p. 4].

2 *Letters*, 21.

3 See Langford, *A Polite and Commercial People*, 258.

4 *York Courant*, 22 Mar. 1743 and 10 Jan. 1749.

5 Turpin was executed on 7 Apr. 1739; see *York Courant*, 10 Apr. 1739 [p. 3].

6 Ibid. 23 Oct. 1739 [p. 3].

7 Ibid. 9 Feb. 1748 [p. 3].

8 Ibid. 19 Dec. 1749 [p. 3].

9 Ibid. 9 July 1745 [p. 3].

10 Drake, *Eboracum*, 241.

11 *York Courant*, 17 July 1739 [p. 3].

12 Thomas Gent, *Life of Thomas Gent* (London, 1832), 192–3.

13 They shared a common grandmother, Elizabeth Clarke, who married twice; first Anthony Light, from which marriage Lydia, the Lumley sisters' mother, was born; and secondly Thomas Robinson, whose son, Matthew, was the father of Elizabeth.

14 Emily J. Climenson, *Elizabeth Montagu: The Queen of the Bluestockings*, 2 vols. (New York: E. P. Dutton and Co., 1906), i. 95–6.

15 Ibid. i. 231.

16 See Daniel Defoe, *Tour*, p. 76; he is quoting John Macky, *A Journey through England in Familiar Letters* (1714–23), i. 4, who was describing the assembly at Bury St Edmunds.

17 Elizabeth Robinson alludes to Elizabeth Lumley's illness in a letter to her sister Sarah; see Climenson, *Elizabeth Montagu*, i. 74. For a useful contextualization of the Sternes' courtship and Elizabeth Lumley's cession of her fortune to her husband's control, see Amanda Vickery, *The Gentleman's Daughter: Women's Lives in Georgian England* (New Haven and London: Yale University Press, 1998), esp. chap. 2.

18 L. P. Curtis, 'New Light on Sterne', *Modern Language Notes*, 76 (June 1961), 499–500.

19 The letter in which this passage occurs is one of the four, printed in *Letters of the late Rev. Mr. Laurence Sterne* (1775) as having been written by Sterne to his wife-to-be in the winter of 1739–40, whose authenticity has been frequently questioned. Most problematic is the letter Curtis prints as Letter 1 in *Letters*, which demonstrably reveals considerable overlap of material with the 'Journal to Eliza', written almost thirty years later. In brief, the principal possibilities are that Sterne copied portions of love letters written to Elizabeth Lumley almost three decades earlier, or that in editing the letters for the 1775 volume the Sternes' daughter Lydia piously misappropriated parts of the 'Journal to Eliza' or (more probably) a now-lost letter from her father to Eliza Draper, and redirected them as though originally written to her mother. Neither of these explanations is altogether devoid of attendant problems. In the former instance, we might wonder how probable it is that Sterne, then in London, had access to love letters written in Yorkshire so long before—to say nothing of *why* he would want to follow these so closely in writing to Eliza Draper (for whom, see below, Chaps. 14 and 15 *passim*). The second explanation is not inherently implausible, for Lydia Sterne (or Lydia de Médalle, as she styled herself following her marriage) was certainly capable of forging, or inciting others to forge, letters from her father

where suitable originals were wanting. Ethical questions aside—and Sterne demonstrably did send virtually identical letters to different female correspondents—the authenticity or otherwise of Letter 1 is of particular interest since in it Sterne employs the term 'sentimental', which he was later to do so much to popularize, a full decade before it became fashionable. The issue has been widely debated without satisfactory resolution. I find Letter 1 suspect and have not quoted from it. Letters 2 to 4 are also problematic, but the characteristic admixture of wistful sentiment and a melancholy awareness of human mortality (especially in Letter 4) leads me to accept them as essentially genuine. For fuller discussion of the issues, see, e.g. Sidney Lee, 'Laurence Sterne', *DNB* xviii. 1099; L. P. Curtis, *Letters*, 10–12, and n.; Erik Erametsa, 'A Study of the Word 'Sentimental' and of Other Linguistic Characteristics of Eighteenth-Century Sentimentalism in England', *Annales Academiae Scientiarum Fennicae*, Ser. B (Helsinki, 1951); Duke Maskell, 'The Authenticity of Sterne's first recorded letter', *Notes & Queries*, 215 (1970), 303–7; Thomson, *Wild Excursions*, 95–8; Cash, *EMY* 81, n. 3; for a different view see Margaret R. B. Shaw, *Laurence Sterne: The Making of a Humorist, 1713–62* (London: The Richards Press, 1957), 38 ff.

20 Curtis, 'New Light on Sterne', 500.

21 Ibid.

22 Climenson, *Elizabeth Montagu*, i. 73.

23 Ibid. 74.

24 *Whitefoord Papers*, 226.

25 LS to Jaques Sterne, letter of 5 Apr. 1751, *Letters*, 39.

26 Borthwick Institute, York; Sutton Parish Book, 77^{v}.

27 Climenson, *Elizabeth Montagu*, i. 74

28 Ibid.

29 Ibid. 73.

30 Ibid.

31 See *Whitefoord Papers*, 226.

Chapter three

1 Holmes, *Augustan England*, 88.

2 Edmund Pyle, *Memoirs of a Royal Chaplain, 1729–63*, ed. Albert Hartshorne (London and New York: John Lane: The Bodley Head, 1905), 266.

3 *DNB* v. 123–4.

4 See above, p. 47.

5 Horace Walpole, *Memoires of the Last Ten Years of the Reign of George the Second*, 2 vols. (London, 1822), i. 75.

6 For Jaques Sterne's involvement in politics in 1727, of which there is no direct evidence, see his letter of 19 Sept. 1752 to the duke of Newcastle, *Letters*, 428.

7 See L. Peter Wenham, *Gray's Court: St. John's College, York* (York, n.d.), 15, 27.

8 The exceptionally ferociously contested 1754 Oxfordshire election, when the Whig duke of Marlborough took on his political opponents in a notoriously Tory county, cost £40,000.

9 Turner had previously served as Member of Parliament for Northallerton between 1715 and 1722.

10 For Jaques Sterne's involvement in the 1734 election, see *Notes and Queries*, 2nd series, 7 (Jan. 1859), 15; Lewis Perry Curtis, *The Politicks of Laurence Sterne* (London: Oxford University Press, 1929), 10; letter of Jaques Sterne to Cholmley Turner [?Apr. 1734], *Letters*, 423; and Forrester, 'Uncle Jaques', 206.

11 *Politicks*, 10–12; J. F. Quinn, 'Yorkshiremen go to the Polls: County Contests in the Early Eighteenth Century', *Northern History*, 21 (1985), 149–55.

12 *York Courant*, 22 Jan. 1740 [p. 3].

13 Ibid. 29 Jan. 1740 [p. 3].

14 For John Burton, see *York Archaeological Journal*, 2 (1877–8), 403–40; Richard Davies, *A Memoir of John Burton*; *York Archaeological Journal*, 2 (1873), ii. 368.

15 See also Kathleen Wilson, 'Urban Culture and Political Activism in Hanoverian England: The Emergence of Voluntary Hospitals', in Eckhart Hellmuth (ed.), *The Transformation of Political Culture: England and Germany in the Late Eighteenth Century* (Oxford: Oxford University Press for the Germany Historical Institute, 1990), 165–84.

16 *York Courant*, 5 May 1741 [p. 3].

17 John Burton, *British Liberty Endanger'd* (1749), 17.

18 *York Courant*, 7 July 1741 [p. 3].

19 Ibid. 21 Apr. 1741 [p. 3].

20 J. F. Quinn, 'York Elections in the Age of Walpole', *Northern History*, 22 (1986), 183.

21 *York Gazetteer*, 15 Dec. 1741 [p. 1].

22 PRO: Assizes. 41.4, cited in Cash, *EMY* 96.

23 While it is reasonable to assume that Sterne's earliest published prose may be found in the first issue (or a subsequent early number) of the *York Gazetteer*, there is no evidence to this effect. The first known issue of the *Gazetteer* is that of 15 December 1741. A number of pieces dating from 1741 to 1747 and published in the London *Daily Gazetteer* or reprinted as handbills were identified as Sterne's by Dr Kenneth Monkman, on the basis of circumstantial evidence or simple assertion; see Monkman, 'More of Sterne's *Politicks* 1741–2', *The Shandean*, 1 (1989), 53–108, and 'Sterne and the '45 (1743–8)', *The Shandean*, 2 (1990), 45–136. If genuine, these political contributions would both fill out Sterne's involvement in the 1741 and 1742 elections and would raise questions concerning his open renunciation of party politics in 1742 (see below, pp. 87–90). Since my subjective reading of the majority of these pieces suggested they were not by Sterne (for an exception, see below, p. 89), they were subjected to computer analysis, involving detailed statistical and lexical evaluation, and compared to a random control sample of Sterne's known writings of the 1740s (five letters: *Letters*, nos. 3, 7, 8, 9, and 10), one piece of political journalism (*York Courant*, 10 Nov. 1741 [p. 1]), and two excerpts from *Tristram Shandy*, written in the 1760s (*TS* VI. xxxix. 378–9 and VII. ii. 386–7). The resulting analysis suggests that the disputed items are extremely unlikely to have been written by Sterne. While the known works by Sterne—of diverse kinds and written many years apart—exhibit a surprisingly high degree of stability in measurements of lexical richness, this stability is not to be found in the anonymous material Monkman attributed to Sterne. Moreover, the greater variability of lexical choice in the attributed material suggests that the pieces were unlikely to have been written by the same author. It is possible that Sterne was trying to disguise his style, but because there is a marked difference between his usual use of closed-set items, of which he was almost certainly unaware, and the use of closed-set items in the attributed pieces, this is unlikely (for 'closed-set' items see E. O. Winter, 'The Statistics of Analyzing Very Short Texts in a Criminal Context', in H. Kniffna (ed.), *Recent Developments in Forensic Linguistics* (Frankfurt: Peter Lang, 1996), 141–79.) This brief summary is based on the conclusions of D. Woolls and S. Wiggins, CFL Software Development, 'Comparison of Known Writings of Laurence Sterne With Anonymous Writing Appearing in the *York Gazetteer*', 30 Sept. 1997. 5 pp. + 7 unnumbered pp. of statistical materials. For their assistance I am much indebted to the authors and to Professor Ian Small of the University of Birmingham.

24 *York Courant*, 9 June 1741 [p. 3].

25 The passage occurs in an item from a lost issue of the *York Gazetteer* for 16 June 1741, subsequently reprinted in a broadside; see Kenneth Monkman and J. C. T. Oates, 'Towards a Sterne Bibliography: Books and Other Material

Displayed at the Sterne Conference', in Arthur H. Cash and John M. Stedmond (eds.), *The Winged Skull: Papers from the Laurence Sterne Bicentenary Conference* (London: Methuen, 1971), 282, item 6 and ill. facing p. 108.

26 See Langford, *A Polite and Commercial People*, 159 and J. M. Beattie, *Crime and the Courts in England 1660–1800* (Oxford: Clarendon Press, 1986), 53; Garbutt was eventually tried and acquitted of the charge; see *York Courant*, 16 and 23 Mar. 1742.

27 Bingley was ennobled as one of the twelve peers Queen Anne created to enable the Tory ministry to force the terms of the Treaty of Utrecht through the House of Lords.

28 Quinn, 'Yorkshiremen go to the Polls', 157, n. 29.

29 *York Courant*, 8 Sept. 1741 [p. 3].

30 Ibid.

31 Ibid.

32 Ibid. 29 Sept. 1741 [p. 3]

33 Ibid. 6 Oct. 1741 [p. 3].

34 Quinn, 'Yorkshiremen go to the Polls', 160.

35 *York Courant*, 20 Oct. 1741 [p. 1]

36 *Query upon Query* would eventually appear in four different versions. On the day following its publication in the *York Courant* it was reprinted, in a slightly expanded form, in the London *Daily Gazetteer*. Revised, and with three additional queries penned by Jaques Sterne, it was published in the *Leeds Mercury* of 3 November, and this revision also appeared separately as a pamphlet. See Curtis, *Politicks*, 47–60; Cedric Collyer, 'Laurence Sterne and Yorkshire Politics: Some New Evidence', *Leeds Philosophical Society Proceedings*, 7:1 (1952), 83–7; Cash, *EMY* 103, n. 3; Monkman, 'More of Sterne's *Politicks*, 1741–2', esp. 63–4.

37 This sentence, almost certainly by Sterne, was omitted in the *York Courant* version, but appears in the London *Daily Gazetteer* printing of the following day: 28 Oct. 1741.

38 *York Courant*, 27 Oct. 1741 [p. 1].

39 In the extended pamphlet version Jaques Sterne drove home this point more forcefully—had Fox not already voted for the Irish woollen manufacture in the bill for importing Irish yarn into England, 'to the Ruin of the Combers, Spinners, &c. of this County'?—in a way unlikely to command much sympathy today from anyone who has read, for example, Swift's accounts of the misery of those employed in the Irish woollen industry in the 1720s and 1730s.

40 The York elections of 1741 and 1742 were notorious for their violence; see Quinn, 'York Elections in the Age of Walpole', 184 and n. 17.

41 See Forrester, 'Uncle Jaques Sterne', esp. 208–9.

42 *York Courant*, 3 Nov. 1741 [p. 3].

43 Ibid.; the lines are appropriated from Pope, *Epistle to Arbuthnot*, ll. 305–8.

44 See Monkman, 'More of Sterne's *Politicks*, 1741–2', 64.

45 Ibid.

46 *York Courant*, 10 Nov. 1741 [p. 1].

47 See J. V. Guerinot, *Pamphlet Attacks on Alexander Pope, 1711–1744* (London: Methuen, 1969), *passim*.

48 *York Courant*, 24 Nov. 1741 [p. 3].

49 Ibid.

50 'To the Rev. Mr. *James Scott* at *Leeds*', 27 Nov. 1741; the broadside is reproduced in Cash and Stedmond (eds.), *The Winged Skull*, facing p. 109.

51 Ibid.

52 Broadside reprinting of an article published in the *York Gazetteer*, 8 Dec. 1741; repr. in Monkman, 'More of Sterne's *Politicks* 1741–2', 72, 73.

53 *York Courant*, 8 Dec. 1741 [p. 4].

54 Ibid.

55 *York Gazetteer*, 15 Dec. 1741 [p. 3].

56 Ibid.

57 *York Courant*, 15 Dec. 1741 [p. 1].

58 Ibid. 5 Jan. 1742 [p. 1].

59 Ibid.

60 Ibid. [p. 3].

61 J. F. Quinn, 'Yorkshiremen go to the Polls', 161.

62 Actually, 8,016 to 7,047: Quinn, ibid.

63 Ibid. 171.
64 Ibid. 173.
65 Even the determined efforts of, especially, L. P. Curtis and Kenneth Monkman have succeeded only in tracking down an incomplete sequence of the political journalism of 1741–2; see Curtis, *Politicks*, *passim*, and Monkman, 'More of Sterne's *Politicks*, 1741–2'.
66 Thomas Gent, *Life of Thomas Gent* (London, 1832), 194.
67 *York Gazetteer*, 19 Jan. 1742; first published in Cash and Stedmond, *Winged Skull*, 284.
68 Quinn, 'Yorkshiremen go to the Polls', 160–1.
69 *York Courant*, 9 Feb. 1742 [p. 3].
70 Ibid. 23 Mar. 1742 [p. 2].
71 Ibid. 27 July 1742 [p. 3].
72 Sidney Smith to J. A. Murray, letter of Aug. 1834: *Letters of Sidney Smith*, ed. Nowell C. Smith (Oxford: Clarendon Press, 1953), 665.
73 Of the items newly attributed to Sterne by Kenneth Monkman in 'More of Sterne's *Politicks* 1741–2', this is the only one which seemed to me likely to be from his pen; computer analysis is not conclusive, but the item conforms more nearly to work known to be by Sterne than any other and I have accepted it as genuine (see also n. 23 above).
74 *York Gazetteer*, 2 Nov. 1742; reprinted in Monkman in 'More of Sterne's *Politicks*, 1741–2', 90–1.
75 Richard Griffith, 'The Ministerial Writer', in *The Posthumous Works of a Late Celebrated Genius, Deceased*, 2 vols. (Dublin, 1770), i. 13–15.
76 *York Gazetteer*, 2 Nov. 1742 [p. 1].

Chapter Four

1 Parish Book of Sutton (PR SUT/F2), Borthwick Institute, York.
2 Ibid.
3 Even when Sterne took a curate to serve Coxwold during his stay in France in the 1760s, after his success with *Tristram Shandy*, he paid him only £30 yearly.
4 For the income attached to the prebends of Givendale and North Newbald, see L. P. Curtis, *Letters*, 9, n. 23.
5 Jonathan Swift and Thomas Sheridan, *The Intelligencer*, ed. James Woolley, no. 3, p. 64.
6 David Hume, 'My Own Life'; see Ernest Campbell Mossner, *The Life of David Hume*, 2nd edn. (Oxford: Clarendon Press, 1980), App. A, p. 613.
7 For Sterne's reply, see *Letters*, 21–2.
8 Returns for thirty Oxford parishes between 1738 and 1788 show a total of just 5.5%: see Rupp, *Religion in England 1688–1791*, 517.
9 Canon Ollard found Sterne's response exceptional among the replies to Archbishop Herring's questionnaire; for the obligation to catechize every Sunday, see Edmund Gibson, *Codex juris ecclesiastici anglicani* (London, 1713), 'Canons of 1603', i. 453. See also Francis Blackburne, *A Charge Delivered to the Clergy of the Archdeaconry of Cleveland at the Visitation held in the Year MDCCLII* (York, 1752).
10 James M. Kuist, 'New Light on Sterne: An Old Man's Recollections of the Young Vicar', *PMLA* 80 (1965), 549.
11 See below, p. 174.
12 Thomas Herring, *Seven Sermons on Public Occasions* (London, 1763), Sermon I, p. 37; see also *Sermons*, v. 59.
13 Kuist, 'New Light on Sterne', 550.
14 Swift, *The Intelligencer*, no. 7, p. 98.
15 *Sermons*, v. 10–11. Though he seems never to have kept one himself, Jonathan Swift commended the use of commonplace books to 'industrious young Divines' in *A Letter to a Young Gentleman Lately enter'd into Holy Orders*; see H. Davis (ed.), *Irish Tracts 1720–23* (Oxford, Blackwell, 1963), 75–6.
16 *A Letter to a Young Gentleman Lately enter'd into Holy Orders*, 70; the connection

between religious and social duty was emphasized by the 82nd Canon of the Canons of 1604, which required the Ten Commandments to be set up on the east end of every church, where they would appear with appropriate sentences from scripture, underneath the royal coat of arms.

17 *York Courant*, 14 June 1743 [p. 3].

18 'Preface' to *Seven Sermons on Public Occasions*, p. iv.

19 For a speculative account of this sermon and Herring's supposed response to Sterne, see Monkman, 'Sterne and the '45 (1743–8)', 47–9.

20 *Memoirs of a Royal Chaplain*, 196.

21 *Whitefoord Papers*, 230–1.

22 Ibid. 231.

23 Ibid.

24 *The Spectator*, no. 112, 9 July 1714, p. 462.

25 Sutton Parish Book, 22^{r}.

26 Ibid.

27 'New Light on Sterne', 550.

28 Tobias Smollett, *The Expedition of Humphry Clinker*, ed. Lewis M. Knapp, rev. Paul-Gabriel Boucé (1966; rev. edn., Oxford and New York: Oxford University Press, 1984), 353.

29 Arthur H. Cash, *EMY* 137–9, has questioned the authenticity of this account, asking how probable it was that the clergyman Elizabeth Lumley *did* marry should turn out already to hold a living adjacent to Stillington, and suggests that Lydia Sterne tampered with this in printing the memoirs; however, since Lydia does not seem otherwise to be engaged in such tampering, and as Professor Cash advances no reason as to why she should have done so in this case, I am inclined to accept Sterne's version.

30 For a computation of the total acreage, see Cash, *EMY* 139 and n. 3.

31 *Whitefoord Papers*, 233.

32 Kuist, 'New Light on Sterne', 550.

33 Ibid.; see also *Whitefoord Papers*, 231–2.

34 *Whitefoord Papers*, 231.

35 'Prologue to the Crazy Tales', *Crazy Tales* (London, 1762), [p. 1].

36 William Hutton, *A Trip to Coatham* (London, 1810), 151.

37 'Prologue to the Crazy Tales', 4.

38 John Hall-Stevenson to John Hall, 17 Feb. 1785, in *Seven Letters Written by Sterne and his Friends*, ed. William Durrant Cooper (London, 1844), 17.

39 See below, pp. 125–7.

40 See *Letters*, 141, citing *Country Magazine* (Nov. 1786), 170.

41 'Epitaph upon a Living Subject', *The Works of John Hall-Stevenson*, 3 vols. (London, 1795), ii. 203; see also *Seven Letters Written by Sterne and His Friends*, 17.

42 Richard Brinsley Peake, *Memoirs of the Colman Family*, 2 vols. (London, 1841), i. 376–7.

43 *The Expedition of Humphry Clinker*, 282.

44 Note to 'Arsinoe: or, Passion Overstrained' ('Old Hewet's Tale'), *The Works of John Hall-Stevenson, Esq.* (London, 1795), iii. 137.

45 See below, p. 301.

46 The 'Demoniacs' is the name Swift gives to the members of the 'Legion Club' or Irish parliament in *A Character, Panegyric, and Description of the Legion Club*; see *Swift: The Complete Poems*, ed. Pat Rogers (Harmondsworth: Penguin, 1983), 550.

47 Sterne to Hall-Stevenson, letters of [June] 1761 and 5 February 1766 (*Letters*, 140, 270).

48 See e.g. Louis C. Jones, *The Clubs of the Georgian Rakes* (New York: Columbia University Press, 1942), esp. chaps. 5 and 6, and pp. 155–63; Constantia Maxwell, *Dublin Under the Georges 1714–1830* (1936; 3rd edn., London: Faber, 1956), 119; and Betty Kemp, *Sir Francis Dashwood: An Eighteenth-Century Independent* (London: Macmillan and New York: St Martin's Press, 1967).

49 For Sterne's later praise of the society at Crazy Castle, see e.g. his letter to Hall-Stevenson of 12 Aug. 1762, *Letters*, 181.

50 See below, p. 251.

51 *Whitefoord Papers*, 231.

52 'To those who are resolved to be criticks in spite of nature, and at the same time have no great disposition to much reading and study, I would recommend them to assume the character of connoisseur. . . . The rememberance of a few names of painters, with their general characters, with a few rules of the Academy . . . will go a great way towards making a very notable connoisseur': *The Yale Edition of the Works of Samuel Johnson*, vol. ii, *The Idler* and *The Adventurer*, ed. W. J. Bate, John M. Bullitt, and L. F. Powell, *Idler* no. 76 (29 Sept. 1759), 236.

53 See Paulson, *Hogarth*, iii. 276–84.

54 *Letters*, 151.

55 *Whitefoord Papers*, 231.

56 Ibid.

57 See Arthur H. Cash, *EMY*, 'Appendix: Portraits of Sterne', 299–316, esp. 299–300 and plate 1 (facing p. 304).

58 *Letters*, 441.

59 See *Catalogue of a Curious and Valuable Collection of Books, among which are included the Entire Library of the late Reverend and Learned Laurence Sterne* (1768); W. G. Day, 'Sterne's Books', *The Library*, 31 (1976), 245–8; Nicolas Barker, 'The Library Catalogue of Laurence Sterne', *The Shandean*, 1 (1989), 9–24; and Kenneth Monkman, 'Books Sterne Owned?', *The Shandean*, 2 (1990), 215–25.

60 Dr John Ferriar was the first to suggest that Sterne was introduced to many of his favourite books by Hall-Stevenson; see *Illustrations of Sterne* (1798), 41.

61 *Whitefoord Papers*, 230.

62 *Letters*, 142.

63 C. B. L. Barr, 'Sterne and York Minster Library',*The Shandean*, 2 (1990), 8–21.

64 Sterne also kept a scrapbook of items of Irish interest, now in the Cambridge University Library, HIB. 3. 730.

65 See Kenneth Monkman, 'Laurence Sterne and the '45 (1743–8)', *The Shandean*, 2 (1990), 45–136; the single exception, which may confidently be attributed to Sterne, is the concluding stanza to the ballad 'The Royal Hunters' March' (see pp. 56–9). One circumstance which tends in particular to throw doubt on the existence of any significant number of poems by Sterne is the fact that he makes no mention of any when casting around in late 1761 for materials which might be published for the benefit of his wife and daughter in the event of his death (see below, pp. 272–3).

66 Thomas Gill, *Vallis Eboracensis* (London and Easingwold, 1852), 199–200 (199).

67 *The Gentleman's Magazine*, 13 (July 1743), 376.

68 An extract from *Night Thoughts*, including this passage, appeared in *the Gentleman's Magazine* eleven months previously; see *The Gentleman's Magazine* 12 (Aug. 1742), 438.

69 *Whitefoord Papers*, 230; the latter is wrongly referred to as 'the Paysanne Parvenue de Marsiaux'.

70 See letter to Robert Dodsley, 5 Oct. 1759, *Correspondence of Robert Dodsley*, p. 4, and *TS*, I. ix. 15.

71 William Hazlitt, 'On John Buncle', *The Round Table* (Edinburgh, 1817), 151.

72 John Seward, *The Spirit of Anecdote and Wit*, 4 vols. (London, 1823), iv. 239–40.

73 Richard Griffith, *A Series of Genuine Letters, between Henry and Frances*, 6 vols. (London, 1786), v. 83.

74 *Thraliana: the Diary of Mrs. Hester Lynch Thrale (later Mrs. Piozzi) 1777–89*, 2 vols., ed. Katharine C. Balderston, 2nd edn. (Oxford, Clarendon Press, 1951), 255.

75 *Whitefoord Papers*, 226.

76 Kuist, 'New Light on Sterne', 549.

77 Ibid.

78 *Whitefoord Papers*, 226.

79 'New Light on Sterne', 549.

80 Ibid. 549.

81 Borthwick Institute, Stillington Records PR STN 2, 23^r.

82 Sutton Parish Book, 23.

83 Ibid. 24.

84 Kuist, 'New Light on Sterne' , 549.

85 *Sermons*, iv. 258.

Chapter five

1 *York Courant*, 27 Aug. 1745 [p. 3].

2 Hardwicke to Herring, 31 Aug. 1745: BL Add. MSS, 35598, fo. 38ʳ.

3 Herring to Hardwicke, 7 Sept. 1745: ibid., fo. 41ᵛ.

4 Ibid., fos. 41ᵛ–42ʳ.

5 Hardwicke to Herring, 12 Sept. 1745: ibid., fo. 45ʳ.

6 *A Speech Made by His Grace the Lord Archbishop of* YORK, *at presenting an Association, enter'd into at the Castle of* YORK, Sept. *24, 1745* (York, [1745]).

7 Herring to Hardwick, 24 Sept. 1745: BL Add. MSS, 35598, fo. 68ʳ.

8 Herring to Hardwicke, 29 Sept. 1745: ibid., fo. 70ʳ.

9 Ibid.

10 'I fear the Greeks, even when they bring gifts' (*Aeneid*, ii. 49); ibid., fo. 70ᵛ.

11 Herring to Hardwicke, 20 May 1747: BL Add. MSS 35598, fo. 242ʳ. (In transcriptions of letters throughout, carets are used to indicate an insertion, and angled brackets to show a cancellation in MS.)

12 Herring to Hardwicke, 27 Sept. 1745: ibid., fo. 70ʳ.

13 Kuist, 'New Light on Sterne', 549.

14 *York Courant*, 29 Oct. 1745 [p. 2].

15 See Monkman, 'Sterne and the '45', 45–136, esp. 52, 135.

16 *Seasonable Advice to the Inhabitants of Yorkshire. By a Yorkshire-Man*, 8; the pamphlet is reproduced in facsimile in *The Shandean*, 2 (1990), between pp. 52–3.

17 See e.g. *York Courant*, 12 Nov. and 13 Dec. 1745.

18 Kenneth Monkman, 'Sterne and the '45', 58 (Fig. 17).

19 *York Courant*, 19 Nov. 1745 [pp. 1–2].

20 Ibid. [p. 3].

21 Herring to Hardwicke, 22 Nov. 1745, BL Add. MSS 35598, fo. 128ʳ.

22 Ibid., fos. 129ᵛ–130ʳ.

23 Burton inherited both his mother-in-law's fortune and that of his father in 1743; see *York Courant*, 11 Jan. 1743 [p. 3] and 4 Apr. 1743 [pp. 2–3].

24 Herring to Hardwicke, 4 Dec. 1745, BL Add. MSS 35598, fos. 135 ff.

25 John Burton, *British Liberty Endangered . . . wherein it is proved, from FACTS, that J.B. has hitherto been a better Friend to the English Constitution, in Church and State, than his Persecutors* (York, 1749); the fullest version of this entire episode appears in Cash, *EMY* 159 ff.

26 Herring to Hardwicke, 4 Dec. 1745; BL Add. MSS, 35598, fo. 136ᵛ.

27 Fitzroy Bell (ed.), *Memorials of John Murray of Broughton*, Scottish History Society Publications, 27 (Edinburgh, 1898), 436.

28 Herring to Hardwicke, 11 Dec. 1745, BL Add. MSS, 35598, fo. 146ʳ.

29 *York Courant*, 14 Oct. 1746 [p. 1].

30 The speculative attribution has been made by Kenneth Monkman; see 'Sterne and the '45', 94–103, and 136.

31 In writing to the earl of Hardwicke, Archbishop Herring thought fit to warn the lord chancellor against taking too seriously any suggestions that Dr Sterne might have made to the effect that the recorder of York was a Jacobite: 'for, tho' yᵉ Recorder is cautious, & in some instances, tender to yᵉ Popish Gentlemen, I think him a perfect honest man': Letter of 11 Dec. 1745; BL Add. MSS, 35598, fo. 147ʳ.

32 Forrester, 'Uncle Jaques Sterne', 216 and 233, n. 33.

33 The paper ran between November 1745 and June 1746.

34 Drake, *Eboracum*, 241; it was perhaps the significant presence of affluent Roman Catholics which led to an unusual performance of Johann Adolf Hasse's Marian setting, *Salve Regina* in the city in 1741; *York Courant*, 10 Feb. 1741 [p. 3].

35 Dorothy M. Owen, 'From the Restoration until 1822', in G. E. Aylmer and Reginald Cant (eds.), *A History of York Minster* (Oxford: Clarendon Press, 1977), 253.

36 *York Journal; or, Protestant Courant*, 1 July

1746, quoted in Kenneth Monkman, 'Sterne, Hamlet, and Yorick: Some New Material', in Cash and Stedmond, *The Winged Skull*, 115.

37 BL Add. MSS 35598, fo. 234[r].

38 Monkman, 'Sterne, Hamlet, and Yorick', 115.

39 *True Patriot*, 3 (19 Nov. 1745), 128, 129.

40 *The Correspondence of Edmund Burke*, ed. Thomas W. Copeland (and others), 10 vols. (Cambridge and Chicago: Cambridge University Press and Chicago University Press, 1969–70), i. 63.

41 'Essay on Ballads', *London Magazine* (1769), 580; quoted by Langford, *A Polite and Commercial People*, 211.

42 Monkman, 'Sterne, Hamlet, and Yorick', 116.

43 Rupp, *Religion in England*, 184.

44 Herring to Hardwicke, 23 Aug. 1746, BL Add. MSS, 35598, fos. 222[v]–223[v].

45 W. E. H. Lecky, *History of England in the Eighteenth Century*, 7 vols. (London: Longman, 1892), iii. 504–5.

46 *The Danger arising to our Civil and Religious Liberty from the Great Increase of* Papists, *and the Setting up* Public Schools *and* Seminaries *for the Teaching and Educating of* Youth *in the pernicious Tenets and Principles of* Popery *consider'd; in a Charge deliver'd to the Clergy of the Archdeaconry of* Cleveland, *in the Visitations held at* Thirsk, Stokesley, *and* Malton, *in the Year 1746* (York, 1747), 9–11*.

47 *York Courant*, 17 Jan. 1749 [p. 3].

48 Ibid. 3 Oct. 1749.

49 See *Letters*, 'Appendix: Letters Pertaining to Sterne and his Family', letter xiii, Jaques Sterne to Mother Elizabeth Stanfield, 19 Nov. 1755, pp. 431–2.

Chapter six

1 *Letters*, 9, n. 25; 44, n. 13; Cash, *EMY* 147, n. 1.

2 Sutton Parish Book, 4[a].

3 *Whitefoord Papers*, 226.

4 Defoe, *Tour*, Letter 9, p. 524.

5 *York Courant*, 18 Apr. [p. 2] and 31 Oct. 1749 [p. 1].

6 *Sermons*, Sermon XLV: 'The Ingratitude of Israel', iv. 422.

7 L. P. Curtis, 'Forged Letters of Laurence Sterne', *PMLA* 50 (1935), 1076–106 (1097).

8 See Arthur H. Cash, 'Sterne as a Judge', in John H. Middendorf, *English Writers of the Eighteenth Century* (New York and London: Columbia University Press, 1971), 17–36.

9 Kuist, 'New Light on Sterne', 550.

10 Toby alludes to 'The Form of Solemnization of Matrimony', *The Book of Common Prayer* (*TS* ix., '**The Eighteenth Chapter**', 526).

11 *Sermons*, iv. 281.

12 Sterne repeated Pauline exhortations to chastity in Sermon XIX, however: '*Felix*'s Behaviour Toward *Paul* Examined', *Sermons*, iv. 177–85.

13 Record of the Stillington Prebendal Court, 10 Aug. 1755; York Minster Library C3[d].

14 Ibid. 25 Aug. 1753; the penance was performed on 2 September, as Sterne confirmed on 8 September.

15 John Howard, *The State of the Prisons in England and Wales*, 3rd edn. (Warrington, 1784), 416.

16 Lawrence Stone, *The Family, Sex and Marriage in England 1500–1800* (1977; rev. and abridged edn., Harmondsworth: Penguin, 1979), 315.

17 *The Bletchley Diary of the Rev. William Cole* (London: Constable, 1931), 9.

18 Stone, *The Family, Sex and Marriage*, 401.

19 *Letters*, 48, n. 2.

20 For a similar case of a young woman imprisoned indefinitely for inability to pay fines levied by an ecclesiastical court, see *Parl. Debates*, xxi. 99, 100, 295–303, quoted by Lecky, *History of England*, iv. 495.

21 Sermon III, 'Philanthropy recommended', *Sermons*, iv. 24.

22 Ibid.

23 *Whitefoord Papers*, 230.
24 Kuist, 'New Light on Sterne', 549
25 Although we are dependent on Sterne's own account here, the fact that he included so much circumstantial—and easily confirmed (or controverted)—information in a letter to his uncle strongly suggests that the account may be trusted without serious reserve, since he would scarcely have given his estranged and unforgiving uncle material which would have enabled him to brand his nephew a liar as well as ungrateful.
26 See above, p. 60.
27 Philip Thicknesse, *Sketches and Characters of the Most Eminent and Most Singular Persons Now Living* (Bristol, 1770), i. 217–19, quoted in Cash, *EMY* 238 n.2.
28 *Letters*, 41, n. 1, quoting *Monthly Repository of Theology and General Literature* (Jan. 1808), 3, 12.
29 *Whitefoord Papers*, 230.
30 Kuist, 'New Light on Sterne', 549.
31 'Walpoliana', *Monthly Magazine*, 7 (May 1799), 300.
32 *Byron's Letters and Journals*, ed. Leslie A. Marchand, 11 vols. (London: John Murray, 1971–83), iii. 229.
33 *The Registers of St. Michael le Belfrey, York*, Part II, The Publications of the Yorkshire Parish Register Society, 11 (1901), 270.
34 *Whitefoord Papers*, 230.
35 *Memoirs*, 13.
36 *Byron's Letters and Journals*, iii. 229.

Chapter seven

1 Whitefoord Papers, 225
2 *York Courant*, 27 Nov. 1744 [p. 3].
3 Ibid. 4 Dec. 1744 [p. 3].
4 Ibid. 9 Apr. 1745, [p. 3].
5 Rupp, *Religion in England*, 373; see also George Lavington, *Enthusiasm of Methodists and Papists Compar'd* (1749–51).
6 *Sermons*, iv. 347.
7 Ibid. 347–8. For Sterne's association of anti-Roman Catholic with anti-Methodist sentiments, see also Sermons XIV and XXV; the lack of references to the Trinity in the sermons generally might even suggest that Sterne followed Blackburne in the Socinianism of which the archdeacon was later to become a leading proponent.
8 Kuist, 'New Light on Sterne', 549
9 Citing remarks by William Warburton and Bernard Mandeville, Melvyn New (*Sermons*, v. 94–5) has suggested that the preaching of charity sermons was not a highly regarded activity; the fact that Archbishop Herring, himself a celebrated preacher, delivered the corresponding sermon the previous year is an indication that this attitude is unlikely to have been widely shared in York, at least during Herring's tenure of the See.
10 The sermon may not, however, be the earliest of the forty-five surviving sermons to have been written, since no firm evidence exists to date many of them.
11 *Sermons*, iv. 40–1.
12 Ibid. 40.
13 The borrowing was first noted by John Ferriar in *Illustrations of Sterne and Other Essays and Verses*, 2nd edn. (London, 1812), i. 126–7; see also Lansing Van der Heyden, *Laurence Sterne's Sermons of Mr. Yorick* (New Haven: Yale University Press, 1948), 127, and *Sermons*, v. 94–111.
14 Sampson Letsome, *The Preacher's Assistant* (London, 1753), part I, p. iii. Such works looked back into the seventeenth century, and particularly to John Wilkins's frequently reprinted and three times revised *Ecclesiastes* (1646) and its successors, including James Arderne's *Directions concerning the Matter and Stile of Sermons* (1671), Joseph Glanvill's *An Essay Concerning Preaching and A Seasonable Defence of Preaching* (1678), and Gilbert Burnet's *Discourse of the Pastoral*

Care (1692; rev. edn., 1713); see Rivers, *Reason, Grace, and Sentiment*, 38 and 49–50.

15 *Sermons*, iv. 47.

16 Ibid. 54.

17 Though the scholarships were established for poor boys, the terms of the archbishop's will were loosely interpreted, and both Jaques Sterne and the younger Richard had held one of the scholarships; the fact that they could have afforded to attend Cambridge University without such aid does not, however, apply to Sterne.

18 *Sermons*, iv. 52–3.

19 Ibid. 51.

20 Ibid. 47.

21 Ibid.

22 *York Courant*, 1 Apr. 1746 [p. 3].

23 This sermon too was printed by Caesar Ward for John Hildyard (though not for any London bookseller).

24 *Sermons*, iv. 255–6.

25 Ibid. 261.

26 Ibid. 266.

27 Ibid. 265.

28 Ibid. 266–7.

29 'Ce qu'on a peut-être jamais dit de mieux sur cette question important se trouve dans le livre comique de Tristram Shandy', Voltaire, *Dictionnaire philosophique* (Paris, 1816), v. 'Conscience', iii. 'De la conscience trompeuse', 134–5.

30 For other possible influences, see *Sermons: The Notes*, 283–98, which, in arguing that Sterne's sermon is to be understood as part of the Anglican establishment's '*necessary* quarrel with Shaftesburian "morality without religion"' (p. 293) offers some particularly interesting passages of a sermon, 'The Connexion of Religion with Morality' published by the Revd John Heylyn, a prebendary of Westminster, in 1749.

31 See also below, pp. 241–4.

32 Wilbur Cross, *The Life and Times of Laurence Sterne*, 3rd edn. (New Haven: Yale University Press, 1929), 242–3.

33 See *Letters*, 148, n. 7 and Cash, *EMY* 224.

34 *Letters*, 52, n.2.

35 Walpole, *Memoires of the Last Ten Years of the Reign of George the Second*, ii. 194.

36 It is easy enough to date *A Political Romance* precisely since the final text breaks into five quite distinct parts. The first and longest alludes to Topham's *Letter* and to Fountayne's *Answer*; the second part makes reference to Topham's second pamphlet contribution to the affair, his *A Reply to the Answer to a Letter lately addressed to the Dean of York*, published in mid-January 1759, evidently after Sterne had written the first part of *A Political Romance*. Sterne's pamphlet—at 1 shilling, twice the price of Topham's—was printed at the end of that same month; the letter Sterne wrote to Caesar Ward, the York printer who was to publish the *Romance*, in which Sterne's letter was finally included, is dated 'Jan. 20, 1759'. See also Sterne's letter of 21–30 January to John Blake, in which he writes that he expects to see the pamphlet 'tomorrow', in Arthur H. Cash, *Laurence Sterne: The Later Years* (London and New York: Methuen, 1986), App. 1, p. 359 (henceforth referred to as '*LY*'.

37 Laurence Sterne, *A Sentimental Journey through France and Italy* with the *Journal to Eliza* and *A Political Romance*, ed. Ian Jack (1968; repr. Oxford: Oxford University Press, 1984), 207; the text of *A Political Romance* occupies pp. 197–230; all future references are to this edition and are given in the text.

38 See *Letters*, 146–7.

39 Swift to Orrery, letter of 17 July 1735: *Correspondence*, iv. 367. Sterne was to invoke this proverb more fully and most memorably in his naming of Uncle Toby's servant in *Tristram Shandy*; see Ian Campbell Ross and Noha Saad Nassar, 'Trim (-tram), Like Master, Like Man: Servant and Sexton in Sterne's *Tristram Shandy* and *A Political Romance*', *Notes & Queries*, 36: 1 (1989), 62–5.

40 Swift to Orrery, letter of 17 July 1735: *Correspondence.* iv. 367.

41 Contrary to Arthur H. Cash's suggestion (*EMY* 276, n. 2), there is no evidence that Sterne went to London himself on this occasion: a reference by Elizabeth Sterne, writing in the autumn of 1761, to her husband's having seen Elizabeth Montagu 'these last two winters', points to exactly the opposite conclusion (the 'last two winters' were those of 1759–60 and 1760–1, when Sterne certainly was in the capital).

42 *European Magazine*, 21 (Mar. 1792), 170.

Chapter eight

1 Letter of 15 Apr. 1760, first published in *St James's Chronicle* (Apr. 1788) and reprinted *European Magazine*; 21 (Mar. 1792), 170.

2 See *The Guardian*, no. 2, and Monkman, 'Sterne, Hamlet and Yorick', 117–23.

3 See Melvyn New, 'Sterne's Rabelaisian Fragment: A Text from the Holograph Manuscript', *PMLA* 88 (1972), 1083–92; New's argument from internal evidence that the 'Fragment' was written in 1759, thereby pre-dating the published version of *Tristram Shandy*, rather than being an early draft of volume IV of the published novel, seems to me wholly convincing.

4 Jonathan Swift, 'Stella's Birthday. March 13. 1726/7', l. 13.

5 *European Magazine*, 21 (Mar. 1792), 170.

6 See above, p. 177, and n. 14 (p. 448).

7 *Seven Sermons on Public Occasions*, Sermon I, p. 13; Herring in fact added wittily: 'though it may perhaps be justly called a new Discovery, that true Religion did indeed consist in the Practice of Moral Virtues' (pp. 13–14).

8 New, 'Sterne's Rabelaisian Fragment', 1088.

9 Yorick reads Rabelais's account of the combat between Triboulet and Gymnast (*Gargantua*, I. xxxv) in *TS* v. xxix.

10 New, 'Sterne's Rabelaisian Fragment', 1089; Sterne's description suggests he may also have had in mind John Gay's *The What d'ye call It* (1715).

11 Ibid. 1089

12 Ibid.

13 Frank T. Boyle, 'Profane and Debauched Deist: Swift in the Contemporary Reponse to *A Tale of a Tub*', *Eighteenth-Century Ireland*, 3 (1988), 25–38.

14 James E. Tierney (ed.), *The Correspondence of Robert Dodsley 1733–1764* (Cambridge: Cambridge University Press, 1988), 415.

15 Most notably in Sterne's parody of the Book of Common Prayer: '*Dearly Beloved Roger, the Scripture moveth thee & me in sundry Places*'; see New, 'Sterne's Rabelaisian Fragment', 1090, n. to line 85

16 *Correspondence of Robert Dodsley*, 415.

17 Ibid.

18 *Whitefoord Papers*, 229.

19 *Correspondence of Robert Dodsley*, 416.

20 There were many different understandings of Sterne's intentions current throughout 1759 and 1760, some quite detailed, suggesting that Sterne himself remained undecided about how to proceed. The anonymous acquaintance of Sterne who later declared that the writer's design had been 'take in all ranks and professions, and to laugh them out of their absurdities', also alleged that 'A system of education is to be exhibited, and thoroughly discussed. For forming his future hero, I have recommended a private tutor, and named no less a person than the great and learned Dr. W[arburton, the Bishop of Gloucester]: Polemical Divines are to come in for a slap. An allegory has been run upon the writers on the Book of Job. The Doctor is the Devil who smote him from head to foot, and G[re]y, P[ete]rs, and Ch[appell]ow his miserable comforters. A group of mighty champions in literature is

convened at Shandy-hall. Uncle Toby and the Corporal are thorns in the private tutor's side, and operate upon him as they did on Dr. Slop at reading the sermon; all this for poor Job's sake; whilst an Irish Bishop, a quondam acquaintance of Sterne's, who has written on the same subject, and loves dearly to be in a crowd, is to come uninvited and introduce himself', *European Magazine*, 21 (Mar. 1792), 169.

21 *Correspondence of Robert Dodsley*, 415.

22 Ibid.

23 Ibid. 421.

24 *Alas! Poor Yorick! or, A Funeral Discourse occasioned by the ... Death of Mr. Yorick* (London, 1761), 20.

25 Kenneth Monkman and James Diggle, 'Yorick and his Flock: A New Sterne letter', *TLS* (14 Mar. 1968), 276.

26 Ibid.

27 *Whitefoord Papers*, 226.

28 *European Magazine*, 21 (Mar. 1792), 170.

29 *Scrapeana*, 2nd edn. (1792), 22.

30 *Whitefoord Papers*, 226.

31 L. P. Curtis, 'New Light on Sterne', *Modern Language Notes*, 76 (June 1961), 501.

32 *Sermons*, iv. 169; Sterne distinguishes in the sermon between the concubine, who 'in Jewish *œconomicks* ... differ'd little from the wife' and 'the more infamous species': ibid.

33 Ibid. 168.

34 Ibid. 169; Sterne was borrowing from John Norris, 'Of Solitude', in *A Collection of Miscellanies*, 2nd edn. (1692), 159; see *Sermons*, v. 208, n. to 169.31–170.6.

35 *Correspondence of Robert Dodsley*, 422.

36 Ibid. 421

37 Ibid.

38 For a detailed account of the printing of the York volumes of *Tristram Shandy*, I–II, see Kenneth Monkman 'The Bibliography of the Early Editions of *Tristram Shandy*, 11–39; for a persuasive view that Robert Dodsley, rather than Ann Ward, should be accounted the *publisher* of these volumes, see *Correspondence of Robert Dodsley*, 416–17, n. 5.

39 See Sterne's letter of 14 Dec. 1759 to the marquess of Rockingham, in Cash, *LY*, App. 1, letter 4, 360.

40 Kenneth Monkman, 'The Bibliography of the Early Editions of *Tristram Shandy*', 22.

41 John H. Harvey, 'A Lost Link with Laurence Sterne,' *Yorkshire Archaeological Journal*, 42 (1967), 103–7.

42 See *Letters*, 77.

43 See *Correspondence of Robert Dodsley*, 417, n. 5 and Anne Bandry, 'Early Advertisements', *The Shandean*, 4 (1992), 244–5; for the publication of the first Irish edition of *Tristram Shandy*, I–II, see Kenneth Monkman, '*Tristram* in Dublin', *Transactions of the Cambridge Bibliographical Society*, 7 (1979), 343–68.

Chapter nine

1 Laurence Sterne to the marquess of Rockingham, 14 Dec. 1759; see Cash, *LY*, App. 1, letter IV, p. 360.

2 *Monthly Review*, 21 (July–Dec. 1759), 'Appendix', 561.

3 The term was first used by William Taylor of Norwich in 1797; see John Brewer, *The Pleasures of the Imagination: English Culture in the Eighteenth Century* (London: HarperCollins, 1997), 541.

4 Ibid. 562.

5 Ibid. 562 n.

6 *Monthly Review*, 571.

7 *Critical Review*, 9 (Jan. 1760), 73.

8 Ibid. 74.

9 In fact there is only the slightest evidence that Sterne was familiar with Smollett's work, though there are undoubtedly similarities between Sterne's characters and Commodore Trunnion, who runs his house like a naval vessel, his lieutenant and servant

Jack Hathaway and Tom Pipes, and a physician distinguished by 'uncouth gravity and supercilious self-conceit'; for Sterne's possible familiarity with *Peregrine Pickle*, see Nicolas Barker, 'The Library Catalogue of Laurence Sterne', *The Shandean*, 1 (1989), 17.

10 *Critical Review*, 9 (Jan. 1760), 74.

11 *London Magazine*, 29, (Feb. 1760), 111.

12 François Béroalde de Verville, *Le Moyen de Parvenir* (?1615; Nouvelle Edition/ Corrigée de diverses fautes qui n'y étoient point & augmentée de Plusieurs autres, ?1700), 44.

13 Half-a-century earlier one of Sterne's own favourite authors, Jonathan Swift, had savaged the changes the proliferation of print culture would bring about, ironically commending index learning as a 'shorter and more prudent Method to become scholars and wits, without the Fatigue of *Reading* and *Thinking*'; *A Tale of a Tub*, ed. A. C. Guthkelch and D. Nichol Smith, 2nd edn. (Oxford: Clarendon Press, 1958), sec. VII, pp. 144–5.

14 Gray to Algarotti, 9 Sept. 1763: *Correspondence of Thomas Gray*, ed. Paget Toynbee and Leonard Whibley, 3 vols. (Oxford: Clarendon Press, 1935), ii. 810–11. For this aspect of Gray's thought, see Suvir Kaul, *Thomas Gray and Literary Authority: Ideology and Poetics in Eighteenth-Century England* (Delhi: Oxford University Press, 1992), *passim.*

15 It was at York, during Race Week, that an acquaintance of Gray's overheard a conversation by three gentlemen, 'whom by their dress & Manner he takes for Lords, say, that I was impenetrable & inexplicable, and they wish'd, I had told them in prose, what I meant in verse, & then they bought me (w[ch] was what most displeased him), & put me in their pocket': *Correspondence of Thomas Gray*, ii. 532.

16 William Mason, *Poems of Mr. Gray* (York, 1775), 335.

17 Ibid. For attitudes towards the professional writer in the first half of the eighteenth century, see Brean S. Hammond, *Professional Imaginative Writing in England, 1670–1740: 'hackney for bread'* (Oxford: Clarendon Press, 1997).

18 Francis Coventry, 'To Henry Fielding, Esq.', *The History of Pompey the Little; or the Life and Adventures of a Lap-Dog*, ed. Robert Adams Day (London: Oxford University Press, 1974), pp. xli–xlii.

19 For the mid-eighteenth-century 'public', see Anne Bermingham, 'Introduction: The Consumption of Culture: Image, Object, Text', in Anne Bermingham and John Brewer (eds.), *The Consumption of Culture 1600–1800: Image, Object, Text* (London and New York: Routledge, 1995), esp. 9 ff.

20 *The History of Tom Jones, A Foundling*, ed. Fredson Bowers, 2 vols. (Oxford: Clarendon Press, 1974), i. 396.

21 *London Magazine*, 29 (Feb. 1760), 111.

22 For a fuller account of these editions, see Monkman, 'Bibliography of the Early Editions of *Tristram Shandy*', 11–39.

23 *Monthly Review*, 21 (1759), App., 568.

24 The possibility that Kenrick was thinking of Herbert is perhaps enhanced by the fact that, in the preface to his novel *The Triumvirate* (1764), Richard Griffith referred directly to Herbert, slightly misquoting the relevant line as 'A tale may catch him who a sermon flies'; see *The Triumvirate* (London, 1764), vol. i, p. xiii.

25 *The Royal Female Magazine*, 1 (1760), 56.

26 L. P. Curtis conjectured the recipient to have been Dr Noah Thomas of Scarborough: see *Letters*, 91 n.

27 *Old England* (7 Apr. 1750), cited by Martin C. Battestin, 'General Introduction' to Henry Fielding, *The History of Tom Jones*, vol. i, p. lvi, n. 2.

28 Samuel Johnson, *The Rambler*, ed. W. J. Bate and Albrecht B. Strauss (New Haven and London: Yale University Press, 1969), no. 4, p. 21.

29 Hugh Kelly, *Louisa Mildmay; or, the Memoirs of a Magdalen* (London, 1767).

30 Richard Griffith, 'Preface', to *The Triumvirate* (1764), vol. i, pp. xiii–xvii.

31 A. D. McKillop, *Samuel Richardson*, 181–2, quoting Forster MS XI, fo. 274, cited in Howes, *Sterne: The Critical Heritage*, 90.

32 James Boswell, *Life of Johnson*, ed. R. W. Chapman, rev. J. D. Fleeman (Oxford: Oxford University Press, 1970), 1125.

33 See e.g. *TS* VII. xxxiv. 422 and *Carteggio di Pietro e di Alessandro Verri*, ed. Francesco Norati and Emanuele Greppi (Milan: L. F. Cogliati, 1911), iii. 460; portraits of Sterne invariably show him in clerical dress.

34 Walpole to Sir David Dalrymple, 4 Apr. 1760: *Walpole's Correspondence* (1952), xv. 66.

35 *Universal Magazine*, 26 (1760), 189–90.

36 Oliver Goldsmith, *The Public Ledger*, 30 June 1760, repr. in *The Citizen of the World*, letter liii, pp. 221–5; James Boswell, in *Boswell Laird of Auchinleck* (1979), 76.

37 *Alas! Poor Yorick*, 20.

38 Thomas Newton to the Revd John Dealtary, 4 Mar. 1760: L. P. Curtis, 'New Light on Sterne', 501.

39 Ibid.

40 See Howes, *Sterne: The Critical Heritage*, 100, citing *Grand Magazine*, 3 (Apr. 1760), 194–8.

41 The extent to which the very notion of authorship was contested in the mid-century may be seen not merely in the extreme case of a writer like Thomas Gray, but also in that of the Irish writer William Chaigneau, author of *The History of Jack Connor* (1752), who endeavoured to confirm his credentials as a gentleman and serious writer by declaring in his preface that he sought no 'pecuniary Indulgence' from the bookseller, a fact thought worthy of mention and comment by the *Monthly Review*. The significance that Cibber's *Letter from Mr Cibber to Mr Pope* held for Sterne is suggested by the fact that Sterne gave a copy of it to his friend Marmaduke Fothergill (*Letters*, 85, n. 2).

42 Sterne's predilection for wit, even in some of his sermons, is so entirely opposed to Warburton's dislike of it, as expressed in the 'Dedication' to *The Divine Legation of Moses* (1738)—of which Sterne made some use in *Tristram Shandy*—that it is easy to believe that Sterne had intended to take Warburton as an example of the solemn clerical writer, as against favourites of his own, such as Rabelais, Béroalde de Verville, and Swift; see *The Divine Legation of Moses*, 'Dedication', pp. i–xliv.

43 *Private Correspondence of David Garrick* (London, 1831), i. 115–16.

44 Walpole to Sir David Dalrymple, 4 Apr. 1760: *Walpole's Correspondence* (1952), xv. 67.

45 Curtis, 'New Light on Laurence Sterne', 501.

46 *European Magazine*, 21 (Oct. 1792), 255–6.

47 Ibid.

48 *Public Ledger*, 20 May 1760, quoted in Cash, *LY* 38.

49 William Fleetwood, 'Epistle Dedicatory' to *The Relative Duties of Parents and Children* . . . , 4th edn. (London, 1732).

50 *Sermons*, iv. 1.

51 Ibid. In truth, the statement is more than a trifle disingenuous. It was not that Sterne believed wit to have no place in sermonizing, but that some of his congregations had evidently been less sure. Certainly, it is noticeable that on one of the rare occasions on which he credits the source of material borrowed for his own sermons—'however, as Arch-bishop Tillotson witily observes upon it' (Sermon XI, *Sermons*, iv. 109)—he seems to be using his eminent predecessor as a shield against attack on himself for undue levity (the archbishop's witticism related to malicious gossip); see also Sermon XXI, which warns against the danger of wit and levity towards religion leading to atheism (ibid. 196–7).

52 *Monthly Review*, 22 (May 1760), 422.

53 Ibid. 424, 422, 423.

54 *The Royal Female Magazine*, 1 (May 1760), 238, quoted in Howes, *Sterne: The Critical Heritage*, 78.

55 *Monthly Review*, 22 (May 1760), 424.

56 See the letter of Georgina, Countess Cowper, to Anne Granville Dewes, 3 Sept. 1760, *Autobiography and Correspondence of Mary Granville, Mrs. Delany*, 1st ser., iii. 602: 'Pray read *Yorick's* sermons, (though *you would not read* Tristram Shandy). They are more like Essays. I like them extremely, and I think he must be a good man.'

57 *Monthly Review*, 22 (May 1760), 425.

58 *The Critical Review*, 9 (May, 1760), 405.

59 Ibid.

60 *Grand Magazine*, 3 (June 1760), 308–11.

61 Boswell, *Life of Johnson*, 1124

62 Ibid.

63 *Sermons*, iv. 1.

64 Ibid. 2

65 Ibid.; for Herring, see above, p. 96.

66 It was one of the characteristics of the seventeenth-century latitude-men to read holy scripture alongside and with reference to classical writings on ethics; see Rivers, *Reason, Grace, and Sentiment*, 35.

67 *Sermons*, iv. 10–11.

68 Ibid. 12.

69 *Monthly Review*, 22 (May 1760), 425 n.

70 *Correspondence of Gray*, ii. 681.

71 *Sermons*, iv. 75.

72 Ibid. 18.

73 Sermon III, *Sermons*, iv. 28–9.

74 Though such 'pathetic' scenes were characteristic of latitudinarian sermonizing generally, Sterne seeks biblical sanction when drawing his congregation's attention to Jeremiah's 'very pathetic representation' of the sorrows of the people of Israel, which served to make all the stronger the impression of change when their possessions and privileges were returned to them; Sermon IX, 'The Character of Herod. Preached on Innocents Day', *Sermons*, iv. 81.

75 Ibid. 18.

76 Ibid. 29.

77 In Sermon IX Sterne offers a sketch of the character of Herod, conscious that scripture 'cuts off in a few words the history of the ungodly', while dwelling 'upon the smallest actions of the righteous'—the advantage of which, says Sterne, 'I suppose' is that it enlarges on no character but 'what is worthy of imitation': ibid. 84–5.

78 Ibid. 65–73.

79 Ibid. 31.

80 Ibid.

81 Ibid. 13.

82 Ibid. 39. It is this scepticism about the very possibility of autobiographical writing which most sets Sterne apart from his great French contemporary Jean-Jacques Rousseau, who, in *The Confessions* (1782–9), begun in 1766, wrote:

> I am commencing an undertaking, hitherto without precedent, and which will never find an imitator. I desire to set before my fellows the likeness of a man in all the truth of nature, and that man myself.
>
> Myself alone! I know the feelings of my heart, and I know men. I am not made like any of those I have seen; I venture to believe that I am not made like any of those who are in existence. If I am not better, at least I am different. Whether nature has acted rightly or wrongly in destroying the mould in which she cast me, can only be decided after I have been read. (London: Dent, 1931), I. i, p. 1.

83 See e.g. Sermon VII: 'The Vindication of Human Nature', where Sterne suggests that however 'we may flatter ourselves with fine-spun notions of disinterestedness and heroism in what we do; that were the most popular of our actions strip'd naked; and the true motives and intentions of them search'd to the bottom; we should find little reason for triumph upon that score'; *Sermons*, iv. 65.

84 Ibid. 103.

85 Ibid. 104; cf. e.g. Montaigne, 'Of the Inconstancy of our Actions': 'If I speak

variously of my self, it is because I consider myself variously. All contrarieties are there to be found . . .'

86 *Sermons*, iv. 74.

87 Ibid.

88 Ibid. 76.

89 'Vid. Tillotson's sermons on this subject'; Sterne does not specify the sermon he has in mind, though it has been suggested that it was Sermon 138, 'The Wisdom of God in his Providence': see *Sermons*, v. 127, and Lansing Van der Heyden Hammond, *Laurence Sterne's Sermons of Mr. Yorick*, 164ff.

90 John Wilkes to Suard, 25 Mar. 1764, quoted by Joel Gold, 'Tristram Shandy at the Ambassador's Chapel', *Philological Quarterly*, 48 (1969), 421–4.

91 See Richard Griffith, *A Series of Genuine Letters between Henry and Frances*, v. 200, and below, p. 414; for a near-contemporary reading of Sterne as a sceptic, see René Bosch, 'Sterne and Voltaire in Purgatory: A Prophecy by W. J. Mickle', *The Shandean*, 8 (1996), 98–112.

92 *Sermons*, iv. 77.

93 *Essay on Man*, i. 266.

94 Pope's uncertain engagement with the problem in his conclusion to the first epistle to the *Essay on Man* (i. 268ff.) brought forth one of William Warburton's longest explanatory notes in Pope's defence; see *The Works of Alexander Pope, Esq.*, 8 vols. (London, 1751), iii. 20–3.

95 *Sermons*, iv. 91.

96 The account of Job offered by Sterne also suggests some affinities with the portrayal of Walter Shandy in *Tristram Shandy*, not least in his suffering over Tristram's own repeated misfortunes and the death of Bobby, though neither the novelist nor preacher finds satisfactory the pretended consolations of classical moralists, in comparison to the solace offered by Christianity; see *TS* v, iii. 282ff. and *Sermons*, iv. 144–5.

97 Sermons, iv. 143.

98 Ibid. 96.

99 Ibid.

100 Ibid. 102.

101 In his sermons Sterne frequently endorses in a wholly orthodox manner, the twelfth and thirteenth of the Thirty-Nine Articles.

102 *Sermons*, iv. 39, 40, 96.

103 Ibid. 6.

104 Even Dr John Ferriar, in indicating some instances of borrowing, declared that 'Charges of Plagiarism in his Sermons . . . I have not been anxious to investigate, as in that species of composition, the principal matter must consist of repetitions': *Illustrations of Sterne* (1798; 2nd edn., London, 1812), i. 123.

105 Jonathan Richardson, *An Essay on the Theory of Painting* (London, 1715), 82–3; Richardson continues in a way which is remarkably appropriate to a modern understanding of Sterne's 'borrowings': 'The Painter that can take a Hint, or insert a Figure, or Groupes of Figures from another Man, and mix these with his Own, so as to make a good Composition, will thereby establish such a Reputation to himself, as to be above fearing to suffer by the share those to whom he is beholden will have in it' (ibid. 83).

106 *Sermons*, iv. 235; the borrowing is documented by Melvyn New in *Sermons: Notes*, 263, n. to p. 234.4–10. Professor New also rightly observes that Sterne's own footnoted referencing of the biblical phrase, in the printed version of the sermon, to 2 Kings 6: 7 is in fact inaccurate (it should be 2 Kings 6: 5); whether or not he knew it—almost certainly not—Sterne's joke was wholly Swiftian: in his 'Verses on the Death of Dr. Swift', Swift had written, in ironic praise of his own verse, 'To steal a line was never known | But what he writ was all his own'—a couplet 'stolen' for the purpose from Sir John Denham's elegy on Abraham Cowley.

107 Samuel Johnson to the Revd Charles Lawrence, 30 Aug. 1780, *The Letters*

of Samuel Johnson, ed. Bruce Redford, 5 vols. (Oxford: Clarendon Press, 1992–4), iii. 311.

108 *Sermons*, iv. 242.

109 *Life of Johnson*, 1060–1.

110 *Sermons*, iv. 2. Sterne here echoes similar sentiments expressed in the 'Dedication to *Elijah and the Widow of Zerephath* (1747); see above, p. 176.

111 These volumes, it is true, were published by T. Becket and P. A. Dehondt who, by 1762, had become Sterne's publishers, but even if there is an element of keeping Sterne's works before the public eye, it can hardly be doubted that the sermons themselves were regarded as superior in style and theologically unexceptionable.

112 *The Practical Preacher: Consisting of Select Discourses from the Works of the Most Eminent Protestant Writers: With Forms of Devotion for the Use of Families*, 4 vols. (London, 1762), vol. i, p. iii. (London: Printed for T. Becket and P. A. Dehondt, 1762).

113 *Correspondence of Thomas Gray*, ii. 670.

114 The last public record of her dates from 4 February 1763, when she had a benefit night in the concert room in Dean Street in Soho; *London Stage*, Part IV, ed. George Winchester Stone, Jr. (1962), 977.

115 *Miscellanies of the Philobiblon Society* (London, 1855–6), ii. 7.

Chapter Ten

1 While such sentiments have a basis in scripture—'Remove far from me vanity and lies; give me neither poverty nor riches', Proverbs 30: 8—they had, by 1760, become one of the most familiar commonplaces of the century; the most celebrated recommendation of the 'middle state' is perhaps that offered to Robinson Crusoe of York, by his father, in the opening pages of Defoe's *Robinson Crusoe* (1719).

2 For a possible reordering of letters 64 and 65 of Curtis's *Letters*, see Cash, *LY* 69, n. 34.

3 *Letters from a Late Eminent Prelate*, 3rd edn. (London, 1809), 335.

4 *Letters*, 217

5 While the idiosyncracy is at least partly due to Sterne, the present attractiveness owes a great deal to Dr Kenneth Monkman, who was responsible for restoration work which did much to save the house from possible total ruin; see also A. Michael Mennim, 'Shandy Hall, Coxwold', *The Shandean*, 4 (1992), 234–43.

6 Robert Midgley to James Erskine of Alva: Coxwold, 29 Sept. 1760: National Library of Scotland, MS 5081, fo. 73.

7 Cash, *EMY* 282–3 and *LY* 65 and n.2

8 *Letters* 120–1.

9 My translation; the original reads: 'nescio quid est materia cum me, sed sum fatigatus & ægrotus de meâ uxore plus quam unquam—& sum possessus cum diabolo qui pellet me in urbem . . . est diabolus amabundus, qui non vult sinere me essere solum; nam cum non cumbendo cum uxore meâ sum mentulatior quam par est—& sum mortaliter in amore—& sum fatuus . . . ' (*Letters*, 124).

10 Letter to Sir William Robinson, 27 June 1760, in Kenneth Monkman, 'Two Sterne Letters, and Some Fragments', *The Shandean*, 1 (1989), 121–2.

11 Sterne to John Hall-Stevenson [?Dec. 1760], *Letters*, 124–5.

12 See also *Letters*, 130, 131–2, 132–3.

13 Thomas Newton to John Dealtary, 26 Feb. 1761; see Curtis, 'New Light on Sterne', 501.

14 Jonas Dennis, *A Key to the Regalia* (London, 1820), 102–3 n.

15 *Monthly Review*, 24 (Feb. 1761), 101.

16 Ibid. 102.

17 Ibid.

18 See e.g. the poet James Grainger:

'Sterne's ravings I have read, and have as often swore as smiled at them. I never relished Rabelais, it was ever too highly relished for me. I cannot therefore admire his shatter-brained successor', letter of 5 June 1761, quoted in John Bowyer Nichols, *Illustrations of the Literary History of the Eighteenth Century* (London, 1848), vii. 276.

19 *The Critical Review*, 11 (Apr. 1761), 316; the identification of Tobias Smollett as reviewer of these volumes was made by James G. Basker; see Basker, *Tobias Smollett: Critic and Journalist* (Newark: University of Delaware Press, 1988), 138, 263.

20 Richard Hurd to the Revd William Mason, precentor of York, 30 Mar. 1761: *The Correspondence of Richard Hurd and William Mason*, ed. Ernest Harold Pearce and Leonard Whibley (Cambridge: Cambridge University Press, 1932), 53.

21 Ibid.

22 Letter of Mark Hildsley to Samuel Richardson, 1 Apr. 1761 (Morgan MSS), quoted in *Letters*, 131, n. 9.

23 Thomas Newton to John Dealtary, 26 Feb. 1761: see Curtis, 'New Light on Sterne', 501.

24 The appearance of *The Life and Opinions of Bertram Monfichet, Esq.* in 1761 suggested that there was still a considerable market for Sternean imitations.

25 *Letters*, 134.

26 Algernon Graves, *The Society of Artists of Great Britain, 1760–91* (London: George Bell, 1907), 93, 208, 211.

27 Ibid. 249; see also Kenneth Monkman, 'Shandean Race Horses', *The Shandean*, 10 (1998), 21–7.

28 *Letters*, 140.

29 *York Courant*, 29 Sept. 1761 [p. 3].

30 Sermon XL, 'Asa: A Thanksgiving Sermon', *Sermons*, iv. 382.

31 Wombwell MSS, Newburgh Priory, Yorks; Historical MSS Commission, *Report on MSS in Various Collections*, ii. 189, quoted in *Letters*, 145, n. 6.

32 See Sterne to Lady ——, 21 Sept. 1761; *Letters*, 143.

33 See below, pp. 326–7 and 420–1.

34 For the slow sale of *Tristram Shandy* V–VI, see below, pp. 297, 299.

35 Monkman, '*Tristram* in Dublin', 349.

36 Monkman, 'Bibliography of the Early Editions of *Tristram Shandy*', id., 'Bibliographical Descriptions', App. 5 of Melvyn and Joan New (eds.), *Tristram Shandy*, 907–38.

37 See Melvyn New, 'A Manuscript of the Le Fever Episode in *Tristram Shandy*', *The Scriblerian*, 23 (1991), 165–74.

38 *Critical Review*, 13 (Jan. 1762), 66.

39 Ibid.

40 Quoted in Howes, *Yorick and the Critics*, 15.

41 *Private Papers of James Boswell*, ed. Geoffrey Scott, 19 vols. (1928–34), i. 127.

42 *Critical Review*, 13 (Jan. 1762), 66.

43 Ibid.

44 Ibid. 68.

45 *Monthly Review*, 26 (Jan. 1762), 32.

46 'Anecdotes by George Steevens', in *Johnsonian Miscellanies*, 2 vols., ed. George Birkbeck Hill (Oxford: Clarendon Press, 1897), ii. 320; it is worth noting that in Murray's *Johnsonia* (1836), 'Sterne' becomes 'Hume'.

47 See Peter Tomory, *Life and Art of Henry Fuseli* (London: Thames and Hudson, 1972), 15.

48 See Kenneth Monkman, 'An Annotated Copy of Sterne's *Sentimental Journey*', *ABA Annual* (1952), 36–9.

49 *Monthly Review*, 26 (Jan. 1762), 41.

Chapter eleven

1 See Arthur H. Cash, 'Some New Sterne Letters', *TLS* (8 Apr. 1965), 284, and *LY* 116–23.

2 *Lloyd's Evening Post*, 12–15 Feb. 1762, p. 158; the poem was later published under the name of its author, Henrietta Pye.

3 Adam Smith to David Hume, 12 Dec. 1763, *The Correspondence of Adam Smith*, ed. Ernest Campbell Mossner and Ian Simpson Ross, 2nd edn. (Oxford: Clarendon Press, 1987), App. E, a, p. 413; for Hume's own preparations for his 1763 visit to France, where his work was already well known, see Ernest Campbell Mossner, *The Life of David Hume*, 2nd edn. (Oxford: Clarendon Press, 1980), esp. chaps. 30 and 31 (pp. 428 ff.).

4 Richard Phelps to Henry Egerton, 12 Feb. 1762: see Cash, 'Some New Sterne Letters'. Voltaire, however, read the first two volumes of *Tristram Shandy* in 1760: 'Have you read Tristram Shandi? T'is a very unaccountable book; an original one. They run mad about it in England': see Voltaire to Algarotti, [Sept. 1760], *Correspondance* (1972), xxii. 119.

5 See Anne Bandry, 'The First French Translation of *Tristram Shandy*', *The Shandean*, 6 (1994), 66–85 *passim.*

6 *Journal Encyclopédique* (1760), 150–1.

7 Richard Phelps to Henry Egerton, 12 Feb. 1762, Cash, 'Some New Sterne Letters', *TLS* 284.

8 For the (possibly overstated) argument that D'Holbach's group was 'a circle of uniform (or nearly uniform) atheists', see Alan Charles Kors, *D'Holbach's Coterie: An Enlightenment in Paris* (Princeton: Princeton University Press, 1976), 4.

9 See Mossner, *Life of David Hume*, 475 ff.; Boswell, *Life of Johnson*, 265.

10 Gibbon, *Memoirs of my Life*, 136.

11 Cash, 'Some New Sterne Letters', *TLS* 284.

12 *Journal Encyclopédique* (May 1761), 132.

13 'The Passport. Versailles', *ASJ* 218

14 See Sterne to Garrick, 31 Jan. 1762: *Letters*, 151.

15 See e.g. Sermon XXXVII, 'Penances', *Sermons*, iv. 347–56.

16 *Mémoires de l'Abbé Baston, Chanoine de Rouen, d'après le manuscrit publié . . . par M. L'Abbé Julien Loth et M. Ch. Verger* (1897; repr. Paris: Librairie Honoré Champion, 1977), 140–9.

17 *Mercure de France*, 82 (Apr. 1762), 224–5.

18 Sermon VI, 'Pharisee and publican in the temple', *Sermons*, iv. 57–64, esp. 62–3.

19 Dominique-Joseph Garat, *Mémoires Historiques sur la vie de M. Suard*, 3 vols. (Paris, 1820), ii. 136.

20 Ibid. 148.

21 'The Passport. Paris', *ASJ* 192.

22 *ASJ* 192–200, 215–29.

23 Ian Simpson Ross, *The Life of Adam Smith* (Oxford: Clarendon Press, 1995), 202.

24 Denis Diderot to Sophie Volland, 26 Sept. 1762, *Correspondance*, ed. Georges Roth and Jean Varloot, 16 vols. (Paris: Editions de Minuit, 1955–70), iv. 172.

25 Sterne was not alone, however, in noting the apparent contentment of the inhabitants of this part of France; David Hume wrote that 'The LANGUEDOCIANS and GASCONS are the gayest people in FRANCE': see *Essays, Moral, Political and Literary*, ed. Eugene F. Miller (rev. edn., Indianapolis: Liberty Classics, 1987), 204.

26 E. Lamouzèle, *Toulouse aux XVIIIe siècle d'après le 'Heures Perdues' de Pierre Barthès* (Toulouse: J. Marqueste, 1914), 212–15.

27 *Sermons*, iv. 100.

28 Voltaire's response was the *Traité sur la tolérance*, written in 1762, though withheld from publication until 1764; Adam Smith introduced Calas's last words into the final edition of his *Theory of Moral Sentiments*, III. ii. 11. See also Theodore Besterman, *Voltaire*, 3rd edn. (Oxford: Blackwell, 1976), esp. chap. 34, 'The Calas case, 1761–1763', 459–71.

29 Lamouzèle, *Toulouse aux XVIIIe siècle*, 227, 230, 237.

30 Ibid. 233.

31 Ibid. 233–7.

32 Ibid. 231–3.

33 Richard Phelps to Henry Egerton, 8 Apr. 1762: Cash, 'Some New Sterne Letters', 284.

34 *York Courant*, 23 Jan. 1750 [p. 3].

35 See Tobias Smollett, *Travels through*

France and Italy, ed. Frank Felsenstein (Oxford: Oxford University Press), 101–2 and nn. 20 and 21.

36 Laurence Sterne to John Mill, 5 Mar. 1763; the text is quoted from Peter De Voogd, 'The Oswald Papers', in *The Shandean*, 10 (1998), 80–91. The five letters Sterne wrote relating to Oswald's death were first published, in a regularized and modernized form by Archibald Bolling Shepperson, 'Yorick as Ministering Angel', *Virginia Quarterly Review*, 30 (1954), 59–60; the manuscript letters are now housed in the Scottish Record Office (ref. GD 213/53) in the Oswald of Auchincruive collection (De Voogd, 'The Oswald Papers', 81, n. 4).

37 *Letters*, 192, n. 2.

38 Cf. 'To the Right Honourable Mr. PITT', *TS* I. [p. 3].

39 *The Tatler*, ed. Donald F. Bond, 3 vols. (Oxford: Clarendon Press, 1987), no. 125 (26 Jan. 1710), ii. 236; see also *The Guardian*, ed. John Calhoun Stephens (Lexington: University Press of Kentucky, 1982), no. 44 (1 May 1713), 178.

40 Smollett, *Travels*, 87.

41 Ibid. 86

42 *Boswell on the Grand Tour: Italy, Corsica, and France 1765–1766*, ed. Frank Brady and Frederick A. Pottle (London: Heinemann, 1955), 269.

43 Smollett, *Travels*, 88

44 *Boswell on the Grand Tour*, 267.

45 Laurence Sterne to Robert Foley, 20 Jan. 1764; the text is that of NLS MS. 2208, fos. 26–7, as given by Peter De Voogd, 'The Letters of Laurence Sterne', *The Shandean*, 4 (1992), 187; contrary to L. P. Curtis's dating of this letter, Lord Rochford was in Montpellier in early November, not in January.

46 Ibid.

47 Smollett, *Humphry Clinker*, 182.

48 Ibid.

49 *Seven Letters*, ed. W. Durrant Cooper, 5.

50 Ibid.

51 Smollett, *Travels*, 89.

52 *Boswell on the Grand Tour*, 269.

53 Smollett, *Travels*, 88.

54 See Joel J. Gold, 'Tristram Shandy at the Ambassador's Chapel', 421–4 and Harlan W. Hamilton, 'Sterne's Sermon in Paris and its Background', *Proceedings of the American Philosophical Society*, 128 (1984), 316–25.

55 The whole episode is rendered more uncertain since William Combe, the supposed recipient of Sterne's account, published it in his forged *Original Letters of the late Reverend Mr. Laurence Sterne* (1788); L. P. Curtis, however, accepts the letter as genuine, as does Harlan W. Hamilton (see 'William Combe and the *Original Letters of the Late Reverend Mr. Laurence Sterne* (1788), *PMLA* 82 (1967), 420–9).

56 *Sermons*, iv. 160.

57 A future acquaintance of Sterne later observed of the consumptive writer that: 'his living for Ten Years past was a Miracle, and that he should live for Twenty Years to come was the only *Miracle*, I fancy, that he believed in': Richard Griffith, *A Series of Genuine Letters between Henry and Frances*, vi. 200.

58 For the pleasures of Hertford's dinners, see Mossner, *Life of David Hume*, 490.

59 *Letters of David Hume*, ed. J. Y. T. Greig, (Oxford: Clarendon Press, 1932), ii. 269.

60 'Montriul', *ASJ* 122.

61 See Adrian Hamilton, *The Infamous Essay on Woman, or John Wilkes seated between Vice and Virtue* (London: André Deutsch, 1972). Shortly after Sterne's death Wilkes would become the centre of commercial exploitation remarkably similar to Sterne's; to profit from the popularity of his radical politics, manufacturers produced Wilkite 'ceramics, bunting, regalia, wigs, brooches, pipes, candlesticks, pots, flagons, tankards, cakes and confections'; see *The Birth of Consumer Society*, 238.

62 Sterne, *Letters*, 212, n. 4, quoting BM Add MSS 30878 fo. 44^{v}.

63 See e.g. Letter 69, to Hall-Stevenson [?Dec. 1760], *Letters*, 124–5 (and above, p. 256) and Letter 83, to David Garrick, 'Paris, Jan. 31, 1762', *Letters*, 151–2.

Chapter twelve

1 See *Letters*, 165, n. 5, quoting Bishopthorpe MSS, Bundle 5, no. 320.

2 *Letters*, 166, n. 5.

3 Ibid., 178.

4 *Humphry Clinker*, 182–3.

5 *Universal Museum and Complete Magazine of Knowledge and Pleasure*, 1 (Jan. 1765), 36; quoted in Howes, *Sterne: The Critical Heritage*, 159.

6 [Jean-Baptiste Suard], *London Chronicle*, 17:1299 (10–18 Apr. 1765), 373, cited in Howes, *Sterne: The Critical Heritage*, 168; the review was translated from that in the *Gazette Littéraire de l'Europe*.

7 [Ralph Griffiths], *Monthly Review*, 32 (Feb. 1765), 124.

8 *Universal Magazine*, quoted in Howes, *Sterne: The Critical Heritage*, 159

9 *Critical Review*, 19 (Jan. 1765), 65.

10 [Ralph Griffiths], *Monthly Review*, 32 (Feb. 1765), 128–30.

11 Ibid. 136.

12 See above, pp. 270–1.

13 *Monthly Review*, 32 (Feb. 1765), 138–9.

14 For a harsh reading of Sterne's sentimental writing, see Leslie Stephen: 'He is a literary prostitute. He cultivates a fineness of feeling with a direct view to the market', *History of English Thought in the Eighteenth Century*, 2 vols. (1876–81; 3rd edn., London: Smith, Elder & Co., 1902), ii. 374–5; for a more sympathetic but overstated view of Sterne's deferral to the authority of periodical reviewers, see Frank Donoghue, *The Fame Machine: Book Reviewing and Eighteenth-Century Literary Careers* (Stanford, Calif.: Stanford University Press, 1996), 5 and 56ff.

15 Josiah Wedgwood to T. Boulton, WMSS.E 18898–26, 19 June 1779; quoted in McKendrick, Brewer, and Plumb, *The Birth of a Consumer Society*, 100.

16 L. P. Curtis suggests the recipient of the letter to have been John Wodehouse: see *Letters*, 256–7; for Thackeray's damning character-sketch, see 'Sterne and Goldsmith', *The English Humourists of the Eighteenth Century*.

17 *York Courant*, *York Courant*, 6 Aug. 1765 [p. 3].

18 See below pp. 420–1.

19 For the inkstand, see above, p. 269.

20 *Critical Review*, 21 (Jan. 1766), 49.

21 Ibid.

22 *Sermons*, iv. 197.

23 *Monthly Review*, 34 (Mar. 1766), 207.

24 William Cower to Joseph Hill, 3 Apr. 1766, *The Letters and Prose Writings of William Cowper*, ed. James King and Charles Ryskamp, 3 vols. (Oxford: Clarendon Press, 1979), i. 135; Cash, *LY* 228, quoting Huntington Library, MO 5319.

25 *Monthly Review*, 34 (Mar. 1766), 207–8

26 *The Letters and Prose Writings of William Cowper*, i. 135.

27 Ibid.

28 'Minor Anecdotes of Dr. Johnson: "By Mr. Wickins"', in *Johnsonian Miscellanies*, edited by George Birkbeck Hill, 2 vols. (Oxford: Clarendon Press, 1897), ii. 429.

29 *Sermons*, iv. 184.

30 Ibid. 243.

31 Ibid. 242, 243.

32 See e.g. Sermon XXI, 'National Mercies considered', *Sermons*, iv. 195–203.

33 Ibid. 206.

34 Ibid. 209.

35 Ibid. 211.

36 Sterne paraphrases the passage elsewhere in the sermons, in No. XXXVII, for example.

37 *Sermons*, iv. 188.

38 See John Locke, *Some Thoughts Concerning Education*, ed. John W. Yolton and Jean S. Yolton (Oxford: Clarendon Press, 1989), secs. 212–16, pp. 262–5; Alexander Pope, *The Dunciad*, iv. 293–322.

39 *Whitefoord Papers*, 228

40 *Sermons*, iv. 193.

Chapter thirteen

1 This aspect of Sterne's creation of a public persona for himself is intriguing; in 1760 James Boswell described Sterne as being 'by fashion's hand completely dressed', but from most other evidence this seems to have been fanciful. It is worth noting that when the Revd John Horne Tooke went to France in 1763 he abandoned clerical dress once across the Channel in favour of more fashionable wear, only to find that D'Alembert, to whom he had acquired an introduction, refused to take him seriously; only when Horne Tooke returned more soberly dressed was D'Alembert prepared to engage him in serious conversation. See Christine and David Bewley, *Gentleman Radical: A Life of John Horne Tooke 1736–1812* (London and New York: Tauris Academic Studies, 1998), 7.

2 Smollett, *Travels*, p. 50.

3 Boswell, *Life of Johnson*, 24 May 1763.

4 Ibid. 28 Apr. 1778.

5 Boswell, 'A Poetical Epistle', 9r.

6 *ASJ* 158

7 Walpole to Thomas Brand, 19 Oct. 1765; *Walpole's Correspondence* (1980), xl. 386.

8 Walpole to George Selwyn, 2 Dec. 1765: ibid., xxx. 207.

9 John Macdonald, *Memoirs of an Eighteenth-Century Footman*, ed. Peter Quennell (London: Century, 1985), 82.

10 See Alex. Stephens (ed.), *Memoirs of John Horne Tooke* (London, 1813), i. 77; Bewley, *Gentleman Radical*, 10.

11 *Boswell on the Grand Tour: Italy, Corsica, and France 1765–1766*, 23.

12 But see below, p. 462 n. 40.

13 Samuel Sharp, *Letters from Italy* (London, 1766), Letter liii, p. 287; see also *Boswell on the Grand Tour*, 23; *The Letters of Edward Gibbon*, ed. J. E. Norton, 3 vols. (New York: Macmillan, 1956), i. 171–2.

14 For Turin, see *Boswell on the Grand Tour*, 21–43.

15 For the politeness of the Torinese to visitors, see Louis Dutens, *Memoirs of a Traveller*, 5 vols. (London, 1806), i. 255–7.

16 A translation into French of extracts from *Tristram Shandy* was published at Venice in 1788, the complete work not becoming available until 1922; two earlier translations of *A Sentimental Journey* preceded Foscolo's, in 1792 and 1812. For Sterne's Italian reception, see Olivia Santovetti, 'The Adventurous Journey of Lorenzo Sterne in Italy', *The Shandean*, 8 (1996), 79–97.

17 *The Letters of Edward Gibbon*, ed. Norton, i. 172.

18 *Boswell on the Grand Tour*, 33.

19 Walpole to Horace Mann, 26 Sept. 1765, postscript of 30 Sept: *Walpole's Correspondence* (1960), xxii. 344.

20 *Carteggio di Pietro e di Alessandro Verri*, I. i. 183.

21 Giancarlo Passeroni, *Il Cicerone*, 6 vols. (Milan, 1768–74), vol. 5, III. xvii. 122.

22 '[C]ioè le vuole fabbricare di pianta', *Carteggio*, I. i. 284.

23 Although this is usually taken as a reference to Gian Battista Martini, it is more likely to have been Sterne's mistake for Gian Battista *Sam*martini, who, unlike the Bologna-based Martini, did organize concerts in Milan in the 1760s.

24 Mann to Walpole, 1 Nov. 1760: *Walpole's Correspondence* (1960), xxi. 446.

25 Ibid. 521; letter of 1 Aug. 1761.

26 *Memoirs*, 141.

27 Dutens, *Memoirs of a Traveller*, iv. 89.

28 See *TS* v. iv. 287.

29 *A Later Pepys*, ed. Alice C. C. Gaussen, 2 vols. (London, The Bodley Head, 1904), i. 279; letter of Sir James McDonald to Sir William Weller Pepys, 5 Jan. 1766.

30 John Thomas Smith, *Nollekens and his Times*, 2 vols. (London, 1828), i. 7.

31 Smollett, *Travels*, 269.

32 Samuel Sharp thought Naples the finest place in Italy: 'above all, I admire the heavens, the earth, and the sea of

Naples', *Letters from Italy*, Letter xvii, p. 67.

33 Gibbon, *Letters*, i. 191.

34 Giacomo Casanova, *Mémoires*, ed. Robert Abirached and Elio Zorzi, 3 vols. (Paris: Gallimard, 1958), iii. 856 and 1188 n.; see also Benedetto Croce, *Aneddoti di varia letterature*, 2nd edn., rev. with additions (Bari: G. Laterza & Figli, 1953), 374–408.

35 Samuel Sharp, *Letters from Italy*, Letter xxvi, p. 109.

36 For Errington as a traveller, see *A Dictionary of British and Irish Travellers in Italy 1701–1800*, compiled from the Brinsley Ford Archive by John Ingamells (New Haven and London: Yale University Press, 1997), 340.

37 For this last letter see Kenneth Monkman, 'Two More Unpublished Sterne Letters', *The Shandean*, 2 (1990), 143–5 (143).

38 Gibbon, *Letters*, i. 190.

39 Sharp, *Letters*, 203; James Boswell spent Easter Sunday 1765 in Rome: Frederick A. Pottle, *James Boswell: The Earlier Years 1740–1769* (London: Heinemann, 1966), 212.

40 The circumstances in which Sterne and Errington separated remain obscure; it seems likely, though, that it was Errington whom Sterne satirized as the joyless traveller, Mundungus, in 'In the Street. Calais' in *A Sentimental Journey* (*ASJ* 119); Gardner D. Stout, Jr. comes close to making this identification, though seeming finally to prefer the more usual identification of Mundungus with Samuel Sharp, who did not, however, as Stout rightly observes, have Errington's 'immense fortune', while the route ascribed to Mundungus ('Rome to Naples—from Naples to Venice—from Venice to Vienna—to Dresden, to Berlin') is very close to that Sterne envisaged taking with Errington (*ASJ* 119, n. to ll. 149–51).

41 But see Sterne's letter of 30 Aug. 1766 to Becket, in which he declared that 'I shall publish the 9th & 10 of Shandy the next winter': *Letters*, 288.

42 M. Dorothy George, *London Life in the Eighteenth Century*, 3rd edn. (1951, repr. Harmondsworth: Penguin, 1976), 140; see also Paul Edwards and Polly Rewt (eds.), *Letters of Ignatius Sancho* (Edinburgh: Edinburgh University Press, 1994); Vincent Carretta (ed.), *Letters of the Late Ignatius Sancho, an African* (Harmondsworth: Penguin, 1998); Paul Edwards, *Black Writers in Britain 1760–1890* (Edinburgh: Edinburgh University Press, 1991); Madeleine Descargues, 'Ignatius Sancho's Letters', *The Shandean*, 3 (1991), 145–66.

43 Carretta (ed.), *Letters*, 73–4; Carretta uses as copy-text the first edition of Sancho's *Letters* (London, 1782), where this letter is misdated 'July, 1776'; for Sterne's version of Sancho's letter, see *Letters*, 282–3.

44 *Sermons*, iv. 99.

45 Carretta, *Letters*, 74.

46 See e.g. Robin Blackburn, *The Overthrow of Colonial Slavery 1776–1848* (London: Verso, 1988), 'Introduction', 1–31 and *passim*.

47 Sterne's formulation is reminiscent of David Hume's discussion of degree; see e.g. *A Treatise of Human Nature*, I. i. 5, 'Of Relations', though his racial attitudes, if not his views on slavery, were certainly in advance of Hume's; see below p. 351.

48 David Hume, 'Of National Characters', *Essays, Moral, Political, and Literary*, I. xxi. 208.; Hume did, however, express his opposition to slavery in 'Of the Populousness of Ancient Nations', ibid., esp. 383 ff.

49 See Blackburn, *The Overthrow*, esp. chaps. 2, 4, and 8.

50 See above, p. 300.

51 See M. Turner, *English Parliamentary Enclosure* (Folkstone, 1980), ch. 3.

52 It is possible that Sterne was writing—or at least seriously intending to write—a further instalment at this time, for he later wrote to William Combe that 'I miscarried of my tenth Volume by the

violence of a fever have just got thro' (*Letters*, 294).

53 See William Combe, *Original Letters of the Late Mr. Laurence Sterne* (London, 1788), and Harlan W. Hamilton, 'William Combe and the *Original Letters of the Late Mr. Laurence Sterne* (1788), *PMLA* 82 (1967), 420–9.

54 Sterne was probably right in his conjecture: see Harlan W. Hamilton, *Doctor Syntax: A Silhouette of William Combe, Esq.* (London: Chatto & Windus, 1969), 23.

55 Casanova, *Mémoires*, iii. 176.

56 Sterne's novel still had sufficient popular appeal, however, to have prompted a spurious ninth volume in 1766, a work which—with its first fifteen pages altered—was cynically reissued in the following year as volume X of *Tristram Shandy*.

57 [Ralph Griffiths], *Monthly Review*, 36 (Feb. 1767), 93.

58 Ibid. 102.

59 *Gentleman's Magazine*, 37 (Feb. 1767), 75–6.

60 *Lloyd's Evening Post*, 20: 1510 (11–13 Mar. 1767), 241.

61 See *Letters*, 300–1, n. 2.

Chapter fourteen

1 Arnold Wright and William Lutley Sclater, *Sterne's Eliza* (London: Heinemann, 1922), 5; unless otherwise indicated, information on Eliza Draper and her family is taken from this source. For Daniel Draper, see also C. Helen Brock, 'Mr Daniel Draper of the East India Company', *The Shandean*, 2 (1990), 137–42.

2 *Sterne's Eliza*, 12.

3 See ibid. 21, 72, 114, 126, and 184.

4 Ibid. 98.

5 Ibid. 138

6 The mercurial shifts in Sterne's moods had, at least in part, a physical source. The present general lack of familiarity with tuberculosis—though the disease is now on the increase once more—has made it harder for us than for our predecessors to read the progress of Sterne's illness between the lines of his letters. A wholly material account of the journal to Eliza may be over-reductive, but it is worth remembering that as late as the mid-nineteenth century aspiring physicians were directed to literary accounts of consumption—in Dickens's *Nicholas Nickleby* (1838–9), ch. 6, for example—as a means of familiarizing themselves with the irregular rhythms of the disease. For a recent account of tuberculosis, see Thomas Dormandy, *The White Death: A History of Tuberculosis* (London and Rio Grande: Hambledon, 1999).

7 Sterne's 'Journal to Eliza' is not to be confused with *Letters from Yorick to Eliza*, published in 1773; the Journal was in fact lost for some sixty years until it was rediscovered by the precocious 11-year-old Thomas Washbourne Gibbs who, while rummaging for spills to light candles, came across the document and, recognizing its significance, preserved it. The *Journal to Eliza*, as it is now known, was first published in Wilbur L. Cross's edition of Sterne's works in 1904.

8 See Henry Fielding *Amelia*, ed. Martin C. Battestin (1752; Oxford: Clarendon Press, 1983), 346 and n. 4, and App. VI, p. 573, n. to p. 346. Dr James's powder had other unhappy literary connections: it was praised by Christopher Smart in his *Hymn to the Supreme Being on Recovery from a Dangerous Fit of Illness* (1756)—the illness being the onset of the mania from which in fact he suffered intermittently thereafter—and was thought to have occasioned the death of Oliver Goldsmith (see e.g. Ralph M. Wardle, *Oliver Goldsmith* (London: Constable, 1957), 280).

9 Sterne mistakenly dated the entry 16

April, though it in fact refers to the previous day.

10 See *Letters*, 342–3.

11 Letter of 21 May 1767: *Letters*, 342.

Chapter fifteen

1 The cancelled '31' in the middle of this entry is one more indication of the extent to which, by this time, Sterne was writing not a literal journal but a carefully fictionalized one.

2 Richard Mead, *A Mechanical Account of Poisons* (London, 1702), Essay iii, 'Of Poisonous Minerals and Plants' (first noted by L. P. Curtis, *Letters*, 349, n. 5).

3 Jonathan Swift, *A Tale of a Tub*, sec. ix, p. 172.

4 Ibid. 174

5 *Letters*, 362 n. For an alternative dating of this letter (to 1765), see Cash, *LY* 218, n. 2; his argument, which rests on his belief that 'Sterne would not carry on simultaneously two public sentimental courtships with well-bred women', does not seem to me sufficiently strong to overturn Curtis's dating.

6 *Monthly Review*, 32 (Feb. 1765), 128.

7 *Carteggio*, I. ii. 244.

8 Elizabeth Montagu to Sarah Scott, 4 Sep. 1768: *Letters*, 439.

9 *A Series of Genuine Letters* ... 6 vols. (1786), v. 83.

10 Ibid. 87.

11 A. C. H. Seymour, *The Life and Times of Selina Countess of Huntingdon*, 2 vols. (London, 1844), i. 280; quoted by Langford, *A Polite and Commercial People*, 246.

12 *Lettters*, 383, n. 8.

13 For Harrogate in the mid-1760s, see Smollett, *Humphry Clinker*, 163.

14 *Sterne's Eliza*, 61.

15 Ibid.

16 Sterne uses an almost identical formulation in describing Tobias Smollett's *Travels*: 'He wrote an account of them, but 'twas nothing but the account of his miserable feelings', *ASJ* 116.

17 *Letters*, 392.

18 See above, p. 368.

19 Whether Sterne understood this as a final entry is tantalizingly uncertain, for, like *A Sentimental Journey*, the journal ends without a concluding full stop.

20 See *ASJ*, 'Note on the Text', 49–54.

21 *A Series of Genuine Letters between Henry and Frances*, v. 200.

22 Crauford's guests included a number of Sterne's friends and acquaintances, including the dukes of Roxburgh and Grafton, the earl of March and Ossory, David Hume, and David Garrick.

23 John Macdonald, *Memoirs of an Eighteenth-Century Footman*, 92.

Epilogue

1 Letter to Doctor *****. [?York,] Jan. 30, 1760: *Letters*, 88.

2 *Monthly Review*, 38 (March 1768), 185.

3 Ibid. 177.

4 Ibid. (Apr. 1768), 311, 309.

5 *Critical Review*, 25 (Mar. 1768), 181.

6 *Political Register*, 2 (May 1768), 383, quoted in Howes, *Sterne: The Critical Heritage*, 201.

7 Horace Walpole to Thomas Gray, 8 Mar. 1768: in *Correspondence of Horace Walpole* (1948), xiv. 183, and to George Montagu, 12 Mar. 1768: ibid. (1941), x. 255.

8 Elizabeth Montagu to ? [1768?]: *Letters*, p. 441.

9 William Warburton to Charles Yorke, 4 Apr. 1768, *Letters from . . . Dr. Warburton . . . to the Hon. Charles Yorke* (1812), quoted in Howes, *Sterne: The Critical Heritage*, 205.

10 *The Works of Vicesimus Knox*, 7 vols. (London, 1824), i. 131.

11 Frances Burney D'Arblay, *Memoirs of Doctor Burney* (1832), quoted in Howes, *Sterne: The Critical Heritage*, 204.

12 Charles Churchill, *The Ghost*, ii. 171: *The Poetical Works of Charles Churchill*, ed. Douglas Grant (Oxford: Clarendon Press, 1956), 84.

13 Charles Kingsley, 'Preface' to Henry Brooke, The Fool of Quality (London, 1859).

14 A rare exception is Thomas Rowlandson's etching, *Yorick Feeling the Grisett's Pulse*, which appeared as the frontispiece to *The Beauties of Sterne*; though presumably not widely understood as such, the illustration is ambiguously open to an eroticized reading.

15 See e.g. Anthony Ashley Cooper, third earl of Shaftesbury, *Characteristicks of Men, Manners, Opinions, and Times* (1711); Francis Hutcheson, *An Essay on the Nature and Conduct of the Passions and Affections with Illustrations on the Moral Sense* (1728; 3rd edn., 1742); David Hume, *A Treatise of Human Nature* (1739–40); Henry Home, Lord Kames, *Essays on the Principles of Morality and Natural Religion* (1751); Adam Smith, *The Theory of Moral Sentiments* (1759); the phrase quoted is from Kames's *Essays* (Edinburgh, 1751), 27. Amid the considerable literature devoted to sensibility, the following selection is particularly valuable in relation to Sterne: Northrop Frye, 'Towards Defining an Age of Sensibility', *English Literary History*, 33 (1956), 144–52; Louis I. Bredvold, *The Natural History of Sensibility* (Detroit: Wayne State University Press, 1962); R. S. Crane, 'Suggestions Toward a Genealogy of the "Man of Feeling"', in *The Idea of the Humanities* (Chicago: University of Chicago Press, 1967); J. C. T. Oates, *Shandyism and Sentiment* (Cambridge: Cambridge Bibliographical Society, 1968); R. F. Brissenden, *Virtue in Distress* (London, 1974); Jean H. Hagstrum, *Sex and Sensibility: Ideal and Erotic Love from Milton to Mozart* (Chicago: Chicago University Press, 1980); David Marshall, *The Surprising Effects of Sympathy: Marivaux, Diderot, Rousseau, and Mary Shelley* (Chicago: University of Chicago Press, 1988); John Mullan, *Sentiment and Sociability: The Language of Feeling in the Eighteenth Century* (Oxford: Clarendon Press, 1988); G. J. Barker-Benfield, *The Culture of Sensibility*; and Tim Parnell, 'A Story Painted to the Heart? *Tristram Shandy* and Sentimentalism Reconsidered', *The Shandean*, 9 (1997), 122–35.

16 See e.g. Barker-Benfield, *The Culture of Sensibility*, esp. pp. 258ff.

17 Mary Wollstonecraft, *A Vindication of the Rights of Woman*, ed. Carol H. Poston (1792; repr. New York and London: Norton, 1975), 9.

18 David Garrick, 'Epitaph on Laurence Sterne', *The Poetical Works of David Garrick*, 2 vols. (London, 1785), ii. 484.

19 *Public Advertiser*, 24 Mar. 1769.

20 Curtis, 'New Light on Sterne', 550.

21 See Isaac Reed, *Diaries, 1762–1804*, ed. Claude E. Jones (Berkeley and Los Angeles, 1946), 156, and Arthur Sherbo, 'The Dissection of Laurence Sterne', *Notes & Queries*, 232 (Sept. 1987), 348.

22 'Maloniana', in Sir James Prior, *Life of Edmond Malone* (London, 1860), 374.

23 See McKendrick, Brewer, and Plumb, *The Birth of a Consumer Society*, 218, 219, 228.

24 The archbishop of York to Mrs Montagu, 26 Mar. 1768: *Letters*, 433.

25 The Revd Andrew Cheap's lengthy and understandably testy memorandum in the Sutton Parish Book begins: 'Be it Remembered That in the Year 1764 during the Incumbency of M^{r}. Laurence Sterne the Vicarage House in this Place was burnt down & entirely destroyed. That he continued Vicar till he died in March 1768 and, tho' he had been frequently admonished and required to rebuild the Vicarage House, he found Means to evade the Performance of it' (64^{v}.); Andrew Cheap costed

the rebuilding of the Vicarage House at £576. 13*s.* 6*d.* (64^{v}, 65^{r-v}).

26 Mrs Montagu to Mrs Sarah Scott [Apr. 1768]: *Letters*, 434.

27 From Mrs Montagu [1768?]: ibid. 440.

28 Lydia Sterne to Mrs Montagu [?5 Apr. 1768]: ibid. 434.

29 See e.g. the letter to the publisher Thomas Becket, probably written in December 1768, which begins: 'Dear S[r][,] I wonder I do not hear from you. I have wrote you two or 3 letters lately which were of consequence' (ibid. 443); in relating John Botham's complaint to Elizabeth Montagu, Lydia excused herself by saying that 'when a person writes on business, there is much less occasion for comp[ts] than for directions', letter of [?5 Apr. 1768], ibid. 434.

30 *Letters*, 434.

31 Ibid.

32 Ibid.

33 The eventual settlement included 10 gns for a picture of Sterne and 6 gns for his bass viol; see ibid. 441.

34 Ibid. 440

35 John Hall-Stevenson subsequently checked up on who had contributed and who had not, and only Lord Irwin appears to have failed to support the Sternes.

36 Lydia Sterne to Elizabeth Montagu, letter of [?5 April 1768]: *Letters*, 435.

37 Ibid.

38 Mrs Montagu to Mrs Sarah Scott, 4 Sept. 1768: ibid. 439.

39 Ibid.

40 Lydia Sterne to Mrs Montagu, [?Jan. 1769]: ibid. 446.

41 Mrs Montagu to Mrs Sarah Scott, 4 Sept. 1768: ibid. 440.

42 Lydia Sterne to Mrs Montagu [?31 Aug. 1768]: ibid. 438.

43 Ibid. 444.

44 Ibid. 445.

45 Lydia Sterne to Mrs Montagu [?31 Aug. 1768]; ibid. 438; as late as January of the following year Lydia was noting that 'we thought we should have done with debts no such matter—a Country man brought a note of hand of M[r] Sterne's & told us of another which we should hear of soon', Lydia Sterne to Mrs Montagu [?Jan. 1769]: ibid. 447.

46 'Advertisement' to 'The ABUSES of CONSCIENCE considered', *Sermons*, iv. 255.

47 John Hall-Stevenson to Lydia Sterne, 18 Nov. 1768: *Letters*, 443.

48 Lydia Sterne to William Strahan [?Winter 1769]: ibid. 447.

49 Lydia Sterne to John Wilkes, 24 Oct. 1769: ibid. 452.

50 Lydia Sterne to Mrs Montagu, 2 Mar. 1770: ibid. 454.

51 Lydia Sterne to Mrs Montagu, 26 Sept. 1771: ibid. 455.

52 Ibid. 456.

53 Lydia's reticence on this subject is suggested by John Croft's misapprehension that Médalle was a Protestant merchant from Normandy, *Whitefoord Papers*, 231.

54 Mrs Montagu to Lydia Sterne [1772], *Letters*, 458.

55 *Archives de la Ville d'Albi*, GG. 26 (Registre 1672–1780); the marriage took place on 28 April 1772.

56 Van R. Baker, 'Laurence Sterne's Family in France', *Notes & Queries*, 22: 3 (1975), 497–501, and 'Whatever Happened to Lydia Sterne?', *Eighteenth-Century Life*, 2 (1975), 6–11.

57 *Letters*, 121 n.

58 *Memoirs of the Life and Correspondence of Mrs. Hannah More*, ed. William Roberts, 4 vols. (London, 1834), i. 67.

59 William Combe, *The Philosopher in Bristol* (1775), 27; quoted in Hamilton, *Dr. Syntax*, 39.

60 *Original Letters of the Late Reverend Mr. Laurence Sterne* (London, 1788).

61 See above, p. 439, n. 19.

62 Lydia Sterne's changes to the 'Fragment in the Manner of Rabelais' are well documented in New, 'Sterne's Rabelaisian Fragment'; her mistranscription of parts of the 'memoirs' are discussed by Kenneth Monkman, in *Memoirs*, pp. xiii–xvi.

63 *The Gentleman's Magazine*, 45 (Apr. 1775), 188.

64 *Monthly Review*, 53 (Nov. 1775), 403–4; With more graciousness than many later critics have shown, Griffiths concluded: 'For us, we really think ourselves obliged to Mrs. Medalle for the entertainment she has procured us' (404).

65 *Letters of the Late Rev. Mr. Laurence Sterne, to his most intimate friends, with a Fragment in the Manner of* Rabelais, *to which are prefix'd, Memoirs of his Life and Family. Written by Himself. And Published by his Daughter, Mrs. Medalle* (London, 1775).

66 Thomas Jefferson to Peter Carr, 10 Aug. 1787: *Writings* (New York: Literary Classics of the United States, 1984), 902.

67 *The Beauties of Sterne* (London, 1782), 'Preface', [p. ix].

68 See David McKitterick, 'Tristram Shandy in the Royal Academy: A Group of Drawings by John Nixon', *The Shandean*, 4 (1992), 85–110; W. G. Day, 'Michael Angelo Rooker's Illustrations to *Tristram Shandy*, *The Shandean*, 7 (1995), 30–42; Peter de Voogd, 'Henry William Bunbury, Illustrator of *Tristram Shandy*', *The Shandean*, 3 (1991), 138–43.

69 Joseph Moser, quoted in Brewer, *The Pleasures of the Imagination*, 463; see also David Alexander, 'Sterne, the 18th-Century Print Market, and the Prints in Shandy Hall', *The Shandean*, 5 (1993), 110–22; Peter de Voogd, 'Sterne All the Fashion: A Sentimental Fan', *The Shandean*, 8 (1996), 133–6.

70 For translations of Sterne, see e.g. Wolfgang Hörner, 'Lorenz Sterne: Early German Translations, 1763–1800', *The Shandean*, 4 (1992), 11–48; Agnes Zwaneveld, 'Laurens Sterne in Holland: The Eighteenth Century' and Peter de Voogd, 'Laurence Sterne in Dutch (18th Century): A Bibliography', *The Shandean*, 5 (1993), 125–49; Bandry, 'The First French Translation of *Tristram Shandy*' and Luis Penegaute, 'The Unfortunate Journey of Laurence Sterne through Spain: The Translations of the Works into Spanish', *The Shandean*, 6 (1994), 66–85 and 150–9; Olivia Santovetti, 'The Adventurous Journey of Lorenzo Sterne in Italy', *The Shandean*, 8 (1996), 79–98'; and Joaquim Mallafrè, 'Sterne in Catalan: Notes on Translation', *The Shandean*, 9 (1997), 109–21.

71 *The Shandean: An Annual Volume devoted to Laurence Sterne and his Works* (1989–), under the general editorship of Peter de Voogd.

72 *The Florida Edition of the Works of Laurence Sterne* (Gainesville, Fla.: University Press of Florida, 1978–), under the general editorship of Professor Melvyn New.

73 Letter of 14 Apr. 1823 to Douglas Kinnaird: *Byron's Letters and Journals*, x. 150.

74 See Eric A. Blackall, *Goethe and the Novel* (Ithaca and London: Cornell University Press, 1976), esp. 201–2. In his diary entry for 5 October 1830 Goethe wrote of Sterne: '[W]ho else in 1759 perceived pedantry and philistinism so clearly and portrayed them with such gaiety [*Heiterkeit*]?' Elsewhere he described Sterne as 'in nothing a model, in everything an indicator and awakener': *Gedenkausgabe der Werke. Briefe und Gespräche*, ed. Ernst Beutler, 25 vols. (Zurich and Stuttgart: Artemis Verlag, 1948–60), viii. 517–18.

75 Friedrich Nietzsche, *Human, All Too Human*, trans. R. J. Hollingdale (1986; new edn. Cambridge: Cambridge University Press, 1996), 238–9.

76 See Eugene Jolas, 'My Friend James Joyce', in Seon Givens (ed.), *James Joyce: Two Decades of Criticism* (New York: Vanguard, 1948), quoted in Richard Ellmann, *James Joyce* (1959; rev. edn. Oxford: Oxford University Press, 1982), 554. Joyce also considered Sterne to be 'my fellow-countryman' and parodied his sentimental manner in *Ulysses*. The very fact of Sterne's Irish birth was largely unknown during his years of fame, but two of his best-known contemporary imitators—Richard Griffith and Henry Brooke—were Irish, as was

Flann O'Brien (Brian O'Nolan), whose metafictional *At Swim-Two-Birds* (1939) owes much to the example of *Tristram Shandy* and whose *The Dalkey Archive* (1964) borrows one of Sterne's best jokes. For accommodations of Sterne within traditions of Irish writing, see e.g. Vivien Mercier, *The Irish Comic Tradition* (London, Oxford, and New York: Oxford University Press, 1962), 245; Ian Campbell Ross, 'Fiction to 1800', in Seamus Deane *et al.* (eds.), *The Field Day Anthology of Irish Writing*, 3 vols. (Derry: Field Day, 1991), i. 682–759; Colm Tóibín, *The Penguin Book of Irish Fiction* (London: Viking, 1999), p. xix.

77 Viktor Shklovsky [Viktor Shkovskiĭ], *Theory of Prose*, trans. Benjamin Sher, 2nd edn. (1929: Normal, Ill.: Dalkey Archive Press, 1990), 'The Novel as Parody', 147–70 (170).

78 Virginia Woolf, 'The *Sentimental Journey*', in *Collected Essays*, 4 vols (London: Hogarth Press, 1966), i. 96.

79 'Il progenitore di tutti i romanzi d'avanguardia del nostro secolo fu senza dubbio il settecentesco *Tristram Shandy* di Laurence Sterne': Italo Calvino, postscript to Laurence Sterne, *Un romanzo politico*, trans. Giuseppe Martelli (Torino: Einaudi, 1981), n.p.

80 'Afterword: A Talk with the Author by Philip Roth', in Milan Kundera, *The Book of Laughter and Forgetting*, trans. Michael Henry Heim (1978; repr. Harmondsworth: Penguin, 1983), 231. Determined as he was to appeal to the widest possible public, regardless of the objections of learned pedants, Sterne would also surely have enjoyed Martin Rowson's witty and splendidly drawn comic book 'interpretation' of *Tristram Shandy* (London: Picador, 1996).

81 In the process Dr Monkman was able to confirm the story that the writer's corpse had been stolen by body-snatchers for dissection.

82 Sterne never referred to his rented house in Coxwold by this name. When he first gave an account of Shandy Hall in volumes I and II of *Tristram Shandy* in 1759 he had not even received the living of Coxwold; subsequently Sterne referred to the house on one occasion as 'this Shandy-castle of mine' (*Letters*, 120), but more usually called it simply his 'cottage' (ibid. 353, 354) or 'thatchd Cottage' (ibid. 335, 346).

List of Works Cited

The following select list of works cited does not include manuscript sources or eighteenth-century periodical and pamphlet literature, details of which will be found in the notes.

Works by Sterne

The Beauties of Sterne: Including all his Pathetic Tales, and most distinguished Observations on Life. Selected for the Heart of Sensibility (London, 1782).

Letters of the Late Rev. Mr. Laurence Sterne, to his most intimate friends, with a Fragment in the Manner of Rabelais, to which are prefix'd, Memoirs of his Life and Family. Written by Himself. And Published by his Daughter, Mrs. Medalle (London, 1775).

Letters of Laurence Sterne, ed. Lewis Perry Curtis (Oxford: Clarendon Press, 1935).

The Life and Opinions of Tristram Shandy, Gentleman, ed. Ian Campbell Ross (1983; rev. edn. Oxford and New York: Oxford University Press, 2000).

—— ed. Melvyn New and Joan New, with Richard A. Davies and W. G. Day, 3 vols. (Gainesville, Fla.: University Press of Florida, 1978–84), volumes i and ii (Text) and iii (Notes) of the *Florida Edition of the Works of Laurence Sterne*.

A Sentimental Journey through France and Italy, ed. Gardner D. Stout, Jr. (Berkeley and Los Angeles: University of California Press, 1967).

A Sentimental Journey through France and Italy with the *Journal to Eliza* and *A Political Romance*, ed. Ian Jack (1968; repr. Oxford: Oxford University Press, 1984).

The Sermons of Laurence Sterne, ed. Melvyn New, 2 vols. (Gainesville, Fla.: University Press of Florida, 1996), volumes iv (Text) and v (Notes) of the *Florida Edition of the Works of Laurence Sterne*.

Sterne's Memoirs: A Hitherto Unrecorded Holograph Now Brought to Light in Facsimile, ed. Kenneth Monkman (Coxwold: The Laurence Sterne Trust, 1985).

Works of Laurence Sterne, ed. Wilbur L. Cross, 12 vols. (London: Jenson Society, 1906).

Other Works Cited

Aylmer, G. E., and Cant, Reginald (eds.), *A History of York Minster*. (Oxford: Clarendon Press, 1977).

Baker, C. H. C. and M. I., *The Life and Circumstances of James Brydges, first Duke of Chandos* (Oxford: Clarendon Press, 1949).

BAKER, Van R., 'Laurence Sterne's Family in France'. *Notes & Queries*, 22:3 (1975), 497–501.
—— 'Whatever Happened to Lydia Sterne?', *Eighteenth-Century Life*, 2 (1975), 6–11.
BANDRY, ANNE, 'Early Advertisements', *The Shandean*, 4 (1992), 244–5.
—— 'The First French Translation of *Tristram Shandy*', *The Shandean*, 6 (1994), 66–85.
BARKER-BENFIELD, G. J, *The Culture of Sensibility: Sex and Society in Eighteenth-Century Britain* (Chicago and London: University of Chicago Press, 1992).
BARKER, NICOLAS, 'The Library Catalogue of Laurence Sterne', *The Shandean*, 1 (1989), 9–24.
BARR, C. B. L., 'Sterne and York Minster Library', *The Shandean*, 2 (1990), 8–21.
BASKER, JAMES G., *Tobias Smollett: Critic and Journalist* (Newark: University of Delaware Press, 1988).
BATE, WALTER JACKSON, *Samuel Johnson* (London: Chatto & Windus, 1978).
BEATTIE, J. M., *Crime and the Courts in England 1660–1800* (Oxford: Clarendon Press, 1986).
BELL, FITZROY (ed.), *Memorials of John Murray of Broughton*, Scottish History Society Publications, 27 (Edinburgh, 1898).
BERMINGHAM, ANNE, and BREWER, JOHN (eds.), *The Consumption of Culture 1600–1800: Image, Object, Text* (London and New York: Routledge, 1995).
BÉROALDE DE VERVILLE, FRANÇOIS, *Le Moyen de Parvenir* (1615? new edn., n.p., 1700?).
BESTERMAN, THEODORE, *Voltaire*, 3rd edn. (Oxford: Blackwell, 1976).
BEWLEY, CHRISTINE and DAVID, *Gentleman Radical: A Life of John Horne Tooke 1736–1812* (London and New York: Tauris Academic Studies, 1998).
BLACKBURN, ROBIN, *The Overthrow of Colonial Slavery 1776–1848* (London: Verso, 1988).
BLACKBURNE, FRANCIS, *A Charge Delivered to the Clergy of the Archdeaconry of Cleveland at the Visitation held in the Year MDCCLII* (York, 1752).
BOSCH, RENÉ, 'Sterne and Voltaire in Purgatory: A Prophecy by W. J. Mickle', *The Shandean*, 8 (1996), 98–112.
BOSWELL, JAMES, *Life of Johnson*, ed. R. W. Chapman, rev. J. D. Fleeman (Oxford: Oxford University Press, 1970).
—— *Boswell on the Grand Tour: Italy, Corsica, and France 1765–1766*, ed. Frank Brady and Frederick A. Pottle (London: Heinemann, 1955).
—— *Boswell Laird of Auchlineck*, ed. Joseph W. Reed and Frederick A. Pottle (London: Heinemann, 1979).
BREWER, JOHN, *The Pleasures of the Imagination: English Culture in the Eighteenth Century* (London: HarperCollins, 1997).
BROCK, C. HELEN, 'Mr Daniel Draper of the East India Company', *The Shandean*, 2 (1990), 137–42.
BROOKE, HENRY, *The Fool of Quality*, with a preface by Charles Kingsley (London, 1859).
BURKE, EDMUND, *The Correspondence of Edmund Burke*, ed. Thomas W. Copeland (and others), 10 vols. (Cambridge and Chicago: Cambridge University Press and Chicago University Press, 1969–70).
BURNET, GILBERT, *History of his Own Time* (London, 1724).
BURTON, JOHN, *British Liberty Endangered . . . wherein it is proved, from FACTS, that J. B. has hitherto been a better Friend to the English Constitution, in Church and State, than his Persecutors* (York, 1749).
CALVINO, ITALO, postscript to Laurence Sterne, *Un romanzo politico*, trans. Giuseppe Martelli (Turin: Einaudi, 1981).
CANNON, JOHN, *Aristocratic Century: The Peerage of Eighteenth-Century England* (Cambridge: Cambridge University Press, 1984).
CASANOVA, GIACOMO, *Mémoires*, ed. Robert Abirached and Elio Zorzi, 3 vols. (Paris: Gallimard, 1958).

CASH, ARTHUR H., 'Some New Sterne Letters', *TLS* (8 Apr. 1965), 284; repr. in *Laurence Sterne: The Later Years*, 116–23.
—— 'Sterne as a Judge', in John H. Middendorf (ed.), *English Writers of the Eighteenth Century* (New York and London: Columbia University Press, 1971), 17–36.
—— *Laurence Sterne: The Early & Middle Years* (London: Methuen, 1975).
—— *Laurence Sterne: The Later Years* (London and New York: Methuen, 1986).
—— and STEDMOND, JOHN M., (eds.), *The Winged Skull: Papers from the Laurence Sterne Bicentenary Conference* (London: Methuen, 1971).
CHAIGNEAU, WILLIAM, *The History of Jack Connor*, 2 vols. (Dublin, 1752).
CHURCHILL, CHARLES, *The Poetical Works of Charles Churchill*, ed. Douglas Grant (Oxford: Clarendon Press, 1956).
CLAY, J. W., 'The Sterne Family', *Yorkshire Archaeological Journal*, 21 (1911), 91–107.
CLIMENSON, EMILY J., *Elizabeth Montagu: The Queen of the Bluestockings*, 2 vols. (New York: E. P. Dutton and Co., 1906).
COLE, WILLIAM, *The Bletchley Diary of the Rev. William Cole* (London: Constable, 1931).
COLLYER, CEDRIC, 'Laurence Sterne and Yorkshire Politics: Some New Evidence', *Leeds Philosophical Society Proceedings*, 7: 1 (1952), 83–7.
COMBE, WILLIAM, *Original Letters of the late Reverend Mr. Laurence Sterne* (London, 1788).
COOPER, WILLIAM DURRANT, (ed.), *Seven Letters Written by Sterne and his Friends* (London, 1844).
COVENTRY, FRANCIS, *The History of Pompey the Little; or the Life and Adventures of a Lap-Dog*, ed. Robert Adams Day (London: Oxford University Press, 1974).
COWPER, WILLIAM, *The Letters and Prose Writings of William Cowper*, ed. James King and Charles Ryskamp, 3 vols. (Oxford: Clarendon Press, 1979).
CRAIG, MAURICE, *Dublin 1660–1800: A Social and Architectural History* (Dublin: Allen Figgis, 1969).
CROCE, BENEDETTO, *Aneddoti di varia letteratura.* 2nd edn. rev. with additions (Bari: G. Laterza & Figli, 1953).
CROFT, JOHN, 'Anecdotes of Sterne vulgarly Tristram Shandy', *The Whitefoord Papers*, ed. W. A. S. Hewins (Oxford, 1898), 223–35.
—— *Scrapeana* (2nd edn., York, 1792).
CROSS, WILBUR L., *The Life and Times of Laurence Sterne*, 3rd edn. (New Haven: Yale University Press, 1929).
CURTIS, LEWIS PERRY, *The Politicks of Laurence Sterne* (London: Oxford University Press, 1929).
—— 'Forged Letters of Laurence Sterne', *PMLA* 50 (1935), 1076–1106.
—— 'New Light on Sterne', *Modern Language Notes*, 76 (June 1961), 498–501.
DAY, W. G., 'Sterne's Books', *The Library*, 31 (1976), 245–8.
DEFOE, DANIEL, *Augusta Triumphans* (London, 1728).
—— *A Tour through the Whole Island of Great Britain*, ed. Pat Rogers (1724–6; repr. Harmondsworth: Penguin, 1971).
DELANY, MARY, *The Autobiography and Correspondence of Mary Granville, Mrs. Delany*, 3 vols., ed. Augusta Waddington Hall, Lady Llanover, 1st series (London, 1861).
DENNIS, JONAS, *A Key to the Regalia* (London, 1820).
DESCARGUES, MADELEINE, 'Ignatius Sancho's Letters', *The Shandean*, 3 (1991), 145–66.
DE VOOGD, PETER 'The Letters of Laurence Sterne', *The Shandean*, 4 (1992), 181–95.
—— 'The Oswald Papers', *The Shandean*, 10 (1998), 80–91.
A Dictionary of British and Irish Travellers in Italy 1701–1800, compiled from the Brinsley Ford Archive by John Ingamells (New Haven and London: Yale University Press, 1997).

DIDEROT, DENIS, *Correspondance*, ed. Georges Roth and Jean Varloot, 16 vols. (Paris: Editions de Minuit, 1955–70).

DODSLEY, ROBERT, *The Correspondence of Robert Dodsley 1733–1764*, ed. James E. Tierney (Cambridge: Cambridge University Press, 1988).

DONOGHUE, FRANK, *The Fame Machine: Book Reviewing and Eighteenth-Century Literary Careers* (Stanford: Stanford University Press, 1996).

DORMANDY, THOMAS, *The White Death: A History of Tuberculosis* (London and Rio Grande: Hambledon, 1999).

DOWNEY, JAMES, *The English Pulpit: A Study of the Sermons of Butler, Berkeley, Secker, Sterne, Whitefield and Wesley* (Oxford: Clarendon Press, 1969).

DRAKE, FRANCIS, *Eboracum: or, the History and Antiquities of the City of York* (London, 1736).

DUTENS, LOUIS, *Memoirs of a Traveller*, 5 vols. (London, 1806).

EAVES, T. C. DUNCAN, and KIMPEL, BEN D., *Samuel Richardson* (Oxford: Clarendon, 1971).

EDWARDS, PAUL, *Black Writers in Britain 1760–1890* (Edinburgh: Edinburgh University Press, 1991).

ERAMETSA, ERIK, 'A Study of the word "Sentimental" and of Other Linguistic Characteristics of Eighteenth-Century Sentimentalism in England', *Annales Academiae Scientiarum Fennicae*, Ser. B. (Helsinki, 1951).

FERRIAR, JOHN, *Illustrations of Sterne and Other Essays and Verses*, 2nd edn. (London, 1812).

FIELDING, HENRY, *Amelia*, ed. Martin C. Battestin (Oxford: Clarendon Press, 1983).

FIELDING, HENRY, *The History of Tom Jones, A Foundling*, ed. Fredson Bowers, 2 vols. (Oxford: Clarendon Press, 1974).

—— *The True Patriot and Related Writings*, ed. W. B. Coley (Oxford: Clarendon Press, 1987).

FITZGERALD, PERCY, *Life of Laurence Sterne*, 3rd edn. (London: Chatto & Windus, 1906).

FLEETWOOD, WILLIAM, *The Relative Duties of Parents and Children*, 4th edn. (London, 1732).

FLUCHÈRE, HENRI, *Laurence Sterne: de l'homme à l'œuvre* (Paris: Gallimard, 1961); trans. and abridged Barbara Bray (Oxford: Clarendon Press, 1965).

FORRESTER, RICHARD, 'Uncle Jaques Sterne', *The Shandean*, 4 (1992), 197–233.

GARAT, DOMINIQUE-JOSEPH, *Mémoires Historiques sur la vie de M. Suard*, 3 vols. (Paris, 1820).

GARRICK, DAVID, *The Poetical Works of David Garrick*, 2 vols. (London, 1785).

—— *Private Correspondence of David Garrick* (London, 1831).

GENT, THOMAS, *Life of Thomas Gent* (London, 1832).

GEORGE, M. DOROTHY, *London Life in the Eighteenth Century*, 3rd edn. (1951, repr. Harmondsworth: Penguin, 1976).

GIBBON, EDWARD, *Memoirs of my Life*, ed. Betty Radice (Harmondsworth; Penguin, 1984).

—— *The Letters of Edward Gibbon*, ed. J. E. Norton, 3 vols. (New York: Macmillan, 1956).

GIBSON, EDMUND, *Codex juris ecclesiastici anglicani* (London, 1713).

GILL, THOMAS, *Vallis Eboracensis* (London and Easingwold, 1852).

GIROUARD, MARK, *The English Town* (New Haven and London: Yale University Press, 1990).

GOLD, JOEL J., 'Tristram Shandy at the Ambassador's Chapel', *Philological Quarterly*, 48: 3 (1969), 421–4.

GOLDSMITH, OLIVER, *The Collected Works of Oliver Goldsmith*, ed. Arthur Friedman, 5 vols. (Oxford: Clarendon Press, 1966).

GORDON, GEORGE, LORD BYRON, *Byron's Letters and Journals*, ed. Leslie A. Marchand, 11 vols. (London: John Murray, 1971–83).

The Grand Juries of the County of Westmeath 1727–1853, 2 vols. (Ledestown, 1853).

GRAVES, ALGERNON, *The Society of Artists of Great Britain, 1760–91* (London: George Bell, 1907).

GRAY, ARTHUR, and BRITTAIN, FREDERICK, *A History of Jesus College, Cambridge* (1960; rev. edn., Cambridge: Silent Books, 1988).

GRAY, THOMAS, *Poems of Mr. Gray*, ed. William Mason (York, 1775).
—— *Correspondence of Thomas Gray*, ed. Paget Toynbee and Leonard Whibley, 3 vols. (Oxford: Clarendon Press, 1935).
GRIFFITH, RICHARD, *The Triumvirate* (London, 1764).
—— *The Posthumous Works of a Late Celebrated Genius, Deceased*, 2 vols. (Dublin, 1770).
—— and GRIFFITH, ELIZABETH, *A Series of Genuine Letters, between Henry and Frances*, 6 vols. (London, 1786).
The Guardian, ed. John Calhoun Stephens (Lexington: University Press of Kentucky, 1982).
HALL-STEVENSON, JOHN, *Crazy Tales* (London, 1762).
—— *The Works of John Hall-Stevenson*, 3 vols. (London, 1795).
HAMILTON, ADRIAN, *The Infamous Essay on Woman, or John Wilkes seated between Vice and Virtue* (London: André Deutsch, 1972).
HAMILTON, HARLAN W., 'William Combe and the Original Letters of the Late Reverend Mr. Laurence Sterne (1788)', *PMLA* 82 (1967), 420–9.
—— *Doctor Syntax: A Silhouette of William Combe, Esq.* (London: Chatto & Windus, 1969).
—— 'Sterne's Sermon in Paris and its Background', *Proceedings of the American Philosophical Society*, 128 (1984), 316–25.
HAMMOND, BREAN, *Professional Imaginative Writing in England, 1670–1740: 'hackney for bread'* (Oxford: Clarendon Press, 1997).
HAMMOND, LANSING VAN DER HEYDEN, *Laurence Sterne's Sermons of Mr. Yorick* (New Haven: Yale University Press, 1948).
HARTLEY, LODWICK, *Laurence Sterne: A Biographical Essay* (Chapel Hill: University of North Carolina Press, 1968).
HARVEY, JOHN H., 'A Lost Link with Laurence Sterne', *Yorkshire Archaeological Journal*, 42 (1967), 103–7.
HELLMUTH, ECKHART (ed.), *The Transformation of Political Culture: England and Germany in the Late Eighteenth Century* (Oxford: Oxford University Press for the Germany Historical Institute, 1990).
HERRING, THOMAS, *Seven Sermons on Public Occasions* (London, 1763).
—— *A Speech Made by His Grace the Lord Archbishop of YORK, at presenting an Association, enter'd into at the Castle of YORK, Sept. 24, 1745* (York, [1745]).
HILL, GEORGE BIRKBECK (ed.), *Johnsonian Miscellanies*, 2 vols. (Oxford: Clarendon Press, 1897).
HOLMES, GEOFFREY, *Augustan England: Professions, State and Society 1680–1730* (London: Allen & Unwin, 1982).
HOME, HENRY, LORD KAMES, *Essays on the Principles of Morality and Natural Religion* (Edinburgh, 1751).
HOWARD, JOHN, *The State of the Prisons in England and Wales*, 3rd edn. (Warrington, 1784).
HOWES, ALAN B., *Yorick and the Critics: Sterne's Reputation in England, 1760–1868* (New Haven: Yale University Press, 1958).
—— (ed.), *Sterne: The Critical Heritage* (London and Boston: Routledge & Kegan Paul, 1974).
HUGHES, EDWARD, *North Country Life in the Eighteenth Century: The North-East, 1700–1750* (1952; repr. London: Oxford University Press, 1969).
HUME, DAVID, *Essays, Moral, Political, and Literary*, ed. Eugene F. Miller (rev. edn., Indianapolis: Liberty Classics, 1987).
—— *Letters of David Hume*, ed. J. Y. T. Greig, 2 vols. (Oxford: Clarendon Press, 1932).
[HURD, RICHARD, and MASON, WILLIAM], *The Correspondence of Richard Hurd and William Mason*, ed. Ernest Harold Pearce and Leonard Whibley (Cambridge: Cambridge University Press, 1932).
HUTTON, WILLIAM, *A Trip to Coatham* (London, 1810).

JEFFERSON, THOMAS, *Writings* (New York: Literary Classics of the United States, 1984).
JOHNSON, SAMUEL, *The Yale Edition of the Works of Samuel Johnson*, ed. W. J. Bate *et al.*, 16 vols. (New Haven and London: Yale University Press, 1958–).
—— *The Letters of Samuel Johnson*, ed. Bruce Redford, 5 vols. (Oxford: Clarendon, 1992–4).
JONES, LOUIS C., *The Clubs of the Georgian Rakes* (New York: Columbia University Press, 1942).
KAUL, SUVIR, *Thomas Gray and Literary Authority: Ideology and Poetics in Eighteenth-Century England* (Delhi: Oxford University Press, 1992).
KEMP, BETTY, *Sir Francis Dashwood: An Eighteenth-Century Independent* (London: Macmillan and New York: St Martin's Press, 1967).
KNOX, VICESIMUS, *The Works of Vicesimus Knox*, 7 vols. (London, 1824).
KORS, ALAN CHARLES, *D'Holbach's Coterie: An Enlightenment in Paris* (Princeton: Princeton University Press, 1976).
KUIST, JAMES M., 'New Light on Sterne: An Old Man's Recollections of the Young Vicar', *PMLA* 80 (1965), 549–53.
KUNDERA, MILAN, *The Book of Laughter and Forgetting*, trans. Michael Henry Heim (Harmondsworth: Penguin, 1983).
LAMOUZÈLE, É., *Toulouse aux XVIIIe siècle d'après le 'Heures Perdues' de Pierre Barthès* (Toulouse: J. Marqueste, 1914).
LANGFORD, PAUL, *A Polite and Commercial People: England 1727–1783* (1989; repr. Oxford and New York: Oxford University Press, 1992).
LECKY, W. E. H., *History of England in the Eighteenth Century*, 7 vols. (London: Longman, 1892).
LEE, SIR SIDNEY, 'Laurence Sterne', *DNB*, xviii. 1086–108.
LETSOME, SAMPSON, *The Preacher's Assistant* (London, 1753).
LOCKE, JOHN, *Some Thoughts Concerning Education*, ed. John W. Yolton and Jean S. Yolton (Oxford: Clarendon Press, 1989).
MACDONALD, JOHN, *Memoirs of an Eighteenth-Century Footman*, ed. Peter Quennell (London: Century, 1985).
MCINTYRE, IAN, *Garrick* (Harmondsworth: Penguin, 1999).
MCKENDRICK, NEIL, BREWER, JOHN, and PLUMB, J. H., *The Birth of a Consumer Society: The Commercialization of Eighteenth-Century England* (London: Europa, 1982).
MASKELL, DUKE, 'The Authenticity of Sterne's first recorded letter', *Notes & Queries*, 215 (1970), 303–7.
MAXWELL, CONSTANTIA, *Dublin Under the Georges 1714–1830* (1936; 3rd edn., London: Faber, 1956).
MENNIM, A. MICHAEL, 'Shandy Hall, Coxwold', *The Shandean*, 4 (1992), 234–43.
MERCIER, VIVIEN, *The Irish Comic Tradition* (London, Oxford, and New York: Oxford University Press, 1962).
MILLER, JAMES, *On Politeness* (London, 1738).
MONKMAN, KENNETH, 'An Annotated Copy of Sterne's Sentimental Journey', *ABA Annual* (1952), 36–9.
—— 'Bibliography of the Early Editions of Tristram Shandy', *The Library*, 5th ser., 25 (1970), 11–39.
—— 'Tristram in Dublin', *Transactions of the Cambridge Bibliographical Society*, 7 (1979), 343–68.
—— 'More of Sterne's Politicks 1741–2', *The Shandean*, 1 (1989), 53–108.
—— 'Two Sterne Letters, and Some Fragments', *The Shandean*, 1 (1989), 121–2.
—— 'Sterne and the '45 (1743–8)', *The Shandean*, 2 (1990), 45–136.
—— 'Two More Unpublished Sterne Letters', *The Shandean*, 2 (1990), 143–5.
—— 'Books Sterne Owned?', *The Shandean*, 2 (1990), 215–25.
—— 'Shandean Race Horses', *The Shandean*, 10 (1998), 21–7.

—— and DIGGLE, JAMES, 'Yorick and his Flock: A New Sterne letter', *TLS* (14 March 1968), 276.

MORE, HANNAH, *Memoirs of the Life and Correspondence of Mrs. Hannah More*, ed. William Roberts, 4 vols. (London, 1834).

MOSSNER, ERNEST CAMPBELL, *The Life of David Hume*, 2nd edn. (Oxford: Clarendon Press, 1980).

NEW, MELVYN, 'Sterne's Rabelaisian Fragment: A Text from the Holograph Manuscript', *PMLA* 88 (1972), 1083–92.

—— 'A Manuscript of the Le Fever Episode in *Tristram Shandy*', *The Scriblerian*, 23 (1991), 165–74.

NICHOLS, JOHN, *Illustrations of the Literary History of the Eighteenth Century*, 8 vols. (London, 1817–58).

OLLARD, S. L., and WALKER, P. C., *Archbishop Herring's Visitation Returns*, 5 vols. (Leeds: Yorkshire Archaeological Society, 1928–31).

PASSERONI, GIANCARLO, *Il Cicerone*, 6 vols. (Milan, 1768–74).

PAULSON, RONALD, *Hogarth*, 3 vols. (Cambridge: Lutterworth Press, 1993).

PEAKE, RICHARD BRINSLEY, *Memoirs of the Colman Family*, 2 vols. (London, 1841).

[PEPYS, WILLIAM WELLER], *A Later Pepys*, ed. Alice C. C. Gaussen, 2 vols. (London, The Bodley Head, 1904).

POPE, ALEXANDER, *The Works of Alexander Pope, Esq.*, ed. William Warburton, 8 vols. (London, 1751).

POTTLE, FREDERICK A., *James Boswell: The Earlier Years 1740–1769* (London: Heinemann, 1966).

The Practical Preacher: Consisting of Select Discourses from the Works of the Most Eminent Protestant Writers: With Forms of Devotion for the Use of Families, 4 vols. (London, 1762).

PRIOR, SIR JAMES, *Life of Edmond Malone* (London, 1860).

PYLE, EDMUND, *Memoirs of a Royal Chaplain, 1729–63*, ed. Albert Hartshorne (London and New York: John Lane: The Bodley Head, 1905).

QUINN, J. F., 'Yorkshiremen go to the Polls: County Contests in the Early Eighteenth Century', *Northern History*, 21 (1985), 149–55.

—— 'York Elections in the Age of Walpole', *Northern History*, 22 (1986), 175–97.

REED, ISAAC , *Diaries, 1762–1804*, ed. Claude E. Jones (Berkeley and Los Angeles: University of California Press, 1946).

REEDY, GERARD, SJ, *The Bible and Reason: Anglicans and Scripture in Late Seventeenth-Century England* (Philadelphia: University of Pennsylvania Press, 1985).

The Registers of St. Michael le Belfrey, York, Part II, Publications of the Yorkshire Parish Register Society, 11 (1901).

RICHARDSON, JONATHAN, *An Essay on the Theory of Painting* (London, 1715).

RIVERS, ISABEL, *Reason, Grace, and Sentiment: A Study of the Language of Religion and Ethics in England, 1660–1780* (Cambridge: Cambridge University Press, 1991).

ROSS, IAN CAMPBELL, 'Fiction to 1800', in Seamus Deane *et al.* (eds.), *The Field Day Anthology of Irish Writing*, 3 vols. (Derry: Field Day, 1991).

—— and NASSAR, NOHA SAAD, 'Trim (-tram), Like Master, Like Man: Servant and Sexton in Sterne's *Tristram Shandy* and *A Political Romance*', *Notes & Queries*, 36: 1 (1989), 62–5.

ROSS, IAN SIMPSON, *The Life of Adam Smith* (Oxford: Clarendon Press, 1995).

RUPP, GORDON, *Religion in England, 1688–1791* (Oxford: Clarendon Press, 1986).

SANCHO, IGNATIUS, *Letters of Ignatius Sancho*, ed. Paul Edwards and Polly Rewt (Edinburgh: Edinburgh University Press, 1994).

—— *Letters of the Late Ignatius Sancho, an African*, ed. Vincent Carretta (Harmondsworth: Penguin, 1998).

SEWARD, JOHN, *The Spirit of Anecdote and Wit*, 4 vols. (London, 1823).
SHAW, MARGARET R. B., *Laurence Sterne: The Making of a Humorist, 1713–62* (London: The Richards Press, 1957).
SHARP, SAMUEL, *Letters from Italy* (London, 1766).
SHEPPERSON, ARCHIBALD BOLLING, 'Yorick as Ministering Angel', *Virginia Quarterly Review*, 30 (1954), 54–66.
SHERBO, ARTHUR, 'The Dissection of Laurence Sterne', *Notes & Queries*, 232 (Sept. 1987), 348.
SMAIL, JOHN, *The Origins of Middle-Class Culture: Halifax, Yorkshire, 1660–1780* (Ithaca: Cornell University Press, 1994).
SMITH, ADAM, *The Correspondence of Adam Smith*, ed. Ernest Campbell Mossner and Ian Simpson Ross, 2nd edn. (Oxford: Clarendon Press, 1987).
—— *The Theory of Moral Sentiments*, ed. D. D. Raphael and A. L. Macfie (Oxford: Clarendon, 1976).
SMITH, JOHN THOMAS, *Nollekens and his Times*, 2 vols. (London, 1828).
SMOLLETT, TOBIAS, *The Expedition of Humphry Clinker*, ed. Lewis M. Knapp, rev. edn., Paul-Gabriel Boucé (1966; rev. edn. Oxford: Oxford University Press, 1984).
—— *Travels through France and Italy*, ed. Frank Felsenstein (Oxford: Oxford University Press, 1979).
The Spectator, ed. Donald F. Bond, 5 vols. (Oxford: Clarendon Press, 1965).
STACPOOLE, ALBERIC, and others (eds.), *The Noble City of York* (York: Cerialis Press, 1972).
STANHOPE, PHILIP, LORD CHESTERFIELD, *Letters from Lord Chesterfield to Alderman George Faulkner, etc., being a Supplement to his Lordship's Letters* (London, 1777).
STERNE, JAQUES, *The Danger arising to our Civil and Religious Liberty from the Great Increase of Papists, and the Setting up Public Schools and Seminaries for the Teaching and Educating of Youth in the pernicious Tenets and Principles of Popery consider'd; in a Charge deliver'd to the Clergy of the Archdeaconry of Cleveland, in the Visitations held at Thirsk, Stokesley, and Malton, in the Year 1746* (York, 1747).
Sterneiana, 21 vols. (New York and London: Garland, 1974–5).
STONE, LAWRENCE, *The Family, Sex and Marriage in England 1500–1800* (1977; rev. and abridged edn., Harmondsworth: Penguin, 1979).
STRAUS, RALPH, *Robert Dodsley: Poet, Publisher & Playwright* (London and New York: John Lane, 1910).
SWIFT, JONATHAN, *The Correspondence of Jonathan Swift*, ed. Harold Williams, 5 vols. (Oxford: Clarendon Press, 1963–5).
—— *A Tale of a Tub*, ed. A. C. Guthkelch and D. Nichol Smith, 2nd edn. (Oxford: Clarendon Press, 1958).
—— and SHERIDAN, THOMAS, *The Intelligencer*, ed. James Woolley (Oxford: Clarendon Press, 1992).
SYKES, NORMAN, *Church and State in the XVIIIth Century* (1935; repr. New York: Octagon Books, 1975).
The Tatler, ed. Donald F. Bond, 3 vols. (Oxford: Clarendon Press, 1987).
THACKERAY, WILLIAM MAKEPEACE, 'Sterne and Goldsmith' in *The English Humourists of the Eighteenth Century* (London, 1856).
THOMPSON, DAVID, *Wild Excursions: The Life and Fiction of Laurence Sterne* (London: Weidenfeld & Nicolson, 1972).
[THORESBY, RALPH], *The Diary of Ralph Thoresby, F.R.S.*, 2 vols. (London, 1830).
THRALE, HESTER LYNCH, *Thraliana: the Diary of Mrs. Hester Lynch Thrale (later Mrs. Piozzi) 1777–89*, ed. Katharine C. Balderston, 2 vols., 2nd edn. (Oxford: Clarendon Press, 1951).
TOMORY, PETER, *Life and Art of Henry Fuseli* (London: Thames and Hudson, 1972).

TOOKE, JOHN HORNE, *Memoirs of John Horne Tooke*, ed. Alex. Stephens (London, 1813).
TURNER, B. N., 'An Account of Dr. Johnson's Visit to Cambridge, in 1765', *New Monthly Magazine*, 10 (1818).
TURNER, MICHAEL, *English Parliamentary Enclosure: Its Historical Geography and Economic History* (Folkstone: Dawson, 1980).
UGLOW, JENNIFER, *William Hogarth: A Life and a World* (London: Faber and Faber, 1997).
VERRI, PIETRO and ALESSANDRO, *Carteggio di Pietro e di Alessandro Verri*, ed. Francesco Norati and Emanuele Greppi (Milan: L. F. Cogliati, 1911).
VICKERY, AMANDA, *The Gentleman's Daughter: Women's Lives in Georgian England* (New Haven and London: Yale University Press, 1998).
WAKEFIELD, GILBERT, *Memoirs of the Life of Gilbert Wakefield* (London, 1792).
[WALPOLE, HORACE], *Horace Walpole's Correspondence*, ed. W. S. Lewis *et al.*, 48 vols. (New Haven: Yale University Press, 1937–83).
—— *Memoires of the Last Ten Years of the Reign of George the Second*, 2 vols. (London, 1822).
WARBURTON, WILLIAM, *The Divine Legation of Moses* (London, 1738).
—— *Letters from a Late Eminent Prelate*, 3rd edn. (London, 1809).
WARDLE, RALPH M., *Oliver Goldsmith* (London: Constable, 1957).
WENHAM, L. PETER, *Gray's Court: St. John's College, York* (York, n.d.).
WINSTANLEY, D. A., *Unreformed Cambridge: A Study of Certain Aspects of the University in the Eighteenth Century* (Cambridge: Cambridge University Press, 1935).
WOLLSTONECRAFT, MARY, *A Vindication of the Rights of Woman*, ed. Carol H. Poston (New York and London: Norton, 1975).
WRIGHT, ARNOLD, and SCLATER, WILLIAM LUTLEY, *Sterne's Eliza* (London: Heinemann, 1922).

Index